COLUMBIA COLLEGE
3 2711 00078 5224
C0-AZE-625

African Americans at War

AFRICAN AMERICANS AT WAR

An Encyclopedia

VOLUME TWO

JONATHAN D. SUTHERLAND

ABC CLIO

Santa Barbara, California   Denver, Colorado   Oxford, England

Library of Congress Cataloging-in-Publication Data
Sutherland, Jonathan.
African Americans at war : an encyclopedia / Jonathan D. Sutherland.
p. cm.
Includes index.
ISBN 1-57607-746-2 (hardcover : alk. paper) ISBN 1-85109-371-0 (eBook)
1. United States—Armed Forces—AfricanAmericans—
Biography—Encyclopedias. 2. African American soldiers—
Biography—Encyclopedias. I. Title.
U52.S88 2003
355'.0092'396073—dc22
2003021501

07 06 05 04 | 10 9 8 7 6 5 4 3 2 1

This book is also available on the World Wide Web as an eBook.
Visit abc-clio.com for details.

ABC-CLIO, Inc.
130 Cremona Drive, P.O. Box 1911
Santa Barbara, California 93116-1911

This book is printed on acid-free paper.
Manufactured in the United States of America

Contents

A

B

C

D

E

F

G

H

I

J

K

L

M

N

O

P

R

S

T

VOLUME TWO

U

V

W

Y

Z

AFRICAN AMERICANS AT WAR

U

Underground Railroad

The Underground Railroad is the name given the legendary means of escape for runaway slaves that operated before the American Civil War. It provided a means by which able-bodied male African Americans could escape to the North, many of them ultimately to fill the ranks of the African American regiments raised during the Civil War.

The Underground Railroad can actually trace its history back to the very beginnings of slavery in North America, although the name is more closely associated with the peak of its activities, commonly held to be between 1830 and 1865. The railroad was neither related to locomotives, nor was it underground. It was rather a cooperative network of abolitionists, sympathizers, and former slaves, all intent on facilitating escape from the South to the Northern states or Canada. There were also routes that took fugitives to Mexico and the West Indies.

The railroad was not formally organized; the majority of the work was carried out by religious groups and a variety of individuals from different ethnic backgrounds. It is almost impossible to estimate the number of fugitives who were helped by the railroad, but the figures must be in the tens of thousands.

Slaves arrived in North America in the early 1600s, and it is widely held that the first Africans arrived as indentured servants at the British colony of Jamestown in 1619. By the mid-1600s, slavery was widespread across New England and the other British colonies, and in 1755 all thirteen colonies had slaves. But it was only in 1793, with the passing of the first Fugitive Slave Act and the invention of the cotton gin, that the need for slave labor in the South rose dramatically and the controls over the institution became more formalized. Cotton production in the South rose from 13,000 bales in 1792 to 5,000,000 in 1860. Slaves were also needed for the other vital cash crops, including tobacco, sugar, rice, and indigo.

In the period 1790 to 1860 the slave population rose from 700,000 to 4 million. Despite this trend, there was always opposition to the institution of slavery, and in the early nineteenth century an abolitionist movement grew strong, calling for emancipation and equal rights for African Americans. Free African Americans and Quakers formed the American Anti-Slavery Society and the New England Anti-Slavery Society. Churches such as the African Methodist Episcopal Zion Church and the Abyssinian Baptist Church, formed by African Americans moving away from white-dominated churches, also became prominent in the cause of abolition.

In another approach to gaining freedom for slaves, the 1820s saw the establishment of two colonies in Africa, Sierra Leone and Liberia; the American Colonization Society organized the transportation of at least 12,000 African Americans to Africa and other places outside of the United States. Prominent African Americans also helped to relocate at least 3,000 African Americans to Africa, the Western Territories, and Canada. However laudable these attempts were, they did nothing to undermine the basic existence of slavery and provided no organized assistance for African American slaves who chose to flee from their masters.

Isolated examples of organized assistance to escaping slaves occurred as early as 1786, when Philadelphia Quakers assisted runaways from Virginia. In 1787 a Quaker named Isaac T. Hopper operated in Pennsylvania and New Jersey, hiding and helping fugitives. By 1831 many of these disparate groups had linked up, albeit informally, and a Kentucky runaway, Tice Davids, is credited with having coined the term "underground road," when he was hidden by a prominent abolitionist, John Rankin, in Ripley, Ohio. Each successful escape spawned more runaways, despite the fact that the only evidence of success visible to their fellow slaves was the fact that they had not been returned to their masters in chains.

The Underground Railroad ran its clandestine operations relying on codes related to railroad jargon, referring to the fugitives as passengers and those who helped them as conductors. James Fairfield, a prominent member of the group and a white abolitionist, traveled into the South and posed as a slave trader in order to free as many people as possible.

By 1849 the group was beginning to include prominent African Americans. In that year Harriet Tubman escaped from Maryland, and she later made almost twenty sorties into the South and freed 300 slaves (including many members of her family and friends). Some of those involved were even more successful, such as John Parker, who, after he had bought his own freedom and become a successful businessman, made frequent boat trips to Kentucky and Virginia to collect runaways from the Ohio River. It has been estimated that he organized the escape of at least 900 individuals. Equally important, three African American abolitionists in the North, William Still, Robert Purvis, and David Ruggles, set up vigilance committees to organize transportation and shelter.

The vast majority of those who escaped were men, largely because they could better endure the physical hardships involved and because it was more usual for male slaves to travel than for women and children. Once one family member had reached freedom, he would attempt to raise funds to buy his family or to organize their escape. Former "passengers" on the railroad included such prominent African Americans as Frederick Douglass.

The Southern states deployed slave catchers, and the slaves' masters themselves swept the area for their lost property. It was therefore necessary for the slaves and their conductors to travel at night and rest during the day. Food and clothing was always a problem, and it was difficult to trust anyone outside of the immediate group for fear that even slaves would turn the fugitives over to the authorities. At the very least, runaways would suffer physical violence, and in many cases males in particular would be lynched and their bodies hung on their master's plantation as a warning to those who might wish to follow in their footsteps.

For the first part of the journey the fugitives were often on their own, as the network tended not to extend deep into the South, and it was only in the Border States and the North that they could expect help from the Underground Railroad. The North Star was the beacon to follow, as it would inevitably take the slave away from the South. They had to travel through wilderness areas, avoiding the main roads, although much later it was possible, with more covert help, to travel by railroad or boat. One of the other major problems was that the fugitives must not look like slaves, which was a challenge, since the fugitives were rarely well clothed. Elaborate disguises were used, sometimes involving the theft of clothing from their masters; women dressed as men, men dressed

Slavecatchers invading a barn that served as a station on the Underground Railroad. The illustration comes from the classic 1872 work Underground Railroad *by the African American abolitionist William Still. (Library of Congress)*

as women, and fairer skinned African Americans posing as whites. Frederick Douglass disguised himself as a sailor to escape to New York, and Henry "Box" Brown had himself nailed into a shipping crate and transported by train from Richmond to Philadelphia.

Once the fugitives reached a member of the Underground Railroad, they were normally passed from station to station, the stations being located between 10 and 30 miles apart. Candles or lanterns were placed in the buildings at night to light the way, and once the fugitives arrived, they would be hidden in cellars, attics, concealed rooms, caves, and even swamps.

By the 1840s there was widespread antislavery feeling in the North; the numbers of runaways had increased, and the abolitionists had become more vocal and visible. In 1850 the U.S. Congress passed a stricter version of the Fugitive Slave Act, effectively ordering federal officials to assist in the capture of runaways; the Northern states could no longer be considered a safe haven for the fugitives. This new law led to widespread kidnapping: slave catchers from the South would take African Americans, regardless of their status, and sell them as slaves in the South. The Underground Railroad had to extend its operations into Canada and similarly, in the South, into Mexico and the West Indies.

By the late 1850s the differences of opinion regarding slavery threatened to tear the nation apart. The Underground Railroad continued to provide assistance and a safe haven for fugitives, and in certain areas, by the end of the decade, plantations were virtually deserted. The Underground Railroad's operations did not cease in 1861 when the American Civil War broke out, but if anything continued with more intensity and purpose. Many of the men who served in the United States Colored Troops were former runaway slaves. Upon reaching the North, under the terms of new laws and conditions established in Washington, they were free men; in the South they were considered initially as contraband, in effect meaning that they were property valuable to the Confederate war effort. Nevertheless, many of these men were keen to return to the South as armed troops and contribute toward the North's war against their former masters. Thus the Underground Railroad made a significant contribution to bringing African Americans into the Union army.

See also American Civil War; Douglass, Frederick; Emancipation Proclamation; Thirteenth Amendment; Tubman, Harriet; United States Colored Troops (APPENDIXES)

References and Further Reading

Bradford, Sarah E. *Scenes in the Life of Harriet Tubman.* 1869. Reprint, Salem, NH: Ayer, 1992.

Fradin, Dennis Brindell. *Bound for the North Star: True Stories of Fugitive Slaves.* Boston: Houghton Mifflin, 2000.

Parker, John P., and Stuart Seely Sprague. *His Promised Land: The Autobiography of John P. Parker, Former Slave and Conductor on the Underground Railroad.* New York: W. W. Norton, 1996.

Ripley, C. Peter, Brenda E. Stevenson, and Larry Gara. *Underground Railroad Handbook.* Washington, DC: National Park Service, 1998.

Still, William. *The Underground Railroad.* Chicago: Johnson Publishing, 1870.

U.S. Air Force

The U.S. Air Force, like other branches of the armed forces, was both slow and reluctant to admit African Americans to its ranks. Nevertheless, once the process of change had begun, it became an unstoppable force, and by the end of the twentieth century, African Americans were at the heart of the service.

Prior to World War I, there was not only a complete lack of opportunity for African Americans to become aviators in their country's armed forces but very little opportunity for anyone to do so; the U.S. Army had only recently established its "Air Service." Perhaps the first African American to seek a connection with what later became the United States Air Force was a maverick named Eugene Jacques Bullard.

Bullard had joined the French Foreign Legion in 1914. He was wounded twice after transferring to a regular French Army unit and then decided to transfer his talents to the French Air Force. He joined a pursuit squadron in May 1917, and on November 7 he shot down a German aircraft, receiving credit for his first confirmed "kill." He offered his services to the U.S. Army on several occasions, but each time it turned him down, as the army did not accept African American pilots in the air service.

The U.S. Army continued to refuse African American pilots until the Tuskegee Institute and several other training facilities around the country had successfully trained African Americans to fly and service aircraft. The government-sponsored Civilian Pilot Training Program began at the Tuskegee Institute in 1939, graduated its first students in May 1940, but it would still be several months before African Americans were finally allowed to fly for their country, despite demonstrated successes in the civilian sector.

As part of a series of announcements by President Franklin D. Roosevelt in September 1940, African Americans were informed that it was the intention of the U.S. Army to allow them to join the Air Corps.

At the beginning of 1941, thirty-three African Americans made the trip from Maxwell Field, Alabama, Fort Devens, Massachusetts, and Fort Bragg, North Carolina, to the Tuskegee Institute in Alabama. They were to begin a five-week aviation course under Capt. Benjamin O. Davis Jr. (an African American West Point graduate) and Capt. Noel Parrish. After successful completion, they attended an advanced course lasting thirty weeks to learn aerobatic skills and

Address of welcome in August 1941 to Army Air Corps cadets in front of the Booker T. Washington Monument on the grounds of the Tuskegee Institute, of which Washington had been the first president. (National Archives)

hone their gunnery abilities. These men formed the nucleus of the 99th Pursuit Squadron, a fighter squadron that became the most famous of the units manned by those who came to be known as the Tuskegee Airmen.

Elsewhere, other African American pilots had to wait somewhat longer. In May 1943, at Selfridge Field, Michigan, under the direction of Col. Robert R. Selway Jr., African Americans began training as bomber crews. By July 1944 Mather Field in California and Hondo Army Airfield, Texas, were training upwards of 100 African Americans as navigators and gunners.

The 99th Fighter Squadron was declared ready for combat in September 1942 and was deployed to Morocco in April 1943. Even though this move lessened the distance between the men and the front, there was no immediate intention to commit them to battle. They became part of the 33d Fighter Group of the 12th Air Force. One of the first combat missions took place on June 2, 1943, when the squadron claimed its first enemy kill. Nonetheless, later in the month the 99th was transferred to the 324th Fighter Group and began to fly escort missions between Tunisia and Sicily.

Generally, however, the U.S. Army was still determined not to use African American fighter crews extensively. The commander of the 33d Fighter Group, William M. Momyer, had not helped the issue when he complained about the 99th Squadron to Maj. Gen. Edwin J. House (12th Air Support Command Headquarters). He had not only accused the squadron of not being aggressive, but claimed that it lacked discipline. He also criticized on Col. Benjamin O. Davis Jr., the squadron's commander, for asking that the men be given a three-day break. Momyer found this request inconceivable, as the squadron had not flown the average seventy

Fliers of a P-51 Mustang Group of the 15th Air Force in Italy relax in the shadow of one of their Mustangs, August 1944. Left to right: Lt. Dempsey W. Morgan Jr., Lt. Carroll S. Woods, Lt. Robert H. Nelson Jr., Capt. Andrew D. Turner, and Lt. Clarence P. Lester. (National Archives)

missions that most of the white pilots in the same fighter group had flown over the preceding nine months. House agreed with Momyer and recommended that the squadron be reassigned to the Northwest African Coastal Air Force. When the suggestion reached the desk of Gen. Henry "Hap" Arnold (commanding general, Army Air Forces), he sought and received Roosevelt's approval, and the 99th was removed from combat.

The squadron's commander, Davis, was shortly afterwards recalled to the United States to train the 332d Fighter Group. Later, defending the 99th, as well as his own request for a brief period of respite, Davis told the Advisory Committee on Negro Troop Policies that the P-40s were not ideally suited to air-to-air combat and that his men had been in action solidly for two months and were down to twenty-six pilots instead of the average thirty-five in the corresponding white units in the fighter group. The advisory committee suspended Arnold's decision to withdraw the 99th and, now under the leadership of Maj. George "Spanky" Roberts, an African American, the squadron was committed to combat over Anzio in January 1944. It protected the invasion force, shooting down at least twelve German aircraft. The unit was awarded a Distinguished Unit Citation, and its success prompted the War Department to commit the all–African American 332d Fighter Group overseas.

Meanwhile the U.S. Army had decided to press ahead with the creation of an African American medium bombardment group, the 477th, also largely as a result of the 99th's performance. The 99th joined the 100th, 301st, and 302d in the newly created 332d Fighter Group, and by the end of the war the 332d had carved itself a considerable reputation. Not only did the flyers of the fighter group never lose a bomber that they had been assigned to escort on raids into Germany, but they also completed 15,000 sorties and 500 dive bombing and strafing missions.

Despite this success, it was not all plain sailing from this point on as far as African American aviators were concerned. Serious incidents threatened the whole process of accepting African Americans as pilots. The first involved the 477th Bombardment Group, in training at Selfridge Field, Michigan. On January 1, 1944, three of the 477th's black officers were told by Col. William L. Boyd, Selfridge's base commander, that they were not to use the officers' club, despite army regulations to the contrary. Boyd was reprimanded, however, and the 477th was transferred to Godman Field, Kentucky. The white officers used the officers' club at nearby Fort Knox, avoiding the issue of integrating the facilities.

The next major changes to affect the Army Air Force were the implications of the recommendations of the Gillem Board, named for its chairman, Lt. Gen. Alvan C. Gillem Jr., which proposed the full integration of African Americans in the U.S. Army in November 1945. Since the Air Force was still an integral part of the U.S. Army at this point, the report of the board, entitled *The Utilization of Negro Manpower in the Post-War Army,* affected this branch of the service as much as the remainder of the army. Although the Army Air Force was soon to become the U.S. Air Force, a separate service, the implications and future was clear.

The issuing of Executive Order 9981 by President Harry Truman on July 26, 1948, officially ended racial segregation in the armed forces. It did not, however, have any major impact on deeply ingrained attitudes. Each service faced the challenge of changing attitudes in order to offer equal opportunity to serve and equal conditions to all Americans, regardless of their color. A long-term consequence was that the executive order effectively eliminated all existing African American units, no matter how impressive their war records.

The abolishment of African American units, however, did not happen immediately. As the United States found itself increasingly embroiled in the conflict between North and South Korea after 1950, a war that eventually claimed over 36,000 American lives, there were still African American units in the armed services. Nonetheless, integration of military units was in progress, and in many respects Korea helped to accelerate the process.

Benjamin O. Davis Jr., who, after a distinguished role in World War II, had become the first African American general in the U.S. Air Force, quite rightly pointed out to the War Department that the air force had been instrumental in blunting the huge infantry assaults against the United Nations forces by the North Koreans and the Chinese. Among the men engaged in air combat over Korea during this time was Maj. Daniel "Chappie" James Jr., a former member of the 477th Bombardment Wing, which had been activated in January 1944. James, like many of the other pilots of his era, had had to make the transition from piston-driven aircraft to jets during the Korean conflict. He was to become the first African American commander of an integrated air force squadron and ultimately an air force four-star general. James was in a perfect position to take full advantage of the air force's moves toward integration in the years immediately after World War II; he had been transferred to the 12th Fighter-Bomber Squadron at Clark Field in the Philippines in September 1949. Over Korea he was known by the call sign "Black Leader," and he flew with professionalism and dash.

After the Korean War, it becomes more and

more difficult to discuss the African American role in the air force as a separate strand of air force history. In general, it is possible to say that, although African American pilots were still in short supply in the 1960s, increasing numbers were attracted to the U.S. Air Force rather than to the U.S. Navy, as it was believed that the former service had a much more progressive attitude. The Vietnam War was the first major conflict in which African Americans were completely integrated into the U.S. armed forces, and a general account of the role of the air force in that war will give an idea of what African American pilots were doing.

In April 1962 Washington finally admitted that U.S. Air Force pilots had been flying combat missions over Vietnam. There was no means of knowing at the time that the fight against the Vietminh, who had now been dubbed the Vietcong, or Vietnamese Communists, would continue for well over a decade.

In 1964 the U.S. Air Force was putting the finishing touches to a plan for an operation, ROLLING THUNDER, that was intended to bomb North Vietnam into submission, as part of President Lyndon B. Johnson's overall strategy of ensuring that South Vietnam did not fall to the Communists. The North Vietnamese attacked a U.S. Navy destroyer in the Gulf of Tonkin on August 2, 1964. On August 5, Johnson ordered the Air Force to attack an oil depot and several other targets in North Vietnam.

On October 22, 1965, Col. Fred V. Cherry of the 35th Tactical Fighter Squadron earned the dubious honor of becoming the first African American to be shot down and captured by the North Vietnamese. He spent a considerable time in the notorious Hanoi Hilton, the North Vietnamese prison that was the principal detention center for captured U.S. air crews, a nightmarish place where U.S. personnel were tortured and starved. He was not to return home until 1973.

By January 1972, President Richard Nixon had initiated negotiations with North Vietnam to end the conflict. It was finally decided in late 1972, that a peace treaty was viable. It was signed in Paris on January 27, 1973, and within sixty days all U.S. troops were out of Vietnam. The last planeload left on March 29, 1973. Beginning prior to the negotiations the U.S. Air Force had been engaged in heavy bombing missions on Hanoi and Haiphong, and even while negotiations were beginning to bear fruit toward the end of 1972, B-52s were flattening military and civilian targets across Vietnam. This continuation of the air war led to a number of American pilots becoming prisoners of war. Even after the last U.S. troops had officially left Vietnam in March, the U.S. Air Force continued to bomb Cambodia until August 14, 1973. Thus U.S. pilots, including African Americans, were still being shot down and were still falling into enemy hands.

The post-Vietnam U.S. Air Force gradually moved from a vast and lumbering service, reliant on draftees, to a far more professional voluntary organization. Recruiters actively sought out African Americans, and by the time the U.S. Air Force deployed for Operations DESERT SHIELD and DESERT STORM prior to and during the 1991 Gulf War, 13 percent of the entire service was African American. Like the other services, the U.S. Air Force, through the commitment of Jimmy Carter to civil rights and the commitment of Ronald Reagan to strengthening the military, had been transformed into an integrated, professional force, attracting highly qualified African Americans as career aviators. With pinpoint precision, the U.S. Air Force contributed to the destruction of Iraq's military machine with a minimum number of casualties to the Allies.

Some time after, as a testament to how far the U.S. Air Force had moved, the wrongs visited on the Tuskegee Airmen were finally put right. In 1945, 101 of the men had been reprimanded for their part in the Freeman Field incident. In 1995 it was decided that these reprimands would be struck from their records. In 1997 at Walterboro, South Carolina, a monument was erected in honor of the Tuskegee Airmen. The town had been extremely hostile to the African American pilots and now made its peace with the men by this tribute. In 1998, at the age of 85, Benjamin O. Davis Jr. finally received his fourth star, after persistent lobbying by men who had served with him during World War II and after.

See also Bullard, Eugene Jacques; Davis, Benjamin Oliver, Jr.; Executive Order 9981; Freeman Field Incident; Gulf War; James, Daniel "Chappie," Jr.; Korean War; National Association for the Advancement of Colored People; 99th Pursuit/Fighter Squadron; Selective Service Acts; Tuskegee Airmen; Vietnam War; World War I; World War II

References and Further Reading

Belknap, Michael R. *The Employment of Blacks by the Federal Government.* New York: Garland, 1991.

Berlin, Ira, Joseph Reidy, and Leslie S. Rowland, eds. *Freedom: A Documentary History of Emancipation, 1861–1867.* Series 2, *The Black Military Experience.* New York: Cambridge University Press, 1982.

Binkin, Martin. *Blacks and the Military.* Washington, DC: Brookings Institution, 1982.

Buchanan, A. Russell. *Black Americans in World War Two.* Santa Barbara, CA: ABC-CLIO, 1977.

Dalfiume, Richard M. *Desegregation of the U.S. Armed Forces: Fighting on Two Fronts, 1939–1954.* Columbia: University of Missouri Press, 1969.

Davis, Lenwood G., and George Hill. *Blacks in the American Armed Forces, 1776–1983: A Bibliography.* Westport, CT: Greenwood Press, 1985.

Department of Defense. *A Pictorial Documentary of the Black American Male and Female Participation and Involvement in the Military Affairs of the United States of America.* Washington, DC: Government Printing Office, 1991.

Donaldson, Gary A. *The History of African-Americans in the Military.* Malabar, FL: Krieger Publishing, 1991.

Ferguson, William. *Black Flyers in World War Two: Prepare for Combat.* Cleveland, OH: William Ferguson, 1987.

Foner, Jack D. *Blacks and the Military in American History: A New Perspective.* New York: Praeger, 1974.

Francis, Charles E. *The Tuskegee Airmen: The Story of the Negro in the U.S. Air Force.* Boston: Bruce Humphries, 1955.

MacGregor, Morris J. *Integration of the Armed Forces, 1940–1965.* Washington, DC: Center of Military History, 1985. http://www.army.mil/cmh-pg/books/integration/IAF-FM.htm#TABLE%20OF%20CONTENTS (accessed September 24, 2003).

Mullen, Robert F. *Blacks in America's Wars: The Shift in Attitudes from the Revolutionary War to Vietnam.* New York: Monad Press, 1974.

Nalty, Bernard C. *Strength for the Fight: A History of Black Americans in the Military.* New York: Free Press, 1986.

Nalty, Bernard C., and Morris J. MacGregor. *Blacks in the Military: Essential Documents.* Wilmington, DE: Scholarly Resources, 1981.

Osur, Alan M. *Blacks in the Army Air Forces during World War Two: The Problem of Race Relations.* Washington, DC: Office of Air Force History, 1977.

Sandler, Stanley. *Segregated Skies: All Black Squadrons of World War Two.* Washington, DC: Smithsonian Institution Press, 1992.

Schlesinger, Arthur M., Jr. *The Age of Roosevelt: The Politics of Upheaval.* Boston: Houghton Mifflin, 1960.

Silvera, John D. *The Negro in World War Two.* Baton Rouge, LA: Military Press, 1964.

Wynn, Neil A. *The Afro-American and the Second World War.* New York: Holmes and Meier, 1975.

U.S. Army

In many respects the experiences of African Americans in the U.S. Army mirrors that of African Americans in all branches of the armed forces. But of all the branches, the army has had the most disparate history with African Americans, alternately banning them and accepting them only to offer them the greatest opportunities in the military during the second half of the twentieth century.

Colonial Practices

The colonists' early experiences with and practices toward African Americans set the tone for later policy in many respects. In times of danger, every able-bodied man was expected to turn out to defend his colony whether that colony was British, French, Spanish, or Dutch. Freed blacks and even slaves were often enlisted to help with colonial defense as the need arose. On the other hand, the fear of slave revolts provided a compelling reason for whites to prevent the arming of African Americans, particularly in the slaveholding areas of the South. In general, each colony enacted its owns rules and regulations regarding African American participation, and even within colonies, these rules and regulations changed dramatically over time.

Regardless of each colony's practices, the forces they raised were colonial militias, not regular armies. The only official armies functioning in North America during the colonial period belonged to the European powers who had established colonies in the New World, and black participation in these bodies was rare, if not nonexistent, on the North American continent.

The American Revolution

The U.S. Army is directly descended from the Continental Army, formed on June 14, 1775, in the opening months of the American Revolution. Each state's militia served in conjunction with the Continental Army, and as during the colonial period, each state established its own policies for its militia, leading to a great deal of variation among militia units.

Initially, the bulk of the soldiers in the Continental Army came from New England, where fighting had first erupted between the British and their colonists, sparking the revolution. Among the troops originally enlisted to fight in the Continental Army were numerous African Americans, many of whom were free men. With the profitability of slavery already declining in the northern colonies, it was not uncommon for slave owners to offer their slaves freedom in exchange for their service in the army, a bargain that northern colonial governments encouraged.

As a result, African Americans fought in the battles of Lexington and Concord in April 1775, and Bunker Hill in June 1775. Commander-in-chief of the army Gen. George Washington banned the enlistment of African Americans in the Continental Army in July of that year, but allowed those already enlisted to remain. In November, the Continental Congress made all African Americans, free or enslaved, officially ineligible for service. However, as the military advantage of arming African Americans became evident, this policy was soon reversed, under Washington's influence, to allow the enlistment of free African Americans.

Prompting the Americans to revise their policy toward African Americans was the British view of black manpower. Early in the war, the British recognized that enlisting blacks in their military would supply much-needed replacements for regular troops while preventing the Americans from using this pool of manpower. In addition, if the blacks were slaves, their enlistment with the British Army would undermine the American economy by depleting the labor force. On November 15, 1775, Virginia's royal governor, Lord Dunmore, issued a proclamation offering freedom to all American bondsmen (slaves or indentured servants) if they fought for the British. Few indentured servants responded to Dunmore's call, but close to 1,000 slaves did. Dunmore's Proclamation came as a rude shock to American leaders, who quickly saw how the loss of African American support could hurt the revolutionary cause. In response, the Continental Congress changed the policy in early 1776, allowing African Americans to serve in the Continental Army but only if they were free.

Throughout this period it seems those African Americans serving with the army were fully integrated and operated within interracial units. What is also clear at this stage is that the recruitment officers, most interested in ensuring that companies and regiments were up to strength, were never averse to signing a man even if he could not prove that he was free. As had been the case prior to the American Revolution, many slaves or poor free men found themselves in either the colonial militias or the Continental Army as replacements for white men who chose not to fight. It seems that African Americans were so common in all units that even the British remarked that they scarcely ever saw an enemy regiment that was all white. At the height of the hostilities, African Americans were serving in both the Continental Army and the state militias, whether as free men, slaves posing as free men, slaves who had been promised freedom for their duty, or slaves serving as substitutes for their masters. A handful reached the rank of sergeant, but none became officers, either in the militias or in the Continental Army.

Integrated units were not universal, however. Although most African Americans were incorporated into regular army units, Rhode Island introduced in January 1778 the first segregated unit after the state had failed to recruit enough white men for the two battalions that Congress had required it to raise. Recruitment focused on slaves because the state's white male population had already been enlisted in other state regiments. With an offer of freedom for slaves, and compensation to their owners, some 250 men joined the regiment. Over the course of the war, the 1st Rhode Island Regiment, led by the white officer Col. Christopher Greene, also included some free African Americans, Native Americans, and whites, the addition of the latter component ending the regiment's short history of segregation. The regiment was particularly commended for its role in the Battle of Long Island.

Connecticut also strove to create an all–African American battalion, but because the state did not offer slaves their freedom in exchange for their service, the battalion did not reach establishment strength until June 1780. Prior to that, Connecticut had a small company of less than sixty African American men operating as the 6th Company. Massachusetts also had an ad hoc African American unit called the Bucks of America, who were apparently deployed to guard parts of Boston during the war.

After the Revolution

In the immediate aftermath of the American Revolution, both the Continental Army and the state militias moved swiftly to divest themselves of African American troops. This move was made in all the states, regardless of the fact that by 1784 Connecticut, Massachusetts, New Hampshire, Pennsylvania, and Rhode Island had all taken steps to abolish slavery, usually through programs of gradual emancipation. The Haitian slave revolt of 1794 panicked Americans so much that free blacks in the North lost their right to vote, and in the South, slaves faced even harsher conditions, thus further discouraging the use of black troops. Even a free black militia unit that had originally been raised as early as 1736 by the French in Louisiana was ordered to disband.

A significant piece of legislation regarding African Americans in the land forces at this time was the Militia Act of 1792. Enacted by Congress to clarify the relationship between the states and the federal government in regards to control of the various state militias, the act passed on May 8, which had undergone several significant revisions in the preceding days, specifically stated that only white men could serve in the militia. In 1798, the War Department extended this decision to all branches of the armed forces and officially excluded African Americans.

The War of 1812 and After

Although much of the fighting associated with the War of 1812 occurred at sea, many significant land battles transpired as well, and almost all of them had African American participants, despite the official policy of the military and the state militias. Once again the British sought to undermine American military effectiveness by offering freedom to any slaves who joined their ranks, a call that brought a few thousand slaves to fight for the British in 1813.

In the South, African Americans also fought in the last major land battle of the War of 1812 at the Battle of New Orleans in early January 1816. Louisiana had already organized a state militia unit of free blacks—the Battalion of Free Men of Color, a unit that had three African American second lieutenants. These men were the first African American commissioned officers in any U.S. state militia. When the battalion officially became part of the U.S. Army just weeks before the battle, Maj. Vincent Populus became the first African American to hold a field grade rank in the army.

Following the War of 1812, once again the U.S. Army discharged many of its troops to limit itself to peacetime strength. With the possible exception of African American laborers, the army became almost exclusively white. In 1820 and again in 1821, U.S. Army Regulations reiterated the ban on recruiting African Americans. Nevertheless, African Americans fought in all three of the Seminole Wars (1816–1858), for both the government (mainly in various state militias) and for the Seminole Indians, who welcomed runaway slaves and encouraged the men to become warriors against the U.S. government.

Between 1846 and 1848 the army fought the Mexican-American War, which involved roughly 1,000 African Americans among the 50,000 volunteers who served in the conflict. Officially the U.S. Army still banned African American participation. Nevertheless, there are records of African Americans serving in the New York 1st Regiment of Volunteers and the 4th Artillery Regiment, as well as the 9th, 10th, 11th, and 13th Infantry Regiments. Notably, following the British pattern, the Mexican Army had attracted a number of runaway slaves, holding out the promise of freedom in return for military service.

The Civil War

Although the American Civil War ostensibly began as a struggle between the ideas of federalism and states' rights, by 1863 and the implementation of the Emancipation Proclamation, it had effectively, in the eyes of African Americans, become a war of liberation. Nevertheless, as with prior conflicts and many of those that followed, both the federal government and most states were initially reluctant to raise African American troops. Given the nature of the conflict, President Abraham Lincoln faced some stark choices. Even though most people in the Northern states did not own slaves, they still did not consider African Americans to be their equals. Even by the latter stages of the war, a minority of Union troops considered the emancipation issue to be what they were fighting for; most simply wanted the restoration of the Union. The trickiest situation regarding the recruitment of African American soldiers involved the border states of Maryland, Kentucky, Delaware, and Missouri, all of which had remained in the Union but had significant slave-owning populations. Lincoln was of the firm opinion that arming African Americans would drive these four states into the arms of the Confederacy. However, African Americans also offered a large potential pool of manpower that could help the North win the war quickly and decisively.

When Lincoln called for 75,000 volunteers in April 1861, large numbers of African Americans offered their services, with African American communities often agreeing to pay for the black troops' expenses. Such offers were made in New York, Pennsylvania, Ohio, and Massachusetts, but in every case, state authorities declined, opting not to enlist African American troops in the opening months of the war. Denied the opportunity of fighting on the front lines, many African Americans created informal home guard units. Some communities decided to employ African Americans as manual laborers, thus freeing white men to serve in combat. For example, in September 1862, Cincinnati formed the Black Brigade to build defenses around the city. But all early requests by African Americans to serve as soldiers were rejected by both the federal government and the U.S. Army.

The role that African Americans would play in the Union war effort was soon complicated by the number of runaway slaves who fled behind Union lines during the war. In the first few months of the war, Union Army officials had returned escaped slaves to the South in accordance with the Fugitive Slave Law of 1850, maintaining that since the federal government did not accept the South's secession from the Union the law was still in effect. But in June 1861, Gen. Benjamin Butler, while commanding the Department of Virginia, seized African American runaways and refused to send them back to the South on the grounds that they were Confederate property and therefore contraband. Butler then put the slaves to work in labor parties, compensating them with a small wage. The net result was to increase the number of African Americans fleeing north, safe in the knowledge that they would not be returned to their masters.

On August 6, 1861, Congress sanctioned Butler's policy by enacting the First Confiscation Act, which decreed that the U.S. government would seize all property of rebelling Southerners, including slaves. As first hundreds and then thousands of runaways fled North, the federal government was increasingly faced with the issue of what to do with them. The army placed these refugees in contraband camps; fed, clothed, and housed them; and employed them in labor details to support the Union war effort. For the first time in its history, the army undertook what proved to be a massive program of social welfare, out of which eventually emerged the Freedmen's Bureau, which helped hundreds of thousands of slaves make the transition to freedom.

The labor supplied by the former slaves in these camps substantially aided the Union war effort. It is believed that nearly 200,000 African Americans operated as laborers for the Union Army during the war, and most of them came from these camps. These men were not formally organized and technically speaking were not enrolled as part of the Union Army.

The First Confiscation Act, however, did not presage a uniform federal policy regarding slavery. When Gen. John C. Frémont attempted to abolish slavery in Missouri, Lincoln quickly and decisively reversed the order and removed Frémont from command. Always, the federal government kept in mind its need of the border states and strove not to adopt policies that alienated them more than necessary to successfully pursue the war. Lincoln also squashed a proposal by Secretary of War Simon Cameron to abolish slavery and employ African Americans as combat troops. Cameron's suggestions were too radical and controversial for an administration that was desperately trying to suppress a rebellion in the South without sparking another rebellion in the North. Americans in neither region were prepared to arm African Americans.

Nevertheless, the ferocity of the war quickly brought about a variety of societal changes that forced many Americans to reexamine their attitudes about both slavery and African Americans. More and more, Northerners began to agree on progessively radical efforts to bring the war to a successful conclusion. On July 17, 1862, Congress enacted the Second Confiscation Act, which authorized the president to deploy contraband slaves for military service. Just one week later, the military governor of the South Carolina Sea Islands, Gen. Rufus Saxton, began raising five African American regiments, totaling 5,000 men. Although the army approved of Saxton's efforts, it did not adopt a wholesale plan to enlist African Americans soldiers.

However, other commanders in the Union Army had also decided to arm African Americans, with or without the sanction of army high command. Butler again proved a path breaker in this area. In the spring of 1862, he had quietly allowed a unit of the Louisiana Native Guards to join his command after he had captured New Orleans, although he proved reluctant to use these troops in combat. In the summer of that year, though, he allowed his subordinate Gen. John W. Phelps to organize five companies of former slaves with the intention of employing these men on the battlefield. Butler subsequently mustered these men into the 1st Regiment of the Louisiana Native Guards on September 27, followed shortly thereafter by the 2d Regiment on October 12 and the 3d on November 24. The same thing was happening in other regions of the war as well. Operating in Kansas, Gen. James H. Lane offered African Americans on August 6, 1862, $10 per month to serve as soldiers. His two regiments consisted of free men from the Northern states and fugitive slaves from Missouri. The 1st Kansas Colored Infantry went into action at Butler, Missouri, on October 29, 1862. In the Department of the South, Maj. Gen. David Hunter created the 1st South Carolina Volunteers, a unit of former slaves that saw action at Darien, Georgia, on November 13, 1862.

With these examples of fighting African American soldiers before them, the federal government and the American public became more accepting of the idea of blacks serving in the Union Army, even as combat troops. Although the Union Army had a much larger manpower pool from which to draw than the Confederate Army, a series of battlefield reversals in late 1862 and early 1863 had caused a sharp drop in morale, leading to more desertions and more difficulties in recruiting new troops to sustain the federal war effort. Also, more Americans began to undergo the ideological transformation that Lincoln underwent during this period: by 1863, it had become apparent to many that too much damage had been inflicted on both sides to ever reconstruct the Union as it had been before the war, even if the Union managed to win the conflict. Therefore, the idea of emancipation became more attractive, as in increasing numbers Northerners began to view slavery as the root cause of the disagreement between the North and South. The best solution to both win the war and rebuild the Union seemed to be to eradicate the bone of contention: slavery. Emancipation would both undermine the Confederates' ability to wage the war and contribute to the Union's ability to win it by making available thousands of additional troops. Consequently, it did not seem unreasonable to many Americans that if the war was about freeing African Americans then they should take an active part in winning it. A secondary benefit of enlisting blacks in the armed forces was the idea that military service would better equip them to deal with their freedom in the future by instilling in them the twin virtues of discipline and order.

The ideas of freeing the slaves and arming blacks did not always go hand in hand, and many Americans supported one idea but not the other. But by the summer of 1863, the tide of public opinion had begun to turn in favor of these proposals, urged on by abolitionists and civil rights leaders who fought for both plans. When Lincoln issued the Emancipation Proclamation on September 22, 1862, freeing all slaves in areas currently in rebellion, he clarified the federal government's policy on slavery and cleared the way for enlisting African Americans in the U.S. military.

Shortly after the Emancipation Proclamation took effect on January 1, 1863, the U.S. Army began actively recruiting African American troops with the assistance of civil rights leaders such as Frederick Douglass and Henry McNeal Turner. State governments also undertook the effort to enlist African American troops, especially states where abolitionist sentiment was strong, such as Massachusetts. On January 26, 1863, Massachusetts Governor John Andrew began raising the 54th Massachusetts Volunteer Infantry. So successful was the recruitment drive that there were sufficient men to raise the 55th as well. African American units from other states quickly followed.

Thousands of African Americans responded to the call to serve, despite rumors that Confederate authorities had vowed to shoot any African American taken prisoner barring arms for the Union. Abolitionists expressed disappointment that more free blacks had not joined, as close to 80 percent of all recruits were former slaves. Some of these slaves were recruited in the most despicable manner, being virtually impressed by Union commanders who forced all adult male slaves in some southern communities to fight for the Union. However, the majority of slaves welcomed the chance to join the Union Army and fight their former masters.

To provide organization for this burgeoning force, the War Department issued General Order No. 143 on May 22, 1863, which estab-

The 26th U.S. Colored Volunteer Infantry on parade at Camp William Penn, Pennsylvania, 1865. (National Archives)

lished the Bureau of Colored Troops. Maj. Charles Foster, a strong supporter of the deployment of African American troops, was appointed the bureau's first chief. The bureau sought to bring a level of professionalization to the newly formed black units, using only professional recruiters and taking steps to make the segregated African American regiments more integrated and uniform in terms of size and training under white officers and some black noncommissioned officers. By December, some 50,000 African Americans had been successfully inducted into more than 70 regiments, a figure that only increased as the Union Army captured more and more Confederate territory. Collectively, the African American units were organized as the United States Colored Troops (USCT).

The first USCT regiment was officially mustered into the Union Army on June 30, 1863. Camp William Penn in Philadelphia became one of the major centers for training the enlisted men, and over ten USCT units were mustered there. White officers and black noncommissioned officers received training at a special school in nearby Philadelphia, and white officers were forced to undergo rigorous examinations before being commissioned in the USCT, although once commissioned, they were more likely to gain promotion than their colleagues who commanded white troops. Gradually all African American regiments were redesignated as USCT units, eventually bringing the USCT to a strength of 135 infantry regiments, 6 cavalry regiments, 12 heavy artillery regiments, and 10 batteries of light artillery. In all, African Americans came to account for roughly 7 percent of the Union Army, representing nearly 200,000 men. Collectively, the units fought in over 250 battles during the Civil War.

The men of the USCT faced far more challenges than their white counterparts, being engaged in a constant battle against discrimination. The Confederacy reacted vehemently to both the Emancipation Proclamation and the subsequent arming of African Americans, with the Confederate Congress issuing legislation on May 1, 1863, stating that white officers of these troops would be summarily executed and that African American enlisted men in uniform would be returned to slavery. As far as the African American troops were concerned, they believed that the Confederates would offer them no quarter. As it turned out, most African American prisoners were treated very much as white captives were. They were exchanged, hospitalized if they needed it, and not shot on sight.

However, there were some notable exceptions, the most infamous of which occurred on April 12, 1864, when Confederate Gen. Nathan B. Forrest stormed the Union outpost at Fort Pillow on the Mississippi River in Tennessee. The exact details of the battle are not only shrouded in mystery, but hotly debated. Many accounts speak of the incident as a massacre, in which wounded African American soldiers were buried or burned alive. When word of the Fort Pillow massacre spread, it served only to make African American soldiers fight more stubbornly and ferociously.

The men also faced discrimination from the Union Army itself. USCT soldiers typically received the dregs of supplies, uniforms, and rations. Black soldiers tended to receive worse medical care than whites and were forced to live in areas of substandard housing and poor sanitation. In the unit's early days, the men had to fight a pay discrepancy that resulted in their wages being one-quarter less than their white counterparts. In protest, many of the men declined their reduced wages, an act that no doubt caused hardship for their families. The dispute continued for nearly a year until Congress, under increasing public pressure, finally agreed to equalize soldiers' pay in June 1864. And finally, despite the formation of the USCT with the goal of putting African American troops into combat, Union officials proved reluctant to deploy the men in battle, assigning them instead to labor duties. The unit's white officers campaigned tirelessly to get their men into action and did finally succeed but only with tremendous effort.

When given the opportunity, African Americans proved anxious to prove themselves in battle, and they did so time and time again, despite lingering prejudices within the army that blacks could not fight. Perhaps the most celebrated turning point in the fortunes of African Americans and their reputation as fighting men needed a tragedy. On July 18, 1863, on Morris Island, South Carolina, the 54th Massachusetts under the command of Col. Robert Gould Shaw dashed themselves against the Confederate bastion of Fort Wagner, which protected the approaches to Charleston. The attack was ruinous but brought the unit significant glory, although Shaw and many of his men did not live to see it and the fort remained in Confederate hands. The American public celebrated the 54th's heroism, however, as soon as reports of the assault began appearing in the newspapers. From that point on, African Americans were increasingly sent into action, notably at Olustee in Florida, Honey Hill in South Carolina, Petersburg in Virginia, and Nashville in Tennessee. The cost was high, though. One estimate claims that some 36,523 enlisted men in the USCT never returned home, many dying of disease or complications from their wounds.

Frontier Duty

Following the end of hostilities and the reestablishment of the Union, the U.S. Army rapidly reduced its forces once more. Nonetheless, many of the African American regiments were still under arms for up to a year after the official end of the war in the spring of 1865. By 1866, the U.S. Congress was actively considering including African Americans in the regular postwar army. For the next forty years or more, the U.S. Army was primarily involved in domestic operations, notably as occupational troops in the South during the period of Reconstruction and also on the western frontier, where disputes with Native Americans had slowed white settlement and development.

In July 1866, the federal government enacted the Army Reorganization Act, which would specify the shape of the post–Civil War army. Recognizing the potential of African American manpower but still unconvinced of blacks' aptitude as soldiers, Congress ordered that just six of the army's sixty regiments be designated as all–African American units: four infantry regiments and two cavalry regiments. In many respects, the duties of the U.S. Army during this period made it more acceptable to use African American troops, despite the reservations of the American public at large. Those troops could be consigned to duties on the western frontier, where racial problems would be limited, as would their interaction with most of American society. Consequently, on August 1, 1866, the 9th and 10th Cavalry and the 38th, 39th, 40th, and 41st Infantry Regiments were officially designated as African American units. Two infantry regiments and both of the cavalry regiments were posted to Texas, while the remaining two infantry units were sent on occupational duties in the South.

In March 1869, after Congress had authorized an additional army reorganization, the 38th and 41st were merged to become the 24th Infantry Regiment, and the 39th and 40th became the 25th Infantry Regiment. The African Americans who served during this period have become popularly known as Buffalo Soldiers, most likely as a result of descriptions emanating from Native Americans who believed the blacks' hair was reminiscent of a buffalo. Whatever the origins of the name were, African American troops soon adopted it with pride. The Buffalo Soldiers served on the western frontier almost continuously from 1866 until 1898, fighting numerous engagements against Native American groups during which they won many battle honors.

Throughout this period the four African American regiments were shifted periodically to cover an enormous frontier, stretching from Texas to California and from Canada to Mexico. Operating in difficult terrain and often with companies deployed in scattered forts and settlements, the men had not only to contend with periodic outbreaks of hostilities arising out of U.S. government policy with regard to Native Americans, but also with a harsh environment that in many respects was almost completely lawless.

For example, the 9th Cavalry was instrumental in subduing the Apache during their six-year assignment in New Mexico in the late 1870s, and it was also involved in the difficult disputes that arose in Oklahoma when white settlers attempted to illegally occupy Indian Territory in the 1880s. In addition, the 9th was present in the summer of 1890 when the Sioux made their last rising against the U.S. government beginning at the Pine Ridge Reservation, before being shipped overseas in 1898, where it served with particular distinction in the Spanish-American War. The experiences of the 10th Cavalry ran along very similar lines, and both the 24th and 25th Infantry Regiments were also involved in some of the most important military campaigns on the western frontier, where they often served as support units for the cavalry.

With the army leadership beginning to accept the idea that African Americans would be a permanent component of its force, an effort began to provide black soldiers on the frontier with the rudiments of education, with the particular goal of educating noncommissioned officers to handle the many administrative duties associated with their rank. There had been regimental schools run by army chaplains to educate men within the African American regiments during the Civil War, and these ventures became the pattern for educating the men in the African American regiments assigned to the frontier. Between 1875 and 1879 in the 25th Infantry alone, around 100 of the men attended classes each day. The army also encouraged the development of other skills among the black troops, including carpentry and blacksmithing. Of great importance were equestrian skills, not only those involved in riding but also the skills involved in the care of their mounts. Although army officials promoted these measures, it was ultimately up to the regimental commanders to determine the scope and breadth of any educational training.

There was no doubt, though, that African American troops received worse treatment than their white counterparts, particularly in terms of supplies. Transporting food, clothing, weapons, ammunition, and other essentials for frontier life posed significant problems for the army's Inspector General's Office, even when those supplies were destined for white troops. The white troops, however, received first priority on these materials, with black troops receiving what was left over. There were instances when the U.S. Army Quartermaster's Department made the decision to send the African American cavalry regiments worn-out nags and saddles that had been discarded by white cavalry units and should have been burned.

When there were problems with the civilian communities, the U.S. Army sometimes acted in support of their men, despite the ingrained racial prejudice embodied in military policies. Nevertheless, severe problems between black troops and white civilians continued. Several African American soldiers were murdered by white citizens, notably in Texas in January 1875. Two African American soldiers were lynched, one in Montana in 1885, another in Wyoming in 1888. There seems to have been a general increase in racial difficulties after 1890, largely as a result of the end of the wars against the Native Americans. With no more frontier to protect, African American troops found themselves posted to more settled areas where they were increasingly likely to interact with the white civilian population.

This period also saw the first African American in the Signal Corps, when W. Hallett Greene was accepted on September 26, 1884, and effectively opened opportunities for African Americans in the hospital and ordnance corps, as well as the quartermaster and commissary departments. Just as significant were the first African Americans at West Point. Although James Webster Smith was the first African American to enter West Point in 1870, he did not graduate. Instead, this honor went to Henry Ossian Flipper, who graduated from the academy in June 1877. Other African American graduates followed, including John H. Alexander in 1887 and Charles Young in 1889. However, Young was the last African American graduate from the academy until 1936.

The Spanish-American War and After

At the close of the nineteenth century, the U.S. Army turned its attention to a new region: the West Indies. Spain had long dominated that area, but by this time, the Spanish Empire was deteriorating and many Spanish colonies began agitating for independence. Chief among them was Cuba, where revolutionaries had been seeking to throw off Spanish control for decades. As Cuba lay so close to American shores and maintained so many commercial ties to the United States, the U.S. government monitored the situation in the colony closely while its own relations with the Spanish government worsened.

On February 15, 1898, the USS *Maine,* a U.S. Navy battleship, exploded while anchored in a Cuban harbor, resulting in the sinking of the battleship. Of the 260 American servicemen who lost their lives, 22 were African American seamen. Lacking evidence to the contrary, Americans quickly decided that the *Maine* had been sabotaged by operatives of the Spanish government, a diplomatic crisis developed that soon led to the outbreak of war. On April 11, 1898, President William McKinley called for the U.S. Congress to authorize the use of armed force to end Spanish oppression of Cuba. On April 20, Congress agreed and declared Cuba to be independent.

At the opening of hostilities, the U.S. Army had some 5,500 African American troops under arms in the four regular army regiments, the 24th and 25th infantries and the 9th and 10th cavalries. These men were later supplemented by the creation of volunteer units. After reorientation, the four regular regiments were assigned to three divisions of the U.S. invasion force.

Even before the troops could be moved to Cuba, though, there were racial problems in Florida that caused the army to deploy all African American troops to Cuba without further delay. They became part of the push toward the Cuban capitol of Santiago, the key objective of the campaign. The 10th Cavalry first saw action at Las Guásimas on June 24, the first American victory of the 114-day war.

African American troops were involved in the most famous engagement of the campaign, popularly known as the Battle of San Juan Hill. The battle actually occurred over three hills, but San Juan became the most famous, in part because of the ferocity of the fighting on that hill and in part because future president Theodore Roosevelt and his troop of Rough Riders played a major role in this fight. As some of the most experienced troops on the battlefield, all four African American regiments performed exceptionally well, earning the respect of their fellow soldiers and the praise of the American public. The 9th and 10th cavalries earned particular distinction for their heroic conduct under fire. Five African Americans were awarded Medals of Honor for their gallantry, and twenty more the Certificate of Merit. Although Roosevelt and the Rough Riders received the lion's share of publicity, the black troops were honored in the United States as well, with books, plays, and songs being written in their honor.

Several thousand African Americans served in state volunteer regiments that were associated with the National Guard, but few of these units arrived in Cuba in time to see any combat. In addition to the state volunteers, the War Department quickly moved to create a number of United States Volunteer Regiments, which were nicknamed "Immune Regiments" because they were supposed to consist of men who had already been exposed to yellow fever, which had proven more deadly than Spanish fire in the contest. Contrary to the belief that these men would be immune, however, a large number of them fell to tropical diseases. Some 4,327 African Americans served in the 7th, 8th, 9th, and 10th U.S. Volunteers. Only the 9th saw active service; while the others remained in the United States.

During the Spanish-American War, the United States had managed to wrest the Philippines from the Spaniards, but native revolutionaries sought true independence for the country, not merely a change in colonial masters. During the insurrection that followed, the four regular army regiments of African American troops saw service in the Philippines. Generally speaking their performance was extremely creditable; notable victories included San Mateo on August 12, 1899, and Iba in January 1900. The African American regulars returned to the United States in 1902, then spent two years between 1906 and 1908 on garrison duties in the Philippines once more.

Between the Spanish-American War and World War I, there were serious racial incidents at Brownsville, Texas, in 1906 involving the 24th and 25th Infantries, and at Houston, Texas, in 1917 involving the 24th Infantry. In both cities, regular army African American soldiers, reacting to what they saw as violence directed against them, took up arms and used them against white civilians and officials, which resulted in loss of life. There were also other less serious incidents between African American soldiers and, most frequently, local police attempting to enforce Jim Crow laws, but the overall effect was to raise the level of concern about the role of African American soldiers, particularly if trained for armed combat. No immediate changes in army policy occurred as a result of these concerns, but the army became increasingly sensitive to how it employed black troops.

Nevertheless, the 10th Cavalry Regiment and some elements of the 24th Infantry Regiment were part of Brig. Gen. John J. Pershing's punitive expedition into Mexico in March 1916, the most significant military engagement for the U.S. Army between the Spanish-American War and World War I. Pershing's expedition had been organized in response to the attack by Mexican revolutionary Pancho Villa and a force of 400 men on the town of Columbus, New Mexico, which had resulted in the deaths of eighteen Americans. The commander of the 10th and long a supporter of the use of African American troops, Pershing was ordered by President Woodrow Wilson to take a military force into Mexico to capture Villa or at least discourage any additional raids across the U.S. border with a show of force. The two-pronged expedition ranged as far as 300 miles into Mexico, but after eleven months, the force was withdrawn without securing Villa. The operation was generally considered a failure, although Villa did not make any more raids across the border.

World War I

On April 6, 1917, the United States entered World War I, which had already been raging on the European continent for three years, bringing horrible devastation and loss of life along the massive front that snaked through much of France. At that time, the U.S. Army numbered just 75,000 men, 20,000 of whom were African American and serving in the four segregated regular army regiments (the 9th and 10th cavalries and the 24th and 25th infantries). To bring the military up to wartime strength, the federal government quickly enacted a draft, passing the Selective Service Act on May 18. By the terms of the act, over 24 million men became eligible for military service, over 2 million of whom were African American.

Throughout the whole of the war, only half a dozen African Americans sat on the draft boards, which critics claimed discouraged African American recruitment. Despite this bias in enlistments, the army was far ahead of other military departments, opening opportunities for blacks to serve in almost every branch except the pilot section of the aviation corps. During World War I, African Americans served in cavalry and infantry regiments; engineer, signal, medical, hospital, ambulance, and veterinary corps; supply and ammunition trains; coast and field artillery; and depot brigades. Blacks also served as regimental adjutants, judge advocates, chaplains, intelligence officers, chemists, surveyors, draftsmen, truck drivers, and mechanics.

The marines, on the other hand, excluded African Americans entirely from their forces. The navy and coast guard, although not barring blacks from serving, discouraged enlistment by bluntly telling them that they would be employed only as mess men, water tenders, and coal passers. Rather than serve in these degrading positions, most African American men went to army recruiting stations in the hopes of serving in a combat unit.

The War Department announced that the best educated and strongest African Americans would be allowed to become combat troops. African Americans who were laborers in civilian life and, perhaps, illiterate, would either not be welcome or be used to create labor battalions. As it turned out some 200,000 African Americans served in the American Expeditionary Force, and some 80 percent of these men found themselves in labor battalions. Although African Americans contributed slightly less than 10 percent to the entire expeditionary force, they provided roughly a third of all the labor troops. Many American leaders clung to the idea that employing African Americans as laborers followed blacks' natural inclinations and would free up white men to fight the war, an opinion that proved hard to alter.

What is perhaps the most perplexing aspect of the U.S. Army's policy was the decision not to deploy its four African American regiments as combat troops overseas, particularly as all four regiments had significant battlefield experience. Initially the explanation was that use of African American troops could spark racial incidents in Europe. Although a handful of experienced men from these units (some 1,600) were reassigned to the new African American units, the 92d and the 93d Infantry Divisions, the majority of the men in the new divisions were inexperienced, or at best had experience serving in the National Guard.

The question of African American officers remained a contentious issue throughout the war. The official army policy of using white officers was based on the belief that African Americans could not command men of their own color, and as a consequence, the new divisions were given a predominantly white command structure. Nonetheless, there was sufficient pressure from civil rights activists and the African American community to bring about the creation of an African American U.S. Army Officer's training facility at Fort Des Moines, Iowa. Between June and October 1917, some 1,250 men attended the facility, with around 250 being prior noncommissioned officers from the regular African American regiments. Some 639 men were commissioned as captains or first or second lieutenants on October 15, 1917, most of whom were assigned to the 92d Division. Other segregated facilities produced another 700 African American officers, which meant that over 1,350 African American officers served at one stage or another during the war, 0.7 percent of all of the U.S. Army's officers. At the same time, 13 percent of draftees were African American.

The lot of African American enlisted men during World War I showed little improvement over the conditions of those who had served during the Civil War. Indeed, some African American troops in Virginia were actually issued mothballed Union uniforms. Poor training, inadequate provisions, and end-of-the-line equipment were commonplace. It was clearly the policy of the War Department and the U.S. Army never to allow any of these men to fight. Still the large numbers of African American noncombatant troops deployed, notably in the supply, signals, and engineer branches of the service, made significant contributions to the overall war effort.

Some African Americans did fight, but only after intense pressure from the African American press and the civil rights movement at home. One result of this pressure was that the 93d Infantry Division was assigned to the French Army, where it was re-equipped and much more fairly handled than would almost certainly have been the case in U.S. service. The division carved out for itself a relatively good reputation and was engaged in some of the bitterest fighting of the last year of the war.

The 92d Infantry Division, however, did not have the advantage of serving with the French Army and thus avoiding many of the discriminatory practices prevalent in the U.S. Army. The 92d was commanded by Gen. Charles C. Ballou as part of the American Second Army under Gen. Robert Bullard. The two men disliked each other intensely, and Bullard had extremely negative opinions about the abilities of African American soldiers. Often elements of the division were deployed or given objectives that they could not reasonably be expected to achieve. Their performance overall was lackluster, but no worse than some white divisions. Unfortunately, there were deliberate, as well as uninformed, attempts to portray the performance of the 92d Division in negative terms, leading to conclusions about the lack of competence of African American officers and soldiers that in turn strongly influenced U.S. Army policy on African Americans for many years.

The Aftermath of World War I

Despite the U.S. Army's treatment of African Americans during World War I, a large number of them opted to reenlist, largely as the result of the poor economic condition of the country after the war. White men, however, tended to leave the army, seeking better pay and employment opportunities elsewhere. Increasingly alarmed that there would be a disproportionate number of African Americans in the army, military authorities imposed a restriction on the enlistment numbers and discouraged as many African Americans as possible from enlisting or re-enlisting. The army did not have the option to disband the four regular African American regiments without the explicit permission of the U.S. Congress. Instead, the army reduced these four long-standing regiments to almost hollow shells and by this means, systematically reduced the number of African Americans in the service.

The U.S. Army's conclusions regarding the value and performance of African American soldiers were based to a large extent on testimony given by those who had commanded African American troops during World War I. In 1919, the assistant commander of the General Staff College requested that all officers who had commanded African American troops during the war comment on their soldiers' performance, evaluate it, and make recommendations about the future use of African Americans in the army. With individuals such as Ballou in prominence, the general consensus seemed to be that African Americans were more of a liability than an asset. Ballou and many others were firmly of the opinion that as most of the African Americans were descendants of slaves, they had inherited cowardice, stupidity, superstition, and lack of initiative. Such racial stereotypes were used to provide explanations of why the 92d Infantry Division in particular had not performed well.

There were dissenting voices, such as Lt. Col. Vernon A. Caldwell, who had commanded African American units in Cuba, the Philippines, and France. He believed that African American troops should be deployed, though he held that they should be organized in units smaller than regimental size. His recommendation was to place an African American company in each of the regular army regiments. A single dissenting voice, however, was not going to sway the U.S. Army, and the plans formulated during the interwar period for using African Americans reflected racist assumptions about the inability of blacks to lead and the perceived danger of forming divisions that would be completely African American. At the same time, the plans were based on the conviction that units smaller than a division must not be integrated, and that most African Americans belonged in labor battalions, not combat units.

World War II

As the United States moved toward involvement in World War II, deeply held beliefs about the racially determined characteristics of African Americans predominated the thinking of the U.S. Army. Even Secretary of War Henry Stimson believed that blacks were incapable of making good officers and that only white officers could make the men excel. Above all, he was determined not to allow integrated units. Army Chief of Staff Gen. George C. Marshall consistently warned President Franklin D. Roosevelt that he should not place too much trust in a race that Marshall insisted had not shown any initiative in battle during previous conflicts.

In May 1940, when Roosevelt requested Congress' permission to expand the armed forces, the industrial psychologist Walter V. Bingham was brought in to resurrect an intelligence test, an early version of the Army General Classification Test (AGCT), which the army used to assess and classify all recruits. The pilot program was run in late 1940, but the War Plans and Training Division failed to incorporate any African Americans in the test study. Equally, the majority of the men who were tested (something in excess of 5,000) all came from the northeast of the United States, which at the time had the highest level of literacy in the country. The results of this program became the standard against which African Americans were measured, consigning the majority of them to support duties and physical labor throughout World War II.

Prior to mass mobilization, regular army African Americans accounted for 4,000 of the army's establishment strength of 118,000. They only accounted for 5 of the commissioned officers in the regular army and 360 of the 100,000 officers in the Army Reserve. Despite the restrictions already in place regarding African American involvement in the U.S. Army, it was the army that absorbed the majority of African American recruits, with substantially fewer blacks going to the other branches of the armed forces.

The National Association for the Advancement of Colored People (NAACP) and many other organizations, such as the Committee on the Participation of Negroes in the National Defense, called on the army to sweep aside segregation, not only on the grounds of reducing discrimination, but also citing the country's best interests. There was continual pressure on the U.S. Army and, as importantly, on Roosevelt himself, who realized that to estrange African

American voters could possibly mean failure in forthcoming elections. On September 5, 1940, the president roundly criticized the U.S. Army, pointing to the adverse publicity it had been receiving from the African American community. He directed the War Department to prepare a statement highlighting equalities of opportunity that would be offered to African Americans in the armed services. Just a week later, Roosevelt was told by the army chief of staff that the army was already planning to create a number of new African American regiments, and that it was perfectly willing to accept African Americans into the service, in proportion to their representation in the population.

From late September, a number of announcements from the White House aimed to reassure the African American community. The first indicated that of the 400,000 men needed for the U.S. Army in the first draft under the terms of the Selective Service Act, some 36,000 would be African American. Despite these announcements, the army's policy on African Americans was still confusing. During a conference in September 1940 a number of key individuals—including executive secretary of the NAACP Walter White, administrator of the Urban League T. Arnold Hill, and African American labor leader A. Philip Randolph—had been assured by the president that he did not favor segregation or blocks on applications to any area of the U.S. Army and the National Guard and that he would work toward an army without segregation. However, the U.S. Army and the War Department were quoted as claiming at exactly the same time that African Americans would not be integrated and that they would have to prove themselves to be dependable before the army would consider using them in combat.

Collectively, around 1.8 million African Americans faced the prospect of being called up, a number roughly in line with the estimate that African Americans constituted 10 percent of the eligible male population. In practice, though, the number of African American men actually drafted proved to be far less than would have been expected based on the number of African Americans in the general population, particularly in the first round of enlistments. Initially, 5 percent of recruits (about 96,000 men) were African American, but by December 1942, the proportion had risen to 17 percent (roughly 420,000 men). Such a disparity points to a discrepancy in the number of eligible recruits and the number of men actually drafted. In the first round of the draft, many African Americans had simply been passed over, selected for service but never called up. Between January and September 1941, only 4,449 African Americans were actually enlisted in the U.S. Army, and by the beginning of 1943, official figures suggested that 300,000 African Americans were still waiting to be inducted (figures drawn from Jefferson 1998). Moreover, in the period from 1941 to 1943, nearly 20 percent of registered African American males failed to report to the induction boards after they had been selected. In May 1943 in Detroit alone, 15 men were imprisoned for draft dodging. By 1946 African Americans accounted for 18 percent of all the draft dodgers who had been prosecuted and imprisoned for draft evasion (figures drawn from Jefferson 1998). To some extent these figures may reflect the fact that the U.S. Army simply could not cope with the vast numbers of men being called into service at that time. In addition, though, army authorities had no clear plan as to how they were going to employ large numbers of African Americans.

By early 1941, though, thousands of African American draftees began arriving at various reception centers throughout the United States. Centers included Fort McPherson, Fort Screven, Camp Blanding, Fort McClellan, Fort Devens, Fort Jackson, Fort Huachuca (which between April and May 1942 took 6,000 men), Fort Benning, Fort Leonard Wood, Fort Knox, Camp Claiborne, Fort Still, Camp Lee, Camp Davis, Fort Riley, Fort Clark, Fort Bragg, and Camp Gruber. The training was intensive and demanding; free time was limited, and in many cases there were few recreational facilities for the men. At various places there were racial problems; men stationed at Fort Jackson barely dared to visit Atlanta for fear of discrimination and violence. In Tampa, Florida, there were incidents of running battles in the streets, and in New York interregimental rivalries had more than a hint of racial overtones.

Two of the more dangerous incidents occurred in Gurdon, Arkansas, when members of the African American 94th Engineer Battalion were involved in a gunfight with state troopers. In January 1942, there was another similar gun battle in Alexandria, Louisiana. Equally worrying was a major skirmish in Bisbee, Arizona, when members of the 369th Infantry Regiment, amounting to nearly 200 men, fought a running battle with 100 military and civilian police. Many of the young African Americans involved were from northern states and had a hard time tolerating the racism that surrounded them in the South. There seemed to be extreme difficulties facing the U.S. Army as they procrastinated in their decision to deploy the men and give them more meaningful duties.

Progress was being made, however. The 93d Infantry Division, after having had basic training at Fort Huachuca, Arizona, spent six weeks on maneuvers in the Louisiana area. They were then moved to Camp Clipper, where the inspector general, Maj. Gen. Virgil L. Peterson, declared the unit ready for combat action overseas. Consequently, after six months of intensive training, the men boarded four transport ships bound for the South Pacific. The 92d Infantry Division, having been trained at various camps in Alabama, Indiana, Kentucky, and Arkansas, also moved to Louisiana for additional training, but they had to wait until June 1944 before they boarded transport ships for Italy. One of the other significant units under training was the 761st Tank Battalion, which was at Fort Hood, Texas, in September 1943. This African American unit was finally committed to Gen. George Patton's 3d Army in mid-1944, where it saw significant action. The 24th Infantry Regiment, along with the African American 76th and 77th Antiaircraft Units, was sent to the New Hebrides in the South Pacific and Guadalcanal in the western Pacific in 1942. They remained in the area until March 1944, when part of the unit was sent to Bougainville, another island in the region.

In short, a few units were deployed overseas, but it was a slow process, and it by no means always resulted in troops having a chance at combat. In the most striking instance of deployment overseas not leading to combat, the 2d Cavalry Division had been posted to North Africa, but as soon as they arrived they were disbanded and reformed as labor units. Surprising results were received from a survey carried out by the War Department on the former members of the African American 2d Cavalry Division. Only 27 percent actually regretted not having been committed to combat (Jefferson 1998). A veteran of the unit later said that the men had experienced so much conflict with their officers that they didn't "have much energy left" for fighting the Germans (cited in Rose 1947, 26–31). The U.S. Army came under severe criticism for its slow deployment of African Americans abroad.

In August 1942, the War Department created the Advisory Committee on Negro Troop Policies, chaired by Assistant Secretary of War John J. McCloy and including Brig. Gen. Benjamin O. Davis, Sr., the first African American general in the U.S. Army who was at this time posted to the Inspector General's Office, and Truman Gibson, a prominent African American lawyer who had become a civilian aide to the secretary of war. After a meeting at the beginning of 1943, they urged the secretary of war to immediately dispatch African American troops to combat zones. This action, they argued, would be the only way to defuse the increasing racial tension caused by keeping these troops in the United States. Stimson chose to ignore their recommendations and instead continued the policy of converting African American troops to service units in order to release white troops for combat duty, a policy that had brought about the dismemberment of the 2d Cavalry Division. The secretary defended his actions by claiming that African Americans were not being committed to combat because of their poor educational attainments and consequent inability to learn how to handle modern weapons. Not surprisingly, Stimson drew the wrath of the African American press, of African American leaders, and of the various civil rights organizations.

In February 1944, the advisory committee met once again and presented recommendations to Stimson to commit African American infantry, artillery, and other units to action. Stimson met with McCloy just a week later and finally agreed that elements of the 92d Division would be committed. At around the same time, elements of the 93d Infantry Division, operating as the 25th Regimental Command Team, were engaged in combat against the Japanese on Bougainville. They performed well, and the 593d Field Artillery Battalion, an integral part of the division, received a special commendation for its efficiency. On New Georgia and the Russell Islands in the Pacific theater, the 368th and the 369th were engaged in running battles with the Japanese.

Prior to these engagements, the 24th Infantry Regiment had been serving on Guadalcanal between March and August 1943. The 1st Battalion had been sent to Bougainville in February 1943, earning the respect of corps commander Gen. Oscar W. Griswold, who commended the unit for its combat prowess. In late 1944, the 1st Battalion was sent to Saipan and Tinian in the Mariana Islands, ostensibly on garrison duty. Saipan in particular, however, was not secure, and many hundreds of Japanese were still at large. The unit was given the responsibility of securing the island. In the summer of 1945, the 24th was sent to the Kerama Islands, where it accepted the surrender of the Japanese garrison, the first formal surrender following the end of hostilities in the Pacific. In Europe, the U.S. Army was beginning to deploy not only increasing numbers of African American support troops, who engaged in such operations as the Red Ball Express following the breakout from the Normandy beaches, but also combat units.

The 92d Infantry Division duly arrived at Naples in August 1944 to become part of the 1st U.S. Armored Division of the IV Corps. The 370th Regimental Combat Team was engaged in action on the Gothic Line, a German defense line, and later elements of the division were assigned to Task Force 92, detailed to capture Massa. Casualties were extremely high, particularly among the 370th. Despite enormous sacrifices, Division Inspector General Gen. Charles Welch claimed that the 370th had shown poor judgment and a basic inability to use combat techniques during the actions in October 1944. The 92d's commander, Edward Almond, proceeded to court-martial, demote, or transfer many of the platoon leaders and noncommissioned officers. A crisis meeting took place in November with Maj. Oscar J. Magee of the Intelligence Division, at which William J. McCaffrey, the 92d's chief of staff, was unequivocal in his condemnation of his men's ability to fight. It was clear from what he said that he had no confidence in the men and that he pitied white officers who had been assigned to the division to lead the men.

Much later, when the situation had been fully investigated, it became clear that Almond's command of the 92d Division had been run on extremely racist lines. African American officers were considered inferior, as were African American noncommissioned officers. Perhaps the statistics speak for themselves, as between October 1944 and May 1945, at Almond's instigation, some 1,800 of his African American men were sent to courts-martial, and 1,500 were transferred out of the division. Col. Howard Green, who commanded the 366th Infantry before he was relieved of his command toward the end of 1944, claimed that, much as Almond had been able to damage his regiment, his men's self-respect had remained intact.

While the 92d struggled to establish its reputation as an effective force, other African American units were being given a better chance to prove their combat prowess. In December 1944, during the last great German counteroffensive of the war, known as the Battle of the Bulge, the 333d and 969th Field Artillery Battalions (African American units of the VIII Corps Artillery) had severely disrupted German attempts to take Bastogne. The 969th received a Distinguished Unit Citation, supported by Maj. Gen. Maxwell D. Taylor, commander of the 101st Airborne Division, which had been aided by the 969th's support.

Another opportunity offered itself as well, this time to an African American armored unit. The 761st Tank Battalion had been assigned to the 26th Division and found themselves under the command of the notoriously blunt and blustery Patton. He made a point of meeting with the men almost as soon as they had been assigned to his command and told them that he was not concerned with what color they were; he had asked for them because they had been recommended to him, and now they must prove to everyone that they could kill Germans effectively. The 761st entered combat near Metz and spent 183 days in combat across France, Belgium, Germany, Luxembourg, and Austria, operating at various times with the 26th, 71st, 79th, 87th, 95th, and 103d Infantry Divisions, as well as the 17th Airborne Division. Its biggest tests came at Morville-les-vic in Alsace, where it engaged a line of German pillboxes successfully, and at Tillet in Belgium in January 1945, where the unit was engaged against the 15th SS Panzer Division for five days. Despite its outstanding performance in these actions, the unit had to wait thirty years before it received its Presidential Unit Citation.

The Aftermath of World War II

By the time World War II ended in 1945, the U.S. Army had recognized the inherent inefficiencies of the existing segregated system for employed African American manpower. The federal government had also reached the conclusion that segregation was no longer in the national interest. The U.S. Army conducted two reviews of African American performance. One, organized by Assistant Secretary of War John McCloy, involved a questionnaire sent to commanders just two weeks after the end of the war in Europe. The results of McCloy's study indicated that the army command structure had found African Americans to have performed unsatisfactorily during the recent war, and many attributed this poor performance to the practice of segregation. A popular suggestion among the officers was to retain only the very best of the African American troops in the peacetime military and to organize them in small units. The second survey was conducted by the civilian aide to the secretary of war, Truman Gibson, and focused more on public perception of African American soldiers. Gibson's report also reported a low perception of African American performance during the war, and civil rights leaders posed a powerful argument placing the blame squarely on the military's policy of segregation. They adamantly maintained that if segregation were eradicated, African American soldiers would perform as well as their white counterparts. In consequence of these reports, McCloy recommended to Secretary of War Robert P. Patterson that an entirely new army policy be framed with regard to African Americans.

Patterson endorsed McCloy's suggestion and organized a review board for that purpose almost immediately. Meeting for the first time on October 1, 1945, and named after the board's chairman Lt. Gen. Alvan C. Gillem, Jr., the Gillem Board was empowered to frame a postwar policy on the use of African American manpower to achieve maximum efficiency in the U.S. Army. Its deliberations included sixty witness interviews and a review of mountains of paperwork. In the end, the board made eighteen recommendations, the most significant of which called for an alteration in the army's segregation policy so that it could make the most effective use of all individuals within its structure regardless of race.

Specifically, the recommendation called for the creation of African American platoons that would service within otherwise white companies, to place African American companies within white battalions, and to incorporate African American battalions into white regiments. The board wanted to scrap quotas for African American officers allowing the army to have a complement of African American officers that could possibly be assigned to command white soldiers. Many civil rights leaders were disappointed in the Gillem Board's recommendations, which stopped far short of full integration, but military authorities were generally receptive to the board's suggestions.

The federal government, however, also felt that the Gillem Board's recommendations had not gone far enough to address the issue. After much debate, President Harry Truman issued Executive Order 9981 on July 26, 1948, officially ending racial segregation within the armed forces. At the same time, Truman also established a presidential committee, named the Fahy Committee after its leader Charles Fahy, to ensure that the order was implemented. Over the next several years, the Fahy Committee worked with the several branches of the armed services to desegregate their forces. The army proved particularly reluctant to implement the policy change, with several senior army officials stating that desegregation simply could not be enacted in the army without destroying its effectiveness. Other army leaders questioned whether the military could not be integrated without greater integration of American society in general and criticized the federal government for making the army the means of social experimentation. Nevertheless, plans for desegregation moved forward under the watchful eyes of the Fahy Committee and civil rights leaders.

The Korean War

As the United States found itself increasingly embroiled in the conflict between North and South Korea from 1950, a war that eventually claimed 140,000 American lives, there were still African American units in all parts of the armed services. Nonetheless integration was under way, and in many respects Korea helped accelerate this process.

The U.S. Army's experience of integrated units during the Korean War showed that those that had undergone the process of integration performed better than those that were all–African American. The still segregated 24th Infantry was especially held to be an example of poor performance by a segregated unit, although the exact nature of its performance is still a matter of controversy. On October 1, 1951, the 24th was deactivated, thus ending the U.S. Army's long tradition of African American combat units. Noncombatant segregated units still existed, however. Despite the order to desegregate, almost half of the U.S. Army's African American manpower remained in units that had not been integrated. The practice of segregation only ended on October 30, 1954, when the secretary of defense was finally able to officially announce that the last of these units had been integrated.

In the decade that followed the Korean War, concrete steps were taken to fully implement Truman's executive order. Although there were individuals who resisted the demand for equality and clung to the concept of segregation, their efforts, although sometimes disruptive and damaging, were in vain. Life on military installations became integrated, from military units to barracks to base schools and housing.

Some problems remained, however, mostly due to actions based on individual prejudices and preconceptions. There was still discrimination in the way that assignments were made, in the way that soldiers were assessed for promotion, and in the way that military justice was applied, but the armed forces led American society in the degree of equality and respect given to African Americans. In this atmosphere, which despite the remaining problems was full of optimism, a number of young African American military officers began careers that would see them rise to the highest level of military positions and civilian service. One of them, Colin Powell, would become chairman of the Joint Chiefs of Staff—America's top-ranking military official—and later, after his retirement from the military, U.S. secretary of state.

Nevertheless, a tremendous problem still existed in many parts of the country in terms of the racial discrimination faced by African Americans, particularly in off-post life. Most pronounced in the south, where Jim Crow laws

Weapons squad leader fighting with the 2d Infantry Division north of the Chongchon River points out the North Korean position to his machine gun crew, November 20, 1950. (National Archives)

remained in effect, but present in varying degrees throughout the country, racial discrimination ranged from relatively subtle discrimination in rental housing or home sales to hotels that refused accommodation to African Americans. Many blacks found the contrast between military and civilian life difficult to accept. During the 1950s, there was a rising chorus of demands that the U.S. government take action to end discrimination in off-base housing, schools, and public accommodations, which contributed to the fledgling civil rights movement that would come to fruition in the 1960s.

The Vietnam War and After

Although the United States had only reluctantly accepted the reestablishment of French colonial rule in Vietnam after the end of World War II, the U.S. government did provide logistical and financial support for the French military effort against the Communist Viet Minh national insurgents seeking an independent Vietnam. With the decisive defeat of the French at Dien Bien Phu on May 7, 1954, the United States assumed a more active role in the governance of Vietnam.

At the Franco-Vietnamese peace conference in Geneva, Switzerland, in 1954, the Viet Minh were forced to accept a temporary division of the country into northern and southern halves. The Viet Minh established the Democratic Republic of Vietnam (North Vietnam) in the north, while the United States was instrumental in establishing the Republic of Vietnam (South Vietnam), and the government of Ngo Dinh Diem, in the south. Elections were planned for 1956 so that the Vietnamese could elect a single government and unite the country, but they never occurred. That, and Diem's policies, led to the rise of an insurgent movement in South Vietnam against Diem's government, a revolution that the North Vietnamese decided to actively support. The first American military advisers to the South Vietnamese arrived in Vietnam in 1955 as the situation in Vietnam began to spiral out of control.

By the end of 1959, the number of American advisers had reached 760, and two advisers had been killed. By the end of 1964, there were 23,300 American military personnel in Vietnam, but 1965 saw the arrival of more than 160,000 additional American soldiers. A steady escalation of American troop strength followed until a peak of 536,100 was reached in 1968.

In the United States, responding to the demands of civil rights leaders and a growing sense of public anger, President John F. Kennedy, at the urging of Secretary of Defense Robert S. McNamara, reactivated the President's Committee on Equal Opportunity in the Armed Forces, chaired by Gerhard Gesell, which was to attempt to find a possible solution to the off-post discrimination faced by members of the U.S. military and to increase the number of qualified African Americans volunteering for military service.

Before the recommendations of the Gesell Committee could be implemented, President Lyndon B. Johnson ordered a massive increase in the number of American soldiers in Vietnam in 1964, and the nature of the war changed with U.S. Army units beginning to actively fight the war. The U.S. Army combat units sent to Vietnam in this early escalation were trained, existing units, with a percentage of African American soldiers higher than the percentage of African Americans in the national population. Many of these soldiers were volunteers who had seen the U.S. Army as an opportunity for advancement denied them in other aspects of American society. A lack of education among these volunteers resulted in a high proportion of them serving in front-line combat units rather than in more sophisticated, technical roles behind the lines.

There was also inequity within the draft. Deferments for college attendance and certain occupations favored middle- and upper-class whites. Consequently, draftees tended to be poor, under-educated, from urban areas, and African American. Draft boards were also overwhelmingly white in composition with seven state boards having no African American members, leading to charges that the boards were unreasonably biased toward enlisting blacks and passing over whites.

A combination of voluntary enlistment and the draft served to place an unusually high percentage of African American soldiers in harm's way during 1965–1968, a fact reflected in the casualty lists. From 1961 to 1965, less than 10 percent of Americans in the military were African American compared to 13 percent of the U.S. population, but almost 20 percent of the combat-related deaths in Vietnam during that period were African American. In 1965 alone, almost 25 percent of the men killed in combat in Vietnam were African American, and in 1968, approximately half of the men in infantry and cavalry units in Vietnam were African American. Starting in 1966, however, the leadership of the army and the Marine Corps worked to reduce the number of African American casualties. They succeeded to the point that by the end of the Vietnam War, the percentage of African Americans killed in combat was roughly in line with national population percentages.

This controversy about African Americans' place within the military occurred against the backdrop of a civil rights movement to end racial discrimination in the United States. Civil rights leaders questioned the role of African Americans in the war, and many suggested that there was a deliberate effort to place African Americans in combat in lieu of whites. Despite the distance between Vietnam and the United States, the racial strife of the period did carry over to Vietnam, becoming most common in rear areas, and the same tensions could be felt in U.S military installations all over the world. The racial tensions of the time were issues of the entire society, not just the army or the army in Vietnam.

U.S. Army Pfc. Jerome Alexander and Sp4c. George Lightfoot, Company B, 2d Battalion, 1st Infantry, 196th Light Brigade, fire at a suspected Viet Cong position during a search-and-destroy mission west of Tay Ninh, South Vietnam. (National Archives)

The army that saw service in Vietnam was an integrated army, a fact that was not lost on African Americans—even while they were sometimes critical. African Americans served with distinction in Vietnam in every department of the army, proving that they could fight as well as their white counterparts and perform successfully in any role, and then re-enlisting at a higher rate than white soldiers.

In the closing days of the Vietnam War, President Richard M. Nixon, responding to overwhelming condemnation of the military draft and charges that those with education, money, and connections could avoid military service through many loopholes, appointed a commission to study the viability of an all-volunteer military force. The commission's report was favorable, and on July 1, 1973, the U.S. government ended the draft and replaced it with an all-volunteer force. Under the new volunteer plan, the percentage of African Americans increased significantly.

In the Persian Gulf War of 1991, 23 percent of all military personnel were African Americans, and 17 percent of total deaths in both combat and non-combat were African Americans. The performance of American military forces, and particularly the army, in the Gulf War led to increased respect for the armed services and increased the willingness of African Americans to volunteer for military service, viewing the military services either as a means to better themselves and their future or as a career.

By the time of the Iraqi War of 2003, African Americans, comprising about 14 percent of the American population, made up 21 percent of military personnel, but only 15 percent of positions considered to be combatant. In fighting in Iraq, to April 10, 2003, some 19 percent of casualties (where race could be determined) were African American, a figure that highlights the nature of hostilities in Iraq, where support troops were suddenly subjected to combat conditions and a significant number of the total casualties were caused by irregular military action.

Honoring African Americans

Starting in the 1980s, the U.S. Army and a succession of White House administrations did their belated best to honor African Americans who had shown exceptional bravery but had never received recognition for their efforts. In May 1991, Cpl. Freddie Stowers of the 371st Regiment finally received a Medal of Honor, which had been recommended back in September 1918 for his bravery during the Champagne Offensive, when 40 percent of his company were killed or wounded. President George Bush bestowed the honor on Stowers' 88-year-old sister and his great-great-nephew, Sgt. Douglas Warren, who was serving in Saudi Arabia with the 101st Airborne Division.

On January 13, 1997, President Bill Clinton officiated at the ceremonies that saw Pvt. George Watson, formerly of the 29th Quartermaster Regiment, who had died after saving several soldiers in the Pacific Ocean in 1944, recognized with a Medal of Honor. Among the other men whose medals were finally presented on this day was 1st Lt. John R. Fox (366th Infantry, 92d Division), Sgt. Ruben Rivers (761st Tank Battalion), Maj. Charles L. Thomas (614th Tank Destroyer Battalion), Sgt. Edward Carter, Jr. (56th Armored Infantry, 12th Armored Division), and Pfc. Willie F. James (415th Infantry Regiment). All of these African American men had died in combat, but they were ably represented by Lt. Vernon Baker (370th Regiment, 92d Division), at 77 the only man left alive of the seven who received their Medals of Honor that day. Baker commented:

> I was a soldier and I had a job to do. I was an angry young man. We were all angry. But we had a job to do, and we did it. I knew things would get better, and I'm glad to say that I'm here to see it—the only thing that I can say to those that are not here with me is, thank you, fellas, well done. And I will always remember you (quoted in Bennett 1997).

See also African American Officers; American Civil War; American Revolution; Antebellum Period; Apache Wars; Baker, Vernon Joseph; Battle Mountain, Korea; Boards of Examination for Officers in United States Colored Troops; Buffalo Soldiers; Bureau of Colored Troops; Carney, William Harvey; Cash, John Anthony, Sr.; Cleburne's Plan; Colonial America; Confederates, African American; Davis, Benjamin Oliver, Sr.; 1812, War of; Flipper, Henry Ossian; Fort Pillow Massacre; Fort Wagner, Battle of; Fox, John R.; Gulf War; Iwo Jima, Battle of; Korean War; Medal of Honor (APPENDIX); Militia Act of 1792; National Association for the Advancement of Colored People; National Guard; Olive, Milton Lee, III; Olustee, Battle of; Pancho Villa Campaign; Philippine Insurrection; Powell, Colin Luther; Red Ball Express; Selective Service Acts; Seminole-Negro Scouts; Service Units of World War II, African American; Smith, James Webster; Sol Legare Island, Battle of; Stowers, Freddie; U.S. Army, Interwar Period; United States Colored Artillery (APPENDIX); United States Colored Cavalry (APPENDIX); United States Colored Troops (APPENDIXES); Vietnam War; West Point; Wham Paymaster Robbery; World War I; World War II; World War II Infantry Replacements; Young, Charles; *individual units*

References and Further Reading

Anderson, Trezzvant. *Come Out Fighting: The Epic of the 761st Tank Battalion, 1942–1945.* Salzburg: Salzburger Druckerei und Verlag, 1945.

Arnold, Thomas St. John. *Buffalo Soldiers: The 92nd Infantry Division and Reinforcements in World War Two, 1942–1945.* Manhattan, KS: Sunflower University Press, 1990.

Barbeau, Arthur E., and Florette Henri. *The Unknown Soldiers: Black American Troops in World War One.* Philadelphia: Temple University Press, 1974.

Belknap, Michael R. *The Employment of Blacks by the Federal Government.* New York: Garland, 1991.

Bennett, James. "Medals of Honor Award at Last to Black World War II Soldiers." *New York Times,* January 14, 1997.

Berlin, Ira, Joseph Reidy, and Leslie S. Rowland, eds. *Freedom: A Documentary History of Emancipation, 1861–1867.* Series 2, *The Black Military Experience.* New York: Cambridge University Press, 1982.

Bigelow, John, Jr. *Reminiscences of the Santiago Campaign.* New York: Harper, 1899.

Binkin, Martin. *Blacks and the Military.* Washington, DC: Brookings Institution, 1982.

Buchanan, A. Russell. *Black Americans in World War Two.* Santa Barbara, CA: ABC-CLIO, 1977.

Bykofsky, Joseph, and Harold Larson. *The Transportation Corps, Operations Overseas: The United States Army in World War Two.* Washington, DC: Government Printing Office, 1957.

Cashin, Herschel V. *Under Fire with the 10th U.S. Cavalry.* New York: Arno Press, 1969.

Coffman, Edward M. *The War to End All Wars: The American Military Experience in World War One.* New York: Oxford University Press, 1968.

Cornish, Dudley T. *The Sable Arm: Black Troops in the Union Army, 1861–1865.* Lawrence: University Press of Kansas, 1987. Originally New York: Longmans Green, 1956.

Dalfiume, Richard M. *Desegregation of the U.S. Armed Forces: Fighting on Two Fronts, 1939–1954.* Columbia: University of Missouri Press, 1969.

Davis, Lenwood G., and George Hill. *Blacks in the American Armed Forces, 1776–1983: A Bibliography.* Westport, CT: Greenwood Press, 1985.

Department of Defense. *A Pictorial Documentary of the Black American Male and Female Participation and Involvement in the Military Affairs of the United States of America.* Washington, DC: Government Printing Office, 1991.

Donaldson, Gary A. *The History of African-Americans in the Military.* Malabar, FL: Krieger Publishing, 1991.

Eaton, Clement. *A History of the Southern Confederacy.* New York: Free Press, 1954.

Fletcher, Marvin. *The Black Soldier and Officer in the United States Army, 1891–1917.* Columbia: University of Missouri Press, 1974.

Foner, Jack D. *The U.S. Soldier between Two Wars:*

Army Life and Reforms, 1865–1898. New York: Humanities Press, 1970.
———. *Blacks and the Military in American History: A New Perspective.* New York: Praeger, 1974.
Foner, Philip S. *Blacks in the American Revolution.* Westport, CT: Greenwood Press, 1975.
Fowler, Arlen L. *The Black Infantry in the West, 1869–1891.* Westport, CT: Greenwood Press, 1971.
Gladstone, William A. *United States Colored Troops, 1863–1867.* Gettysburg, PA: Thomas Publications, 1990.
Glatthaar, Joseph T. *Forged in Battle: The Civil War Alliance of Black Soldiers and White Officers.* New York: Free Press, 1990.
Glass, Edward L. N. *History of the 10th Cavalry, 1866–1921.* 1921. Reprint, Fort Collins, CO: Old Army Press, 1972.
Hargrove, Hondon. *Buffalo Soldiers in Italy: Black Americans in World War Two.* Jefferson, NC: McFarland, 1985.
Heywood, Chester D. *Negro Combat Troops in the World War: The Story of the 371st Infantry.* Worcester, MA: Commonwealth Press, 1928.
Jefferson, Robert F. "African Americans in the U.S. Army during World War II." In *A Historic Context for the African-American Military Experience.* Edited by Steven D. Smith and James A. Ziegler. U.S. Army Corps of Engineers, 1998. https://www.denix.osd.mil/denix/Public/ES-Programs/Conservation/Legacy/AAME/aame4.html#Race,%20Labor,%20and%20War:
Johnson, Charles, Jr. *African American Soldiers in the National Guard: Recruitment and Deployment during Peacetime and War.* Westport, CT: Greenwood Press, 1992.
Johnson, Jessie J., ed. *A Pictorial History of Black Soldiers (1619–1969) in Peace and War.* Hampton, VA: Hampton Institute, 1969.
Kaplan, Sidney, and Emma Nogrady Kaplan. *The Black Presence in the Era of the American Revolution.* Amherst: University of Massachusetts Press, 1989.
Leckie, William H. *The Buffalo Soldiers: A Narrative of the Negro Cavalry in the West.* Norman: University of Oklahoma Press, 1967.
Lee, Ulysses. *The Employment of Negro Troops.* Washington, DC: Office of the Chief of Military History, 1966.
Little, Arthur W. *From Harlem to the Rhine: The Story of New York's Colored Volunteers.* New York: Covice Friede, 1936.
Lord, Francis A. *They Fought for the Union.* New York: Bonanza Books, 1960.
MacGregor, Morris J. *Integration of the Armed Forces, 1940–1965.* Washington, DC: Center of Military History, 1985. http://www.army.mil/cmh-pg/books/integration/IAF-FM.htm#TABLE%20OF%20CONTENTS.
McGuire, Phillip, ed. *Taps for a Jim Crow Army: Letters from Black Soldiers in World War Two.* Santa Barbara, CA: ABC-CLIO, 1983.
McPherson, James M. *The Negro's Civil War.* New York: Pantheon, 1965.
Mays, Joe H. *Black Americans and their Contribution towards Union Victory in the American Civil War, 1861–1865.* Lanham, MD: University Press of America, 1984.
Motley, Mary P. *The Invisible Soldier: The Experience of the Black Soldier in World War Two.* Detroit: Wayne State University Press, 1975.
Mullen, Robert F. *Blacks in America's Wars: The Shift in Attitudes from the Revolutionary War to Vietnam.* New York: Monad Press, 1974.
Nalty, Bernard C. *Strength for the Fight: A History of Black Americans in the Military.* New York: Free Press, 1986.
Nalty, Bernard C., and Morris J. MacGregor. *Blacks in the Military: Essential Documents.* Wilmington, DE: Scholarly Resources, 1981.
Patton, Gerald. *War and Peace: A Black Officer in the American Military, 1915–1941.* Westport, CT: Greenwood Press, 1981.
Quarles, Benjamin. *The Negro in the Civil War.* Boston: Little, Brown, 1953.
———. *The Negro in the American Revolution.* Chapel Hill: University of North Carolina Press, 1961.
———. *The Negro in the Making of America.* New York: Collier Books, 1964.
Redkey, Edwin S. *A Grand Army of Black Men: Letters from African-American Soldiers in the Union Army, 1861–1865.* New York: Cambridge University Press, 1992.
Rose, Arnold M. "Army Policies toward Negro Soldiers—A Report on a Success and a Failure." *Journal of Social Issues* 3 (Fall 1947): 26–31.
Schubert, Frank N. *On the Trail of the Buffalo*

Soldier. Wilmington, DE: Scholarly Resources, 1995.

Scipio, L. Albert. *The Last of the Black Regulars: A History of the 24th Infantry (1869–1951).* Silver Spring, MD: Roman Publications, 1983.

Scott, Emmett J. *Scott's Official History of the American Negro in the World War.* 1919. Reprint, New York: Arno Press, 1969.

Shapiro, Herbert. *White Violence and Black Response: From Reconstruction to Montgomery.* Amherst: University of Massachusetts Press, 1988.

Silvera, John D. *The Negro in World War Two.* Baton Rouge, LA: Military Press, 1946.

Utley, Robert M. *Frontier Regulars: The United States Army and the Indian, 1866–1891.* New York: Macmillan, 1973.

Wilson, Joseph T. *The Black Phalanx: A History of the Negro Soldiers of the United States in the Wars of 1775–1812, 1861–1865.* 1890. Reprint, New York: Arno Press, 1968.

Wynn, Neil A. *The Afro-American and the Second World War.* New York: Holmes and Meier, 1975.

U.S. Army, Interwar Period (1918–1941)

Despite the wholesale deployment of African American troops in the front line and in service units during World War I, the policies of the armed services toward racial minorities had changed little by the beginning of the interwar period. By the end, though resistance to using African Americans was still strong, changes were at least planned. It had proved to be impossible to simply return to the status quo before the war, partly because of the movement of increasing numbers of African Americans from the South to northern cities in search of manufacturing jobs. The pressure was on. It was in the U.S. Army that the most important changes took place; the other services tended to take their cue from the army.

The Dilemma after World War I

Despite the (rather belated) acceptance and involvement of African Americans in the army in the latter stages of World War I, relatively few African Americans were able to choose the U.S. Army as a career path after the war. With limited economic opportunities at home, the army was still seen as an honorable profession by African Americans, and it fell to the African American press and civil rights organizations to press the army to see to it that African American citizens received full recognition and were able to achieve their potential in the organization.

The general African American public fully expected that the courage and the loyalty of the 404,348 African American troops who had served during World War I would be taken as ample demonstration of their patriotism and loyalty to the country. The two African American divisions, the 92d and the 93d, had received considerable public and official attention during the conflict. Not all of the press was complimentary, but on the other hand, it was not only the African American press that contained examples of bravery under fire. Newspapers in Boston and Pittsburgh, for example, featured stories from which the African American public and U.S. citizens in general derived inspiration. What had shocked and dismayed African Americans across the country was the abuse from white officers, the discriminatory treatment, and the rumor that African American troops were being used as either shock troops or as laborers. Rumors were also rife of arrests, courts-martial, and examples of cowardice. The enforced retirement of a respected and successful African American officer, Col. Charles Young, on the eve of what he and many others expected to be his appointment to a field command, brought universal astonishment. As evidence later attested, the court-martial figures and the accusations of misconduct were much inflated. Without doubt, the command structure of the African American units, the men's own inexperience, the lack of equipment, and the contradictory orders they received, all taken together made the extent to which their performance was adequate even more remarkable under the circumstances. But those who were in the position of making the decisions seemed to be unable to realize how well the men had done.

It became a common feeling among those in command that in the event of another war, African American troops should not be deployed in combat. They should be used either as laborers or as support units for white units. If that turned out to be the case, any freedom, or at least relative lack of restriction, that had been seen during World War I would be much more curtailed in future conflicts.

In 1917, when the United States entered World War I, there was no distinct policy as to the employment of African Americans. The army, however, was determined to frame its own policy, and it was to the testimony of commanders in the field that the planners turned after the war. The testimony related to the 92d Division, the only African American division to operate as part of American forces in France. Testimony was from regimental and higher level commanders who condemned both African American officers and enlisted men. The evidence these commanders gave supported the conclusion that African American troops should not be assigned to combat duty. This conclusion was reinforced by similar evidence from the 93d Division, although it was at variance from the opinions of the French, with whom the regiments of the 93d served. The testimony of officers in the field who praised the performance of African Americans was ignored. The commanders of the four regular African American regiments (two cavalry, two infantry) that had not seen service in France were not consulted. Decisions were made based on the performance of non-regulars (volunteers, National Guardsmen, second draftees) by officials who had not actually led them in battle.

The War Department recognized that in the event of a major war, a considerable number of African Americans would have to be mobilized. What they had to decide was how these troops could be deployed into militarily efficient units. Since their plan was to use as few African Americans as possible in the peacetime army, the vast majority of those who were used in a major war would have little army experience. One approach was to ensure that, where deployed, African Americans would have white officers and noncommissioned officers. This was the proposal favored by the War Department; the alternatives were far more drastic. On the one hand the number of African Americans mobilized could be reduced to such a small figure that there would be no complications. Alternatively, instead of creating all–African American units, the army could integrate.

The first alternative would simply bring the same problems that had been prevalent in almost every regiment ever since African American units had been mobilized. Racial prejudices would be reinforced, and African Americans could quite rightly claim lack of opportunity and incentive, since they could not hope to become officers. The other two options were politically dangerous. If African American involvement were to be diminished, that would mean disbanding the four African American regiments, and white units would have to be created to replace them. As for integration, at this stage of U.S. history, African Americans invariably held subordinate positions in society. It was unthinkable that an African American would have a superior rank to a white man, yet in a fully integrated army, that would be inevitable.

Lack of Opportunity for African Americans

In 1866 and 1869, four African American regiments were firmly established by Congress. Four infantry regiments were merged into two in 1869, but the status of the two cavalry regiments and the two infantry regiments that remained was further reinforced by the Revised Statutes of 1878. The National Defense Act of 1920 stated that regular African American regiments were no longer required, but it was successfully argued that the 1920 defense act did not repeal the legislation governing their existence. The four regiments were retained. Legislative action would be required in order to deactivate the African American regiments; therefore the judge advocate general suggested a simple compromise. The regiments would be reduced in size, as had been the case in 1890. By 1921 six troops of the 9th and seven of the 10th had been demobilized or inactivated. Effectively, only African Americans who had been in the U.S. Army before April 1917 were retained. On June 30, 1922, it was the turn of the 24th Infantry to be reduced, yet the number of those offering themselves for reenlistment on the same day that they had been discharged was still high. The expedient hit upon was to cease new enlistments, and the net result was that opportunity to join or to gain promotion in African American regiments was rare.

In 1926 an expansion of the Air Corps had been ratified by U.S. Congress, which took place, incrementally, over the next five years, but overall, the army continued to shrink. The fifth increment, in 1931, meant that existing forces would have to be cut, resulting in further cuts to the four Regular Army units. The Air Corps did not accept African American enlistment, and so there was nowhere for the men to go. Comparatively speaking, the regiments were overstrength. With the economic depression of the 1930s, more African Americans wished to join the U.S. Army, but there was nowhere for them to be deployed. There were now calls for equality, and the National Association for the Advancement of Colored People (NAACP), in particular, saw the reductions in the African American regiments as incompatible with the army's claim that they were not discriminating against African American soldiers. By gradual reduction the four regiments were effectively withering away, mere skeletons of what they had once been.

Even the resumption of enlistment in 1934 did little to practically help African Americans join up. The four regiments were posted to remote locations, and enlistment required the physical presence of the volunteer to inquire whether there were any vacancies. The army did not help, as they did not provide funds for recruits to travel to these distant locations. In order to join the 25th, a trip to southeastern Arizona, where the regiment was stationed, was necessary. Under such conditions, the regiments themselves found it difficult to find and train qualified and fit young African American men. The opportunities for training were few, as each regiment had numerous elements on detached duties and there were few opportunities for anything other than routine work.

There had been a major change starting in the 1890s, in that African American units had been created for the National Guard, but during World War I, only the 369th Infantry (established as the 15th Infantry Regiment, New York National Guard on June 2, 1913) reached its full strength. Many suffered the fate of the 372d, which, although it consisted of two battalions and the nucleus of a third, was split between the District of Columbia, Massachusetts, and Ohio, with a further unit created in 1940, based in New Jersey. Any hope of training the 372d as a cohesive combat unit was in vain.

Elsewhere, the Reserve Officers' Training Corps (ROTC) for the most part only accepted African Americans at Howard University in Washington, D.C., and Wilberforce University in Ohio. At some northern universities, a few African Americans were allowed into ROTC, but only a few. African American reserve officers eligible for service numbered just 353 in 1940, and the consequence was that the only African American reserve regiment that was close to a full staff was the 428th Infantry in the District of Columbia.

In 1940, Junior ROTC facilities were established at the Hampton Institute, Virginia, the Tuskegee Institute, Alabama, Prairie View College, Texas, and North Carolina Agricultural and Technical College. There were other facilities in Washington and Chicago. Citizen's Military Training Camps had been authorized by Congress in 1920 to provide training for young men in the summer, but like the National

Guard units, these camps were largely unknown to the African American public, and as a result, comparatively few African American citizens offered their services.

Army Attempts to Solve the Problem

The army sought to deal with the thorny problem of how African Americans would be deployed in the event of a war in a 1922 plan, which effectively remained at the core of army thinking until the development of a new plan in 1937. According to the 1922 plan:

1. There would be no expansion of the four regular army regiments.
2. Since the states would retain control of the National Guard, the 1922 plan was limited to considering units in the Organized Reserves on a federal level.
3. Each corps area commander was to submit a plan for utilizing African American personnel in his area. Each corps area was expected to plan for use of approximately half of the African Americans in the corps area.

It seems that these policies were based on the following assumptions:

1. That the army recognized that policy had to appear to be fair but recognized the fact that a readily acceptable solution might not be forthcoming.
2. That in principle African American troops would be used in combat, but only because the white population, if African American troops were not used, would unfairly have to shoulder all the losses in a war.

In the plan itself, the authors of the plan explained some of their assumptions as follows:

> That the Negro is a citizen of the United States, entitled to all of the rights of citizenship and subject to all of the obligations of citizenship; that the Negro constitutes an appreciable part of our military manhood; that while not the best military material, he is by no means the worst; that no plan of mobilization for the maximum effort can afford to ignore such a fraction of the manhood, especially in these times when war makes demands upon the physical defectives and the women; and finally, that in a democracy such as ours political and economic conditions must be considered, and that decision must rest upon these two considerations alone (quoted in Lee 1966, 32–33).

The studies upon which the plan was formulated addressed the three most challenging issues: (1) the use of African Americans as combat troops, (2) the size and home stations of African American units, and (3) the race of officers for African American units.

As far as the use of African Americans as combat troops was concerned, psychological test data from World War I were used to indicate the probable intelligence of potential recruits. The test data were interpreted to mean that African Americans were less intelligent than their white counterparts. Nonetheless, the results showed a spread of intelligence across all of the recognized grades. It was therefore concluded that, although the tests indicated that large numbers of African Americans would be barred from combat duty by testing, this was no reason in itself not to use psychological tests in order to sift the entire population.

With regard to the size and deployment of African American units, the plan suggested that generally speaking these units should be smaller than their white counterparts. It was not deemed advisable to group these units as divisions, but to scatter them among white divisions, based on the evidence that African American units had performed well when grouped with white units in the past.

The third issue, which really focused on African American officers, was again considered on the basis of testimony from World War I that blamed African American officers for the comparative lack of success of the 92d and the 93d Divisions. The inference was that white officers would provide "proper" leadership, which African American troops would not receive from African American officers. On the other hand, the study did not rule out the possibility of African American officers:

> It is not reasonable to accept that the Negro will be willing to serve in the ranks with no hope of a commission. Moreover, it cannot be fairly stated that no Negro possesses the necessary qualities of leadership to make him an efficient officer. Not all our white officers are selected from the ranks of the most intelligent. As a matter of fact, we commission many white officers of only average intelligence. It follows that there must be some Negroes of intelligence equal to some of the whites who we commission. The trouble in the past has been that we have not demanded from the Negro the same standard of intelligence, grade for grade, as from the white (quoted in Lee 1966, 33–34).

The corps commanders were explicitly told not to create African American units if they did not have qualified African American officers to command them. Effectively this would mean that corps commanders had carte blanche not to accept African Americans. The plan was approved on December 23, 1922, and sent to the corps commanders on December 27. The corps commanders in turn were required to submit their mobilization plans, which were approved on July 12, 1923. The question of the use of African American manpower remained a sensitive issue, and, as a result, corps commanders were advised not to circulate the information contained in the plans. African American units were barely mentioned, even in the War Department's own plans, and in 1928 corps commanders were still not allowed to show their mobilization plans to units that would have African American troops. This order was not rescinded until 1938.

A plan based on a new set of studies came into existence in 1931. The fundamental assumptions remained the same:

1. That potential African American manpower was around 10 percent.
2. That African Americans should bear their share of responsibility in a war.
3. That military realities had to be the basis for policy, unlike World War I where political and racial issues took precedence over what could be considered to be sound military policy.
4. That unless the War Department had sound policies for the use of African Americans in combat units, prior to the outbreak of a war, they would be forced to use them as combat troops by necessity or political pressure once hostilities had gotten under way.

One major difference was that the 1931 plan stipulated that African American units would not be deployed in combat roles until after war had broken out and hostilities had begun. This would mean that competent officers could be deployed in white regiments rather than having to be reserved for African American ones.

It was hoped that for at least the first year of hostilities, the responsibility of combat would rest on the shoulders of white troops. After this period African American units would be mobilized, and large African American formations would only be created once the smaller units had demonstrated their ability to conduct combat operations.

The 1933 plan of mobilization showed that African Americans would account for only 31,245 of the 1,526,380 men in the initial mobilization. In other words, this figure was just 2.05 percent of the available total American manpower; proportionately, it should have been 9.45 percent, or approximately 144,000 men.

The War Department began another study of manpower in 1937; they hoped to avoid the problems that had arisen during World War I. In

1917 the first manpower registration of African Americans and whites between twenty-one and thirty years had identified 9,562,581, or 89.87 percent, whites, and 1,078,333, or 10.13 percent, African Americans. A widely disproportionate number of African Americans had been placed in the Class 1 category for unlimited service: Some 556,917 of the Class 1, or 51.65 percent of the available men, were African American, while 3,110,659, or 32.5 percent of the available men, were white. From early June to early September 1917 just 4,000 African Americans were called up, as opposed to 650,000 whites, which caused numerous complaints from the white population. Between September and December, however, the situation was reversed, and large numbers of African Americans were drafted, which led to complaints, both from the African American community and from white farmers, who were losing their agricultural workers.

The 1937 plan aimed to mobilize African Americans and whites proportionately and to call up the correct proportions from day one. However, due to the low numbers of African Americans in military units prior to mobilization, a disproportionate draft would have to be instituted to redress this imbalance before proportional call-ups could go into effect. The problem was readily apparent, in that African Americans only accounted for 1.8 percent, or 6,500, of the total of 360,000 in the regular army and the National Guard. Calculations were made on the basis of mobilizing a million men, which meant that 88,000 African Americans would have to be called up, in addition to the 552,000 whites to achieve the correct overall proportion. It was further recommended that African American combat units have half again as many company officers as white units. It was still widely believed that African Americans needed more training, closer supervision, and better-qualified noncommissioned officers in order to become effective soldiers.

The 1937 plan and the studies on which it was based were kept quiet, and publication and circulation suppressed. The Army War College and the War Department seem to have firmly believed that if the 1.8 percent African American manpower became public knowledge, it would lead to the call for either the creation of new African American regiments, or the replacement of white regiments with African American ones.

The mobilization regulations of 1937 took a significant period of time to be processed and published, and when they were, they included clear instructions as to how matters relating to African Americans were to be expressed:

1. African American manpower was to be indicated in the mobilization plans at a percentage of the total mobilized strength equal to the correct ratio of African American manpower to total manpower.
2. Each corps was to provide African American manpower that reflected the ratio of African Americans to the total manpower of their area's male population, and each corps would therefore have different African American ratios.
3. As much as possible, consistent with defense needs, African Americans were to serve in combat units, as opposed to service units, in the same proportion as whites.
4. African American units would be mobilized to full wartime strength as early as possible where that was believed to be useful for purposes of training.
5. Excluding African Americans assigned to labor pools and the like, African Americans were to be assigned to African American formations, and the warrant officers and enlisted men of those formations should all be African American.
6. Reserve officers for African American units of the Organized Reserves could be African American. Chaplains for African American Regular Army units could

be African American. Officers for African American organizations in garrison could be African American. National Guard units would have some positions in their African American units that could be filled by African Americans. All such assignments would depend on the availability of qualified African American personnel.

7. African American officer candidates would only be recruited in proportion to the number of replacements needed, and these candidates must be fully qualified.
8. The ratio of African Americans assigned to service command and the War Department (rather than to regiments) in an area should be at least in proportion to their representation in the population of that area.

The War Department fixed percentages of African Americans for each of the nine corps areas based on the white and African American populations:

1st Corps	1.26 percent
2d Corps	4.26 percent
3d Corps	11.25 percent
4th Corps	33.37 percent
5th Corps	6.45 percent
6th Corps	4.25 percent
7th Corps	5.58 percent
8th Corps	10.52 percent
9th Corps	1.03 percent

African American troops were to be assigned primarily to reserve infantry, cavalry, or artillery regiments, harbor defense units, ammunition trains, engineer/general service regiments, the quartermaster service, ordnance companies, service command units, and the War Department overhead installations. What is particularly significant is that the Protective Mobilization Plan of 1940, which arose from the 1937 policy, shows that instead of the African American manpower percentage of between 9 and 10 percent (as a proportion of the total manpower), only 5.81 percent of enlisted men were African American. Most of these men, as can be seen in the Protective Mobilization Plan, were assigned to the infantry, the engineers, and the quartermasters. All other areas of the army either had no African American units or very small ones. An analysis of the disposition of African American units in the Protective Mobilization Plan shows that the vast majority of African Americans were to be assigned to noncombat service units.

The War Department's Organization and Training Division (G-3) undertook a further examination of the provisions of the Protective Mobilization Plan in the summer of 1940. Some of the units no longer existed or were no longer required, and their absence would cause an imbalance between African Americans in combat units and service troops. G-3 recommended that African Americans be allowed to join all arms and services of the U.S. Army, with the exception of the Air Corps and the Signal Corps. Separate African American battalions would provide harbor defense and antiaircraft units, and would initially be commanded by African American officers. These could later be replaced with white officers if necessary. Splitting African American units into such small groups would make it very difficult to incorporate these battalions into a larger formation, while at the same time it would deal with the problem of deploying African American officers. The War Plans Division and the Personnel Division disagreed with G-3 with regard to exempting African Americans from the Air Corps and Signal Corps. The War Plans Division gave this explanation:

> It is neither desirable nor practicable in a major mobilization to exclude Negro manpower per se from any Arm or Service. Furthermore, it is the opinion of this Division that Negro manpower can be as successfully employed in some capacities in both the Air Corps and the Signal Corps as it is in the other Arms and Services. Any limitation in the use of Negroes in the Arms and Services must be predicated

A group of African American men enlist in the United States Army Air Corps, March 24, 1941. They will be assigned to the 99th Pursuit Squadron at Chanute Field, Illinois. This is the first time the Army Air Corps has opened its enlistment to African Americans. (Bettmann/CORBIS)

> upon the actual availability of personnel with required qualifications rather than upon any arbitrary elimination of the Negro as a whole on the grounds of lack of technical capacity. Our greatest difficulty with the Negro troops in the World War came not primarily from a lack of technical capacity, but from psychological factors and from faulty leadership (quoted in Lee 1966, 46–47).

The Personnel Division held that excluding African Americans from the Air and Signal Corps would make it impossible to maintain correct racial proportions within the U.S. Army, and would mean that African Americans would not incur their share of the risks of war. Nevertheless, the Air and Signal Corps, as far as G-3 was concerned, were not going to employ African Americans. G-3 pointed out that the chief of the Air Corps had taken a firm stand against using African Americans, at least until a complete African American unit could be established. Congress had already established that the Air Corps was not to train African Americans as pilots; the Civil Aeronautics Authority was given the responsibility of training African American pilots. These pilots, however, could not be used by the Air Corps. The inherent problem was that pilots were officers, and it was considered unthinkable that African American officers should have authority over white enlisted men.

The Signal Corps based its opposition on the grounds that it would be difficult to recruit competent African Americans, although they were willing to consider a separate African American stream of companies or battalions to service an African American division, if one were ever to be organized.

There were other major considerations. If African American troops were to be assigned to white divisions, as the Personnel Division had also recommended, this would mean that in each of the active divisions in the regular army and the National Guard, an African American regiment would supplant a white regiment. It was G-3's view that this would inhibit the combat efficiency of the units who had already trained together, and they doubted whether a mixed division would be efficient in combat.

As far as the African American media and public were concerned, the mobilization regulations were unknown; nevertheless, it was widely believed that African American troops would both be segregated and probably be used as laborers in the event of war. Those who did have some knowledge of the proposals did not feel that the plans were equitable. The War Department found itself in a difficult position; their Public Relations Bureau wrote on October 11, 1939:

> The War Department has given serious thought to questions involving the induction of Negroes into the military service. However, the War Department is not an agency which can solve national questions relating to the social or economic position of the various racial groups composing our Nation. The War Department administers the laws affecting the military establishment: it cannot act outside the law, nor contrary to the will of the majority of the citizens of the Nation (quoted in Lee 1966, 49).

On the eve of the greatest expansion of the U.S. Army in American history, the War Department had the following less than adequate position:

1. African Americans would be mobilized in proportion to the percentage they represented of men of military age.
2. African Americans would be mobilized early in order to build up and maintain the correct 9 to 10 percent figure.
3. They would be trained longer, if necessary, in order to ensure that they were fully trained.
4. African Americans would be assigned to all arms and services as long as they qualified.
5. African American troops would be used in combat, and the same ratio of African Americans would be assigned to combat units as was true of whites so that, statistically, an African American soldier would have as much chance as a white soldier of being assigned to a combat unit. This was the official position of the War Department, despite the fact that not all branches of the armed services had agreed to this, nor was it likely to be technically possible in all types of combat units.
6. Initially, African Americans would be assigned to all–African American units. These would be kept deliberately small and could be assigned to larger, white formations if necessary.
7. Larger African American troop units would only be routinely deployed into combat-ready units after smaller units of African Americans had proved themselves in combat.
8. Some positions for officers within African American units could be either African American or white, but African American officers would have to meet the same standards as white officers and be similarly trained.
9. In African American units it would be desirable to have 50 percent more officers than in white units.

10. African American officers could only command African American troops.
11. Initially, African Americans would be assigned to the Reserve and National Guard units and various service units.
12. As it turned out, these well-laid plans underwent a number of changes, many of which would not fit easily with accepted aspects of the use of African American troops. Various parts of the U.S. Army and the other services fought tooth-and-nail to retain the vestiges of policy that had been in place since World War I. Only the urgent need for more troops during World War II led to significant steps toward integration.

See also National Association for the Advancement of Colored People; Selective Service Acts; U.S. Army; World War I; World War II; Young, Charles

References and Further Reading

DuBois, William E. B. *The Gift of Black Folk.* Boston: Stratford, 1924.

Lee, Ulysses. *The Employment of Negro Troops.* Center of Military History United States Army: Washington, DC. 1966.

MacGregor, Morris J. *Integration of the Armed Forces, 1940–1965.* Washington, DC: Center of Military History, 1985. http://www.army.mil/cmh-pg/books/integration/IAF-FM.htm#TABLE%20OF%20CONTENTS.

MacGregor, Morris J., and Bernard C. Nalty, eds. *Blacks in the United States Armed Forces: Basic Documents.* 13 vols. Wilmington, DE: Scholarly Resources, 1977.

Scott, Emmett J. *Scott's Official History of the American Negro in the World War.* Chicago: Homewood Press, 1919.

U.S. Coast Guard

As the smallest of the five armed services, the U.S. Coast Guard has had a complex and long-standing relationship with African Americans. Initially, the Coast Guard discouraged African Americans, slave or free, from participating. During World War II, though, the organization led all the branches of the armed services in integrating its ranks. Surprisingly, after the war, the Coast Guard lagged behind the rest of the military in ensuring that African Americans were accorded opportunities to serve in all ranks.

On August 7, 1789, the first session of the U.S. Congress established the Coast Guard to combat smuggling and ensure the safety of ships in American waters. Originally named the Revenue Marine when it came into service on August 4, 1790, it soon became known as the Revenue Cutter Service. From the very beginning, the ships had a number of African American slaves on board in the roles of cooks, stewards, and seamen. Even the first commissioned officer of the Revenue Cutter Service, Hopley Yeaton, was accompanied on many of his voyages by his slave, Senegal.

After Congress banned the international slave trade in 1807, the Revenue Cutter Service took on the added responsibility of policing U.S. waters for those attempting to violate the law and import slaves from Africa or the West Indies. During the first ten years after the act had been passed, Revenue Cutter Service vessels stationed in Southern ports intercepted literally dozens of ships and recovered around 500 slaves.

Until 1843, both slaves and free blacks were employed in the Revenue Cutter Service, although their participation was discouraged by the organization's leadership and they were relegated to low-level jobs as cooks, stewards, and ordinary seamen. On November 2, 1843, the service enacted a new regulation that specifically prohibited slaves from working aboard its vessels. Slaves were barred "from ever being entered for the Service, or to form a complement of any vessel of the Revenue Marine of the United States" (cited in U.S. Coast Guard Historian's Office).

While both the army and navy changed their policies toward African Americans dramatically during the Civil War, the Revenue Cutter Service continued to treat blacks as they always had. The first sign of change came in March 1865, when President Abraham Lincoln awarded Michael Healy a commission as a third lieutenant, making him the first African American officer in the service. Healy enjoyed a long and successful career with the service, being promoted to second lieutenant in 1866 and first lieutenant in 1870. Sailing mostly in the northern seas around Alaska, Healy was appointed commanding officer of a vessel in 1877—the first African American to command a ship in the armed forces. He was considered to be one of the finest sailors ever to sail in the treacherous seas in the north and continued to receive promotions for the rest of his career. Stationed in Alaska, he was responsible for seizing sealers, drawing maps, dispensing justice, and carrying out a wide variety of missions. Through these many functions, he became one of the most distinguished individuals in Alaska at that time.

At the close of the nineteenth century, the United States became embroiled in a diplomatic wrangle with Spain, primarily over the status of the Spanish-held colony of Cuba, which had been agitating for its independence. Diplomacy quickly failed, and the United States found itself at war with the ailing Spanish Empire. With the island of Cuba lying so close to U.S. waters, the Revenue Cutter Service played a significant role in the naval portion of the Spanish-American War, with one battle involving a naval vessel receiving more attention than any other. On May 11, 1898, the Revenue Cutter *Hudson* sailed into the Spanish-held Cardenas Bay, along with two U.S. Navy gunboats and a torpedo boat. The service's two-gunned *Hudson* was to take part in a raid on the Spanish defenses, picking its way through the minefield, toward the seemingly defenseless Spanish gunboats lashed to the sugar wharves.

The U.S. torpedo boat, the *Winslow,* accompanied the *Hudson* as they closed with the Spanish ships and instantly the *Winslow* came under fire from the Spanish land batteries. In the first 20 minutes the *Hudson* fired 135 shells, its guns ably manned by, among others, an African American steward called Savage. With the Spaniards firing at the U.S. vessels from five different points in a period of around 30 minutes, the *Winslow* eventually suffered a critical hit; its boiler was destroyed, and the crew could no longer steer it. Gradually, the *Winslow* drifted toward the shore. The Spaniards then turned their attention to the *Hudson,* which was maneuvering to tow the *Winslow* out of danger. The *Hudson*'s commanding officer, 1st Lt. Frank H. Newcomb wrote in his report:

> Each and every member of the crew from the boatswain down to Moses Jones, the colored boy who attached himself to the after gun and never failed to have a shell ready when it was needed, did his whole duty cheerfully and without the least hesitation. This appears more the remarkable in view of the fact that none of them had ever been under fire before, and that the guns were without protection or shelter of any kind. They deserve the most substantial recognition in the power of the Government for their heroic services upon this occasion (quoted in U.S. Coast Guard Historian's Office).

On the recommendation of President William McKinley, Congress passed the following resolution:

> In the face of a most galling fire from the enemy's guns, the reserve cutter *Hudson* commanded by First Lieutenant Frank H. Newcomb, United States Revenue Cutter Service, received the disabled *Winslow,* her wounded commander and remaining crew. The commander of the *Hudson* kept his vessel in the very hottest fire of the action, although in constant danger of going ashore on account of the shallow water, until he finally got a line fast to the *Winslow* and towed that vessel out of range of the enemy's guns, a deed of special gallantry.
>
> I recommend that, in recognition of the single act of heroism of First Lieutenant Frank H.

> Newcomb, United States Revenue Cutter Service, above set forth, the thanks of Congress be extended to him, and to his officers and men of the *Hudson,* and that a gold Medal of Honor be promised to Lieutenant Newcomb, and a silver Medal of Honor to each of his crew who served with him at Cardenas (quoted in U.S. Coast Guard Historian's Office).

After the war ended, the Revenue Cutter Service returned to its normal peacetime duties, which had not changed much over the preceding 100 years, being charged with patrolling American waters for smugglers and helping ships and sailors in distress. In 1915, Congress ordered the merger of the Revenue Cutter Service with the Life-Saving Service, naming the new organization the U.S. Coast Guard. The Life-Saving Service had only existed since 1878, and African Americans seemed to have enjoyed relative equality with their white counterparts during that time. The men in this service were responsible for patrolling the beaches in search of floundering ships or sailors in distress, manning lifeboats and buoys, and maintaining lifesaving stations. The first African American lifesaving station keeper was Richard Etheridge, who was appointed in 1880 as keeper of the Pea Island Life-Saving Station in North Carolina. This station was also manned exclusively by African Americans.

When the United States entered World War I in April 1917, the newly formed U.S. Coast Guard assisted the U.S. Navy, both in providing homeland defense and in manning vessels sent into the war zone to transport troops, supplies, weapons, and ammunition. Many African Americans participated in this effort, although they were still generally held to low-level positions. No other African American officers had been commissioned after Healy, and African Americans were found almost exclusively in the lowest ranks and the worst jobs, such as cooks, stewards and messmen. Notably, the vast majority of African Americans in the Coast Guard served on shore duty, particularly in positions requiring large amounts of manual labor.

In the spring of 1942, shortly after the United States entered World War II, the Coast Guard was compelled to reevaluate the way in which it employed African Americans. In April of that year, the navy announced that African Americans would be admitted into the general service of the U.S. Navy, the U.S. Marines, and the U.S. Coast Guard, but this announcement did not offer as many opportunities for African Americans as it seemed to on first appearance. Other than in the capacity of messmen, blacks did not have many opportunities to serve aboard U.S. ships, as authorities strictly adhered to a program of segregation. So although African Americans would be more encouraged to join the Coast Guard by the navy's announcement, they would be restricted mostly to shore duties.

Compelled by the urgency of war, the Coast Guard moved quickly to implement the new policy, enlisting 150 African American volunteers later that spring and sending them to Manhattan Beach Training Station in New York. Although the classes were integrated, the barracks and messes were still segregated. Those who qualified after the four weeks of basic training could then go on to train for a variety of roles in the service, including radiomen, coxswains, electricians, yeomen, and pharmacists. But before officials had a chance to evaluate the success or failure of this new policy, the federal government declared that all recruitment for the branches of the military would occur through the draft. The Selective Service Act, which mandated the terms of the draft, included a provision for racial quotas, which brought many more African Americans into the Coast Guard.

Initially, the majority of the African American volunteers and draftees were assigned to shore duties, which remained strictly segregated but allowed for promotion, even to officer ranks. Those serving aboard ships as messmen had assigned battle stations that they might be required to take during combat situations but were otherwise restricted to menial positions. Only a handful of all–African American vessels existed in the Coast Guard at this time, one of which provided material assistance in sinking a German U-boat (submarine) in 1943.

The question of whether or not the Coast Guard should integrate its ships remained at the forefront of the minds of the organization's leaders. The general shortage of manpower meant that white sailors rotated off their ships for shore duty for periodic breaks from combat were not easily replaced with other white sailors. African American sailors were the obvious replacements, but authorities feared heightened racial tensions among an integrated crew. Therefore, blacks were stuck with shore duty, while whites had trouble getting their share of shore duty. The problem lay in two contradictory policies: segregation and rotating sea and shore duties. Coast Guard authorities were convinced that both policies were essential to maintaining vessels' combat effectiveness.

Nevertheless, the Coast Guard began to experiment with desegregation in 1943. In June of that year, Lt. Charlton Skinner proposed to captain a ship with an integrated crew. Coast Guard authorities approved the plan in November, and Skinner compiled his crew aboard the weather ship, USS *Sea Cloud*. Of the 173 men aboard, the crew included 4 African American officers and 50 African American petty officers and seamen. The *Sea Cloud* saw service off the coasts of France, Greenland, and Newfoundland and assisted in the sinking of a German U-boat in June 1944. Throughout these assignments, there had been remarkably little racial tension among the crew, marking the experiment a success. One other Coast Guard vessel, the USS *Hoqulan*, operated with an integrated crew and had a similar experience.

By July 1944, some 25 percent of African Americans in the U.S. Coast Guard were officers, the highest percentage in all of the armed services, even though African Americans only accounted for 2.1 percent (5,000 men) of the total manpower of the Coast Guard. The war also saw other advancements by African Americans in the Coast Guard. In 1944, Lt. (JG) Clarence Samuels became the first African American to command a major U.S. Coast Guard vessel (Light Vessel No. 115) since Michael Healy. In the same year, Ens. Harvey Russell became the first African American graduate of the Coast Guard Officer Candidate School in Yorktown, Virginia. In 1945, Olivia Hooker, D. Winifred Byrd, Julia Mosley, Yvonne Cumberbatch, and Aileen Cooke became the first African American women to enter the SPARs, the women's reserve of the Coast Guard, established in 1942. The U.S. Coast Guard's successful integration policy during World War II prompted the U.S. Navy to begin integration, which it did in 1945 with its auxiliary fleet.

Within a few years of the war's end in 1945, the Coast Guard had become fully integrated, officially adopting a policy of merit-based assignments and promotion. It served as a model for integration when the other branches of the armed services adopted, or were forced to adopt, policies of integration after President Harry Truman signed Executive Order 9981 on July 26, 1948, officially ending segregation.

However, African Americans still faced discrimination. At his inauguration parade in January 1961, President John F. Kennedy noted that there were no African American cadets in the Coast Guard Academy unit. He immediately called Secretary of the Treasury Douglas Dillon and ordered him to ensure that African Americans were enrolled in the next academy class. In 1966, Merle Smith became the first African American to graduate from the academy; the first African American women graduates were Angela Dennis and Daphne Reese in 1983.

Likewise, African Americans were slow to rise to the top ranks of the organization. In 1977, Bobby C. Wilks became the first African American to reach the rank of captain in the Coast Guard. In the following year, Manson K. Brown became the first African American to command the Cadet Brigade in the Coast Guard Academy's history. Not until 1998 did the Coast Guard commission its first African American admiral, Erroll M. Brown. These milestones occurred noticeably later than in other branches of the armed forces, despite the Coast Guard's initial acceptance of integration.

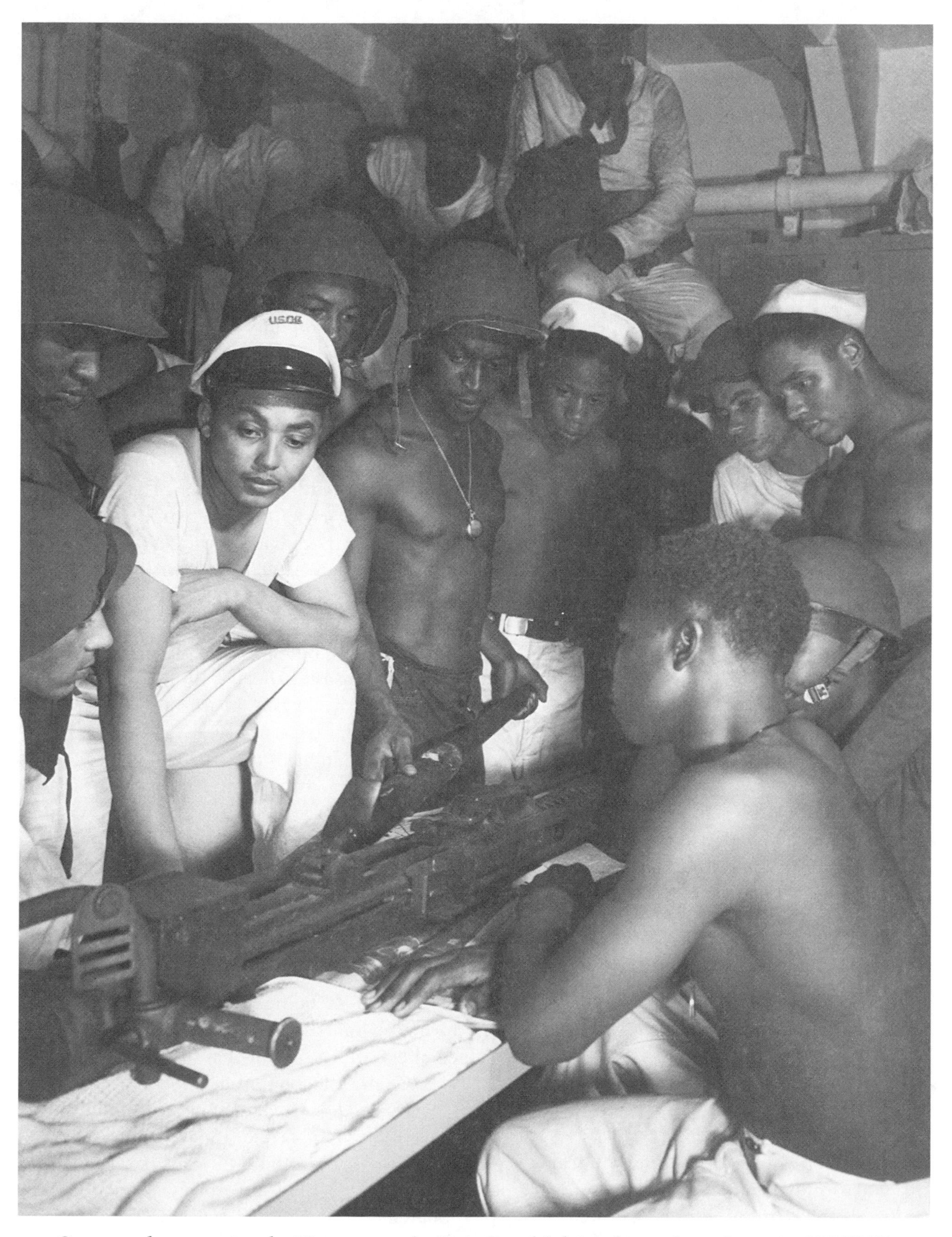

Crew members manning the 20 mm guns of a Coast Guard fighting ship in the early 1940s. (CORBIS)

See also Healy, Michael Morris; Selective Service Acts; Spanish-American War; U.S. Navy; World War II

References and Further Reading

Carbone, Elisa. *Storm Warriors.* New York: Alfred A Knopf, 2001.

Greene, Robert E. *Black Defenders of America, 1775–1973.* Chicago: Johnson Publishing, 1974.

MacGregor, Morris J. *Integration of the Armed Forces, 1940–1965.* Washington, DC: Center of Military History, 1985.

Strobridge, Truman R. *Blacks and Lights: A Brief Historical Survey of Blacks and the Old U.S. Lighthouse Service.* Washington, DC: U.S. Coast Guard Historians Office, 1975.

Townsend, Linda E., and Dupree Davenport. *A History of Blacks in the Coast Guard from 1790.* Washington, DC: Department of Transportation, 1977.

U.S. Coast Guard Historian's Office. "A History of African Americans in the Coast Guard." January 1999. http://www.uscg.mil/hq/g-cp/history/h_Africanamericans.html (accessed August 8, 2003).

United States Colored Troops

See Bureau of Colored Troops; U.S. Army; United States Colored Artillery (APPENDIX); United States Colored Cavalry (APPENDIX); United States Colored Troops (APPENDIXES); *individual units*

United States Colored Troops of Kentucky (Civil War)

African Americans from Kentucky provided significant numbers of men to serve in various units of the United States Colored Troops (USCT), as the African American regiments that fought for the Union in the Civil War were called. At least 23,703 men from Kentucky served in two cavalry, four heavy field artillery, and seventeen infantry regiments.

The first unit to be created was the 4th U.S. Colored Field Artillery (Heavy) in June 1863, and the last, the 125th U.S. Colored Infantry, was formed at Louisville, Kentucky, between February 12 and June 2, 1865. The men served across Kentucky, as well as fighting in a number of engagements elsewhere. Notably, those who stayed on garrison duty within the state saw action against Confederate guerrillas at Ghent, Haddix's Ferry, Harrodsburg, Lexington, and Owensboro.

African Americans from Kentucky also saw action in Virginia at Saltville, Marion, Petersburg, Richmond, Fort Harrison, Hatcher's Run, Portsmouth, and Bermuda Hundred; in Tennessee at Union City, Fort Donelson, Johnsonville, and Nashville; in North Carolina at Fort Fisher, Sugar Loaf Hill, Federal Point, Fort Anderson, Wilmington, Kinston, Goldsboro, Cox's Bridge, Raleigh, and Bennett's House; and in Arkansas at Duvall's Bluff.

The 109th, 114th, 116th, and 117th U.S. Colored Infantry witnessed the surrender of Robert E. Lee at Appomattox Courthouse on April 9, 1865. In the aftermath of the war a number of the regiments were sent to Texas and were engaged in operations along the Rio Grande until September 1866. The regiments involved in these operations to discourage French interference in Mexico were the 109th, 114th, 116th, 117th, 118th, and 122d. The 125th U.S. Colored Infantry not only had the distinction of being the last regiment to be formed when the unit ceased to exist on December 20, 1867, but it also became the last U.S. Colored Troop unit in the U.S. Army.

The 5th U.S. Colored Cavalry Regiment was created on October 24, 1864, and initially saw action in Virginia and Kentucky. It was engaged in Burbridge's Raid into southwestern Virginia (September 20–October 17, 1864) and later in Stoneman's Raid (December 10–29, 1864).

Throughout the first eight months of 1865 the regiment operated in Kentucky and Tennessee; it was transferred to the Department of Arkansas in August 1865, where it remained until it was mustered out on April 20, 1866.

The 6th U.S. Colored Cavalry Regiment also saw action during Stoneman's Raid, and in January it was transferred to Camp Nelson and Paducah, Kentucky. From March to May 1865 the regiment was in operations in Tennessee.

In addition to the 4th U.S. Colored Field Artillery (Heavy) Regiment, Kentucky also provided men for the 8th and the 12th regiments. The 4th had formerly been known as the 2d Regiment Tennessee Heavy Artillery (African descent). It operated in Kentucky, Tennessee, and Arkansas until it was mustered out on February 25, 1866. The 8th was first designated 1st Regiment Kentucky Heavy Artillery (African descent), then the 7th, and finally the 8th. The regiment operated largely from Paducah, Kentucky, but saw action at Haddix's Ferry, on August 27, 1864. The regiment was mustered out of service on February 10, 1866. The 12th saw postings exclusively in Kentucky, most frequently at Camp Nelson and at Bowling Green. The regiment was mustered out of service on April 24, 1866.

See also American Civil War; United States Colored Artillery (APPENDIX); United States Colored Cavalry (APPENDIX); United States Colored Troops (APPENDIXES)

References and Further Reading

Brown, Kent Masterson. *The Civil War in Kentucky: Battle for the Bluegrass State.* Mason City, IA: Savas Publishing, 2000.

Colling, Benjamin Franklin. *Fort Donaldson's Legacy: War and Society in Kentucky and Tennessee, 1862–1863.* Knoxville: University of Tennessee Press, 1997.

Harrison, Lowell H. *Civil War in Kentucky.* Lexington: University Press of Kentucky, 1995.

Sears, Richard D. *Camp Nelson, Kentucky: A Civil War History.* Lexington: University Press of Kentucky, 2002.

U.S. Marine Corps

Although now a fully integrated service of the armed forces, the U.S. Marine Corps was the last to accept African American enlistment into its ranks during World War II. Nevertheless, there is evidence to suggest that African Americans have been present in the Marine Corps since April 1776.

Early History

According to the few still existing muster and pay rolls of the American Revolutionary period, three African Americans served in the ranks of the Continental Marines (the U.S. Marine Corps predecessor) and ten others were marines with the state navies of Connecticut, Massachusetts, and Pennsylvania. Evidence suggests that a slave belonging to William Marshall from Wilmington, Delaware, was recruited into the Continentals by a Capt. Miles Pennington in April of 1776 to serve on the vessel *Reprisal.* The man, variously known as Keto and John Martin, had joined with the permission of his master. His service was cut short when the ship went down with nearly all hands off the coast of Newfoundland in October 1777. Two other contemporaries were definitely fighting troops. The first was Isaac Walker, who appears on the muster rolls of Capt. Robert Mullan's company of Continental Marines at Philadelphia on August 27, 1776. He is clearly identified as being an African American. On October 1, he was joined by an individual intriguingly described as "Orange . . . Negro" (quoted in Shaw and Donnelly 1975, ix). Both of the men remained on the musters until at least April 1, 1777, which suggests that they may have fought at the second battle of Trenton on January 2, 1777, and at the battle of Princeton on January 3, 1777.

The Continental Marines ceased to exist in 1784, but ten years later Congress agreed to the building of six frigates, which were each to contain a complement of marines. An order from the secretary of the navy on March 16, 1797, effectively barred African Americans from serving on board these new ships within the marine companies. On July 11, 1798, Maj. William Ward Burrows was appointed the commandant of the newly reformed Marine Corps. Burrows reiterated the secretary of the navy's instruction not to recruit African Americans, as evidenced in a letter to Lt. John Hall, who was a Marine Corps recruitment officer operating in Charleston, South Carolina: "You may enlist as many Drummers and Fifers as possible, I do not care what Country the D & Fifers are of but you must be careful not to enlist more Foreigners than as one to three natives. You can make use of Blacks and Mulattoes while you recruit, but you cannot enlist them" (quoted in Shaw and Donnelly 1975, ix).

Few records related to the nineteenth century detail the recruitment and muster rolls of the fledgling U.S. Marine Corps. Although it was acceptable practice for African Americans to serve as seamen on board ships where marines were also deployed, it is not clear whether African Americans in any number managed to be accepted into the Marine Corps itself. It is probable that those who were recruited were musicians, along the lines of the instructions from Burrows, not strictly speaking fighting men, but that is not to say that they did not face the same dangers and deprivations as the other men in the Marine Corps. Still, officially the Marine Corps was for whites only.

World War II

One hundred and fifty years of whites-only tradition came under threat June 25, 1941, with President Franklin D. Roosevelt's Executive Order No. 8802, which forbade racial discrimination in the defense industries and the government and established the Fair Employment Practices Commission, and the Selective Service Act of 1940, which outlawed discrimination in selection and training in the armed forces. Brig. Gen. Thomas E. Watson was given the task by the U.S. Marine Corps Commandant Maj. Gen. Thomas Holcomb to implement Executive Order No. 8802. The Corps, however, as the service most resistant to change, took the position that African Americans were utterly unsuited to become marines. Generally, the requirements of the order were considered an unnecessary nuisance, given the fact that the Corps was preparing for their inevitable involvement in a new world war.

After Pearl Harbor in December 1941, Holcomb gave evidence at a General Board of the Navy on January 23, 1942, and stated that the efficiency of the Corps would be impaired if they were forced to take African Americans into the service. Holcomb, however, realized that he was fighting against a tide of opinion that he could not stem and added additional reasons for not wanting to accept African Americans into the Corps at that time. He first referred to the question of the availability of officers to train the African Americans, stating that he would need "the best type of officer on this project, because it will take a great deal of character and technique to make the thing a success, and if it is forced upon us we must make it a success." But the numbers of available officers were limited: "They simply can not be spared if we are going to be ready for immediate service with the fleet." From the Corps perspective, his concluding remarks are particularly telling: "The Negro race has every opportunity now to satisfy its aspirations for combat, in the army—a very much larger organization than the Navy or Marine Corps—and their desire to enter the naval service is largely, I think, to break into a club that doesn't want them" (cited in Shaw and Donnelly 1975, 1).

Roosevelt, Congress, and African Americans in general would have none of this, and the pressure mounted on Holcomb and the Corps to institute plans for the acceptance of African Americans without any further delay. Though the navy still drew criticism because it allowed African Americans only into the steward service or auxiliary roles, and the other services because they still maintained very strict segregation, at least the U.S. Army, Navy, and Air Force had already put plans into action. The Corps was lag-

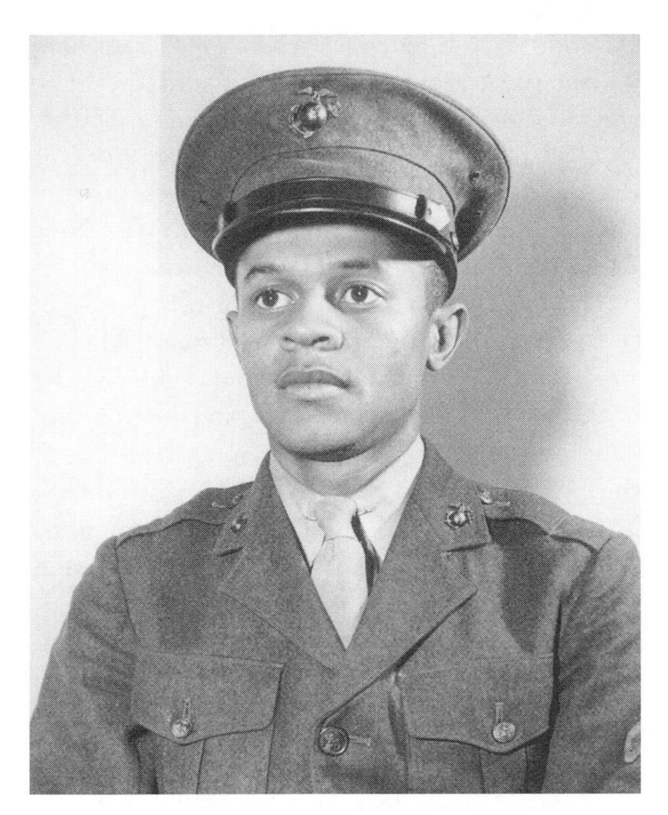

Howard P. Perry, the first African American to enlist in the U.S. Marine Corps. Breaking a tradition of 167 years, the Marines started enlisting African Americans on June 1, 1942. (National Archives)

ging behind in developing a plan, and it was inevitable that they drew the greatest criticism from the administration, the press, activists, and the African American population.

On April 7, 1942, in a statement from the secretary of the navy, Frank Knox, it was announced that the Marine Corps, the navy, and the coast guard would all be recruiting African Americans as soon as was practicable once training facilities were in place. The navy moved first, on June 1, by recruiting 1,000 African Americans per month for general service, with no restrictions on the branches of the navy open to African Americans. A century and a half of opposition from the Marine Corps ended with the statement that in July 1942 a full battalion of African Americans would be created. Future general Ray A. Robinson told the story this way:

> When the colored came in, we had the appropriations and the authority, and we could have gotten 40,000 white people. It just scared us to death when the colored were put on it. I went over to Selective Service and saw General Hershey, and he turned me over to a lieutenant colonel—that was in April and he was one grand person. I told him, "Eleanor [Roosevelt] says we gotta take in Negroes, and we are just scared to death; we've never had any in; we don't know how to handle them; we are afraid of them." He said, "I'll do my best to help you get good ones. I'll get the word around that if you want to die young, join the Marines. So anybody that joins [has] got to be pretty good!" And it was the truth. We got some awfully good Negroes (quoted in Shaw and Donnelly 1975, 1–2).

Holcomb appointed the South Carolinian Col. Samuel A. Woods Jr. to lead the training of the African American marines. He had had twenty-five years service in the Corps, and he became the first commanding officer of the 51st Composite Defense Battalion and the Montford Point Camp, which would serve as the training center for the men. Woods presented his plans in April 1942; with a budget of $750,000, he proposed the establishment of a new camp that would take 1,000 African Americans for a six-month training program culminating in the establishment of the first battalion. The officers of the battalion would be white, but the non-commissioned officers would be eventually drawn from the best of the recruits.

On May 15, Holcomb sent out letters of instruction to the Recruiting Divisions (Central, Eastern, and Southern), with the public announcement of the recruitment drive being made five days later. Men started reporting to the recruiters on June 1. Interestingly, Holcomb had decided to ensure that the first African American battalion should contain representatives from all parts of the United States, and he allotted recruitment targets to each of the three divisions. Five hundred of the men would come from the South, while the eastern and central regions would provide 200 each.

Although the Corps had accepted that African American recruitment was inevitable, it is clear that the intention from the outset was not to create an integrated force. The men would be required to have the same aptitudes and fitness required of white recruits, but they would not only be set apart in segregated units, their role would be restricted by the terms of their enlistment. The recruits would be designated as Class III(c) of the Marine Corps Reserve, and therefore assigned to inactive duty in a General Service Unit; moreover, their contracts were stamped with the word "Colored." The first two African Americans to enlist on the first day of the recruitment at Pensacola, Florida, were Alfred Masters and George O. Thompson.

The first batches of recruits were specifically chosen for abilities that qualified them to help get the camp ready for the main influx of men. Most of the recruits had a burning desire to join what they figured was the best fighting service, and many also simply wanted to be the first to break down the final barrier in the armed forces. Some of the men were not averse to lying in order to be accepted into the Corps, such as a young Bostonian named Obie Hall who claimed to be a truck driver when questioned by a recruiting sergeant. In fact he was not, but the white lie ensured that Hall would become the first man of the first squad of the first platoon when he reported to Montford Point on September 2, 1942.

The battalion was officially activated on August 18, 1942, and the first three recruit platoons consisted of forty men each, with several newly designated members of the Special Enlisted Staff (SES), a unit specifically assigned to each of the platoons. There was a shortage of white noncommissioned officers, and it was hoped that African Americans qualified to become NCOs could quickly be identified from the initial batch of recruits. The 51st Composite Defense Battalion was to consist of 1,200 men, who would continue to arrive at Montford Point until the target had been reached. There was a good deal of sifting out, and the attrition rate was around 50 percent. The facility consisted of a headquarters building, a chapel, two warehouses, a theater, a barbershop, a beer hall, a dispensary, a mess hall, quarters for the SES, a generator plant, a motor transport compound, an officers' club, and 120 prefabricated huts for the men. The nearest town was Jacksonville, and as the camp was located beside the New River, the men were plagued by mosquitoes.

The most colorful character of this period in the history of the African American Marine Corps was a man who had been a regular in the 25th Infantry Regiment and a navy mess attendant and steward, Gilbert Johnson. At the age of thirty-seven he had volunteered to join the U.S. Marine Corps; he later became known as "Hashmark" Johnson. There were other men who had considerable previous service, including George A. Jackson, who had been a lieutenant in the 10th Cavalry. He and Johnson went on to become well-known drill instructors. Among the other men were a number of college graduates, including Charles F. Anderson, who became the first African American sergeant major in the Marine Corps, and Charles W. Simmons, a man with postgraduate qualifications who also became a sergeant major. Two men emerged as expert exponents of hand-to-hand combat, Arvin L. Ghazlo, who was a former bodyguard, and Ernest Jones.

The first recruits finished their initial training at the end of November and were sent to Camp Lejeune for live fire training. Of the first group nearly 200 of the men now proudly wore their marksman or sharpshooter badges. On November 19, sixteen men were made private first class, and these men were the first among many who would remain at Montford Point in order to see the rest of the battalion through their training. There was a rude awakening in December 1942, when the men were first given a short period of leave that enabled them to visit Jacksonville, only to find the town, warned of their coming, virtually closed. The Montford Point authorities rallied to their aid and organized trucks to take them to larger towns outside the state, but on their return they encountered the full Jim Crow discrimination. They were made to sit at the back of buses or refused a ride altogether. On at least one occasion the marines banded together, threw off the bus driver, and drove the bus back to Montford Point themselves.

By late December some of the men were being trained to use artillery pieces, and by now the rifle company of the 51st had been created. Again when the men were allowed leave over the Christmas period, several were arrested for impersonating marines: so little was known of their existence.

In January 1943, under the terms of the Selective Service Act, the Marine Corps was required to increase African American recruitment up to the statutory 10 percent. This meant that among the 99,000 men the corps would recruit during 1943, nearly 10,000 would need to be African American. It was, therefore, proposed that a stepped-up recruitment system be instituted, calling for 400 recruits in February and March, 800 in April, 1,300 in May, and 1,000 for each month for the rest of the year. This meant that Montford Point had to be enlarged, and in keeping with the policy of segregation, part of the solution was not to draft troops into Composite Defense Battalions but to create a stewards branch, which was authorized on January 1, 1943. It was agreed that the February and March intake would be absorbed into the 51st, a new camp would be established, and a Mess Attendant's School and an Officers, Cooks, and Stewards School would be formed. The vast majority of Montford Point marines were relegated to noncombat battalions. The first batches of the previous year's recruits enjoyed the advantages of promotion and the promise of some kind of combat duty.

On March 11 the Headquarters and Service Company, Headquarters Battalion, was created and the recruit Depot Battalion was activated. Colonel Woods, who had commanded the Montford Point camp, was replaced by Lt. Col. W. Bayard Onley, and by April hundreds of new recruits were pouring in. The majority of the white drill instructors had left Montford Point by the end of April, to be replaced with African American drill instructors, including Hashmark Johnson. If anything, the new African American drill instructors made the new recruits' lives more miserable than their white predecessors had done. Johnson even referred to himself as an ogre; he was determined that every single man who graduated from the camp would bring glory to the Corps and honor to his race. With the arrival of prominent musicians such as Lt. Robert Troup Jr., the camp established a rich reputation for its music. By the closing months of 1943, the 51st and other depot companies were preparing to embark for the Pacific, and a number of stewards were ready to take up positions in officers' messes around the world.

There had been a change of plan regarding the 51st, and it was recommended that it become a heavy defense battalion and that the rifle company and the 75 mm Howitzer battery be detached to form an infantry battalion. The men still believed that they would be used only for labor duties, but on June 7, 1943, the word "composite" had been dropped from the unit's title, and a machine gun group and an artillery group had been added. The men still continued their training throughout 1943, and by July the company had reached 1,700 men; it was now clear that the unit would be split, and the 52d Defense Battalion was slated to begin organization at the beginning of 1944.

On August 20, 1943, the U.S. Marine Corps suffered its first African American casualty, Cpl. Gilbert Fraser Jr., who died in a fall. The main road from the camp to the artillery area was named after him. The battalion left Montford Point and took over the Camp Knox site in September 1943; here they continued with their combat training. An inspection of the unit, which included Secretary of the Navy Frank Knox and the commandant of the Marine Corps, General Holcomb, indicated that the men were ready for action.

Lt. Col. Floyd A. Stephenson sought orders for his 51st and discovered that their embarkation instructions had been delayed, but that he would have to lose 400 men in December to begin the formation of the 52d. At around the same time, white noncommissioned officers and instructors were transferred out of the 51st and replaced with African Americans, which meant that embarkation was imminent. Finally, in early January preparations began, and by January 19 the majority of the 51st had finally left for their embarkation ports. Shortly before the departure, there was a potentially serious incident involving some of the last of the 51st still at Montford Point, who became involved in a brawl with military police. Cpl. Rolland J. Curtiss was wounded in the melee, but it could not be established who fired the shot. Nevertheless, the majority of the men were now at San Diego and proudly wearing their United States Marine Corps badges, with the 51st emblazoned above.

Even here, at Camp Elliott, the men faced discrimination when they were told to sit at the back of the cinema. It was here, too, that they lost Lieutenant Colonel Stephenson, who was replaced by Col. Curtis W. LeGette, who had been in the Marine Corps since 1910.

On February 11 the troops left for the Ellice Islands to relieve the 7th Defense Battalion. They were to provide garrisons for Nanomea Island, Funafuti, and Nukfeteau. The first detachment was landed on February 25 and the remainder on February 27. The islands were something of a backwater, and although the bases needed to be protected, they were rarely used except for emergencies and repairs. The period was dominated by continued practice and boredom, interrupted only by a few shots at an enemy submarine on March 28. The efficiency of the battalion, despite constant training, was a grave concern to the new commander, but by July the battalion was involved in preparations to move to a more forward area of the theater.

The 51st sailed on September 8 and headed for Eniwetok Atoll, a major support base for the Mariana Islands. They arrived on September 14, and took over responsibility for a number of islands. Again they trained and retrained. On December 13, 1944, LeGette was replaced by Lt. Col. Gould P. Groves, who had known the battalion since 1943. Again the men lapsed into boredom, and although there were a number of alerts, they failed to see the enemy.

On June 12, 1945, elements of the battalion were detached and sent to Kwajalein, but still they saw no combat. In late November the battalion was replaced, and they sailed for Pearl Harbor, docking at San Diego on December 10. The battalion was formally disbanded on January 31, 1946.

Meanwhile, the 52d, based on its cadre of 400 men from the 51st, was entrusted to Col. Augustus W. Cockrell, who had been commissioned into the corps in 1922. The 52d did not suffer the same difficulties in training that had inevitably been present at first, and the men proved to be quickly proficient. After some reorganization in the summer of 1944, on July 12, Lt. Col. Joseph W. Earnshaw took over the battalion, and in August training was completed at Montford Point. After further reorganization on August 15, the battalion was ready for embarkation. By August 19 effectively two different parts of the battalion had been established, and by August 24 the 52d had arrived at Camp Pendleton, California.

On September 21, 1944, the battalion left San Diego for Pearl Harbor, then sailed on to the Marshall Islands on October 8. Their destination was the Majuro Atoll. Here part of the battalion was disembarked on October 17, but the remainder sailed on, landing at Kwajalein Atoll on October 22. Both groups were engaged in test firing.

Potentially, they could face the enemy, who still occupied a number of the islands in the area. A detachment was deployed to reconnoiter and clear some of the smaller atolls of Japanese troops, and in December the battalion took their first Japanese prisoners. By April 1, 1945, the fluid front line of the Pacific War had moved closer to Japan, and the 52d was identified as a unit to become engaged in the Okinawa operations.

The first detachments landed at Guam on March 24, and here there were still hundreds of Japanese troops who had become isolated after the main fighting had ceased. The 52d sent out patrols and laid ambushes and claimed their first enemy kill on April 1. On April 13 more enemy soldiers were encountered, and this pattern continued throughout the month and into May. On May 5, after all of the battalion had been reunited, they started intensive training for another move forward, now under the command of Lt. Col. Thomas C. Moore. A date of June 15 was given. It was clear to the corps that the men had performed extremely well on Guam and that they were experienced enough to deal with more aggressive opposition. As it turned out, the move was delayed, and although loading had started on July 9, the movement order was cancelled and they remained on Guam. This was a great disappointment to the men, but they continued their patrols and engagements with pockets of Japanese resistance. In the event, movement orders did come, but the movement took them farther away from combat. The 52d sailed to Kwajalein and Eniwetok to relieve the 51st.

After the end of the hostilities many of the men who had been in the battalion long enough to warrant a return to the United States were given permission at the beginning of February 1946. Many of the other men were transferred to Saipan to form the Heavy Anti-Aircraft Group (Provisional). The troops arriving back in San Francisco who had been with the original volunteers in 1942 were processed and discharged through Camp Pendleton. On March 13, 1946, the remaining men still part of the 52d Defense Battalion embarked at Guam and headed for San Diego, arriving there on March 26, where they were discharged at Camps Pendleton and Lejeune. By May 15, 1946, after the last discharges were completed, the 52d Defense Battalion ceased to exist. The unit was redesignated the 3d Anti-Aircraft Artillery Battalion (Composite) and was finally disbanded on May 15, 1947. The remaining men were temporarily transferred into provisional depot companies, and some were sent to join the headquarters company at Montford Point.

While the 51st and 52d Defense Battalions waited impatiently for combat opportunities, it was the units who had not been designated as combat units that found themselves in the firing line and suffered casualties during the war. Those soldiers who found themselves in combat came from the troops that were originally designated as labor units, such as those in the depot and ammunition companies. It was these men who accounted for most of the 7 African American Marines who were killed in combat, the 78 who were wounded, the 9 who suffered from combat fatigue (probably what is now designated post-traumatic stress disorder), and the 35 who died from a variety of other causes.

Given the nature of the type of war facing the United States in the Pacific, it was necessary to have a sophisticated means of supplying, supporting, and reinforcing the combat units. It was essential that all forms of transportation be smoothly organized in a foolproof way. The enormous distances between each area of contact with the enemy meant difficulties that must not be underestimated, and the logistical headaches involved required the deployment of an almost equal number of men to those who were actually engaged in combat. The U.S. Marine Corps established a system by which each support unit was responsible for dealing with specific types of supplies. They were also responsible for the salvaging and recycling of equipment when possible and appropriate.

Initially, the Marine Corps lacked their own stevedores and had to use combat troops to perform this function. By 1943 the increasing numbers of African American troops entering the U.S. Marine Corps offered a solution to the supply problem. Many thousands of the men who graduated from Montford Point were transferred into supply units. The first unit, the 1st Marine Depot Company, was activated at Montford Point on March 8, 1943, commanded by Capt. Jason M. Austin Jr. It consisted of two platoons and a headquarters, amounting to 3 officers and 110 enlisted men. Initially, as was the pattern with most of the African American units, they had white noncommissioned officers, but these were replaced with African American noncommissioned officers as men moved up through the ranks. By 1944 all of the depot companies leaving Montford Point had their full complement of African American NCOs. This process of replacing white NCOs with African Americans was formalized on March 14, 1943, in a set of instructions issued by the commandant of the Marine Corps known as Letter of Instruction 421. It instructed unit commanders to find African Americans "having the requisite qualities of intelligence, education and leadership to become non-commissioned officers" (quoted in Shaw and Donnelly 1975, 30).

Between March and September 1943, ten depot companies were created. It was then decided that a different form of unit structure would be created, a form that became known as a marine ammunition company. These companies would work alongside white ordnance companies in field and base depots. It was the ammunition company's role to load, unload, and guard ammunition. They would be responsible for moving the ammunition from its point of arrival to the front line. The first such unit, the 1st Marine Ammunition Company, was again created at Montford Point, under 2d Lt. Placido A. Gomez on October 1, 1943. The training of these units was fairly basic, and the men were given just two months to become proficient in handling ammunition. The units were given a white staff noncommissioned officer and eight officers to help instill in the men the safety requirements of the role they were fulfilling. Each of the ammunition companies consisted of four platoons, with a total of 251 enlisted men. The emphasis was on teamwork, as the men were very reliant upon one another, due to the dangerous nature of the work involved.

Between October 1943 and September 1944 one ammunition company and two depot companies were created each month at Montford Point. The last of the twelve ammunition companies was activated on September 1, 1944, and the last of the marine depot companies was activated on October 1, 1945, by which time there were fifty-one in existence.

There were considerably different attitudes about these men who were being posted into these two different sorts of unit. The officers of the depot companies did not expect their men to see combat, and so often only required the men to have strong backs and stamina; the officers of the ammunition companies knew their men were likely to find themselves under fire, and so took the infantry training very seriously. Still, all of these men were armed and trained (to some extent) with rifles and side arms.

The 1st Marine Depot Company left Montford Point just three weeks after it had been organized, arriving at San Diego on April 5, 1943. On April 16 they boarded the USS *Hunt* and two days later sailed for New Caledonia. This became the route taken by most of the depot and ammunition companies en route to the Pacific. The 1st was bound for the 1st Base Depot, which was supporting the U.S. Marine operations in the Solomons, where they had just ended the battle of Guadalcanal. A second depot company, the 4th, was created in New Caledonia in April, which absorbed existing quartermaster personnel. They were moved to the island of Banika, north of Guadalcanal, to help support U.S. Marines as they pushed into the Solomons. A number of the following units, both depot and ammunition companies, also moved into this area by the middle of 1944 in the final operations aimed at eliminating Japanese resistance in New Britain.

When the 1st Marine Depot Company arrived in Noumea in May, it provided vital relief to the hard-pressed troops on the base. By June 30, the 2d and 3d companies, which had been formed at Montford Point in April, also arrived at Noumea. The 4th Marine Depot Company accompanied the 1st to Guadalcanal on board the USS *Crescent City*, leaving on August 5 and arriving on August 12. They were then shipped on to Banika, arriving on August 13. From then on for a short period they experienced Japanese bombing raids. Other African American units were transferred straight from Montford Point to Hawaii, Samoa, the Gilberts and Marshalls, and Pearl Harbor itself.

By the spring of 1944 African American U.S. Marine units were spread across the whole of the Pacific from Hawaii to Guadalcanal. On June 15, 1944, the U.S. Marine Corps turned its attention to Saipan in the Marianas. The 7th Field Depot was assigned to deal with supplies for the 2d and 4th Marine Divisions of the V Amphibious Corps. These included the 3d Marine Ammunition Company and the 18th, 19th and 20th Marine Depot Companies. Simultaneously the 5th Field Depot, based on Guadalcanal, was to provide support for the 3d Marine Division and the 1st Provisional Marine Brigade (III Amphibious Corps), who were due to attack Guam. The 5th Field Depot included the 2d and 4th Marine Ammunition Companies.

African American Marines landed on Saipan on D-Day (June 15, 1944). Here the 3d Marine Ammunition Company came under intense Japanese artillery fire but escaped without injury. Pfc. Leroy Seals, in another African American unit, was wounded and died of his injuries the following day. Although the support troops were not designated as combat units, they were forced to assist in the defense of the beachhead perimeter and beat off Japanese counterattacks. Depot companies also landed on June 15, with both the 18th and 20th in support of the 4th Marine Division and the 19th in support of the 2d. They unloaded ammunition and equipment under heavy fire near Charan Knoa, and four of the 18th's men were wounded by mortar fire. During the night of June 15, Japanese infiltrators managed to slip through a gap between the 23d and 8th Marines, and the 18th Depot Company assisted in dealing with them.

The exploits of the depot companies and ammunition companies are amply evidenced by a contemporary press account by the commander of the 20th Marine Depot Company, Capt. William C. Adams:

> My company landed about 2 P.M. on D-Day. We were the third wave, and all hell was breaking when we came in. It was still touch and go when we hit shore, and it took some time to establish a foothold. My men performed excellently. I had previously told them: "You are the first Negro troops ever to go into action in the Marine Corps. What you do with the situation that confronts you, and how you perform, will be the basis on which you, and your race, will be judged. . . ." They did a swell job. . . . Among my own company casualties, my orderly was killed. My men are still living in foxholes (quoted in Shaw and Donnelly 1975, 34).

June 15 also saw the death of the first African American U.S. Marine as a direct result of close enemy combat. Pvt. Kenneth J. Tibbs died of wounds received on D-Day.

Other African American units continued to be fed in to Saipan, and several more men were hit and wounded while performing their arduous work. The fighting wore on, as the Japanese continued to press the U.S. Marines, seemingly without respite. The contributions of the African American troops were already being felt, and the Commandant, Gen. Alexander A. Vandergrift, remarked: "The Negro Marines are no longer on trial. They are Marines, period" (quoted in Shaw and Donnelly 1975, 35).

The next target for the marines was Tinian, which was assaulted at the end of July 1944. The 3d Ammunition Company was deployed with the assault troops, but took no casualties. By this time the 3d Ammunition Company, the 18th, 19th, and 20th Depot Companies had all received Presidential Unit Citations for their support of the 4th Marine Division.

The final target in the Marianas for the Marines was the island of Guam. It had been intended that the assaults would be made on June 18, 1944, but due to the stubborn resistance of the Japanese on Saipan, the operation was delayed for over a month, and the landings went in on July 21. Again African American support units were deployed, with the 2d Marine Ammunition Company supporting the 3d Marine Division and the 4th Marine Ammunition Company supporting the 1st Provisional Marine

Brigade. The marines and the supporting naval vessels pulverized Guam prior to the landings, but they still ran into determined Japanese resistance, which threatened to break up Marine assaults as they formed on the beaches. On D-Day itself one African American was wounded, and the same night the 4th Ammunition Company foiled a Japanese attack on their ammunition dump. They suffered no casualties but killed fourteen of the enemy. On July 24 three of their numbers were wounded by Japanese artillery fire. The island was finally secured on August 10.

However, despite the official proclamation that Guam was secure, there was still Japanese at liberty on the island. As late as September 27, 1944, two members of the 4th Ammunition Company were wounded by the enemy on the island. In December 1944, Pfc. Luther Woodward followed footprints near the ammunition dump he had been posted to guard. He discovered a group of six Japanese hiding in a native hut. He opened fire, killing one and wounding another, and the survivors ran. Woodward returned to his unit and persuaded five other men to help him find the Japanese. Woodward killed another of the enemy, as did a colleague, and for his gallantry Woodward received the Bronze Star on January 11, 1945. This was later upgraded to the Silver Star.

African American support units were also involved in other U.S. Marine operations, notably the battle for the island of Peleliu in the Palau Islands. The 11th Marine Depot Company and the 7th Marine Ammunition Company were assigned to the 16th Field Depot, which was supporting the 1st Marine Division. Operations against the Palau Islands began at the end of August, and on September 15 U.S. Marines landed on Palau itself. Here the men faced near fanatical resistance, and the African American Marines were involved on the beaches for the first few days and were then assigned to moving the ammunition to the ebbing front line. A number of the men were wounded between September 20 and 24. The last casualty suffered by African American Marines on the island was that of Cpl. Charles E. Cane, who was wounded on October 9.

The commander of the 1st Marine Division, Maj. Gen. William H. Rupertus, was delighted with the way in which the men had supported his division and, in letters of commendation to the commanding officers of the 7th Ammunition Company and the 11th Marine Depot Company, stated: "The Negro race can well be proud of the work performed . . . as [the men involved] have demonstrated in every respect that they appreciate the privilege of wearing a Marine uniform and serving with Marines in combat. Please convey to your command these sentiments and inform them that in the eyes of the entire division they have earned a 'Well Done'" (quoted in Shaw and Donnelly 1975, 37).

The 8th Ammunition and 36th Depot Companies were present at the largest U.S. Marine amphibious operation in the Pacific against the island of Iwo Jima. The deceptively tiny volcanic island saw intense and ruinous fighting from the moment V Corps landed on February 19, 1945. The two African American units landed on D-Day and under constant artillery fire managed to avoid casualties until February 22. A white officer and an African American corporal were wounded on that day, and on February 25 six of the men were wounded, two of whom later died of their injuries.

As the fighting moved to the north of the island, it seemed that the conflict was beginning to draw to a close. A few further casualties to the African Americans occurred in early March, and then, just as it appeared that the fighting was about to end, came a vicious Japanese counterattack. On March 26 an ad hoc group of up to 300 Japanese launched an attack on the beaches in the west. Understandably the Marines, having been assured ten days earlier that the island was secure, were not expecting this assault. In the pitch black there was chaos, and the 36th Marine Depot Company was in the thick of the fighting. Two of their men were later awarded Bronze Stars. Once the fighting was finally ended, again the African Americans drew praise, this time from the commander of the 8th Field Depot, Col. Leland S. Swindler. Not only was he delighted with their performance and danger awareness, not to mention courage, but he was also particularly impressed with their reluctance to claim any attention for their roles. Directly after the final securing of Iwo Jima, the African American troops returned to the Hawaiian Islands to prepare for the next major offensive.

The largest concentration of African American U.S. Marines to become directly involved in combat occurred at Okinawa, starting on April 1, 1945. Okinawa was a key island, close to the Japanese homeland, and the invasion of Okinawa was the last conventional invasion before the dropping of the atomic bombs on Japan. The 1st, 3d, and 12th Ammunition Companies, together with the 5th, 18th, 37th, and 38th, all attached to the 7th Field Depot, arrived on D-Day, April 1, 1945. Before hostilities ended on the island, the 9th, 10th and 20th had also arrived.

The 1st and 3d Ammunition Companies, together with the 5th, 37th, and 38th Depot Companies, took part in the landing on the southeast of the island with the 2d Marine Division. This attack was a feint, as the main thrust was on the western coast, consisting of the III Amphibious Corps and the U.S. Army's XXIV Corps. By April 3 the bulk of the African American Marines had landed on the island, and they were supporting the 1st and 6th Marine Divisions. Initially the Marines swept inland and occupied most of the northern parts of the island, with the Japanese concentrating in the south. Casualties among the African American troops began to mount during April, as they were operating close to the front lines. When the U.S. forces moved south, the difficulties in resupplying the men became more acute. Again casualties began to rise during May and June. Other African Americans operating as stewards in the U.S. Marine Corps were deployed as stretcher bearers, and a number of these were killed or wounded while retrieving wounded men from the battlefield. Henry Shaw and Ralph Donnelly, in their official history, *Blacks in the Marine Corps,* estimate that more than 2,000 African Americans who had passed through Montford Point served on Okinawa.

Officially hostilities ended on the island on June 22, but as Okinawa was so strategically placed, the African American units had much to do to help build up the enormous supply dumps that were being established. When the war ended in August 1945, many of the men traveled to Kyushu as part of the occupying army. Preparations had been made for an offensive against the island, but of course the Japanese did not resist the occupation of the island or the major Japanese naval port of Yokusuka.

The 24th, 33d, 34th, 42d, and 43d Depot Companies, along with the 6th, 8th, and 10th Ammunition Companies, landed at Sasebo between September 22 and 26, 1945, with the 36th Marine Depot Company arriving in late October. The United States had been prepared for the worst, not expecting the Japanese to accept the occupation without entering into hostilities. As it was, the Marine Corps was able to begin demobilization of its troops as early as November, with the 24th Depot Company and 6th Ammunition Company disappearing first. By January 1946 more African American units were on their way back to Guam for demobilization, while others made the voyage back to Montford Point for disbandment in June 1946. The 8th Ammunition Company, however, remained on Guam for the time being. Even units that had only been in existence for a year, such as the 42d and 43d Depot Companies, were disbanded on March 14 in Japan. When the 10th Ammunition Company boarded the SS *Dashing Wave* on April 5, 1946, they were the last African American unit to leave Japan. They were disbanded at Montford Point in May.

Other units had been sent to Northern China, and they found an altogether different state of affairs, as there was a civil war being fought between the Chinese Nationalist and Communist forces. The role of the U.S. Marines was to repatriate Japanese nationals. The 1st Ammunition Company and the 5th, 37th, and 38th Depot Companies started landing at Tangku on September 30. The Chinese reacted to the African Americans with wariness. The vast majority of Chinese had never seen anyone of African descent; they firmly believed that the men had either painted their skins or had been in the sun for too long. For a period of time they were convinced that if the men washed the color would come off. After their initial reserve, the Chinese took to the African Americans, and there were no instances of problems.

Over the first few months, hundreds of thousands of Japanese were repatriated, and by January 1946 it became clear that the U.S. Marine contingents could be downsized. Three companies left on January 7, 1946, and were officially disbanded on February 21. The last African Americans to leave China were the 37th and 38th Depot Companies and the 12th Ammunition Company in early March. They were disbanded at the beginning of April at Montford Point.

World War II had seen twenty-four of the sixty-three African American units in the Marine Corps engaged in combat across the Pacific. In most of these units, the soldiers had worked six days a week on twelve-hour shifts, ensuring that the supply channels of the U.S. Marines remained efficient and that the combat troops were never short of supplies or ammunition. As the operations became more numerous and strenuous, the workload only increased.

As for the relationship between the white Marines and the African Americans, there were a number of racial incidents as late as December 1944, which were extensively investigated by a court of inquiry, whose findings ran to 1,200 pages. Many of these incidents occurred while the troops were based on Guam. In general, the findings of the court of inquiry were that African American marines had for the most part not been involved in the worst incidents, but rather the clashes had been between white marines and African Americans from the U.S. Navy. The morale and discipline of African American marines was found to be good, though there was some resentment of policies that discriminated against African Americans.

The Postwar Years

By the summer of 1946 all that remained of the African American units were the 8th Ammunition Company and the 49th Depot Company. They were officially deactivated on September 30, 1947, by which time both of the units were down to skeleton strength. The men who had served during World War II had indeed been Marines in the truest sense of the word, despite the fact that they had often found themselves stranded in backwaters, dealing with hundreds of thousands of tons of supplies, and guarding them against an enemy that never came.

The U.S. Marine Corps had not managed to raise the 10 percent of African Americans it had promised in 1943. The paper strength of the U.S. Marine Corps in October 1944 was 475,000, of whom 15,131 were African American. What had happened, however, was that the Marine Corps was steadily moving toward having African American officers. In the summer of 1944, the first batch of enlisted men with a college or university education were admitted into the U.S. Navy's V-12 Program. It was still the intention that African American officers should not be put in command of white troops. Nevertheless, three African Americans were selected to attend officer training by March 1945; these were Sgt. Maj. Charles F. Anderson, Sgt. Maj. Charles W. Simmons, and 1st Sgt. George F. Ellis Jr. None of the three passed the course, one being given a medical discharge and the other two failing for academic reasons. It is interesting to note that Anderson later became a lawyer, Ellis a doctor, and Simmons a college professor and author.

The breakthrough finally occurred with former Pfc. Frederick C. Branch, who was commissioned as a second lieutenant in the U.S. Marine Corps Reserve on November 10, 1945. He later saw active service in Korea. Three more African Americans joined the V-12 Program in 1946, two of whom returned to active service as officers.

There were still grave questions surrounding the role of African Americans in the Marine Corps in the wake of World War II, above all concerning the men who wished to reenlist. The Bureau of Naval Personnel officially announced in a circular letter on February 27, 1946, that there would be no more restrictions on the grounds of race. The Marine Corps had a proposed postwar establishment strength of 100,000, and it was proposed that African Americans should account for 2,800 of these men, most of whom would be assigned to the stewards branch. A proposal to allow African Americans into the Aviation Branch was reversed in June 1946. In May 1946 the Marine Corps declared that it was not its responsibility to settle matters of racial discrimination without clear guidelines from the government. During 1946, African American recruitment into the Marine Corps was, officially at least, suspended.

Montford Point was again chosen as the training center for any potential African American recruits, and preparations were under way to install the necessary drill instructors, including Hashmark Johnson, to handle the volunteers. The first men started arriving in June 1946. Further training facilities were required, and McAlester, Oklahoma, was chosen as an additional center. Here the men suffered a great deal of discrimination from the locals and were restricted to the east end of the town of McAlester on their infrequent visits. It was quickly realized that the African Americans should be removed from McAlester and sent to an area that had a large existing number of African American civilians. To this end, Port Chicago, California, and Earle, New Jersey, were chosen, and by January 1947 these bases were in operation.

Meanwhile, the projected number of African Americans had been cut progressively from 2,800 to 1,500, and on July 1, 1947, African American enlistment was suspended. By mid-1947 African American strength in the Marine Corps had reached 2,200, including stewards. Plans were considered to transfer the vast majority of those men who were not already stewards directly into the stewards branch, but, under pressure, the Marine Corps reconsidered.

Events elsewhere were to take the decision away from the U.S. Marine Corps, as on November 23, 1947, the Committee Against Jim Crow in Military Service and Training was established, thus beginning a push for effective integration of African Americans into the military in all arms of the service. By March 17, 1948, President Harry Truman, in the wake of asking Congress for a peacetime draft, began to realize that African Americans would not accept segregation any longer. The peacetime draft was signed into law on June 24, and Executive Order 9981 passed on July 26. With it was set up the Fahy Committee, which was intended to ensure that the Marine Corps, along with the other services, instituted a policy of equal treatment and opportunity.

On June 23, 1949, an order to the whole navy, ALNAV 49447, was issued by the secretary of the navy, Francis P. Matthews. It is considered the landmark declaration of racial policy aimed at ending segregation and discrimination for the U.S. Navy and Marine Corps. It expressly forbade inequality on the basis of race, color, or religion; it mandated that there be no more segregation or separate facilities and that advancement and training be offered without prejudice.

By November 18, 1949, the U.S. Marine Corps had overturned all of its previous regulations relating to African American Marines, including the requirement of segregated units. From then on African Americans were deployed in the Marine Corps on the same terms as whites. This effectively ended Montford Point's existence as a segregated training facility. This landmark year also saw the first African American woman join the U.S. Marine Corps Women Reserves, and on September 9, Montford Point was finally deactivated, with the 200 or so men there being transferred to other units. The U.S.

Marine Corps had come a long way in seven years, from accepting its first African Americans and putting them in segregated units to becoming a fully integrated service. Despite its tardiness in accepting African Americans, the Marine Corps could not resist the overwhelming pressure, not to mention legislation, which demanded its full integration.

The Korean War

When the Korean War broke out in 1950, some 1,500 African Americans were serving in the Marine Corps, and the corps as a whole only amounted to 74,279. By 1953, African American strength in the corps had risen to 14,731 out of a total strength of 249,219, effectively increasing African American membership of the corps from 2 to 6 percent. It is also significant to note that in 1950 a quarter of African Americans were in the stewards branch, but of the 1953 total, only just over 500 were in this section of the corps.

African Americans were present with the 1st Provisional Marine Brigade, manning the Pusan perimeter in July 1950. More men arrived throughout August and September to engage in the attack on Inchon and the liberation of Seoul. African Americans were being posted to units both individually and wholesale and performed every function across the corps.

As integration progressed, it becomes increasingly more difficult to identify the exact movements and combat actions of African Americans. Some of the men stand out for their displays of valor, such as Pfc. A. C. Clark, who was wounded twice in action while evacuating two wounded marines on December 13, 1952. Clark was serving with H Company, 3d Battalion, 5th Marines, and during his action he destroyed an enemy machine-gun post, killing the three-man crew, and was awarded the Silver Star. In the previous August he had already been awarded the Bronze Star after saving his wounded platoon leader.

Elsewhere African American NCOs were brought in and commanded white platoons. Even Hashmark Johnson arrived in Korea and was given a series of jobs, which only months before would never have been open to a man of his color. African American officers were also beginning to filter into Korea, the first of which was Lt. William K. Jenkins. He had the distinction, while serving as platoon leader for Company B, 1st Battalion, 7th Marines, of being the first African American Marine Corps officer to lead troops into combat. Frank E. Petersen became the first African American to be commissioned into the Marine Corps from the Naval Aviation Cadet Program. He flew sixty-four combat missions, winning six Air Medals and a Distinguished Flying Cross, and by 1973 had reached the rank of lieutenant colonel.

Edgar R. Huff, who had had a long association with Montford Point, also served in Korea, and in September 1952 he became the first African American to become a battalion sergeant major.

Toward Full Integration

Directly after the Korean War, Marine Corps strength dropped from 205,275 in 1954 to 154,242 in 1960, but the numbers of African Americans in the corps remained at around 12,500, both male and female. The stewards branch itself had a number of African Americans who reached ranks as high as warrant officer, but on March 1, 1954, the policy of accepting steward-only enlistments was finally ended. It was expected that many of the African Americans in the stewards branch would opt for general Marine Corps service, but in fact the branch only lost about 10 percent of its men. A real stigma had been attached to serving white officers during the 1940s, but that was no longer the case.

Not all of the integration was as smooth as in the combat units, and it was only with the increase in pressure for integration in all areas of society, symbolized by the historic *Brown v. Board of Education* ruling by the Supreme Court on May 17, 1954, that segregated schools and housing on bases was ended. Officially desegregation of these facilities occurred throughout the armed forces on September 1, 1955.

As the Marine Corps entered the 1960s, there were a number of violent clashes between African American and white members of the corps. Rising African American consciousness led many of the newer recruits to openly challenge aspects of Marine Corps life that had been accepted by the older veterans. There were signs that aspects of the Marine Corps had not been effectively integrated. By 1962, for example, several Marine Corps bases, including Bridgeport, California, and Charleston, South Carolina, had no African Americans due to housing considerations. Equally there were no African American recruitment officers. Again there was considerable pressure from the White House, this time from the Kennedy administration, demanding that Robert S. MacNamara, the secretary of defense, ensure true equal opportunity in the armed forces.

One of the difficult problems facing the corps and the other sections of the armed forces was that local communities, particularly in the South, were still resistant to allowing African Americans to use civilian facilities or services. Steps had to be taken, for example, to place areas near military bases off-limits if they still maintained segregated housing. If such a move went into effect, it would effectively wreck the local economy, which was dependent on the dollars spent by servicemen. This, if nothing else, would force local communities to reconsider their discriminatory opinions and practices. A large number of landmark court cases proceeded during the 1960s on issues involving housing and education. When movement was not swift or white communities balked at the changes being imposed, a number of racial incidents occurred. A series of racial incidents at Camp Lejeune in 1969 led to armed conflict between African American and white Marines and locals, ending in a large number of arrests.

The conclusions of a House of Representatives subcommittee of the Armed Services Committee proved to be very embarrassing for the Marine Corps. The corps and its commandant, Gen. Leonard F. Chapman Jr., were forced to accept that they had problems. By this time the United States was deeply involved in Vietnam, and many of the so-called fragging incidents that happened there, when soldiers threw fragmentation grenades in officers' tents, were in all probability racially motivated. That race hatred was behind much of the fragging was certainly a common belief among white officers. The corps was also grappling with two less serious problems associated with African American behavior and appearance. There was a trend during this period for African Americans to grow their hair long, and the corps was at pains to point out that Afro hairstyles should not exceed 3 inches and that sideburns were prohibited. More difficult were the clenched-fist salutes associated with Black Power. Although the corps outlawed these during official ceremonies, it accepted the practice in other circumstances as being a way of expressing unity and a greeting between African American marines.

By May 1967 only 155 of the 23,000 officers in the Marine Corps were African American, and steps were beginning to be made to increase this proportion. By September 30, 1973, the number of African American officers on active duty had risen to 378, an increase achieved by focusing on recruiting college graduates. African American enlisted men now accounted for 17.41 percent of the corps. Much of this increase could be attributed to Lt. Col. Frank E. Petersen Jr., who filled the role of special assistant to the commandant for minority affairs.

During the Vietnam War, some 448,000 U.S. Marines served in the theater between 1965 and 1973; 41,000 were African Americans. African Americans were involved in the war from the very beginning, not only in the role of enlisted men, but as officers and noncommissioned officers at squad, platoon, and company level. African Americans also served in the Marine Corps as aviators. They were present at many of the major engagements, including Khe Sanh and Da Nang, as well as during the Tet Offensive. Many thousands of the men were awarded Navy Crosses, Silver Stars, Distinguished Flying

U.S. Marines of the Special Landing Force approach the beach in Rung Sat swamp, South Vietnam. (National Archives)

Crosses, Bronze Stars, and other medals, including the Purple Heart. Five African Americans from the U.S. Marine Corps were awarded Medals of Honor, including Pfc. James Anderson Jr., who was killed at Cam Lo on February 28, 1967, while serving with Company F, 2d Battalion, 3d Marines. Anderson has the distinction of being the first African American U.S. Marine to win a Medal of Honor. Other Medal of Honor winners were Sgt. Rodney M. Davis, Pfc. Ralph H. Johnson, Pfc. Oscar P. Austin, and the last man to win a Medal of Honor in Vietnam, Pfc. Robert H. Jenkins Jr.

Although the men who have served in integrated units from Korea to the present day have showed their own gallantry, valor, and dedication to the corps, it is the men who reported to Montford Point in August 1942 that began the African American association with the U.S. Marine Corps. It is, therefore, understandable that individuals such as Sgt. Maj. Gilbert H. "Hashmark" Johnson retain the respect and affection of the men who followed him. A living endorsement of Johnson's importance was poignantly made on April 19, 1974, when a ceremony reactivated Montford Point as Camp Gilbert H. Johnson.

See also Desegregation of Armed Forces (APPENDIX); Gifu; Korean War; Medal of Honor (APPENDIX); Petersen, Frank E; Vietnam War; World War II

References and Further Reading

Garand, George W., and Truman R. Strobridge. *History of the U.S. Marine Corps Operations in World War Two.* Vol. 4, *Western Pacific Operations.* Washington, DC: Historical Division, 1971.

Hough, Frank O. *Pearl Harbor to Guadalcanal: History of the U.S. Marine Corps Operation in*

World War Two. Washington, DC: Headquarters U.S. Marine Corps, 1958.

Middlebrook, Lewis F. *History of Maritime Connecticut during the American Revolution, 1775–1783.* 2 vols. Salem, MA: Essex Institute, 1925.

Shaw, Henry I., Jr. *The United States Marines in North China, 1945–1949.* Washington, DC: Historical Branch, 1968.

———. *The United States Marines in the Occupation of Japan.* Washington, DC: Historical Branch, 1969.

Shaw, Henry I., Jr., Bernard T. Nalty, and Edwin T. Turnbladh. *Central Pacific Drive: History of the U.S. Marine Corps Operations in World War Two.* Vol. 3. Washington, DC: History and Museums Division, U.S. Marine Corps, 1966.

Shaw, Henry I., Jr., and Ralph W. Donnelly. *Blacks in the Marine Corps.* Washington: U.S. Marine Corps. 1975. http://www.mcu.usmc.mil/ftw/files/black.txt (accessed August 8, 2003).

Stillman, Richard J., II. *Integration of the Negro in the U.S. Armed Forces.* New York: Praeger, 1968.

U.S. Navy

African Americans have always been an integral part of American naval operations, and up through the Civil War they took their place in combat, forming a more substantial part of that branch of the service than of any other. Then, as whites began to find the navy more attractive, African Americans came to be limited to service positions, and between the two world wars discouraged from serving even there. It took World War II to really open the navy to African Americans again, and even then old practices hung on, at least until the Vietnam War.

Before the American Revolution

Before 1775, the British colonies that later made up the United States did not have a navy. The vessels that were eventually pressed into action by both the Continental Navy and the navies of the various colonies during the American Revolution probably already had a considerable number of African American sailors. Life on board ship was not especially appealing; not only was it hazardous, but also the living conditions were poor and the food even worse. Any sea captain would be prepared to take any man who presented himself, and no questions were asked of a man who might very well have been a runaway slave. Poor African Americans, even if they were free, were often left with no alternative but to seek employment at sea. As a result, the early naval experiences of African Americans were wholly on integrated vessels.

The American Revolution

The early U.S. Navy basically consisted of any vessel that could be pressed into service against the British. Consequently, to support the Continental Navy, which had approximately fifty vessels of various types, there were the colonial, or state, navies, some of which were almost as large as the Continental Navy itself. Supporting these two more official types of navies were the numerous privateers, who operated under letters of marque received from the Continental Congress or individual colonies. Judging from the names on manifests and lists of ships' crews, there were African Americans in each of these three categories and on nearly every vessel, even in the British Navy.

Given the choice, African Americans opted to serve in the state navies rather than the Continental Navy, since the pay was better and the opportunities more varied. In the Continental Navy African Americans were often relegated to the lowest positions on the vessel. Both the state navies and the privateers were much more egalitarian. African Americans were also involved in naval duties in the dockyards, and increasingly the skills of African American artisans were needed to ensure the vessels remained afloat.

African Americans in either an American or British vessel faced an uncertain future if captured. Those discovered on British ships tended to be pressed into service on American vessels, and African Americans on American ships captured by the British were often transported to the West Indies as slaves.

The Continental Navy was disbanded after the American Revolution, and any ships that it had were sold. It was not until the United States became involved in an undeclared naval war with France in 1798, known as the Quasi War, that the U.S. Navy Department was finally established, and it is certain that African Americans fought in that war. Again, with difficulties in attracting white sailors, the navy enlisted African Americans as a means of filling the crews.

The War of 1812

In June 1812 the United States declared war on Great Britain, and according to official records African Americans accounted for between 10 to 20 percent of all naval personnel, at least in some theaters. There were mixed feelings about their performance; individual captains were either concerned about the numbers in their crews or perfectly happy with their competence. Capt. Oliver Hazard Perry, who led the U.S. fleet in the Battle of Lake Erie, had 100 African Americans spread among the 400 sailors who manned his 10 vessels. He at first complained about the presence of African Americans in the reinforcements he had been sent, but their performance during the battle prompted him to write to the secretary of the navy, praising their courage and hard work. Working alongside the U.S. Navy at this time were a number of privateers. Again these vessels probably had a considerable number of African Americans among their crews.

The U.S. Navy, after the War of 1812, still continued to enlist free African Americans. However, in 1816 the service banned any employment of slaves. There were continual concerns, particularly from the Southern states at this time, regarding the numbers of African Americans in the navy. As a consequence, in 1839, enlistments of African Americans were pegged at 5 percent, a figure that remained in force until the Civil War.

The Civil War

During the Civil War, while the federal government and the U.S. Army dragged their heels or outright rejected offers from African Americans to serve in the army, there was no such discrimination as far as the navy was concerned. On September 25, 1861, the U.S. Navy officially sanctioned the enlistment of African Americans. Its greatest problem, however, was dealing with the thousands of slaves who presented themselves to their vessels as soon as they were spotted. Certainly in the early years of the war, having been rejected by the army, African Americans were keen to make some contribution, and as a result the secretary of the navy, Gideon Welles, began to address the problem in September 1862. He recognized that the high numbers of would-be sailors could not be ignored and that commanders should employ them for basic duties aboard vessels.

As in all previous conflicts, the navy found it difficult to attract white sailors. The Northern states were not keen for their men to join the navy, as any that did were not counted in the recruiting quotas. The fugitive slaves offered to fill the gap in manpower. Any physically fit man would find employment and $10 a month. There was no segregation, due to the conditions on board the vessels, and it is believed that by the end of the war between 19,000 and 30,000 African Americans had served in the Union Navy, a full 25 percent of the entire strength. This is a much more significant figure, proportionately, than the 7 percent of the Union army who were African Americans.

Perhaps the most celebrated early contribution of African Americans occurred on May 12, 1862, when a twenty-three-year-old slave, Robert Smalls, hijacked the Confederate steamer *Planter* and, under the noses of the Confederate artillery protecting Charleston harbor, guided the vessel to the Union blockade lines. Smalls was later awarded a bounty for the vessel by the U.S. Congress, and in the aftermath of the war he entered politics.

Also during the Civil War, many African Americans formed labor details, loading and unloading supplies and equipment for the navy. A handful became navigators or engineers, and in the latter stages of the war most of the sailors were trained to fight, rather like Marines. A number of African American seamen were particularly adept at handing the heavy artillery pieces on board the ships, which helped prompt the U.S. Army into deploying African American artillery units. African Americans on board naval vessels served in all ranks below petty officer.

Three African American sailors won Medals of Honor at the battle of Mobile Bay in August 1864, including John Lawson, who was serving aboard the USS *Hartford* in its attack on the *Tennessee, Fort Morgan,* and other Confederate vessels. Lawson, although he was wounded and the rest of his gun crew were out of action, continued to man the artillery piece throughout the whole action. It is believed that around 800 African American sailors were killed in action during the American Civil War, and another 2,400 are believed to have died from diseases.

Landsman John Lawson of the U.S. Navy, who was one of three African Americans awarded the Medal of Honor for heroism aboard the USS Hartford *during the Battle of Mobile Bay, August 5, 1864. (U.S. Naval Historical Center)*

New Restrictions after the Civil War: A White Man's Navy

Directly after the Civil War the U.S. Navy chose to reverse its integration policy toward African American sailors. Although the past 100 years had seen considerable African American recruitment and employment within the U.S. Navy, the policy now was to restrict their deployment solely to the stewards branch.

By 1917, the number of African Americans in the navy had dropped to less than 7,500. Gradually, in the fifty years between the end of the Civil War and World War I, the U.S. Navy had transformed itself into what was called in 1907 the "Great White Fleet." The old, antiquated wooden vessels had been completely replaced by a steam-driven steel navy, symbolized by the sixteen battleships, painted white, that were displayed in 1907. The navy had become far more attractive to white recruits. Those African Americans who remained were restricted to serving as laborers and servants, and in other low-ranking positions. The men were segregated and excluded from all of the key roles on board ships and in the dockyards.

During Reconstruction, when African American political power was at a high point, three African Americans did attempt to work their way through the United States Naval Academy at Annapolis, Maryland, despite its known rigors; the four-year program failed at least 30 percent of all midshipmen. African Americans had to contend with extreme racial prejudice as well. James H. Conyers from South Carolina was the first African American candidate; he failed on academic grounds. Alonzo McClen-

Cooks on the deck of the USS Ossipee, *1887. After the Civil War African Americans were almost completely restricted to positions of cooks and stewards in the navy. (U.S. Naval Historical Center)*

Mess attendants on board the USS Bushnell *(AS-2) during World War I. (U.S. Naval Historical Center)*

nan, who was also from South Carolina, chose to abandon his studies at the academy and study medicine instead. The third African American candidate, from Mississippi, Henry E. Baker, was unfairly dismissed from the academy and chose to become a clerk in the U.S. Patent Office, although he was offered reinstatement.

In the latter stages of the nineteenth century and the beginning of the twentieth, African Americans were finding it increasingly difficult to gain entrance to or even to remain in the stewards branch. It was the U.S. Navy's view that Asian Americans were far better at the job and made better servants than African Americans. This trend was accelerated when the United States effectively gained control over the Philippines, and by the time the country joined World War I in 1917, Filipinos outnumbered African Americans in the U.S. Navy.

Even though over 2.2 million, or 9.63 percent of all the registered males eligible to serve during World War I were African American, the U.S. Navy sought to discourage their enlistment. They were told that they would only be deployed as mess men or as laborers. As a direct consequence of this policy, the vast majority of African Americans chose to join the army rather than the navy. This preference accounts for the fact that only 1 percent of the navy's manpower during the whole of World War I was black. African Americans were barred from enlisting in the navy from 1919 to 1932; after that they could join only as mess men.

The small number of African American sailors in 1919, who served in racially mixed crews, were allowed to remain until retirement. One such sailor, John Henry ("Dick") Turpin, had become the first African American chief petty officer (the highest enlisted rank) in 117. He had been in the navy since 1896 and survived the sinking of the USS *Maine* in 1898. He retired in 1925.

World War II

Despite a few relatively minor changes during the interwar period, on Sunday, December 7, 1941, the U.S. Navy was a predominantly white service. The Japanese bombing of the U.S. Pacific fleet and the subsequent destruction of or damage to 19 vessels, in addition to the 150 aircraft and 2,335 men lost, meant one thing: war had come, and with it a growing need for the U.S. Navy to radically rethink its entire recruitment policy. Manpower was undoubtedly a major concern, but changes in military policy toward African Americans also owed much to the lobbying of civil rights leaders and the related desire of President Franklin D. Roosevelt and other politicians to garner votes from a growing African American constituency.

War was officially declared against Japan the following day. The existing African American servicemen were restricted at this stage to the stewards branch or labor duties in naval dockyards. The U.S. Navy lacked a single African American officer. All that would change by the end of the war. Theoretically, at least, in four years time, any position in the U.S. Navy would be open to African Americans.

On that day when Japanese aircraft flew unchecked over U.S. soil, the first African American act in the U.S. Navy had also been played out. Dorie Miller from Texas was a steward on board the *West Virginia,* and after having helped to evacuate wounded men from the burning battleship, he ran to man an antiaircraft machine gun. Although the mythology that has gathered around Miller has made for exaggerated claims, the fact remains that the untrained machine-gunner accounted for at least two and possibly as many as six Japanese aircraft. The U.S. Navy, in typical style, referred to Miller in their reports as "an unnamed Negro Messman" (Reddick 1947, 205). Finally, in March 1942 Miller was publicly recognized, and in May he was awarded the Navy Cross. Miller died on board the *Liscome Bay* on November 24, 1943.

The accelerated changes that swept through the U.S. Navy during World War II must be put in the context of the position that African Americans had found themselves in, in the immediate aftermath of World War I. At the close of hostilities of World War I the U.S. Navy had a total complement of 435,398 men, of whom 1.2 percent, or 5,328, were African American (Reddick 1947, 203). This figure gradually reduced until the early 1930s, largely as a result of Filipinos joining the U.S. Navy. Then Filipino recruitment dropped, and by 1932 African Americans were again recruited, but only as mess men, members of the stewards branch. Rigid segregation was thus achieved, and due to the poor conditions and lowly status of mess men, very few of the men ever served more than one term of enlistment.

By June 1940 the African American complement in the U.S. Navy had climbed to a little over 2 percent (Mueller 1945, 112), and it was around this time that there was a call for 200 additional African Americans to serve as stewards and fulfil similar duties. The attitude toward African Americans at this time is best summed up by Frank Knox, who was then secretary of the navy: "I am convinced that it is no kindness to Negroes to thrust them upon men of white race. One branch of the Navy is reserved exclusively for negroes, and that is messmen" (letter to Senator Arthur Capper, August 1, 1940, quoted in Krawczynski 1998).

In September 1940 Walter White (secretary of the National Association for the Advancement of Colored People [NAACP]), A. Philip Randolph (president of the Brotherhood of Sleeping Car Porters), and T. Arnold Hill (National Youth Administration) coauthored a memorandum to Roosevelt, Knox, and the assistant secretary of war, Robert P. Patterson, asking them to improve the lot of African Americans within the national defense program. They threatened that 100,000 African Americans would march on Washington. Patterson framed new proposals, which Roosevelt immediately accepted; from now on African Americans in the military would represent their equivalent proportions in the population, every service would accept African Americans, and African Americans would be accepted as officers. The conditions were that it might take some time, particularly in the event of war, and that segregation within the military would continue.

It took Secretary Knox until June 1941 to commission a committee to look at African American opportunities, both in the U.S. Navy and in the U.S. Marine Corps. After six months of work the committee recommended that no change be made to the policy of limiting African Americans in the navy to the mess service.

Early 1942 saw Japanese fortunes in the ascendant; the brunt of the defense of the Pacific Islands fell to the U.S. Navy and the U.S. Marine Corps. There was an immediate need to enlarge the armed forces, but Knox still refused to consider allowing African Americans into the U.S. Navy in roles other than mess men, despite continuous pressure from the NAACP and other civil rights organizations. In frustration, the NAACP wrote directly to the president and asked him to intercede, and on January 9, 1942, he ordered Knox to find other forms of employment for African Americans in the navy. Knox asked the navy's General Board to accept 5,000 African Americans for general service, but on February 3 the board's recommendation was that African Americans remain only in the stewards branch, arguing that white personnel would not accept African Americans in any other role.

Roosevelt refused to accept the position, suggesting that the board find special posts and assignments for African Americans that would not cause racial tension within the service. Finally, on February 25, 1942, the board recommended that African Americans be allowed to enlist for general service, but that they not be assigned to the main fleets. Segregation was to be maintained. Roosevelt agreed, and on March 31, 1942, he and Knox ordered the navy to institute the new policy. Knox could now announce that African American volunteers would be accepted for general service in the U.S. Navy from June 1, 1942. There was no intention, however, of curtailing the numbers of African Americans who were being tucked away in the stewards branch.

The general service enlistment quota of 277 men per week would provide just over 14,000 African American sailors in the first year. Segregated training camps were established to handle the men at the Great Lakes Training Center in Illinois. The largest, Camp Robert Smalls, named after a black Civil War hero, provided special morale-building activities along with the standard military training. Men who qualified for specialist training either remained in segregated schools at Great Lakes or were transferred to the Hampton Institute in Virginia. A handful of the men were also sent to the Navy Technical Training Station in Memphis, Tennessee, to train as aviation machinist mates. A few other men went to Camp May, New Jersey, to attend the Soundman School there, or to the Messmen's School, based in Bainbridge, Maryland.

The U.S. Navy faced a considerable problem with the large numbers of illiterate African Americans, whom they would have normally sent directly into the stewards branch. However, the branch was virtually full, and the navy had to establish educational facilities that would run alongside the basic naval training. It is believed that up to 15,000 African American recruits attended the series of twelve-week courses, designed to reach the fourth-grade reading level required for general service positions.

Most of the new recruits were sent to segregated construction battalions (CB Special Battalions—hence the name Seabees). These men worked as stevedores and underwent basic training in segregated facilities at Camps Bradford and Allen, outside Norfolk, Virginia. The units were not intended to be deployed as combat troops. Nonetheless, there were a number of occasions when African American Seabees had to join in the fighting.

Up until the issuance of Executive Order 9279, which placed the U.S. Navy, along with the other armed services, within the Selective Service system, the navy had accepted volunteers only. From December 5, 1942, they were now expected to increase their African American complement to 10 percent. By this stage the navy was already taking 1,500 African Americans per month into the stewards branch and a further 1,200 into general service. There now seemed to be no other alternative than to consider using mixed crews, but the Bureau of Naval Personnel, Knox, and even Roosevelt were opposed to this move.

According to the Bureau of Naval Personnel, from February 1943 until June 1945 African American strength in the U.S. Navy rose from 26,909 to 165,500, while the percentage of African Americans serving in the stewards branch fell from 68 percent to 45 percent. Although theoretically the new racial policies opened up a vast number of naval professions to African Americans, the majority of the men were still being assigned to shore duties or, at the very best, small segregated coastal vessels, and many of them had still not been given the opportunity to serve overseas. They were still living under strictly segregated conditions and were very tightly controlled in terms of their leave and locations they could or could not visit during leave. They rarely received promotions in rank.

When African American Seabees protested mistreatment in a discriminatory navy, they often faced severe punishment. In July 1943, 19 members of the 80th Construction Battalion received dishonorable discharges for lodging a complaint with their commanding officer. A year later 44 African American stevedores at Port Chicago were sent to prison for refusing to work in dangerous conditions after two ammunition-laden ships exploded, killing 300 men. In both case the charges were revoked following sustained lobbying from the civilian African American community.

Although the U.S. Navy was reluctantly assigning African Americans to the general service, the authorities were far less willing to make rapid steps in terms of African American officers. In September 1943 the assistant secretary of the navy, Adlai E. Stevenson, pointed out to Secretary Knox that the U.S. Navy was going to have difficulty explaining why the navy had 60,000 African Americans in the service and were enlisting black men at a rate of 12,000 a month, yet they had no African American officers. In November 1943 Knox finally bowed to the inevitable and proposed to commission twenty-two African Americans as officers. Twelve of them would have line duties, and ten would be assigned as staff officers. The screening process was designed to exclude any man who had ever professed strong civil rights convictions.

The Golden Thirteen, as the first African American officers were known, twelve line officers and a warrant officer, received their segregated training at the Great Lakes Training Center, begun on January 1, 1944. Notably, none of the men were allowed to serve overseas. The navy then selected ten African American civilians to be trained as staff officers in the summer of 1944; three eventually found employment in the supply corps, three in the medical corps, and two each in the chaplain's corps, the dental corps, and the civil engineer corps. This move was a very belated and token effort on the part of the U.S. Navy, as collectively these men accounted for a large proportion of the sixty African American officers who ultimately served in the U.S. Navy during the war.

The U.S. Navy was beginning to realize that it would not be able to continue assigning African Americans to essentially segregated support functions—that it was inevitable that the call would come for African Americans to be assigned to seagoing naval vessels. As was its normal practice, it attempted to preempt this call. To forestall criticism of continued segregation and its policy of ensuring that no African Americans outranked white servicemen, the navy decided to experiment with predominantly African American crews. On January 29, 1944, the U.S. Navy commissioned the USS *Mason,* which was to have a complement of 183 men, of whom all but 40 would be African American. The destroyer escort vessel would have white officers and a predominantly African American crew. Within two months a second vessel had been identified, the *PC-1264,* which was to become engaged in convoy escorts between New York and Cuba; 50 of its 61 sailors were African American.

The major difference between the *PC-1264* and the USS *Mason* was that the plan for the former vessel proposed to replace all of the white petty officers, once African Americans had been trained sufficiently to take up the posts. This process took six months, and for fifteen months the *PC-1264* was the only U.S. naval vessel with a complete complement of African American enlisted men. The venture convinced the navy that African Americans were capable of serving and running modern vessels.

Peace celebrations at the Naval Amphibious Base, Manus, Admiralty Islands, August 15, 1945. Members of the 22d Special Naval Construction Battalion cheer the news of Japan's acceptance of peace terms. (National Archives)

Neither of the vessels actually engaged the enemy; nevertheless, they were fully trained and perfectly capable of protecting themselves and whatever vessels they were escorting. However, the experiment also showed that maintenance of a segregated navy was inefficient and expensive.

Forrestal Begins a Period of Rapid Change

A major change in U.S. Navy policy occurred in the immediate aftermath of the death of Secretary Knox on April 28, 1944. A far more pragmatic man, James A. Forrestal, who had been the undersecretary of the navy since August 1940, took over. He expanded the experiments with African American sailors by integrating the crews of twenty-five larger auxiliary vessels. The project's success prompted the Bureau of Naval Personnel on March 6, 1945, to officially begin assigning African Americans to the general service personnel of the auxiliary. In turn, on July 1, 1945, segregated training at Great Lakes ceased, and from that time on African Americans were trained alongside white recruits.

In March 1945 Forrestal appointed another individual who was to have a marked impact on integration within the U.S. Navy. Lester B. Granger of the National Urban League covered over 50,000 miles and visited nearly sixty-seven naval centers in six months, collecting information regarding the experiences of African Americans in the service. He found that commanders adhering to the 1944 pamphlet *Guide to Command of Negro Naval Personnel,* which recommended policies to boost morale among and ensure fair treatment of African American servicemen, reported fewer racial problems. Granger suggested a number of key policies that assisted the transition that was under way in the U.S. Navy.

The Gillem Board, appointed to study the question of integration in the armed services, which delivered its findings in November 1945, had carefully studied the U.S. Navy's progress in terms of integration. In the immediate aftermath of World War II the U.S. Navy had begun to integrate African Americans into their officer schools and specialist training facilities. They had also taken steps to ensure that integration was under way in their recruit training centers and in the WAVES. The secretary of the navy, James Forrestal, officially ended segregation within the U.S. Navy in February 1946; this was formalized in Circular Letter 48–46, issued by the chief of Naval Operations: "Effective immediately, all restrictions governing types of assignment for which Negro naval personnel are eligible are hereby lifted. Henceforth, they shall be eligible for all types of assignments in all ratings in all activities and in all ships of the naval service." Thus the U.S. Navy moved into the postwar years with what has been called "the most progressive African American policy of all the armed forces" (quotations from Krawczynski 1998).

But if the official policy was integration, the reality was rather different. After the war, even though African Americans served in all branches, opportunities for African Americans shrank as the number of available positions decreased. Most African Americans still served in the (unofficially) segregated stewards branch, and only a handful of officers were African

Americans. Morris MacGregor, in his *Integration of the Armed Forces, 1940–1965*, suggests that the navy had simply returned to its old pre–World War I tradition of white officers, nonwhite servants, and an integrated general service. That much was easy; beyond that, the navy had no real desire to go. However that may be, the navy was proud of its integration policy and explained the apparent inconsistencies on the grounds of the high standards required for running the navy and the fierce competition for available positions. The navy was perhaps thus less concerned than the other branches of the armed services by Executive Order 9981, issued by President Truman on July 26, 1948, which officially ended racial segregation in the armed forces.

More pressure to change the reality of the situation came during the years after Truman's order, and the stewards branch was generally seen as the biggest problem. In 1949, 66.12 percent of the African Americans in the navy were still in the stewards branch. As for the racial makeup of the branch, according to MacGregor, "In 1949 it had 10,499 Negroes, 4,707 Filipinos, 741 other nonwhites, and 1 white man" (chap. 16). The standards for admission were lower, rising to high rank was impossible, and the men were treated like servants. Lt. Dennis D. Nelson, who had been one of the Golden Thirteen and who was a powerful voice for reform, made an appeal that shows the depth of the problem. In a memo to the Public Relations Department sent in March of 1948, he urged that all members of the service should "refrain from the use of 'Boy' in addressing Stewards. This has been a constant practice in the Service and is most objectionable, in bad taste, shows undue familiarity and pins a badge of inferiority, adding little to the dignity and pride of adults" (quoted in MacGregor 1985, chap. 9). Small wonder that educated African Americans, the kind the navy wanted to attract in order to meet demands for a higher proportion of African Americans as both regular enlisted men and officers, were put off, seeing the navy as basically still a white man's world.

The stewards branch was the biggest problem, but the simplest way of resolving it was constantly rejected. The commissary was predominantly white, and merging the two branches would have meant instant integration. Instead, all sorts of measures were taken to improve the status of the stewards, and the proportion of African Americans in the navy who served in the stewards branch did drop to 23.35 percent by 1958 (MacGregor 1985, chap. 16). However, those who replaced the African Americans were also nonwhite, from the Philippines or other parts of the western Pacific. The image of racial segregation remained.

Toward Full Integration

The Korean War (1950–1953) was the first U.S. war in which all the services were at least nominally integrated, and it was clear that African Americans looked on the war as a test of the government's commitment to ending segregation. In the navy practice was far from declared policy. In the early 1950s African Americans accounted for just 4 percent of naval personnel, with the highest number serving as stewards. African Americans still tended to be assigned to the "lower decks" in support functions, but they were increasingly being integrated into defensive roles on board, manning guns and antiaircraft positions. The first African American naval pilot was Ens. Jesse Brown, assigned to the USS *Leyte*. He was killed in the early months of the war on a combat mission over Changjin Reservoir in North Korea. In 1955, well after the Korean War, the navy was still assigning the majority of African Americans to the steward branch of the service, a circumstance that did not begin to change until the following year, when the navy assigned nearly 75 percent of its African American sailors to general duties.

By the time the U.S. Navy faced its next major challenge in the Vietnam War, it was a much more completely integrated service. The navy received its first harsh awakening to the implications of this new conflict on August 2, 1964, when North Vietnamese patrol boats attacked a naval destroyer in the Gulf of Tonkin. The U.S. Navy played an important role in interdicting enemy attacks and launching air offensives against the Vietnamese throughout the conflict.

Integrated or not, the navy had clearly not solved all its racial problems, and it saw its share of the difficulties that became so marked throughout the country after the assassination of Martin Luther King Jr. on April 4, 1968. It was at a naval installation at Cam Ranh Bay in South Vietnam that hooded sailors with a burning cross raised a Confederate flag soon after the assassination. In 1970, a potential battle between African American and white sailors at the Great Lakes Naval Base in Illinois was avoided by an officer who was able to make peace. In that same year, Adm. Elmo R. Zumwalt began to work on ending various still common discriminatory practices and on increasing the percentage of African Americans in the ranks and in the officer corps. Nevertheless, racial violence broke out in 1972 on the USS *Kitty Hawk* and the USS *Constellation*.

Progress continued to be made, if slowly, toward fully incorporating African Americans into all ranks in the navy. In 1971 Samuel L. Gravely Jr., who had been a sailor on board the USS *PC-1264* during World War II, became the first African American admiral. It was not until 1996 that an African American, J. Paul Reason, reached the rank of four-star admiral; he commanded the Atlantic Fleet from 1996 to 1999, when he retired. In 2001 there were nine African Americans with the rank of admiral. By the mid-1990s the percentage of African Americans in the navy as a whole, only about 5 percent in 1970, had risen to 18 percent, exceeding that in the air force.

Still, as in the rest of the armed services and in American society as a whole, full equality for African Americans was still more promise than fact. As the navy became increasingly technical, underrepresentation of African Americans in more technical fields and the elite forces continued. For example, in 1997 only 9 percent of navy SEALs were African American, half their overall proportion in the navy. But at the end of the twentieth century, after over two centuries of African American participation in the navy, there were encouraging signs that discrepancies in opportunities for specialization and promotion were continuing to diminish—probably at a faster rate than in the civilian economy.

Seaman Daniel J. Lewis stands watch as lookout on the bridge of the submarine USS John Adams *(SSBN-620), December 1969. (U.S. Navy)*

See also African American Officers; American Civil War; American Revolution; Antebellum Period; Brashear, Carl Maxie; Brown, Jesse LeRoy; Brown, Wesley Anthony; Colonial America; Desegregation of the Armed Forces (APPENDIX); 1812, War of; Executive Order 9981; Golden Thirteen; Gravely, Samuel Lee, Jr.; Guam Incident; Gulf War; Korean War; Lake Erie, Battle of; *Mason,* USS; Miller, Dorie; Mulzac, Hugh; National Association for the Advancement of Colored People; *PC-1264,* USS; Philippine Insurrection; Port Chicago Mutiny;

Selective Service Acts; Smalls, Robert; Spanish-American War; Trinidad Disturbance; Vietnam War; Women Accepted for Volunteer Emergency Services; World War I; World War II; Z-Gram 66

References and Further Reading

Belknap, Michael R. *The Employment of Blacks by the Federal Government.* New York: Garland, 1991.

Berlin, Ira, Joseph Reidy, and Leslie S. Rowland, eds. *Freedom: A Documentary History of Emancipation, 1861–1867.* Series 2, *The Black Military Experience.* New York: Cambridge University Press, 1982.

Binkin, Martin. *Blacks and the Military.* Washington, DC: Brookings Institution, 1982.

Buchanan, A. Russell. *Black Americans in World War Two.* Santa Barbara, CA: ABC-CLIO, 1977.

Byers, Jean. *A Study of the Negro in Military Service.* Washington, DC: Department of the Navy, 1947.

Coffman, Edward M. *The War to End All Wars: The American Military Experience in World War One.* New York: Oxford University Press, 1968.

Dalfiume, Richard M. *Desegregation of the U.S. Armed Forces: Fighting on Two Fronts, 1939–1954.* Columbia: University of Missouri Press, 1969.

Davis, Lenwood G., and George Hill. *Blacks in the American Armed Forces, 1776–1983: A Bibliography.* Westport, CT: Greenwood Press, 1985.

Department of Defense. *A Pictorial Documentary of the Black American Male and Female Participation and Involvement in the Military Affairs of the United States of America.* Washington, DC: Government Printing Office, 1991.

Donaldson, Gary A. *The History of African-Americans in the Military.* Malabar, FL: Krieger Publishing, 1991.

Foner, Jack D. *Blacks and the Military in American History: A New Perspective.* New York: Praeger, 1974.

Foner, Philip S. *Blacks in the American Revolution.* Westport, CT: Greenwood Press, 1975.

Harrod, Frederick S. *Manning the New Navy: The Development of a Modern Naval Enlisted Force, 1899–1940.* Westport, CT: Greenwood Press, 1978.

Kaplan, Sidney, and Kaplan, Emma Nogrady. *The Black Presence in the Era of the American Revolution.* Amherst: University of Massachusetts Press, 1989.

Krawczynski, Keith. "African American Navy, Marine, Women's Reserves, and Coast Guard Service during World War II." In *A Historic Context for the African-American Military Experience.* Edited by Steven D. Smith and James A. Ziegler. U.S. Army Corps of Engineers, 1998. https://www.denix.osd.mil/denix/Public/ES-Programs/Conservation/Legacy/AAME/aame3a.html#7%20African%20American%20Navy (accessed August 9, 2003).

MacGregor, Morris J. *Integration of the Armed Forces, 1940–1965.* Washington, DC: Center of Military History, 1985. http://www.army.mil/cmh-pg/books/integration/IAF-FM.htm#TABLE%20OF%20CONTENTS (accessed August 9, 2003).

Mueller, William R. "The Negro in the Navy." *Social Forces* 24 (1945): 110–115.

Mullen, Robert F. *Blacks in America's Wars: The Shift in Attitudes from the Revolutionary War to Vietnam.* New York: Monad Press, 1974.

Nalty, Bernard C. *Strength for the Fight: A History of Black Americans in the Military.* New York: Free Press, 1986.

Nalty, Bernard C., and Morris J. MacGregor. *Blacks in the Military: Essential Documents.* Wilmington, DE: Scholarly Resources, 1981.

Nelson, Dennis D. *The Integration of the Negro into the U.S. Navy.* New York: Farrar, Strauss and Young, 1951.

Quarles, Benjamin. *The Negro in the Civil War.* Boston: Little, Brown, 1953.

———. *The Negro in the American Revolution.* Chapel Hill: University of North Carolina Press, 1961.

———. *The Negro in the Making of America.* New York: Collier Books, 1964.

Reddick, L. D. "The Negro in the United States Navy during World War II." *Journal of Negro Education* 32 (1947): 210–219.

Silvera, John D. *The Negro in World War Two.* Baton Rouge: Louisiana Military Press, 1964.

Wilson, Joseph T. *The Black Phalanx: A History of the Negro Soldiers of the United States in the Wars of 1775–1812, 1861–1865.* 1890. Reprint, New York: Arno Press, 1968.

Wynn, Neil A. *The Afro-American and the Second World War.* New York: Holmes and Meier, 1975.

Ute War (1879)

The Ute War, also called the "Meeker Massacre," deserves special mention in any treatment of the role of African Americans in the military because African American cavalrymen, known as "Buffalo Soldiers," were so deeply involved in the conflict. In spite of the racial prejudice and discrimination endured by African Americans after the Civil War, the Buffalo Soldiers of the 9th and 10th Cavalry regiments fought in skirmishes and battles on the western frontier for twenty-four years and earned a reputation as outstanding soldiers. Capt. Francis S. Dodge and the D company of the 9th Cavalry Regiment, an all–African American unit created by the Army Reorganization Act of 1866, saved besieged white soldiers during the Ute War, a Native American uprising on the White River of northwest Colorado.

Trouble had been developing on the three Ute reservations, as the Indian Department and white settlers put increasing pressure on the dwindling lands of the Utes. In September 1879, tension mounted when Nathan C. Meeker, the U.S. government Indian agent for the Ute White River Reservation, attempted to culturally transform the Native Americans into pious farmers. When Meeker plowed a Ute pony racetrack, the Indians retaliated and publicly beat the Indian agent. Meeker sent two couriers requesting military support, one to Maj. Thomas T. Thornburgh, commandant at Fort Frederick Steele, Rawlins, Wyoming, and another to Capt. Francis S. Dodge commander of the 9th Cavalry camped near the Grand River. When the Ute Indians learned that he had called for federal reinforcements they attacked the White River Agency in late September 1879, killed Meeker and several of his assistants, and captured his wife and daughter. News of the incident cause a national outrage against Native Americans and encouraged the government to relocate the Ute tribes to Utah reservations.

Meanwhile, on September 29, 1879, Thornburgh and nearly 200 men from the 4th Infantry and 5th Cavalry and 25 wagons entered the reservation boundaries near Milk Creek. As the soldiers watered their horses, the Utes under Chief Colorow ambushed the soldiers. Thornburgh and twelve other men were instantly killed, and the troops, now under the command of Capt. J. Scott Payne (5th Cavalry), formed a barricade with the wagons and were put on the defensive for several days.

Meeker's courier found Dodge on October 1, 1879. The captain and company D of the 9th Cavalry and approximately forty Buffalo Soldiers and their officers immediately set out for the White River Reservation to assist Thornburgh's men. He issued 225 rounds per man to the Buffalo Soldiers. Dodge and his men covered seventy miles on the first day and arrived within sight of Payne's command just before first light on October 2.

As Dodge and his men rode into the defensive perimeter, they found the troops there in a pitiful plight. Over the next three days, the Utes continued their attacks, often taunting the Buffalo Soldiers with cries of "Black-whitemen!" and at other times singing: "Soldiers with black faces, you ride into battle behind the white soldiers; But you can't take off your black faces, and the white-face soldiers make you ride behind them" (quoted in Emmitt 1954, 219–220).

During the siege, all but four of D company's horses were killed and forty-two men of Thornburgh's former command were wounded, but the arrival of the Buffalo Soldiers raised the morale of the troops, and all hoped that fresh reinforcements would arrive.

On October 5, 1879, Col. Wesley Merritt arrived with five companies of the 5th Cavalry, the vanguard of some 2,000 men who had entrained from Cheyenne, Wyoming, to Rawlins and then covered 160 miles in forty-eight hours. Another force of around 1,000 men was moving up from New Mexico.

As Merritt's men appeared, the Utes withdrew with the 5th in pursuit. Within days peace negotiations brought military operations to a close. For their bravery, both Captain Dodge and African American Sgt. Henry Johnson received Medals of Honor. Dodge was later to say of his men that they had "proven themselves good soldiers and reliable men" (quoted in Santala 1994, 63).

See also Buffalo Soldiers; Johnson, Henry (1824–1904); Medal of Honor (APPENDIX); 9th Cavalry

References and Further Reading

Amos, Preston E. *Above and Beyond in the West: Black Medal of Honor Winners, 1870–1890.* Washington, DC: Potomac Corral, The Westerners, 1974.

Emmitt, Robert. *The Last War Trail: The Utes and the Settlement of Colorado.* Norman: University of Oklahoma Press, 1954.

Leckie, William H. *The Buffalo Soldiers: A Narrative of the Negro Cavalry in the West.* Norman: University of Oklahoma Press, 1967.

Santala, Russel D. *The Ute Campaign: A Study in the Use of the Military Instrument.* Fort Leavenworth, KS: U.S. Army Command and General Staff College, 1994.

Schubert, Frank N. *Black Valor: Buffalo Solders and the Medal of Honor, 1870–1898.* Wilmington, DE: Scholarly Resources, 1997.

V

Vietnam War (1954–1975)

The Vietnam War marked a significant change in the way that African Americans contributed to America's military efforts. African Americans who served in a military capacity during the colonial period often did so as volunteers in an unofficial capacity or with a local militia. From the Civil War through the Korean War, segregated African American units, usually officered by whites, performed in both combat and support capacities. In 1948 President Harry Truman ordered the military establishment to desegregate. Although the navy and air force accomplished integration by 1950, the army, with the vast majority of African American servicemen, did not achieve desegregation until after the Korean conflict. Vietnam, then, marked the first major combat deployment of an integrated military and the first time since the turn of the century that African American participation was actually encouraged.

In 1962 President John F. Kennedy reactivated the President's Committee on Equal Opportunity in the Armed Forces. Chaired by attorney Gerhard Gesell, and known as the Gesell Committee, the panel explored ways to draw qualified African Americans into military service. In 1964 African Americans represented approximately 13 percent of the U.S. population but less than 9 percent of the nation's men in arms. The committee found uneven promotion, token integration, restricted opportunities in the National Guard and Reserves, and discrimination on military bases and their surrounding communities as causes for low African American enlistment. Before the government could react to the committee's report, the explosion of U.S. involvement in Southeast Asia, previously limited to financial aid and military training and advisers, changed the problem. As U.S. forces were introduced into Vietnam in ever-increasing numbers in the mid-1960s, the expanded military, a discriminatory draft, and other government programs brought not only increased African American participation but accusations of new forms of discrimination.

U.S. involvement in Vietnam unfolded against the domestic backdrop of the civil rights movement. From the outset, the use, or alleged misuse, of African American troops evoked charges of racism. Civil rights leaders and other critics, including the formidable Dr. Martin Luther King Jr., came to view the Vietnam conflict as racist—"a white man's war, a black man's fight." King maintained that black youths represented a disproportionate share of early draftees and that African Americans faced a much greater chance of seeing combat than did their white counterparts.

The draft did pose a major concern. Selective

Marine in the 3d Marine Division searches for snipers north of Con Thien, which overlooked a principal North Vietnamese infiltration route into South Vietnam. (National Archives)

Service regulations offered deferments for college attendance and a variety of essential civilian occupations that favored middle- and upper-class men, who were overwhelmingly white. "Safe havens" from service in Vietnam existed in the National Guard and the reserves, but slots in these institutions were even more subject to discrimination and favoritism. The vast majority of draftees were poor, undereducated, and urban—blue-collar workers or unemployed. Furthermore, African Americans were woefully underrepresented on local draft boards; in 1966 blacks accounted for only slightly more than 1 percent of all draft board members, and seven state boards had no African American representation at all.

"Project 100,000," a program launched in 1966 that was part of President Lyndon Johnson's Great Society, was aimed at enhancing the opportunities of underprivileged youths from poverty-stricken urban areas by offering more lenient military entrance requirements. It largely failed. More than 350,000 men enlisted under Project 100,000 during the remainder of the war; 41 percent were African American and 40 percent drew combat assignments. Casualty rates among these soldiers were twice those of other entry categories. Few Project 100,000 inductees received training that would advance military careers or create better opportunities for civilian life.

Some reforms were introduced into the draft system in 1967, when deferments for graduate students and teachers were eliminated, raising the proportion of college-educated personnel in Vietnam from 6 percent in 1966 to 10 percent four years later. A national lottery, a much fairer system implemented in early 1970, had little effect on who served in Vietnam, as U.S. personnel needs there were already being drastically reduced. Likewise, the implementation in 1973 of the all-volunteer armed forces, which eliminated the unfair aspects of the draft, came too late in the war to have much impact.

African Americans often did supply a disproportionate number of combat troops, a high percentage of whom had voluntarily enlisted. Although they made up less than 10 percent of American men in arms and about 13 percent of the U.S. population between 1961 and 1966, they accounted for almost 20 percent of all combat-related deaths in Vietnam during that period. In 1965 alone African Americans represented almost one-fourth of the army's killed in action. In 1968 African Americans, who made up roughly 12 percent of army and Marine total strengths, frequently contributed half the men in front-line combat units, especially in rifle squads and fire teams. Under heavy criticism, army and Marine commanders worked to lessen black casualties after 1966, and by the end of the conflict, African American combat deaths amounted to approximately 12 percent—more in line with national population figures. Final casualty estimates do not support the assertion that African Americans suffered disproportionate losses in Vietnam, but this in no way diminishes the fact that they bore a heavy share of the fighting burden, especially early in the conflict.

Destructive racial disturbances in many American cities in the mid-1960s had negative effects on the military, but the widespread violent reaction to the 1968 assassination of Martin Luther King brought the greatest racial turmoil to the armed forces. Racial strife, rarely an issue among combat units because of shared risk and responsibility, became most evident in rear areas and on domestic installations. At the Navy base at Cam Ranh Bay in South Vietnam, white sailors donned Ku Klux Klan–like outfits, burned crosses, and raised the Confederate flag. African American prisoners, many of whom were jailed for violent crimes, rioted at the U.S. Army stockade at Long Bình; one white soldier was killed and several others were wounded during the upheaval, which spread over weeks. The Marine base at Camp Lejeune, North Carolina, and the army's Fort Benning, Georgia, Fort Bragg, North Carolina, and Camp Pendleton, California, were among the important domestic posts to witness serious racial problems.

These disturbances, with their implications not only for equity and fairness but also for military effectiveness, prompted the military to undertake a study to determine the cause of racial unrest in the armed services. Air Force Col. Lucius Theus, an African American career officer who had worked his way up through the ranks, having entered the Army Air Corps as a private in 1942, chaired the committee. Theus had broad administrative experience in the air force and had served as deputy base commander at Cam Ranh Bay in Vietnam. The committee's work resulted in "The Report of the Inter-Service Task Force on Education in Race Relations" (July 31, 1970), which recommended education in race relations for all military personnel and a race relations education board to set policy and approve curricula for the program. As a direct result of the Theus Committee report, the Defense Race Relations Institute (DRRI) was established at Patrick Air Force Base, Florida, in June 1971—probably not coincidentally, just a month after another racial disturbance at Travis Air Force Base in California.

It was clear, however, that education by the DRRI to make all military personnel aware of racial difficulties would be only a beginning; the "impersonality, insensitivity, and indifference [to racial problems] of commanders at various levels of the chain of command" that were observed after the Travis riots would require "commitment to change, strong leadership at all levels, sensitivity to problems, and the resolve to take action when necessary." A month after another disturbance at Laredo Air Force Base in Texas, Air Force Chief of Staff General John D. Ryan sent a letter to all commands clearly stating: "I desire that you, your commanders and supervisors support the USAF Equal Opportunity and Race Relations Education program with the same vigor and enthusiasm as that given the flying mission" (quotations from Osur 2001).

Other measure were taken to address racial problems in the services. Particularly during the

Seaman Lawrence W. Overton loading magazines for his M-16 rifle from 5.56 x 45mm ammunition stripper clips, as he assumes the watch on the USS Harnett County *(LST-821), May 1969.* Harnett County *was then operating on the Vam Co Dong River, South Vietnam. (U.S. Navy/ Ed Nelson)*

tenure of Adm. Elmo Zumwalt, who became chief of naval operations in June 1970, the navy attempted to deal with discrimination within its ranks and to actively recruit more African Americans into the enlisted ranks as well as increase the numbers of black midshipmen at the U.S. Naval Academy. The other service academies also undertook more aggressive recruiting of African Americans in order to augment the small number of African American officers. Zumwalt issued a number of so-called Z-grams, general communications to the navy dealing with issues of racial discrimination. By 1974 his policies were beginning to bear fruit: African Americans accounted for more than 8 percent of naval personnel, up from 5.5 percent a few years earlier.

African Americans played a major role in Vietnam. Contrary to popular impression, a large proportion of African American servicemen were well-trained, highly motivated professionals; some twenty received the Medal of Honor, and a number of the African American officers who served there became general officers—the most notable example being Colin Powell. Despite the likelihood of seeing hazardous duty, African Americans reenlisted at substantially higher rates than whites. In 1964 blacks represented less than 9 percent of all U.S. armed forces; by 1976 they made up more than 15 percent. The percentage of African American officers doubled between 1964 and 1976, yet they still accounted for less than 4 percent of the total. These statistics suggest that although full equality was far from being achieved, participation by African Americans in the Vietnam War strengthened their position in the armed forces beyond what had been achieved in most sectors of civilian society at the time.

See also African Americanization; Joel, Lawrence; Medal of Honor (APPENDIX); National Association for the Advancement of Colored People; Olive, Milton Lee, III; U.S. Air Force; U.S. Army; U.S. Marine Corps; U.S. Navy; Z-Gram 66

References and Further Reading

Binkin, Martin, Mark J. Eitelberg, et al. *Blacks in the Military.* Washington, DC: Brookings Institution, 1982.

Cash, John. *Seven Firefights in Vietnam.* Washington, DC: Office of the Chief of Military History U.S. Army, 1970.

Coffey, David. "African American Personnel in U.S. Forces in Vietnam." In *Encyclopedia of the Vietnam War: A Political, Social, and Military History,* ed. Spencer C. Tucker. Santa Barbara, CA: ABC-CLIO, 1998.

Dougan, Clark, Samuel Lipsman, et al. *A Nation Divided.* Boston: Boston Publishing, 1984.

Foner, Jack D. *Blacks and the Military in American History.* New York: Praeger, 1974.

Goff, Stanley, and Robert Sanders, with Clark Smith. *Brothers: Black Soldiers in the Nam.* Novato, CA: Presidio Press, 1982.

Hauser, William L. *America's Army in Crisis: A Study of Civil-Military Relations.* Baltimore: John Hopkins University Press, 1973.

Nalty, Bernard C. *Strength for the Fight: A History of Black Americans in the Military.* New York: Free Press, 1986.

Osur, Alan M. "Black-White Relations in the U.S. Military, 1940–1972." http://www.airpower.maxwell.af.mil/airchronicles/aureview/1981/nov-dec/osur.htm (created November 13, 2001; accessed September 24, 2003).

Terry, Wallace. *Bloods: An Oral History of the Vietnam War by Black Veterans.* New York: Ballantine Books, 1984.

Walker, William (d. 1864)

During the Civil War, Sgt. William Walker (Company A, 3d South Carolina Colored Infantry) was tried and executed for leading a mutiny in the ranks at Camp Bennett, Hilton Head, South Carolina. It was claimed that on November 19, 1863, Walker took command of his company and led the men into the tent of Col. Augustus Bennett, their company commanding officer, who later testified against Walker during the soldiers' January trial. Walker told the men to stack their arms and announce that they would no longer serve duty for $7 per month. The colonel told the men to take their weapons and return to duty or be shot. Walker then instructed Company A to leave its arms and return to quarters. The root cause of the action was the Union Army's decision to pay African Americans $7 per month instead of the same pay issued to white soldiers. According to William Walker's court martial statement written in January 1864, he voluntarily entered the regiment after he was promised the same wages and allowances as were issued to all U.S. soldiers. After the soldiers of Company A learned that lower wages were issued to African Americans, they allegedly refused further duty. Walker insisted that he exercised no command over the other men.

Nevertheless, a military court was convened at Hilton Head, South Carolina, from January 9–12, 1864, in which Walker was charged with several counts, including mutinous conduct, conduct prejudicial to good order and military discipline, mutiny, and breach of arrest.

Not only were the men in the 3d South Carolina Colored Infantry paid unequal wages, the regiment did not receive proper training, and was largely used for labor duties (against General Gilmore's instructions). Like Walker, the men had enlisted on the basis that they would be paid the full rate. Likewise, the soldiers in the 3d South Carolina Volunteers were not read the Articles of War, and therefore did not realize that their actions contrary to the army laws and regulations (i.e., that they constituted mutiny, which was punishable by death).

Walker was found guilty on a majority verdict, and before the case could be referred to the president, the sentence of death was carried out on March 1, 1864. Walker's case was specifically mentioned during the U.S. Senate debate on the payment of African American troops and used as an example to buttress the case for reform.

See also American Civil War; United States Colored Troops (APPENDIXES)

References and Further Reading

Buckley, Gail. *American Patriots: The Story of Blacks in the Military from the Revolution to Desert Storm.* New York: Random House, 2001.

Hamilton, William J., III. "The Court Martial of William Walker, 3rd SC Colored Infantry." http://www.awod.com/gallery/probono/cwchas/walkertr.html (accessed August 13, 2003).

Westwood, Howard C. *Black Troops, White Commanders, and Freedmen during the Civil War.* Carbondale: Southern Illinois University Press, 1992.

WALLER, CALVIN (1937–1996)

Gen. Calvin Waller of the U.S. Army, an African American, was the deputy commander during Operation DESERT STORM in the Gulf War (1991).

Waller, commander in chief Gen. Norman Schwarzkopf, and the chairman of the Joint Chiefs of Staff, Colin Powell, had all crossed paths on numerous occasions prior to their involvement in the Gulf War. Waller, like his two contemporaries, was a career soldier and had been, like them, a young officer in Vietnam. He had shared training at Fort Leavenworth with Schwarzkopf and had worked closely with Powell at the Pentagon during the 1970s and 1980s in the Defense Department. Waller was considered to be something of a genius in terms of logistics, and he came to Desert Storm with the unenviable task of dealing with 540,000 troops. He had been personally requested for the job by Schwarzkopf during the latter's buildup in Saudi Arabia, known as Operation Desert Shield.

Waller was among the first generation of African American officers to rise to high command in the U.S. Army in the wake of the Vietnam War. He served as deputy commander of Fort Lewis under Schwarzkopf between 1986 and 1987 and then commanded the 8th Infantry Division in Germany in 1989.

Waller arrived in Saudi Arabia in December 1990 and had precious little time to prepare the troops for the impending ground offensive. It was widely believed that Waller was one of the few men who could deal with Schwarzkopf's brusque manner and volatile temper. It is significant that it was Waller who called Schwarzkopf on February 28 to inform him that President George Bush had decided to announce a ceasefire after just 100 hours of the offensive. Waller's message did cause friction between the two men, as Schwarzkopf believed that it would allow considerable numbers of Iraqi troops to extract themselves unmolested.

Waller was very vocal in the war against drugs and constantly agitated for action to dissuade African American youth from using drugs and to encourage them to attend school regularly. Waller retired in 1991 and moved into private life as a senior vice president in industry. He was a strong supporter of the belief that every American citizen should perform two or three years' service to the country and that some form of mandatory public service should be instituted, very much along the lines of the Civilian Conservation Corps, which had been run by the U.S. Army during the 1930s. At the age of fifty-eight Calvin Waller suffered a heart attack and died.

See also Gulf War; Powell, Colin Luther

References and Further Reading

Atkinson, Rick. *Crusade.* Boston: Houghton Mifflin, 1993.

Gordon, Michael R., and Bernard Trainor. *The Generals' War.* Boston: Little Brown, 1995.

Powell, Colin L., with Joseph E. Persico. *My American Journey.* New York: Random House, 1995.

WALLEY, AUGUSTUS (1856–1938)

Augustus Walley served in the 9th Cavalry and saw action on the frontier and in Cuba and the

Philippines during the Spanish American War, winning a Medal of Honor in 1881.

Walley was born into slavery on March 10, 1856, in Reisterstown, Maryland. After the Civil War he worked as a laborer until November 26, 1878, when he joined Troop I of the 9th Cavalry at Baltimore. He remained with the regiment until he was discharged on November 25, 1883.

On August 16, 1881, Walley saw action against Apaches in the Cuchillo Negro Mountains, New Mexico, where he saved the life of Private Burton, whose horse had bolted and then thrown him. Despite the presence of Apaches who continually fired at him, Walley saved the trooper, and he was recommended for a Medal of Honor by Lt. George R. Burnett.

Walley received his Medal of Honor on October 1, 1890, and was additionally awarded a Certificate of Merit on the recommendation of Col. Edward Hatch, the regiment's commander.

Walley saw action in Cuba, where at the battle of Las Guásimas (June 24, 1898), he rescued Major Bell of the 1st Cavalry, who had been shot through the leg on the battlefield. Walley was awarded another Certificate of Merit for this gallantry. By now Walley was serving with the 10th Cavalry, having re-enlisted November 26, 1883, the day after his initial enlistment ended. He continued to serve until 1907, completing twenty-nine years in the army. He was recalled to active service on May 1, 1918, and finally retired on March 8, 1919. Augustus Walley died in Baltimore on April 9, 1938.

See also Apache Wars; Buffalo Soldiers; Las Guásimas, Battle of; Medal of Honor (APPENDIX); 9th Cavalry; Spanish-American War; 10th Cavalry

References and Further Reading

Beer, W. F., and O. F. Keyed. *Deeds of Valor: How America's Heroes Won the Medal of Honor.* Detroit: Perrien-Keydel, 1903.

Leckie, William H. *The Buffalo Soldiers: A Narrative of the Negro Cavalry in the West.* Norman: University of Oklahoma Press, 1967.

Wanton, George Henry (1868–1940)

George Wanton was an African American career soldier who served with the 10th Cavalry for thirty-six years. He was born in Paterson, New Jersey, on May 15, 1868, and enlisted in Troop M of the 10th U.S. Cavalry in 1889. In 1892, he received a promotion to corporal (he had been demoted to private by the time he won the Medal of Honor). Prior to his enlistment in the U.S. Army he had joined the U.S. Navy in 1884, and after four years of enlistment he was discharged in 1888.

As a member of the 10th Cavalry, Wanton was sent to Cuba during the Spanish American War. On June 30, 1898, units of the 10th Cavalry aboard the USS *Florida* attempted a landing at Tayabacoa on the east coast of Cuba to link up with General Maximo Gomes's Cuban insurgents. The landing took place near a Spanish-held blockhouse, and the U.S. troopers were ambushed. The bulk of the men were evacuated, but some sixteen or so wounded were abandoned and were captured by the Spaniards.

Back on board ship, volunteers were called to help free the prisoners, despite the fact that several attempts had already been made and had failed. Privates Wanton, Dennis Bell, Fitz Lee, and William H. Thompkins volunteered and put ashore on a launch. Wanton and the others surprised the Spanish forces and rescued the prisoners, managing to get them back to the USS *Florida* and safety. For this deed, Bell, Lee, Thompkins, and Wanton were all awarded the Medal of Honor on June 23, 1899, the citation for each reading: "Voluntarily went ashore in the face of the enemy and aided in the rescue of his wounded comrades; this after several previous attempts at rescue had been frustrated."

Wanton was subsequently promoted to sergeant in 1898 and continued to serve with the 10th Cavalry until he retired from service in 1925. Wanton served as an honorary pallbearer at the burial of the Unknown Soldier of World War I at the ceremony at the Memorial

Amphitheater of the Arlington National Cemetery in 1921.

Master Sgt. George Henry Wanton died on November 27, 1940, at Walter Reed Hospital in Washington, D.C. He was buried with full military honors in Arlington National Cemetery.

See also Spanish-American War; 10th Cavalry

References and Further Reading

Fletcher, Marvin. *The Black Soldier and Officer in the United States Army, 1891–1917*. Columbia: University of Missouri Press, 1974.

Freidel, Frank. *The Splendid Little War.* Boston: Little, Brown, 1958.

Funston, Frederick. *Memories of Two Wars: Cuban and Philippine Experiences.* New York: Charles Scribner's Sons, 1911.

Halstead, Murat. *Full Official History of the War with Spain.* New Haven, CT: Butler and Alger, 1899.

Lee, Fitzhugh, ed. *Cuba's Struggle against Spain. With a Story of Santiago by T. Roosevelt. A Description of the Destruction of the "Maine" by R. Wainwright.* New York: American Historical Press, 1899.

WARREN, JOHN E., JR. (1946–1969)

1st Lt. John E. Warren Jr., U.S. Army, Company C, 2d Battalion (Mechanized), 22d Infantry, 25th Infantry Division was killed in action in Tay Ninh Province, Republic of Vietnam, January 14, 1969. The citation for his Medal of Honor read:

> For conspicuous gallantry and intrepidity in action at the risk of his life above and beyond the call of duty. 1st Lt. Warren distinguished himself at the cost of his life while serving as a platoon leader with Company C. While moving through a rubber plantation to reinforce another friendly unit, Company C came under intense fire from a well-fortified enemy force. Disregarding his safety, 1st Lt. Warren with several of his men began maneuvering through the hail of enemy fire toward the hostile positions. When he had come to within 6 feet of one of the enemy bunkers and was preparing to toss a hand grenade into it, an enemy grenade was suddenly thrown into the middle of his small group. Thinking only of his men, 1st Lt. Warren fell in the direction of the grenade, thus shielding those around him from the blast. His action, performed at the cost of his life, saved 3 men from serious or mortal injury. First Lt. Warren's ultimate action of sacrifice to save the lives of his men was in keeping with the highest traditions of the military service and reflects great credit on him, his unit, and the U.S. Army.

Warren was born in Brooklyn, New York, on November 16, 1946, entered service in New York, and started his tour of duty in Vietnam on September 7, 1968. Warren was platoon leader of Company C, when they were ambushed west of Dau Tang, Tay Ninh (Caw Koin), at a rubber plantation. The Medal of Honor was presented to Warren's family at the White House by President Richard Nixon on April 7, 1970. He is buried at the Long Island National Cemetery, Farmingdale, Long Island.

See also Medal of Honor (APPENDIX); Vietnam War

WASHINGTON, WILLIAM G. (D. 1952)

Six years before the integration of the U.S. Army, William Washington became the first African American commanding officer in the U.S. Army when he arrived at Aberdeen Proving Ground in November 1942. Major Washington became the commander of Company D, 2d Regiment; he had joined the U.S. Army as an enlisted man in 1914 and had spent twenty-eight years as such before he was made an officer.

Washington was known as a perfectionist, determined to work his way through the segregated environment of the U.S. Army. The fact that Washington survived in the U.S. Army during the deep cuts of the period between the two world wars amply shows his ability and commitment to the service.

Washington was initially assigned to Fort Douglas, Arizona, after basic training, and from 1916 to 1922 he served in the Philippine Islands. Upon his return to the United States he became post ordnance sergeant of harbor defense at the Columbia River, later serving in the same position at the Presidio in San Francisco. Washington had another tour of duty in the Philippine Islands from 1931 to 1933, then served in San Francisco, and was later transferred to Savannah, Illinois.

Washington was promoted to captain in May 1942 and briefly served as a captain at Fort Sill, Oklahoma, before being transferred to the Aberdeen Proving Grounds in 1942 and promoted to major. He retired two years later after having served thirty years in the U.S. Army. In a letter of praise, Col. James W. Mosteller Jr., his commander at Daniel Field, Georgia, said of Washington: "During this entire period your record was without a blemish, and such a period of enlisted service without one instance of company punishment is unusual and exceptional. Upon your relief from active duty I desire to commend you for your long and efficient service, and the excellent record that you have earned" (quoted in Heimbach).

When he left the U.S. Army in 1944, the South Carolinian moved to California to become a farmer. He died in 1952.

See also U.S. Army; U.S. Army, Interwar Period

References and Further Reading

Heimbach, Meghan. "William B. Washington was APG's First African American Company Commander." *Aberdeen Proving Ground News,* n.d. http://www.defenselink.mil/specials/AfricanAm2003/apg.html/ (accessed August 14, 2003).

WATSON, GEORGE (1915–1943)

One of the seven African Americans who fought in World War II who were finally recognized with Medals of Honor in 1997, Pvt. George Watson was born in Birmingham, Alabama, and drafted into the U.S. Army in September 1942, training at Fort Benning, Georgia. He was assigned to the 2d Battalion, 29th Quartermaster Regiment, and was posted to the Pacific Theater.

On March 8, 1943, Watson and his unit were on board the USAT *Jacob* near Porloch Harbor, New Guinea, when they came under attack from Japanese aircraft. The vessel was hit several times, and the order to abandon ship was given. Watson swam back and forth, retrieving those who could not swim or who were injured, dragging them onto life rafts. Unfortunately, as the vessel finally sank beneath the waves, the swell pulled Watson under, and he was never seen again. Watson was a good swimmer, and he had willingly passed his own life preserver to another man.

For his gallantry he was awarded the Distinguished Service Cross, the first African American winner of the award during World War II. A memorial was set up to him at Manila American Cemetery on the Philippines and another at the George Watson Memorial Field at Fort Benning. On January 13, 1997, Watson's award was upgraded to the Medal of Honor and bestowed posthumously by President Bill Clinton at the White House.

Watson died with no known next of kin, and his Medal of Honor and citation are now housed at the U.S. Army Quartermaster Museum, Fort Lee, Virginia. In 1997 the Navy christened the USNS *Watson* (T-AKR-310) in his honor.

See also Medal of Honor (APPENDIX); World War II

Wereth Massacre (December 17, 1944)

Eleven African American prisoners of war were tortured and executed by German SS troops in Wereth, Belgium, on December 17, 1944. The story did not surface until 1996, when a television news show reported what had happened and the men began to receive belated recognition.

On December 16, 1944, a surprise German counterattack in the Ardennes area of Belgium, beginning what is known as the Battle of the Bulge, hit U.S. and Allied troops in the midst of snowstorms. S.Sgt. Thomas James Forte of the 333d Field Artillery Battalion and ten other African American enlisted men were separated from the unit by the sudden German attack.

Initially, Forte and the men were hidden in a farmhouse by Belgian civilians, but an SS patrol captured them. After the patrol disarmed the Americans, they were temporarily held captive and then marched out of Wereth, never to be seen alive again. Medical reports on the bodies showed that the men had been systematically tortured before being murdered. The case remained classified for many years after the war as one of the 268 atrocities committed by SS troops during the Ardennes offensive.

In 1998, Maj. Gen. James W. Monroe, commander of the U.S. Army Industrial Operations Command, presented posthumous awards to Sergeant Forte's relatives. Listed as murdered in 1944, in addition to Sergeant Forte, were Cpl. Mager Bradley, Pfc. George Davis, Pfc. George Motten, Pfc. Due Turner, Pfc. Jim Leatherwood, Privates Curtis Adams, Nathaniel Moss, and W. E. Pritchett, Technician 4th Class James Stewart, and Technician 5th Class Rob Green. Monroe said of the men at the ceremony:

> Staff Sergeant Forte and his fellow soldiers risked their lives and epitomized the Army core values with their exemplary behavior, efficiency and fidelity during their military service. It is for this reason—we are honoring, remembering and recognizing the acts of Staff Sergeant Forte. We owe a great debt of gratitude for the ultimate sacrifice he made. He and the other 10 courageous soldiers shared the common bonds of the Armed Forces which is duty and sacrifice (quoted in Whistine).

See also Bulge, Battle of the; World War II

References and Further Reading

Whistine, Bob. *Army News Service,* April 20, 1998. Available in abbreviated form as "World War II Veteran Killed in Action Receives Posthumous Purple Heart." *The Edge Online* 6, no. 2 (Summer 1998). http://www.osc.army.mil/ea/edge/sum1998.htm (accessed August 14, 2003).

West Point

The most elite army training institution in the country, the U.S. Military Academy at West Point resisted the introduction of African American cadets until the second half of the twentieth century. Those who attended the school before that time faced widespread discrimination, as administrators, teachers, and fellow students all attempted to discourage them from completing their degrees. With the dramatic social changes wrought in both the army and American society since 1950, though, West Point has finally welcomed African American cadets, providing them with the education and training to excel as army officers.

Founded in 1802 on the site of a strategically important fort during the American Revolution, West Point was long a bastion of elitism, even among whites. Cadets were nominated into the academy by U.S. senators and representatives from the candidates' respective states and were subjected to rigorous entrance examinations that included both academic and physical components. The academic tests included an assessment of candidates' skills in mathematics, grammar, history, and geography. The physical examination was carried out in order to eliminate the possibility that any cadet was carrying either an infectious or chronic disease. Those who gained admittance faced five years of grueling coursework from their instructors, exacting training from their officers, and humiliating hazing from their peers. Upon graduation, cadets were commissioned second lieutenants in the U.S. Army. With the prestige of West Point backing them up, many went on to illustrious military careers.

For the first sixty years of the school's existence, the question of whether or not to admit African Americans was moot. Since blacks were banned from service in the army, they were obviously not eligible for enrollment at West Point. The Civil War, though, marked the reversal of this prohibition of African Americans from the military. With thousands of black soldiers in arms by 1865, the issue of African American officers emerged as a major controversy among military authorities, political figures, and the general public. Most Americans disdained the idea that blacks could command white troops, and thus very few African Americans were elevated to the officer corp.

Nevertheless, some African Americans strove to break this racial barrier, particularly during the period of Reconstruction, when Americans' views regarding racism were challenged continuously in both the North and the South. With the passage of the Thirteenth (1865), Fourteenth (1868), and Fifteenth (1870) Amendments abolishing slavery, conveying citizenship on African Americans, and granting them the right to vote, respectively, critics of the idea of commissioning African American officers had less ground on which to stand. Consequently, the first African American cadet was nominated and accepted to West Point in 1870.

Admission to West Point, however, did not presage acceptance. In fact, the cadet, a South Carolinian named James Webster Smith, faced tremendous discrimination on all fronts during his time at West Point and was almost completely isolated during his tenure. He was forced to repeat his freshman year as a punishment for arguing with a cadet who had stepped on his toes, part of a systematic campaign of harassment. He eventually began to have academic problems and was dismissed in 1874. It is clear that his time at West Point was extremely difficult; he was both humiliated and viciously treated by his fellow students.

Shortly after Smith's departure, another African American cadet faced even more severe treatment. Johnson Chestnut Whittaker faced the same program of harassment and discrimination that prevented him from earning his degree, but although he completed his five years of course work on schedule in 1880, he was beaten and tortured before he could take his final examinations. In an episode that has never been adequately explained by anyone in authority at West Point, Whittaker was found in his room, "bleeding and insensible, bound hand and foot to his bedstead. His head was partly shaved, and his feet and hands slashed" (Marszalek 1994).

Despite the racism prevalent at all levels of American society, the incident sparked a public outcry and massive press coverage, leading to a congressional investigation. At the resulting court of inquiry, school authorities accused Whittaker of inflicting the injuries himself in order to avoid the final examinations. He was consequently court-martialed and dishonorably discharged. Although a subsequent court reversed this decision, Whittaker was never allowed to take his examinations and thus failed to graduate from West Point.

Not until 1877 did the first African American graduate from West Point. Former slave Henry Ossian Flipper from Thomasville, Georgia, endured a difficult five years at the academy, during which he lived as a social outcast among the other cadets, much as Smith and Whittaker had done before him. Indeed, he had roomed with both Smith and Whittaker during his first few years at the school, having enrolled in 1872. Unlike his roommates, though, he was allowed to graduate with his class, receiving his commission and taking up his assignment with the all–African American 10th Cavalry, with whom he spent several years on frontier duty. Perhaps the public furor over Whittaker's treatment had discouraged fellow cadets or school authorities from preventing Young's graduation.

Exactly ten years later, Flipper was followed by another African American West Point graduate, John H. Alexander. After graduation, he was assigned to a post at Fort Robinson, Nebraska, and then became a military instructor at Wilberforce University. His career proved brief,

John Hanks Alexander, who graduated from the U.S. Military Academy at West Point in 1887. He served with the Buffalo Soldiers in the West. (CORBIS)

however, as he died of a heart attack only seven years after graduating from the academy.

The third African American to graduate from West Point was Charles Young, who followed Alexander by two years, graduating in 1889. Young embarked on what was to become an exemplary career, but he was the last African American to graduate from West Point until 1936. Although Congress had nominated twenty-seven African Americans for admission to the academy between 1870 and 1889, only twelve had passed the entrance examinations, and of those twelve, only two—Young and Alexander—finished their degrees. West Point had a notoriously high attrition rate even among white cadets, but blacks cadets faced additional challenges that proved to be insurmountable for all but a few.

Between 1889 and 1936, several African Americans attended West Point but none graduated. Finally, cadet Benjamin O. Davis Jr. bridged the racial gap by graduating in June 1936. He too had received harsh and almost unbearable treatment from his peers during his time at West Point. He roomed alone, was forced to eat his meals at a separate table, and was spoken to by his fellow students only when it was absolutely necessary to convey orders. Davis eventually became the leader of the Tuskegee Airmen and the first African American to be promoted to the rank of general in the Air Force. His graduation also blazed a trail for the graduation of other African American cadets, although there were still only a handful of them.

As the U.S. Army underwent the massive process of desegregation in the late 1940s and early 1950s, West Point experienced similar changes, finally lifting the prohibition on African Americans participating in social functions and sports teams in 1951. Although African American officers continued to represent just 2 percent of the U.S. Army's officer corps until well into the 1960s, the weakening of racial barriers was slowly but inexorably occurring at West Point as well as in the rest of the army and American society, spurred forward by a powerful civil rights movement. Although change has been gradual at the academy since the 1950s, the outward signs of hostility toward African Americans have now passed into uncomfortable memory, and African American cadets receive the same treatment as their white peers. Like all U.S. military institutions, the academy now represents a microcosm of U.S. society, with a representative group of African Americans, and its administration works hard to eradicate any lingering remnants of discrimination.

The rise of affirmative action programs in the United States in the 1970s caused West Point officials to reexamine the academy's admissions procedures, particularly after school administrators publicly stated the desirability of a diverse student population. Officials rejected the adoption of a quota system, which would admit a specified number of African Americans regardless of their ability to pass the entrance examinations. Instead, the administration opted to set a goal of 10–12 percent for African American admissions, striving to meet this goal not by reducing standards for black cadets but by devoting more time to recruiting blacks so that the pool of initial candidates for admission would be larger and therefore more likely to produce acceptable applicants. Race, however, is not factored into the admissions policy, and all cadets, black or white, must meet the same tough admission standards. Officials confidently maintain that this policy will eventually bring about the desired results. In 2003, 8 percent of the academy's student body was African American, making West Point the most ethnically diverse of all three military academies. However, African Americans represent roughly 13 percent of the American population, a discrepancy that illustrates how far West Point still has to go before it reaches its goal of truly representing American society.

As for those first African American cadets who faced such hardships in their efforts to graduate, the federal government finally took steps to rectify the wrongs done to them at West Point. In 1995, President Bill Clinton posthumously awarded Whittaker his degree from West Point. Two years later, at the urging of South Carolina's Democratic Congressmen John Spratt and Jim Clyburn and Republican Senator Strom Thurmond, Clinton did the same for Smith.

See also Buffalo Soldiers; Davis, Benjamin Oliver, Jr.; Flipper, Henry Ossian; Smith, James Webster; Young, Charles

References and Further Reading

Ambrose, Stephen E. *Duty, Honor, Country: A History of West Point.* Baltimore: Johns Hopkins University Press, 1996.

Atkinson, Rick. *The Long Gray Line.* Boston: Houghton Mifflin, 1989.

Flipper, Henry Ossian. *Black Frontiersman: The Memoirs of Henry O. Flipper, First Black Graduate of West Point.* Ed. Theodore D. Harris. Fort Worth: Texas Christian University Press, 1997.

Flipper, Henry Ossian. *The Colored Cadet at West Point.* Ed. with intro. by Quintard Taylor Jr. Lincoln: University of Nebraska Press, 1998.

Grant, John, James L. Lynch, and Ronald H. Bailey. *West Point: The First Two Hundred Years.* Guilford, CT: Globe Pequot Press, 2002.

Gray, Valerie A. *The Court Martial Trial of West Point Cadet Johnson Whittaker: A Headline Court Case.* Berkeley Heights, NJ: Enslow Publishers, 2001.

Marszalek, John F. *Assault At West Point: The Court-Martial of Johnson Whittaker.* New York: Prentice-Hall, 1994.

Washington, Wayne. "West Point and White House Go Opposite Ways on Diversity," *Boston Globe,* February 2, 2003.

Wham Paymaster Robbery (May 11, 1889)

During the Wham Paymaster Robbery in Arizona, Buffalo Soldiers, as the African American troops who served on the frontier were called, faced an outlaw ambush. Ten of the soldiers won medals or certificates for the bravery they showed in the encounter.

For twelve years Maj. Joseph W. Wham had organized the payroll deliveries to U.S. Army garrisons in the area. When he left Fort Grant with his assistant Hamilton Lewis (B Company, 24th Infantry), his escort was made up of nine infantrymen of the all–African American 24th Infantry and two soldiers of the all–African American 10th Cavalry; they were detailed to guard the $28,345.10 that Wham was carrying in an Army ambulance. Sgt. Benjamin Brown (Company C of the 24th) led the detail, accompanied by Cpl. Isaiah Mays (B Company), Squire Williams (K Company), Benjamin Burge (E Company), Julius Harrison (B Company), Oscar Fox, George Arrington, George Short, and James Young, all of the 24th, and Thornton Harris and James Wheeler of the 10th.

The payroll was bound for Fort Thomas, due north, but the route went northwest, edging along the western slopes of the Graham Mountains, traveling through Cedar Springs. The portion of the route passed was bordered by cliffs on the right and rocky terrain on the left. As the two wagons, the second carrying the escort, crested the low hill, it was clear that the trail had been blocked by a boulder. As Brown and the escort advanced toward the obstructions, a shot rang out. In the next half an hour, the twenty or so outlaws fired nearly 500 shots at the men. Despite their wounds, nearly all of the men continued firing back, but they were pinned down. The outlaws scrambled from their cover and seized the sacks of gold before Corporal Mays managed to walk and crawl 2 miles to Cottonwood ranch to raise the alarm. Fort Grant dispatched K Company of the 24th Infantry to track down the outlaws, but after three days they gave up the hunt.

Wham recommended that Brown and Mays should receive the Medal of Honor and that the other eight men should be awarded Certificates of Merit. He believed that two of the men, Fox and Short, had hidden themselves for the duration of the fight, but in fact they had been wounded.

The 10th's commander, Lt. Col. George C. Hunt, merely passed the commendations on but the 24th's colonel, Zenas Bliss, published a regimental order expressing appreciation for their actions. There was some debate from higher ranking officers in Washington on account of the fact that the payroll had been lost, but the awards were finally approved by Redfield Proctor, the secretary of war, on February 1, 1890.

Arrington, Wheeler, Lewis, and Young were no longer in the army by the end of 1890. Corporal Mays stayed in the army until the summer of 1893. By then, after an argument with his commanding officer, he had been reduced to a private, fined $10, and reassigned to D Company in Fort Bayard, New Mexico.

Sergeant Brown later qualified as a distinguished marksman and by 1904 was ranked fifty-fourth best shot in the entire army. He suffered a stroke that year while assigned to Fort Assiniboine, Montana, and died in Washington, D.C., the next year.

See also Apache Wars; Buffalo Soldiers; 10th Cavalry; 24th Infantry Regiment

References and Further Reading

Dowsey, Fairfax D. *The Buffalo Soldiers in the Indian Wars.* New York: McGraw-Hill, 1969.

Schubert, Frank N., ed. *On the Trail of the Buffalo Soldier: Biographies of African Americans in the U.S. Army, 1860–1917.* Wilmington, DE: Scholarly Resources, 1995.

———. *Black Valor: Buffalo Soldiers and the Medal of Honor, 1870–1898.* Wilmington, DE: Scholarly Resources, 1997.

Williams, Cathay (1842–1892?)

Cathay Williams was a remarkable woman. Posing as a man, "William Cathey" (as she called herself) served in the African American 38th Infantry Regiment from November 1866 to October 1868—the only female Buffalo Soldier.

Williams was born to a slave mother (her father was a freeman) near Independence, Missouri, in about 1842. Her mother worked for planter William Johnson, who moved the family to Jefferson City when Williams was a little girl. When the war broke out the Union Army came to Jefferson City and took Williams and other African Americans with them as paid servants. She became a cook, ultimately working for Gen. Philip Sheridan in Washington and during Union raids in the Shenandoah Valley. At the end of the war she was employed at the Jefferson Barracks in Missouri.

On November 15, 1866, Williams enlisted in the army for a three-year term in St. Louis. Her story, in her own words, appeared ten years later in the St. Louis *Daily Times* (January 2, 1876). One reason she gave for having enlisted was that she wanted to make her own living and not be dependent. "Only two persons," she said, "a cousin and a particular friend, members of the regiment, knew that I was a woman." They never betrayed her; she passed what must have been a cursory fitness exam and her sex was not revealed until October 1868 when she was given a medical discharge.

During her time with the 38th Infantry, Williams performed all the duties of a soldier, standing guard, carrying her pack and rifle, and marching with her company from Fort Riley, Kansas, to Fort Harker and later to Fort Union, New Mexico. In September her company was sent to Fort Cummings and finally to Fort Bayard, New Mexico, a 47-mile trek accomplished in one day. There is no record of the regiment engaging in combat during Williams's enlistment.

Williams's health apparently deteriorated in the army. She was hospitalized on at least five occasions with different illnesses. On the recommendation of an assistant surgeon and of her own captain, Williams received a certificate of disability and was discharged at Fort Bayard on October 14, 1868.

Having left the army, she traveled to Fort Union and worked as a cook until 1870, then as a laundress in Pueblo, Colorado. After two years she moved on to Las Animas County, where she spent another year before finally settling down in Trinidad, Colorado.

In June 1891 she applied for an invalid pension based on her military service. Her application, which was sworn to before a county clerk, claimed that she was the William Cathey who had served as a private in Company A, 38th U.S. Infantry. She asked for an invalid pension on account of her deafness, rheumatism, and neuralgia. On September 9, 1891, she was examined by a doctor from the Pension Bureau; among other things he noted that all of her toes had been amputated. In February of the following year the Pension Bureau rejected her claim.

Nothing is known concerning Cathay Williams after the rejection of her invalid pension claim. She is not listed in the 1900 census for Trinidad, and it must be assumed that she either died prior to the census or moved to another location. What is known about Williams is that, under the name of "William Cathey," she was the only documented African American woman to serve in the U.S. Army before women were officially permitted in the service.

See also African American Women in the Military; American Civil War; Buffalo Soldiers; 9th Cavalry; 10th Cavalry

References and Further Reading

Blanton, DeAnne. "Cathay Williams: Black Woman Soldier, 1866–1868." *Minerva* 10 (1992): 1–12. http://www.buffalosoldier.net/CathayWilliamsFemaleBuffaloSoldierWithDocuments.htm (accessed August 14, 2003).

Wilson, William Othello (1867–1928)

William Wilson is the only known deserter to be awarded the Medal of Honor for bravery. As a corporal in the 9th Cavalry, Wilson won his Medal of Honor during the Pine Ridge Campaign (1890–1891).

Wilson enlisted on August 21, 1889, at the age of twenty-two. He had been born in Hagerstown in western Maryland and was promoted to the rank of corporal in December 1890 with a reputation for being one of the best marksmen in his unit. He also had a reputation for wearing a long, black leather coat, a broad-brimmed, white hat, and a large pair of spurs on his boots. His flamboyant appearance seems to have been accepted by his officers.

On December 30, 1890, a day after the massacre at Wounded Knee Creek, Wilson was with troops D, F, I, and K of the 9th, protecting a supply train. Shortly after first light a large band of Sioux attacked the troops. The cavalry, under Capt. John S. Loud, formed a circle with the wagons and decided to send a rider to seek reinforcements. Wilson offered to carry the dispatch, and as he sped out of the encampment he was pursued by eight or ten warriors. He outran them with help from his fellow cavalrymen, who opened fire on his pursuers from the encampment, and found Maj. Guy V. Henry, who saddled up his men and rode off to relieve the besieged wagon train. After a brief skirmish the Sioux broke off, and the wagons were successfully driven to their destination.

On New Year's Day, acting on the orders of Major Henry, his adjutant described Wilson's ride as "one involving much risk as the Indians knowing what was intended would endeavor to intercept the messenger, and overwhelmed by numbers certain death would follow" (quoted in Schubert 1997, 126). A copy was sent to Regimental Headquarters at Fort Robinson.

Wilson stayed with the regiment in Pine Ridge throughout the freezing winter until March 1891. A few days before the regiment was due to leave Wilson decided to head to Chadron, Nebraska, where he stayed in a hotel. He was immediately recognized, and the army had him arrested for desertion. He was also charged with the theft of a rifle and the forgery of a civilian name on checks in the amount of $200. Wilson denied the desertion charge and said: "My reason for being in Chadron was a drinking spell and while I was under the influence of drink I found myself in Chadron having been constantly on duty for about four months as acting commissary sergeant at Pine Ridge Agency and Battalion 9th Cavalry in the field which was the most mental strain to which I have been subjected to in my life" (quoted in Schubert 1997, 127).

Wilson was locked up at Fort Robinson, and in May a court martial was convened. In the event, he was found guilty only of absence without leave and check forgery. He was sentenced to four years' hard labor and forfeiture of pay, and he lost his corporal's stripes. But because the reviewing authority, Gen. John R. Brooke, did not believe the forgery charge to be accurate, the sentence was rejected except for the demotion in rank.

Rather than being daunted by this setback, Wilson asked to be awarded the Medal of Honor, and his officers were still prepared to support him. Lt. Powell wrote: "It is with pleasure that I commend the very gallant conduct of the within named applicant and invoke the bestowal upon him of a Medal of Honor to which in my judgement he is unquestionably entitled" (quoted in Schubert 1997, 129). Within a month the Medal of Honor was on its way to Wilson.

In August 1893, as a private in H Troop based at Fort Duchesne, Wilson set off for Bellvue near Omaha, Nebraska, to represent the regiment in the annual marksmanship contest. He attended, but he only made it back as far as Denver. He claimed that he had lost his train fare and asked for a duplicate ticket and money to pay for his meals. It was at that point that Wilson disappeared with his carbine and revolver. Wilson made no attempt to hide; he went back to his native Hagerstown, where he married, had seven children, and worked as a teacher, a cook, and a carpenter. The army never seemed to be interested in dragging him before a court martial again, and he remained in Hagerstown until he died in Washington County Hospital on January 18, 1928. It was only after his death that it became public knowledge that he had won the Medal of Honor, as he had never spoken of it since he had made his decision to desert the army.

See also Buffalo Soldiers; Medal of Honor (APPENDIX); 9th Cavalry

References and Further Reading

Schubert, Frank N. *Black Valor: Buffalo Soldiers and the Medal of Honor, 1870–1898*. Wilmington, DE: Scholarly Resources, 1997.

Women's Army Auxiliary Corps

The official entry of African American women into the U.S. Army was made possible by the work of those women who, during World War II, were able to bring about the creation of the Women's Army Auxiliary Corps, later called the Women's Army Corps.

Shortly before the Japanese attack on Pearl Harbor, Representative Edith Nourse Rogers of Massachusetts introduced a bill to the House of Representatives with the intention of setting up a semimilitary organization of 25,000 women. The organization was to be called the Women's Army Auxiliary Corps (WAAC), and it was hoped that these women would fill U.S. Army noncombat posts and free men to fight.

The proposal had the approval of army chief of staff George C. Marshall. As it turned out, the U.S. Congress had more pressing concerns during 1941 (the lend-lease bill, price controls, war plant production, and so on). Rogers therefore introduced another bill in January 1942, suggesting the creation of the corps with a projected strength of some 150,000.

Unlike the previous attempt, this new bill also included an amendment providing that the women should be enlisted and given the same status as men in the U.S. Army. This amendment provoked vigorous debate; although Congress recognized the need to mobilize women for the war effort, many were averse to giving women military status and the accompanying privileges of servicemen.

Nonetheless, the basic premise was accepted, and Congress approved the creation of the corps on May 14, 1942, without the amendment. On the following day President Franklin D. Roosevelt signed the compromise bill, and the Women's Army Auxiliary Corps was created. The bill initially authorized the U.S. Army to enlist 150,000 officers and enlisted women, aged twenty-one to forty-five. They were to be noncombatants and organized separately in terms of pay, housing, supply, training, and medical care. There was no stipulation that they could not serve overseas.

In order to stress the separation between the corps and the U.S. Army, the grades were created in such a way as to ensure that there would be no direct comparisons. The WAAC grades of third officer, second officer, first officer, field director, assistant director, and director are broadly comparable to the U.S. Army's second lieutenant to colonel. For the enlisted women, the grades of auxiliary, junior leader, leader, staff leader, technical leader, first leader, and chief leader can be seen as parallel to U.S. Army grades from private to master sergeant. Until November 1, 1942, whatever the equivalence of the grades, the WAAC personnel drew lower pay, but after this date the pay structure was equalized.

As a result of Congress and the U.S. Army being clear about the fact that the WAAC was not a military organization, the personnel were not governed by the usual Articles of War; consequently, the director of the WAAC drew up the WAAC regulations covering appointment, enlistment, promotion, discipline (a code of conduct with punishments for breaches), training, uniforms, pay, and discharge. The new regulations mirrored those in the U.S. Army, and in fact issues not covered in the WAAC regulations were referred to U.S. Army regulations.

The first WAACs arrived at Fort Des Moines on July 20, 1942; included in this first batch were some 440 officer candidates (who would attend the WAAC Officer Candidate School). Graduates were commissioned as third officers after a six-week training program. Around 150 women arrived every two weeks to attend the WAAC Officer Candidate School (OCS). The first 125 WAAC enlisted personnel arrived on the same day to begin a four-week training course, but as the problems were ironed out in the training and new facilities were constructed, the size of these drafts was increased. From the outset, the quality of the officer candidates was high; around 40 percent were college graduates, with the average age of thirty. The enlisted personnel, with an average age of twenty-four, had some 60 percent high school graduates.

Initial recruitment figures (to June 30, 1943) had been set at 25,000, but this figure was reached by November 1942. The secretary of war, Henry L. Stimson, increased the target for June 30, 1943, to the full 150,000, while ensuring that additional training facilities were in place. Shortly before the end of 1942, at Daytona Beach, Florida, a second WAAC training facility was up, followed by Fort Oglethorpe, Georgia; Fort Devens, Massachusetts; and Camp Ruston, Louisiana.

Practical issues now came into play, with renewed calls for the WAAC to be granted full military status. WAACs serving overseas were not entitled to enhanced terms of pay, nor were they covered under the government's life insurance. If any WAACs, such as the 200 or more who were serving in Gen. Dwight D. Eisenhower's North African theater in Algeria, became sick or was wounded, they would not receive veterans' hospitalization, neither would their parents receive death gratuities. One of the other major concerns was the status and fate of the women should they fall into enemy hands; under the terms of their enlistment, they would have no protection under international agreements related to prisoners of war.

Representative Rogers and Director Oveta Culp Hobby received the approval of Marshall for their draft of a bill to present to Congress (January 1943), but it was not fully approved by the two houses and signed by the president until July 1, 1943. The act now called for the official creation of a Women's Army Corps within the U.S. Army. Thus the WAAC now became the WAC. No limitations were set on the size of the corps, and the age range of those eligible for enlistment was extended from twenty to forty-nine.

The old WAAC grades disappeared, translated into equivalent grades in the U.S. Army. The maximum grade available was colonel, but this was restricted to the director of the corps. Otherwise the highest rank possible was lieutenant colonel, while enlisted women could rise to the highest rank, that of master sergeant. There were still inconsistencies in the system, and the women who had served in the WAAC could not count this time toward their overall length of service. From this point forth, however, the WAC was subject to all of the conditions, regulations, codes, and privileges of the U.S. Army.

As for African American women, they were as determined to serve the country as their male counterparts. Back in 1940, there had been a policy adopted by the War Department to accept African Americans on a quota basis (10 percent as a reflection of their percentage of the population). Also in 1940, the Selective Service Act specifically prohibited discrimination on the grounds of color or race. The U.S. Army, however, was reluctant to undertake what it saw as an experiment in social change, and this reluctance was coupled with the fact that segregation was ingrained in the service. If the U.S. Army was to accept African Americans, then it would be on an equal but separate basis. This was intended, of course, to include the training, but by 1942 African Americans and whites were training at the same officer candidate schools, and they were training together at specialist and technical training schools. While these developments were taking place, basic training remained segregated; it was under these conditions that the WAAC and later the WAC began to develop their racial policies.

In England, Maj. Charity Adams Earley and Capt. Abbie N. Campbell inspect the first contingent of African American members of the Women's Army Corps assigned to overseas service, February 15, 1945. (National Archives)

The first WAAC OCS class of 440 women that arrived at Fort Des Moines in July 1942 had just 40 African Americans. Initially, training of these women was segregated, but this practice was changed in November 1942 after continued pressure from the National Association for the Advancement of Colored People (NAACP). Training, housing, and messes were desegregated for officer candidates, although the enlisted women were still segregated. The women in both groups were assigned to segregated units, and all training of African American enlisted women was carried out by African American officers and noncommissioned officers.

There was no limitation, however, to the specialist areas to which the African American women could be assigned, and at specialist training schools the races were mixed. The major problem arose when the women were assigned to units. It was usually the case that each U.S. Army post had one women's unit, officially either African American or white. In practice, however, women were assigned to these units regardless of their color, and expedience meant that they would not be segregated once they had arrived on post.

Despite these gradual moves, the number of African American women in either the WAAC or the WAC never approached the recommended figure of 10 percent. The total number of African American women who entered the services (July 1, 1942–June 30, 1945) managed to reach just 5.1 percent (a total of 6,527 women).

AFRICAN AMERICANS IN THE WOMEN'S ARMY CORPS, 1945–1978

	African American Officers	*Total Officers*	*African American Warrant Officers*	*Total Warrant Officers*	*African American Enlisted*	*Total Enlisted*	*Total African Americans*	*Total*
1945	117	5,733	0	44	3,732	90,180	3,849	95,957
1946	15	1,793	0	18	658	16,699	673	17,896
1947	9	1,035	0	5	310	7,094	319	8,134
1948	4	611	0	42	121	4,699	125	5,352
1949	12	626	0	23	340	4,260	352	4,909
1950	18	686	1	22	629	6,551	648	7,259
1951	30	1,010	1	39	1,015	10,883	1,046	11,932
1952	40	1,171	1	57	1,291	10,228	1,332	11,456
1953	38	1,109	0	55	1,131	8,760	1,169	9,924
1954	31	964	0	52	838	6,787	869	7,803
1955	29	876	0	48	954	7,716	983	8,640
1956	32	847	0	44	1,029	7,770	1,061	8,661
1957	28	808	0	43	937	7,156	965	8,007
1958	24	740	0	39	909	7,074	933	7,853
1959	27	732	0	39	1,015	7,837	1,042	8,608
1960	28	735	0	39	1,155	8,279	1,183	9,053
1972	52	901	5	19	2,396	12,349	2,453	13,269
1973	56	1,073	4	21	3,184	16,457	3,188	17,551
1974	63	1,249	6	19	5,450	26,328	5,519	27,596
1975	85	1,446	6	22	8,031	37,703	8,122	39,171
1976	98	1,921	6	31	9,681	44,461	9,785	46,413
1977	236	2,409	8	45	11,293	46,094	11,537	48,548
1978	264	2,636	12	68	14,412	50,292	14,688	52,996

Notes: Figures refer to ends of fiscal years; end of fiscal year changed from June 30 to September 30 in 1977. No statistics were maintained on African American personnel from 1961 to 1971.

Source: Strength of the Army Reports (STM-30), 1945–1959 and (DCSPER 46), 1960–1978; Report, ODCSPER, Ten Year Review of Equal Opportunity in the Army, 10 December 1974, Tables 9, 17; Third Annual Assessment of Army Equal Opportunity Programs, March 1979.

After the war, women continued to serve in the WAC while Congress debated the permanent role of women in America's armed forces. The Women's Armed Services Integration Act, signed by President Harry S. Truman in June 1948, changed the status of the WAC and made its members eligible for both the Regular Army (WAC RA) and the Army Reserve. The WAC played a significant role in the U.S. Army through both the Korean and Vietnam wars as well as in its other operations and peacetime responsibilities.

In 1978, in order to end the discrimination implied by women's separate status in the U.S. Army, the WAC was officially disbanded and women became full and equal members of the army and the Army Reserve.

See also African American Women in the Military; World War II

References and Further Reading

MacGregor, Morris J., Jr. *Integration of the Armed Forces, 1940–1965*. Washington, DC: Government Printing Office, 1981.

Morden, Bettie J. *The Women's Army Corps,*

1945–1978. Washington, DC: Center of Military History, 2000. http://www.army.mil/cmh-pg/books/wac/index.htm (accessed September 16, 2003).

Sparrow, John C. *History of Personnel Demobilization in the U.S. Army.* Department of the Army Pamphlet 20–210. Washington, DC: Center for Military History, 1954.

Treadwell, Mattie E. *The Women's Army Corps.* Washington, DC: Government Printing Office, 1954.

Women's Reserve of the U.S. Navy (WAVES)

The creation of the Women's Reserve of the U.S. Navy, known as the WAVES (Women Accepted for Volunteer Emergency Service), in July 1942 potentially represented an opportunity for African American as well as white women. Initially, however, the secretary of the navy, Frank Knox, refused to allow African American women to be accepted. This decision was overturned on July 28, 1944, largely as a result of accusations by Thomas E. Dewey, the Republican presidential candidate in the 1944 election, that Roosevelt's administration was discriminating against African American women. It was therefore decided in October 1944 that African American women would be admitted into the U.S. Navy, the U.S. Coast Guard, and the U.S. Marine Corps.

The first commander of the WAVES was Capt. Mildred McAfee (later Mildred McAfee Horton), who took a leave of absence from the presidency of Wellesley College to accept this post. She, together with noted African American educator Mary McLeod Bethune, helped the secretary of the navy push through the decision to admit African American women to the WAVES.

However, the process facing African American women wishing to enter naval service was somewhat difficult and protracted, and by the end of World War II there were still only 72 African American women in the WAVES, of a total of over 90,000 women serving or in training.

In December 1944 the first two African American female naval officers, Lt. Harriet Ida Pickens and Ens. Frances Wills, graduated from the Naval Reserve Midshipmen's School at Northampton, Massachusetts, and received their commissions. They were the only African American WAVES officers to serve during World War II.

Enlisted WAVES received "boot camp" training at Iowa State Teachers College in Cedar Falls and later at Hunter College in New York City. From boot camp they went for specialized training to Oklahoma A&M University in Stillwater and Indiana University in Bloomington.

WAVES, who by law served only in the United States (including Hawaii), played a very important part in the navy's mission. The constituted 55 percent of uniformed personnel serving at Navy Department headquarters in Washington handled 80 percent of the navy's mail service, and played an integral part in naval communications and logistics. WAVES also performed a variety of other specialized tasks, such staffing aircraft control towers and providing instrument flight training to male pilot trainees. Although WAVES did not receive the same benefits as male naval personnel, could not serve overseas, and were limited as to the rank they could obtain, they made a distinguished name for themselves during the war and paved the way for women to enter naval service in the postwar world.

After the defeat of Japan in September 1945, the Navy moved to demobilize; all WAVES were to be discharged within six months. Many WAVES re-enlisted in the Naval Reserve during this period, however, while Congress was petitioned to pass legislation making women a permanent part of the U.S. Navy. In July 1948 President Truman signed the Women's Armed Services Integration Act, which made it possible for women in the Naval Reserve to apply for the entrance into the regular Navy.

Frances Wills (left) and Harriet Ida Pickens are sworn in as apprentice seamen by Lt. Rosamond D. Selle, New York City. In December 1944, Wills and Pickens became the navy's first African American WAVES officers. (U.S. Navy)

See also African American Women in the Military; World War II

References and Further Reading

MacGregor, Morris J., Jr. *Integration of the Armed Forces, 1940–1965*. Washington, DC: Center of Military History, 1985. http://www.army.mil/cmh-pg/books/integration/IAF-FM.htm#TABLE%20OF%20CONTENTS (accessed August 16, 2003).

World War I (1914–1918)

World War I offered the first real opportunity for large numbers of African Americans to serve their country in a time of war after the American Civil War. The African American presence in the armed forces since 1865 had gradually become smaller, and despite significant contributions during the Indian Wars, the Spanish American War, the Philippine Insurrection, and the punitive expedition against Pancho Villa, the African American held a poor reputation as a fighting man. Unfortunately, with the U.S. Army decision not to deploy the 20,000 men of the four existing African American regular units (9th and 10th Cavalry and 24th and 25th Infantry), which were probably the most experienced in the army, the opportunity fell only to inexperienced African American National Guardsmen, volunteers, and draftees. Moreover, due to the army's reluctance to deploy African American troops in Europe, coupled with the fact that the United States joined the war only toward the end, in 1917, the opportunity was limited, and the army establishment's view of the men was mixed, to say the least.

Making Ready for War

In the United States few African Americans served in the armed forces, and those that did so faced segregation and discrimination. At the same time, the U.S. government and public could not fail to notice that since the outbreak of the war, some of the major belligerents were using significant numbers of troops from both Africa and Asia. The French alone deployed over 275,000 troops from Africa and another 260,000 from North Africa. Unfortunately, in the early years, these men like so many others faced a new form of warfare, one that pitted human flesh against mass machine guns and massed artillery. The use of colonial troops in the role of shock or assault troops had resulted in a higher casualty rate than for white units.

U.S. opinion of the worth of troops of color was divided strictly along racial lines. The majority of African Americans were most struck by what they read of the extreme gallantry shown by African troops fighting for the French and for the British. They noted that the Germans were offering rewards for the capture of any African soldiers, whom they believed to be the most proficient in the use of edged weapons. As far as the Woodrow Wilson administration and the bulk of the white population were concerned, however, the occasions when African colonial troops failed to perform or fled in combat, even though their failures were no more marked than those of their white counterparts, served to reinforce existing beliefs about the capabilities of black soldiers.

In the months preceding the U.S. declaration of war against Germany, the U.S. Army had already put plans in place to draft African Americans. Indeed, twelve days before the American declaration of war on April 6, 1917, the First Separate Battalion (Colored) of the District of Columbia National Guard was mobilized in order to guard strategic positions in the capital. It is widely believed, however, by those scholars who question the motives behind this decision, that the act was based, not on any recognition of the abilities of African Americans, but on the belief that the Germans would find it much more difficult to infiltrate an agent into an African American unit than a white one.

The African American population was on the eve of responding as positively as it had done during the Civil War to the call to fight for their country, even against a backdrop of continued discrimination, racism, and the ever-present lynching. The year 1916 had seen over fifty lynching incidents, and a similar number in 1917, the majority, but not all, taking place in the racially segregated South. The growing problem was recognized by President Woodrow Wilson, who also recognized the fact that the lynching could undermine the war effort and the participation in every respect of the vastly important African American population. His hands were tied, however, as the lynching issues were state business. In the summer of 1917 new racial clashes flared across the country, notably in East St. Louis, Illinois. After four days of rioting, over a hundred African Americans had been murdered or seriously injured, as had at least eight whites. The press roundly condemned the rioting, but on July 28 over 25,000 African Americans took part in demonstrations in New York.

African Americans in the U.S. Army were not immune to racial discrimination and intimidation either, but both in and out of uniform, the large percentage of African Americans who had never experienced slavery were not prepared to suffer the same kind of indignities their forbears had. They asked to be treated as Americans, and despite racial tensions, they wanted to serve their country, but they were more likely to resist injustice.

The U.S. Army had extensively used the four regular African American units in its wars of expansion in the latter half of the nineteenth century. The units were not deployed abroad, but consigned to distant and desperately isolated posts on the frontier. Whenever they came into contact with civilian U.S. society, they encountered the Jim Crow laws, which still shaped the lives of African Americans, especially in the South, but they would not accept this treatment and habitually chose to confront it or seek revenge, as the circumstances dictated. Both the Brownsville incident (August 1906) and the Houston riot (August 1917) did much to tarnish the already stained reputation of African American regular soldiers, and their behavior during the riots served to confirm the white South in its beliefs about the inferiority, even savagery, of African Americans and to justify unequal treatment.

On the eve of America's entrance into the Great War, the 20,000 men in the four regular regiments of African American troops could have been posted fairly quickly directly to France. African American National Guardsmen would require considerable training before deployment. The third group, African American civilians, would clearly take the largest period of preparation and training, as would any men without military experience. When the Selective Service Act of May 18, 1917, was passed, it required that all males between twenty-one and thirty-one register, regardless of race. There was little African American opposition to the draft, but in the South, white factory and plantation owners were concerned that if conscription affected both whites and blacks, a severe labor shortage could result.

From the beginning those who were called to be processed faced discrimination. The effect of this discrimination, which also involved all-white draft boards, seems to have been that African Americans were actually more likely to be drafted, perhaps partly because whites believed that the African Americans would largely be used as laborers, as indeed turned out to be the case. To take one example, in Fulton County, Georgia, of the 202 African Americans examined, only 6 were given exemptions, while 526 of the 815 white draftees were turned down on medical grounds.

Some 2,290,527, or 9.6 percent of those drafted, were African American. Of the 1,078,331 African Americans examined in June, 51.6 percent, or 556,917, were put into Class I, which meant that they were immediately available. In stark contrast, 3,110,659, or 32.5 percent, of whites were placed in the same category. Of the Class I draftees, 24 percent of whites were inducted and 36 percent of African Americans. Throughout the war, although African Americans accounted for 10.19 percent of those registered, they provided 12.6 percent of those inducted. The figures were more striking in the South, where African Americans accounted for between 30 and 58 percent of the inducted draftees. Technically, under the draft laws, those who refused or failed to register, or who failed to appear when selected by lottery for industries were considered as deserters. Taken together with those who deserted while in service, African Americans deserted at a rate of 9.81 percent, compared to a white desertion rate of 3.86 percent (Barbeau and Henri 1974, 36).

Those African Americans who worked for white employers were more likely to be exempted, whereas African Americans who ran their own farms or businesses were much more likely to be inducted. Equally, there were a number of instances when notices of induction were deliberately lost or intercepted so that "friends" of those involved in the registration process could collect the bounty for turning in a deserter.

When the African American conscripts were called for training, there was grave concern as to where this training should take place. White Southerners in particular were uncomfortable with the prospect of having large numbers of uniformed and armed African Americans concentrated in their midst. It was proposed by South Carolina, among other states, to send all Southern African American draftees into training camps up North. The Houston riot of 1917 had unnerved the South, and the War Department suggested that a "safe ratio" be applied to determine the number of whites and African Americans in each training camp. This approach, it was felt, would ensure that the African American draftees were outnumbered by two to one. The approach had logistical problems, however, as white draftees would have to be called up first and assigned to training camps, and then the appropriate number of African Americans assigned to that camp.

A large majority of the men found themselves in segregated camps, at least initially following induction, where the isolation and lack of facilities caused enormous hardships. Fortunately, they were supplied with some of the essentials by a segregated YMCA, both in the United States and later in France. Also involved in ensuring that recreational facilities were available were the far more racially liberal Knights of Columbus and the Salvation Army. The Red Cross, although segregated, involved itself in ensuring that African American sick and wounded were properly looked after in hospitals and in towns and cities that they passed through. African American chaplains were organized by the Federal Council of Churches, and the War Camps Community Service, despite a severe lack of funds, tried to provide recreational facilities and activities.

The training of the troops presented an even greater challenge, given the still dominant racist attitude that branded African Americans as having a blood lust or being at a different stage of evolution from whites. Senior military advisors even believed that African Americans were morally weak, were riddled with character deficiencies, and were naturally cowards. Taking the varying views on African American training into account, the Army chief of staff, Tasker Bliss, in August 1917 offered six plans for dealing with African American draftees.

Plan one suggested that African American troops would be stationed in the same areas as whites but in a segregated part of the camp. This first plan would at least ensure that African American draftees would receive the same levels of training as their white counterparts and that they would be sent to camps with white men and other African Americans from their own states. The second plan was to assign 48,000 African Americans into combat units, one with each of the sixteen National Army Cantonments, with the rest of the African American draftees being used as laborers. The inevitable consequence of this option was that considerable numbers of African Americans from the South would be sent into northern states to be organized in regiments. The third plan suggested that African American troops be stationed in segregated facilities at least one mile from existing white camps. This plan was potentially the most expensive and, for that reason alone, it was never seriously considered.

Plan four suggested the creation of two African American training facilities in the South that would handle all African American draftees. Again, this was never a viable option, particularly if the camps were built in Southern states. Plan five recommended that eight northern training camps handle all African American draftees and that they not receive full training or weapons until they reached France. The logistics of moving thousands of African Americans from the South to northern states was a major consideration in the rejection of this plan.

The sixth plan proposed the delaying of the African American draft and, when it did come, that the draftees be sent to the training facility nearest to their homes, where they would receive basic training and then be immediately shipped to France in support roles only and not as combat troops. This was the option that Tasker Bliss favored; nevertheless, in conversations with W. E. B. Du Bois, a prominent African American intellectual and activist and one of the founders of the National Association for the Advancement of Colored People (NAACP), Secretary of War Newton D. Baker reportedly indicated that 30,000 African Americans would be used as combat troops and 50,000 would serve in labor and supply functions. No clear plan was ever worked out. The troops for the two African American divisions were trained at either existing facilities or facilities being built primarily for white troops. The majority of African American soldiers were used as labor and trained in similar locations (Barbeau and Henri 1974, 42–43).

Pseudo-scientific evidence was used to support the notion that African Americans were not suitable for combat. It was held that African Americans generally were not mentally or physically capable of being combat troops and should be confined to labor duties. Psychologists saw the mass drafts of World War I as an excellent opportunity to carry out extensive intelligence tests to discover whether these widely held racialist convictions were valid. The base results of the comparative studies of white draftees and African American draftees seemed to provide strong evidence to support the notion that African Americans were mentally inferior to whites. With the advantage of hindsight, it is now clear that these early mass intelligence tests were not administered in an even-handed manner and that the test batches of individuals were unrepresentative and chosen in a biased way. At the time, however, the results were accepted as showing that the average African American draftee had a mental age of 10.1 years compared to 13.15 years for whites.

Even at the time, however, the extent to which the results said anything about the natural intelligence of African Americans was called in question. Col. Robert M. Yerkes of the U.S. Army collated many of the intelligence test results and published them with his conclusions in 1921. From the bare figures, Yerkes showed that both African Americans and whites in the north outscored their counterparts in the South, and that Northern African Americans tended to score higher than white draftees from the South. In 1917, however, most observers who looked at the tests saw them as confirming that African Americans were in general not intelligent enough to be combat soldiers.

As far as the physical suitability of African American draftees was concerned, many African Americans were accepted as being suitable, despite having disabilities that would have disqualified a white man. Then their relative lack of physical fitness was used to prove that African Americans were not capable of combat duty. Undoubtedly the most important factor affecting the physical condition of the men, both African American and white, was comparative economic prosperity. Nevertheless, any evidence that suggested that African Americans were inherently not fit to be combat troops was exploited by opponents of African American advancement.

Writing for the *Proceedings of the National Academy of Sciences,* in the March 5, 1919, issue, two U.S. Army doctors, A. G. Love and C. B. Davenport, reported that African American combat troops were 19 percent more likely to report sick than white troops. They overlooked the fact that hygiene, medical inspections, and hospital facilities in African American camps were extremely poor compared to the facilities offered to white troops and that the draft boards had accepted African Americans who were already chronically ill. None of the weaknesses of this study and other similar studies were realized at the time. Rather they served to reinforce the generally held view that African

Americans should serve as laborers and not soldiers.

While the draftees faced their own peculiar problems in being accepted, graded, assigned, and trained for their roles as either laborers or combat soldiers, equally challenging problems faced African Americans who applied to become officers. The vast majority of African Americans deemed to have officer potential came from the Northern states, the middle class, and the college educated. Nevertheless, they still had to face the racist convictions of a predominantly white world.

The first officer training camp (OTC) was established at Plattsburgh, New York, soon followed by thirteen others. These camps were not, however, open to African Americans. It fell to Gen. Leonard Wood to propose that a separate African American OTC be established, and from the outset individuals such as the African American writer and NAACP associate, James Weldon Johnson, and the NAACP president, Joel E. Spingarn (a white man), urged the very best African Americans to come forward; they contended that the U.S. Army wanted the camp to fail and wanted the African American officers to prove the army wrong. Howard University, a primarily African American institution, managed to convince 1,500 students to volunteer, and at the same time offered facilities at the university for the new African American OTC. Instead, a decision was made on May 12, 1917, to establish a camp in Des Moines, Iowa. The army set the age bracket at twenty-five to forty, but the bulk of the early volunteers were college students under the age of twenty-five.

Although the army leadership did not believe that African Americans could successfully command in combat, it accepted the inevitable, while placing restrictions not applied to white officer candidates on the African American officer trainees. Despite the fact that 13 percent of the draftees who would form the rank and file were African American, no more than 2 percent of the officer candidates were to be African American. This 2 percent figure was in fact not achieved; only 0.7 percent of officers serving during World War I were African American. Those who made it through OTC to serve with a regiment faced far more stringent and regular tests of their competence than did whites, along with the prospect of being removed from command for the slightest indiscretion or hesitation. The final proviso was that African American army officers should not attain a field rank, which effectively capped promotion at the rank of captain.

When the Des Moines officer training camp opened in July 1917, of the 1,250 candidates, around 250 were noncommissioned officers from the four existing African American regular regiments. The balance consisted of 1,000 civilian volunteers. The 24th Infantry Regiment's second in command, Gen. Charles Ballou, was transferred to command the camp. Initially, the men were trained for ninety days, but this was later increased by a month. Graduation was deferred because the men would have no troops to lead, as the induction of African Americans had been postponed.

The first graduations took place on October 15, with 639 commissions—all that remained of the original batch of candidates. Of that number, 204 became second lieutenants, 329 first lieutenants, and 106 captains. The majority of the captains were former regular army noncommissioned officers. Most of the officers were eventually assigned to the 92d Division, although some, not posted to the infantry regiments, found themselves in field artillery, engineer, signal, or machine gun units. The bulk of these men had received no training in these auxiliary units, and when they found themselves posted to France with their regiments, they quickly had to learn their new duties. The net result for the artillery officers, for example, was that their white commanding officers considered the African Americans unsuited to the task and asked for them to be replaced by white men. Over a period of months the majority of these officers were replaced, as were a number of the captains assigned to infantry regiments.

The Des Moines course closed immediately after the graduation of the first class of African

American officers. The training of African American officer candidates had to take place at established, white officer training centers, where the training of the African Americans was delegated to the existing camp staff. The reception accorded the African Americans varied widely, with some centers practicing strict segregation in all things while others integrated the courses of instruction, albeit usually for practical reasons. The number of additional African Americans commissioned as officers through the other centers was about 700. The following examples should indicate the different environments that African American officer candidates encountered.

A class of ninety-six artillery officers, out of which only forty-four graduated, began training at Camp Meade, Maryland, but were then relocated to Camp Taylor, Kentucky, where they moved from one area to another, six different times. Similarly, only six of the twenty-four African American artillery officer candidates completed their course at Fort Sill, Oklahoma, whereas at Camp Hancock, Georgia, forty-three of the fifty-six who were trained by British and French officers to be machine-gun specialists completed their program.

Many of those who graduated were initially assigned as replacements, but the prejudice against having African Americans outrank white soldiers made their lives difficult. Some of the new officers were warned not to expect white subordinates to salute them, but to be prepared to watch those same soldiers salute white officers of inferior rank. White officers tended to believe that African Americans needed a white officer to direct them and that African American troops would not readily accept orders from a black officer.

African American regiments found themselves officered by predominantly white men, usually from the South. The most outstanding African American officer of the period, the 10th Cavalry's Col. Charles Young, was a West Point graduate who had served with great distinction throughout his entire career. In 1917 he was recommended for promotion, but was ordered to the military hospital in San Francisco for a physical examination. The examination determined that he was unfit for active duty and he was retired from active service on the day before other colonels, junior to him in seniority, were elevated to the rank of brigadier general. Young had been diagnosed previously with Bright's Disease and high blood pressure, which may have afforded the army leadership a way to avoid promoting an outstanding officer to a very visible rank. If nothing else, the cruel way in which Young's hopes for a command were disappointed highlights the fact that the U.S. Army had a distinct political agenda in their opposition to African American officers, and that opposition had little to do with their actual competence. As it turned out, any problems with African American officers during World War I were primarily the result of inadequate training.

The Combat Units

The two largest African American formations during World War I were the 92d and 93d Divisions. It is important to note that the 93d was designated as a provisional division, as initially it consisted of three infantry regiments of the National Guard and one regiment made up from draftees. The three National Guard units had already been rejected for racial reasons by white divisions; they consisted of the 15th New York Regiment, the 8th Illinois, the 1st Separate Battalion of Washington, D.C., the 9th Separate Battalion of Ohio, and individual companies from as far afield as Connecticut, Maryland, Massachusetts, and Tennessee. Most of the formations that made up the division were understrength; some had only white officers, and only African American officers, and some had a mix.

The story of the 15th New York, which later became the 369th Infantry Regiment, is typical of the experience of these troops, of the discrimination and racism they suffered. The unit was formed in the autumn of 1916 by William Hayward, who became the colonel of the regiment. Initially the unit comprised 650 men, but

A 1918 poster by Charles Gustrine entitled "True Sons of Freedom: Colored Men—The First Americans Who Planted Our Flag on the Firing Line" celebrates the role of African Americans in World War I. (Library of Congress)

by the spring of 1917 this number had grown to over 1,400. The officers were white, and in the early months the officers were understrength by at least two-thirds. Although the regiment boasted the fact that both James Reese Europe and Noble Sissle, legendary jazz musicians, were leaders of their 44-man regimental band, they had nowhere to train, nor did they have sufficient weapons or any assistance from outside the regiment. In May 1917, with just 250 rifles for 2,000 men, they began training at Camp Whitman, New York, but they lacked uniforms, equipment, and supplies.

No sooner had they completed their training than they were scattered on guard duty throughout New York, New Jersey, and Pennsylvania. It was therefore impossible for Hayward to institute any form of additional training, but in the autumn of 1917 the regiment was finally sent to Spartanburg in South Carolina for further training. They were met with the most severe forms of racism, and local spokespersons predicted that these northern African Americans would only bring trouble to South Carolina and that they could not expect the locals to behave toward them in any different way than the local African American population. Although steps were taken from the outset to prevent tensions and potential incidents, there were numerous ugly scenes. If nothing else, the tensions in Spartanburg hastened the 15th's transition from a New York National Guard unit to the 369th Infantry Regiment and its embarkation to France.

The 8th Illinois National Guard was mobilized in March 1917 and proceeded to Camp Logan for its training, narrowly missing the Houston riots. It therefore arrived in Texas at a time of high racial tension, and once again this hastened the unit's transition and embarkation to Europe as the 370th Infantry Regiment.

Among the smaller units that later became part of the 93d, additional difficulties existed. The 1st Separate Battalion of Washington, D.C., was placed on guard duty around the capital, and Kentucky Representative Robert Y. Thomas wrote to Wilson's secretary, Joseph Tumulty:

> You had better take these nigger soldiers away as guards of the tunnel and put some white men there. The nigger soldiers spend a good deal of their time socially at night, in talking to nigger women who congregate around that place. I do not know whether you know it or not; but I know that a nigger knows nothing about patriotism, love of country, or morality, and if in the army at all, should be commanded by white officers. If they are not they are going to make trouble wherever they go (National Archives RG165, Item 9397–13, July 6, 1917; quoted in Barbeau and Henri 1974, 78).

At Camp Sheridan, Montgomery, Alabama, a member of the 9th Separate Battalion of Ohio was kidnapped by white racists, prompting other members of the unit to go out and search for him. Thirty-five of them were arrested by white military police, and the battalion was confined to barracks.

It was decided to merge all of the various smaller units into the 372d Infantry Regiment, and all of the men were ordered to present themselves at Camp Stuart, Virginia, in January 1918. The first battalion consisted of the men from Washington, and the second battalion contained the Ohio, Maryland, Tennessee, Massachusetts, and Connecticut National Guardsmen. In order to bring the unit up to full strength, 250 African American draftees from Illinois, Michigan, and Ohio also joined the regiment. The regiment had a mix of African American and white officers, but all of the senior positions were exclusively reserved for white men. The regiment sailed for France on March 30, 1918.

The final unit of the 93d Division, the 371st Infantry Regiment, consisted of 3,380 men organized at Camp Jackson in October 1917. These were predominantly draftees from North and South Carolina, with considerable numbers from Alabama, Florida, and Georgia. Again the majority of the officers were white and from the South. Most of the men had come directly from the harsh conditions in the Southern economy, and of the initial batch two-thirds of the men were replaced on the grounds that they were unfit for duty.

The 92d Division initially consisted of 40,000 men who, after weeding out, were reduced to 26,000, 4,000 of whom were sent to Tuskegee and Hampton, among other technical schools, for further training. Most of the African American officers had come from Des Moines, while the balance consisted of white National Guardsmen officers who were not needed elsewhere. Gen. Charles C. Ballou was given command of the division, and even in the early months he realized the uphill struggle that he and his men would face, with a lack of equipment and lack of opportunity to train. The division was never concentrated in one place while on U.S. soil.

The first regiment of the 92d, the 365th, had drawn its men largely from Oklahoma and Texas; the 366th were mainly from Alabama. The 367th were New Yorkers, and the 368th were from Maryland, Pennsylvania, and Tennessee. Alongside the three infantry regiments were three field artillery regiments, which were severely undertrained; they remained at home when the division sailed for France on June 10, 1918. Members of the division suffered from racial abuse at their various training posts as they prepared for embarkation; when they did sail, they had not completed their training, and their officers, whether African American or white, were arguably ill prepared.

The Labor Units

Although the men in the two infantry divisions eventually saw combat, the vast majority of African American draftees were simply transferred into a temporary existence that resembled the chain gang. African Americans accounted for at least 30 percent of laborers in the army, reflecting the commonly held belief that they were not only inferior but that they should be barred from the most important task of fighting. Their availability for labor was seen as an ideal opportunity to release white men to fight in the war. A confidential memorandum of October 1917 suggested that 70 percent of all African American draftees should be used in labor units. Here they could carry out all the menial tasks, releasing white men to deal with the real matter in hand.

By September 1917, 83,400 men had reported to National Army Camps as part of the first draft call. To begin with they were organized into stevedore regiments, but later, in January 1918, 3,500-man labor battalions were formed. The men in these battalions were to carry out a variety of labor duties in the United States. If the quality of the white officers was poor in the fighting divisions, then the army found the very worst white officers to command these men. As late as March 1918 African Americans were restricted to the rank of corporal. White noncommissioned officers tended to be housed separately, and it was not until the last months of 1918 that African Americans were promoted to the rank of sergeant. It was difficult for these soldiers to accept the fact that they had been called to arms yet would not have any prospect of seeing combat. The training was along strict military lines with weapons and drills, yet the army discipline was nothing but discipline; it never led to combat duty.

In September 1918 it was recognized that at least a third of the units were capable of combat action, but they lacked weapons, and there was no real will to prepare additional African American soldiers for the battlefield. For the men and the African American population at large, this situation was simply a return to the mistreatment and humiliation of slave period existence. On several occasions the men were hired out to contractors to build roads or other projects, with their officers pocketing their wages, making them feel even more strongly that they were being treated like slaves.

The few African Americans assigned to labor units who did make the voyage across the Atlantic to the war in Europe eventually found themselves in labor battalions collectively called the Services of Supply (SOS) in the later stages of the war. They operated in the forty-six engineer service battalions, forty-four labor battalions, twenty-four labor companies, fifteen pioneer infantry regiments, three stevedore regiments, two stevedore battalions, and two butchery companies. The stevedores were responsible for ensuring that the American Expeditionary Force was in a fit state to march off the transport ships and straight to the front line, if required. Their ability to deal with vast amounts of equipment staggered the Allies, especially the French. In September 1918 at Bordeaux, African American stevedores dealt with 800,000 tons of materials, and at Brest they unloaded food supplies at a rate of 2,000 tons per day. Elsewhere African Americans were felling trees, building and repairing roads and railroads, and burying the dead. Some operated close to the front lines and received casualties from enemy artillery fire.

Despite their sterling work, they were generally despised, and most senior officers had a very low opinion of them. It is true that, at least on paper, these units no longer had the disadvantage of being labeled labor battalions, with all the connotations of punishment and discipline. But dressing the units up as SOS did little to change the boredom and frustration of being assigned to what was still essentially a manual labor role.

Experience in Combat

The 369th Infantry Regiment, being the first African American unit to land in France, found itself initially assigned to the SOS. They had had just three weeks of training and barely knew how to fire a rifle, yet they were designated as combat troops; they were not wanted. As the year turned, and still the general staff debated as to what to do with them, it was initially decided to make them pioneer infantry, which effectively meant that they would be battlefield laborers. Eventually a compromise of sorts was reached, with the arrival of the balance of the 93d Division. The French were desperate for more combat units, and it was decided that they would be lent to the French, which the U.S. Army considered an ideal solution; it was believed that the French, having experience in dealing with African troops, would be better suited to working with African American soldiers.

True, there was a cultural, administrative, and equipment-based problem with the integration, and there was still the difficulty that the units had not been adequately trained, but on the whole the experiment was a success. The French replaced the Springfield rifle with their own Lebel and intended to use the troops, just as they did their own French Africans, as charging infantry, reliant on the bayonet. Apart from French helmets, the regiments retained their American uniforms but everything else was French, as, too, was the enormous improvement in the rations.

Within the French Army, the African Americans found equality of a kind they had never encountered while serving in the U.S. Army. The American Expeditionary Force headquarters wrote a confidential document aiming to explain the position of the African American in the United States, entitled "Secret Information Concerning Black American Troops." It was penned by a Colonel Linard, a French officer serving at American Expeditionary Force (AEF) headquarters, and beseeched the French to ensure that the African Americans be kept separate from whites in order to prevent "race mongrelization." French officers were implored not to eat with African American officers, not to encourage familiarity, and, above all, only to praise the men when absolutely necessary. It was implied in the document that the 15 million African Americans in the United States represented a very real threat to the continued domination of the whites at home (Aptheker 1956, 119). When the document was read to the French National Assembly in July 1919, it was universally condemned. The French Chamber of Deputies reaffirmed their desire to ensure that all men, regardless of race or religion, should be treated on an equal basis and therefore condemned the American attitude out of hand.

It was the men of the 369th who saw action first, when they charged at Chateau-Thierry and at Belleau Wood. When the rest of the 93d arrived in France in April 1918, they, too, saw action within three months. All suffered high casualties at Argonne and Champagne, and by the time the war had ended, some 32 percent of the entire division had been killed or wounded. The experience of these men within the French army was wholly different from that of the African American draftees who formed the 92d Division.

From the beginning the relationship between General Ballou, who commanded the 92d, and Gen. Robert Bullard, who was the commanding officer of the American Second Army, colored the men's entire experience. Ballou, for his time, was relatively fair, and he jealously protected his division against his commanding officer. Bullard's attitude to the men was influenced by the fact that they were not only draftees but also African American, and he wanted the men to be used purely in the SOS. Bullard believed all of the stereotypes prevalent about African American men at the time and was not ready to risk them in combat. His position was supported by the majority of white officers within the division.

When the regiment arrived in France it was grossly underequipped and typically undertrained. Ballou was caught between the dictates of the U.S. Army and the needs of his division. The troops were required to muster every hour of the day in order to check that none were missing or engaged in activities disapproved of by the authorities.

By August 1918 the 92d joined French troops close to the German border, in the Saint-Dié sector, and on August 31 the men saw their first action at Frapelle, when the Germans tried to assault their lines. By mid-September they had successfully defended against eleven enemy attacks, and they were now redeployed to become part of the American push in the Argonne region. They were taken out of the Saint-Dié line and into the new front.

The 368th Infantry Regiment was brigaded with the 11th Cuirassiers and assigned to an 800-yard gap between the American 77th Division and the nearest unit of the French Fourth Army. The 368th had traveled over 100 miles in open railway flat cars in the pouring rain and moved into their trenches on September 25. The regiment and a dismounted French cavalry regiment were combined into a taskforce-type organization, Groupement Durand, which was to be responsible for maintaining the cohesion of the offensive line. The 368th lacked the training, experience, and equipment to carry out the task. Unsurprisingly, there was a breakdown in communications and, without heavy-duty wire cutters to cut through the barbed wire, the regiment found it impossible to make headway when the offensive was under way on September 26, although the night of September 27, they had taken the town of Binarville, and on the following day, after a five-hour artillery barrage, the regiment found itself almost isolated, with pockets of German resistance to their rear. During the fighting, the confusion was often intense, communications were poor, and at times various units retreated without permission. Fortunately, Allied successes elsewhere led the Germans to pull back, and by September 30 they had advanced 6 miles beyond Binarville. The regiment had suffered over 250 casualties.

The confusion on the battlefield, due in part to the regiment's inexperience and the complexity of its mission, had marked its performance as a failure, and, together with the other three regiments of the division, the 368th was withdrawn on October 5. The U.S. Army decided that African American officers and noncommissioned officers had been the root cause of the failure of the regiment to fulfil its role. Courts martial were instituted, and five of the leaders were found guilty of cowardice on the battlefield and sentenced to death. They were later exonerated by a War Department investigation, which concluded that the regiment had performed as well as could be expected, given its inexperience and lack of equipment. It was also suggested that contradictory orders had been given to the lead units, which added to the chaos. The 368th was not the only American unit to perform badly during the offensive. The white 35th Division had also descended into chaos, yet no action was taken against its leaders. The 92d Division was then moved to the Marbache sector on October 8, and the division suffered over 450 casualties during the next month.

Certainly Gen. Bullard saw only the negative side of the story, as evidenced in a diary entry he wrote on November 1, 1918:

> The Negro Division seems in a fair way to be a failure. It is in a quiet sector, yet can hardly take care of itself, while to take any offensive action seems wholly beyond its powers. I have been here now with it three weeks and have been unable to have it make a single raid upon the enemy. Their Negro officers have an inadequate idea of what is expected of soldiers, and their white officers are too few to leaven the lump (Bullard 1925, 294–295).

Objective evidence contradicts Bullard entirely. During this period the 366th defeated a German attempt to capture a strategic bridge, supporting artillery effectively ended German offensive actions in the area, and continued patrols were being carried out, capturing enemy prisoners and leading to the decoration of a number of the troops.

November 10 found the division on either side of the Moselle River and part of the last Allied offensive of the war; the target was Metz. The 365th and 366th were deployed on the East Bank and the 367th on the West, with the 368th in reserve. The three regiments performed well, and by the time news of the armistice filtered through to them the following day, they had reached their objectives, at the cost of 500 killed or wounded. Total casualties for the division during the war had reached 1,700. Again Bullard criticized the division, despite their best attempts to prove their combat prowess. He accused the division of wasting time and not attacking in an effective manner, and he considered their performance to be inferior to the actions of the other American divisions to their left and right. But still he could not deny that the division had met its objectives.

Thanks to Bullard's negative reports, it was considered in U.S. Army circles that African Americans were inherently cowardly. Even those who recognized that the African American officers were doing their level best in a difficult situation suggested that their efforts were largely aimed at contributing to the progress of their race rather than fulfilling the wishes of their country.

African American troops did have their supporters, and most of the senior white officers at regimental level recognized that the men consistently performed well under fire and generally accepted any hardships without question. Given the fact that the 92d, in particular, had lacked any serious training and had never had the opportunity to serve together until they arrived in France, their performance, by and large, was considerably better than that of the majority of white units under similar circumstances.

Even after the armistice on November 11, 1918, African American units still remained active in Europe. The 369th was moved into Germany to occupy enemy towns and was the last to leave the area on December 10, when it rejoined the rest of the American troops in France.

To the west of the Moselle River, for the very first time, the 92d assembled as a division. It was largely a question of ensuring that all of the combat troops did not get themselves into difficulties now that the hostilities had ended. Huge numbers of African American SOS were deployed throughout France to deal with the thousands of bodies that lay unburied on the battlefields. Equally there were millions of unexploded shells and thousands of miles of barbed wire. These would all have to be dealt with in order to ensure that the French soil was ready for the spring harvest. In the Romagne region alone, some 6,000 African Americans reburied 23,000 corpses.

Despite all of their combat sacrifices and contributions to the war effort, none of the African American troops were allowed to march in the Victory Parade in Paris. Significantly, however, black troops who had served with the French and the British were included in the parade. African American servicemen had donated 300,000 francs to the War Orphan's Fund, despite the fact that many of the men had had their pay withheld.

As the men began to assemble for embarkation to the United States, there was almost a pathological terror among the American authorities, who feared that the African Americans would cause problems among the French population. The African American units were largely restricted to barracks and denied any opportunity to meet with women. There was also a fear emanating from the American Expeditionary Force headquarters, as evidenced in a secret report written at the end of January 1919, that the African American officers in particular would cause future problems at home, now that they had seen the equality of French Africans. This tension was heightened when it was learned that W. E. B. Du Bois, who was considered a radical, planned to meet the 92d Division in January. Du Bois had traveled to France to represent the NAACP at the peace conference and to monitor the treatment of African American troops. Intelligence officers were instructed to report on all of his movements and conversations with African American officers and to forward the confidential information immediately to the intelligence services.

The military police, as they had been throughout the period, were astonishingly brutal toward African American troops, and there was a Senate investigation into the execution of sixty-two men, many of whom were African Americans. The U.S. Army denied that any illegal executions had taken place, and there was little recorded evidence that any firing squads or hangings had been authorized during the short period African Americans were in Europe. However, the Graves Registration Service testified that they had reburied men who had been hanged, and an officer came forward to testify that he had supervised the execution of two African Americans at a base in France in January 1919. No real conclusions were reached, and the investigations petered out.

When the men began returning home, it was the 369th, parading along Fifth Avenue in New York, that was given the best reception accorded African American servicemen. Marching on the streets of New York in French phalanx formation to French martial music, played by the 369th band under the leadership of James Reese Europe, the 369th was then entertained at the 71st New York Infantry armory by the city's officials. As for those returning to the South, it was reported that several of the men had their uniforms taken away from them at railroad stations and that in Missouri African American troops refused to take the last place in the parade line. For the most part the men were eager to return to their normal lives, but still the debate about their contribution raged.

Col. Allen J. Greer, the chief of staff of the 92d Division, was still corresponding with likeminded individuals, charging that the division's African American officers and men were cow-

New York's African American 369th (old 15th) Regiment (the Harlem Hellfighters) marched along Fifth Avenue in a victory parade to the beat of its famous band. Regimental hero Henry Johnson, the first American to be awarded the French Croix de Guerre with Gold Palm, is standing in the open automobile holding a bouquet. (National Archives)

ards. Osceola McKaine, an African American lieutenant who had served with the 92d, complained to the War Department about the libels that Greer was spreading. The onus was put on McKaine to prove that Greer had written libelous documents. Again the issue gradually subsided as more and more of the men involved returned to civilian lives.

Although a large number of African American officers had served during World War I, it was considered by the U.S. Army that it would not be a sound policy to retain very many of them. Those who were retained joined (or rejoined) the four regular African American regiments, but only until those regiments reached establishment strength. The majority of American veterans returning to the United States and the uncertainties of civilian life were supported by the veterans' organization, the American Legion, but, particularly in the South, African Americans were virtually barred from the organization. Although sometimes allowed to form segregated posts, African American veterans were not eligible to hold national posts in the American Legion or to attend national conventions.

For the veterans who returned to the South, an altogether more sinister environment awaited them. The concept of having uniformed African Americans within the population, men who had been exposed to the "liberal attitudes" of the

French, was intolerable to the racists and the Ku Klux Klan. There were a number of incidents in Alabama, Kentucky, Mississippi, South Carolina, Texas, and Wyoming. Lynching went on an upward spiral from 1917, and in 1918 more than fifty African Americans were murdered in this way. There were other cases of lynching in Georgia, Louisiana, and North Carolina, and by the end of 1919, more than seventy African Americans had been lynched, eleven of whom had been burned alive. Several Southern politicians condoned the lynching incidents, claiming that the men had been rapists and therefore deserved this summary justice. Amongst the victims of 1919 were at least ten African American veterans, one of whom, Daniel Mack, was taken by a mob from a jail in Sylvester, Georgia, and beaten to death. In Pine Bluff, Arkansas, another veteran was chained to a tree and shot for refusing to step off a pavement when ordered to do so by a white woman.

There were also a number of riots in the summer of 1919, believed to have exceeded thirty-eight across the whole of the country; the period was dubbed the Red Summer, as a result of the blood that was spilled during that time. The general attitude seems to have been that the African American veterans had been "spoiled" by seeing how a society that did not fear "mongrelization of the races" treated those of African descent, and that they had returned to the United States determined not to be treated in the same way as they had been before their service in Europe. They were deemed to be defiant and, above all, capable for the first time of defending themselves physically. It was therefore simply a question of the white population defending themselves against these arrogant African Americans.

There was also considerable criticism from the African American veterans of individuals within their own community who had for many years championed their cause, but now found themselves superficially accepted by the establishment. Among those singled out for criticism were Emmett Scott and Robert Moton. The former had asked that evidence of the army's discrimination be suppressed, and Motom had called upon the African American veterans not to do anything that would destroy their newly found reputation as fighting troops who were loyal to their country. While these men and many other leaders called for patience, much of the African American press called for direct action. The African American publication *Challenge* wrote of the race riots in October 1919:

> We are fully ignored by the President and law makers. When we ask for a full-man's share they cry "insolent." When we shoot down the mobist that would burn our properties and destroy our lives, they shout "Bolshevist." When a white man comes to our side armed with the sword of righteousness and square dealing, they howl "Nigger-lover and bastard." If we take our grievances to Congress they are pigeon-holed, turned over to moths. We are abandoned, cast off, maligned, shackled, shoved down the hills toward Golgotha in "The Land of the Free and the Home of the Brave" (quoted in Barbeau and Henri 1974, 179–180).

There was much talk about the "new Negro," and certainly the war seems to have produced a more intense feeling of solidarity among the African American population. African Americans had answered the nation's call to fight in the first major conflict since the American Civil War, but rather than seeing them as proving their loyalty to the nation, the white population had simply viewed their contribution as part of a growing danger. The French had given them a kind of recognition their own countrymen for the most part denied them; the armed forces moved to use African Americans as little as possible as soon as the war was over.

See also Champagne Offensive; Chateau-Thierry, Battle of; Croix de Guerre; Du Bois, William Edward Burghardt; Europe, James Reese; Houston Riots; Marne, Second Battle of the; 92d Division; 93d Division; Spartanburg Incident; 370th Infantry Regiment; 371st Infantry Regiment; 372d Infantry Regiment;

369th Infantry Regiment; U.S. Army; U.S. Army, Interwar Period; Young, Charles

References and Further Reading

Aptheker, Herbert. *Toward Negro Freedom.* New York: New Century, 1956.

Barbeau, Arthur E., and Florette Henri. *The Unknown Soldiers: Black American Troops in World War I.* Philadelphia: Temple University Press, 1974.

Bullard, Robert L. *Personalities and Reminiscences of the War.* New York: Doubleday, 1925.

Farwell, Byron. *Over There.* New York: W. W. Norton, 1999.

Hagood, Johnson. *The Services of Supply.* Boston: Houghton Mifflin, 1927.

Krawczynski, Keith. "World War I." In *A Historic Context for the African-American Military Experience.* Edited by Steven D. Smith and James A. Ziegler. U.S. Army Corps of Engineers, 1998. https://www.denix.osd.mil/denix/Public/ES-Programs/Conservation/Legacy/AAME/aame3.html (accessed August 15, 2003).

Little, Arthur. *From Harlem to the Rhine.* New York: Corvici, 1936.

Mason, Monroe, and Arthur Furr. *The American Negro with the Red Hand of France.* Boston: Cornhill, 1920.

Scott, Emmett J. *Scott's Official History of the American Negro in the World War.* Chicago: Homewood Press, 1919.

Sweeney, W. Allison. *History of the American Negro in the Great World War.* Chicago: Cuneo-Henneberry, 1919.

World War II

While fighting the greatest war in history, the U.S. armed forces also faced concerted pressure to end segregation and unequal treatment and opportunity for African Americans. Because of that pressure and because of the needs of the armed services, some changes did occur, and the results of those changes were enough that the ground was prepared for the full integration of the armed services in the decade following the war. This entry is not primarily concerned with the achievements of African Americans during the war or with telling the story of what happened during the war chronologically; that material will be found in the entries on the various branches and individual units and people. Rather it looks at each branch of the armed services, discussing the forces for change, the forces that worked against change, and the extent of what was gained.

African American leaders embodied their calls for change in the Double V campaign, V for victory abroad against fascism and V for victory at home against all forms of discrimination. Civil rights leaders felt that if the U.S. Army and the other armed services could be persuaded to end inequality, then civilian institutions and businesses would be forced to follow. The U.S. Army especially came under extraordinary pressure, as it was in process of becoming the largest employer in the United States, and the stage was set for major confrontation. On the other hand, by comparison the U.S. Army was the most progressive of all of the armed services, at least in the sense that it had regular African American units, something no other service had.

The U.S. Army

From the outset, the U.S. Army recognized that it was expected to lead the way, but army leaders spoke in strong terms of the army's reluctance to engage in what they described as social experiments. Claiming that they had a war to fight first and foremost, the army leaders hoped to avoid the pressing demands that were being made to end segregation. They would certainly make no move unless supported, or better yet, ordered by Congress; accordingly, though important changes did happen, the lot of African Americans within the service changed much less than those who pressed for change hoped.

Mobilizing for War

The U.S. Army's mobilization policy was firmly based on its leaders' attitudes to the experience

Members of the African American 9th Cavalry Regiment (Buffalo Soldiers) at Fort Riley, Kansas, ride in the army's new speedy vehicle, which became famous as the jeep, in May 1941. On the eve of World War II the army was the only branch of the U.S. military that had any African American units. (U.S. Army)

of World War I. The traditionalists pointed to what they saw as the lackluster performance of wholly African American units such as the 92d Division during the last war, making it the main support of their resistance against the increasing calls from civil rights activists to eliminate a repeat of the 1917 mobilization policy. The U.S. Army recognized the fact that it would have to mobilize African Americans, but it proposed to use them as segregated units only. Above all, the U.S. Army constantly referred to issues such as military efficiency and claimed that integration would impair the service's ability to fight the war.

President Franklin D. Roosevelt and the Washington establishment found themselves in the unenviable position of having to placate both the civil rights activists and the War Department (not to mention taking into account the sensibilities of the white Southerners who formed an important segment of the Democratic Party). Given the impending U.S. involvement in the war, there was little time to force the two parties together and reach a compromise. Roosevelt met with African American representatives on September 27, 1940, but rather than waiting for a policy to be imposed upon them, U.S. Army leaders quickly released a policy statement on October 9. The U.S. Army promised that with the expansion of the service, it would recruit and utilize African Americans in proportion to their population in the country. This would mean that some 10 percent of the U.S. Army would be African American, and what was more, they would be employed in both combat and noncombat roles. The army would not, however, countenance the integration of African Americans in mixed units. All African Americans, including both the officers and the enlisted men, would be used solely in segregated units. The army went on to claim that the practice of segregation was well founded and that it worked; it saw no convincing reason to amend its policies in that respect.

As far the U.S. Army was concerned, it had presidential approval for this stance, and indeed Roosevelt had not made it clear that segregation was unacceptable. Unfortunately for Roosevelt, the call to end segregation in the armed services came at a time when he was embroiled in a presidential campaign to secure a third term, and he was dependent on the support of urban African Americans, as well as of the white Southern wing of the Democratic Party. His opponent, Wendell L. Willkie, had come out solidly behind the civil rights demands, and Willkie had begun to attract considerable numbers of the voters upon whom Roosevelt had been relying in order to win a third term. Roosevelt could afford neither to distance himself entirely from the U.S. Army, nor to appear to fully support their mobilization policy. His resulting actions were seen by many as just tinkering with the system and not addressing the fundamental problems.

Part of his immediate reaction involved elevating Col. Benjamin O. Davis Sr., Col. Campbell C. Johnson, and Judge William H. Hastie to positions of power and importance. Davis became a brigadier general, the first African American ever to hold this rank. Colonel Johnson was promoted from his post at Howard University (where he had commanded the Reserve Officers Training Course) to special aide to the director of the Selective Service. Judge Hastie, then dean of Howard University, became the civilian aide to the secretary of war.

Hastie faced the most difficult role; on the one hand the War Department wanted to use him as a public relations representative to deflect criticism, a role like that Emmett J. Scott had played during World War I. On the other hand, the civil rights activists expected Hastie to force through rapid changes. In the event, Hastie not only had his own agenda, but his own method of handling the seemingly incompatible calls for his time and support. Hastie knew that a quick fix would never solve the long-term, underlying problems; what he had to prove was that segregation was not efficient. For the first ten months or so, Hastie busied himself with observing the situation from the ground up. He quickly noted that segregation was certainly counterproductive in terms of building morale in the African American troops. His second major observation was that using African Americans only in segregated units did not make the best use of their talents. Above all, he believed that segregation and discrimination were fundamentally at odds with the nation's championship of democracy, which all claimed to be defending in this war; in a word, segregation was hypocritical. Hastie began to frame a proposal for progressive integration; he began with calls to assign individual African Americans with particular talents and expertise without regard to their race.

Hastie met strong resistance in the form of Henry L. Stimson (secretary of war) and Gen. George C. Marshall (chief of staff). They both supported the tradition of segregation, stating that it had been in place since 1863 and that they saw no reason to place faith in African Americans, who they believed showed little initiative in combat. They said as much to Roosevelt, as can be seen in Stimson's diary (October 25, 1940, quoted in MacGregor 1985, chap. 2). Stimson's attitudes were typical of the times in being contradictory in the extreme; on the one hand he claimed that he supported the civil rights of all Americans, while on the other he opposed integration. As late as January 1942, Stimson was noting in his diary that social equality would never be achieved, as widespread interracial marriages would never become common (January 24, 1942; quoted in MacGregor 1985, chap. 2).

Marshall's objections to Hastie's proposals centered on the expected impact of integration on the efficiency of the armed services. He claimed that the U.S. Army was not the place, nor was the war the time to tackle a fundamental social problem such as integration. On a more practical level, he recognized the inherent problems of training African Americans in the Southern U.S. Army recruitment centers, where they would be subject to Southern laws and customs with their own distinctive approach to race. Marshall also seems to have believed that African Americans were not as intelligent or as skilled as whites and that his massive task of preparing the U.S. Army for war would be hindered if he was forced to put African Americans in roles to which they were not suited. As far as senior U.S. Army officials were concerned, to allow the passage of integration at this crucial time, when the nation was on the verge of entering the hostilities, would put the country at risk of a social revolution and with it the destruction of a system that had already been proven.

Marshall was present at a conference on December 8, 1941, the very day that the United States entered the war. Addressing the assembled African American editors and publishers, he told them that there would be changes and that he was not altogether satisfied with the progress made so far. On the other hand, Col. Eugene R. Householder, the adjutant general, also addressed the conference, and his words expressed the real consensus among army leaders:

> The Army is made up of individual citizens of the United States who have pronounced views with respect to the Negro just as they have individual ideas with respect to other matters in their daily walk of life. Military orders, fiat, or dicta, will not change their viewpoints. The Army then cannot be made the means of engendering conflict among the mass of people because of a stand with respect to Negroes which is not compatible with the position attained by the Negro in civil life. . . . The Army is not a sociological laboratory; to be effective it must be organized and trained according to the principles that will insure success. Experiments to meet the wishes and demands of the champions of every race and creed for the solution of their problems are a danger to efficiency, discipline and morale and would result in ultimate defeat (quoted in MacGregor 1985, chap. 2).

In effect, although the civil rights activists did not know it, this was the army's last word. Despite the feeling shared by many that segregation was on a par with Nazi racial policies, the U.S. Army had spoken and was immobile. John J. McCloy, the assistant secretary for war, was ready to accept this position; the issue of African Americans serving in segregated or integrated units was not, he believed, the paramount concern. In any case, he felt, the vast majority of U.S. citizens would not countenance integration. His primary worry was that African Americans were more concerned with the integration issue than winning the war, and if the Allies lost the war, the question of African American equality was a lost cause. He urged the African American community to rally around the flag and trust that changes would be forthcoming when victory was achieved. The same argument had been used in World War I, and real integration had not come. If integration did come soon after World War II, it was partly because the changes the army accepted under political pressure had enough impact to make it clear that segregation was a completely inefficient way of using manpower, partly because African Americans had more of a chance to prove themselves in combat, and partly because society was changing.

The Problems of Deployment

Just one year after the nation entered the war, 399,454 African Americans were under arms in the U.S. Army, a full 7.4 percent of the enlisted men. The problem was what to do with them. Under pressure from Roosevelt, the army had agreed to open all arms of the service to African Americans but had insisted on keeping them in segregated units. In theory, all arms of the service were to have African Americans in numbers proportionate to the national population, which was about 10 percent.

Opening all components of the U.S. Army to African Americans proved to be a more difficult process than had been anticipated. In addition to opposition from within the service itself, it was simply not practical to create or realign units with specific functions in order to reach the 10 percent figure. Although the army increased the number of African Americans in the service, African Americans were unevenly distributed; the Air, Signal, and Medical Corps each had just 2 percent, the infantry had reached 5 percent—all under the 10 percent that had been promised. The bulk of African Americans found themselves attached elsewhere, or rather unattached: unassigned and miscellaneous detachments had 27 percent African American membership. A full quarter of the Engineer Corps was African American and 15 percent of the

Quartermaster Corps. What this meant was that most African Americans were either in support units or simply unwanted, being kept unused and becoming more and more discontented.

The disproportionate nature of the assignments can be traced partly to a deeper form of discrimination and inequality; they were not simply the result of overt racism within the U.S. Army, even though the insistence by the army on segregation exacerbated the problem. Segregated and inferior education was the basic problem. In March 1941, the U.S. Army had introduced the Army General Classification Test (AGCT). The system placed all of the enlisted men in one of five categories. Officers and specialists were taken from the top three groupings, and what were in reality unskilled laborers from the bottom two.

These test results pointed to an underlying problem. Beneath the veneer of equality of opportunity in the United States lay the fact that the majority of African Americans had come from neighborhoods where, educationally, economically, and culturally, they were disadvantaged. Numerically speaking, more whites than African Americans scored in the lower categories, but since they were a much lower percentage of the whole and could be assigned anywhere, the U.S. Army could absorb almost any number of poorly rated white soldiers, whereas the large percentage of low-rated African Americans had to be assigned to the limited number of African American units. A secondary problem was the assignment of the well-educated African Americans; they too would have to be assigned to units that would have a preponderance of poorly rated men. The inevitable outcome would be that their talents would be wasted.

From the outset, the segregation policy caused other enormous unforeseen problems; not only was segregated housing for the men at a premium, but also there was a distinct lack of experienced officers and noncommissioned officers to train them. As a result, many of the men remained unassigned or awaiting training. The Bureau of Selective Service increased the pressure by pointing to many African Americans who should have been called up but who had been passed over, suggesting that the quota system be scrapped altogether and urging the army to accept more African Americans. The army's response was to create new African American units to absorb more men, even though many of the units had no clear role or purpose and the army could not train them at the time.

The U.S. Army Air Forces

Of all of the components of the U.S. Army, the U.S. Army Air Forces (USAAF) was the most resistant to accepting African Americans. In the 1940 mobilization plans, the USAAC (U.S. Army Air Corps, as it was known from 1926 to 1941) had avoided having an allotment of African Americans. It would take time to train African American ground crews, and in the meantime African American pilots could not be used, because these pilots would outrank the white men in the ground crews. The chief of the USAAF, Maj. Gen. Henry H. Arnold, had explained in a memo in May of 1940 that African American pilots were out of the question, "since this would result in having Negro officers serving over white enlisted men. This would create an impossible social problem" (quoted in MacGregor 1985, 26). When it came to the mobilization plans of 1941, the War Department insisted that the Army Air Force accept African Americans. Recruitment was to be accelerated, and the chief of staff set targets, the result of which was some 77,500 African Americans in the USAAF by 1943. Initially, the USAAF decided to establish some nine squadrons, which were to be primarily concerned with the maintenance of their airfields. On January 16, 1941, however, Undersecretary of War Robert P. Patterson announced the creation of an African American fighter squadron. The men who trained for that squadron faced segregated training facilities at Tuskegee, Alabama, which did not equal the white facilities that had been established at Maxwell Airfield.

The training facility at Tuskegee created far more African American pilots than could easily

Newly commissioned officers from Officer Candidate School, Fort Benning, Georgia, May 29, 1942. During World War II African Americans continued to be woefully underrepresented in the officer corps. (National Archives)

be absorbed into a single fighter squadron. The net result was the creation of the 332d Fighter Group, encompassing a further three African American squadrons, all of which were in a combat theater by 1944. By late 1943, the USAAF had decided to create the 477th Bombardment Group; now the deficiencies of the segregated training facilities came home to the service. Tuskegee had been supremely efficient in turning out quality fighter pilots, but it lacked the facilities to deal with the additional demands of training bombing crews. Equally, the disproportionate numbers of African Americans who found themselves graded low in the AGCT meant that the available African American manpower to fill the 477th was limited. As a result of these two factors, the 477th did not become operational until after hostilities had ended. The pilots, navigators, and bombardiers who served in this unit had had to be temporarily assigned to previously white-only training facilities even to achieve this level of training; that they were so assigned was a singular example of the USAAF's ability to place expedience over tradition.

Nonflight African American officers were initially destined for segregated training facilities, despite the fact that Robert A. Lovett (assistant secretary of war for air) promised Hastie that the training would be integrated. When the Technical Training Command announced the creation of a segregated training program in 1942, even though the decision was quickly rescinded, it brought about Hastie's resignation. In January 1943, the Army Air Force made another promise, this time to Lovett, that African American officer candidates would be posted throughout the schools regardless of their color. In practice, the majority found themselves at either Tuskegee or Godman Fields, although some were assigned to an integrated facility at Miami Beach. While the Army Air Force was struggling to cope with African American pilots and officers, it used the tried and tested creation of temporary units and unassigned status to absorb the masses of enlisted men. From 1943, literally hundreds of training squadrons, quartermaster and engineer companies, as well as base security units, were created. By the end of the war, there was practically no Army Air Force base in the world without its contingent of African Americans doing service work.

Problems in Deployment in the Infantry and Cavalry

The challenge of what to do with all the African American units that were being formed in the infantry and cavalry was complicated by the decision that had been made following World War I not to create segregated African American divisions. The U.S. Army capped the largest African American infantry unit at regimental level; elsewhere, African American armored and artillery units consisted of either squadrons or battalions. In October 1940, the two regular African American cavalry regiments, the 9th and the 10th, were combined with white regiments to form the 2d Cavalry Division. This continued to be the formula used; African American units were incorporated as parts of predominantly white formations.

Prior to World War II, African American leaders had agreed with the policy of not creating wholly African American divisions. They did not share the mistaken belief of the military establishment that the World War I divisions had not fought well, but they believed that separate divisions would perpetuate segregation in the U.S. Army. In the early weeks of the war, individuals such as Walter White, executive secretary of the NAACP, called on the U.S. Army to create an integrated division of volunteers, an action that would at one stroke raise the morale and participation of African Americans and counter the accusations of discrimination from abroad. His suggestion drew the support of the NAACP, but the implacable opposition of the U.S. Army, for many of the reasons already mentioned.

Despite this outright opposition, by the end of 1942 the U.S. Army was considering assigning some African Americans to white units. The proposal came from Col. Edwin W. Chamberlain (Organization-Mobilization Group of G-3); it did not, however, reflect any belief in real integration, nor would it have promoted equal treatment. He argued:

1. Units of African American troops were less useful to the U.S. Army than units of white soldiers, given that the majority of African American soldiers scored poorly on the AGCT.
2. It was therefore a waste of resources and manpower to concentrate these men into wholly African American units; moreover, these segregated units only perpetuated the divisions between African Americans and white troops.
3. The creation of African American units should therefore be halted, and African Americans in categories IV and V of the AGCT should be assigned to white units (on a ratio of one African American to nine whites).
4. These men would provide the 10–20 percent of the unit that only required the most basic of training, and they would serve as drivers, cooks, orderlies, and the like.
5. African Americans with higher AGCT scores could then be concentrated in the existing African American units, where their superior intellect would increase the overall efficiency of the unit.

Although Chamberlain strongly denied any racial discrimination in his overall proposal, the underlying attitude behind his approach can be best summed up by his own statement in a memo that his ideas involved no more racial in-

Troops of the 10th Cavalry, a Buffalo Soldier regiment, present arms while in bivouac at Fort Riley, Kansas, May 1941. Despite the regiment's long combat history, it was combined with the 9th Cavalry to form the all–African American 2d Cavalry Division, which was then converted to a service rather than combat role in 1944. (U.S. Army)

tegration than "the employment of Negroes as servants in a white household" (quoted in MacGregor 1985, 29).

In the event, Chamberlain's proposals were not adopted, and another solution was sought to absorb the increasing numbers of African Americans in the U.S. Army. In any case, Chamberlain's ideas had already drawn considerable opposition from both the civil rights movement and the armed forces. Reluctantly, the U.S. Army turned its policy, active since the end of the previous war, on its head and authorized the creation of all–African American divisions, hoping that they would absorb the enormous numbers of unassigned men. In the spring of 1942, the 93d Division was reactivated, followed by the 92d later in the year. In February 1943, the 2d Cavalry Division became an all–African American organization. The process was under way, and each of the three divisions could absorb 15,000 African Americans.

By 1943, however, the quota system was being challenged in a new way. Paul V. McNutt, chairman of the War Manpower Commission, wanted to abolish the quota system; he doubted whether it was legal, and he was responding to increasing criticisms that African Americans were not being called up in sufficient numbers. The critics pointed out that white men regardless of their marital status found themselves drafted, while large numbers of young African Americans were overlooked by the draft. Stimson defended the legality of the system, in part by explaining that African Americans could only be inducted into the services at the rate that the services could handle. He also explained that since few African Americans were assigned to combat duties, their casualty rates would be lower, and thus more white men would have to be called up as replacements.

McNutt planned to abandon the quota system once the backlog of African American inductees had been cleared and set the date for the end of the quota system as January 1944. In fact, the quota system remained in place throughout the war because of a fundamental change in the manpower equation. Before March 1943, the problem was that more African Americans were available than the army could accommodate, necessitating a quota to keep the percentage of African Americans to the level the army considered manageable. In March, however, the situation changed. The manpower requirement necessitated by the magnitude of the war began to affect African Americans as well as whites, and the U.S. Army began to require more African Americans than were immediately available. This meant the quota system could no longer be perceived as keeping African Americans out of the army. By September 1944 African Americans accounted for some 9.6 percent (701,678) of the U.S. Army. African American women had peaked at 6 percent of the volunteer Women's Auxiliary Corps (later the Women's Army Corps), despite the fact that a target of 10 percent had been set (MacGregor 1985, chap. 2).

The U.S. Army had to face the manpower shortages squarely and adopt a radical new plan. The attempt to maintain a balance for African Americans between combat troops and service troops was abandoned. Immobile stateside African American combat units, unwanted by combat commands abroad, were converted into service troops in order to free white troops for combat. The most notorious example of this policy was the treatment of the 2d Cavalry Division, which included the 9th and 10th Cavalry, African American regiments with a ninety-year record of service. The units of the division were inactivated and converted to service troops after arriving in North Africa in March 1944. Responding to growing criticism of the policy, Stimson deepened a growing controversy by claiming that African American combat units had not been able to master modern combat techniques, hence their conversion from combat to service operations. In spite of some commitment of African Americans to combat, designed to alleviate political pressure (see below), the army continued to assign most African Americans to service units for the rest of the war.

The Demoralizing Effects of Segregation

From the beginning of the war African American soldiers suffered a gradual deterioration in morale as a result of the U.S. Army's overall policy of keeping them in segregated units and marginalizing them as combat-ready troops. The net result was a vicious circle of poor morale, poor performance, and poor discipline. Moreover, the bulk of African American soldiers were based in camps in the South, and whenever they left the camps they were subject to the often draconian laws that controlled the lives of the local African American populations. Segregation in the camps themselves had never been the avowed policy of the U.S. Army, but the practice of segregating all facilities soon became common there too. African Americans found themselves assigned to poor-quality barracks and substandard facilities, particularly in terms of recreation. Hastie summed up the problem in a memo to the secretary of war: "The traditional mores of the South have been widely accepted and adopted by the Army as the basis of policy and practice affecting the Negro soldier. In tactical organization, in physical location, in human contacts, the Negro soldier is separated from the white soldier as completely as possible" (September 22, 1941, quoted in MacGregor 1985, 35).

In November 1941, the Red Cross blood banks became segregated. The U.S. Army's surgeon general defended the policy, despite the fact that the Red Cross admitted that there were no reasonable scientific grounds for such segregation. As it turned out, the Red Cross retained its segregated blood banks throughout the war, regardless of the constant pressure from African American groups and civil rights activists, including the NAACP. The net result was yet another cause of demoralization for African Americans, both in the military and in the public at large, and this at a time when the Red Cross was calling for ever more donors to cover the inevitable demands of combat casualties.

The nature of the officers who commanded African American units was another contributing factor in the demoralization of African American troops. By 1942, only 0.35 percent of African Americans in the U.S. Army were officers, despite the fact that there were severe shortages of officers in all of the African American units (MacGregor 1985). Steps were put in place to increase the number of African American officers, but given the prejudices of white commanders, that did not solve the problem. It was clear that many of the senior white officers of the units did not consider that African Americans were capable of filling the role of officer. The lack of segregated facilities for African American officers ruled out postings to many U.S. Army bases, coupled with the fact that many local communities openly campaigned to keep African American officers away from their area. Even when there were facilities for the African American officers, another major concern undermined their positions. The U.S. Army had a long tradition of not allowing African American officers to outrank or command white officers serving in the same unit, the net result being that the enlisted men did not consider African American officers to be full-fledged superiors, which adversely affected the credibility and effectiveness of black officers.

The white officers assigned to African American units tended to be Southerners, following a tradition that could be traced back through many of the conflicts since the end of the American Civil War, a tradition that was based on the belief that Southerners knew how to handle African Americans. These Southerners in many cases came from rural backgrounds and tended to collide culturally with the predominantly urban African Americans. To add to the problem, many of the white officers were of low caliber, assigned to African American units because they were unwanted elsewhere.

In August of 1942, Stimson acceded to the demands that a permanent body be set up to monitor racial issues, suggest reforms, and address the thorny problem of training and use of African American troops. Assistant Secretary McCloy had been placed in charge of the Advisory Committee on Negro Troop Policies. In the beginning, however, the committee did little but collect and pass on information.

An attempt was made to have more African Americans sent overseas, which seemed the most hopeful way of defusing the situation. In May 1942, the War Department issued a directive to the U.S. Army (Air, Ground, and Services Forces). African American troops were now to be sent overseas in proportion to the percentages of men in the three sections of the U.S. Army. Each of the theater commanders would be informed that African Americans were to be dispatched to their commands, and they were not to be given the opportunity to refuse them. At this point in the war, the majority of the men were to be sent to Great Britain, and the initial batches were to be service troops.

Although Great Britain did not object to the dispatch of African American troops, other foreign nations lodged complaints. In the case of some of the West Indian islands, they feared that well-paid African Americans would undermine the local economies by stimulating calls for higher rates of pay within the islands. Panamanian authorities objected to the deployment of a single African American unit. Both Chile and Venezuela refused to have African Americans on their soil. Even Alaska complained of African American deployment, but since Alaska was a U.S. territory, all objections were overruled. A compromise of sorts was reached in the case of Iceland, Greenland, and Labrador, since Stimson stated that northern climates were probably not suitable for African Americans anyway. As a result of these objections, a policy of sorts was established of assigning no African Americans either to bases in the far north or to countries that lodged objections.

Although theater commanders had no choice but to accept African Americans whether they wanted them or not, it was still up to the commanders to decide who would be sent into combat. In many cases, the commanders resorted to not asking for troops as reinforcements in order to avoid having African Americans sent to their commands. While the overseas commanders avoided racial tensions and problems by effectively keeping African American units at home, the pressure cooker threatened to explode on the U.S. bases dotted around the country. There were widespread disciplinary problems arising out of dull routines and severe local laws, problems that often led to violence, either instigated by the African American troops or in response to violence meted out to them by a hostile local population and law enforcement system. There was a continuous merry-go-round of disciplinary charges, investigations, exonerations, and attempts at reform, but little was done that actually cut to the heart of the matter. The men felt underused and sidelined, despite all the talk of their being used in proportion throughout all of the commands of the U.S. Army.

It also seems that wherever a little piece of the United States was exported to a foreign land, along with it went Jim Crow, an ever-present specter of military discrimination. Despite local laws and mores accepting the presence of African Americans, the U.S. Army did its best to impose segregation, and nowhere more than in Great Britain. Here, the African Americans were warmly welcomed as allies, in what had been some of the bleakest and loneliest times for a country set against the Axis forces since 1939. In the United States, the attitude toward African Americans was most often one of intolerance, which led to situations that threatened to become riots. Disciplinary problems that spilled out of the camps were less than skillfully handled by military police. The most serious incidents in the United States during the summer of 1943 occurred in camps in California, Georgia, Kentucky, Mississippi, and Texas. Elsewhere, in U.S. Army camps across the world, smoldering resentment threatened to erupt into violence, much to the alarm of the Advisory Committee on Negro Troop Policies, the War Department, and local military commanders.

At the same time, support for continuing the policy of segregation came from an unlikely source. The Office of War Information commissioned a survey in 1943, the results of which were published in July, asking respondents in five cities in the United States for their views on segregation. *The Negroes' Role in the War: A Study of White and Colored Opinions* showed that some 25 percent of the African American public supported segregation in the U.S. Army (quoted in MacGregor 1985). The Special Service Division Research Branch commissioned two U.S. Army surveys, *What the Soldier Thinks* (December 1942) and *Attitudes of the Negro Soldier* (July 1943). A staggering 38 percent of African American soldiers actually approved of segregated units, a low percentage compared to the 88 percent of white troops who approved, but still surprisingly high, and over half of the African Americans surveyed preferred separate facilities on the bases (MacGregor 1985). How these findings squared with the resentment toward segregation can be explained by an observation made by the Special Services Division: "Many of the Negroes and some of the whites who favor separation in the Army indicate by their comments that they are opposed to segregation in principle. They favor separation in the Army to avoid trouble or unpleasantness" (quoted in MacGregor 1985, 44).

Efforts at Reform and Some Successes

In December 1943, some twenty-five civil rights groups met to frame their demands on the presidential candidates in the coming year's election. Hastie had already resigned, discouraged with the lack of progress so far, and joined in the attacks on the U.S. Army and its segregation policies; he was replaced by Truman K. Gibson Jr. Gibson too was a lawyer, a graduate of the University of Chicago, and had become Hastie's assistant in 1940. Following Hastie's resignation on January 29, 1943, Gibson became the acting civilian aide, officially replacing Hastie on September 21, 1943. Gibson urged the president and the U.S. Army to act before political pressure forced changes and warned them that what they did or did not do would affect the result of the election. The civil rights groups had made the following demands:

1. Full integration (at the very least in volunteer units)
2. Abolition of racial quotas
3. Institution of a race relations education program in the U.S. Army
4. More assignment of African Americans to combat duties

5. Removal of African American troops from areas in which discrimination or violence had occurred
6. Abolition of the blood plasma segregation system in the Red Cross
7. Abolition of segregated facilities in the U.S. Army

With vociferous support from the African American media as well as anti-administration newspapers such as the *Chicago Tribune*, it seemed possible that a negative response from the administration and the U.S. Army would mean that marginal states could be lost to the president, giving Gibson some powerful leverage. Gibson was no less opposed to racial segregation than Hastie had been, but he advocated practical changes that could be made one step at a time rather than global policy change. He was able to make himself heard in the War Department, and he worked closely with the Advisory Committee on Negro Troop Policies, led by McCloy.

The Advisory Committee on Negro Troop Policies was convinced that the root cause of the racial problems the army was encountering was the failure of local commanders to take the issue seriously and in general to take full responsibility for discipline and morale. Marshall incorporated some of the committee's recommendations in a letter to field commanders, making clear that any commander who did not deal adequately with racial issues would be removed from his post. He did not, however, follow the committee's advice to have individual commanders report back to him on the steps they had taken. Most importantly, he ignored the committee's recommendation that African American troops should be sent into combat zones, even though the committee considered that the best way to improve the morale of African American troops.

The committee then addressed the problem of the African American press, which had not followed the example of such important leaders as Hastie in criticizing the army judiciously, but had actually heightened racial tension by its inflammatory coverage of any story that put the army's handling of race relations in a bad light. There had already been calls from some sections of the U.S. Army to censor the African American press in the belief that the constant criticisms were detrimental to army morale. Marshall was urged by the Army Service Forces to warn the African American press in July 1943 that they should show a little more caution in their reporting and in their editorials, since running material that could be construed as being incitement could well bring charges of sedition against the newspaper. Marshall shied away from a direct confrontation and appointed African Americans to the Bureau of Public Relations to help ensure that positive stories related to African Americans in the U.S. Army received the due attention of African American journalists. Although the move was in some ways effective, in that more accurate and positive stories were reported in the African American press, the editorial coverage was still highly critical of the basic policy of segregation and the refusal of the War Department to send African American combat units overseas.

In March 1944, the committee was again pressing Stimson to commit African Americans to combat and to ensure that any necessary retraining was undertaken at the earliest opportunity. Above all, the committee believed that African American troops needed to feel that they were an asset and not an impediment to the U.S. Army. In a memo, McCloy directly addressed the army's usual argument:

> There has been a tendency to allow the situation to develop where selections are made on the basis of efficiency with the result that the colored units are discarded for combat service, but little is done by way of studying new means to put them in shape for combat service.
>
> With so large a portion of our population colored, with the example of the effective use of colored troops (of a much lower order of intelligence) by other nations, and with the many imponderables that are connected with the situation, we must, I think, be more affirmative about the use of our Negro troops. If present methods do not bring them to combat efficiency, we should change those methods.

> That is what this resolution purports to recommend (quoted in MacGregor 1985, chap. 2).

On March 4, 1944, with the blessing of Stimson, the committee met with the U.S. Army staffers to work out possible combat assignments for the African American 92d and 93d Divisions. Regimental combat teams were to be selected, with the 92d providing a team of volunteers and the 93d an existing unit. In this way, the fighting qualities of both ordinary African American troops and volunteers could be assessed. It was hoped that the experiences gained in the close monitoring of their performance would provide a blueprint for the deployment of greater numbers of African Americans in the not too distant future.

Even while steps were being taken to prepare the 92d and 93d Infantry Divisions for overseas deployment, African American units already overseas, but assigned to service or labor duties, were being returned to a combat-capable status. In January 1944, the 1st Battalion, 24th Infantry Regiment, which was performing service command duties for the New Georgia Group Service Command, moved from Guadalcanal to Bougainville, where it undertook the work of unloading ships. The 1st Battalion was the last African American battalion that had all white officers. In response to the War Department's message urging the prompt use of African American ground combat units, it was transferred from service duties to the role of regimental reserve for the 148th Infantry Regiment. On March 11, 1944, while reinforcing two battalions of the 148th, two men of the 1st Battalion were killed. The following night, the 1st Battalion conducted its first combat patrol and encountered a Japanese patrol of eight men. In the firefight that followed, the 1st Battalion's patrol lost one man and killed one Japanese soldier—the first enemy casualty inflicted by African American ground troops. Later in March, African American artillery units began missions in support of operations near Bougainville.

The 93d Infantry Division, comprising the 368th Regimental Combat Team (RCT), the 369th RCT, and the 25th RCT, whose personnel had been chosen in preparation for an early combat role, had arrived in the Solomon Islands by the end of February 1944. The division moved to Guadalcanal, but the 368th and 369th quickly moved on to occupation and security assignments throughout the New Georgia Group of islands. The men of the 25th RCT, however, underwent refresher training before departing on March 22, 1944, for the southern region of Bougainville, where the 1st Battalion, 24th Infantry was already deployed. On March 30, the 25th RCT went under the operational control of the U.S. Army's Americal Division and began operations with the Americal within twenty-four hours. Each of the regiment's battalions was attached to one of the Americal Division's regiments, and the 25th's supporting artillery and the separate 594th Artillery were attached to the Americal Division Artillery. The 93d Divison's supporting units were also attached to the Americal Division as appropriate.

The 370th RCT was selected to be the advance unit for the division and was formed at Fort Huachuca, Arizona, on April 4, 1944. It sailed from Virginia for the Italian front on July 15 and arrived at Naples, Italy, on July 30, 1944. It immediately began a series of exercises and evaluations, assigned to IV Corps (and shortly afterward, also the 1st Armored Division) and working closely with white staff of the corps headquarters and the 1st Armored Division. One of its artillery units, the 598th Field Artillery, undertook its first fire mission on August 29. The following day, troops of the 370th began offensive operations and captured its first prisoners of war.

The rest of the 92d Infantry Division arrived during October and November. The 371st RCT arrived by October 18, the 368th RCT by November 8, and the last divisional support units by November 22. The infantry and artillery units of the 92d Division became available for combat operations soon after their arrival; the 371st RCT began combat operations on October 31, 1944.

Gradually the process of converting inactive

African American units into combat-ready troops got under way, helping to alleviate the tensions in the United States. Realizing that many of the officers in these units were not effective leaders, Lt. Gen. Lesley J. McNair (head of Army Ground Forces) declared that officers graded "excellent" would be replaced, if it was practicable, before their unit shipped abroad. It was, of course, often not practicable.

This process was a slow one; for the most part African American troops were still jammed into inadequate camps around the United States and subjected to the same levels of discrimination from the U.S. Army and the local communities as ever, despite Marshall's letter urging commanders to deal with issues of discrimination. A month before part of the 93d was committed to Bougainville, the War Department finally responded to the urging of the Advisory Committee on Negro Troop Policies and issued clear guidelines to the local commanders on the official U.S. Army racial policies, along with instructions on how to develop African American leadership within the units still in camp. In terms of what had gone before, *Command of Negro Troops* (War Department Pamphlet 20–6, February 29, 1944) was a major breakthrough and served as the blueprint for later policies adopted by the other armed services. Above all, the pamphlet was objective and looked at African American rights within the context of the U.S. Army. The pamphlet clearly reflected the committee's aim of improving the conditions of African American troops by demanding that commanders take greater responsibility, asserting unequivocally that all races could fight equally well provided they were properly led.

Another publication in October of 1944 conveyed the same basic message; Army Service Forces Manual M-5 (*Leadership and the Negro Soldier*) stated:

> War Department concern with the Negro is focused directly and solely on the problem of the most effective use of colored troops. . . . The Army has no authority or intention to participate in social reform as such but does view the problem as a matter of efficient troop utilization. With an imposed ceiling on the maximum strength of the Army it is the responsibility of all officers to assure the most efficient use of the manpower assigned (quoted in MacGregor 1985, 35).

As long as the army persisted in using only segregated units, of course, full efficiency could not possibly be achieved. But segregation of camp facilities was another matter. On March 10, 1943, the War Department had issued a directive ordering those in charge of armed service facilities to remove signs labeling facilities as being for either black or white troops. It had been a forlorn hope to expect that the signs would be torn down overnight, and in any case certain units and camps were exempt from the edict. A reinterpretation was issued on July 8, 1944, instructing commanders that they could allocate particular facilities to a named unit, but that facilities such as post exchanges and theaters should be available to all troops regardless of color. Most significant in the changes was that government-owned transport was now to be fully opened to all U.S. Army troops and that no local color bars would be imposed on African American soldiers using government vehicles.

Unfortunately, as had been the case with the previous directive, there was a distinct lack of will to impose the changes. For the most part the directive was ignored or fudged to convert color bars into unit bars, effectively the same thing under the current conditions of African American segregated units. The impact was not felt in many of the camps, and continued restrictions led to incidents such as the one that occurred at the officers' club at the Indiana base, Freeman's Field, when African American officers were arrested when they tried to assert their right to enter a still segregated facility.

That incident prompted the committee to reiterate the directive in clearer terms to the commanders of bases, who were told that segregation was not acceptable in the cases of clubs and messes; in effect this meant that the only acceptable form of segregation officially sanctioned by the U.S. Army was segregation by unit. There would still be segregated African American units, but in operational respects the U.S. Army was to be integrated. Acting Secretary Patterson explained the thinking in a letter to Governor Chauncey Sparks of Alabama:

> The War Department has maintained throughout the emergency and present war that it is not an appropriate medium for effecting social readjustments but has insisted that all soldiers, regardless of race, be afforded equal opportunity to enjoy the recreational facilities which are provided at posts, camps and stations. The thought has been that men who are fulfilling the same obligation, suffering the same dislocation of their private lives, and wearing the identical uniform should, within the confines of the military establishment, have the same privileges for rest and relaxations (September 1, 1944; quoted in MacGregor 1985, chap. 2).

By this stage, the committee had succeeded in dragging the U.S. Army further than would have been thought possible and could take pride in the fact that many of the discrimination issues had been resolved. There were, however, major race tensions and still some examples of racial incidents occurring here and there. One problem, of course, was that African American soldiers now experienced an intolerable duality of legal systems. On bases and in government-owned vehicles the U.S. Army racial policy would apply, but the moment the troops stepped out of the camps or boarded a local bus, the local Jim Crow laws would be in effect. The other problem was that segregated units were still the norm.

Two Experiments in Integration

In at least two areas, however, enough integration was achieved to make it easier to move toward full integration after the war. One of these areas was officer training, the other, the approach to integration in Europe in 1945, caused by the desperate need for men.

As far as officer training was concerned, the army's policy at the beginning of the war reflected the experience of World War I. In 1917, an African American officer candidate training facility had been established in Des Moines, Iowa. The army had operated an African American officer training course at Fort Des Moines, Iowa, from June to October 1917. Although 1,250 men attended the course, there was only one graduating class of 639 officers on October 15, 1917. The Des Moines African American training course was then closed and the training of African American officers was delegated to the existing officer training centers, where the reception of African Americans varied widely. Some of the centers practiced strict segregation while others integrated their courses (usually for practical reasons). The number of additional African Americans commissioned as officers through the other centers was small, only about 700.

Whether the army deliberately admitted unqualified candidates to the Des Moines course to ensure failure of the program and to bolster support for the belief than African Americans were incapable of being trained or functioning as officers has long been debated. Clearly, different admission standards did apply. White officer candidates had to be college graduates, while African American officer candidates only had to be high school graduates. In addition, the army's personnel system proved unwilling or unable to route African American college graduates to Des Moines, sending many of them to labor units. There had also been charges that the training at Des Moines was irrelevant to the realities of combat in World War I, but that statement was true of all of the officer candidate centers. Most significantly, the Des Moines school did not address the gap of life experiences separating most African American men from white men in 1917, and did begin to prepare them to lead men and react to life-or-death situations without delay.

The goal for African American leadership in the military had been different in 1917. At that time, the goal had been to ensure that as many

African American men as possible were trained to serve as officers in African American military units. African American leaders had called for a segregated officer training course because they thought it more likely to be established rather than a program of integration and because they feared that African American officer candidates would be harshly and unfairly treated if they were attending a white officer training center. By World War II, African American leaders saw integration of officer training programs as both the goal of sound officer training for African Americans and as an important civil rights goal.

The U.S. Army collectively maintained the firm opinion that African Americans were simply not suited for the officer corps. If the U.S. Army was to be required to train African American officers, then they should be schooled alongside white candidates and held to the same standards, so that only the very best graduated.

According to the mobilization plans of 1937, African American officers were assumed, but only as many as necessary to provide officers for the African American units designated to have African American officers. They were, however, to be trained in integrated facilities. When a large number of officer training schools were established in 1941, General Davis assumed that integration was agreed and that schools would provide, not African American or white officers, but American officers, officers whose status rested firmly on their abilities.

If the War Department and Davis had expected race not to be an issue in the training of officers, they were mistaken. What seems to have happened was that commanders, having a bias against African American officers, made it hard for African Americans to apply and succeed. Certainly, few African Americans were selected for officer training. Of the nearly 2,000 candidates between July 1941 and October 1941, only 17 were African American. By the end of the year, the figure had risen by just 6 students.

A quota system seemed to some civil rights leaders to be the answer, and in fact Hastie had suggested one before the schools were established. The U.S. Army claimed that the imposition of quotas would be a political gesture, would result in unqualified men being commissioned as officers, and could be seen as discriminating against worthy white candidates. In fact, explicit quotas turned out not to be necessary; the wholesale rejection of African American candidates terminated when the authorities made it clear that considerable numbers of African Americans were expected to present themselves at the schools for training. Local commanders now began approving applications and ensuring that increasing numbers of potential African American candidates had access to the relevant paperwork.

This meant real integration, and it naturally raised some objections. In Florida, for example, some members of the House of Representatives objected when the Air Corps School at Miami became integrated. In a letter to Representative John J. Sparkman of Alabama, the White Supremacy League's president, Horace Wilkinson, complained that at Fort Benning white candidates had to eat and sleep with African Americans, calling such treatment "the most damnable outrage that was ever perpetrated on the youth of the South" (August 24, 1943; quoted in MacGregor 1985, chap. 2).

The War Department gave a neutral answer to this and other complaints, stating that it was simply impractical to separate the two races all of the time, due to the small numbers of African Americans involved. It was both efficient and economical to end segregation in this case, an argument that set an important precedent.

The second significant breakthrough came with the infantry replacement crisis that began to become acute in the European theater in the summer of 1944. Ground Force Replacement Command had been converting service units into infantry for a time, but African Americans had not been involved. The process needed to be accelerated when the Germans launched their Christmas offensive in the Ardennes, the Battle of the Bulge, which cost the United States more than 41,000 killed, wounded, or missing. Lt. Gen. John C. H. Lee's Communication Zone contained thousands of African Americans, and his proposals to Gen. Dwight D. Eisenhower to use these men as infantry replacements was accepted. On December 26, 1944, Lee sent out a call for African American volunteers to join combat units (limited to privates in the top four AGCT categories). Any noncommissioned officers would have to accept a drop in rank to be considered. In Lee's own words: "It is planned to assign you without regard to color or race to the units where assistance is most needed, and give you the opportunity of fighting shoulder to shoulder to bring about victory. Your relatives and friends everywhere have been urging that you be granted this privilege" (letter to Commanders of Colored Troops, quoted in MacGregor 1985, chap. 2).

Although the need for infantry replacements was crucial to the continued prosecution of the war, Supreme Headquarters, Allied Expeditionary Force (SHAEF) was afraid that if Lee's call came to be known to civil rights activists, it would lead to increased demands for total integration. Eisenhower issued a revised version of the letter that was a general appeal for volunteers, not a call to African Americans specifically, and that dropped the promise of individual assignment on a nonracial basis.

The response from African American service troops was overwhelming, placing severe strain on the continued operations of the service units in which they had served and the ability of the army to retrain them. Accordingly, only 2,500 were assigned to combat duties; a further 3,000 were turned down. By January 1945, the men assembled for six weeks of intensive training, at the end of which some fifty-three platoons were created (each with a white lieutenant and a sergeant). All but two of the platoons were assigned to infantry divisions (the other two being sent to armored divisions). Sixteen of the platoons were sent to the Sixth Army Group and the remainder to the First and Seventh Army Groups. In the First Army, the African American platoons were deployed on the basis of three per division, but in the Seventh Army, the platoons were grouped into provisional companies and assigned to armored divisions to serve in the infantry battalions. The general performance of the men seemed better when they were used at platoon level; the company-sized units failed to live up to expectations, partially because they had not been trained to operate like this and lacked the command structure and experience.

When the hostilities ended, the African American infantry replacements found themselves reassigned to African American units. The integration of platoons into companies had been only an experiment, and as an experiment it was evaluated. During May and June 1945, the Research Branch of the Information and Education Division (attached to Eisenhower's headquarters) carried out a survey to see how the overall deployment of the African American units had worked. Some 250 men from seven divisions were interviewed; these white company officers and platoon sergeants were asked about the combat performance of the African Americans. A further 1,700 questionnaires were distributed to enlisted men to elicit their attitudes toward the African Americans. Not one African American was asked about his views, his recollections of the experience. The main results of the interviews and the questionnaires can be summarized as follows:

1. According to more than 80 percent of the officers and noncommissioned officers, the African Americans had performed well in combat.
2. Some 69 percent of the officers and 83 percent of the noncommissioned officers believed that there was no reason why African Americans could not be as effective as infantry as white soldiers, given the same training and experience.
3. The enlisted men for the most part admitted that they had disliked the idea of serving with African Americans, but some 75 percent had discovered, once they actually went into combat together, that their misgivings had been unfounded.
4. Some 77 percent of the officers and noncommissioned officers felt more fa-

vorably toward African Americans after working closely with them. The more intense the combat and pressure, the better the relationships that had developed.

5. The camaraderie between white troops and African Americans had been much better than had been expected. Early distrust had largely changed into mutual respect and even friendliness.
6. Many of the officers stated that the inclusion of African American platoons in white companies was useful because African Americans and whites competed with one another.
7. Generally, only those enlisted men who had not actually had contact with African Americans still felt suspicion and hostility (figures and facts drawn from MacGregor 1985, chap. 2).

The Army Service Forces commanding general, Brehon B. Somervell, thought it inadvisable to release the findings of the investigations, seeing the test as inadequate and fearing that it would give the civil rights movement the ammunition to demand integration in the Pacific theater. He believed that this would adversely affect operations, but more significantly he felt that accelerating the integration progress would alienate many sections of the media who had so far supported the War Department and that they could, in turn, influence the American public to oppose universal military training after the war.

Like Somervell, Gen. Omar N. Bradley believed that the experiment should not be used as a basis for significant conclusions. He believed that not only were the African American troops used as infantry atypical (in the sense that they were selected from the higher AGCT categories), but that they had only participated in the last stages of the war when German resistance had already been broken. He also believed that once the common enemy, the Germans, had been defeated, there was considerable risk of racial friction if close associations between African American and white troops were continued. Bradley suggested that continued experiments with African Americans be carried out with more typical troops and that whole companies be assigned to white regiments to maintain a degree of segregation, as a way of avoiding racial friction once combat was over.

At the least, what had been proved was that a significant number of African Americans had been willing to risk their lives even in the closing stages of the war when they could have enjoyed comparative safety and comfort in the areas to the rear. The volunteers had shown that they were willing to respond patriotically when called and that they were capable of performing well in combat. Above all, the incorporation of segregated African American platoons into white companies had not proved to be the grave danger so often feared by the U.S. Army; it had not led to racial and social turmoil, but to mutual respect.

By the end of the war it was clear that the Double V campaign had not achieved all its goals as far as the U.S. Army was concerned. Progress had been made in opening specialized training to African Americans, in removing the barriers of segregation in army facilities, and in providing integrated training to African American officers; the integration of African American platoons in white companies had been successful. Nevertheless, segregated units were still official policy, with all their attendant disadvantages. By the end of World War II there was good reason to hope that the days of the U.S. Army being able to continue to protect their segregation policy were over and that in the postwar years, integration would prove to be an inevitable step forward.

The U.S. Navy

Before the war, the navy was essentially the preserve of whites, with African Americans present almost exclusively as servants. By the end of the war, not only had the numbers of African Americans in the general service become significant, experiments in integration had convinced the navy that integration was practical, and after the war, the navy was the first of the major branches to adopt integration as an official policy. Full integration and real equality were still many years away, but a beginning had been made.

The Prewar Navy: A Policy of Exclusion

In June 1940 African Americans in the U.S. Navy made up just 2.3 percent of the establishment strength of 170,000, or 4,007 men (MacGregor 1985, chap. 3). Of that number, 4,001 were members of the stewards branch; the other 6 were regular navy men, specifically retained in that status when changes to navy enlistment regulations in 1922 required that all African Americans enlisting or re-enlisting in the navy join the stewards branch. Over the next few years the African American regular navy, except for these six, left the navy. Although officially this policy ended in 1932, in practice the navy did not welcome African Americans except as stewards.

The stewards branch had its own uniform and insignia with the maximum rating of chief steward and no authority over men in the mainstream of the U.S. Navy. The men's duties were to work in the officers' mess and take care of menu plans, quarters, and supplies. Even though they were not part of the regular U.S. Navy structure, the men were assigned battle stations. Thus Dorie Miller, an African American and the first hero of World War II, after finding his battle station on the USS *Arizona* at Pearl Harbor on December 7, 1941, wrecked by a Japanese torpedo, went on deck, where he manned a machine gun and is credited with shooting down at least two Japanese aircraft.

By the time Miller was surrounded by fire and incoming enemy aircraft, African Americans in the U.S. Navy had been increased slightly to 2.4 percent (5,026) all of whom were assigned to the stewards branch.

In July 1940, Frank Knox had become the new secretary of the navy. Unfamiliar with the service, he had little choice but to rely on the advice of the senior navy leadership, who upheld the status quo. Knox seems himself to have believed that real change was not practical in a time of war. Those who worked with him, James V. Forrestal, Ralph A. Bard, and Adlai E. Stevenson, were a different matter, especially Forrestal and Stevenson, who both played important roles in the changes of the war years. The real force for change, however, was President Franklin D. Roosevelt.

When Knox had been less than two weeks behind the secretary's desk, the Bureau of Navigation (which at the time had the principal role in personnel issues), asked him to sign a letter to New York's lieutenant governor, Charles Poletti, effectively endorsing the current naval policy on race issues. The letter made the following points:

1. Exclusion of African Americans from any role other than mess man was the only practical solution, as segregation was not practicable on board ship.
2. From the U.S. Navy's experience, African Americans were incapable of maintaining discipline, particularly if they had command over white sailors.
3. All–African American units or crews were not an acceptable solution, as the service needed men who could be assigned anywhere.
4. In the U.S. Navy's opinion and based on experiments with crews made up of other races, all–African American crews would not be effective.

Agreeing with these points, Knox suggested that the better home for the African American was in the U.S. Army. Knox drew considerable criticism for his statement, and in September 1940 he requested that the navy's General Board prepare reasoned arguments why African Americans should not be enlisted in the service. The result was an extension of the points raised in the letter to Poletti, fully endorsed by the chief of Naval Operations and the Bureau of Navigation.

A conference at the White House on June 18, 1941, simply confirmed this position, in the presence of the president and representatives from the African American community. Knox reiterated the position that African Americans could not be used for general service in the U.S.

Navy "because men live in such intimacy aboard ship that we simply can't enlist Negroes above the rank of messman" (quoted in MacGregor 1985, chap. 3).

Where Knox and Roosevelt differed was on the question of whether African Americans should be admitted into general service in the U.S. Navy at all. They both agreed that integration was impractical, particularly in a time of war, but Roosevelt felt that there could be a compromise and that African Americans could be accepted, but segregated. His first suggestion was to put some "good Negro bands" aboard the battleships and see how things developed from there (quoted in MacGregor 1985, chap. 3). Knox did not respond to Roosevelt's suggestion to deploy African Americans musicians as a means of promoting good will between the races, but it was clear that the issue was not going to go away.

In response to increasing protests against the navy's policy, within weeks Knox appointed a new committee to conduct an investigation, a committee consisting of personnel officers from both the U.S. Navy and the U.S. Marine Corps. It took some six months to carry out its deliberations. The majority report brought forward many arguments and finally concluded that no change needed to be made, since "within the limitations of the characteristics of members of certain races, the enlisted personnel of the Naval Establishment is representative of all the citizens of the United States." In the same set of recommendations, the minority report suggested that a limited number of African Americans could be deployed for general duties "on some type of patrol or other small vessel assigned to a particular yard or station" (Letter, Chief, Bureau Navy, to Chairman, General Board, January 22, 1942, quoted in MacGregor 1985, 63). The minority report went on to suggest that this limited experiment would silence African American criticisms of the U.S. Navy by using African Americans as something other than servants, and that useful information on how well they performed could be gleaned without wholesale recruitment.

The War Begins: Pressures for Change

The majority report was of course accepted, but the NAACP petitioned the president, demanding that the issue be taken up in light of the massive recruitment campaign that had followed Pearl Harbor. President Roosevelt turned to the Fair Employment Practices Committee, whose chairman, Mark Abridge, entered into discussions with Assistant Secretary Bard. Abridge pointed out to Bard that the U.S. Navy had actually regressed in terms of racial policy and that it was inconceivable that African Americans should be excluded from general service, given that they had served in the last world war. Abridge, however, had no power to enforce the committee's view, and Knox still clung to the notion that now was not the time to radically change the structure of the navy. One reason Knox gave for rejecting the idea of segregated general service was that the African American population could not provide him with even a single vessel's complement of competent sailors. Roosevelt, however, was adamant, and on January 15, 1942, he instructed Knox to find a way of using African Americans in the U.S. Navy in roles other than stewards. The job of framing such a system was passed on to the General Board, with instructions to create a plan that would allow some 5,000 African Americans to be accepted into general service.

The General Board met on January 23, 1942. Inspector General of the Navy Rear Adm. Charles P. Snyder, who had clearly been won over by the minority report, suggested that African Americans should be admitted into the Musician's Branch and the Aviation Branch, as well as on auxiliary ships, transports, and other smaller vessels. Snyder went on to suggest that segregated training schools be established and that the notion of segregated general service be accepted, since some form of change was inevitable. Snyder's suggestions were spurned by the Bureau of Navigation; their spokesman, Capt. Kenneth Whiting, replied: "The sponsors of the program desire full equality on the part of the Negro and will not rest content until they obtain it" (quoted in MacGregor 1985, 65).

Even more vociferous was Maj. Gen. Thomas Holcomb (commandant of the Marine Corps):

> If we are defeated we must not close our eyes to the fact that once in they [African Americans] will be strengthened in their effort to force themselves into every activity we have. If they are not satisfied to be messmen, they will not be satisfied to go into the construction or labor battalions. Don't forget the colleges are turning out a large number of well educated Negroes. I don't know how long we will be able to keep them out of the V-7 class. I think not very long (quoted in MacGregor 1985, 65).

As far as Holcomb was concerned, the entry of African Americans into general service in the U.S. Navy would be "absolutely tragic"; he saw them as trying "to break into a club that doesn't want them" (quoted in MacGregor 1985, 65). His views, profoundly felt, were echoed by the Bureau of Aeronautics, the Bureau of Yards and Docks, and, to some extent, the U.S. Coast Guard.

As a consequence of this stiff opposition from all quarters, the General Board reported on February 3, 1942, that it was unable to submit a workable plan and that it recommended the proposals to recruit African Americans into the general service be abandoned. If the U.S. Navy policy of admitting African Americans only as mess men was discrimination, then the navy was merely reflecting the norms of discrimination in society in general.

A Policy of Segregation

Roosevelt did not feel that integration was practicable during the war years, but at the same time he refused to accept that exclusion was the only alternative. The General Board was sent instructions to keep looking for a solution; forced to come up with a compromise, the board asked all areas of the U.S. Navy to submit lists of assignments and stations (other than the stewards branch) that could accept African Americans. Based on those recommendations, the board recommended the establishment of a battalion of African American marines and one of African American Seabees (members of construction battalions, or CB Special Battalions), all–African American crews in some of the Coast Guard cutters, and the assignment of a considerable number of African Americans to shore defense craft and other base-related duties.

On April 7, 1942, Knox declared that African American volunteers would be accepted into the U.S. Navy at the rate of 277 per week and that they would be eligible for general service, including all areas of the Navy, Coast Guard, and the Marine Corps. The target figure for the first year was set at 14,000. As far as the African American community was concerned, the reaction was mixed. The NAACP was cautiously optimistic that this would be the first stage toward equality; the National Negro Congress was delighted with Knox's announcement. On the other hand, the limitations were obvious: African Americans would be segregated, only able to reach the rank of petty officer, and unable to serve at sea on any of the navy's major vessels in the fleet (with the exception of members of the stewards branch). Critics of the policy condemned it as just another instance of the system that had caused so much trouble in the U.S. Army and in society at large.

On April 21, 1942, Knox approved plans for the construction of Camp Barry (later renamed Camp Robert Smalls), part of the vast Great Lakes Training Center. Although the new camp was on the land of the main center, it reflected the U.S. Navy's overall policy toward African Americans; it was a part of the larger whole, but still segregated. An advanced training school at Hampton, Virginia, was also earmarked for the recruits. The enlistments got under way on June 1, 1942, with the promised targets of men (277 per week) starting at Great Lakes later in the month. Simultaneously, the doors were opened for additional mess men and Seabees.

A somewhat controversial figure was placed in command of the Camp Smalls facility—the son of the founder of the Hampton Institute. Lt. Cmdr. Daniel Armstrong had submitted a proposal to Knox in April 1942 suggesting ways that African Americans could be used in the U.S. Navy and offering ideas as to how they should be trained. Knox was clearly impressed with Armstrong, but the lieutenant commander's approach to training came under severe criticism for its somewhat paternalistic approach. Armstrong believed that African Americans needed to receive vocational training, which would suit their culture. Segregated education, away from the influences of the white-dominated society would produce well-trained men, in his view. From the point of view of the better-educated African Americans who passed through the facility, as well as of outside commentators, this was just another form of discrimination.

To begin, before the draft swelled the number of African Americans assigned to the camp, the course lasted twelve weeks; this was later reduced to eight. About a third of the men graduated as Class A, which meant that they were eligible for specialist occupations (e.g., electricians, mechanics, signalmen). Those who achieved this grading either remained at Camp Smalls for advanced training or were transferred to Hampton. The rest were sent to naval stations or local defense or district vessels where they replaced white sailors (seamen, third class). Around eighty of each of the intakes were assigned as unskilled laborers at ammunition depots.

Compared to the thousands of men that the U.S. Army had to handle as a result of the Selective Service, the small numbers of volunteers the U.S. Navy had to cope with were manageable; indeed, at times it appeared that there would be difficulty in even reaching the modest numbers of under 300 men per week. Part of the problem was that around half of the men who did apply were turned down for physical reasons. In addition, there was obviously severe competition from the U.S. Army, and it seemed that African Americans on the whole preferred the U.S. Army to the U.S. Navy.

Chief of Naval Personnel Rear Adm. Randall Jacobs was concerned that as the months passed the U.S. Navy was becoming even less attractive to young African Americans. Various reasons were suggested, including the notion that African Americans were afraid of the sea; the real cause was probably the U.S. Navy's reputation since the beginning of the century as a white man's preserve. African American reservists of World War I vintage were wheeled out to visit the recruitment centers around the country and assure the young men of the opportunities in the U.S. Navy. Gradually, by this process, the recruitment fortunes of the U.S. Navy began to change. The opportunities were, however, still limited; by February 1, 1943, of the 26,909 African American volunteers (2 percent of the total enlisted figure), some 19,227 had been placed in the stewards branch against just 6,662 in general service and 2,020 in the Seabees (MacGregor 1985, chap. 3).

While the U.S. Navy worked on recruiting more African American volunteers, the U.S. Army had been complaining that they were forced to take a higher percentage of African Americans than the navy. Others criticized the reliance on volunteer recruitment on the grounds of efficiency. On December 5, 1942, Roosevelt mandated that volunteer recruitment should no longer be an option for any man between eighteen years and thirty-eight years old to be subject to the draft, effective February 1943. This policy not only meant the end of volunteer recruitment, it placed the Selective Service under the control of the War Manpower Commission.

The Impact of the Draft

Under the new recruitment conditions, the U.S. Navy would be able to designate the number of African Americans required each month on a quota basis, but the Bureau of Naval Personnel proposed to keep the figures roughly in line with the numbers they had been recruiting up to this point from volunteers. In other words, with the support of Knox, they proposed to continue to accept 1,200 or so a month for general service and 1,500 for the stewards branch; otherwise they argued, it would be necessary to have mixed crews in the fleet. Roosevelt conceded that this was not policy and that Knox should so inform the director of Selective Service, Maj. Gen. Lewis B. Hershey.

Under the terms of the Selective Service Act, which prohibited racial discrimination, it was actually illegal to make separate demands for African Americans or whites. Paul V. McNutt, the chairman of the War Manpower Commission, told Knox that men should be called up on the basis of their order number and not their color. Moreover, the net percentage of African Americans in all services had only reached 6 percent, a little more than half of their component part of the population (MacGregor 1985, chap. 3), and the navy was clearly doing much less than the army to reach the 10 percent figure. On February 22, 1943, Roosevelt wrote the following memorandum to Knox:

> I guess you were dreaming or maybe I was dreaming if Randall Jacobs is right in regard to what I am supposed to have said about employment of negroes in the Navy. If I did say that such employment should be stopped, I must have been talking in my sleep. Most decidedly we must continue the employment of negroes in the Navy, and I do not think it the least bit necessary to put mixed crews on the ships. I can find a thousand ways of employing them without doing so.
>
> The point of the thing is this. There is going to be a great deal of feeling if the Government in winning this war does not employ approximately 10 percent of negroes—their actual percentage of the total population. The Army is nearly up to this percentage but the Navy is so far below it that it will be deeply criticized by anybody who wants to check into the details.
>
> Perhaps a check by you showing exactly where all white enlisted men are serving and where all colored enlisted men are serving will show you the great number of places where colored men could serve, where they are not serving now—shore duty of all kinds, together with the handling of many kinds of yard craft.
>
> You know the headache we have had about this and the reluctance of the Navy to have any negroes. You and I have had to veto that Navy reluctance and I think we have to do it again (February 22, 1943; quoted in MacGregor 1985, 80).

Knox ordered the Bureau of Naval Personnel to produce new quota figures that would raise the number of African Americans in the U.S. Navy as soon as possible. The bureau, desperate to maintain some form of control over the men admitted into the service, offered a rise to 5,000 a month in April 1943; after that for each month of the year it would increase to 7,350. This was a significant increase, given the 2,700 currently being accepted. In order to defuse the potential challenges from McNutt, the U.S. Navy through Knox promised him that 10 percent of the men inducted for the rest of the year would be African American, a total of 71,900 for the year. This offer fell far short of what was needed to bring the African American contingent in the U.S. Navy to 10 percent and to accommodate the backlog of registered African American inductees. McNutt's own revised figures called for the U.S. Navy to draft some 125,000 African Americans before January 1944; the U.S. Navy agreed to the increase, and from this time on appears to have accepted all the African Americans the Selective Service could send them. The navy never reached 10 percent of African Americans in their total enlisted strength, but by the end of the war, African Americans accounted for 11.1 percent of the total the U.S. Navy had drafted (MacGregor 1985, chap. 3).

What remained was the problem of assigning the vast new numbers of African Americans, given the fact that segregation was still in place. Twenty-seven new African American Seabee battalions were created for overseas deployment, many African Americans were assigned to harbor craft and local defense units, and the rest were sent to guard shore stations (up to 50 percent of the strength in the posts). The U.S. Navy was concerned with the possible racial problems that might arise from the sudden influx and set out the following two operating rules governing the deployment of the men: African Americans would be assigned only where they were needed; and as far as possible, African Americans from the Northern states would not be posted to Southern commands.

In addition, the Bureau of Naval Personnel would determine the number and the roles of African Americans assigned to a particular post rather than leaving it to the discretion of the local commander. Once the men were assigned, the local commander could not change their duties without prior consultation with the bureau. Bureau representatives would also be sent to naval stations to ensure that local commanders were complying with the instructions

Suggestions regarding the assignment of African Americans to the larger vessels in the fleet were rejected by the U.S. Navy, despite the fact that they feared that concentrating the men on shore stations might make trouble. And in fact, there were already rumblings of discontent from the men, who felt that they were marginalized and assigned to backwaters with little hope of combat or promotion. As far as African American women were concerned, they were still excluded from the WAVES and the Women's Reserve of both the Coast Guard and the Marine Corps, as well as the Nurse Corps. Eleanor Roosevelt pressed the U.S. Navy on the question in November 1943, but as the Bureau of Medicine and Surgery explained, African American nurses were not needed, despite the fact that there were shortages, as 500 white nurses were being trained who would fill the vacancies.

There was room for 7,700 African Americans in the small craft service; some 38,000 men (by mid 1944) were still consigned to service in the stewards branch, the ultimate symbol of being a second-class member of naval personnel. With the massive leap in combat-ready vessels had come an increased need for stewards, and recruitment offices had often assigned African Americans with superior education and training to the stewards branch. Unsurprisingly, these men did not make the best servants. In an attempt to raise standards in the stewards branch, the navy built training schools for stewards at Norfolk, Virginia, and at Bainbridge, Maryland, but these if anything made the problem worse by making the men feel more isolated. The white-officered 7,000 Seabees and 5,000 laborers or construction workers were assigned to the Pacific theater, where most of the men labored long and hard loading and unloading vessels. Most assignments for African Americans in the U.S. Navy were in the United States. Most of the men were commanded by less than satisfactory white officers. By 1943, only the U.S. Coast Guard had African American officers; in the navy only a limited number of petty officer positions were available in the few shore posts, and the competition for those positions was intense.

The smoldering resentment of many of the better-educated African Americans began to bubble to the surface, largely as a result of the fact that many had been assigned to unskilled labor duties and had no chance of promotion. Not only did they bitterly resent the fact that they were expected to do these jobs and that they would not have the opportunity to fight, but they were articulate, and their resentment affected others.

The basic problem, of course, was segregation. Not only did it limit the positions African Americans could hold, it affected every aspect of their lives. Many who came from Northern states were now experiencing it for the first time, both in all the facilities in their camps and when they ventured out into civilian society, particularly if they were stationed in the South, where segregation was rigidly enforced by both the military and the civilian police forces.

Given these factors and the frustration they created, racial strife was inevitable. The first serious incident took place at St. Julien's Creek, Virginia, in June 1943. Some 640 African Americans were serving at the ammunition depot there, and about half of them rioted over segregated seating for a radio show. A month later in the Caribbean, over 700 men in the 80th Construction Battalion conducted a protest regarding transport segregation. The U.S. Navy placed the blame on poor leadership, and at least one of the commanding officer was relieved of his command.

The Special Programs Unit: New Attempts at Reform

After these incidents, the Bureau of Naval Personnel set up the Special Programs Unit to oversee everything connected with African American enlistment, theoretically including taking over from the Enlisted Division the responsibility of assigning African Americans. When it was established in August 1943, however, only three officers were assigned to the unit; nonetheless, they did good work, and from these small beginnings eventually came the blueprint for the full integration of the U.S. Navy.

The unit worked on the problem of the large concentrations of men in the United States, and more were sent overseas. The unit established a new training center for illiterate African American draftees at Camp Robert Smalls; some 15,000 men passed through the twelve-week course (providing the equivalent of a fifth-grade education), before it was merged with a similar facility for white draftees toward the end of the war. The unit also took on the problem of better-educated African Americans who had received some form of specialist training but were not being assigned appropriately. These mismatched assignments were particularly prevalent in the South. In December of 1943 the Bureau of Naval Personnel solved the problem by accepting the unit's recommendations that African American sailors should not be assigned to what could be described as civilian duties (i.e., stevedores and maintenance crews). The only exceptions in the United States were the supply facilities at Boston and Norfolk.

The only really effective way to ease racial tension, however, was to open the fleet to African Americans, and the unit pressed for the chance to prove that African Americans were up to the job. Finally, toward the beginning of 1944, the bureau assigned some 196 African Americans and 44 white officers and petty officers to the USS *Mason,* a new destroyer. At the same time, the *PC-1264,* a patrol vessel was assigned 53 African American seamen and 14 white officers.

The USS *Mason* was considered satisfactory on its shakedown cruise, and those petty officers who were African American were considered competent, although it was charged that discipline could have been better. The experiment revealed that the African American enlisted men were perfectly capable of handling the vessel and that integration could work. The white noncommissioned officers lived closely with the men, yet there were no signs of racial tension.

The Special Programs Unit also worked on opening up more opportunities for advancement to African Americans, urging that African Americans be promoted in accordance with their abilities and in greater numbers. The Bureau of Naval Personnel responded by speeding up the process of promoting African Americans, even stating that it was acceptable to promote those who were qualified, whether or not the unit to which they were assigned already had a full complement of noncommissioned officers. Initially, local commanders chose to interpret the instructions in a detrimental manner to African Americans, as they took the view that since the men could not qualify for sea duty then, ipso facto, they were not qualified. It took a further, more explicit order from the bureau in January 1944 to close this loophole in the interpretation.

The bureau was motivated by the growing realization that African American units would have better discipline and better morale if they had more African Americans in positions of power. They set up an African American leadership course at the Great Lakes training facility, with the aim of assigning two men to each of the African American base companies operating abroad. Twelve African Americans who had worked in education and public relations as civilians were also assigned to the recruitment centers around the country. The African American petty officer training program was expanded, and the bureau was considering the training of African American commissioned officers.

The crew of the U.S. Navy submarine chaser PC-1264 *salutes the U.S. flag as the 173-foot-long escort vessel is commissioned, May 1, 1944. The* PC-1264 *was one of two navy vessels during World War II with largely African American crews. The experiment of segregated vessels, although it proved administratively inefficient, helped overcome the resistance to integration. (National Archives)*

Knox argued that the U.S. Navy needed a large well-trained force of African American enlisted men before it could possibly consider commissioning African American officers, but his objections were overcome by the arguments of his special assistant Adlai Stevenson. In a memo to Knox in September of 1943, Stevenson argued that, given the induction of some 12,000 African Americans each month, the U.S. Navy could not ignore the inevitable calls from the African American community and the administration for African American officers. He reasoned that the higher the proportion of African Americans in the navy, the greater the pressure and accusations of discrimination would be. Stevenson recommended that they should immediately commission ten or a dozen of the very best African Americans and that they should not make a great issue of the matter, treating it as a matter of course.

In theory, African Americans could become commissioned officers in the U.S. Navy in any of the three usual ways. The U.S. Naval Academy in Annapolis, however, had no African Americans enrolled, and the V-12 program, an accelerated officer training program that was part of the Naval Reserve Officers Training Corps, had only twelve African Americans enrolled in the integrated colleges around the country. No African Americans had been selected from the final route, a direct commission from the enlisted ranks or civilian life—in fact this route was rarely used. The V-12, which produced some 80,000 officers over the course of the war, was the preferred route as far as the U.S. Navy was concerned. In December 1943, the bureau sent out a circular to all commanders asked for African American enlisted men to be transferred to the program, but the bureau realized that few African American officers would be produced in time.

On December 15, 1943, Knox finally approved the selection of twelve line and ten staff officers from a list of enlisted men. He was reluctant to repeat the procedure and wanted to review the progress of the men before he approved any more commissions for African American enlisted men. Sixteen men reported for segregated training at Great Lakes on January 1, 1944; only twelve of the men were granted commissions, even though all successfully completed the course, because the bureau made a last-minute decision to commission only twelve African Americans. One of the noncommissionees had performed so well in the course that he was made a warrant officer (he lacked a college degree). The Golden Thirteen, as they became known, entered the U.S. Naval Reserve as line officers on March 17, 1944. The Bureau of Naval Personnel designated the new ensigns as "Deck Officers Limited–Only," a category usually given to men who had physical or educational deficiencies. None of the men had disabilities of any kind, and all of them were professionals in civilian life.

By the end of the summer, another ten African Americans had been commissioned as staff officers, this time after having trained alongside white officers. The bureau had recognized that maintaining segregated training facilities made no economic sense. These men had been recruited from civilian professions to serve in the Chaplain, Civil Engineer, Dental, Medical, and Supply Corps. The African American officers now numbered twenty-two, just over a third of the sixty African Americans who would be commissioned during the war.

The small numbers of African American officers did little to help with the problems of officering the large numbers of African American sailors. For the most part, the bureau had been assigning white officers from the Southern states, according to the old notion that they understood African Americans and how to handle them. Worse yet, when asked by the bureau to supply men suitable for duty with African American units, commanders took the opportunity to divest themselves of officers who were neither performing well nor popular. There had to be another way of approaching the situation, and the Special Programs Unit looked at the noncommissioned officers currently working at the Great Lakes training facilities. Not only had these men been working with African Americans for some time, but they tended to be experienced and capable; as a result a program was instituted in January 1944 to commission some of the men and assign them to African American units.

Nevertheless, most of the officers would still be inexperienced in working with African Americans, and the Special Programs Unit decided to tackle the attitudes of these officers directly. The message of equality was the focus of the *Guide to the Command of Negro Naval Personnel* (Bureau of Naval Personnel, February 1944). Even having the pamphlet published had been a struggle; many key figures in the U.S. Navy wanted to ignore the whole issue of racial tensions, and others dismissed the work of the Special Programs Unit as sociological tinkering. The pamphlet's wording pulled no punches:

> The idea of compulsory racial segregation is disliked by almost all Negroes, and literally hated by many. This antagonism is in part a result of the fact that as a principle it embodies a doctrine of racial inferiority. It is also a result of the lesson taught the Negro by experience that in spite of the legal formula of "separate but equal" facilities, the facilities open to him under segregation are in fact usually inferior as to location or quality to those available to others. . . . The Navy accepts no theories of racial differences in inborn ability, but expects that every man wearing its uniform be trained and used in accordance with his maximum individual capacity determined on the basis of individual performance (quoted in MacGregor 1985, 83).

Forrestal Takes Over and Real Integration Begins

Things were about to change irrevocably, and the traditionalists in the U.S. Navy had clearly lost the initiative. One crucial factor in increasing the pace of change was the sudden death of Frank Knox on April 28, 1944, and his replacement by Undersecretary James Forrestal. Forrestal was not a radical, he was a realist, and he was able to impress on the service the fact that segregation was inefficient, that integration would be genuinely efficient, and that it was necessary for fairness, a factor that the U.S. Navy had ignored for many years.

A full year before Knox died, the Planning and Control Activity personnel had suggested that African Americans be assigned to the larger vessels in the fleet. At the time Admiral Jacobs had said, "You couldn't dump 200 colored boys on a crew in battle" (quoted in MacGregor 1985). This suggestion and several more during 1943 had met with similar comments. Forrestal, ever the realist, and not prepared to sacrifice the efficiency of the fleet, reasoned that it might not be practicable to introduce integration on ships actually engaged in combat, but he was determined to tackle the problem of the vast numbers of African Americans on shore duty.

On May 20, 1944, Forrestal proposed his plan to integrate some of the fleet auxiliary vessels in a memo to the president, forcefully pointing out the drawbacks of the situation as it stood: "From a morale standpoint, the Negroes resent the fact that they are not assigned to general service billets at sea, and white personnel resent the fact that Negroes have been given less hazardous assignments" (quoted in MacGregor 1985, 84).

Forrestal received Roosevelt's blessing to assign African Americans to the large auxiliary vessels, up to a limit of 10 percent of the crews. If the experiment worked, he would assign more African Americans to other vessels as the opportunities arose. In early August of 1944, official word went out from Adm. Ernest J. King, the chief of Naval Operations, to the commanding officers of twenty-five of the largest fleet auxiliaries that African Americans would soon be assigned to them. The plan was to have 15 percent of the men be third-class petty officers (as much as possible volunteers culled from long-term shore duty), 43 percent from Class A schools, and 42 percent from recruit training (MacGregor 1985, chap. 3).

King instructed the commanding officers to ensure equality of assignment, promotion, and training, and he advised that the white sailors be fully informed of the situation and trained in order to prevent racial tension. The experiment was a success; the African Americans were not separately berthed, and the men were assimilated into the crews without incident. It was now decided that all of the auxiliary fleet could be integrated. In March of 1945 the chief of Naval Personnel submitted a plan to gradually assign African Americans to all of the auxiliary vessels, up to a limit of 10 percent, and King approved it.

In April, the Bureau of Naval Personnel took the next step—assigning African American officers to the integrated vessels, the first man being sent to the USS *Mason*. Although the bureau issued clear instructions to the commanders of the vessels regarding the priming of their crews to expect African American officers, the process was not always followed. Still, the reasons for that neglect were not always resistance to change; in fact, the words of the commander of the USS *Chemang* to a new African American officer provide a glimpse of the changing attitudes of the fleet: "I'm a Navy Man, and we're in a war. To me, it's that stripe that counts—and the training and leadership that it is supposed to symbolize. That's why I never called a meeting of the crew to prepare them, to explain their obligation to respect you, or anything like that. I didn't want anyone to think you were different from any other officer coming aboard" (quoted in MacGregor 1985, chap. 3).

Forrestal was also concerned about the WAVES (Women Accepted for Volunteer Emergency Service; the Women's Reserve of the U.S. Navy), whose director, Capt. Mildred H. McAfee (who had been president of Wellesley College), had been recommending the recruitment of African American women for some two years. She hoped that accepting African Americans into the women's auxiliary would deflect some of the criticisms leveled at the U.S. Navy.

The Bureau of Naval Personnel had been firmly opposed to the recruitment plan, on the grounds that the women in the auxiliary were designed to free their male counterparts for other positions. The bureau argued that there were already sufficient African American males to fill all of the posts available to them, and so African American women were unnecessary.

Tentative plans had been made in April 1943 to induct some 5,000 African American women into the WAVES, but the plan was never seen through, and Knox seems basically to have opposed and tried to delay any admission of African Americans. Shortly before his death, the Congress of Industrial Organizations (CIO) was pressing him hard to change his stance on the issue, but it fell to Forrestal to sort out the policy.

Acting with the advice of McAfee, the Bureau of Naval Personnel, and the Special Programs Unit, Forrestal made his recommendations to the president on July 28, 1944. He called for integrated training for African American WAVES and assignment to continental U.S. bases, preferably where there were already a significant number of African American males. The president, hoping to avoid controversy during his election campaign, told Forrestal not to put the plan into effect yet, but then Thomas E. Dewey made a speech in Chicago, accusing the White House of discriminating against African American women. Swiftly, Roosevelt told Forrestal to get the recruitment under way.

On December 21, 1944, the first two African American WAVES officers graduated from Smith College, with enlistment beginning just a week later. By July 1945, the U.S. Navy had managed to train only seventy-two African American WAVES at the Hunter College Naval Training School, but they had been trained in a completely integrated program, and the Special Programs Unit considered the integration of the WAVES one of their greatest accomplishments. It not only worked, it served as a blueprint for the future integration of male recruitment.

Forrestal was clearly pleased with the progress that had been made so far, but as a realist, he knew that he would have to have the support of the high command of the U.S. Navy before any major and lasting changes could be made.

In a Columbia University oral history interview, Lester Granger (an official with the National Urban League in charge of industrial relations, who later became Forrestal's special representative on racial matters) recalled a meeting between Forrestal and Admiral King:

> He [Forrestal] said he spoke to Admiral King . . . and said "Admiral King, I'm not satisfied with the situation here—I don't think that our Navy Negro personnel are getting a square break. I want to do something about it, but I can't do anything about it unless the officers are behind me. I want your help. What do you say?" He said that Admiral King sat for a moment, and looked out the window and then said reflectively, "You know, we say that we are a democracy and a democracy ought to have a democratic Navy. I don't think you can do it, but if you want to try, I'm behind you all the way." And he told me, "And Admiral King was behind me, all the way, not only he but all of the Bureau of Personnel. They've been bricks" (quoted in MacGregor 1985, chap. 3).

With the news that King and Admiral Jacobs (chief of Naval Personnel) had promised their support, many of the Special Programs Unit's ideas received much more attention. In August 1944, King stated that he wished all commands to pay close attention to the qualifications of officers who commanded African American units; in December he focused on the Pacific Command (where there were high concentrations of African American base companies) to ensure that the employment and advancement of African Americans was reformed.

Back in March 1944, the Bureau of Naval Personnel had authorized African American cooks and bakers to be eligible for duty in other commissary branches of the service, and in June all of the cooks and stewards were told to wear chief petty officer uniforms, which they had not been eligible to wear until this point. (This order was not without its drawbacks, since it meant that the enlisted men in the stewards branch were the only ones left wearing uniforms that distinguished them from other naval personnel.) On February 21, 1945, the Bureau ordered that the ammunition depots, both in the United States and abroad, limit the African American component to 30 percent, a move designed to break up the large concentrations of the men languishing on routine duty. The base companies in the Pacific were also given a more appropriate military structure.

In terms of segregated training, the Bureau made a number of major changes, primarily to reduce costs by closing duplicate facilities for the training of specialists. The last of the all–African American training facilities was officially closed in June 1945, by which time African Americans were training alongside their white counterparts in dozens of schools and training facilities.

It took a considerable amount of time for some of the policies and plans to work their way through the U.S. Navy's cumbersome bureaucratic systems, and some never made it. A plan to integrate the whole of the logistical support system floundered and was eventually rejected, as was the suggestion that repair units attached to the amphibious program be racially mixed. On August 30, 1944, King himself rejected the idea that net tenders and mine vessels be integrated, on the grounds that the vessels needed to have the most expert seamen and the most experienced officers. Also in August, the Bureau of Naval Personnel authorized commanders to look for African American recruits in the general service to transfer into the stewards branch. In the rush to accept as many African Americans into general service, there had been a severe dip in the numbers of men entering the stewards branch, and this part of the service was desperately undermanned.

Later, in July 1945, an example of the U.S. Navy's old ways came to the surface when it was discovered by the bureau that the African American trainees at Bainbridge Naval Training Center were being organized into all–African American companies. The basis of this regressive step was that in the past the smaller numbers of African Americans had had to be integrated (as per instructions and for practical and economic reasons), but when numbers increased, and African Americans began arriving in company-sized classes, the training center simply kept the companies intact.

Thus, although progress had been made, full integration was by no means achieved, and many African Americans were still assigned to menial jobs. Three major incidents in the last twelve months of the war seemed to express the frustrations African Americans still felt. The first, at Port Chicago, California, gained national attention.

On July 17, 1944, at Port Chicago (located on an arm of San Francisco Bay currently part of the Concord Naval Weapons Station), while two ammunition ships were being loaded, an explosion killed some 300 people, of whom 250 were African Americans from a segregated labor battalion. Unsurprisingly, many of the men who survived the disaster refused to work on the vessels and the docks under the same conditions. Fifty of the men were charged with mutiny and sentenced to long terms of imprisonment. It took the intervention of Thurgood Marshall (then national counsel for the NAACP) and Lester Granger (of the National Urban League), supported by the African American press and various African American organizations, to have the sentences set aside and the men returned to active duty.

In December 1944, on the Pacific island of Guam, bubbling resentment and months of interracial problems between African American seamen and white U.S. Marines boiled over into violence. On December 24, 1944, a series of shootings in the town of Agana claimed the lives of one African American and a white marine. Mistakenly believing the dead African American to be a sailor, African Americans from the Naval Supply Depot commandeered vehicles and drove into the town in force and confronted the military police. As it happened, no further violence occurred that night, but on Christmas Day two trucks full of armed African Americans drove onto the marine base, sparking a riot. In the aftermath, some forty-three of the African Americans were charged and sentenced to up to four years imprisonment. Several of the white marines were also court-martialed and sentenced.

This time, NAACP head Walter White went to Guam to investigate the situation, appearing as a witness before the Marine Court of Inquiry. White was able to show the court that the men had suffered from discrimination for many months and were poorly led. With the aid of civil rights lawyers, the men were released in early 1946.

In California at Port Hueneme in March 1945, a Seabee battalion chose an entirely different approach to highlight the problems that it had been facing. A thousand men went on a hunger strike for two days but continued to work. The resulting publicity forced the navy to investigate. The investigation led to the commander being removed and the unit assigned to new duties abroad.

Rather belatedly, even those most bound by tradition in the U.S. Navy began to realize that one of the principal ways of avoiding repetition of these incidents was to integrate and disperse African Americans throughout the service, thus removing the main weapons African American sailors had used hitherto, solidarity and collective action. Adm. Chester W. Nimitz (commander in chief of the Pacific Fleet) was quoted by Walter White as advising a captain of an attack cargo vessel: "If you put all the Negroes together they'll have a chance to share grievances and to plot among themselves, and this will damage discipline and morale. If they are distributed among other members of the crew, there will be less chance of trouble. And when we say we want integration, we mean Integration" (quoted in MacGregor 1985, chap. 3).

Forrestal continued to press for steadily increasing integration. In March 1945, Lester Granger of the National Urban League began work with the Department of Defense. Granger concentrated on potential and actual racial problems in the service, a continuation of his work with the Urban League. Granger brought his practical approach to integration to the issue of African American equality in the U.S. Navy, and he was able to adjust his argument to each of the target groups in the service and touch the concerns each had.

Granger recognized that the discussions should begin with issues of survival, of comfort, and of security, rather than the question of justice. As far as the members of the command structure of the U.S. Navy were concerned, he focused on efficiency; he talked to them about the risks to their goals and objectives that came from not using the men under their command in the most efficient manner. As far as African Americans in the U.S. Navy were concerned, Granger focused on instilling in their minds the need to take advantage of all opportunities for training in order to improve themselves and ultimately make themselves invaluable to the service; in this way they would be accepted and needed and would attain equality.

Granger urged Forrestal to create an advisory council consisting of representatives from each of the branches of the U.S. Navy to oversee the service's racial policies, and to appoint an African American as an executive agent for the council working out of Forrestal's own offices. Forrestal was reluctant to add another formal organization, even though the Special Programs Unit was too busy to do the whole job. Instead of adopting Granger's suggestions, Forrestal opted for an informal committee and asked Granger to join it.

Forrestal seems to have been content with the reforms that were already in progress, and with some reason. In March 1945, the surgeon general announced that the service would be accepting and recruiting African American nurses. In June, the Bureau announced that recruitment and training of men assigned to general duties would be integrated in the name of efficiency. In July, the service began integrating training for submariners and naval aviators. All through this period, Granger was visiting facilities around the country, aiming to get as many commanders on his side as possible.

By August 15, 1945, V-J Day, the U.S. Navy was clearly moving toward becoming fully integrated. By that date, some 164,942 African Americans were enlisted in the U.S. Navy. Admittedly that was still only 5.3 percent of the total enlisted strength, well below the 10 percent figure that had been specified as reflecting the proportion of African Americans in the U.S. population at large (MacGregor 1985, chap. 3). Nonetheless, it did represent a doubling of the percentage of African Americans who had been in the service before the opening of hostilities. A more important problem was that most of this number had not yet been affected by the new integration policies. Only a handful were officers: sixty, including six women, four nurses, and two WAVES. Of the 164,942, around 68,000 were still in the stewards branch; 58,000 were ordinary seamen, but large numbers of them were still in segregated labor or base battalions and companies.

These figures represented the wartime navy, swelled by draftees, and did not tell the whole story. As far as the regular U.S. Navy was concerned, the figures were even less impressive. There were just 7,066 African American regulars, accounting for 2.14 percent of the total, and most of them were in the stewards branch. If African American reservists wanted to remain in the service, then they would have to compete with the many thousands of white sailors in what would be a vastly reduced postwar U.S. Navy. Once the majority of the wartime reservists and draftees were released by the U.S. Navy, there was a grave danger that the service would return to its old ways and that African American involvement would be both limited and, in effect at least, segregated.

Nevertheless, Forrestal felt that the rapid changes during the war had been sufficiently successful that the command structure of the U.S. Navy was now convinced that an integrated postwar navy was both desirable and efficient. Only about six months after the war, Forrestal officially declared the U.S. Navy an integrated service, the first of the branches of the armed services to take this step. African American involvement would be from top to bottom, with no further restrictions either on assignment or promotion. World War II had changed the navy forever, though the full realization of the promise of integration and equal treatment still took many years.

U.S. Marine Corps

Legally, the Marine Corps came under the Department of the Navy, and the U.S. Marine Corp's Commandant, Maj. Gen. Thomas Holcomb, whose frank opposition to allowing any African Americans in all-white Corps has already been quoted, was under the command of the secretary of the navy in larger matters that involved general policy, such as racial policy. How that policy was carried out was left to the commandant. Accordingly, the story of the place of African Americans in the Marine Corps was quite different from that of the navy; while the U.S. Navy moved from segregation to at least a measure of real integration, the Marine Corps, a small, elite, traditionally all-white service, moved from complete exclusion of African Americans to acceptance, but rigid segregation.

The New Policy of Segregation

Holcomb was quite frank, at least during meetings with the U.S. Navy's General Board. He told them, when Marine Corps expansion was discussed in April 1941, "If it were a question of having a Marine Corps of 5,000 whites or 250,000 Negroes, I would rather have the whites" (quoted in MacGregor 1985, chap. 4). He did not voice these views in public, but he was firm in his opposition to including African Americans, calling it impractical because the Corps was too small to have racially segregated units. At the same time, he gave instructions to his medical examiners that if any African Americans were to apply to the Corps, they should be turned down on medical grounds.

As discussed earlier, under pressure from Roosevelt, Knox had by April of 1942 promulgated a plan for admitting African Americans into general service in the U.S. Navy, including the Marine Corps. Forced to take some step, Holcomb offered to recruit 1,000 African Americans for a segregated composite defense battalion. The unit would incorporate artillery (antiaircraft and seacoast), a light tank platoon, a rifle company, and other supporting units. The men would be trained in a segregated camp and assigned to a remote location where they would operate on their own as a fully independent unit.

As far as the Navy's General Board was concerned this step seemed acceptable, and Knox was informed that it was the only option, as it was impractical to assign African Americans to an amphibious combat unit. The official position was that men in such units had to be able to be reassigned from one unit to another when necessary because of casualties, and that could not be done with African Americans without destroying segregation. Also, the Corps had a distinct lack of the kind of experienced noncommissioned officers who would be needed in a combat unit and to assign any number to an African American unit would be a waste of the talents of this limited number of men.

Enlistment got under way on June 1, 1942, with the first men beginning their training on August 26 at Montford Point (part of the Marine Barracks reserve at New River, North Carolina—now Camp Lejeune). These men eventually became the 51st Composite Defense Battalion under the command of Col. Samuel A. Woods Jr.

The major problem facing African Americans and their involvement in the Marine Corps was the fact that the service had had no experience or knowledge of them. The Marine Corps had been exclusively white by tradition, and frankly the Corps was frightened and alarmed at what was happening. A senior official in the Division of Plans and Policies, Gen. Ray A. Robinson, recalled his feelings in 1942 in an oral history interview in 1968:

> It just scared us to death when the colored were put on it. I went over to Selective Service and saw Gen. Hershey, and he turned me over to a lieutenant colonel [Campbell C. Johnson]—that was in April—and he was one grand person. I told him, "Eleanor [Mrs. Roosevelt] says we gotta take in Negroes, and we are just scared to death, we've never had any in, we don't know how to handle them, we are afraid of them." He said, "I'll do my best to help you get good ones. I'll get the word around that if you want to die young, join the Marines. So anybody that joins is got to be pretty good!" And it was the truth. We got some awfully good Negroes" (quoted in MacGregor 1985, chap. 4).

Roosevelt's abolition of volunteer enlistments and the establishment of quotas in December 1942 meant that Holcomb could expect to have to cope with a further 15,400 African Americans in 1943. In actuality, the Corps only managed to process some 9,916 inductees during the year, but by 1946 (when the draft was terminated) the Corps had around 16,000 African Americans. Considering the overall throughput of African Americans during the whole of the period, this figure rises to 19,168, of whom 3,129 were volunteers, making roughly 4 percent of the enlisted men (MacGregor 1985, chap. 4).

Even though the percentage was not high, the insistence that all must be put in strictly segregated units made these numbers a major challenge to deal with, and that challenge was intensified by the fact that an estimated 70 percent of these men scored in the two lowest categories of the General Classification Test (GCT). In terms of numbers, more whites than African Americans scored in these low categories, but the whites could be scattered throughout the service, whereas the perceived need to keep African Americans segregated meant that all segregated units were burdened with many low-scoring men. Equally, those who scored higher were kept in these units, with no chance of going into combat or becoming officers.

Finding Assignments for African Americans

The service struggled to find assignments for all these men. The Division of Plans and Policies suggested creating more defense battalions, a messmen's (stewards) branch, and new units to provide messengers and chauffeurs, clerks and janitors. That last suggestion was dropped because it would have made such bad press. As many men as possible were absorbed into new defense battalions, but any expansion in the number of defense battalions was limited by the number of available African American officers and noncommissioned officers. It was felt that noncommissioned officers in particular had to be African American, as the army's experience was held to show that any integration at that level would cause racial tensions in the service. White noncommissioned officers were unavoidable at first, but they should be replaced by African Americans as soon as possible to avoid racial tensions and improve African American morale.

This solution followed the same path as the U.S. Army—Southern noncommissioned officers were employed, as the Corps felt that they understood how to supervise African Americans. General Holcomb was not satisfied with this solution, yet at the time there seemed to be no other option. As soon as was practicable, he wanted the Southern white sergeants removed from the African American units and replaced. Certainly Holcomb wanted the experiment of enlisting African Americans to be a success, and he proclaimed that "all Marines are entitled to the same rights and privileges under Navy Regulations" and expected African American marines to "become a credit to the Marine Corps" (quoted in MacGregor 1985, chap. 4). He told his commanders to keep him informed as to how the African American marines were settling into the Corps and their duties. At the same time, in May 1943 he expressed this conviction to those in command: "It is essential that in no case shall there be colored non-commissioned officers senior to white men in the same unit, and desirable that few, if any be of the same rank" (quoted in MacGregor 1985, chap. 4). In effect, this meant that African American corporals on the eve of promotion to sergeant would be transferred out of any unit that still had white corporals.

The new messmen's branch was established in January 1943. The Corps already had a mess branch, which of course was all white, but that was now entitled the commissary branch. As for the messmen's branch, it was soon redesignated the stewards branch in conformity with the U.S. Navy. Men were only supposed to enter this service if they freely volunteered, according to Secretary Knox's instructions. In direct contravention to this edict, recruiters were told to persuade around half of the African Americans recruited in the early months of the war to sign up for the stewards branch, as it had been assessed that a steward would be needed for every six officers (though this ratio was later scaled down). By July 5, 1944, African Americans in the stewards branch had reached a high point and accounted for some 14 percent of all African Americans in the Corps. This figure of around 1,400 remained static for the remainder of the war.

By that time that the bulk of the defense battalions had been deployed in the Pacific, the course of the war had unmistakably changed in favor of the Allies. The Japanese were on the defensive, unable to launch any meaningful offensive actions. The need for the defense battalions had passed. What was needed were men to support the huge logistical problems of conveying war materials to the fluid fronts; equally large numbers of men were needed to replace losses from the costly amphibious assaults on each of the ever more tenaciously held islands, as the Allies closed in on the enemy's mainland.

It was therefore decided that special units should be created to support the logistical efforts, and the Division of Plans and Policies authorized the establishment of fifty-one depot companies and twelve ammunition companies of African Americans. Although many of the units served in base and service depots, a considerable number of them were deployed under fire. Their role was to move supplies into a new battle zone directly after the landings, secure supply dumps, and make certain that the wounded were safely evacuated. Up to 8,000 African Americans served in these units, accounting for some 40 percent of the enlistment numbers. These men had not been specifically trained for combat, whereas the African Americans in the composite defense battalions, who had received combat training, were never used in that capacity. The support troops won a number of combat citations, not to mention praise from other marines and commanders in the field.

Training and Deploying African Americans

Training was completely segregated at Montford Point. After the initial eight-week training period, men assigned to the defense battalions were sent off for specialist training, and sixty men from each of the ammunition companies attended ammunition and camouflage school (after which they were promoted to the rank of corporal). Ammunition companies had white sergeants (ordnance specialists), since the Corps felt that more experienced men were needed in these positions; the depot and defense units followed the general rule of having African American noncommissioned officers. All specialist training was segregated, white instructors being replaced by African Americans as quickly as possible.

The depot companies, as labor units, might find themselves assigned to a Pacific post after as little as two weeks of training. By comparison, the 51st Defense Battalion had spent some two months on intensive training before they were committed to the Pacific theater. By the time the 51st and the 52d were ready to be committed to the Pacific, the Corps had decided to begin to dismantle the composite battalions. Unlike the eighteen white defense battalions, all but one of which were retrained and reassigned as anti-aircraft artillery battalions to serve with amphibious assault groups, the 51st and the 52d were assigned to the Marshalls and Guam, respectively, now relegated by the course of the war to distant backwaters, though the 52d did engage successfully with pockets of Japanese resistance.

Among all of the services of the armed forces, the Corps was the last to make significant changes to its racial policies. The Corps seemed impervious to criticism and complaints from the African American press and civil rights groups, not to mention the comments of the men already within the Corps. Each time, the Corps explained that due to its size, duplicate facilities were untenable and uneconomical, and integration was not an option. It took President Harry S. Truman's order in March of 1948 to desegregate the whole armed forces, with the legislation that followed, to bring about integration—World War II had only brought the Corps from rigid exclusion to rigid segregation.

The U.S. Coast Guard

Unlike the Marine Corps, the U.S. Coast Guard had had a long tradition of African American involvement in the service prior to World War II, and it was, albeit on a small scale, the most successful of the services in its treatment of African Americans, demonstrating to the others how efficient and trouble-free real integration could be.

Like the Marine Corps, the Coast Guard was not simply part of the U.S. Navy; nominally at least, it was part of the Treasury Department, but in 1915 a statute was issued that stated that the Coast Guard would become an effective part of the U.S. Navy when the president deemed it necessary and it would, at this point, come under the jurisdiction of the secretary of the navy. Accordingly, the U.S. Coast Guard was placed under the secretary of the navy on November 1, 1941, and it remained so until the order was rescinded on January 1, 1946.

Thus the Coast Guard came under the Chief of Naval Operations in terms of cooperating and contributing to the operations of the U.S. Navy, but it was still expected to carry out its normal duties (port security, ice-breaking, navigational aid to shipping, and the like). The Chief of Naval Operations, therefore, had to make sure that his calls on the Coast Guard did not impede their ability to carry out these tasks. This duality of purpose and responsibility was recognized formally by Secretary Knox in March 1942. In terms of recruitment, training, and assignment of Coast Guard personnel, the service maintained its administrative independence, embodied in the Commandant's Advisory Board and the Personnel Division. On the other hand, the Coast Guard came under the jurisdiction of the U.S. Navy when parts of its service operated under U.S. Navy control.

The Background

The Coast Guard, like the U.S. Navy, had a tradition of enlisting African Americans in its general service, and unlike the navy it had continued that tradition in the twentieth century. On the other hand, it had restricted the numbers of African Americans and curtailed the opportunities open to them in the service. Still, in 1939, cadres of African Americans were present in the service. A group served at Pea Island, North Carolina, operating a lifesaving station; others served at lighthouses and on tenders on the Mississippi River. All of these men had been part of the Lighthouse Service, which was transferred to Coast Guard control that year. A handful of African Americans were serving in integrated crews; some notable individuals were even commanding vessels. Other African Americans were in the stewards branch, which in the small vessels of the Coast Guard meant close contact with the rest of the crew. On the whole, though, African Americans served in segregated conditions, and the whites who to a great extent made up the Coast Guard came from backgrounds (the Eastern Shore of Maryland and Virginia, the Outer Banks of North Carolina) that made them unlikely to be happy with integration.

The Policy of Segregation and Its Drawbacks

In January 1942, when discussions began about formally accepting African Americans into the general service of the naval establishment, the initial reaction of the Coast Guard, voiced by Commander Lyndon Spencer, mirrored what had been said by the service's larger partners, the U.S. Navy and U.S. Marine Corps. It was not practical to take African Americans into the general service because segregation could not be maintained on a ship, and integration was not something to be undertaken in wartime. In fact, he believed that due to the size of the vessels in the Coast Guard, maintaining segregation would be even more difficult; nevertheless, he added, "if we have to we will take some of them" (quoted in MacGregor 1985, chap. 4).

When it was clear that taking African Americans was unavoidable, Coast Guard commandant Rear Adm. Russell R. Waesche suggested a plan that called for the enlistment of some 500 African Americans into the general service. He told the chairman of the General Board, Vice Adm. Walton R. Sexton, that 300 of the men would serve on the smaller vessels and the balance would be deployed on shore duties. He made no suggestions with regard to training petty officers, but told Sexton that as over half of the men serving on the smaller vessels were of this rank, it was assumed that some of the African Americans would over time apply and be accepted as petty officers.

On February 24, 1942, Waesche identified some eighteen vessels (tenders and patrol boats) that would have African American crews. Training would take place at the Manhattan Beach Training Station, New York, although he believed that the men would need a longer period of basic training than was usually the case. Advanced training would then follow, when the men would be grouped into units to take over everything except petty officer duties on a given vessel.

It was proposed that a cap of 150 would be enlisted in the first instance and that the program would then be frozen until the first group had been trained and assigned, and had served on board long enough for meaningful conclusions to be drawn from the overall experience. In this way, the commandant would have the flexibility to amend the program in the light of what was discovered. A substantial number of other African Americans would be assigned to port duty.

Despite the objections of the General Board to the plan, which did not seem to them to allow for adequate segregation, the first 150 men were duly sent to Manhattan Beach, and formed into a separate training company. Due to the size of the facility, the men were trained on an integrated basis, but housed and messed in segregated facilities.

Four weeks later, the qualified men went off for further training, while the rest were assigned to the captains of the ports for shore duties. By August 1942, around three hundred African Americans had been recruited, trained, and then assigned to general duties; simultaneously several hundred African Americans were joining the stewards branch.

The Impact of the Draft

Up until December 1942, all the Coast Guard had to deal with was a small number of African American volunteers. Then, like the rest of the naval establishment, it had to deal with larger numbers coming in through the draft. These numbers were of course not as large for the Coast Guard; it only inducted 15,296 draftees in all between 1943 and 1946. Of these, 13 percent (1,667) were African American. By the end of the war, around 5,000 African Americans had served in the Coast Guard, recruited at a rate of 137 against 1,000 whites per month in 1943 alone.

As opposed to the U.S. Navy and the U.S. Marine Corps, the Coast Guard could not deal with this influx by forming large segregated units. The stewards branch already had 1,500 African Americans in place as of January 1943, and could only absorb half of those who entered. The rest of the men had to be assigned to general service.

By the end of the war, some 2,500 African Americans had served in the U.S. Coast Guard Stewards Branch, performing similar duties to those assigned to the U.S. Navy and the U.S. Marine Corps. Given the small size of the vessels, however, stewards were assigned to important battle stations, giving them more of a chance to play significant roles. For example, in February 1943 a steward who was also a gun captain on board the cutter *Campbell* led a group of stewards in manning a gun and helping to sink an enemy submarine. The group won a citation for their efforts.

The size of the ships also made it possible for some African Americans to move out of the stewards branch and into general service, largely as a result of the fact that the vessels' white officers had a much better opportunity to see the African American stewards at work and how they performed on battle stations. Still, about 63 percent of African Americans in the Coast Guard were stewards (in other words, servants) for the whole war.

As for African Americans in general service, the majority of them were assigned to captains of the ports, district commanders, and headquarters units. These men operated security and labor details, were assigned to stores or radio operations, and were assigned to local Coast Guard stations, a second all–African American base being established at Tiana Beach, New York. African Americans also served in beach patrols, which had been created in 1942; these outposts accounted for around 11 percent of all of the Coast Guard manpower and were designed to watch out for enemy infiltration along the coastlines. African Americans also staffed a number of segregated horse and dog patrols.

The overall manpower policy of the Coast Guard called for a rotation of all guardsmen from shore to sea and sea to shore. Given that the policy of the Coast Guard was segregation and that segregation could not be maintained on board ship, the 2,400 African Americans on shore duty stayed on shore duty. This practice threatened to cause racial problems, since it meant African Americans were denied sea duty and whites had less chance for promotion on land.

Experiments in Integration

Lt. Carlton Skinner recommended changing this policy, perhaps partly because of his own firsthand experience of the limitations of the racial policy at work. Skinner had served for two years on board the USCGC *Northland,* and as executive officer he had recommended that an African American steward who was a qualified mechanic be promoted to a motor mechanic petty officer. The request had been turned down on racial grounds, but Skinner appealed on the man's behalf and won. In June 1943, Skinner recommended creating a completely integrated ship, in which African American seamen could be given experience at sea. Despite the fact that his immediate superior marked Skinner's request as "disapproved," Adm. Russell Waesche, the Coast Guard commandant, decided to approve the training.

In November 1943, Skinner was transferred to the USS *Sea Cloud (IX 99),* operating in the North Atlantic. Skinner was by now a lieutenant commander, and Waesche approved the transfer of African American apprentice seamen to the vessel in batches of twenty every time the vessel put into port. The men came direct from the Manhattan Beach training facility. Skinner was appointed captain of the *Sea Cloud* on the second patrol, and gradually began building an integrated crew. The experiment was a success, and although the vessel was decommissioned in November 1944, the *Sea Cloud* had met all fleet and operational requirements and was officially credited with helping to sink a German submarine in June 1944.

Four African American officers and 50 petty officers and seamen had been part of the 173-man crew, as an integrated unit, yet there had been no racial problems on board ship. The only racial tension occurred when the vessel put into the Boston Navy Yard, and then it consisted merely of hostility from some departments of the yard. Skinner had ensured that his African American officers were accepted in the officers' clubs, and when the men had served on shore duties, they were sent as integrated groups.

Despite Skinner's and the *Sea Cloud*'s undoubted successes, at least one officer charged that the experiment was simply a means of answering criticism of the Coast Guard's refusal to use African Americans at sea. However that may be, Waesche did not have the experiment publicized, following Skinner's original suggestion to avoid publicity in order to make the experiment a more valid one.

Skinner's original hope was that African Americans could be used throughout the fleet and treated according to their ability rather than their race, but in fact the only other completely integrated vessel to serve during the war was the destroyer escort *Hoquim,* which operated from the base at Adak on the Aleutian Islands in 1945, also commanded by Skinner. Again the experiment was a success. It seems likely that Skinner and the lessons learned from the *Sea Cloud* and the *Hoquim* helped to hasten the integration of the U.S. Navy's auxiliary fleet. It is certain that at least one of Forrestal's assistants consulted Skinner on his views during the integration process.

What most distinguished the U.S. Coast Guard from the other armed services during World War II was their lack of concern as to whether African Americans outranked whites. By the end of the war, around 965 African Americans served as petty officers or warrant officers, many of them in situations where they outranked whites. It was a question of expedience; the service simply did not have the capacity to assign all the African American petty officers to segregated positions. At the same time, a few African Americans became commissioned officers and two commanded integrated crews.

The Coast Guard also recruited a few African American women into their SPARs, as the women's reserve was called, joining with the

U.S. Navy at the specific request of the President to do so in the latter stages of 1944. Given the fact that recruitment for the Women's Reserve was suspended on November 23, 1944, it was not a great surprise that only five African American women had been recruited. These women trained at the Manhattan Beach facility and were assigned to Coast Guard district offices without any regard to their color.

Of course it is true that the experience of African Americans in the Coast Guard needs to be seen in the context of the larger-scale recruitment, training, and deployment that was under way during the war. Comparatively, the service was tiny, and the percentage of African Americans was never higher than 2.1 percent, significantly lower than in the other services, and of course well below the 10 percent of the population of the United States that was generally held to be African American at that time. Nevertheless, the Coast Guard set an important example of how well integration could work, once the world war and the political pressures of the time forced it to change.

World War II as a Turning Point

From the initial period leading up to the United States joining the Allies in the hostilities, it was clear that the president and many of his well-placed and senior advisors knew that African American involvement, to a greater or lesser degree, was essential in the prosecution of and the continued support for a major world war. It was also essential because of political pressure; the president could not afford to alienate African American voters, who formed a significant part of his political base. Unfortunately, political pressure also came from Southern whites, who played so large a role in the Democratic Party of that time. Given this situation, as well as the resistance to change within the armed services, it is not surprising that the first steps involved making greater use of African Americans, but maintaining segregation and keeping African American participation in combat to a minimum.

Many factors led to increased change: continued pressure from the leaders of the African American community, the African American press, and the broader civil rights movement; increased need for manpower as the war dragged on; the basic inefficiency of segregation; racial incidents that pointed up the frustrations of those who were underused or misused, as well as discriminated against. Although more African Americans were finally sent overseas and into combat, sometimes even in integrated units, integration remained an occasional experiment or the result of unavoidable necessity.

When given the opportunity, often at the last moment and in many cases hopelessly undertrained and badly equipped, African Americans were determined to prove their value to their country. Those who had the best chance to do so are still celebrated: the Tuskegee Airmen, the Montford Point Marines, the crews of the USS *Mason*, and the integrated Coast Guard vessels. Many more—in adverse conditions, sometimes coming under fire, still completely segregated, with virtually no hope of going into combat or winning advancement—toiled ceaselessly to load and unload ammunition and supplies and to support the war effort in many other thankless jobs, whether in the continental United States, in Europe, or in the Pacific. Given the reluctance of the U.S. military to accept African Americans at any level in the armed forces, their contribution seems all the more remarkable.

See also African American Enlistment; African American Officers; African American Women in the Military; Desegregation of Armed Forces (chronology); Double V; Golden Thirteen; Guam Incident; Iwo Jima, Battle of; Jim Crow Military; Miller, Dorie; Montford Point Marines; National Association for the Advancement of Colored People; Port Chicago Mutiny; Segregation and Racism in the Military; Selective Service Acts; *PC-1264*, USS; Tuskegee Airmen; U.S. Air Force; U.S. Army; U.S. Army, Interwar Period; U.S. Coast Guard; U.S. Marine Corps; U.S. Navy; Women's Auxiliary Army Corps;

Women's Reserve of the U.S. Navy; World War II Infantry Replacements

References and Further Reading

Francis, Charles E. *The Tuskegee Airmen: The Story of the Negro in the U.S. Air Force.* Boston: Bruce Humphries, 1955.

Furer, Julius Augustus, Charles Eddison, and Ernest McNeill Elder. *Administration of the Navy Department In World War II.* Washington, DC: Department of the Navy, 1959.

Ginzberg, Eli. *The Negro Potential.* New York: Columbia University Press, 1956.

Greene, Robert E. *Black Defenders of America, 1775–1973.* Chicago: Johnson Publishing, 1974.

Hastie, William H. *On Clipped Wings: The Story of Jim Crow in the Army Air Corps.* New York: NAACP, 1943.

Kaplan, Hyman R. *This Is the United States Coast Guard.* Cambridge, MD: Cornell Maritime Press, 1971.

King, Samuel. *Marginal Man and Military Service: A Review.* Washington, DC: Government Printing Office, 1966.

Lee, Ulysses. *The Employment of Negro Troops.* United States Army in World War II: Special Studies. Washington, DC: Center of Military History United States Army, 1966. http://www.army.mil/cmh-pg/books/wwii/11–4/index.htm#contents (accessed August 22, 2003).

MacGregor, Morris J., Jr. *Integration of the Armed Forces, 1940–1965.* Washington, DC: Center of Military History, United States Army, 1985. http://www.army.mil/cmh-pg/books/integration/IAF-fm.htm (accessed August 16, 2003).

Mandelbaum, David G. *Soldier Groups and Negro Soldiers.* Berkeley: University of California Press, 1952.

Motley, Mary P., et al. *The Invisible Soldier: The Experience of the Black Soldier, World War II.* Detroit: Wayne State University Press, 1975.

Murray, Florence, ed. *Negro Handbook, 1946–1947.* New York: A. A. Wyn, 1948.

Osur, Alan M. *Blacks in the Army Air Forces during World War II: The Problem of Race Relations.* Washington, DC: Government Printing Office, 1977.

Purdon, Eric. *Black Company: The Story of Subchaser 1264.* Washington, DC: Luce, 1972.

Shaw, Henry I., Jr., and Ralph W. Donnelly. *Blacks in the Marine Corps.* Washington, DC: Government Printing Office, 1975.

Stouffer, Samuel A., et al. *Studies in Social Psychology in World War II.* Vol. I, *The American Soldier: Adjustment during Army Life.* Princeton, NJ: Princeton University Press, 1949.

Strobridge, Truman R. *Blacks and Lights: A Brief Historical Survey of Blacks and the Old U.S. Lighthouse Service.* Washington, DC: Office of the USCG Historian, 1975.

Treadwell, Mattie E. *The Women's Army Corps.* Washington, DC: Government Printing Office, 1954.

World War II Infantry Replacements

By December 1944, the U.S. Army was facing something of a manpower crisis in the European theater. There was a gap between numbers of casualties and the numbers of infantrymen available to replace them. The Ground Force Replacement Command (GFRC) put a program in place in July 1944 to bridge the gap; it aimed to retrain men from other arms of the service as infantrymen. Progress was slow, and the problem was exacerbated by the falling numbers of men being sent from the United States to Europe.

In early December 1944 it was estimated that by the end of the month, the army would be short about 29,000 riflemen. Just a week later, the Germans launched their last great counteroffensive in the west, the Ardennes offensive, which made the situation even worse. Even without the casualties that the Ardennes offensive caused, the army's own offensive operations would have been seriously impaired. Plans had been laid to deal with the shortages, and it had been proposed that all physically fit service personnel would be redeployed as infantrymen. Notably, Lt. John C. H. Lee's Communications Zone units could provide some 20,000 men. Men from new divisions, straight from basic training, would be posted into veteran divisions as a matter of course, and limited-assignment men (that is, less-able soldiers) would fill the service positions.

Lee also consulted Gen. Dwight D. Eisenhower, among others, proposing that African American men who were physically qualified be deployed to serve as infantrymen. The level of panic and crisis helped override many of the anticipated objections to the move, and Eisenhower, Gen. Omar N. Bradley, and the other army commanders agreed with the proposition. Lee now needed assistance to swing the operation into force, and he consulted with Brig. Gen. Henry J. Matchett (of the GFRC) and the African American Brig. Gen. Benjamin O. Davis Sr. (special adviser and coordinator to the theater commander on Negro troops). Unsurprisingly, Davis was very enthusiastic, and by Christmas Day 1944, a plan had been formed to train African American volunteers as infantry replacements. The call went out on December 26, and by the twenty-seventh it had been relayed to all of the troops. It read:

> 1. The Supreme Commander desires to destroy the enemy forces and end hostilities in this theater without delay. Every available weapon at our disposal must be brought to bear upon the enemy. To this end the Commanding General, Com Z, is happy to offer to a limited number of colored troops who have had infantry training, the privilege of joining our veteran units at the front to deliver the knockout blow. The men selected are to be in the grades of Private First Class and Private. Non-commissioned officers may accept reduction in order to take advantage of this opportunity. The men selected are to be given a refresher course with emphasis on weapon training.
>
> 2. The Commanding General makes a special appeal to you. It is planned to assign you without regard to color or race to the units where assistance is most needed, and give you the opportunity of fighting shoulder to shoulder to bring about victory. Your comrades at the front are anxious to share the glory of victory with you. Your relatives and friends everywhere have been urging that you be granted this privilege. The Supreme Commander, your Commanding General, and other veteran officers who have served with you are confident that many of you will take advantage of this opportunity and carry on in keeping with the glorious record of our colored troops in our former wars.
>
> 3. This letter is to be read confidentially to the troops immediately upon its receipt and made available in Orderly Rooms. Every assistance must be promptly given qualified men to volunteer for this service (Letter, Headquarters Com Z to Commanders of Colored Troops, December 26, 1944, quoted in Lee 1966, 689).

Initially only 2,000 men would be accepted, both because this was the maximum capacity of the GFRC and because it would not be too heavy a toll on the service units, whose functions could not be impaired by a sudden depletion in manpower. The highest-scoring and best-qualified men would be chosen first, and no one below grade IV on the Army General Classification Test would be taken. The volunteers would be chosen by January 9, 1945, and would be expected to report to the 16th Reinforcement Depot (in Compiègne, France) by the next day. There they would be unassigned and attached to the GFRC. Once retrained, the men would be assigned to combat units without regard to their race. This was a remarkable innovation, for up to this point in the history of the U.S. Army, no official move had ever been made to mix African American soldiers into white units. Equally important was the fact that the men would be assigned on an individual basis, replacing men lost without any regard to a quota system.

A copy of the letter circulated to the troops eventually found its way onto the desk of Lt. Gen. Walter B. Smith at the Supreme Headquarters, Allied Expeditionary Force (SHAEF). He felt that the letter was explosive and that the War Department would never agree to the plan.

He asked Lee to change the contents of the letter, but Lee demurred. Consequently, Smith fired off a letter to Eisenhower:

> Although I am now somewhat out of touch with the War Department's Negro policy, I did, as you know, handle this during the time I was with General Marshall. Unless there has been a radical change, the sentence which I have marked in the attached circular letter [the sentence "It is planned to assign you without regard to color or race to the units where assistance is most needed, and give you the opportunity of fighting shoulder to shoulder to bring about victory"] will place the War Department in very grave difficulties. It is inevitable that this statement will get out, and equally inevitable that the result will be that every negro organization, pressure group and newspaper will take the attitude that, while the War Department segregates colored troops into organizations of their own against the desires and pleas of all the negro race, the Army is perfectly willing to put them in the front lines mixed in units with white soldiers, and have them do battle when an emergency arises. Two years ago I would have considered the marked statement the most dangerous thing that I had ever seen in regard to Negro relations.
>
> I have talked with Lee about it, and he can't see this at all. He believes that it is right that colored and white soldiers should be mixed in the same company. With this belief I do not argue, but the War Department policy is different. Since I am convinced that this circular letter will have the most serious repercussions in the United States, I believe that it is our duty to draw the War Department's attention to the fact that this statement has been made, to give them warning as to what may happen and any facts which they may use to counter the pressure which will undoubtedly be placed on them.
>
> Further, I recommend most strongly that Communications Zone not be permitted to issue any general circulars relating to negro policy until I have had a chance to see them. This is because I know more about the War Department's and General Marshall's difficulties with the negro question than any other man in this theater, including General B. O. Davis whom Lee consulted in the matter—and I say this with all due modesty. I am writing this as I may not see you tomorrow morning. Will talk to you about it when I return (Smith, letter to Eisenhower, January 3, 1944, quoted in Lee 1966, 690).

An amended letter was sent, with a covering note that ordered the destruction of the original communication. The new version read:

> 1. The Supreme Commander desires to destroy the enemy forces and end hostilities in this theater without delay. Every available weapon at our disposal must be brought to bear upon the enemy. To this end the Theater Commander has directed the Communications Zone Commander to make the greatest possible use of limited service men within service units and to survey our entire organization in an effort to produce able bodied men for the front lines. This process of selection has been going on for some time but it is entirely possible that many men themselves, desiring to volunteer for front line service, may be able to point out methods in which they can be replaced in their present jobs. Consequently, Commanders of all grades will receive voluntary applications for transfer to the Infantry and forward them to higher authority with recommendations for appropriate type of replacement. This opportunity to volunteer will be extended to all soldiers without regard to color or race, but preference will normally be given to individuals who have had some basic training in Infantry. Normally, also, transfers will be limited to the grade of Private and Private First Class unless a noncommissioned officer requests a reduction.
>
> 2. In the event that the number of suitable negro volunteers exceeds the replacement needs of negro combat units, these men will

> be suitably incorporated in other organizations so that their service and their fighting spirit may be efficiently utilized.
>
> 3. This letter may be read confidentially to the troops and made available in Orderly Rooms. Every assistance must be promptly given qualified men who volunteer for this service (letter Headquarters Com Z, December 26, 1944).

Unfortunately, the revised letter appeared too late, and many of the commanders of African American units had already received the original on December 28, 1944, and had distributed copies to relevant sections of their commands. It is worth noting that there were no African American infantry units in Europe; that African American artillery, tank, and tank destroyer units (such as the 333d Field Artillery Battalion and the 761st Tank Battalion) were desperate for replacements; and that the revised letter implied volunteers would find themselves primarily in these units.

The situation was becoming muddy and confused. After-the-fact interpretations suggest that it was not Eisenhower's intention to place African Americans in white units. It seems that Eisenhower's preferred solution was to deploy African American volunteers into existing African American units first and then to use any excess volunteers to create new trainee units that could be assigned to any army group; the initial goal would be to establish a full battalion. These African American units "could be substituted for white units in order that white units could be drawn out of line and rested" (Supreme Headquarters American Expeditionary Force G-1, January 8, 1945).

But the bulk of the volunteers had already answered the call by the time the revised letter was in common circulation. By February 1945, 4,562 African American troops had volunteered, including many noncommissioned officers who were prepared to take the drop in rank.

The first batch of 2,800 volunteers was ordered to report to the GFRC throughout January and in early February. This group was a mix of men, dominated by some 38 percent from the engineers. Of the rest, 29 percent were former quartermasters, 20 percent came from transportation, 9 percent were signalmen, 2 percent came from ordnance, and the remaining 2 percent came from all other branches of the service. About 63 percent had been truck drivers, duty soldiers, longshoremen, basic soldiers, construction foremen, and cargo checkers. Only 10 percent of the first batch were over the age of thirty. Some 22 percent were high school graduates, higher than the 18 percent of African Americans in the army as a whole who were high school graduates.

The men were formed up into the 47th Reinforcement Battalion, 5th Retraining. Training was under the command of Col. Alexander George at the 16th Reinforcement Depot based at Compiègne. It was apparent from the outset that the men were well motivated, and the absenteeism and discipline records were excellent. Toward the end of January 1945, the retraining was coming to a close, and the problem of deploying the men needed to be cleared up. The GFRC was only really geared to provide individual replacements for units; it was not able to create a battalion from scratch. There was now an added complication: Responsibility for these men transferred from Lee to the newly arrived Lt. Gen. Ben Lear. Lear's new instructions, which he received from Lee, were that Eisenhower "now desires that these colored riflemen reinforcements have their training completed as members of Infantry rifle platoons familiar with the Infantry rifle platoon weapons." Lee told him, "It is my feeling that we should afford the volunteers the full opportunity for Infantry riflemen service. Therefore we should not assign them as Tank or Artillery reinforcements unless they express such preference. To do otherwise would be breaking faith, in my opinion" (Lee, memo to Lear, February 1, 1945).

In any event, forty-five to forty-seven overstrength platoons could be created, and the first of the 2,253 men considered ready on March 1 were organized as thirty-seven platoons. Of these, twenty-five would be transferred to the command of Twelfth Army Group and the balance to the command of the Sixth Army Group. Each of the platoons was met by a platoon leader and sergeant at the depot, and the army groups were given the discretion to use the men as they saw fit, either as platoon-sized reinforcements or as larger groups, and eventually as whole battalions as more men became available.

Of the men assigned to the Twelfth Army Group, three platoons were given to each of the divisions, and each division gave one platoon to each of their regiments, reinforcing one of the regiment's companies. Brig. Gen. Charles Latham, speaking shortly after the war, said of the new divisions, "They had had some sort of training before they joined us, but we wanted to make sure they knew all the tricks of infantry fighting. We assigned our best combat leaders as instructors. I watched those lads train and if ever men were in dead earnest, they were" (before American Council on Race Relations, New York City, July 12, 1946; quoted in Lee 1966, 695).

Most of the divisions welcomed the men with open arms. They were personally addressed by the divisional commander and given the division's patches. The general experience was that they were incorporated and accepted quickly and used just like any other platoon. The army and theater headquarters were especially interested in the performance and casualty rate of the platoons. For the most part, average casualty figures were the same as or in some cases slightly higher than those of similar white platoons.

There were inherent contradictions between the way the original letter said the men would be used and the way they were eventually used, and now those contradictions came back to haunt the army. All of the men were privates; some had been noncommissioned officers willing to lose their rank to fight. Now the platoons had no real rank structure, and the divisional commands struggled with grades and promotions. Some of the men were clearly eligible to be promoted to noncommissioned officers, and others showed the aptitude for officer training.

By the end of March, the divisions were beginning to realize that the men were very credible replacements, and for the most part, the combat élan of the platoons was exceptional. Several of the men had already been recommended for the Bronze Star. General Davis made a tour of the divisions to collect his own impressions of the men's first month. At Twelfth Army Group, General Bradley was well satisfied; Gen. Courtney Hodges (of the First Army) reported that his African American troops were excellent. The general impression, from army group to regimental level, was that the new platoons were functioning well. The experience of the African American platoon assigned to the 60th Infantry Regiment was typical of the approach of these men, who had been thirsting for action ever since they had arrived in Europe. On April 5, 1945, the African American platoon had taken part in the capture of Lengenbach, running into stiff opposition from the die-hard German defenders. On April 9, Pfc. Jack Thomas was awarded the Distinguished Service Cross for leading his squad against an enemy force that had blocked a road. Under heavy fire, he scattered the Germans with grenades and fired a rocket at a solitary German tank. Not content with this, he then scooped up a member of the rocket launcher team who had been wounded and carried him to cover.

The 104th Infantry Regiment gave General Davis the following report:

> Morale: Excellent. Manner of performance: Superior. Men are very eager to close with the enemy and to destroy him. Strict attention to duty, aggressiveness, common sense and judgment under fire has won the admiration of all the men in the company. The colored platoon after initial success continued to do excellent work. Observation discloses that these people observe all the rules of the book. When given a mission they accept it with enthusiasm, and even when losses to their platoon were inflicted the colored boys accepted these losses as part of war, and continued on their mission. The Company Commander, officers, and men

> of Company "F" all agree that the colored platoon has a calibre of men equal to any veteran platoon. Several decorations for bravery are in the process of being awarded to the members of colored platoons (letter, Davis to GI Inspection Section, April 25, 1945).

Maj. Gen. Edwin F. Parker, commander of the 78th Division at Remagen, told Davis that he wanted more African American platoons. The 99th Division reported that their African American troops

> performed in an excellent manner at all times while in combat. These men were courageous fighters and never once did they fail to accomplish their assigned mission. They were particularly good in town fighting and were often used as the assault platoon with good results. The platoon assigned to the 393d Infantry is credited with killing approximately two Germans and capturing 900. During this action only three of their own men were killed and fifteen wounded (Headquarters 99th Division, letter to Commanding General XII Corps, June 21, 1945).

Not all of the reports were complimentary; the twelve platoons that had been assigned to the Seventh Army were handed over to the 12th Armored Division, whose lack of infantry had become critical. The unit had already had a less-than-ideal experience with the 827th Tank Destroyer Battalion, an African American unit, and great things were not expected of the new African American infantry platoons. The platoons' new role was to support tank operations, for which they had no experience. They were assigned to the armored infantry battalions of the division and soon picked up the fundamentals of this form of combat. On March 26 four more platoons arrived from Sixth Army Group and joined the 14th Armored Division, attached to the Combat Command Reserve and designated as the Seventh Army Provisional Infantry Company No. 1 attached to the 56th Armored Infantry Battalion. When the 14th moved to the Third Army on April 23, the company moved with them.

Four days earlier, General Davis had visited the battalion and discovered that the company had not yet been deployed as a whole unit, but detachments had already been committed to combat. A notable episode had occurred on March 23 at Speyer: African American Sgt. Edward A. Carter Jr. led three men across a field toward an enemy position after coming under heavy fire. Two of his men were killed and a third wounded, but the sergeant continued to move in on the German position. He was forced to take cover after receiving five wounds, but when eight Germans attempted to capture him, he killed six of them and captured the other two. Using the prisoners as a shield, he recrossed the field and delivered the prisoners for interrogation.

The men attached to the 14th Armored Division were in continual combat from April 5 to May 3, 1945, as the division moved through Bavaria. The first real opportunity for combat came as two of the platoons took Mainz. At Creussen on April 15, the 94th Reconnaissance Squadron found itself surrounded by enemy troops and called for reinforcements, which it received in the form of part of the 25th Tank Battalion and one African American infantry platoon. As the reinforcements approached Gottsfeld at around 11:45 a.m., they came under fire from German antitank guns, and two tanks were knocked out. The African American platoon dismounted from the tanks and, under heavy fire, managed to clear the Gottsfeld by 3 p.m. The tanks were able to move forward once again, knocking out five enemy tanks; the combined force was able to enter Creussen at 5 p.m. The African American platoons of the Combat Command Reserve operated in the area until about April 17, patrolling the area and capturing large numbers of German prisoners. As far as the 14th were concerned, the African American troops had proved themselves.

Gen. Alexander Patch was still unconvinced, and he complained to General Davis that the men were not suited to be used as armored infantry. Davis carefully explained that the men had been trained as riflemen and were learning on the job and that in his opinion they were performing well above expectations. This was an issue that required a solution, and a series of communications between Generals Davis and Lear and Gen. Jacob L. Dever and General Patch suggested that the men be used only in infantry divisions commensurate with their training. Alternatively, it was suggested that they receive additional training for use in armored divisions. The result was that Maj. Gen. Roderick Allen (commander of the 12th Armored Division) visited General Patch on May 12 to discuss the matter. But by then the hostilities were over, for Patch had decided on May 11 that the issue need not be pursued and that Allen would arrange for the men to receive company training.

The men's morale and performance were undoubtedly affected by the size and nature of their deployment. The larger groups, of company size, felt somewhat distanced from the units they fought alongside. The smaller groups, operating at either platoon or even squad level, had become integral parts of the units to which they were assigned. For the most part, the experiment simply proved that integration of African Americans was positive and that continued segregation was counterproductive. Examples of the benefits of integrating the smaller formations were widespread, and platoon and company commanders were generally very positive and complimentary. What had also been a decisive factor in the success of the program was the lack of friction or instances of racial problems. Time and time again, the African Americans had proved firsthand to their white counterparts that they were not afraid to take the same risks. When opportunities arose for rest and recreation, the races mixed, eating together and socializing. One company commander was quoted as saying, "The premise that no soldier will hold black skin against a man if he can shoot his rifle and does not run away proved to be substantially true. Most of the white men of the company soon became highly appreciative of the Negroes' help and warmly applauded their more colorful individual and combat exploits" (Lewis 1945, 4).

With hostilities in Europe now giving way to occupation, with its very different requirements and function, there were some concerns about retaining the African American elements with the white units. The African Americans, as redeployment got underway, feared they would be transferred back into service units. A large group of the men were transferred to a combat engineer battalion and began work on constructing redeployment camps. Redeployment was based on a points system throughout the army, and the majority of the African Americans had fewer points than did white troops because they had only been deployed as combat troops since the beginning of 1945. Those with higher point totals (about 1,000 men) were sent to the 69th Infantry, which was bound for America. Another group was sent to the 350th Field Artillery Battalion, an African American unit with a low redeployment status, which meant that the men were able to retain their status as combat troops. The African American combat troops feared that they would not have the opportunity to return to the United States along with the divisions in which they had fought. They would lose the honor of returning home as acknowledged combat troops, and given that many of the men hoped discrimination in the army was coming to an end, this was a matter of great concern.

The use of African American rifle platoons had dealt with the last major hurdle in the army: No longer would these men be considered only worthy of driving a truck or digging latrines. World War II proved that African Americans could be deployed for longer and in more varied roles than they had ever before been permitted. By the end of the war, some 10 percent of the army's total manpower were African Americans. What remained was to review the deployment and make sure that the lessons were not forgotten.

The McCloy Committee was already at work to establish a clearer postwar policy on the deployment and use of African Americans, but on October 4, 1945, the War Department appointed Lt. Gen. Alvan C. Gillem Jr. to head a board of officers to investigate and prepare a new policy on the employment of African Americans in the army. The tide had now begun to turn inexorably toward integration. In the summer of 1945 the chief historian of the army, Dr. Walter L. Wright Jr., wrote to Col. John M. Kemper:

> With your general conclusion regarding the performance of Negro troops, I tend to agree: They cannot be expected to do as well in any Army function as white troops unless they have absolutely first-class leadership from their officers. Such leadership may be provided, in my opinion, either by white or by Negro officers, but white officers would have to be men who have some understanding of the attitude of mind which Negroes possess and some sympathy with them as human beings. What troubles me is that anybody of real intelligence should be astonished to discover that Negro troops require especially good leadership if their performance is to match that of white troops. This same state of affairs exists, I think, with any group of men who belong to a subject nationality or national minority consisting of under-privileged individuals from depressed social strata. American Negro troops are, as you know, ill-educated on the average and often illiterate; they lack self-respect, self-confidence, and initiative; they tend to be very conscious of their low standing in the eyes of the white population and consequently feel very little motive for aggressive fighting. In fact, their survival as individuals and as a people has often depended on their ability to subdue completely even the appearance of aggressiveness. After all, when a man knows that the color of his skin will automatically disqualify him for reaping the fruits of attainment it is no wonder that he sees little point in trying very hard to excel anybody else. To me, the most extraordinary thing is that such people continue trying at all.
>
> The conclusion which I reach is obvious: We cannot expect to make first-class soldiers out of second or third or fourth class citizens. The man who is lowest down in civilian life is practically certain to be lowest down as a soldier. Accordingly, we must expect depressed minorities to perform much less effectively than the average of other groups in the population. So far as the war in progress is concerned, the War Department must deal with an existing state of affairs and its employment of Negroes must parallel the employment of the same group in civilian American society. Yet, it is important to remember that the civilian status of Negroes in this country is changing with a rapidity which I believe to be unique in history; the level of literacy is rising steadily and quickly and privileges other than educational are being gained every year (personal letter to Kemper, July 3, 1945, quoted in Lee 1966, 704).

Wright's words were prophetic, and before another ten years had elapsed segregation in the military would be over. Progress toward desegregation had been helped by the sacrifices of the men who volunteered when the U.S. Army was in dire need in Europe from the end of 1944 through 1945.

See also: Carter, Edward Allen, Jr.; Davis, Benjamin Oliver, Sr.; Double V; Segregation and Racism in the Military; U.S. Army; World War II

References and Further Reading

Carter, Joseph. *The History of the 14th Armored Division.* Atlanta, GA: Love, 1946.

Hoegh, Leo A., and Howard J. Doyle. *Timberwolf Tracks: The History of the 104th Infantry Division, 1942–1945.* Washington, DC: Infantry Journal Press, 1946.

Lee, Ulysses. *The Employment of Negro Troops.* U.S. Army in World War II; Center of Military History

Publication 11/4. Washington, DC: Government Printing Office, 1966.

Lewis, Robert. "Negroes under Fire." *The Progressive and LaFollette's Magazine* 9 (September 9, 1945): 4.

Mittelman, Joseph B. *Eight Stars to Victory: A History of the Veteran Ninth U.S. Infantry Division.* Columbus, OH: 9th Infantry Division Association, 1948.

Star, Shirley. "Negro Soldiers." In *The American Soldier: Adjustment during Army Life,* ed. Samuel A. Stouffer et al. Princeton, NJ: Princeton University Press, 1949.

Young, Charles (1864–1922)

Charles Young was the third African American to graduate from West Point (in 1889) and the first to attain the rank of lieutenant colonel in the U.S. Army. He was born in Maylick, Kentucky, in 1864 and graduated from high school in Ripley, Ohio.

He was first assigned duty in the 10th Cavalry at Fort Robinson, Nebraska, and he spent the remainder of his military career attached to all–African American regiments. An accomplished linguist, with a good command of Latin, Greek, French, Spanish, and German, Young served as professor of military science at Wilberforce University.

From 1894 and throughout the Spanish American War (1898) he commanded the 9th Ohio Volunteer Infantry and was brevetted major. In 1903 he was acting superintendent of parks at Sequoia and General Grant National Parks in California, and married Ada Barr, with whom he had two children, Charles Noel, born in 1907, and Marie, born in 1909.

Young was one of the first military attachés, controlled by the Military Information Division, at the U.S. legation in Port au Prince, Haiti. He made extended military reconnaissance of the country and the neighboring Republic of Santo Domingo and produced detailed maps of the local terrain between 1904 and 1907.

In 1908 he was sent to the Philippines to command a squadron of two troops, following which time he went to Liberia for more attaché duty. His responsibility there was to advise the Liberian constabulary and to supervise the construction of roads. For his efforts and achievements in Liberia, Young received the Spingarn Medal. The Spingarn Medal, founded in 1914, has been awarded annually by the National Association for the Advancement of Colored People (NAACP) to an African American who has demonstrated distinguished merit and achievement during the year.

During the 1916 punitive expedition in Mexico, Young commanded a squadron of the 10th Cavalry. On March 9, 1916, at Agua Caliente, Mexico, Major Young led a squadron in a cavalry pistol charge against the Villista forces, routing the 150 men led by General Francisco Beltran; Young's squadron received no casualties. On April 12 his squadron relieved the wounded Maj. Frank Tompkins at Hacienda Santa Cruz de la Villegas, an action that may have prevented a war with Mexico. Young was promoted to the rank of lieutenant colonel in 1916 for his operations in Mexico, eventually rising to the rank of colonel the following year and for a short time in command of Fort Huachuca.

Young was expected to become the first African American general to take part in World War I, as General Pershing had included him on the list of officers to be considered for brigade or higher command. But prior to the outbreak of this war he appeared before the American Expeditionary Force promotion board and was found to be physically unfit to serve overseas.

In a determined attempt to prove his fitness and gain permission to command his black troopers in France during World War I, Young rode on horseback from Ohio to Washington, D.C., to press his claim to serve during the war. When his medical records were finally released they showed that he suffered from chronic nephritis (Bright's disease), but these were hardly debilitating conditions and did not preclude his being recalled later to serve in Africa, reinforcing the suspicion that the army had enforced Young's retirement so as not to allow an African American to reach the rank of general.

Young was later recalled to serve once more as military attaché in Liberia, and he died while on a research expedition in Lagos, Nigeria, on April 8, 1922. His body was returned to the United States and is buried in Arlington National Cemetery; his home in Ohio is a registered National Historical Landmark.

W. E. B. Du Bois, historian and one of the founders of the National Association for the Advancement of Colored People (NAACP), wrote of his longtime friend Young in an issue of *The Crisis* after the colonel's death:

Maj. Charles Young of the 10th Cavalry, 1916. In 1916, Young played a key role in the campaign against Pancho Villa, which prompted his promotion to lieutenant colonel and then full colonel in 1917. (National Archives)

> The life of Charles Young was a triumph of tragedy. No one ever knew the truth about the Hell he went through at West Point. He seldom even mentioned it. The pain was too great. Few knew what faced him always in his army life. It was not enough for him to do well—he must always do better; and so much and so conspicuously better, as to disarm the scoundrels that ever trailed him. He lived in the army surrounded by insult and intrigue and yet he set his teeth and kept his soul serene and triumphed. He was one of the few men I know who literally turned the other cheek with Jesus Christ. He was laughed at for it and his own people chided him bitterly, yet he persisted. When a white Southern pigmy at West Point protested at taking food from a dish passed first to Young, Young passed it to him first and afterward to himself. When officers of inferior rank refused to salute a "nigger," he saluted them. Seldom did he lose his

temper, seldom complain. . . . He is dead. But the heart of the Great Black Race, the Ancient of Days—the Undying and Eternal—rises and salutes his shining memory: Well done! Charles Young, Soldier and Man and unswerving friend (quoted in Finley 1993).

See also Buffalo Soldiers; 9th Cavalry; Pancho Villa Campaign; Philippine Insurrection; Spanish-American War; 10th Cavalry; West Point; World War I

References and Further Reading

Chew, Abraham. *A Biography of Colonel Charles Young*. Washington, DC: Pendleton, 1923.

Cox, Clinton. *The Forgotten Heroes*. New York: Scholastic, 1993.

Finley, James P. "Roll Call: Colonel Charles Young—Black Cavalryman, Huachuca Commander, and Early Intelligence Officer." *Huachuca Illustrated: A Magazine of the Fort Huachuca Museum,* vol. 1, 1993. http://www.lib.byu.edu/~rdh/wwi/comment/huachuca/HI1-19.htm (accessed September 16, 2003).

Leckie, William H. *The Buffalo Soldiers: A Narrative of the Negro Cavalry in the West*. Norman: University of Oklahoma Press, 1967.

Scott, Edward Van Zile. *The Unwept: Black American Soldiers and the Spanish-American War.* Montgomery, AL: Black Belt Press, 1995.

Z

Z-Gram 66 (December 17, 1970)

The so-called Z-Grams were policy directives issued by Adm. Elmo Russell Zumwalt Jr. while he was chief of naval operations between July 1, 1970, and July 1, 1974. Z-Grams are more properly known as Z-NavOps. During Zumwalt's period in office, he issued 121 Z-Grams, the most important of which, as far as African Americans were concerned, was Z-Gram 66, which was issued on December 17, 1970. Z-Gram 66 was written as a result of the gradual reduction in African American participation in the Vietnam War.

Following is the full transcript of Z-Gram 66:

Z-gram #66: (Equal Opportunity);
dated December 17, 1970
Equal Opportunity in the Navy

1. The purpose of this NavOp is to express my wholehearted support of the policies on equal opportunity strongly reaffirmed by the secretary of the Navy in AlNav 51, to express my general guidance for implementation of these policies, and to direct implementation of a few of the actions we can take immediately.
2. Last month, [Navy] Secretary [John H.] Chafee and I, along with other senior officials of the Navy Department, met on one occasion with representative black Navy officers and their wives and later with a representative group of black enlisted men and their wives. Prior to these meetings, I was convinced that, compared with the civilian community, we had relatively few racial problems in the Navy. However, after exploring the matter in some depth with these two groups, I have discovered that I was wrong—we do have problems, and it is my intention and that of Secretary Chafee to take prompt steps toward their solution.
3. What struck me more than anything else was the depth of feeling of our black personnel that there is significant discrimination in the Navy. Prior to these meetings, I sincerely believed that I was philosophically prepared to understand the problems of our black Navy men and their families, and until we discussed them at length, I did not realize the extent and deep significance of many of these matters.
4. There are two keys to the problem. First, we must open up new avenues of communication with not only our black personnel, but also with all minority groups in the Navy so that we may learn what and where the areas of friction are. Second, all of us in the Navy must develop a far greater sensitivity to the problems of all our minority groups so that

we may more effectively go about solving them. Our meetings here in Washington were a beginning, but no more than that. Much remains to be done.

5. For example, I am particularly distressed by the numerous examples of discrimination black Navy families still experience in attempting to locate housing for their families. This situation and others like it are indicative in some cases of less than full teamwork being brought to bear by the whole Navy team on behalf of some of our members and failure to use existing authority and directives to enforce their rights (SecNav Inst 5350.12). In some places housing personnel are tacitly contributing to discrimination in housing.
6. Secretary Chafee and I have asked our staffs to begin work with other members of the Navy Department to make an in-depth investigation of this problem and present to us within 60 days proposals which will help alleviate the most acute housing problems. Meanwhile, there are many things that can be acted upon immediately. Therefore, by 15 January 1971 I expect action to be taken as follows:

A. Every base, station and aircraft squadron commander and ship commanding officer shall appoint an aware minority group officer or senior petty officer as his special assistant for minority affairs. This officer or petty officer should have direct access to the commander/commanding officer and will be consulted on all matters involving minority personnel. Excepting those commands already having minority-affairs officer billets, the initial assignment will be on a concurrent duty basis. (I carefully weighed this item with my desire, as expressed in Ref A, to reduce collateral duty assignments. However, after discussing this with several black officers I became convinced that they would in fact cherish this as a collateral duty.)

B. All shore based commanders shall ensure that a minority group wife is included in the Navy wives ombudsman concept set forth in Ref B.

C. The programs already begun by ComNavSupSysCom to ensure that the special needs of minority groups are recognized and provided for shall be expedited, namely:

1. Suitable cosmetics and other products for black personnel and their dependents will be stocked in Navy exchanges.
2. Ship's stores will stock black grooming aids.
3. Every base and station will employ, as soon as possible, at least one qualified black barber/beautician in major barber and beauty shops, and will work toward the goal of having sufficient barbers/beauticians qualified in hair care for black personnel to provide service for all black patrons.
4. All major commissaries shall stock foods and produce frequently requested by minority groups. As a minimum, specific recommendations should be solicited from minority personnel and their families and acted upon by local commissary managers.

D. Special services officers which deal in discount tickets for various entertainment programs will also obtain discount tickets to events of special interest to minority groups whenever such tickets are available.

E. A representative selection of books, magazines and records by and about black Americans will be made available in Navy libraries, wardrooms, clubs and other reading areas.

Any of the above which can't be accomplished within the time specified above will be reported via chain of command together with a summary of circumstances preventing timely implementation.

7. In order that I may reach a more complete understanding of the problems experienced by our minority personnel, in addition to SecNav/OpNav/BuPers team visits I am directing my special assistant for minority affairs, LCdr Norman, to visit major naval activities within CONUS to meet with individual commanding officers and with minority military personnel and their dependents. By learning in depth what our problems are, I believe we will be in a better position to work toward guaranteeing equal opportunity and treatment for all of our Navy people.
8. This is the first of my reports to you on minority affairs. Secretary Chafee and I will be looking into all areas of minority affairs and will be issuing further reports as our problems become more clear and their solutions become more apparent. It is evident that we need to maximize our efforts to improve the lot of our minority Navymen. I am convinced that there is no place in our Navy for insensitivity. We are determined that we shall do better. Meanwhile, we are counting on your support to help seek out and eliminate those demeaning areas of discrimination that plague our minority shipmates. Ours must be a Navy family that recognizes no artificial barriers of race, color or religion. There is no black Navy, no white Navy—just one Navy—the United States Navy.

E. R. Zumwalt, Jr., Admiral, U.S. Navy
Chief of Naval Operations

See also U.S. Navy; Vietnam War

References and Further Reading

Naval Historical Center Web site. "Z-Gram # 66." http://www.history.navy.mil/faqs/faq93-66.htm.

Zumwalt, Elmo, Jr. *On Watch: A Memoir.* New York: Quadrangle/New York Times, 1976.

Zumwalt, Elmo, Jr., and Elmo Zumwalt III. *My Father, My Son.* New York: Macmillan, 1986.

Chronology

1639

Virginia passes the first legislation excluding African Americans from the militia forces.

1652

Massachusetts passes a law requiring African Americans and Native Americans living with, or servants to, English settlers to be given military training in case of Native American attacks.

1656

Massachusetts repeals the 1652 law in response to fears of African or Native American uprisings.

1660

Connecticut excludes African and Native Americans from military call-up.

1676

Nathaniel Bacon of Virginia offers freedom to slaves joining his rebellion to seize Native American lands. Virginia suppresses the revolt, known as Bacon's Rebellion, without recruiting slaves for its forces.

1689

During King William's War, African Americans in the regular militia are forced to fight against France and its Native American allies.

1703

Slaves are enlisted in South Carolina to fight in Queen Anne's War (1702–1713). Freedom is offered for killing enemy soldiers or taking them prisoner.

1705

Virginia passes legislation preventing African Americans from holding military office.

1707

South Carolina passes legislation requiring militia captains to ensure that each white militiaman brings with him an armed African American slave.

1708

South Carolina recruits African American slaves to protect Charleston against Native American raids.

1715

A Native American tribe, the Yamasee, lead an uprising in the Carolinas. Despite North Carolina's misgivings about arming African American slaves, many African American militiamen help crush the rebellion.

1719

South Carolina rescinds the law offering freedom to slaves who kill or capture the enemy; a cash bounty is offered instead.

1723

Virginia allows recruitment of African Americans to serve as trumpeters, drummers, and laborers.

1729

French Louisiana recruits African American slaves for a border war with Native Americans.

1735

Free African Americans serve as officers for Louisiana, leading African American slave units in wars against Native Americans.

1744–1748

During King George's War, both freed and enslaved African Americans serve in militia units from New Hampshire, Rhode Island, and Connecticut. African Americans also serve on privateers operating out of Boston.

1747

South Carolina authorizes enlistment of half the able-bodied slave population between sixteen and twenty years of age to serve in the militia in times of emergency.

1754–1763

During the French and Indian War many African Americans see service in militia from across New England; notable individuals, including Benjamin Negro and George Gire, receive recognition of their service in the form of a pension.

1770

Runaway slave Crispus Attucks is killed in the Boston Massacre (March 5). He is shot after he attacks a British officer and knocks the musket from the hands of a grenadier.

1774

Massachusetts begins recruiting African Americans into their militia companies. British general Gage turns down the offer of slaves in Boston to enlist in loyal militias in return for their freedom. New York offers freedom to slaves who serve in the militia for three years.

1775

Massachusetts decrees that only free African Americans may serve in the militias.

African Americans Pomp Blackman and Prince Estabrook fight in the Battles of Lexington and Concord (April 19).

May. Several African Americans participated in the storming of Fort Ticonderoga by Ethan Allen's Green Mountain Boys.

June. After assuming command of the Continental Army, George Washington issues orders not to recruit African Americans. He later rescinds the instruction to allow the enlistment of freemen.

African Americans Peter Salem, Salem Poor (Poore), and Cuff Whittemore all serve in the Battle of Bunker Hill (June 17). Peter Salem allegedly shoots a British major, John Pitcairn. Salem Poor receives a commendation for his bravery in the battle (December 5).

July. American general Horatio Gates instructs his recruiting officers not to enlist African Americans, free or slave.

September 26. South Carolina's Edward Routledge's proposal to dismiss all African Americans already enlisted in the Continental Army or militias is defeated in the Continental Congress. Washington agrees to recruit only white troops from this point.

October 8. In a change of policy, Washington announces that only free African Americans will be considered for enlistment, this is ratified by the Continental Congress.

November 7. The Dunmore Proclamation is released offering freedom to male slaves who would serve in loyalist regiments. Over 500 African Americans respond (only 300 are recruited) and the Ethiopian Regiment is formed in Virginia. They fight in the defense of Norfolk (December 11) but are beaten. Some six months later, the 300-man regiment has been halved following a smallpox epidemic.

November 28. The Continental Congress establishes the Continental Navy; free and slave African Americans are welcome to enlist.

December 30. George Washington issues a general order encouraging the enlistment of free African Americans in recognition of large numbers offering their service.

1776

Virginia officially welcomes free African Americans

into the militia; Massachusetts and New Hampshire follow suit. South Carolina, and later many of the other Southern states, pass legislation decreeing the death penalty for slaves who join the British army or navy.

February 21. Washington issues an order reminding recruiters that slaves are not to be enlisted in the Continental Army.

June. Charleston faces British attack and press-gangs all African Americans to work on field defenses. The South Carolina Committee of Safety pays slave masters ten shillings per day to lease their African Americans; in the event of death or maiming, slave owners are compensated.

September 26. African American hangman Bill Richmond executes Connecticut officer Nathan Hale in New York for spying.

1777

Virginia announces that African Americans will be enlisted only if they can show a Certificate of Freedom. Maryland and other Northern states, to ensure that they meet the Continental Congress's new recruitment quotas, allow slaves to enlist.

The widespread use of African American slaves does not become a substitute for white men being called up. Rhode Island establishes that all African American battalions be commanded by white officers. There slaves are offered equal pay and freedom.

Edward Hector, serving in the 3d Pennsylvania Artillery, fights at the Battle of Brandywine (September 11). He is given a cash reward for his bravery.

October. Connecticut issues a proclamation freeing slaves who sign up for the state militia.

1778

April. Massachusetts votes to continue integrating African Americans into militia units despite pleas to create segregated units.

June 10. The Rhode Island Assembly halts African American recruitment in response to fears about the loss of slaves in Newport and how it would affect the economy.

June 28. At the Battle of Monmouth in New Jersey, over 700 African American soldiers fight in the engagement.

August. Over 300 slaves, recruited by Continental Army officers under Washington's orders, enlist and fight in the unsuccessful attempt to seize Newport.

August 24. In a report by Adj. Gen. Alexander Scammell of the Continental Army, he claims that some 755 African American soldiers are serving in fourteen brigades.

Quamino Dolly, an African American slave, acts as a guide and scout for Lt. Col. Archibald Campbell, helping his British force seize Savannah, Georgia.

1779

South Carolina becomes the first state to object to the Continental Congress's approval of the recruitment of slaves as soldiers and seamen for the duration of the war.

Austin Dabney, the only African American present at the Battle of Kettle Creek in Georgia (February 14), shows great courage in the fighting.

March. South Carolina and Georgia reject the Continental Congress's call to recruit 3,000 African American slaves to serve in segmented units. Congress suggests that the slaves be given $50 and their freedom after the war, and that the slave owners be compensated. Later, Gen. Nathanael Greene's plan to recruit African Americans is defeated by the objections of South Carolina's John Laurens, formerly Washington's aide-de-camp and liaison officer between America and France.

The African American slave Pompey, an American spy, obtains a British password that allows Gen. Anthony Wayne's troops to capture the enemy fort at Stony Point, New York.

June. British general Sir Henry Clinton offers freedom to all African American slaves who join loyalist militias. This action signals an increase in African American recruitment by both sides during the war.

June 21. After declaring war on Britain, Spanish Louisiana troops, including freemen and slaves of African descent led by black officers, help capture Pensacola and Mobile from the British. Several black soldiers and officers later are awarded medals for bravery.

During the siege of Savannah, Georgia (September 3–October 28), over 500 freemen from Haiti serve in the French fleet under Adm. Jean Baptiste d'Estaing. Around 14 percent of the 3,600-member French expeditionary force are African Americans, including the future ruler of an independent Haiti, Henry Christophe.

1780

June. An all–African American unit, the Connecticut Colonials, is formed. The unit will serve for two years, finally being disbanded in November 1782. At that point, some fifty-two freemen and slaves are incorporated into white units.

September 23. Two African Americans are instrumental in the capture and later execution (October 2) in New York of the British spy Maj. John André, an adjutant to General Clinton.

1781

The New York General Assembly allows slaves to join the military. In return for three years' service, they will gain their freedom.

June. Maryland passes legislation enabling free African Americans to enlist; some 750 answer the call.

October 19. After General Cornwallis surrenders at Yorktown, Virginia, it is revealed that his African American spy, James Armistead, was in fact a double agent.

1782

The British free all African Americans who enlisted before November 30.

1783

Responding to the reenslavement of African American veterans in the South, Virginia passes legislation guaranteeing them freedom for their military service.

September 3. Hostilities end between America and Britain with the signing of the Treaty of Paris. By the end of the war some 5,000 African Americans have served in the Continental Army and an additional 5,000 in state militia units.

1786

In recognition of their services during the war, Austin Dabney is granted his freedom by Georgia and James Armistead receives his from Virginia.

1791

Congress reexcludes African Americans and Native Americans from the regular army.

1792

May. Congress restricts militia enlistment to white citizens only; state militia laws follow suit.

1798

Secretary of War James McHenry and Secretary of the Navy Benjamin Stoddert issue directives prohibiting the enlistment of African Americans in the U.S. Navy and the U.S. Marine Corps. Despite the racial enlistment policy, many African Americans serve in the naval war against France (1798–1800). The war against France was only a war in name—it was carried out only at sea and involved U.S. and French vessels harassing one another. African Americans were already in the U.S. Navy and therefore served as they had always done.

1800

Caesar Lloyd Cummings, employed as a clerk and messenger, is the sole surviving African American in the U.S. Marine Corps.

The African American population reaches 1,002,037, or 18.9 percent of the population. Ninety percent of these are slaves.

African American slave Gabriel Prosser begins organizing a slave rebellion in Virginia.

August 20. Prosser musters hundreds of slaves to march on Richmond, six miles from his owner's property. The plan fails due to poor weather and treachery.

September. Prosser is arrested after being turned in by a slave in Norfolk. He and thirty-five others are hanged for insurrection.

1801

Spain cedes Louisiana to France, which has existing African American militia.

1802

In Henrico County, Virginia, a slave called Arthur writes a recruiting leaflet to start another rebellion. A copy of the leaflet is passed to the authorities by a slave.

1803

Haitian rebel leader Toussaint L'ouverture dies in a French prison and Napoleon Bonaparte restores slavery to the island, as well as Martinique and Guadeloupe. Former slave Jean-Jacques Dessalines (1758–1806) defeats the French and forces the sale of Louisiana to the United States.

In New Orleans, free African American militiamen offer their services to the U.S. Army; they are turned down.

1807

President Thomas Jefferson signs a bill stating that the United States will no longer engage in the slave trade beginning January 1, 1808.

June 22. Three African American sailors—William Ware, David Martin, and John Strachan—are forcibly removed from the USS *Chesapeake* by British troops from the HMS *Leopard* three miles off the Virginia coast. The British arrested the men as deserters. Two of the sailors are eventually returned to the United States and the third dies in England.

1811

A slave rebellion led by African American Charles Deslondes, originally from Santo Domingo, flares up in New Orleans. Local militia hang the captured rebels on the spot. African American militia are involved in the mopping-up exercises.

1812

The War of 1812 breaks out between the United States and Great Britain.

The British recruit slaves for the Royal Navy and arm runaway slaves in Florida.

The U.S. privateer *Governor Tompkins* is attacked by a British frigate. John Johnson and John Davis, both African Americans, are mortally wounded in the engagement.

Louisiana passes legislation to allow free African Americans to serve in the state militia.

The African American population reaches 1.4 million, of whom 84 percent are slaves.

1813

March 3. The U.S. Navy, due to severe manpower shortages, authorizes the enlistment of free African Americans.

September 10. The Battle of Lake Erie ends in a U.S. victory, with approximately 25 percent of Adm. Oliver Hazard Perry's sailors being African American.

1814

Sir Alexander Cochrane's British fleet anchors in Chesapeake Bay, offering freedom to African American slaves who bear arms for the Crown. Up to 5,000 respond and Rear Adm. George Cockburn creates the Black Marines.

May. Escaped African American slaves in the service of the British Royal Marines, under Acting Ens. William Hammond, fight their first action as they storm a U.S. coastal defense battery at Pungoteague, Virginia.

August. The Black Marines fight at the Battle of Bladensburg in Maryland.

August 2. Around 1,000 New York African Americans assist in the construction of defense works at Brooklyn Heights to defend the city against the British.

September. Philadelphia authorities enlist the support of African American clergy to recruit African Americans for help in the building of defenses around the city in the wake of the British capture of Washington, D.C. The African Americans build defense works to the south of Philadelphia, on the west bank of the Schuylkill River.

September 11. African American troops take part in the Battle of Plattsburg, which aims to protect the Hudson Valley and New York City.

September 21. Gen. Andrew Jackson pleads for free African Americans in Louisiana to join his army. He offers equal pay and the same bounty and land grants given to white volunteers. African Americans join segregated units officered by white men and African American noncommissioned officers.

October. New York authorizes the creation of two African American militia units to be led by white officers. Freemen will receive equal pay, and slaves who join with the permission of their masters are offered freedom at the termination of hostilities.

December 12. Two African American battalions raised by Col. Michel Fortier, Sr., one of which is led by 2d Lt. Isidore Honoré, form in New Orleans. Vincent Populus becomes the first African American field-grade officer.

1815

Although the Battle of New Orleans is fought two weeks after the Treaty of Ghent (which officially ends the War of 1812), Gen. Andrew Jackson deploys in the engagement two battalions of African American troops, amounting to 430 men. For the British, African American troops and West Indians also take part in the engagement. Also present is freed African American Maj. Joseph Savary, leading 200 freemen to fight for the Americans.

March 3. Following the end of hostilities, Congress votes to exclude African Americans from the military and establishes a peacetime army of 10,000 men. The War Department issues a statement criticizing the value and conduct of African Americans during the war.

1816

The U.S. Navy decides to exclude African American slaves from serving on their vessels or in their dockyards.

1817

November–December. The U.S. Army mounts an expedition to destroy the Negro Fort (on the Apalachicola River in Spanish Florida), which is manned by African American runaway slaves. The fort is captured and destroyed, putting an end to attacks on U.S. settlements in the wake of the War of 1812.

1818

A number of African American runaway slaves ally with Seminole Indians and fight against the U.S. Army during the First and Second Seminole Wars.

1819

Joseph Savary, who had recruited free African Americans from St. Domingue and Cuba, receives a pension for his war service.

1820

Congress decides to exclude free African Americans from enlisting in the U.S. Army. State militias follow suit.

The Missouri Compromise declares that all land north of the Ohio River, with the exception of Missouri, shall not be slave-owning.

Harriet Tubman is born in Maryland. Her slave name is Araminta, or Minty.

1821

New U.S. Army regulations are announced that limit recruitment to free white males.

Austin Dabney, a free African American veteran of the American Revolution is finally rewarded for his military service by being granted a 112-acre farm by the Georgia legislature.

December. Denmark Vesey begins organizing his African American slave rebellion in the Charleston, South Carolina, area.

1822

May 30. Peter Devany, a slave, betrays Vesey.

June 22. Vesey is captured and later hanged along with thirty-six other African Americans.

1827

John B. Russwurm starts *Freedom's Journal,* the first African American newspaper.

1829

September. David Walker, an African American abolitionist and publisher from Boston, publishes "Walker's Appeal" in *Freedom's Journal.*

1830

African Americans are excluded from the Ohio state militia.

David Walker flees to Canada after death threats from the South and dies mysteriously.

1831

Texans begin their war of independence against Mexico. A free African American, Greenbury Logan, is one of the first to settle in Texas and fight in this conflict.

January. Militant white abolitionist William Lloyd Garrison publishes the first edition of the *Liberator* on New Year's Day.

August. Nat Turner's rebellion takes place in Southampton County, Virginia. Turner and about seventy followers kills sixty white slave owners. The rebellion is brutally put down.

1833

Great Britain abolishes slavery and compensates former slave owners with £20 million. The United States now stands alone as the only major slave-owning country.

1834

The New Orleans Free Men of Color, who had fought during the two previous wars, are disbanded.

The Liberator's readership is now 75 percent African American.

1835–1843

The Second Seminole War takes place. Continued resistance from the Seminole Indians and their African American allies prolongs the conflict. The war ends in victory for the U.S. Army at a cost of $40 million and 1,800 deaths.

1836

The U.S. Congress passes the notorious gag rule, which disallowed debate on slavery and the slave trade.

African American fifer Peter Allen is listed among the dead when 300 Texans are massacred after surrendering to Mexican forces at Goliad. Allen was a musician in Captain Wyatt's company.

1837–1838

African American Josiah Henson serves with the British in the Colored Volunteers during the Canadian Rebellion.

1838

Frederick Douglass becomes a free man after escaping from slavery in Baltimore, Maryland. He changes his name to Douglass from Frederick Augustus Washington Bailey.

The Underground Railroad is established. It also becomes known as the Business of Egypt on account of Canada being dubbed "the promised land."

1839

The U.S. Navy establishes a quota of 5 percent for the number of African Americans recruited into naval service following complaints from white sailors regarding the number of African Americans in the navy. The restrictions are announced in a circular by the acting secretary of the navy, Isaac Chauncey.

The Liberty Party is founded by James G. Birney, a former slave owner from Alabama and member of the Anti-Slavery Society.

1840

Richard Hildreth publishes *Despotism in America,* a highly influential antislavery text.

1842

The Senate debates and passes a bill put forward by Senator John C. Calhoun of South Carolina to exclude African Americans from the U.S. Navy, except in the capacity of manual laborers. The bill is passed in the Senate but not brought to a vote in the House.

1844

The Liberty Party holds a convention in Buffalo, where a runaway slave, the Reverend Henry Highland Garnet, calls for a general strike and a slave revolt.

1845

The gag rule of 1836 is abolished.

Abolitionist Frederick Douglass publishes *Narrative of the Life of Frederick Douglass* in Boston.

John L. O'Sullivan (1813–1895), who helps direct the purpose of the nation for the next fifty years, coins the term "manifest destiny," calling for the annexation of continental North America, including California, Texas, western Canada, and Alaska. Integral is the concept of liberty for all.

1846–1848

President James K. Polk initiates the Mexican-American War for the possession of Texas and California. The war culminates with U.S. victories at the Battles of Buena Vista and Veracruz in Mexico. African Americans in the U.S. Navy assist in the capture of California.

1846

The Wilmot Proviso is passed by the U.S. Congress, prohibiting the introduction of slavery into any new territories gained by the United States.

April 24. The Mexican-American War begins. The war breaks out following a skirmish between Mexican cavalry and U.S. troops blockading a Mexican town. African Americans are largely excluded from the war due to increasing tensions over the race issue, except in the roles of service and support. However, over 1,000 African Americans serve in the U.S. Navy during the war in blockades of Mexican ports.

1847

For two years after the publication of his book, Frederick Douglass is forced into exile in Great Britain and Ireland because he is still officially a wanted man for being a runaway slave. Funds are raised by Ellen Richardson to buy his freedom.

1850–1859

An estimated 3,000 African American and white Underground Railroad "conductors" smuggle approximately 75,000 runaway slaves into Canada.

1850

California applies to join the Union as a free state.

The Fugitive Slave Act encourages the kidnapping of African Americans because alleged runaways can be seized in any state, cannot testify, cannot call for witnesses, and can be immediately transported to their supposed master, regardless of the period that has elapsed between their escape and their capture.

1851

Harriet Tubman begins her long association with the Underground Railroad.

1852

Harriet Beecher Stowe publishes *Uncle Tom's Cabin.*

1853

Harriet Beecher Stowe publishes *A Key to Uncle Tom's Cabin,* which is based on a conversation with a former slave and now Canadian resident, Josiah Henson.

1854

The Kansas-Nebraska Act allows new territories to decide whether they shall be a slave-owning state.

1855

In Kansas, proslavery and abolitionist groups clash, forming their own militias. In May, abolitionist John Brown joins the Liberty Guards, a guerrilla band that killed five during the Pottawatomie Massacre.

1856

James Buchanan becomes president. Senator Charles Sumner, an abolitionist, is physically attacked in the U.S. Senate by South Carolina representative Preston Brooks.

May. Following a proslavery attack on Topeka, Kansas, John Brown and his sons are part of a group that massacres proslavers at nearby Pottawatomie Creek.

1857

Dred Scott v. Sandford. Scott, who was born a slave, had been taken to the non-slave owning part of Louisiana by his master. When his master died, Scott applied for freedom on the grounds that slavery was outlawed in the territory. A Missouri court rejected his claim, but Scott's supporters asked the Supreme Court to make a ruling. The Supreme Court ruled that Scott did not have the rights of a free citizen to sue in a federal court and that he was property and nothing more. The ruling, which overturned the decision of the circuit court of St. Louis, excluded all African Americans from U.S. citizenship and drove a larger wedge between the proslavery lobby and the abolitionists.

1858

The Oberlin Rescue takes place when local inhabitants of Oberlin, Ohio, rescue an escaped slave, John Price, from the local marshal and take him to Canada. Those involved later give themselves up and are met with substantial acclaim.

1859

August. The violently fervent abolitionist John Brown plans his attack on the arsenal at Harpers Ferry, Virginia, to seize the weapons to arm African Americans for a slave revolt.

October 16. John Brown's Provisional Army of the United States meets at a farm five miles from Harpers Ferry. There are seventeen whites and five African Americans.

October 17. En route to the armory, Brown's men shoot and kill African American Hayward Shepherd. By noon, militia have arrived, later joined by Lt. Col. Robert E. Lee and Lt. J. E. B. Stuart, who assume command.

October 18. Now surrounded, Brown receives a note from Lee demanding his surrender. Brown refuses and Stuart leads the assault. Shortly after dawn, the raid is over.

October 25. Brown and his men are indicted by a grand jury. Their trial begins the next day.

November 2. Brown is found guilty and sentenced to hang in a month.

December 2. John Brown is hanged, with future Confederate commanders Robert E. Lee, J. E. B. Stuart, and Thomas "Stonewall" Jackson present.

December 8. Brown is buried in New York.

1860

November 6. Abraham Lincoln is elected president.

December 20. South Carolina secedes from the Union.

1861

The Civil War starts. Free African Americans begin to petition Abraham Lincoln for the right to bear arms in defense of the Union. Initially they are ignored.

Julia Ward Howe writes the words of the "Battle Hymn of the Republic" to the same tune as the popular "John Brown's Body."

At the outbreak of the war, African American slaves account for 3,950,511 of the South's population of

8,099,674; the North's white population is 18,901,917.

January–February. Mississippi, Florida, Alabama, Georgia, Louisiana, and Texas secede from the Union.

January 21. New York and other non-slave-owning states pledge allegiance to the Union.

January 29. Kansas joins the Union.

February 4–8. The first Confederate convention is held in Montgomery, Alabama, and adopts a constitution.

February 9. Jefferson Davis is elected president of the Confederate States of America.

March 4. Abraham Lincoln is inaugurated as president of the United States.

April. Free African Americans in New Orleans, Louisiana, form their own Native Guard battalion, officered by African Americans. The state government approves African American commissions, and informs Confederate authorities in Richmond in November. Like most state militias, service conditions prohibit deployment outside of the state. After the capture of New Orleans by the Union, many of the men would later fight in the United States Colored Troops (USCT).

April 12. Fort Sumter, South Carolina, is attacked by Confederate troops.

April 15. Lincoln officially declares a state of insurrection. He pleads for the enlistment of 75,000 men to serve for a period of three months. The U.S. Army refuses to accept African American volunteers, and Lincoln concedes the point in an attempt to placate the border states. The U.S. Navy authorizes the enlistment of escaped slaves into service.

April–May. Virginia, Arkansas, and North Carolina secede from the Union.

April 19. Frederick Douglass begins his drive to convince the federal government to enlist African American troops.

May 24. The term "contraband" (referring to refugee slaves) is first used by Gen. Benjamin Butler at Fort Monroe, Virginia.

June. Tennessee announces that free African Americans between the ages of fifteen and fifty are welcome to enlist for military service. They are offered $8 per month plus clothing and rations.

July. After the First Battle of Bull Run, President Lincoln calls for 50,000 African Americans to serve in the war effort as auxiliary workers.

July 22. In the Crittenden Resolution, the U.S. House of Representatives states that it is not the intention or desired outcome of the war to end slavery but to preserve the Union.

July 25. The U.S. Senate approves the Crittenden Resolution.

August 6. Congress passes legislation to confiscate property of military value to the Confederacy. This includes slaves being used in support functions and as construction labor, creating the "contraband" class of African Americans.

August 30. Operating in St. Louis, Missouri, Capt. John C. Frémont confiscates Confederate property and frees slaves.

September. The U.S. secretary of the navy officially authorizes the enlistment of African Americans into the service. The U.S. Marine Corps makes a statement suggesting that African Americans will be enlisted, but in practice, enlistments are rare.

October. Brig. Gen. Thomas W. Sherman lands on the South Carolina coast with his troops and vows not to interfere with the slavery tradition.

After the Union defeat at Ball's Bluff, Virginia, Frederick Douglass complains that the U.S. Army still refuses to accept African Americans. He declares that African Americans were good enough to fight for George Washington but not for George B. McClellan, the Union commander in chief.

November. General McClellan instructs his army commanders to return runaway slaves to their owners.

African American sailors are part of Comdr. Samuel F. DuPont's forces that capture Port Royal Island and the South Carolina Sea Islands, 50 miles from Charleston.

1862

Union General David Hunter raises a regiment of African Americans to help defend the coastline of

South Carolina, Georgia, and Florida. Hunter becomes known as "Black David" because of his attempts to emancipate and arm all able-bodied male African Americans. Hunter's first African American casualty is the volunteer John Brown.

January 15. The U.S. War Department receives a request from Gen. Thomas W. Sherman to provide teachers for the Port Royal area of South Carolina to begin an education program for former slaves.

February 4. The Virginia House of Delegates discusses the possibility of recruiting free African Americans into the Confederate army, but nothing is agreed upon.

March. U.S. Congress forbids the return of runaway slaves.

April. President Lincoln ratifies the abolition of slavery in Washington, D.C., and authorizes funds to facilitate voluntary emigration of African Americans to Haiti or Liberia.

May. The 1st South Carolina Volunteer Infantry is created at Beaufort by Maj. Gen. David C. Hunter.

May 13. The Confederate gunboat *Planter* is hijacked by African American Robert Smalls in the Charleston harbor and surrendered to the U.S. Navy.

June. Sen. James H. Lane of Kansas creates the 1st Kansas Colored Volunteers, consisting of runaways and African Americans confiscated from their owners in Missouri and Arkansas.

July 17. Congress authorizes the Militia Act and the Second Confiscation Act, which authorize the U.S. Army to use African Americans as combat troops. In practice, the majority at this point remain in support functions.

August. Hunter's 1st South Carolina Volunteer Infantry is officially accepted by the War Department.

Lane's 1st Kansas Colored Volunteers swells to 500 ex-slaves and begins training at Fort Leavenworth.

Col. James Montgomery forms a battalion of troops, Montgomery's Brigade, containing African Americans, Native Americans, and whites.

August 11. From his headquarters in Corinth, Mississippi, Gen. Ulysses S. Grant orders the use of fugitive slaves for army support functions.

August 14. At a meeting of free African Americans, Lincoln suggests that African Americans be relocated in Central America.

August 21. Jefferson Davis issues a statement denouncing generals David Hunter and John Phelps for their determination to recruit slaves into the Union army.

August 25. U.S. Secretary of War Edwin M. Stanton authorizes Brig. Gen. Rufus Saxton to raise 5,000 African American troops on equal pay and rations following the failure of McClellan's Peninsular Campaign.

September. African Americans are recruited into segregated Louisiana Native Guard regiments by Gen. Benjamin F. Butler, Union commander of the Department of the Gulf.

Confederate troops marching through Maryland are said to include at least 3,000 African Americans among their 64,000 men.

September 16. Lincoln's colonization suggestion of August 14 is rejected by Frederick Douglass.

September 22. The Emancipation Proclamation is announced by Lincoln.

September 27. The 1st, 2d, and 3d regiments of the Louisiana Native Guard become the first all–African American regiments to be officially mustered into the Union army.

October 10. At the request of Jefferson Davis, Virginia drafts 4,500 African Americans as laborers to build defense works around Richmond.

October 27–28. During the Battle of Island Mound in Missouri, 225 African Americans of the 1st Kansas Colored Volunteers acquit themselves well in the two-day engagement, suffering ten killed and twelve wounded.

October 28. Montgomery's Brigade defeats Confederate guerrillas at Butler, Missouri.

November 3–10. At St. Helena Island during an expedition led by Lt. Col. O. T. Beard, Company A of the 1st South Carolina Negro Regiment participates in what is probably the first African American combat engagement of the Civil War.

December 23. Davis signs a proclamation ordering the execution of captured white officers in command of African American troops. Enlisted African Americans falling into Confederate hands will be dealt with by the state from which they are perceived to have originated.

1863

U.S. Secretary of War Edwin M. Stanton, decrees that African American troops are to be considered as auxiliaries and paid $10 per month, less $3 for clothing, compared to $13 for white troops.

William Wells Brown, a former Kentucky slave, publishes *The Black Man,* a frank description of life as a slave.

The son of David Walker, the first African American abolitionist publisher, is elected to the Massachusetts legislature.

January 1. President Lincoln's Emancipation Proclamation enters into effect. Former Confederate slaves will now be welcomed into the Union Army.

January 12. Jefferson Davis's proclamation of December 23, 1862, is approved by the Confederate Congress.

January 20. Stanton gives Governor John Andrew of Massachusetts authorization to recruit African American troops.

January 31. Company A, 1st South Carolina Negro Regiment unofficially becomes the first unit of former slaves to join the U.S. Army.

February 9. Governor Andrew orders the creation of the African American 54th Massachusetts Volunteers.

February 21. At Camp Meigs in Readville, Massachusetts, the first twenty-five volunteers enlist with the 54th Massachusetts Volunteers.

Lincoln writes to Andrew Johnson, the military governor of Tennessee, "the bare sight of 50,000 armed and drilled black soldiers upon the banks of the Mississippi would end the rebellion at once."

Thomas Wentworth Higginson's 1st and 2d South Carolina Volunteers, composed of African Americans, capture Jacksonville, Florida.

March 3. Congress passes the Conscription Act, calling for all males between the ages of twenty and forty-five to be enlisted. The act does not exclude African Americans enlisting or being used as substitutes. A payment of $300 will avoid conscription.

March 14. The Battle of Port Hudson involves five African American regiments from Louisiana. Despite gallant fighting, the attacks on the fortified position fail and heavy casualties are inflicted on the regiments.

March 21. Frederick Douglass issues his "Men of Color, to Arms" declaration.

March 26. Adj. Gen. Lorenzo Thomas receives orders from Stanton to muster African American regiments in the Mississippi Valley area.

March 30. The 54th Massachusetts Volunteers are officially mustered into the Union army.

May. Massachusetts orders the creation of the 55th Massachusetts Volunteers, which will also be composed only of African Americans.

Camp William Penn in Pennsylvania is established as a base for training African American enlistees.

May 1. The Corps d'Afrique is established under General Order No. 40 by Maj. Gen. Nathaniel P. Banks. It is proposed that the corps will have eighteen regiments of all arms.

The Confederate Congress decrees that white officers commanding African American troops will be hanged as inciters of servile insurrection. Confederate General Nathan Bedford Forrest, a former slave trader, offers $1,000 for the head of "a commander of a nigger regiment."

May 18. At Sherwood, Missouri, the 1st Kansas Colored Volunteers are involved in an engagement with Confederates.

May 22. The War Department issues General Order No. 143, opening the door for African Americans to become part of the regular U.S. Army. The order creates the United States Colored Troops, into which nearly all African American regiments will be absorbed.

May 27. The 1st Louisiana Native Guard makes six charges against the Confederate defense works at Port Hudson, Louisiana.

May 28. The 54th Massachusetts Volunteers leave camp bound for South Carolina.

June. The Combahee River raid in South Carolina takes place, led by Col. James Montgomery and Harriet Tubman, successfully freeing 800 slaves and destroying millions of dollars of Confederate property.

June 3. The 54th Massachusetts Volunteers march through Beaufort, South Carolina.

June 6. Under General Order No. 47, the Louisiana Native Guard regiments are redesignated infantry regiments of the Corps d'Afrique. Existing African American officers in three of the regiments are replaced with white officers.

June 28. At the Battle of Milliken's Bend in Vicksburg, Mississippi, African American troops successfully hold off large Confederate forces with the support of U.S. gunboats.

July. Union Gen. Quincy A. Gillmore issues an order stating that there will be no distinction between African American and white troops under his command.

July 4. The 1st Louisiana Native Guard takes part in the final assault on Vicksburg.

July 13–16. Draft riots occur in New York, predominantly involving Irish Americans. Union troops restore order after the lynching of several African Americans and widespread destruction of property. African Americans are blamed for starting the Civil War by the rioters.

July 17. The 1st Kansas Colored Volunteers take part in the Battle of Honey Springs, Indian Territory.

July 18. The Battle of Fort Wagner takes place in South Carolina, with the 54th Massachusetts Volunteers earning praise despite their failed attempts to storm a Confederate fort protecting Charleston. The unit's commander, Robert Gould Shaw, is killed along with 116 enlisted men; 156 are wounded or captured. For his bravery during the battle, Sgt. William Carney becomes the first African American to be awarded the Medal of Honor.

August. African Americans begin to be enlisted by Iowa to help meet the state's quota for military recruits.

August 23–24. In two letters, the first to Lincoln and the second to the adjutant general, Gen. Ulysses S. Grant acknowledges the value of African American troops as soldiers and their potential contribution to the war effort.

August 29. General Order No. 64 charges the provost marshal general with the task of recruiting African Americans into the Corps d'Afrique, following disappointing enlistment numbers under General Banks's direction.

September 6. Fort Wagner is occupied by Union forces after Confederate forces evacuate.

September 17. General Order No. 77, issued by General Gillmore, declares that African American troops should not be used to carry out ancillary duties for white soldiers.

October 11. The African-descent regiment, first the Iowa Volunteers, which consists of nine complete companies, is mustered into the Union army.

1864

January 2. Confederate officers in the Army of the Tennessee propose to recruit African Americans into the army in exchange for their freedom.

January 8. Massachusetts senator Henry Wilson introduces a bill to encourage African American enlistment. The bill also proposes to deal with the pay differentials between African American and white volunteers.

February, 1. The South Carolina Volunteer Infantry is redesignated the 33rd United States Colored Troops (USCT).

February 20. The Battle of Olustee in Florida ends in defeat for the Union army. Present at the engagement are the 8th and 35th USCT and the 54th Massachusetts Volunteers.

March 11. African American 1st Sgt. Stephen A. Swails of the 54th Massachusetts Volunteers is commissioned a second lieutenant by Governor John Andrew.

April. The first regiment of the Corps d'Afrique is redesignated the 7th Regiment, USCT.

April 8. The U.S. Senate approves the Thirteenth Amendment.

April 12–13. Around 300 African American and white soldiers are killed by Confederate troops led by Gen. Nathan Bedford Forrest in the so-called Fort Pillow massacre in Kentucky.

April 18. The 1st Kansas Colored Volunteers takes part in a campaign south of Little Rock, Arkansas, under Maj. Gen. Frederick Steele. When the expedition runs into Confederate opposition, it retreats and the 1st Kansas suffers high casualties when wounded or surrendered men are massacred.

May 24. Under the command of Gen. Edward A. Wild, African American troops garrisoning Fort Pocahontas, or Wilson's Landing, roughly handle the lead elements of a Confederate army driving into Virginia.

June 15. Congress finally agrees to pay African American troops on an equal basis with whites. They also free any still-enslaved wives and offspring of African American soldiers serving in the Union army.

The U.S. House of Representatives fails to approve the Thirteenth Amendment.

June 19. While serving aboard the USS *Kearsarge* off the coast of France, Joachim Pease, an African American sailor, wins the Medal of Honor for his gallantry during the sinking of the Confederate raider *Alabama.*

July 8. The Thirteenth Amendment is officially supported by President Lincoln.

July 30. The infamous "crater" is created in the Confederate defense works at Petersburg, Virginia. Over 1,300 African American troops die during the Petersburg campaign.

August 1. The U.S. War Department announces that African American troops, providing they were free men on April 19, 1861, will receive full pay backdated to January 1, 1864.

August 5. The Battle of Mobile Bay takes place, and African American John Lawson, despite injuries sustained onboard the USS *Hartford,* keeps firing his gun throughout the engagement and is later awarded the Medal of Honor.

September. Gen. William T. Sherman complains to the Federal government that he does not want the organization of African American troops under his command.

The U.S. paymaster gives $170,000 in back pay to the 54th Massachusetts Volunteers.

September 12. Jefferson Davis receives a letter from Gen. Robert E. Lee requesting that African Americans be used in support functions for the army.

September 28. The Battle of Fort Harrison takes place, with African American troops helping take the key defensive position.

September 29. The Battle of Chaffin's Farm (New Market Heights) is fought in Virginia. Thirteen of the USCT regiments are engaged in the battle and thirteen African American infantrymen would later be awarded the Medal of Honor.

November–December. Despite Sherman's protestations about the presence of African American troops, they take part in his "March to the Sea" through Georgia and are involved in the raids and destruction of Confederate war assets.

November 7. Davis suggests that the Confederate army buy slaves of its own and free them after a period of service. They would be used in support functions.

November 8. Lincoln is reelected president of the United States.

November 30. The Battle of Honey Hill, South Carolina, takes place. Five African American regiments are present, including the 54th and 55th Massachusetts Volunteers.

December. The 1st Kansas Colored Volunteers becomes the 79th Regiment, USCT.

December 3. The first all–African American U.S. Army Corps, the 25th, is created. It will be the only one.

December 6. Lincoln asks Congress to revisit the Thirteenth Amendment.

December 18. Jefferson Davis authorizes the use of African Americans to build defense works to shield Atlanta from Sherman's advancing Union army.

December 21. The 3rd U.S. Colored Cavalry begins its wartime participation in raids toward Vicksburg, Mississippi.

1865

Martin R. Delany becomes the first African American to be promoted to the rank of major in the U.S. Army.

President Abraham Lincoln proposes to grant the vote to educated or veteran African Americans.

Zimri Lew, a veteran of the 55th Massachusetts Volunteers and great-grandson of the American Revolution veteran Barzillai Lew, dies in South Carolina of dysentery.

January 1. The U.S. House of Representatives debates the Thirteenth Amendment for a second time.

January 11. Gen. Robert E. Lee writes a letter in which he recommends granting immediate freedom to African Americans who enlist in the Confederate army, and freeing their families either at the end of their service, at the end of the war, or at their death.

January 15. The 1st Regiment of the United States Colored Troops (USCT) are involved in the amphibious attack on Fort Fisher, guarding the harbor of Wilmington, North Carolina.

January 31. The U.S. House of Representatives passes the Thirteenth Amendment.

February. Singing abolitionist and pro-Union songs, the 54th and 55th Massachusetts Volunteers are the first Union regiments to enter Charleston, South Carolina.

February 18. In a letter, Lee not only agrees with proposals to enlist free African Americans and former slaves to fight for the Confederacy, but also concedes that they would make good soldiers.

March 3. Under pressure, the War Department rescinds its statement of August 1, 1864, which discriminated against those who were not freed men before April 19, 1861. Now all African American soldiers will receive equal back pay from their day of enlistment.

March 4. Lincoln is inaugurated as president of the United States for a second term.

March 13. Jefferson Davis authorizes legislation to recruit 300,000 slaves into the Confederate army, with the promise of freedom if they are honorably discharged.

March 31–April 9. The Battle of Fort Blakely, Alabama, takes place. Eleven USCT regiments take part in the engagement.

April 2. The Confederate capital, Richmond, Virginia, is abandoned and African American troops of the 5th Massachusetts Cavalry are among the first to enter the city.

April 3. Enlistment of African Americans into the Confederate army officially begins.

African American residents of Richmond warmly welcome a visit by Lincoln to their city.

April 9. After taking part in the Petersburg and Richmond campaigns, African Americans are present to witness Lee's surrender at Appomattox Court House. Among the Confederates paroled in the aftermath are thirty-six African Americans.

April 14. John Wilkes Booth, a Confederate fanatic, shoots Lincoln at Ford's Theatre in Washington, D.C.

April 15. Lincoln dies and is replaced by his vice president, Andrew Johnson.

May 11–14. The Battles of White's Ranch and Palmetto Ranch take place in Texas. The 62d Colored Infantry Regiment takes part in the latter engagement, the last battle of the Civil War.

May 12. Gen. Oliver O. Howard becomes head of the new Freedmen's Bureau, which assists in the postwar settlement of African Americans.

August. The 54th Massachusetts Volunteers is mustered out.

December 18. The Thirteenth Amendment is ratified by twenty-seven states, with only Delaware, Kentucky, New Jersey, and Mississippi rejecting the amendment.

1866

Across the South, in the aftermath of the Civil War, states recruit large numbers of African Americans to ensure Republican control of the states and to maintain law and order. Twenty-two states and the District of Columbia create African American National Guard units, with black company and field-grade officers, unlike the majority of existing federal units.

May 1–3. Race riots in Memphis, Tennessee, claim the lives of forty-six African Americans. Houses, schools, and churches are burned by whites. These events prompt the creation of Fort Pickering, to be garrisoned by African American troops who will patrol the city.

July 28. Against severe opposition, Republican congressmen manage to establish the concept that African Americans would serve in the armed forces during peacetime. The ensuing reorganization of the U.S. Army creates six African American regiments, four infantry and two cavalry. The 9th and 10th Cavalry, as well as the 38th, 39th, 40th, and 41st Infantries, of African Americans are excluded from the artillery, as it was believed that they lacked the necessary technical experience and skills.

1867

August. Riding out of Fort Arbuckle, Kansas, Company F of the 10th Cavalry engages Sioux Indians.

September 19. Troop G of the 9th Cavalry engages Native Americans 45 miles from Fort Hays, Kansas.

1868

February. The 10th Cavalry engages in patrols against Comanche and Kiowa Indians.

June. Gen. Philip Sheridan orders the 10th Cavalry to Fort Gibson, Nebraska, for future operations against the Comanche and Kiowa.

September 15. Troop I, 10th Cavalry, holds off 700 Lakota and Cheyenne warriors for eight days, until they are relieved by Troop H at Arikaree Island, Republican River, Nebraska.

October. Troop I, 10th Cavalry, is attacked by 500 Native Americans en route to Beaver Creek, Nebraska.

1869

The four African American regular army regiments (38th, 39th, 40th, and 41st) are reorganized into two infantry regiments, the 24th and 25th.

African American Robert Brown Elliot becomes adjutant general of South Carolina. His militia are charged with the task of dealing with the Ku Klux Klan.

June 11. Native Americans attack Camp Wichita, Texas, in an attempt to drive off 10th Cavalry horses.

1870

Robert Brown Elliot becomes the first African American to command the South Carolina National Guard.

May 20–21. For his efforts during an action with the Kickapoo Indians in Texas, Sgt. Emanuel Stance of the 9th Cavalry is awarded the Medal of Honor.

July. James W. Smith from South Carolina becomes the first African American to be admitted to the U.S. Military Academy at West Point.

July 4. Maj. Zenas R. Bliss recruits Seminole Negro (mixed African American and Seminole Native American blood) scouts to operate with the army against Native Americans in Texas. Four of the scouts will later be awarded the Medal of Honor.

1871

January 24. Comanche Indians kill African American frontiersman Britton "Brit" Johnson and two African American cowboys.

May. The 10th Cavalry escorts Gen. William T. Sherman to arrest Native American leaders at Fort Sill, Indian Territory (Oklahoma).

September 19. Troop B of the 10th Cavalry is attacked by a large Native American war party at Fort Sill.

1872

John Henry Conyers from South Carolina becomes the first African American to be admitted to the U.S. Naval Academy at Annapolis. He later resigns without completing his studies.

December 26. The Medal of Honor is awarded to seaman Joseph B. Noil after he saves a colleague who had fallen overboard.

1874

June 26. After suffering four years of racism and ostracism, James Webster Smith leaves West Point without completing his studies.

August 22–23. The 10th Cavalry fights off 400 Comanche and Kiowa at the Wichita Agency.

1875

April–December. Companies of the 24th and 25th Infantry and the 10th Cavalry survey the Great Plains.

April 6. Elements of the 10th Cavalry escorting the Cheyenne Indian leader Black Horse are ambushed at Cheyenne Agency, Indian Territory. They chase the Native Americans for 400 miles.

April 25. Pompey Factor, Isaac Payne, and John Ward win the Medal of Honor for their actions at Eagle's Nest Crossing, Pecos River, Texas, while serving with the Seminole Negro scouts.

July 14. The 10th Cavalry and the 24th and 25th Infantry, with Seminole Negro scouts, begin their four-month tour with Shafter's Expedition into the Staked Plains, Texas.

October 19. Seminole Negro scouts discover and destroy a large Native American camp near Laguna Sabinas, Texas.

November. Shafter's Expedition ends after a 2,000-mile journey.

1876

June 25. While operating as an interpreter with the U.S. Army, African American Isaiah Dorman is reputedly killed at the Battle of the Little Bighorn along with elements of Gen. George Armstrong Custer's 7th Cavalry.

July 30. Seminole Negro scouts are attacked by Lipan and Kickapoo Indians at Saragossa, Mexico.

1877

March. At St. Angela, Texas, cowboys cut the sergeant's stripes from the uniform of an African American sergeant in the 10th Cavalry. In the ensuing fight one soldier is killed and another wounded and three of the cowboys are shot and killed. Nine Buffalo Soldiers, the generic name given to African Americans in U.S. Army, probably by Native Americans, are indicted for murder.

March 2. Rutherford B. Hayes becomes president of the United States, and in a deal with the Democrats the military reconstruction period is terminated.

April 24. Many African American National Guard units in the Southern states are deactivated following the withdrawal of federal troops from Louisiana.

June 10. Elements of the 10th Cavalry and Seminole Negro scouts intercept Mexican revolutionaries at Devil's River on the Rio Grande.

June 15. African American Henry O. Flipper, a former Georgia slave, becomes the first African American to graduate from West Point.

July. Forty members of the 10th Cavalry march 400 miles in eighty-six hours without water, in search of Native Americans.

September 28. Seminole Negro scouts and Buffalo Soldiers cross the Rio Grande into Mexico.

October–December. Seminole Negro scouts cross and recross the Rio Grande and search the Santa Rosa Mountains for Native Americans.

1879

Henry O. Flipper joins the 10th Cavalry.

September 4. Apache Indian chief Victorio attacks Company E of the 9th Cavalry, killing five of the Buffalo Soldiers.

September 16. Two companies of the 10th Cavalry are ambushed by Victorio in the Black Range mountains in New Mexico.

1880

January–May. The 9th Cavalry carries out operations in southern New Mexico against Apache Indian leader Victorio.

May 12. Mescalero warriors are chased to the Rio Grande by the 10th Cavalry.

July. Lt. Henry O. Flipper of the 10th Cavalry rides

100 miles in twenty-one hours after spotting Victorio's scouts.

August 6. The Battle of Rattlesnake Springs, Texas, takes place. Victorio is ambushed by the 10th Cavalry but flees under cover of darkness.

August 11. The 10th Cavalry continues its pursuit of Victorio to the Rio Grande.

1881

Tennessee is the first Southern state to segregate its public transportation.

1882

Henry O. Flipper is court-martialed for embezzling funds.

The Medal of Honor is awarded to African American Thomas Boyne, a member of the 9th Cavalry, for his bravery in two actions with Native Americans in New Mexico.

1886

Former slave Allen Allensworth joins the U.S. Army as a chaplain. He later establishes schools for African American soldiers and their children at Fort Supply, Indian Territory, and Fort Bayard, New Mexico.

1887

African American John Alexander of Ohio becomes the second African American graduate of West Point.

1889

African American Charles Young becomes the third African American to graduate from West Point.

May 11. The Wham Paymaster Robbery takes place; Sgt. Benjamin Brown and Cpl. Isaiah Mays are later awarded the Medal of Honor for defending the paymaster from robbery.

1891

May 25. Troop K of the 9th Cavalry becomes the first African American troops to serve east of the Mississippi River when they are ordered by the secretary of war to move from Fort Myer in Washington, D.C., to Nebraska.

1892

Troopers of the 9th Cavalry shoot up Suggs, Wyoming, after enduring racial harassment.

1893

Members of the 9th Cavalry open fire in a saloon near Fort Concho, Texas, after Texas Rangers make several physical attacks on African American soldiers.

Soldiers of the 9th Cavalry save an African American Civil War veteran from being lynched in Crawford, Nebraska.

1896

The "worthies" of Salt Lake City, Utah, send a delegation to Washington complaining about the deployment of the 24th Infantry at Fort Douglas.

Lt. James Moss leads a detachment of the 25th Infantry on a 1,000-mile cycling maneuver.

1897

Lt. James Moss and twenty-four volunteers of the 25th Infantry cycle 1,900 miles from Fort Missoula to St. Louis, Missouri.

1898

Benjamin O. Davis Sr. joins the District of Columbia National Guard as a lieutenant.

February 15. Twenty-two African American sailors are among the 250 men killed when the USS *Maine* is blown up in the Havana harbor.

April 19. The 24th Infantry leaves Salt Lake City, Utah, en route to Cuba via Tampa, Florida, to fight in the Spanish-American War. They are given a rousing farewell.

April 21. The Spanish-American War begins. All four African American regular army regiments will see action. Sixteen regiments of African American volunteers are recruited. One of the regiments will see action.

May 1. John Jordan, an African American gunner's mate on board the USS *Olympia,* participates in firing the first shell at the Spanish fleet during the Battle of Manila Bay.

June 6. In Tampa, Florida, shortly before embarking for Cuba, the 24th and 25th Infantry are involved in brawls with the 2d Georgia Volunteer Infantry and racist local businessmen as a result of the rumor that Ohio volunteers had used an African American child for target practice.

June 24. The Battle of Las Guásimas takes place. In the first major engagement of the Spanish-American War, the 10th Cavalry is among those engaged under the command of former Confederate general Joseph Wheeler.

July 1–2. The Battles of San Juan Ridge, Kettle Hill, and El Caney take place. The 24th Infantry and the 9th and 10th Cavalry are involved in these major engagements. Edward Baker, Jr., wins the Medal of Honor for his bravery during these battles.

1899

African American National Guard units from Virginia are inactivated following President William McKinley's instruction to attach the 1st and 2d Infantry battalions to the 6th Virginia Infantry. African American officers' ability to command is questioned and the officers resign.

The 9th Cavalry becomes the first African American unit to be assigned as part of the regular garrison of the Washington Presidio.

March. The 9th U.S. Volunteer Infantry, an African American unit, arrives in Cuba.

March 2. The 9th and 10th Cavalry and the 48th and 49th Volunteer Infantry are ordered to the Philippines.

May 15. L Company of the 24th Infantry becomes the first African American unit to be stationed in Alaska.

July. The 24th Infantry is transferred from the Washington Presidio to fight in the Philippine Insurrection with the other three existing African American regular regiments. Two regiments of African American volunteers, the 48th and 49th, will also see service in the Philippines.

November 17. David Fagan, an African American enlisted man in the 24th Infantry, deserts the army and joins the Filipino rebels.

November 17–18. The 25th Infantry storms the island of Luzon in the Philippines.

1900

Congress authorizes the creation of ten new U.S. Army regiments; none will be open to African Americans.

January. The 25th Infantry frees American prisoners near Mount Arayat in the Philippines.

1901

The U.S. Navy decides on a new policy that precludes encouraging the recruitment of African Americans. Current African American servicemen are reduced to support roles.

February. In the immediate aftermath of the capture of the Filipino rebel leader Emilio Aguinaldo, the 48th and 49th Volunteer Infantry are sent back to the United States and disbanded.

April. Charles Young, the third African American to graduate from West Point, is sent to the Philippines for an eighteen-month tour of duty.

May 19. Benjamin O. Davis Sr. becomes the first African American enlisted man to be commissioned as a second lieutenant in the regular U.S. Army.

December. David Fagan, the 24th Infantry deserter, is killed by a bounty hunter.

1902

Following the reduction in federal control of the National Guard under the terms of the Militia Act, African Americans are excluded from what had been the state militias, with the exception of six states and the District of Columbia.

1903

African American cavalry become the first black troops to patrol California national parks, while

Capt. Charles Young of the 9th Cavalry is appointed acting superintendent of Sequoia National Park for the duration of the summer.

During Theodore Roosevelt's visits to San Francisco and the Presidio, members of the 9th Cavalry become the first African Americans to be part of a presidential honor guard.

1906

A study by the U.S. Army War College is initiated that will conclude that African Americans have neither the intelligence nor the technical skills to be allowed to join artillery units.

Chaplain Allen Allensworth becomes the first African American lieutenant colonel in the regular U.S. Army.

The U.S. Army now has only four African American officers, including Charles Young and Benjamin O. Davis, Sr.

August 13. A brief but violent riot by members of the 25th Infantry takes place in Brownsville, Texas, during which one white man is killed and another wounded.

November 6. One hundred sixty-seven members of the 25th Infantry (three companies) are dishonorably discharged for their involvement in the Brownsville riot.

1907–1908

The 25th Infantry carries out operations in the Philippines against Moro tribesmen.

1908

November. Fourteen of the men dishonorably discharged from the 25th Infantry in November of the previous year are allowed to reenlist.

1909

April. African American Matthew Henson, Adm. Robert E. Peary's assistant, accompanies Admiral Peary and four Eskimos on an expedition to reach the North Pole.

1916

March. Following a raid into New Mexico by Pancho Villa, the Mexican bandit leader, President Woodrow Wilson sends two African American regiments as part of Brig. Gen. John J. Pershing's force to capture Villa.

October. African American Eugene Jacques Bullard, having served in the French Foreign Legion and the French infantry, joins the French Air Service. He will fly over twenty combat missions, receiving a number of French decorations for gallantry.

1916–1917

African Americans account for 2 percent, or 20,000 men, of all regular army and National Guard units. Only three African Americans are commissioned officers.

1917

Dr. Lewis T. Wright serves as a first lieutenant in the Medical Corps. He pioneers the injection of smallpox vaccines, which later becomes common practice for the regular U.S. Army.

Qualified African American nurses are excluded from the American Red Cross on the basis that the U.S. Army will not accept African American women.

African American Lloyd A. Hall is appointed the assistant chief inspector of powder and explosives at the U.S. Ordnance Department.

Col. Charles Young, the highest-ranking African American officer, is forced to retire due to ill health. This is on the eve of the possibility of his being placed in command of an all–African American unit, which was vigorously opposed by Washington authorities.

Vertner W. Tandy becomes the first African American officer in the New York National Guard. He joins as a first lieutenant and is later promoted to the rank of major. Later, he becomes a prominent architect.

Alton Augustus Adams becomes the first African American bandleader in the U.S. Navy.

March 25. African American major James E. Walker's District of Columbia National Guard is assigned the task of protecting Washington, D.C.

April. The American Negro Loyal Legion informs Washington that 10,000 African American volunteers are standing by for an immediate draft into the army.

April 4. Following President Woodrow Wilson's request to Congress to declare war on Germany, the U.S. Senate agrees.

April 6. The U.S. House of Representatives agrees with the war declaration on Germany.

May 18. In the Selective Service Act, Congress authorizes the registration and drafting of all males between twenty-one and thirty years of age. On the first day 700,000 African Americans volunteer.

May 19. Fourteen officer-training camps are established by Congress for white officers. The first all–African American officer-training school is established at Fort Des Moines, Iowa.

May 21. Leo Pinckney becomes the first African American to be drafted into the U.S. Army for World War I.

June. Four hundred African American merchantmen are among those first shipped to France.

June 5. The first of four registrations for World War I begins. Some 2,290,527 African Americans would register, accounting for 9.63 percent of the total registration.

June 15. African American officer-training classes begin at Fort Des Moines. Two hundred and fifty of the initial class are noncommissioned officers from the 24th and 25th Infantry and the 9th and 10th Cavalry.

August 23. The Houston Riots take place when African Americans of the 24th Infantry from Camp Logan attack a police station, killing sixteen citizens and police and wounding twelve others. The riots are the culmination of several weeks of intense racial harassment. Many of the soldiers will be given life sentences and twenty-nine are condemned to hang.

October. The African American 92d Infantry Division (known as the Buffalo Division, comprising the 365th, 366th, 367th, and 368th Infantry Regiments) is activated, composed of draftees.

October 5. Emmett J. Scott, the former secretary of Booker T. Washington, becomes special assistant to the U.S. secretary of war. His responsibility is to ensure that there is no discrimination in the application of the Selective Service Act.

October 15–17. The first 639 African American officers are commissioned from Fort Des Moines. The school will eventually produce 1,400 commissioned officers.

December. The 93d Infantry Division (the 369th, 370th, 371st, 372d Infantry Regiments) is created.

December 11. Without prior notification, the first African American to be condemned to die as a result of the Houston Riots is executed.

December 12. The 369th Infantry Regiment (known as the Harlem Hellfighters) becomes the first African American unit to be sent to Europe. Prior to their embarkation, members of the regiment are involved in the Spartanburg incident in South Carolina.

1918

The Committee on Public Information accredits Ralph Waldo Tyler as the only African American war correspondent with the responsibility to report specifically on African American war news.

In Manhattan, Kansas, a theater owner is fined after refusing to allow an African American sergeant to enter the premises.

March 10. The 369th Infantry Regiment is transferred to the French 16th Division.

April. The 372d Infantry Regiment arrives in France and is later attached to various French divisions.

June. The 371st Infantry Regiment is attached to the French 157th Red Hand Division.

July. W. E. B. Du Bois writes an editorial in *The Crisis,* the publication of the National Association for the Advancement of Colored People, calling on African Americans to close ranks with white Americans to support the combat troops in France.

The 370 Infantry Regiment joins the French 36th Division on the Meuse-Argonne front.

July 6. The 369 Infantry faces a German attack at Minacort.

July 18. The 369th Infantry is involved in the Marne counteroffensive.

July–August. The 370th is involved in the Oise-Aisne offensive.

August. The 92d Infantry Division is sent to the front, where they will remain under fire until November 1918.

The 369th Infantry's band is ordered to the rear to undertake a tour of camps and hospitals to help raise morale.

August 7. A confidential memorandum is written by French liaison officers at the American Expeditionary Force headquarters, advising French officers how they should deal with African American troops. They are advised to keep their distance from African American men, only give praise when absolutely essential, and ensure that they have no opportunity to meet French women.

August 12. The 92d Division moves to the front line at St. Dié to the southeast of Metz.

August 24. The commander of the 372d Division requests that his African American officers be replaced with white men.

August 30. The 92d Division defeats a German counterattack at Frapelle.

September. African American servicemen in Services of Supplies (SOS) units unload an average of 25,000 tons of military supplies per day.

The Black Yankees, the 809th Pioneer Infantry, suffer enormous losses from a Spanish influenza epidemic during their fourteen-day voyage to France.

September 3. African American troops are the target of propaganda leaflets from the Germans, urging them to turn their backs on the Allies and fight for Germany.

September 14. The 371st Division is ordered to Somme Bione, Champagne, to take part in the Meuse-Argonne offensive.

September 16. Six more African Americans are executed as a result of the Houston Riots.

September 20. The 368th Infantry Regiment of the 92d Division is moved to engage German forces in the Argonne Forest region.

September 26–October 5. The 369th Infantry takes part in the Meuse-Argonne offensive.

September 28. The 372d Infantry joins the Champagne offensive and takes Bussy Farm.

October 1. The 372d Infantry relieves the 371st Infantry at Trieres Farm and captures the railroad center at Monthois.

October 7. The 372d Infantry is relieved by the French 125th Division.

The 92d Division is transferred to the Marbache sector.

November. Charles Young is reinstated by the U.S. Army after having ridden a horse from Ohio to Washington, D.C., to prove his fitness. He is not given the command he craves and instead is sent to Fort Grant, Illinois, to train African American recruits.

The 1st Battalion, 367th Infantry Regiment, is awarded the Croix de Guerre for its combat performance and bravery at Metz.

The 369th Infantry is the first Allied force to reach the Rhine River.

November 7. The 92d Division suffers 500 casualties but takes its objective before the armistice is declared.

November 10. The 92d Division is ordered to take the heights to the east of Champeny.

November 11. The 370th Infantry fights in the last engagement of World War I when they capture a German train moments before the armistice.

November 13. Following the flu epidemic, the Army Nurses Corps admits eighteen African American nurses; half are sent to Camp Grant, Illinois, and the others assigned to Camp Sherman, Ohio. They will live in segregated housing but will work in integrated hospitals.

1919

African American veterans of World War I return home and with the exception of the 369th Infantry Regiment, which parades in New York with white soldiers, all others are mustered out with little acclaim.

Major rioting about race occurs in Illinois, Nebraska, Texas, and Washington, D.C., during which ten war veterans are among the seventy-five African Americans lynched by white mobs.

The U.S. War Department imposes restrictions on the enlistment of African Americans into the army, only welcoming reenlistments.

February. W. E. B. Du Bois travels to Paris to represent the National Association for the Advancement of Colored People at the peace conference. He goes on to organize the Pan-African Congress.

March 15. The American Legion, a veterans group, is formed in Paris, France. African American veterans are allowed to join, but in segregated positions.

May 9. James Reese Europe, a famous African American musician and composer who had been in the 369th Infantry during World War I, is murdered by Herbert Wright.

July 14. African American soldiers are banned by the U.S. Army from taking part in the victory parade on Bastille Day in Paris.

July 28. African American veterans meet at the 370th regimental armory in Chicago, determined to protect themselves with weapons during the height of the Chicago race riots.

1920

June. The four regular African American regiments, the 9th and 10th Cavalry and 24th and 25th Infantry, survive an army downsizing after Congress passes the National Defense Act.

1921

The 3d Battalion, 24th Infantry Regiment, is disbanded, having languished in New Mexico after the 1917 Houston Riots.

1922

Joseph H. Ward becomes the first African American to head a Veterans' Bureau hospital as the chief medical officer at Tuskegee, Alabama.

The 24th Infantry Regiment, now stationed at Fort Benning, Georgia, is reduced in size to just over 800 men.

Former Canadian Air Corps African American veteran Hubert Julian hits the headlines by parachuting onto the rooftop of a Harlem optician's store for publicity.

January 8. Col. Charles Young, the U.S. Army's highest-ranking African American officer, dies while on military liaison duty in Nigeria.

Bessie Coleman, the first African American licensed female pilot, makes her first exhibition flight in Chicago.

1923

Bessie Coleman makes a flight in the largest aircraft yet flown by a woman.

The U.S. Navy ceases recruitment of African American stewards, preferring Filipinos.

1924

Hubert Julian parachutes onto the roof of City College, New York.

July 4. Julian fails in his attempt to fly from Harlem to Liberia.

1925

A report from the Army War College recommends that African Americans should not be used as military pilots due to their inherent cowardice and lack of intelligence.

1926

Bessie Coleman dies when her aircraft crashes during an exhibition flight at Jacksonville, Florida.

1929

Alonzo Parham joins the U.S. Military Academy at West Point. He is the first African American candidate to join since Charles Young. Parham leaves after one year.

1932

African Americans are now able to enlist in the U.S. Navy, ending a restriction that had been in place since the end of World War I. The majority are admitted into the Filipino Steward's Branch.

Benjamin O. Davis Jr., son of Benjamin O. Davis Sr., who both go on to become generals, arrives at West Point. He would become a significant influence in World War II when African American combat pilots were deployed.

1936

Benjamin O. Davis Jr. graduates from West Point. He is only the fourth African American to graduate and the first to receive his commission in the twentieth century.

The U.S. Naval Academy admits James Johnson, but due to ill health he resigns after eight months.

December. The first African American volunteers leave New York bound for the Spanish Civil War.

1937

The U.S. Naval Academy admits George Trivers as a cadet; he leaves after one month due to academic problems.

Willa B. Brown becomes the first African American woman to obtain a commercial pilot's license.

African Americans join the Abraham Lincoln Battalion and head to Spain to fight in the civil war.

February 23. The Abraham Lincoln Battalion fights its first battle of the Spanish Civil War at Pingarron Hill.

March. Salaria Kee, a nurse from Harlem, sails for Spain. She will be the only African American nurse to serve in Spain.

July 5. African Americans are involved in the Brunete offensive in Spain.

December 1937–February 1938. African Americans are involved in the long-running Battle of Teruel in Spain.

1938

Willa B. Brown and her former flight instructor, Cornelius R. Coffey, found the National Airmen's Association of America and establish the Coffey School of Aeronautics. The school will train African American pilots and act as a preliminary training base for the Tuskegee Airmen.

Benjamin O. Davis Sr. becomes commander of the 369th Infantry Regiment.

October 4. Republicans decide to withdraw the International Brigades from Spain.

October 29. The last of the 200 U.S. members of the International Brigade leave Spain via Barcelona.

1939

The number of African American troops in the U.S. Army drops to 4,000. In response the army mounts a campaign to increase its African American component to 10 percent, which would reflect the black percentage of the general U.S. population.

By this year some 100 African Americans have become certified civilian pilots.

The 47th and 48th Quartermaster Regiments are created by the U.S. Army. They are wholly African American.

Wyoming senator Harry Schwartz begins his attempts at persuading the secretary of war to allow African Americans into the Army Air Corps.

May. African American Rayford W. Logan heads the newly formed Committee for the Participation of Negroes in National Defense. The committee is instrumental in inserting nondiscriminatory clauses in the 1940 Selective Training and Service Act.

The African American newspaper *Chicago Defender* and the National Airmen's Association of America support black pilots Chauncey Spencer and Dale White in their attempts to convince Congress to include African Americans in the Civilian Pilot Training Program. Missouri senator Harry S. Truman is among those who support their efforts.

June 27. The Civilian Pilot Training Program is created by Congress. Only one of the existing schools participating in the program will accept African American pilots. Willa B. Brown lobbies the Army Air Corps to include African Americans. The Army Air Corps continues to exclude African American pilots, but seven other schools enroll African Americans for flight training.

September 3. Following the German invasion of Poland, Great Britain and France declare war on Germany. The United States reiterates its neutrality.

1940

The U.S. War Department begins preparations for the country's inevitable involvement in World War II, suggesting a 6 percent quota for African American troops in the armed forces, despite African Americans accounting for 10 percent of the population.

Benjamin O. Davis Sr. becomes the first African American brigadier general and given command of the 4th Brigade of the 2d Cavalry Division at Fort Riley, Kansas, which includes the 9th and 10th Cavalry.

August 1. The first chemical decontamination company, an all–African American unit, is created by the U.S. Army as part of its continuing attempts to absorb increasing numbers of African American recruits.

August 15. The 41st General Service Engineer Regiment is created, another all–African American U.S. Army unit.

September 15. The Selective Training and Service Act is signed by President Franklin D. Roosevelt. It calls for the first peacetime draft in American history.

September 17. African American leaders and spokespersons present a seven-point mobilization program to the secretary of the navy and the assistant secretary of war. Among many issues raised are the desegregation of the armed forces and the inclusion of African Americans in flight training.

September 27. President Roosevelt meets with prominent African American leaders on the issue of segregation and the entrance of African Americans into the branches of the military.

October. The War Department confirms its segregation policy and establishes a quota for African American enlistment.

October 1. Dr. Charles Richard Drew, an African American, becomes the director of the First Plasma Division, Blood Transfusion Association. He is a blood plasma pioneer who created the blood-bank system.

October 9. Roosevelt issues a statement claiming that desegregation would not be in the interest of national security and defense.

November 1. African American William H. Hastie, the dean of Howard University Law School, is appointed civilian aide to the secretary of war in matters of black rights.

December 18. The U.S. Army Air Corps finally concedes on the issue of flight training for African Americans by formulating plans to set up a specialist facility at the Tuskegee Institute in Alabama.

1941

The 366th Infantry Regiment is activated by the U.S. Army and becomes the first regular army unit to have African American officers.

Willa B. Brown is appointed the training coordinator for the Civil Aeronautics Administration and becomes a teacher in the Civilian Pilot Training Program.

By the end of the year some 97,725 African Americans are serving in either the European or Pacific theaters in World War II.

January. Ernest Calloway becomes the first African American to refuse to be inducted into the U.S. Army on the grounds of segregation. The labor organizer and civil rights spokesperson is a member of the group Conscientious Objectors against Jim Crow. He is imprisoned and becomes the first of 400 African Americans classified as conscientious objectors during World War II. Others refuse on religious grounds or due to the quota system.

A. Philip Randolph, the labor and civil rights leader and founding president of the Brotherhood of Sleeping Car Porters, proposes a march on Washington, D.C., to protest against both military discrimination and labor practices. The march is set for July 1941.

January 9. Henry L. Stimson, the secretary of war, approves the foundation of the flight-training program at the Tuskegee Institute in Alabama.

January 13. The first African American armored unit, the 78th Tank Battalion, is created.

February. The 1st Battalion, 351st Field Artillery Regiment, is activated at Camp Livingston, Louisiana. It will later be designated the 351st Field Artillery Battalion.

March. The 78th Tank Battalion begins its training program at Fort Knox, Kentucky.

May 8. The 78th Tank Battalion is redesignated the 758th Tank Battalion and later becomes one of the three African American tank battalions (together with the 761st and 784th) that will form the 5th Tank Group. The battalions consist of African American enlisted men and white officers.

June. An investigative committee is set up to examine African American opportunities in the U.S. Navy and U.S. Marine Corps.

June 25. Roosevelt issues Executive Order 8802, aiming to end discrimination in the war industry. It establishes the Committee on Fair Employment Practice and aims to defuse the call for a march on Washington.

June 29. Brig. Gen. Benjamin O. Davis Sr. is assigned to the U.S. Army Inspector General's Office to carry out inspections of African American troops.

July. The U.S. Army establishes its integrated officers' cadet schools. In the first six months over 2,000 are admitted; only 21 are African American.

July 19. At the Tuskegee Institute, African American pilots begin their training with the U.S. Army Air Corps.

August 4. At Huntsville Arsenal, Alabama, construction begins on a factory that will manufacture colored smoke munitions, toxic gases, and incendiary weapons. The factory will employ large numbers of African Americans. The ceremony is led by commanding officer Col. Rollo C. Ditto.

August 25. At the Tuskegee Institute, African Americans begin their flight instruction phase of training.

September. Fourteen percent of U.S. Army recruits, and 25 percent of those drafted, are African American.

September 2. Capt. Benjamin O. Davis Jr. becomes the first African American in the U.S. Army Air Corps to complete a solo flight.

October. Frank Knox, the secretary of the navy, confirms U.S. Navy policy to admit the majority of African Americans into the Steward's Branch.

October 25. At the Redstone Arsenal in Alabama, the Ordnance Corps begins construction of a chemical ammunition, rifle grenade, and bomb factory that will employ large numbers of African Americans.

December 7. At Pearl Harbor, U.S. Navy messman Dorie Miller, an African American, is one of those killed during the preemptive Japanese attack on the U.S. naval facility. He is credited with shooting down several Japanese aircraft while manning a machine gun on the USS *Arizona*.

1942

The U.S. Army combines the African American 9th and 10th Cavalry into the 2d Cavalry Division and at Fort Huachuca, Arizona, creates the first World War II African American infantry division, the 93d.

Following a number of critical articles in African American newspapers about treatment of African Americans in the United States and black participation in the war effort, the U.S. Justice Department threatens to take action against twenty editors and charge them with sedition.

Lt. Della H. Raney becomes the first African American chief nurse in the U.S. Army Nurse Corps while serving at the Tuskegee Army Air Field, Alabama.

January 9. The U.S. Navy and U.S. Marine Corps are instructed by President Franklin D. Roosevelt to accept African Americans into their regular military units.

January 17. In Alexandria, Louisiana, African American soldiers are involved in a fight with local law enforcement officers.

February. Plans are approved for the construction of the Alcan Highway through Canada to Alaska, enabling a link from the United States to its most threatened region. The African American 93d, 95th, and 97th Engineer General Service Regiments will help build this road link.

The commandant of the U.S. Coast Guard, Rear Adm. Russell R. Waesche, proposes the enlistment of 150 African Americans, to be trained at Manhattan Beach, New York.

February 3. The U.S. Navy's General Board presents its proposal to enlist 5,000 African Americans in positions not within the Steward's Branch. It is rejected by President Roosevelt and U.S. Navy Secretary Frank Knox because they wanted integration, not a compromise.

February 25. The U.S. Navy's General Board resubmits its African American enlistment plans.

March. John Roosevelt (Jackie) Robinson is drafted and attends basic training at Fort Riley, Kansas. He applies for the Officers Candidate School and is rejected. Robinson, a superb athlete who later broke the color bar in major league baseball, needs the contacts and influence of African American boxer Joe Louis to reverse the decision.

At Manhattan Beach, New York, the first 150 African American volunteers for the U.S. Coast Guard begin training.

African American civilians account for less than 3 percent of those employed in war production.

March 7. Capt. Benjamin O. Davis Jr. and four other African Americans graduate from the Tuskegee airfield program. They are assigned to the 99th Pursuit Squadron.

March 31. Roosevelt and Knox approve the U.S. Navy's plans to allow African Americans into general service positions.

April. The African American 91st and 96th U.S. Army Engineer Battalions arrive in Australia to build allied airfields.

April–May. Fort Huachuca receives 6,000 men who are eventually assigned to the 93d Infantry Division.

April 1. The 761st Black Panther Tank Battalion, an African American unit, is activated at Camp Claiborne, Louisiana, with predominantly African American officers.

April 2. After being assigned to the 93d Infantry Division, the 24th Infantry Regiment leaves Fort Benning for San Francisco prior to embarkation to the Pacific.

April 7. The U.S. Navy announces the opening up of its General Service Branch to African Americans. In practice African Americans are still restricted to steward and labor duties, or shore installations and harbor craft.

May. The U.S. Coast Guard begins accepting African American recruits into all areas of the service.

May 4. The 24th Infantry Regiment is assigned to garrison duty in the New Hebrides.

May 15. The Women's Auxiliary Army Corps (WAAC) is created, changing to the Women's Army Corps (WAC) in 1943. Charity Adams Earley later becomes the first African American woman to be commissioned.

May 22. The 332d Fighter Group, consisting of the 100th, 301st, and 302d Fighter Squadrons, is activated at Tuskegee Army Air Field.

June. The first of 167,000 African Americans are inducted into the U.S. Navy under the terms of the Selective Service Board. The first African American trainees report to Camp Robert Smalls at the Great Lakes Naval Training Station. The first African American man to report is Doreston Carman Jr.

June 1. The U.S. Marine Corps breaks its 167-year tradition of being a whites-only section of the armed forces. Howard P. Perry is the first of 20,000 African Americans to serve in the marines during World War II. They will all be trained at Montford Point, North Carolina.

June 18. Harvard University medical student Bernard W. Robinson becomes the first African American to be given a reserve commission as a doctor in the U.S. Navy.

July 20. At Fort Des Moines, Iowa, the first forty African American women recruits begin officer training. Although the women are trained alongside white officer trainees, they live in segregated facilities.

July 30. Roosevelt signs and enacts the necessary legislation to create the Women Accepted for Volunteer Emergency Service (WAVES) military unit. Initially the secretary of the navy excludes African American women on the grounds that there are few African American men serving on U.S. Navy vessels.

August. Following the successful incorporation of the first 150 African Americans into the U.S. Coast Guard, more are recruited and trained, with 300 posted on active duty.

August 26. Howard P. Perry reports to Montford Point as the first-ever African American member of the U.S. Marine Corps. Some 12,738 African American marines will serve overseas during World War II.

The U.S. Marine Corps creates the first two African American combat units, the 51st and 52d Defense Battalions. They are placed under the command of Samuel A. Woods Jr. to form the 51st Composite Defense Battalion. By the end of World War II African Americans would account for just 2 percent of the U.S. Marine Corps' total manpower, including 8,000 serving as ammunition loaders and stevedores.

The Advisory Committee on Negro Troop Policies is formed, chaired by Assistant Secretary of War John J. McCloy. Also on the committee is Brig. Gen. Benjamin O. Davis Sr., who is now with the Inspector General's Office.

September. The War Shipping Agency appoints Hugh Mulzac as captain of the SS *Booker T. Washington*. He had been asking for his own ship for twenty-five of his thirty-five-year naval service.

Two hundred African Americans from Chicago report to Fort Leonard Wood, Missouri, to attend the Engineer Replacement Center for combat engineer training.

October. The first thirty-six African American women graduate from the officer-training facility at Fort Des Moines, Iowa, and are inducted into the WAAC.

The U.S. Navy accepts the first African Americans into the new Construction Battalions. Training begins at Camps Bradford and Allen in Virginia.

October 15. The 92d Infantry Division is reactivated by the U.S. Army at Fort McClellan, Alabama. Some 12,000 enlisted men and 600 African American officers will serve in the division during World War II. Two hundred of the 92d Infantry officers are white.

November. In Bisbee, Arizona, 200 men of the 369th Infantry are involved in a gun battle with 100 military and civilian police. Two of the men are killed and 15 wounded. Two hundred are arrested and some will receive 50-year prison sentences.

November 20. The Alcan Highway opens to U.S. Army traffic.

November 23. Congress creates the SPARs (Semper Paratus, Always Ready), the U.S. Coast Guard Women's Reserve. In the early months of the unit, African American women are excluded.

December. Assistant Secretary of War John J. McCloy, chairing the Advisory Committee on Negro Troop Policies, recommends the creation of an African American parachute battalion.

The U.S. Coast Guard terminates its limited African American volunteer enlistment and begins shifting to general recruitment.

December 5. Roosevelt signs Executive Order 9279, which compels the military to accept at least 10 percent African Americans into the armed forces.

1943

Clarence Samuels becomes the first African American to be commissioned by the U.S. Coast Guard and is eventually assigned to captain the cutter *Sweetgum*.

The U.S. Marine Corps sends the first African American unit, the 1st Marine Depot, overseas.

William Baldwin becomes the first African American to be recruited into the U.S. Navy for general service.

The first African American military doctors and nurses are sent overseas to Liberia.

John Roosevelt Robinson is commissioned as a second lieutenant in the U.S. Army.

The U.S. Office of War Information appoints its first African American photojournalist, Gordon A. Parks Sr.

By the end of the year 504,000 African American troops are serving either in the European or Pacific theaters.

January 5. As a result of continuing segregation and discrimination in the armed forces, Judge William H. Hastie resigns his post as a civilian aide to the secretary of war.

February. African American personnel in the U.S. Navy reaches 26,909.

From February until November 1943, African Americans account for 13 percent of U.S. Coast Guard recruits. Some 5,000 will serve in the coast guard during the war (2 percent of the total number).

February 13. The Women's Marine Corps is created and becomes the only auxiliary service to continue throughout the war to exclude African Americans.

February 22. African Americans, while serving as stewards onboard the U.S. Coast Guard cutter *Campbell*, ram and sink a German U-boat. The African American gun crew commander is awarded the Bronze Star and other members of the crew receive decorations.

February 25. The 555th Parachute Infantry Company (known as the Triple Nickels), an African American unit, is created under the orders of U.S. Army Chief of Staff George C. Marshall.

March. The African American 93d Infantry Division begins maneuvers in Louisiana.

March 8. African American private George Watson saves several fellow soldiers before drowning when their ship is sunk by Japanese aircraft off New Guinea. He is one of six African Americans to posthumously receive their Medals of Honor at a ceremony on January 13, 1997.

April 1. The 784th Tank Battalion is activated, bringing the African American 5th Tank Group up to full strength.

April 24. The 99th Pursuit Squadron deploys in Morocco for further training.

May. Sgt. Gilbert Hashmark Johnson, formerly of the 25th Infantry Regiment, replaces the last white U.S. Marine Corps drill instructor at Montford Point.

African American pilots receive training at Selfridge Field, Michigan, including Daniel "Chappie" James, who will become a four-star general.

May 27. The U.S. government announces that all businesses operating in a discriminatory manner will be excluded from war contracts.

June. Ohio congresswoman Frances Payne Bolton introduces an amendment to the Nurses' Training Bill that bans racial discrimination. This allows over 2,000 African American women to enroll in the Cadet Nurse Corps.

The U.S. Coast Guard cutter USS *Seacloud* becomes the first integrated vessel following Lt. Comdr. Carlton Skinner's proposals. Half of its crew are African American as well as four of its officers.

The 616th–619th Bombardment Squadrons become the all–African American 477th Bombardment Group.

June 2. The 99th Pursuit Squadron flies its first combat mission from Tunisia over the Mediterranean.

June 20. A race riot in Detroit, Michigan, claims the lives of twenty-five African Americans and nine whites, and is only put down when federal troops take control. The riot erupted as a result of white resentment to Southern African Americans taking an increasing number of war industry jobs.

July. Fourteen African American members of the 80th Construction Battalion are discharged after disturbances in Trinidad.

July 2. Lt. Charles Buster Hall claims the first enemy aircraft kill for the 99th Pursuit Squadron.

July 25. The USS *Harmon* becomes the first U.S. Navy vessel to be named after an African American, Leonard Roy Harmon, who was posthumously awarded the Navy Cross. The vessel is launched at Quincy, Massachusetts.

August. The Special Unit of the U.S. Navy's Bureau of Naval Personnel is established to help with full integration.

August 21. The WAC appoints its first African American major, Harriet M. West, who later serves at the WAC headquarters' Bureau Control Division in Washington, D.C., as chief of planning.

September. Despite calls from the African American press since Pearl Harbor, the U.S. Army decides not to create a volunteer integrated division.

Adlai E Stevenson, the assistant secretary of the navy, suggests in a letter to Navy Secretary Frank Knox that African Americans be commissioned in the U.S. Navy.

October. Col. Benjamin O. Davis Jr. takes command of the 332d Fighter Group at Selfridge Field, Michigan.

November. The USS *Seacloud,* under Lt. Carlton Skinner, begins operations in the North Atlantic.

November 9. Brig. Gen. Benjamin O. Davis Sr. writes a memorandum calling for the end of Jim Crow practices in the U.S. Army.

November 30. The 79th Fighter Group accomplishes a record twenty-six missions, nine having been flown by the 99th Pursuit Squadron.

December. The number of African Americans in the U.S. Navy breaks the 100,000 barrier by 1,573.

The first units of the 93d Infantry head for the South Pacific.

December 15. At Fort Hood, Texas, the 761st Tank Battalion begins advanced armor training in medium tanks.

December 19. The first African American paratrooper is enlisted. Walter Morris is the first volunteer who will join the 555th Parachute Infantry Company, now authorized by Army Ground Forces Headquarters.

December 30. The 555th Parachute Infantry Company is officially activated at Fort Benning, Georgia.

1944

The U.S. Marine Corps promotes its first African American warrant officer, James E. Johnson, and its first sergeant major, Charles F. Anderson.

African American civilians now account for 8 percent of the workforce engaged in war production.

Brig. Gen. Benjamin O. Davis Sr. acts as a consultant, Stuart Heisler as the director, and Carlton Moss as the writer for Frank Capra's U.S. Army training film *The Negro Soldier.* The movie meets with critical acclaim, highlighting the contributions of African American troops in the army, and is credited with helping to quicken the pace of desegregation.

African American soldiers, largely in segregated units, now account for nearly 9 percent of the U.S. Army.

Segregation and the use of African American troops in the U.S. Army becomes a key issue in the presidential campaign.

January 1. The first thirteen African American enlisted men are selected as line officers for the Great Lakes Naval Training Station. They will become known as the "Golden Thirteen."

January 27–28. The 99th Pursuit Squadron shoots down twelve enemy aircraft over Italy. Capt. Clarence Jamison's flight accounts for five kills in just five minutes.

January 29. The U.S. Navy commissions the USS *Mason,* which will have a predominantly African American crew.

February. The 51st Defense Battalion becomes the first African American combat unit for the U.S. Marines to be sent to the Pacific. Although the battalion does not see combat, it is assigned to guard duty on the Ellice and Marshall Islands.

The U.S. Navy publishes *Guide to Command of Negro Naval Personnel,* which discourages segregation and focuses on promoting equal opportunities.

February. The Advisory Committee on Negro Troop Policies requests and recommends that African American units be committed to combat.

The 99th Pursuit Squadron is engaged in the Allied air assault on Monte Cassino, dropping bombs on the Benedictine monastery.

February 23. The Bureau of Naval Personnel's Special Unit succeeds in convincing the U.S. Navy to create two all–African American vessels commanded by white officers.

March. The Golden Thirteen become the first thirteen African Americans to be commissioned in the U.S. Navy. Forty-seven more will be commissioned during World War II by the navy.

Subchaser *PC-1264* is commissioned by the U.S. Navy with a predominantly African American crew.

The 366th Infantry Regiment leaves Camp Patrick Henry, Virginia, bound for North Africa.

March 11. The first battalion of the 24th Infantry Regiment is placed under the command of the 148th Infantry Regiment and becomes the first African American unit to go into combat in World War II. Soldiers of the 24th Infantry fight the Japanese on their first day on Bougainville in the Solomon Islands. Privates Leonard Brooks and Annias Jolly are the first African American infantrymen to be killed in ground combat in World War II.

March 17. The 100th, 301st, and 302d Fighter Squadrons, forming the 332d Fighter Group, first see combat action. In July 1944 the 99th Fighter Squadron will join the group and collectively the squadrons will fly 1,578 missions and 15,533 sorties. For the loss of 66 men, they will destroy 261 enemy aircraft and damage an additional 148.

March 20. The USS *Mason* becomes the first largely African American warship in the U.S. Navy. Its captain, Lt. Cmdr. William M. Blackford, and the crew ensure that despite detractors, their war service is successful.

March 28. The 93d Infantry Division, of which the African American 25th Infantry Regiment is included, engages the Japanese at Bougainville.

April 4. The 93d Infantry suffers its first casualties during an ambush on Bougainville.

May. The 366th Infantry Regiment arrives in Italy and is assigned to guard air bases.

May 10. Having arrived in Europe, the 2d Cavalry Division, consisting of the 9th and 10th Cavalry, are deactivated and the troops are reassigned to various units in North Africa.

June. The USS *Seacloud* helps sink a German submarine in the North Atlantic.

The first troops of the 92d Infantry Division pass through Camp Patrick Henry, Virginia, and leave for northern Italy.

June 6. The 320th Negro Anti-Aircraft Barrage Balloon Battalion is the only African American unit to take part in the initial D-Day landings. An African American, Pvt. Warren Capers, is also present on D-Day and wins a Silver Star for his contribution in setting up a dressing station that treats over 300 wounded men. African American infantry medic Bruce M. Wright lands on Omaha Beach as part of the third wave and earns a Purple Heart for his actions.

June 15. The 3d Marine Ammunition Company and the 18th and 20th Depot Companies, African American units, land on Saipan. The 3d Marine helps beat back a Japanese counterattack. These units become the only African American auxiliary marines to unexpectedly see combat action.

June 25. Capt. Wendell Pruitt and Lt. Gwynne Pierson, both African Americans, sink a German destroyer in Trieste Harbor with their machine guns. Pruitt receives the Air Medal with six Oak-leaf Clusters and the Distinguished Flying Cross.

June–July. Staff Sgt. Timerlate Kirven and Cpl. Samuel J. Love, Sr., of the 2d Marine Division become the first African Americans to be awarded Purple Hearts by the U.S. Marine Corps after being wounded on Saipan.

July. The 99th Fighter Squadron is assigned to the 332d Fighter Group.

The subchaser *PC1264* becomes the first vessel of its kind to be crewed by African Americans. Officers are white, but the first African American officer is assigned to the vessel in 1945.

African Americans now account for 25 percent of commissioned officers in the U.S. Coast Guard, the highest percentage of African American officers in the armed forces.

July 6. Following his refusal to sit at the rear of a military bus at Fort Hood, Texas, Lt. John Roosevelt Robinson, an African American officer in the 761st Tank Battalion, is arrested and court-martialed. He is later acquitted because the War Department recognizes that the U.S. Army has violated its order to prohibit racial discrimination.

July 12. African American Capt. Joseph Elsberry shoots down three enemy aircraft in a single mission over Germany.

July 15. The 370th Regimental Combat Team of the 92d Infantry Division leaves for Europe.

July 17. At Port Chicago, California, the *E. A. Bryan* and the *Quinalt Victory* explode while sailors are loading ammunition. Of the 320 killed, 202 are African American. A large number of the 390 injured are also African American. This one event accounts for 15 percent of all African American casualties during World War II.

July 30. The 370th Regimental Combat Team of the 92d Infantry Division joins the Fifth Army in the Mediterranean. It later becomes part of IV Corps of the Fifth Army.

August. Following the U.S. Navy's Special Unit recommendations, the secretary of the navy, James V. Forrestal, approves the integration of African American sailors on twenty-five auxiliary ships.

The 92d Infantry Division is deployed to face the German-held Gothic Line. They make several assaults and begin to chase the retreating Germans deeper into northern Italy.

August 9. At Port Chicago, California, orders are given to recommence ammunition loading onto vessels. Over 250 African American sailors refuse to obey orders. Fifty of the men are later court-martialed by the U.S. Navy and 208 are convicted of lesser offenses.

August 25. African Americans, accounting for 75 percent of the drivers, begin the Red Ball Express military operation, a logistics mission to bring much-needed fuel, ammunition, and supplies to the front from the depot areas in France.

August 27. The 370th Regimental Combat Team of the 92d Infantry Division first sees action on the Arno River, Italy.

October. The 371st Regimental Combat Team of the 92d Infantry Division arrives in Europe.

During offensive operations against the German-held Gothic Line in Italy, the 92d Infantry Division, under Maj. Gen. Edward M. Almond, is forced to retreat, giving ammunition to the U.S. press regarding misgivings about African American combat efficiency.

The 52d Defense Battalion, the second U.S. Marine Corps African American combat unit, arrives in the Pacific to serve in the Marshall Islands, Guam, Eniwetok, and Kwajalein.

The U.S. Coast Guard's SPARs announce the immediate admission of African American women. By mid-1945 it will only have five African American members.

October 10. The 761st Tank Battalion lands at Omaha Beach, Normandy, France, and is assigned to the 26th Infantry Division, XII Corps, of Lt. Gen. George S. Patton's Third Army.

October 13. African American private Ernest A. Jenkins is awarded the Silver Star by Patton for his gallantry during the liberation of Chateau Dun in France.

October 18. While protecting convoy NY-119, the USS *Mason* runs into a storm off the British coast. The ship is instrumental in saving a number of smaller vessels by escorting them safely into port.

October 19. The WAVES are opened to African American women, but fewer than a hundred will serve in the auxiliary during World War II. The first seventy-two include two women who will later become officers (Lt. Harriet Ida Pickens and Ens. Frances Wills). The first African American WAVE is Bessie Garret.

October 20. The U.S. Coast Guard's SPARs begin enlisting African American women. The first is Olivia J. Hooker.

November. The 365th Regimental Combat Team of the 92d Infantry Division arrives in Europe.

Elements of the 92d Infantry Division use mortar fire to contribute to the destruction of a number of enemy defensive positions in Italy.

The first African American woman war correspondent, Elizabeth B. Murphy Moss (Phillips), receives her certification but is forced to return to the United States due to ill health before she can post her first report.

November 8. During an assault on the towns of Moyenvic and Vic-Sur-Seille, the 761st Tank Battalion becomes the first African American armored unit in combat. For his role in the action, Staff Sgt. Ruben Rivers is awarded a Silver Star for his gallantry and leadership.

November 15. Staff Sgt. Ruben Rivers is wounded in action but refuses to be evacuated.

November 16. The Red Ball Express military

operation ends, having transported 412,193 tons of supplies from Normandy to the Rhine in 6,000 trucks.

November 19. Staff Sgt. Ruben Rivers is killed in action and posthumously receives the Medal of Honor in January 1997.

November 25. The 555th Parachute Infantry Company, now renamed Company A, 555th Parachute Infantry Battalion, begins training at Camp Machall, North Carolina.

November 30. The 366th Infantry Regiment is assigned to the 92d Infantry Division.

December. The 24th Infantry Regiment is posted to Saipan and Tinian, ostensibly as garrison troops but it is engaged in clean-up operations to snuff out remaining Japanese resistance.

December 14. At Climbach, France, Lt. Charles L. Thomas receives multiple wounds while storming the village under heavy enemy fire. He later dies of his wounds and is one of the seven African Americans awarded the Medal of Honor in January 1997.

December 16, 1944–January 16, 1945. The Battle of the Bulge takes place. During the engagement, the U.S. Army forms ad hoc integrated units comprised of 2,500 African American volunteers in 40-man platoons that are attached to white units. They fight to repulse a major German counter-offensive in the Ardennes. The U.S. Army grudgingly acknowledges that the emergency experiment is successful.

December 26. While serving as a forward artillery observer, 1st Lt. John R. Fox of the 366th Infantry Regiment, 92d Infantry Division, calls down friendly fire on his own position at Sommocolonia in Italy to stop a determined German counteroffensive. He is posthumously awarded the Medal of Honor in January 1997.

December 31, 1944–February 2, 1945. After the failure of the German Ardennes offensive, the U.S. Army resumes offensive operations in the Ardennes area. Among those at the forefront of the attacks to relieve Bastogne is the 761st Tank Battalion, which manages to penetrate the German positions in three places.

1945

Although the 761st Tank Battalion is nominated for a Presidential Unit Citation, it does not receive the award until 1978.

At Godman Field, Kentucky, Col. Benjamin O. Davis Jr. assumes command of the 477th Composite Group. He becomes the first African American placed in command of a U.S. Army Air Forces base. The 477th Composite Group consists of members of the 332d Fighter Group and the 477th Bombardment Group.

By the summer, the U.S. Navy ends its policy of maintaining segregated training facilities.

January. The 761st Tank Battalion fight a five-day engagement with the German 15th SS Panzer Division around Tillet, Belgium.

January 12. The Stilwell Road, a strategic military route connecting India, Burma, and China, opens for the first convoy of supplies to Chiang Kai-shek's Nationalist Chinese troops. Several thousand African American troops are involved in the building of the overland route.

January 23. The U.S. Army Nurse Corps bows to pressure from the National Association of Colored Nursing to end its racial restrictions.

January 25. The U.S. Navy Nurse Corps begins to allow African American women to enlist.

February. The 6888th Central Postal Directory Battalion, under the command of African American Maj. Charity Adams Earley, becomes the only African American WAC unit to be posted abroad. It will serve in Birmingham, England, and Rouen and Paris, France, with personnel working seven days a week and handling over 65,000 letters and packages per shift.

February 8. Gen. Mark W. Clark, commander of the Fifth Army, restructures the 92d Infantry Division.

Harry S. McAlpin becomes the first African American accredited to attend a White House press conference. He represents the *Atlanta Daily World.*

February 19–March 25. The Battle of Iwo Jima takes place and claims at least twelve African American casualties out of the 6,000 marines killed and 20,000 wounded.

March. The white 442d and 473d Infantry Regiments are assigned to the 92d Infantry Division after the 365th and 366th have their numbers stripped to reinforce the 370th. This makes, for the first time, the 92d Infantry Division an integrated division.

The 365th and 366th Infantry Regiments of the 92d Infantry Division advance across the Serchio Valley in Italy and capture the Cinquale Canal.

Lester B. Granger of the National Urban League is appointed by the secretary of the navy, James V. Forrestal, to investigate the treatment of African Americans in the U.S. Navy. Granger will cover 50,000 miles and visit sixty-seven naval bases in six months. His recommendations to assign African Americans to sea duties, i.e., to assign more to general service, not just to Steward's Branch or shore duties, are ordered to be implemented by Forrestal.

March 6. The Bureau of Naval Personnel announces that African Americans will be assigned to fleet auxiliary ships.

March 9. Ens. Phyllis Mae Dailey becomes the U.S. Navy's first African American nurse.

March 14. The 366th Infantry Regiment is deactivated as a combat unit and becomes two service units.

March 20–23. The 761st Tank Battalion breaks through the Siegfried Line, the last major German defense position in the west. They capture seven German towns in their assault.

March 23. African American Staff Sgt. Edward A. Carter is wounded by German troops near Speyer, Germany, but manages to kill six Germans and capture two others. For his actions he would be posthumously awarded the Medal of Honor in January 1997.

March 24. The 332d Fighter Group is awarded a Presidential Unit Citation for its operations in escorting bombers over Germany.

April. Pilot Wendell Pruitt dies while performing a victory roll over the Tuskegee airfield.

April 1–June 21. The Battle of Okinawa takes place. The African American 1st, 3d, and 12th Ammunition Companies and the 5th, 18th, 37th, and 38th Depot Companies of the U.S. Marine Corps are engaged. Fourteen men are wounded during the engagements.

April 5. After being arrested for breaking illegal color bars (the base barred African American officers from using facilities), at Freeman Field, Indiana, 101 African American members of the 477th Bombardment Group are accused of mutiny. Despite official policy, the base commander had continued to enforce segregation. Three African American officers are court-martialed and the other men are given reprimands. The actions taken against the men are set aside or removed from their records by the U.S. Air Force in 1995.

April 5–6. During fighting near Viareggio, Italy, 2d Lt. Vernon J. Baker is awarded the Medal of Honor for destroying two enemy defensive positions, ensuring wounded men are evacuated, and leading an assault against the enemy through a minefield. He is the only African American still alive in January 1997 when he and six others are belatedly awarded their decoration.

April 7. Operating as a scout, Pfc. Willy F. James Jr. is killed during an attempt to retrieve his platoon leader in Lippoldsberg, Germany, and is posthumously awarded the Medal of Honor in January 1997.

April 11. African American troops of the Third Army are present at the liberation of the Buchenwald concentration camp in Germany. It is likely that these were members of the 761st Tank Battalion.

April 26. The 332d Fighter Group claims the last four enemy aircraft kills in the Mediterranean. By this time the unit had flown 1,578 combat missions, shot down 111 enemy aircraft, and destroyed 150 planes on the ground.

April 30. The Italian campaign comes to an end, with the 92d Infantry Division having suffered 25 percent casualties. Among the 12,000 decorations are 95 Silver Stars, 2 Distinguished Service Crosses, a Distinguished Service Medal, and 16 Legions of Merit.

May. The 555th Parachute Infantry Battalion is assigned to the western United States to deal with Japanese incendiary bombs attached to paper balloons landing in Oregon and California. During their period of service they make over 1,000 parachute jumps.

May 5. The 761st Tank Battalion joins up with Russian forces at Steyr, Austria.

June. The U.S. Naval Academy in Annapolis, Maryland, accepts Wesley A. Brown as a cadet. He will become the first African American to graduate and be commissioned in June 1949.

July. The 24th Infantry Regiment is posted to Okinawa to carry out similar duties performed in Saipan and Tinian.

July 1. The chief of naval personnel discontinues the training program for African American recruits at the Great Lakes Naval Training Station as part of the navy's integration policy.

August. The 24th Infantry Regiment is posted to Ryukya to carry out similar duties performed in Okinawa, Saipan, and Tinian.

August 22. The 24th Infantry Regiment, commanded by Col. Julian G. Herne Jr., accepts the first Japanese surrender of ground units, on Aka Island.

September. By this time over 695,000 African Americans are serving in a wide variety of roles in the U.S. Army.

September 1. Secretary of War Robert P. Patterson appoints a board of three general officers to investigate the U.S. Army's policy with respect to African Americans. They are to prepare a new policy for the integrated and efficient use of African Americans. Heading the board as chairman is Gen. Alvan C. Gillem Jr. The board will become known as the Gillem Board.

September 22. The 758th Tank Battalion is deactivated at Viareggio, Italy.

October. The 555th Parachute Infantry Battalion becomes part of the 82d Airborne Division when it is moved from Camp Machall to Fort Bragg, North Carolina.

October 1. The Gillem Board holds its first meeting and continues its deliberations for the next four months.

November 10. Pfc. Frederick C. Branch becomes the first African American commissioned as a reserve officer in the U.S. Marine Corps.

1946

February. Aiken, South Carolina, police attack African American World War II veteran Isaac Woodard, who is blinded as a result of the attack after an argument with a bus driver.

April. The Gillem Board publishes its report, *Utilization of Negro Manpower in the Postwar Army Policy.* The report recommends that the U.S. Army's future policy should eliminate, at the earliest practicable moment, any special consideration based on race. African American commentators and activists are stunned that the board does not challenge the issue of segregation in the army. Later, Secretary of the Army Kenneth Royall will describe the proposed policy as "equality of opportunity on the basis of segregation."

July. In Monroe, Georgia, two African American veterans and their wives are dragged from their car by a racist white mob that then riddles their bodies with sixty bullets.

July 30. U.S. Attorney General Tom Clark announces that President Harry S. Truman has instructed the Justice Department to proceed with all its resources to investigate the Monroe, Georgia, atrocity and other crimes of oppression so as to ascertain if any federal statute can be applied.

September 12. Truman writes to the National Urban League, stating that government has an obligation to see that the civil rights of every citizen are fully and equally protected.

December 6. The President's Committee on Civil Rights is established.

1947

John W. Lee becomes the first African American to hold a commission in the regular U.S. Navy.

May. President Harry S. Truman is presented with a report from the President's Advisory Commission on Universal Training. It concludes that "nothing could be more tragic for the future attitude of our people, and for the unity of our Nation, than a program [the proposed Universal Military Training program] in which our Federal Government forced our young manhood to live for a period of time in an atmosphere that emphasized or bred class or racial difference."

October. The National Association for the Advancement of Colored People presents "Statement on the Denial of Human Rights to Minorities in the Case of Citizens of Negro Descent in the USA; and an Appeal to the United Nations for Redress" to the United Nations.

October 29. The President's Committee on Civil Rights issues its report, *To Secure These Rights.* The committee roundly condemns segregation, specifically in the armed forces. The report concludes with the opinion that only legislative or administrative action will be able "to end immediately all discrimination and segregation based on race, color, creed or national origin in . . . all branches of the Armed Services."

November. Truman receives a memorandum from Clark Clifford, special counsel to the president (1946–1950), stating his opinion that the president, in order to win the 1948 presidential election, will have to focus on civil rights and the issues affecting African Americans in particular.

The Committee Against Jim Crow in Military Service and Training is established by labor and civil rights leader A. Philip Randolph and black Republican Grant Reynolds.

1948

January. After considering his options, President Harry S. Truman determines that segregation in the armed forces and the civil service can only be ended by administrative action in the form of an executive order, rather than through the legislative process.

February 2. Truman tells Congress that he has instructed the secretary of defense to take steps to have the remaining instances of discrimination in the armed services eliminated as rapidly as possible.

March 22. Truman has a meeting with leading African Americans who try to convince him to insist on desegregation amendments to legislation being considered in Congress regarding the reintroduction of the draft.

March 27. The "Declaration of Negro Voters" is issued by twenty African American organizations meeting in New York. The declaration demands that every vestige of segregation and discrimination in the armed forces be forthwith abolished.

March 30. As the representative of the Committee Against Jim Crow in Military Service and Training, A. Philip Randolph testifies before the Senate Armed Services Committee. He contends that African Americans will refuse to serve in the armed forces if legislation does not end segregation.

April 26. A delegation of some sixteen African American leaders informs Secretary of Defense James V. Forrestal that African Americans are likely to react very aggressively if segregation is not outlawed in the armed forces.

May. Truman's staff considers advising the president that it may be prudent to establish a committee to oversee the integration program in the armed forces.

June 25. The creation of the League for Nonviolent Civil Disobedience Against Military Segregation is announced by Randolph.

June 29. Randolph tells Truman that unless he issues an executive order to end segregation in the armed forces, it is probable that African Americans will seek to resist the draft.

July 13. Minneapolis mayor Hubert H. Humphrey, a member of the platform committee at the Democratic National Convention, proposes that the party call for the abolition of segregation in the armed forces. The proposal is rejected, despite the support of Truman and his advisors. A more moderate stance is adopted in order not to alienate the Southern delegates and supporters.

July 14. Delegates at the Democratic National Convention overwhelmingly vote to overrule the platform committee and the Truman administration's moderate approach. They vote for a more liberal policy that incorporates the desegregation of the armed forces. Truman's staff works on drafting an executive order to end segregation, while the president decides to follow the suggestion of his advisors and set up a committee to oversee the desegregation program in the armed forces.

July 26. Truman signs Executive Order 9981, establishing the President's Committee on Equality of Treatment and Opportunity in the Armed Services as the overseeing body to monitor the implementation of the desegregation program. Due to the ambiguity of the executive order, some army staff officers leak to the press that they do not consider that 9981 forbids segregation.

July 27. Gen. Omar N. Bradley, the army chief of staff, states that in his opinion a desegregated army will only come into existence when American society is no longer segregated itself.

July 29. Truman is forced to make it clear at a press conference that Executive Order 9981's primary purpose is to end segregation in the armed forces.

August 2. A. Philip Randolph and other representatives of the League for Nonviolent Civil Disobedience Against Military Segregation meet with J. Howard McGrath, the chairman of the Democratic National Committee. McGrath assures them that the President's Committee on Equality of Treatment and Opportunity in the Armed Services will end segregation in the armed forces as intended by Executive Order 9981. Convinced of his sincerity and given reassurances, Randolph and the other representatives issue a statement ending the organization's civil disobedience campaign.

August 14. Secretary of the Army Kenneth Royall admits to the press that "segregation in the army must go." He is not convinced that it will happen immediately.

September 18. The members of the President's Committee on Equality of Treatment and Opportunity in the Armed Services are announced by the White House. The chairman is Charles Fahy and subsequently the committee is known as the Fahy Committee. The body will have five members, two of whom are African American.

October 9. Preemptively, the U.S. Navy announces that it will be continuing and extending its policy of integration that it began in the last few months of World War II.

December. Secretary of Defense Forrestal receives a proposal from Royall that an experimental integrated unit be established in the army. In this way, the U.S. Army could assess the process and effects of integration. Stuart Symington, the secretary of the air force, presents Truman with an integration plan for the U.S. Air Force. It proposes to assign African Americans to units on the basis of merit and not on the basis of color or creed.

1949

Sfc. Edward Carter, a veteran of the Abraham Lincoln Brigade and World War II, is dishonorably discharged because he was seen as a communist. The American Civil Liberties Union takes up his case.

Col. Benjamin O. Davis Jr. attends the U.S. Air Force's Air War College.

Wesley Brown becomes the first African American to complete the U.S. Naval Academy's program at Annapolis.

January 12. President Harry S. Truman has his first meeting with the Fahy Committee. Also present are the secretaries of the army, navy, air force, and defense.

January 13. Representatives of the armed services are called to the first of the hearings set up by the Fahy Committee. Secretary of the Army Kenneth Royall defends the U.S. Army's segregation policy; the U.S. Marine Corps follows suit and admits that only 1 of its 8,200 officers is African American. Secretary of the Navy John L. Sullivan admits that only 5 of the U.S. Navy's 45,000 officers are African American, but states that the Navy is committed to a policy of integration. Secretary of the Air Force Stuart Symington also agrees to institute a policy of desegregation.

January 22. The U.S. Air Force prematurely announces to the press that it has completed its plans for a desegregated service.

March 28. The Fahy Committee calls the secretaries of the army, navy, and air force to testify. The secretary of the U.S. Air Force and the secretary of the U.S. Navy testify that they are opposed to segregation in their services and confirm that policies are in place or are being developed to achieve integration. The secretary of the U.S. Army testifies that he wishes to maintain a segregated service and states that the army is not an instrument for social evolution.

April 1. Secretary of Defense Louis Johnson issues directives to Symington, Sullivan, and Royall clearly stating his department's commitment to equality of opportunity and employment in the armed services.

May 11. Johnson decides to approve the U.S. Air Force integration plan, but flatly rejects those proposed by Sullivan and Royall for the U.S. Navy and U.S. Army, respectively. The Fahy Committee makes additional recommendations to the army and navy, including the army ending its 10 percent African American enlistment quota and desegregating all of its units.

June 7. The revised U.S. Navy integration plan is accepted by Johnson. The U.S. Army revised plan is rejected once more and Johnson makes a formal statement to the U.S. Army insisting that it incorporates the recommendations of the Fahy Committee before he approves the plan.

July 5. Gordon Gray, the new secretary of the army, and Gen. Omar N. Bradley, the army chief of staff, make the formal presentation of a revised U.S. Army plan to the Fahy Committee. The army still proposes to maintain segregation and the 10 percent African American recruitment quota.

July 25–27. Speaking as the representative of the Fahy Committee, Charles Fahy tells Truman, Johnson, and Gray that the U.S. Army plan for integration will not be accepted until the army embraces the spirit of Executive Order 9981.

August–September. Fruitless discussions continue between the Fahy Committee and representatives of the U.S. Army to resolve the disparity of the army's integration plan to those of the other two services.

September. Daniel "Chappie" James joins the 12th Fighter-Bomber Squadron at Clark Air Base in the Philippines.

September 27. The U.S. Army sends a copy of its revised plan to Johnson. The Fahy Committee is apprised of the dispatch, but does not receive a copy of its own.

September 30. Johnson approves the revised U.S. Army plan, which still incorporates the maintaining of segregated units and the 10 percent African American enlistment quota.

October 6. For public relations purposes, Truman announces to the press that the U.S. Army plan is a "a progress report" and not a completed and approved document. He reaffirms his commitment to ensuring that the U.S. Army follows the lead of the other two services and ends segregation.

October 11. Truman receives a letter from Fahy stating that the revised U.S. Army plan would not end segregation in the service.

November. The U.S. Army again revises its integration plan, which still includes segregated units and the 10 percent recruitment quota. The Fahy Committee warns the U.S. Army that it has no hope of having the plan approved and that it is the intention of the committee to release a statement to the press roundly condemning the plan.

December. Truman and the White House ask the Fahy Committee not to issue a condemnation of the U.S. Army plan to the press. Instead, they ask that the Fahy Committee reissue recommendations to the U.S. Army with advice as to steps needed to modify the plan to achieve the goal of approval.

African American Bradley Biggs, formerly of the 555th Parachute Battalion and the 82d Airborne Division, becomes a company commander at Gifu, Japan.

December 15. The White House is presented with the Fahy Committee's recommendations and suggested modifications to the U.S. Army integration plan. The Fahy Committee stands by the phasing out of segregation and the termination of the recruitment quota.

December 27. Gray and Fahy meet and discuss the issue. Gray concedes on the point of segregated units, but reserves the right to institute this as a rolling program over a period of time

1950

January 14. The U.S. Army's integration plan is finally approved by the Fahy Committee. The 10 percent African American recruitment quota remains an issue to be dealt with at a later date.

January 16. President Harry S. Truman is apprised of the approval of the U.S. Army's integration plan by the Fahy Committee. The plan is officially issued as Special Regulations No. 600–629–1 by the U.S. Army.

February 1. The continuing operation of the Fahy Committee is approved by Truman until such a time that the U.S. Army formally accepts the abolition of the 10 percent recruitment quota for African American enlistments.

March 1. Gordon Gray, the secretary of the army, discusses the matter of the 10 percent recruitment quota with Truman. He tells the president the U.S. Army will abolish the 10 percent recruitment quota, but if there is a larger than 10 percent influx of African Americans into the army that the president had already stated that the army would have the right to reinstate the quota. He bases his assumptions on the long discussions held over the past several months with the president on this issue.

March 13. Seemingly assured by Truman's conversation with Gray, the U.S. Army agrees to abolish its 10 percent recruitment quota for African Americans. The change of policy will enter into effect in April 1950.

March 27. Truman thanks Gray for the change of policy and tells him: "I am sure everything will work out as it should."

May 22. Freedom To Serve, the last report of the Fahy Committee, is published and submitted to Truman. In thanking the committee, the president expresses hopes that the recommendations are carried out and "within the reasonably near future, equality of treatment and opportunity for all persons within the armed services would be accomplished." With this, the Fahy Committee effectively completes its work.

June. The U.S. Army encounters severe difficulties as it tries to predict the levels of recruitment for African Americans. Training camps are told, unofficially, that training should be integrated. Meanwhile in Korea, the problem of replacing white border casualties in combat units and the sudden influx of African American recruits speeds up the integration process as African American replacements are assigned to previously segregated, white-only units.

June 24–25. North Korea crosses the 38th parallel and invades South Korea.

June 27. Truman orders the Seventh Fleet into the Strait of Taiwan and commits air support for South Korean forces.

June 29. The U.S. administration realizes that the South Koreans are incapable of dealing with the North Korean invasion without U.S. ground troops.

July. The 24th Infantry Regiment, the 159th Field Artillery Battalion, the 77th Engineer Combat Company, and the 512th Military Police Company, all African American units, are sent to Korea.

July 2. Gen. Douglas MacArthur is given command of Korean military operations and asks for ground troops.

July 6. Truman officially winds up the operations of the Fahy Committee, despite the fact that members of the committee feel there is still work to be done in monitoring the implementation of the integration plans in the three services.

July 10. The four African American units land at Pusan, South Korea.

July 20. The 25th Infantry Division (which includes the 24th Infantry Regiment, the 77th Engineer Combat Company, and the 159th Field Artillery Battalion) begins a sixteen-hour battle to recapture Yechon to the north of Pusan.

July 21. Future Lt. Col. Charles M. Bussey mans 2 machine guns during the Yechon offensive and kills 258 North Koreans despite being wounded twice.

July 31. 1st Lt. Leon A. Gilbert, an African American, acting commander of Company A, 24th Infantry Regiment, is charged with desertion in the face of the enemy. He is initially sentenced to death but this is commuted to fifty years imprisonment.

August. After having won a Distinguished Service Medal in the spring following his rescue of a fellow pilot from an aircraft accident, Daniel "Chappie" James rejoins his squadron in Korea.

August 6. Pfc. William H. Thompson, of the 24th Infantry Regiment, covers the retreat of his company by manning a machine gun. He is mortally wounded and is the first soldier to win a Medal of Honor in Korea. It is the first African American Medal of Honor to be awarded since the Spanish-American War.

August 31. The 24th Infantry Regiment is forced to withdraw from Battle Mountain (Hill 625); it is later accused of cowardice.

September 15. MacArthur masterminds landings at Inchon behind enemy lines.

September 16. The 9th Infantry Regiment, led by

white Lt. Col. Cesido Butch Barberis and including a battalion of African Americans, crosses the Naktong River.

October. James is awarded the Distinguished Flying Cross for close ground support at Namchonjom, North Korea.

November. Truman reduces Gilbert's sentence from fifty years to twenty years' imprisonment, following pressure from senators, congressmen, and civil rights groups.

November 23. The 25th Infantry Division faces two-and-a-half enemy divisions while en route to Yalu.

November 25. U.S. troops face an enormous counteroffensive by the North Korean and Chinese forces.

December. James completes his 100th Korean combat mission.

1951

Project Clear, a U.S. Army study, claims that integration would improve efficiency.

January. In Korea, the Eighth Army unofficially adopts the policy of integrating African Americans into white-only units once the all–African American units have reached official combat strength.

March 18. The Department of Defense announces that all basic training in the armed services will be integrated from this point onward.

April. The commander of the United Nations Command in Korea, Gen. Matthew B. Ridgway, requests that the U.S. Army approve the integration of African Americans into all units under his command.

June 2. Sgt. Cornelius H. Charlton, an African American, is killed while leading three assaults on an enemy ridge near Chipo-Ri. He is awarded a posthumous Medal of Honor.

July 26. The U.S. Army approves Ridgway's request and makes an announcement that within six months all units assigned to Japan, Korea, and Okinawa will be integrated.

October 1. The 24th Infantry Regiment is deactivated because of desegregation.

1952

African American pilot Daniel "Chappie" James is promoted to the rank of major.

1953

Daniel "Chappie" James becomes the first African American officer to lead an integrated fighter squadron when he assumes command of Otis Air Force Base, Massachusetts.

The American Civil Liberties Union finally ends Edward Carter's appeal to rejoin the U.S. Army, the former sergeant having been branded as un-American by the Establishment.

Lawrence Chambers becomes the second African American to graduate from the U.S. Naval Academy in Annapolis, Maryland.

April. Lt. Frank E. Petersen, only the fourth African American to complete the Naval Aviation Cadet Program, begins his Korean tour of duty. He will fly sixty-four combat missions.

July 27. The Korean armistice is signed.

September. President Dwight D. Eisenhower sends a military and economic task force to Saigon, concluding that the French will win the war in Vietnam.

October. The U.S. Army makes an official announcement that 95 percent of African Americans serving in the army are now in fully integrated units.

1954

The last segregated support units are desegregated.

May 7. French-held Dien Bien Phu in Vietnam falls to the Viet Minh after a fifty-six-day siege.

May 17. The U.S. Supreme Court rules that segregated schools are unconstitutional, ending a twenty-year court battle by the National Association for the Advancement of Colored People.

1955

January. The United States establishes the Military Assistance and Advisory Group in Saigon and begins training South Vietnamese troops.

August 13. African American World War II veteran Lamar Smith is murdered in Mississippi for registering African American voters.

October. Ngo Dinh Diem declares himself president of the Republic of Vietnam.

1957

Daniel "Chappie" James is posted at the Pentagon as a lieutenant colonel.

African American Colin Powell reports to the Reserve Officers' Training Corps facility at Fort Bragg, North Carolina.

Ngo Dinh Diem's repression in South Vietnam triggers guerrilla action by the Viet Minh.

September 4. The so-called Little Rock Nine case hits the headlines as nine African American teenagers are prevented from entering a school in Arkansas. Eventually the Little Rock Nine will be given bodyguards from the 101st Airborne Division.

1959

Colin Powell graduates from City College of New York, and enters the U.S. Army.

Benjamin O. Davis Jr. is promoted to the rank of brigadier general.

1960

Daniel "Chappie" James becomes director of operations for the 81st Tactical Fighter Wing in Great Britain.

As a lieutenant, Colin Powell commands a company of the 3d Armored Division.

February 1. In Greensboro, North Carolina, four African American college students, one of whom is wearing a Reserve Officers' Training Corps uniform, are refused service at a segregated lunch counter. This triggers nationwide civil rights protests and thousands of arrests.

1961

Colin Powell is transferred to Fort Devens, Massachusetts, with the 1st Battle Group, 4th Infantry, of the 2d Infantry Brigade.

1962

Colin Powell receives word of his transfer to Vietnam.

December. Powell arrives in the A Shau Valley near Vietnam's border with Laos. He is a field adviser to the Army of the Republic of Vietnam.

1963

January 2. The Battle of Ap Bac takes place in the delta region of Vietnam and ends in disaster.

February 7. Colin Powell and his Army of the Republic of Vietnam battalion help initiate Operation GRASSHOPPER to clear out North Vietnamese troops.

April 3. An enemy mortar attack nearly kills Powell.

November 1. Now holding the rank of captain, Powell reports to Tan Son Nhut Airport to travel to the Infantry Officer's Advanced Course at Fort Benning, Georgia.

Ngo Dinh Diem's government is overthrown by Gen. Duong Van Minh. Diem, his brother, and chief adviser are murdered the next day.

1964

Lt. Gen. Benjamin O. Davis Jr. becomes chief of staff for U.S. forces in Korea and chief of staff for the United Nations Command.

1965

African American Capt. John Cash begins his first tour of duty in Vietnam.

May. Colin Powell completes the Infantry Officer's Advanced Course at Fort Benning and becomes an instructor at the school.

October. Col. Fred V. Cherry of the 35th Tactical Fighter Squadron is shot down over North Vietnam. He is the first African American to be captured by the North Vietnamese and is later sent to the infamous Hoa Lo prison, nicknamed the Hanoi Hilton.

October 22. Pfc. Milton L. Olive III sacrifices his own life while with the 173d Airborne Brigade in order to save other soldiers. He becomes the first

African American enlisted man to win a Medal of Honor in Vietnam.

1966

Defense Secretary Robert S. McNamara launches Project 100,000, aiming to admit 100,000 unemployed and poorly educated U.S. citizens into the armed forces.

1967

Colin Powell is assigned to the Army Command and General Staff College at Fort Leavenworth, Kansas.

African Americans in the U.S. Army are reenlisting at a rate twice that of their white counterparts.

October 31. Capt. Riley Leroy Pitts is killed in action at Ap Dong and becomes the first African American officer to ever win a Medal of Honor. He is one of 9,300 Americans killed in Vietnam in 1967.

1968

U.S. forces suffer 14,592 dead throughout the year. African Americans account for 20 percent of combat troops and 14.1 percent of casualties.

April 1. The Tet offensive in Vietnam is launched by the North Vietnamese.

July. Colin Powell returns to Vietnam as the executive officer of the 3d Battalion, 1st Infantry, 11th Infantry Brigade, Americal Division. He is based in Quang Ngai.

November. Powell is almost killed in a helicopter crash in Vietnam.

1969

Daniel "Chappie" James is in command of Wheelus Air Force Base in Libya when he confronts Libyan dictator Col. Muammar Khadafy, who is leading a column of half-tracks to seize the military facility. James confronts Khadafy face-to-face and says, "Move your hand away from that gun!" The Libyan leader and the column of half-tracks withdraw.

Forty-five African Americans enter West Point as first-year cadets.

Over 160 violent racial attacks take place throughout the year at Camp Lejeune, North Carolina.

1970

Daniel "Chappie" James is awarded his first general's star.

Forty African Americans enter West Point as first-year cadets.

March. African American airmen react violently when white servicemen are rumored to be setting up a Ku Klux Klan group at the air base at Goose Bay, Labrador. Charges are brought against African Americans and the National Association for the Advancement of Colored People helps to defuse the situation.

July 10. Racial disturbances occur at the Great Lakes Naval Training Center, Illinois, and later are investigated by the Bureau of Naval Personnel and the Office of the Secretary of the Navy. Sweeping changes are made in the wake of these incidents.

December 17. Adm. Elmo R. Zumwalt, the chief of naval operations for the U.S. Navy, issues the directive "Equal Opportunity in the Navy."

1971

The U.S. Navy launches its BOOST Program to raise educational levels of minority groups in the service.

March. The mayor of Berlin, Germany, criticizes residents for discriminating against African American servicemen.

May 21. Racial fighting at Travis Air Force Base, California, leads to the arrest of 135 men.

June 24. The Defense Race Relations Institute is established at Patrick Air Force Base, Florida.

November. Gen. Michael S. Davison, commanding general of U.S. Army, Europe, launches an African American educational literacy program supported by Maj. Gen. F. E. Davison, the second-highest-ranking African American in the U.S. Army. They meet with representatives of the National Association for the Advancement of Colored People and the National Urban League at Berchtesgaden, West Germany.

1972

Capt. John Cash returns to Vietnam.

African Americans account for 7.3 percent of enlisted men and 1 percent of officers in the U.S. Navy and 13.7 percent of enlisted men and 1.5 percent of officers in the U.S. Marines. In the U.S. Air Force, African American enlisted men amount to 12.6 percent and officers 1.7 percent.; in the U.S. Army, the figures are 17.1 percent and 3.9 percent.

Fifty-one African Americans enroll at West Point as first-year cadets.

October 12. African American and white sailors brawl onboard the USS *Kitty Hawk.* Twenty-seven African Americans are charged.

October 16. African American and white sailors fight each other on the USS *Hassayampa.* Eleven African Americans are charged.

November 3. Racial violence breaks out on the USS *Constellation* during a training exercise off the coast of California.

1973

January 27. The United States and Vietnam sign a peace treaty in Paris. Prisoners of war will be exchanged and the United States agrees to leave Vietnam within sixty days.

March 29. The last aircraft containing U.S. troops leaves Vietnam.

August 14. U.S. bombing in Vietnam is officially ended by order of Congress.

1975

Daniel "Chappie" James becomes the first African American four-star general and takes command at North American Aerospace Defense Command (NORAD) in Colorado.

1976

Colin Powell becomes a colonel and is placed in command of the 2d Brigade, 101st Airborne Division, based at Fort Campbell, Kentucky.

1977

Clifford L. Alexander becomes the first African American secretary of the army. He is appointed by President Jimmy Carter. There are nine African American generals at this time.

1978

January. Gen. Daniel "Chappie" James retires.

February. James dies and is buried at Arlington National Cemetery.

December. Colin Powell reaches the rank of brigadier general.

1979

July. The Defense Race Relations Institute becomes the Defense Equal Opportunity Management Institute.

1981

Clifford L. Alexander leaves office as secretary of the army. There are now thirty African American generals, including Colin Powell and Hazel Winifred Johnson, the first African American woman general.

Col. Fred V. Cherry retires from the U.S. Air Force.

African Americans account for 33.2 percent of enlisted men and 7 percent of officers in the U.S. Army, 12.2 percent of enlisted men and 2.7 percent of officers in the U.S. Navy, 22 percent of enlisted men and 4 percent of officers in the U.S. Marine Corps, and 14.4 percent of enlisted men and 4.8 percent of officers in the U.S. Air Force.

1982

Colin Powell becomes the deputy commanding general of the U.S. Army Combined Arms Combat Developments Activity, based at Fort Leavenworth, Kansas.

December. African Americans account for 4.4 percent of officers and 19.4 percent of enlisted men in the National Guard or reserve units.

1983

Colin Powell chairs Project 14 to investigate the U.S. Army's future over the next four years.

December 4. African American Robert O. Goodman Jr., an electronics warfare officer, is shot down over Lebanon by Syrian forces and is taken prisoner. He is later released due to a visit to Syria by the Rev. Jesse Jackson.

1985

Colin Powell warns Caspar Weinberger of the Iran-Contra Affair.

African Americans account for an average of 8 percent of West Point cadets.

1986

July. Colin Powell becomes a three-star general and is placed in command of V Corps in Frankfurt, Germany.

1987

Brig. Gen. Fred A. Gordon becomes the first African American commandant of West Point.

November. Colin Powell becomes the first African American National Security Adviser.

1988

A campaign is launched by supporters to award the Medal of Honor to Sgt. Henry Johnson and Dorie Miller, Ship's Cook, 3d Class, African American veterans of World War I and World War II, respectively.

1989

Former African American veteran Duery Felton of the 1st Infantry Division becomes the curator of the Vietnam Veterans Memorial Collection.

August. Colin Powell becomes chairman of the Joint Chiefs of Staff.

1990

Thousands of African American soldiers are among those who lose their jobs when the armed services downsize.

December 1. 184,000 allied troops are in place in Saudi Arabia for Operation Desert Shield. African Americans account for 20 percent of U.S. troops (30 percent in the U.S. Army, 22 percent in the U.S. Navy, 17 percent in the U.S. Marine Corps, and 13 percent in the U.S. Air Force) in the Persian Gulf region.

1991

January 21. African American Lt. Phoebe Jeter is the first African American woman to direct a Patriot missile battery to shoot down Iraqi Scud missiles.

February 28. President George Bush announces a cease-fire in the Gulf War. Of the 266 U.S. soldiers killed, some 15 percent are African American. Among the dead, the youngest is Pvt. Robert D. Talley (eighteen years) and the oldest is 1st Sgt. Joseph Murphy (fifty-eight years), both African Americans.

May. Bush awards African American World War I veteran Freddie Stowers's sister his posthumous Medal of Honor.

May 1. Maj. Gen. Marcelite J. Harris becomes the first African American woman in the U.S. Air Force to become a two-star general.

1994

July. A memorial is dedicated in Concord, California, to the sailors killed in the accidental explosion of two ships at Port Chicago in July 1944.

1995

Johnson C. Whittaker posthumously receives his U.S. Army commission over 100 years after being dismissed from West Point after an incident that was probably racially motivated.

The official reprimands of African American members of the 477th Bombardment Group following the Freeman Field incident in 1945 are stricken from their service records.

Shaw University (named after Robert Gould Shaw, colonel of the 54th Massachusetts Regiment, who was killed in the assault on Fort Wagner), North Carolina, is nominated to investigate potential African American Medal of Honor recipients and the fact that no African Americans received the Medal of Honor in World War I or World War II.

December. Two white soldiers, neo-Nazis and supporters of the racist National Alliance, stationed at Fort Bragg and a third man murder an African American couple. James Burmeister and Malcolm Wright, both of the 82d Airborne Division and a third soldier, Randy Meadows, carried out the murders. Burmeister and Wright were convicted and sentenced to life. Meadows pleaded guilty to conspiracy and being an accessory.

1996

African Americans account for 9.8 percent of U.S. Marine Corps personnel, with 6.5 percent of the officers and three men with the rank of general.

1997

In Walterboro, South Carolina, a monument to the Tuskegee Airmen is dedicated.

African Americans account for 17.4 percent of total U.S. Navy personnel, with 5.9 percent of the officers and 2.2 percent of the admiral class.

January 13. Vernon Baker is the only living recipient of the Medal of Honor conferred on African American veterans by President Bill Clinton in a ceremony at the White House. Baker, a member of the 370th Regiment, 92d Division, is awarded his medal for gallantry at Castel Aghinolfi, Italy, in 1945. Posthumous awards are given to Pvt. George Watson (a member of the 29th Quartermaster Regiment who had already been the first African American to win the Distinguished Service Cross in World War II), 1st Lt. John R. Fox (a member of the 366th Infantry Regiment, 92d Division, who was killed in 1944 at Serchio, Italy), Staff Sgt. Ruben Rivers (a member of the 761st Tank Battalion who was commended for his action at Guebling, France, in 1944), Maj. Charles L. Thomas (a member of the 614th Tank Destroyer Battalion who received the medal for his bravery at Climbach, France, in 1944), Staff Sgt. Edward Carter, Jr. (a member of the 56th Armored Infantry Regiment, 12th Armored Division, who was awarded the medal for his numerous acts of bravery in Germany in 1945), and Pfc. Willy F. James (a member of the 415th Infantry Regiment who displayed bravery at Lippoldsberg, Germany, in 1945).

February 22. Maj. Gen. Marcelite J. Harris retires from the U.S. Air Force.

1998

Master Chief Vincent Patton III, an African American, is appointed as the principal adviser to the commandant of the U.S. Coast Guard.

February 1. Lillian Fishburne is promoted to the rank of rear admiral, becoming the first female African American flag officer in the U.S. Navy.

July 23–24. Five African American troops who fought during the Battle of the Bulge are belatedly granted their Bronze Stars: 1st Sgt. Vincent R. Malveaux; Sgt. J. C. Wade; Pfc. Andrew W. Nix Jr.; T5g. Mate Montgomery; and former Sgt. Marteller Pollock Jr.

1999

February. West Point's first African American graduate, Henry O. Flipper, receives a presidential pardon, more than 100 years after his court-martial for misappropriation of funds.

2000

November. More than 100 U.S. Navy divers and their families attend the premiere of the movie *Men of Honor,* which chronicles African American navy diver Carl Brashear's struggle against racism.

2001

January 20. Retired general Colin Powell becomes the first African American secretary of state.

May 25. Senate Resolution 97, referred to the Judiciary Committee, resolves that the Senate (1) honor the bravery and dedication of the Buffalo Soldiers throughout United States and world history, (2) honor one of the Buffalo Soldiers' most distinguished heroes, Col. Charles Young, for his lifetime achievements, and (3) recognize the continuing legacy of the Buffalo Soldiers throughout the world.

2002

March 6. U.S. District Judge Royce C. Lamberth says written directions by the U.S. Army to promotion boards urging that they consider "past personal or institutional discrimination" are unconstitutional because they give preference to one race or gender over another.

July 4. Gen. Benjamin O. Davis Jr., 89, the legendary commander of the Tuskegee Airmen, dies at Walter Reed Army Medical Center. Davis is buried at Arlington National Cemetery and his memory is honored with a heritage flyover.

2003

Colin Powell leads the accusations against Iraq, claiming that it has been less than candid regarding its disclosures concerning weapons of mass destruction. In his address to the United Nations Security Council on February 5, Powell outlines U.S. intelligence data on Iraq's weapons programs.

United States Colored Artillery, Formation and Service Records of

Independent Battery, United States Colored Light Artillery

Date Raised
December 23, 1864

Muster Point(s)
Leavenworth, Kansas

Date Disbanded
July 22, 1865

Place Disbanded
Fort Leavenworth, Kansas

Movement Orders and Attachments
Attached to District of North Kansas, Department of Kansas, to July 1865.

Engagements and Campaigns
Duty at Leavenworth and Fort Leavenworth, to July 1865.

1st Regiment, United States Colored Heavy Artillery

Date Raised
February 20, 1864

Muster Point(s)
Knoxville, Tennessee

Date Disbanded
March 31, 1866

Place Disbanded
District of East Tennessee

Movement Orders and Attachments
Attached to 2d Brigade, 4th Division, XXIII Corps, Department of Ohio, to February 1865. 2d Brigade, 4th Division, District of East Tennessee, Department of the Cumberland, to March 1865.
1st Brigade, 4th Division, District of East Tennessee, to March 1866.

Engagements and Campaigns
Duty at Knoxville, to January 1865. Operations against Wheeler in East Tennessee, August 15–25, 1864. Operations in northern Alabama and East Tennessee, January 31–April 24, 1865. Stoneman's operations from East Tennessee into southwestern Virginia and western North Carolina, February–April 1865. At Greenville and in District of East Tennessee, to March 1866.

3d Regiment, United States Colored Heavy Artillery

Date Raised
March 11, 1864

Muster Point(s)
Organized from 1st Tennessee Heavy Artillery (African Descent). Designated 2d United States Colored Heavy Artillery, March 11, 1864, and 3d Heavy Artillery, April 26, 1864.

Date Disbanded
April 30, 1866

Place Disbanded
District of West Tennessee

Movement Orders and Attachments
Attached to District of Memphis, Tennessee, Department of Tennessee, to June 1864. Memphis, Tennessee, District of West Tennessee, to July 1865. 2d Infantry Brigade, District of West Tennessee,

to September 1865. District of West Tennessee to April 1866.

Engagements and Campaigns
Served as garrison at Fort Pickering and in defenses of Memphis, Tennessee, and in District of West Tennessee, to April 1866.

4th Regiment, United States Colored Heavy Artillery

Date Raised
March 11, 1864

Muster Point(s)
Organized from 2d Tennessee Heavy Artillery (African Descent). Designated 3d Heavy Artillery, March 11, 1864, and 4th Heavy Artillery, April 26, 1864.

Date Disbanded
February 25, 1866

Place Disbanded
Pine Bluff, Arkansas

Movement Orders and Attachments
Attached to District of Columbus, XVI Corps, Department of Tennessee, to August 1864. District of Columbus, Department of Ohio, to June 1865. Department of Arkansas, to February 1866.

Engagements and Campaigns
Garrison duty at Fort Halleck, Columbus, Kentucky, to June 1865. Union City, Tennessee, September 2, 1864. Near Fort Donelson, Tennessee, October 11, 1864. Moved to Arkansas, June 1865, and duty at Pine Bluff, to February 1866.

5th Regiment, United States Colored Heavy Artillery

Date Raised
March 11, 1864

Muster Point(s)
Organized from 1st Mississippi Heavy Artillery (African Descent). Designated 4th Heavy Artillery, March 11, 1864, and 5th Heavy Artillery, April 26, 1864.

Date Disbanded
May 20, 1866

Place Disbanded
Vicksburg, Mississippi

Total Casualties
Lost during service 4 officers and 124 enlisted men killed and mortally wounded, and 697 enlisted men to disease.

Movement Orders and Attachments
Attached to 1st Division, United States Colored Troops, District of Vicksburg, to February 1865. Unattached, Post of Vicksburg, Department of Mississippi, and Department of the Gulf, to May 1864.

Engagements and Campaigns
Garrison duty at Vicksburg, to May 1866. Expedition from Vicksburg to Rodney and Fayette, September 29–October 3, 1864. Expedition from Vicksburg to Yazoo City, November 23–December 4, 1864.

6th Regiment, United States Colored Heavy Artillery

Date Raised
March 11, 1864

Muster Point(s)
Organized from 2d Mississippi Heavy Artillery (African Descent). Designated 5th Heavy Artillery, March 11, 1864, and 6th Heavy Artillery, April 26, 1864.

Date Disbanded
May 18, 1866

Place Disbanded
Department of the Gulf

Movement Orders and Attachments
Attached to Post of Natchez, Mississippi, District of Vicksburg, Mississippi, Department of Tennessee, and Department of Mississippi, to February 1865. Post of Natchez, Department of Mississippi, to April 1865. Department of the Gulf, to May 1866.

Engagements and Campaigns
Duty at Natchez, Mississippi, and Vidalia, Louisiana, to May 1866. Skirmish near Vidalia, July 22, 1864. Attack on steamer *Clara Bell,* July 24, 1864. Expedition from Natchez to Gillespie's Plantation, Louisiana, August 4–6, 1864. Concordia

Bayou, August 5. Expedition from Natchez to Buck's Ferry and skirmish, September 19–22, 1864. Expedition from Natchez to Waterproof and Sicily Island, September 26–30, 1864. Expedition from Natchez to Homichitto River, October 5–8, 1864. Expedition from Vidalia to York Plantation, Louisiana, October 26–27, 1864. Skirmish at Black River, October 31–November 1, 1864.

8th Regiment, United States Colored Heavy Artillery

Date Raised
April 26, 1864

Muster Point(s)
Paducah, Kentucky

Date Disbanded
February 10, 1866

Place Disbanded
Department of Kentucky

Movement Orders and Attachments
Attached to Paducah, District of Columbus, Kentucky, XVI Corps, Department of the Tennessee, to August 1864. Paducah, District of Columbus, Kentucky, Department of the Ohio, to February 1865, and Department of Kentucky, to February 1866.

Engagements and Campaigns
Garrison duty at Paducah, to February 1866. Operations against Confederate general Nathan Bedford Forrest in Kentucky, March 16–April 14, 1864. Action at Fort Anderson, Kentucky, March 25, 1864. Expedition from Paducah to Haddix Ferry, July 26–27, 1864. Skirmish near Haddix Ferry, August 27, 1864.

9th Regiment, United States Colored Heavy Artillery

Date Raised
October 8–November 1, 1864

Muster Point(s)
Clarksville and Nashville, Tennessee

Date Disbanded
May 5, 1865

Place Disbanded
Department of the Cumberland

Movement Orders and Attachments
Attached to District of Nashville, Department of the Cumberland, to May 1865.

10th Regiment, United States Colored Heavy Artillery

Date Raised
April 4, 1864

Muster Point(s)
Organized from I Corps d'Afrique Heavy Artillery. Designated 7th Regiment Heavy Artillery, April 4, 1864, and 10th Regiment Heavy Artillery, May 21, 1864.

Date Disbanded
February 22, 1867

Place Disbanded
New Orleans, Louisiana

Movement Orders and Attachments
Attached to defenses of New Orleans, Department of the Gulf, to October 1864. 1st Brigade, 3d Division, United States Colored Troops, Department of the Gulf, to November 1864. Defenses of New Orleans, to February 1867. Expedition to Lake Verret, Grand Bayou, and the Park, April 2–10, 1865 (Company G).

Engagements and Campaigns
On garrison duty at New Orleans and in the Department of the Gulf during entire term.

11th Regiment, United States Colored Heavy Artillery

Date Raised
April 4, 1864

Muster Point(s)
Organized from 14th Rhode Island Colored Heavy Artillery. Designated 8th Heavy Artillery, April 4, 1864, and 11th Heavy Artillery, May 21, 1864.

Date Disbanded
October 2, 1865

Place Disbanded
New Orleans, Louisiana

Movement Orders and Attachments
Attached to defenses of New Orleans, Department of the Gulf, to October 1865.

Engagements and Campaigns
Garrison duty at New Orleans and other points in the defenses of that city, to October 1865.

12th Regiment, United States Colored Heavy Artillery

Date Raised
July 15, 1864

Muster Point(s)
Camp Nelson, Kentucky

Date Disbanded
April 24, 1866

Place Disbanded
Department of Kentucky

Movement Orders and Attachments
Attached to 2d Brigade, 1st Division, District of Kentucky, Department of the Ohio, to January 1865. Military District of Kentucky and Department of Kentucky, to April 1866.

Engagements and Campaigns
Garrison duty in District of Kentucky, at Bowling Green, Camp Nelson, and other points, to April 1866.

13th Regiment, United States Colored Heavy Artillery

Date Raised
June 23, 1864

Muster Point(s)
Camp Nelson, Kentucky

Date Disbanded
November 18, 1865

Place Disbanded
Kentucky

Movement Orders and Attachments
Attached to Military District of Kentucky, Department of the Ohio, to February 1865, and to Department of Kentucky, to November 1865.

Engagements and Campaigns
Garrison duty at Camp Nelson, Smithland, Lexington, and other points in Kentucky, to November 1865.

14th Regiment, United States Colored Heavy Artillery

Date Raised
March 17, 1864

Muster Point(s)
Organized at New Bern and Morehead City, North Carolina, from 1st North Carolina Colored Heavy Artillery

Date Disbanded
December 11, 1865

Place Disbanded
Department of North Carolina

Movement Orders and Attachments
Attached to defenses of New Bern, Department of Virginia and North Carolina, to January 1865. Subdistrict of New Bern, Department of North Carolina, and Subdistrict of Beaufort, North Carolina, Department of North Carolina, to December 1865.

Engagements and Campaigns
Garrison duty at New Bern and other points in the Department of North Carolina, to December 1865.

References and Further Reading

Beecham, Robert K. *As If It Were Glory: Robert Beecham's Civil War from the Iron Brigade to the Black Regiments,* ed. Michael E. Stevens. Madison, WI: Madison House, 1998.

Cornish, Dudley Taylor. *The Sable Arm: Black Troops in the Union Army, 1861–1865.* Lawrence: University Press of Kansas, 1987.

Current, Richard Nelson. *Lincoln's Loyalists: Union Soldiers from the Confederacy.* New York: Oxford University Press, 1992.

Denney, Robert E. *The Civil War Years: A Day-by-Day Chronicle.* New York: Gramercy Books, 1992.

Dyer, Frederick H. *A Compendium of the War of the Rebellion.* 3 vols. New York: Thomas Yoseloff, 1959.

Gladstone, William A. *United States Colored Troops, 1863–1867.* Gettysburg, PA: Thomas Publications, 1990.

Glatthaar, Joseph T. *Forged in Battle: The Civil War Alliance of Black Soldiers and White Officers.* Baton Rouge: Louisiana State University Press, 2000.

Hansen, Joyce. *Between Two Fires: Black Soldiers in the Civil War.* New York: Franklin Watts, 1993.

Higginson, Thomas Wentworth. *Army Life in a Black Regiment.* Williamstown, MA: Corner House Publishers, 1984.

McPherson, James M. *Marching Toward Freedom: Blacks in the Civil War, 1861–1865.* New York: Knopf, 1968.

———. *The Negro's Civil War: How American Blacks Felt and Acted during the War for the Union.* New York: Pantheon, 1965.

Redkey, Edwin S., ed. *A Grand Army of Black Men: Letters from African American Soldiers in the Union Army, 1861–1865.* New York: Cambridge University Press, 1992.

Wilson, Joseph T. *The Black Phalanx: A History of the Negro Soldiers of the United States in the Wars of 1775–1812, 1861–1865.* 1890. Reprint, Salem, NH: Ayer Company Publishers, 1992.

United States Colored Cavalry, Formation and Service Records of

1st Regiment, United States Colored Cavalry

Date Raised
December 22, 1863

Muster Point(s)
Camp Hamilton, VA

Date Disbanded
February 4, 1866

Place Disbanded
Texas

Movement Orders and Attachments
Attached to Fort Monroe, Va., Department of Virginia and North Carolina, to April 1864. Unattached Williamsburg, Va, Department of Virginia and North Carolina, to June 1864. 1st Brigade, 3d Division, 18th Corps, Army of the James, to August 1864. Defenses of Portsmouth, Va., District of Eastern Virginia, to May 1865. Cavalry Brigade, 25th Corps, Department of Virginia and Department of Texas, to February 1866.

Engagements and Campaigns
Duty at Fort Monroe and Williamsburg, Va., until May 1864. Reconnaissance in Kings and Queens County February 1864. Butler's operations on south side of James River and against Petersburg and Richmond May 4–28. Capture of Bermuda Hundred and City Point May 5. Swift Creek May 8–10. Operations against Fort Darling May 12–16. Actions at Drury's Bluff May 10–14–15 and 16. In trenches at Bermuda Hundred until June 18. Baylor's Farm June 15. Assaults on Petersburg June 16–19. Siege of Petersburg until August. Action at Deep Bottom July 27–28. Ordered to Fort Monroe August 3. Duty at Newport News and at Portsmouth and in District of Eastern Virginia until May 1865. Cos. E and I detached at Fort Powhatan and Harrison's Landing August 1864 to May 1865. Moved to City Point, Va., thence sailed for Texas June 10. Duty on the Rio Grande and at various points in Texas until February 1866.

2d Regiment, United States Colored Cavalry

Date Raised
December 22, 1863

Muster Point(s)
Fort Monroe, VA

Date Disbanded
February 12, 1866

Place Disbanded
Texas

Movement Orders and Attachments
Attached to Fort Monroe, Va., Department of Virginia and North Carolina, to April 1864. Unattached Williamsburg, Va, Department of Virginia and North Carolina, to June 1864. 2d Brigade, 3d Division, 18th Corps, Army of the James, to August 1864. Unattached 3d Division, 18th Corps, to December 1864. Unattached 25th Corps, Department of Virginia, to May 1865. Cavalry Brigade, 25th Corps, Department of Virginia and Department of Texas, to February 1866.

Engagements and Campaigns
Duty at Fort Monroe, Portsmouth, and Williamsburg, Va., until May 1864. Demonstration

on Portsmouth March 4–5. Action near Suffolk March 10. Reconnaissance from Portsmouth to the Blackwater April 13–15. Butler's operations on the south side of James River and against Petersburg and Richmond May 4–28. Capture of Bermuda Hundred and City Point May 5. Swift Creek May 8–10. Operations against Fort Darling May 10–16. Actions at Drury's Bluff May 10–16. Near Drury's Bluff May 20. Duty in trenches at Bermuda Hundred until June 13. Point of Rocks June 10. Richmond Campaign June 13–July 31. Baylor's Farm June 15. Assaults on Petersburg June 16–19. Siege of Petersburg and Richmond June 16, 1864, to February 18, 1865. Duty before Petersburg until July 1864. Moved to Deep Bottom July 25. Action at Deep Bottom July 27–28. Strawberry Plains, Deep Bottom, August 14–18. Actions at Deep Bottom September 2 and 6. Chaffin's Farm September 29–30. Darbytown Road October 7. Battle of Fair Oaks, Darbytown Road October 27–28. Near Richmond October 28–29. Duty in trenches north of James River until February 1865. Ordered to Norfolk February 18. Duty in District of Eastern Virginia at Norfolk, Suffolk, etc., until May. Ordered to City Point, Va.; thence sailed for Texas June 10. Duty on the Rio Grande and at various points in Texas until February 1866.

3d Regiment, United States Colored Cavalry

Date Raised
March 11, 1864

Muster Point(s)
Organized from 1st Mississippi Cavalry (African Descent)

Date Disbanded
January 26, 1866

Place Disbanded
Department of Mississippi

Movement Orders and Attachments
Attached to 1st Brigade, United States Colored Troops, District of Vicksburg, Miss., Department of the Tennessee, to April 1864. Winslow's Cavalry Brigade, District of Vicksburg, to December 1864. 3d Brigade, Cavalry Division, District of West Tennessee, to January 1865. Unattached Cavalry, District of West Tennessee, to June 1865. 1st Brigade, Cavalry Division, District of West Tennessee, to January 1866.

Engagements and Campaigns
Duty at Vicksburg, Miss., and in that district until December 1864. Action at Roach's Plantation, Miss., March 30. Columbus, Ky., April 11 and 13 (detachment). Expedition from Haines' Bluff up Yazoo River April 19–28. Near Mechanicsburg April 20. Expedition from Vicksburg to Yazoo City May 4–21. Benton May 7 and 9. Yazoo City May 13. Near Vicksburg June 4. Expedition from Vicksburg to Pearl River July 2–10. Jackson July 7. Utica July 13. Grand Gulf July 16. Bayou Tensas, La., August 26. Expedition from Goodrich Landing to Bayou Macon August 28–31. Expedition from Vicksburg to Deer Creek September 21–26. Near Rolling Fork September 22–23. Expedition from Vicksburg to Rodney and Fayette September 29–October 3. Expedition from Natchez to Woodville October 4–11. Fort Adams October 5. Woodville October 5–6. Operations in Issaqueena and Washington Counties October 21–31. Steele's Bayou October 23. Expedition from Vicksburg to Gaines' Landing, Ark., and Bayou Macon, La., November 6–8. Rolling Fork November 11. Expedition from Vicksburg to Yazoo City November 23–December 4. Big Black River Bridge November 27. Moved to Memphis, Tenn. Grierson's Expedition from Memphis, Tenn., to destroy Mobile & Ohio Railroad December 21, 1864–January 5, 1865. Franklin Creek December 21– 22, 1864. Okolona December 27. Egypt Station December 28. Franklin January 2, 1865. Moved to Memphis from Vicksburg, Miss., January 5–10. Duty there and in District of West Tennessee until April. Expedition from Memphis to Brownsville, Miss., April 23–26. Moved to Vicksburg April 29–May 1 and operating about Natchez for the capture of Jeff Davis May. Operations about Fort Adams May 3–6. Duty in District of West Tennessee and Department of Mississippi until January 1866.

4th Regiment, United States Colored Cavalry

Date Raised
April 4, 1864

Muster Point(s)
Organized from 1st Corps d'Afrique Cavalry

Date Disbanded
March 20, 1866

Place Disbanded
Department of Mississippi

Movement Orders and Attachments
Attached to defenses of New Orleans, La., Department of the Gulf, to August 1864. District of Port Hudson, La., Department of the Gulf, to October 1864. 1st Brigade, 2d Division, United States Colored Troops, Department of the Gulf, to December 1864. District of Port Hudson, La., Department of the Gulf, to July 1865. Department of Mississippi to March 1866.

Engagements and Campaigns
Duty in the defenses of New Orleans, La., at New Orleans, Carrollton, Camp Parapet, and Donaldsonville, District of LaFourche, until August 1864. Ordered to Baton Rouge, La., August 8, and duty in the defenses of that post until July 1865. Expedition to Clinton August 23–29, 1864. Action at Olive Branch, Comite River, August 25. Expedition from Port Hudson to Jackson April 11–13, 1865. Duty at various points in the Department of Mississippi until March 1866.

5th Regiment, Massachusetts Cavalry (Colored)

Date Raised
May 5–8, 1864

Muster Point(s)
Camp Meigs, Readville, MA

Date Disbanded
October 31, 1865

Place Disbanded
Texas

Movement Orders and Attachments
At Camp Stoneman, Giesboro Point, Md., May 8–12. Dismounted and moved to Camp Casey, near Fort Albany, May 12. 2d Battalion moved to Washington May 6–8, and to Camp Casey May 9. 3d Battalion moved to Washington May 8–10, and to Camp Casey May 11. Regiment moved to Fortress Monroe, Va., thence to City Point, Va., May 13–16. Attached to Rand's Provisional Brigade, 18th Army Corps, Department of Virginia and North Carolina, May 1864. Hinks' Colored Division, 18th Army Corps, to June 1864. 1st Brigade, 3d Division, 18th Army Corps, to July 1864. Point Lookout, Md., District of St. Mary's, 22d Army Corps, to March 1865. Unattached, 25th Army Corps, Department of Virginia, to June 1865. Department of Texas to October 1865.

Engagements and Campaigns
Duty at City Point, Va., as infantry until June 16, 1864. Before Petersburg June 16–19. Siege of Petersburg June 16–28. Moved to Point Lookout, Md., June 30, and duty there guarding prisoners until March 1865. Ordered to the field and duty near Richmond, March; near Petersburg, April; near City Point, May; and at Camp Lincoln until June 16. Ordered to Texas and duty at Clarksville until October.

5th Regiment, United States Colored Cavalry

Date Raised
October 24, 1864

Muster Point(s)
Camp Nelson, KY

Date Disbanded
March 20, 1866

Place Disbanded
Department of Arkansas

Total Casualties
Regiment lost during service, 35 enlisted men killed and mortally wounded and 1 officer and 151 enlisted men to disease. Total 187.

Movement Orders and Attachments
Attached to 1st Division, District of Kentucky, Department of Ohio, to February 1865. Military District of Kentucky and Department of Arkansas, to March 1866.

Engagements and Campaigns
Participated in Burbridge's Raid from Kentucky into southwestern Virginia September 20–October 17, 1864. Action at Saltville, Va., October 2. At Lexington, Ky., October 19. Harrodsburg, Ky., October 21. Stoneman's Raid into southwestern Virginia December 10–29. Near Marion December 17–18. Capture of Saltville and destruction of salt

works December 20–21. Duty at Ghent, Paducah, LaGrange, Crab Orchard, and Camp Nelson until August 1865 and in the Department of Arkansas until March 1866.

6th Regiment, United States Colored Cavalry

Date Raised
October 24, 1864

Muster Point(s)
Camp Nelson, KY

Date Disbanded
April 15, 1866

Place Disbanded
Duvall's Bluff, AK

Movement Orders and Attachments
Attached to 1st Division, District of Kentucky, Department of Ohio, to February 1865. Military District and Department of Kentucky to December 1865 and Department of Arkansas to April 1866.

Engagements and Campaigns
Stoneman's Raid into southwestern Virginia December 10–29, 1864. Capture and destruction of lead mines December 17. Near Marion December 17–18. Saltville December 20–21. At Camp Nelson and Paducah, Ky., until March 1865. At LaGrange, Tenn., until May. At Camp Nelson, Wild Cat, and Danville, Ky., until July. At New Haven and Catlettsburg, Ky., until October. At Covington, Ky., until December. At Louisville, Ky., and Helena, Ark., until January 1866.

References and Further Reading

Beecham, Robert K. *As If It Were Glory: Robert Beecham's Civil War from the Iron Brigade to the Black Regiments,* ed. Michael E. Stevens. Madison, WI: Madison House, 1998.

Cornish, Dudley Taylor. *The Sable Arm: Black Troops in the Union Army, 1861–1865.* University Press of Kansas, 1987.

Current, Richard Nelson. *Lincoln's Loyalists: Union Soldiers from the Confederacy.* New York: Oxford University Press, 1992.

Denney, Robert E. *The Civil War Years: A Day-by-Day Chronicle.* New York: Gramercy Books, 1992.

Dyer, Frederick H. *A Compendium of the War of Rebellion.* 3 vols. New York: Thomas Yoseloff, 1959.

Gladstone, William A. *United States Colored Troops, 1863–1867.* Gettysburg, PA: Thomas Publications, 1990.

Glatthaar, Joseph T. *Forged in Battle: The Civil War Alliance of Black Soldiers and White Officers.* Baton Rouge: Louisiana State University Press, 2000.

Hansen, Joyce. *Between Two Fires: Black Soldiers in the Civil War.* New York: Franklin Watts, 1993.

Higginson, Thomas Wentworth. *Army Life in a Black Regiment.* Williamstown, MA: Corner House Publishers, 1984.

McPherson, James M. *Marching Toward Freedom: Blacks in the Civil War, 1861–1865.* New York: Knopf, 1968.

———. *The Negro's Civil War: How American Blacks Felt and Acted during the War for the Union.* New York: Pantheon, 1965.

Redkey, Edwin S., ed. *A Grand Army of Black Men: Letters from African American Soldiers in the Union Army, 1861–1865.* New York: Cambridge University Press, 1992.

Wilson, Joseph T. *The Black Phalanx: A History of the Negro Soldiers of the United States in the Wars of 1775–1812, 1861–'65.* Hartford, CT: American Publishing Company, 1890. Reprint Salem, NH: Ayer, 1992.

United States Colored Troops, Formation and Service Records of

1st Regiment,
South Carolina Infantry (Colored)

Date Raised
January 31, 1863

Muster Point(s)
Beaufort, South Carolina

Date Disbanded
February 8, 1864

Movement Orders and Attachments
Attached to District of Beaufort, X Corps, Department of the South, to January 1864. Barton's Brigade, District of Hilton Head, South Carolina, X Corps, to February 1864. Designation of regiment changed to 33d United States Colored Troops.

Engagements and Campaigns
Before muster, three companies on expedition along coasts of Georgia and Florida, November 3–7 (Company A), and Doboy River, November 8. Duty at Beaufort, and Port Royal Island, to March 1863. Expedition from Beaufort up St. Mary's River in Georgia and Florida, January 23–February 1. Skirmish at Township, January 26. Expedition from Beaufort to Jacksonville, Florida, March 6–10. Occupation of Jacksonville, March 10–31. Camp Jackson, March 10. Operations near Jacksonville, March 23–31. Skirmish near Jacksonville, March 29. At Beaufort, to January 1864. Expedition up South Edisto River, July 9–11, 1863. Action at Williston Bluff, Pon Pon River, July 10. Expedition to Pocotaligo, South Carolina, November 23–25, (Companies E and K). Skirmish near Cunningham's Bluff, November 24. (Companies C and K at Hilton Head, South Carolina, to September 1863, then moved to Beaufort, October 2.) Regiment moved to Hilton Head, January 1864. Expedition to Jacksonville, February 6–8.

1st Regiment,
United States Colored Infantry

Date Raised
May 19–June 30, 1863

Muster Point(s)
District of Columbia

Date Disbanded
September 29, 1865

Place Disbanded
North Carolina

Total Casualties
Regiment lost 4 officers and 67 enlisted men killed and mortally wounded, and 1 officer and 113 enlisted men to disease. Total: 185.

Movement Orders and Attachments
Attached to U.S. forces, Norfolk and Portsmouth, Virginia, Department of Virginia and North Carolina, July–October 1863. U.S. forces, Yorktown, Virginia, Department of Virginia and North Carolina, to April 1864. 1st Brigade, Hincks's Colored Division, XVIII Corps, Army of the James, Department of Virginia and North Carolina, to June 1864. 1st Brigade, 3d Division, XVIII Corps, to December 1864. 1st Brigade, 1st Division, XXV Corps, to December 1864. 1st Brigade, 3d Division, XXV Corps, to March 1865. 1st Brigade, 3d Division, X Corps, Department of North Carolina, to August 1865.

Engagements and Campaigns
Duty at Norfolk, Portsmouth, and Yorktown, Virginia, to April 1864. Expedition from Norfolk to South Mills, Camden Court House, etc., North Carolina, December 5–24, 1863. Gen. Benjamin F. Butler's operations south of James River and against Petersburg and Richmond, Virginia, May 4–June 15. Action at Wilson's Wharf, May 24. Assaults on Petersburg, June 15–18. Siege of Petersburg and Richmond, June 16–December 7, 1864. Explosion of mine, Petersburg, July 30. Demonstration on north side of James River, September 28–30. Battle of Chaffin's Farm, New Market Heights, September 28–30. Fort Harrison, September 29. Battle of Fair Oaks, October 27–28. Expedition to Fort Fisher, North Carolina, December 7–27. Second expedition to Fort Fisher, January 7–15, 1865. Capture of Fort Fisher, January 15. Sugar Loaf Hill, January 19. Sugar Loaf Battery, February 11. Fort Anderson, February 18–20. Capture of Wilmington, February 22. Northeast Ferry, February 22. Campaign of the Carolinas, March 1–April 26. Advance on Goldsboro, March 6–21. Occupation of Goldsboro, March 21. Cox's Bridge, March 23–24. Advance on Raleigh, April 9–13. Occupation of Raleigh, April 13. Surrender of Gen. Joseph E. Johnston and his Confederate army at Bennett's House, April 26. Duty in Department of North Carolina, to September.

2d Regiment, United States Colored Infantry

Date Raised
June 20–November 11, 1863

Muster Point(s)
Arlington, Virginia

Date Disbanded
January 5, 1866

Place Disbanded
Florida

Total Casualties
Regiment lost 3 officers and 24 enlisted men killed and mortally wounded, and 11 officers and 135 enlisted men to disease. Total: 173.

Movement Orders and Attachments
Ordered to Department of the Gulf, December 1863. Attached to District of Key West, Florida, Department of the Gulf, February 1864–July 1865. Department of Florida, to January 1866.

Engagements and Campaigns
Duty at New Orleans, Louisiana, and Ship Island, Mississippi, to February 13, 1864. Ordered to Key West, February 13. Affair at Tampa, Florida, May 5. Operations on west coast of Florida, July 1–31. Expedition from Fort Myers to Bayport, July 1–4. Expedition from Cedar Key to St. Andrew's Bay, July 20–29. Fort Taylor, August 21. Station No. 4, February 13, 1865. Attack on Fort Myers, February 20. Operations in vicinity of St. Marks, February 21–March 7. East River Bridge, March 4–5. Newport Bridge, March 5–6. Natural Bridge, March 6. Duty in District of Florida, to January 1866.

3d Regiment, United States Colored Infantry

Date Raised
August 3–10, 1863

Muster Point(s)
Camp William Penn, near Philadelphia, Pennsylvania

Date Disbanded
October 31, 1865

Place Disbanded
Florida

Movement Orders and Attachments
Ordered to Department of the South. Attached to 4th Brigade, Morris Island, South Carolina, X Corps, Department of the South, to November 1863. 3d Brigade, Morris Island, X Corps, to January 1864. Montgomery's Brigade, District of Hilton Head, South Carolina, X Corps, to February 1864. 2d Brigade, Vogdes's Division, District of Florida, Department of the South, to April 1864. District of Florida, Department of the South, to October 1864. 4th Separate Brigade, District of Florida, Department of the South, to July 1865. Department of Florida, to October 1865.

Engagements and Campaigns
Siege of Forts Wagner and Gregg, Morris Island, August 20–September 7, 1863. Action at Forts Wagner and Gregg, August 26. Capture of Forts Wagner and Gregg, September 7. Operations against Charleston from Morris Island, to January

1864. Moved to Hilton Head, and Jacksonville, Florida, February 5–7, and duty there as Heavy Artillery, to May 1865. (One company at Fernandina, Florida.) Expedition from Jacksonville to Camp Milton, May 31–June 3, 1864. Front Creek, July 15. Bryan's Plantation, October 21. Duty at Tallahassee, Lake City, and other points in Florida, May–October, 1865.

4th Regiment, United States Colored Infantry

Date Raised
July 15–September 1, 1863

Muster Point(s)
Baltimore, Maryland

Date Disbanded
May 4, 1866

Place Disbanded
North Carolina

Total Casualties
Regiment lost 3 officers and 102 enlisted men killed and mortally wounded, and 1 officer and 186 enlisted men to disease. Total: 292.

Movement Orders and Attachments
Moved to Fort Monroe, Virginia, October 1, 1863; then moved to Yorktown, Virginia. Attached to 2d Brigade, U.S. forces, Yorktown, XVIII Corps, Department of Virginia and North Carolina, to April 1864. 2d Brigade, Hincks's Colored Division, XVIII Corps, to June 1864. 2d Brigade, 3d Division, XVIII Corps, to December 1864. 2d Brigade, 1st Division, XXV Corps, to January 1865. 2d Brigade, 3d Division, XXV Corps, to March 1865. 2d Brigade, 3d Division, X Corps, Department of North Carolina, to August 1865. Department of North Carolina, to May 1866.

Engagements and Campaigns
Duty at Yorktown, to May 1864. Expedition from Yorktown to Matthews County, October 4–9, 1863. Wistar's Expedition against Richmond, February 6–8, 1864. New Kent Court House, February 8. Expedition to Bottom's Bridge in aid of Kilpatrick's cavalry, March 1–4. Expedition into King and Queen County, March 9–12. Expedition into Matthews and Middlesex Counties, March 17–21. Gen. Benjamin F. Butler's operations south of James River and against Petersburg and Richmond, May 4–June 15. Skirmish at Bermuda Hundred, May 4. Duty at Spring Hill on Appomattox River, to June. (Built Fort Converse on Bermuda Hundred line.) Attack on Fort Converse, May 20. Before Petersburg, June 15–18. Siege operations against Petersburg and Richmond, June 16–December 7. Mine explosion at Petersburg, July 30. Dutch Gap, September 7. Battle of Chaffin's Farm, New Market Heights, September 28–30. Battle of Fair Oaks, October 27–28. First expedition to Fort Fisher, North Carolina, December 7–27. Second expedition to Fort Fisher, January 7–15. Assault and capture of Fort Fisher, January 15. Sugar Loaf Hill, January 19. Sugar Loaf Battery, February 11. Fort Anderson, February 18–20. Capture of Wilmington, February 22. Northeast Ferry, February 22. Campaign of the Carolinas, March 1–April 26. Advance on Goldsboro, March 6–21. Occupation of Goldsboro, March 21. Cox's Bridge, March 23–24. Advance on Raleigh, April 9–18. Occupation of Raleigh, April 14. Surrender of Gen. Joseph E. Johnston and his Confederate army at Bennett's House, April 26. Duty in Department of North Carolina, to May 1866.

5th Regiment, United States Colored Infantry

Date Raised
August–November 1863

Muster Point(s)
Camp Delaware, Ohio

Date Disbanded
September 20, 1865

Place Disbanded
Carolina City, North Carolina

Total Casualties
Regiment lost 4 officers and 77 enlisted men killed and mortally wounded, and 2 officers and 166 enlisted men to disease. Total: 249.

Movement Orders and Attachments
Moved to Norfolk, Virginia, November 1863. Attached to U.S. forces, Norfolk and Portsmouth, Virginia, Department of Virginia and North Carolina, to January 1864. 2d Brigade, U.S. forces, Yorktown, XVIII Corps, Department of Virginia and North Carolina, to April 1864. 2d Brigade, Hincks's

Colored Division, XVIII Corps, Army of the James, Department of Virginia and North Carolina, to June 1864. 2d Brigade, 3d Division, XVIII Corps, to December 1864. 3d Brigade, 1st Division, XXV Corps, to December 1864. 3d Brigade, 3d Division, XXV Corps, to March 1865. 2d Brigade, 3d Division, X Corps, Department of North Carolina, to August 1865. Department of North Carolina, to September 1865.

Engagements and Campaigns
Duty at Norfolk and Portsmouth, to January 1864. Wild's Expedition to South Mills and Camden Court House, North Carolina, December 5–24, 1863. Action at Sandy Swamp, North Carolina, December 8. Moved to Yorktown, January 1864, and duty there until May. Wistar's Expedition against Richmond, February 6–8. Expedition to New Kent Court House in aid of Kilpatrick's cavalry, March 1–4. New Kent Court House, March 2. Expedition into King and Queen County, March 9–12. Expedition into Matthews and Middlesex Counties, March 17–21. Gen. Benjamin F. Butler's operations on south side of James River and against Petersburg and Richmond, May 4–June 15. Capture of City Point, May 4. Fatigue duty at City Point and building Fort Converse on Appomattox River, to June 15. Attack on Fort Converse, May 20. Before Petersburg, June 15–18. Bailor's Farm, June 15. Siege operations against Petersburg and Richmond, June 16–December 6. In trenches before Petersburg, to August 27. Mine explosion at Petersburg, July 30. Moved to Deep Bottom, August 28. Battle of Chaffin's Farm, New Market Heights, September 28–30. Fort Harrison, September 29. Battle of Fair Oaks, October 27–28. In trenches before Richmond, to December. First expedition to Fort Fisher, North Carolina, December 7–27. Second expedition to Fort Fisher, January 7–15. Assault and capture of Fort Fisher, January 15. Sugar Loaf Hill, January 19. Federal Point, February 11. Fort Anderson, February 18–20. Capture of Wilmington, February 22. Northeast Ferry, February 22. Campaign of the Carolinas, March 1–April 26. Advance on Kinston and Goldsboro, March 6–21. Occupation of Goldsboro, March 21. Cox's Bridge, March 23–24. Advance on Raleigh, April 9–14. Occupation of Raleigh, April 14. Surrender of Gen. Joseph E. Johnston and his Confederate army at Bennett's House, April 26. Duty at Goldsboro, New Berne, and Carolina City.

5th Regiment, Massachusetts Cavalry (Colored))

Date Raised
May 5–8, 1864

Muster Point(s)
Camp Meigs, Readville, Massachusetts

Date Disbanded
October 31, 1865

Place Disbanded
Texas

Total Casualties
Regiment lost 7 enlisted men killed and 116 enlisted men to disease. Total: 123.

Movement Orders and Attachments
1st Battalion moved to Washington, D.C., May 5–8, 1864. At Camp Stoneman, Giesboro Point, Maryland, May 8–12. Dismounted and moved to Camp Casey, near Fort Albany, May 12. 2d Battalion moved to Washington, D.C., May 6–8, and to Camp Casey, May 9. 3d Battalion moved to Washington, D.C., May 8–10, and to Camp Casey, May 11. Regiment moved to Fort Monroe, Virginia, then to City Point, Virginia, May 13–16. Attached to Rand's Provisional Brigade, XVIII Corps, Department of Virginia and North Carolina, May 1864. Hincks's Colored Division, XVIII Corps, to June 1864. 1st Brigade, 3d Division, XVIII Corps, to July 1864. Point Lookout, Maryland, District of St. Mary's, XXII Corps, to March 1865. Unattached, XXV Corps, Department of Virginia, to June 1865. Department of Texas to October 1865.

Engagements and Campaigns
Duty at City Point as infantry until June 16, 1864. Before Petersburg, June 16–19. Siege of Petersburg, June 16–28. Moved to Point Lookout, June 30, and duty there guarding prisoners until March 1865. Ordered to field and duty near Richmond, March; near Petersburg, April; near City Point, May; and at Camp Lincoln until June 16. Ordered to Texas and duty at Clarksville until October.

6th Regiment, United States Colored Infantry

Date Raised
July 28–September 12, 1863

Muster Point(s)
Camp William Penn, near Philadelphia, Pennsylvania

Date Disbanded
September 20, 1865

Place Disbanded
North Carolina

Total Casualties
Regiment lost 8 officers and 79 enlisted men killed and mortally wounded, and 5 officers and 132 enlisted men to disease. Total: 224.

Movement Orders and Attachments
Moved from Philadelphia to Fort Monroe, Virginia, October 14; then to Yorktown, Virginia. Attached to U.S. forces, Yorktown, Department of Virginia and North Carolina, to January 1864. 2d Brigade, U.S. forces, Yorktown, XVIII Corps, Department of Virginia and North Carolina, to April 1864. 2d Brigade, Hincks's Colored Division, XVIII Corps, Army of the James, to June 1864. 2d Brigade, 3d Division, XVIII Corps, to August 1864. 3d Brigade, 3d Division, XVIII Corps, to December 1864. 2d Brigade, 1st Division, XXV Corps, to December 1864. 2d Brigade, 3d Division, XXV Corps, to March 1865. 3d Brigade, 3d Division, X Corps, Department of North Carolina, to August 1865. Department of North Carolina, to September 1865.

Engagements and Campaigns
Duty at Yorktown, to May 1864. Wild's Expedition to South Mills and Camden Court House, North Carolina, December 5–24, 1863. Wistar's Expedition against Richmond, February 2–6, 1864. Expedition to New Kent Court House in aid of Kilpatrick's cavalry, March 1–4. New Kent Court House, March 2. Williamsburg, March 4. Expedition into King and Queen County, March 9–12. Expedition into Matthews County, March 17–21. Gen. Benjamin F. Butler's operations south of James River and against Petersburg and Richmond, May 4–June 15. Capture of City Point, May 4. Fatigue duty at City Point and building Fort Converse on Appomattox River, to June 15. Attack on Fort Converse, May 20. Before Petersburg, June 15–18. Bailor's Farm, June 15. Siege operations against Petersburg and Richmond, June 15–December 17. In trenches before Petersburg and fatigue duty at Dutch Gap Canal, to August 27. Moved to Deep Bottom, August 27. Battle of Chaffin's Farm, New Market Heights, September 29–30. Fort Harrison, September 29. Battle of Fair Oaks, October 27–28. In trenches before Richmond, to December. First expedition to Fort Fisher, North Carolina, December 7–27. Second expedition to Fort Fisher, January 7–15. Bombardment of Fort Fisher, January 13–15. Assault and capture of Fort Fisher, January 15. Sugar Loaf Hill, January 19. Sugar Loaf Battery, February 11. Fort Anderson, February 18–20. Capture of Wilmington, February 22. Northeast Ferry, February 22. Campaign of the Carolinas, March 1–April 26. Advance on Kinston and Goldsboro, March 6–21. Occupation of Goldsboro, March 21. Cox's Bridge, March 23–24. Advance on Raleigh, April 9–14. Occupation of Raleigh, April 14. Surrender of Gen. Joseph E. Johnston and his Confederate army at Bennett's House, April 26. Duty in Department of North Carolina.

6th Regiment, Louisiana Infantry (Colored)

Date Raised
July 4, 1863

Muster Point(s)
New Orleans, Louisiana

Date Disbanded
August 13, 1863

Place Disbanded
New Orleans

Movement Orders and Attachments
Duty at New Orleans.

7th Regiment, United States Colored Infantry

Date Raised
September 26–November 12, 1863

Muster Point(s)
Baltimore, Maryland

Date Disbanded
November 15, 1866

Place Disbanded
Baltimore

Total Casualties
Regiment lost 1 officer and 84 enlisted men killed and mortally wounded, and 1 officer and 307 enlisted men to disease. Total: 393.

Movement Orders and Attachments
Duty at Camp Benedict, Maryland, to March 1864. Ordered to Portsmouth, Virginia, March 4, then to Hilton Head, South Carolina, March 7–10, and to Jacksonville, Florida, March 14–15. Attached to post of Jacksonville, District of Florida, Department of the South, to July 1864. District of Hilton Head, Department of the South, July 1864. Jacksonville, District of Florida, Department of the South, to August 1864. 1st Brigade, 3d Division, X Corps, Army of the James, Department of Virginia and North Carolina, to December 1864. 1st Brigade, 2d Division, XXV Corps, to January 1866. Department of Texas, to October 1866.

Engagements and Campaigns
Duty at Jacksonville, to June 1864. Cedar Creek, April 2. Near Jacksonville, May 6. Near Camp Finnegan, May 25. Near Jacksonville, May 28. Expedition to Camp Milton, May 31–June 3. Camp Milton, June 2. Moved to Hilton Head, June 27. Expedition to North Edisto River and John's and James Islands, July 2–10. Near Winter's Point, July 3. King's Creek, July 3. Skirmishes on James Island, July 5 and 7. Burden's Causeway, John's Island, July 9. Moved to Jacksonville, July 15. Expedition to Florida Camp, Gulf Railroad, July 22–August 5. Moved to Bermuda Hundred, Virginia, August 6–11. Siege operations against Petersburg and Richmond, August 1864–April, 1865. Demonstration north of James River, August 16–20. Russell's Mills, August 16. Strawberry Plains, August 16–18. Battle of Chaffin's Farm, New Market Heights, September 28–30. Darbytown Road, October 13. Battle of Fair Oaks, October 27–28. Near Richmond, October 28. In trenches before Richmond, to March 27, 1865. Appomattox Campaign, March 27–April 9. Hatcher's Run, March 29–31. Fall of Petersburg, April 2. Pursuit of Confederate general Robert E. Lee, April 3–9. Appomattox Court House, April 9. Surrender of Lee and his army. Moved to Petersburg, April 11, and duty there until May 24. Moved to Indianola, Texas, May 24–June 23. Duty on Rio Grande and at various points in Department of Texas, to October 1866. Moved to Baltimore, October 14–November 4.

7th Regiment, Louisiana Infantry (Colored)

Date Raised
July 10, 1863

Muster Point(s)
New Orleans, Louisiana

Date Disbanded
August 6, 1863

Place Disbanded
New Orleans

Movement Orders and Attachments
Duty at New Orleans.

8th Regiment, United States Colored Infantry

Date Raised
September 22–December 4, 1863

Muster Point(s)
Camp William Penn, Philadelphia, Pennsylvania

Date Disbanded
December 12, 1865

Place Disbanded
Philadelphia

Total Casualties
Regiment lost 4 officers and 115 enlisted men killed and mortally wounded, and 132 enlisted men to disease. Total: 251.

Movement Orders and Attachments
Left Philadelphia for Hilton Head, South Carolina, January 16, 1864. Attached to Howell's Brigade, District of Hilton Head, Department of the South, to February 1864. Hawley's Brigade, Seymour's Division, District of Florida, Department of the South, to April 1864. District of Florida, Department of the South, to August 1864. 1st Brigade, 3d Division, X Corps, Army of the James, Department of Virginia and North Carolina, to December 1864. 2d Brigade, 2d Division, XXV Corps, to April 1865. 1st Brigade, 2d Division, XXV Corps, and Department of Texas, to November 1865.

Engagements and Campaigns
Expedition from Hilton Head, to Jacksonville, Florida, February 5–6, 1864. Occupation of Jacksonville, February 7. Advance into Florida, February 8–20. Camp Finnegan, February 8. Battle of Olustee, February 20. Retreat to Jacksonville and duty there until April. Moved to St. John's Bluff, April 17, and duty there until August. Raid on Baldwin, July 23–28. Moved to Deep Bottom, Virginia, August 4–12. Action at Deep Bottom,

August 12. Duty at Deep Bottom and in trenches before Petersburg, to September 27. Battle of Chaffin's Farm, New Market Heights, September 28–30. Fort Harrison, September 29. Darbytown Road, October 13. Battle of Fair Oaks, October 27–28. In trenches before Richmond, to March 27, 1865. Appomattox Campaign, March 28–April 9. Hatcher's Run, March 29–31. Fall of Petersburg, April 2. Pursuit of Confederate general Robert E. Lee, April 3–9. Appomattox Court House, April 9. Surrender of Lee and his army. Moved to Petersburg, April 11, and duty there until May 24. Sailed from City Point for Texas, May 24. Duty at Ringgold Barracks and on Rio Grande, Texas, to November, 1865.

9th Regiment, United States Colored Infantry

Date Raised
November 11–30, 1863

Muster Point(s)
Camp Stanton, Maryland

Date Disbanded
November 20, 1866

Place Disbanded
New Orleans, Louisiana

Total Casualties
Regiment lost 1 officer and 46 enlisted men killed and mortally wounded, and 2 officers and 266 enlisted men to disease. Total: 315.

Movement Orders and Attachments
Duty at Benedict, Maryland, to March 1864. Moved to Port Royal, South Carolina, March 3–7. Attached to District of Hilton Head, South Carolina, Department of the South, to April 1864. District of Beaufort, South Carolina, Department of the South, to August 1864. 1st Brigade, 3d Division, X Corps, Army of the James, Department of Virginia and North Carolina, to December 1864. 2d Brigade, 3d Division, XXV Corps, to January 1865. 2d Brigade, 1st Division, XXV Corps, to January 1866. Department of Texas, to November 1866.

Engagements and Campaigns
Duty at Hilton Head, to April 1864, and at Port Royal, to June. Ashepoo Expedition, May 24–27. Expedition to John's and James Islands, June 30–July 10. Engaged, July 7 and 9. Duty at Beaufort, to August. Moved to Bermuda Hundred, Virginia, August 4–8. Siege operations against Petersburg and Richmond, August 1864–April 1865. Demonstration on north side of James River, August 13–18. Skirmishes at Deep Bottom, August 14–15. Russell's Mills, August 16. Moved to Bermuda Hundred front, August 18, then to Petersburg, August 24, and duty in trenches until September 26. Demonstration on north side of James River, September 26–30. Battle of Chaffin's Farm, New Market Heights, September 28–30. Fort Gilmer, September 29. Darbytown Road, October 13. Battle of Fair Oaks, October 27–28. In trenches before Richmond, to April 1865. Occupation of Richmond, April 3. Duty at Richmond, Petersburg, and City Point, to June. Moved to Brazos Santiago, Texas, June 7–July 1, then to Brownsville. Duty at Brownsville and on Rio Grande, Texas, to October 1866.

10th Regiment, United States Colored Infantry

Date Raised
November 18, 1863

Muster Point(s)
Virginia

Date Disbanded
May 17, 1866

Place Disbanded
Texas

Movement Orders and Attachments
Attached to Drummondstown, Virginia, Department of Virginia and North Carolina, December 1863–April 1864. 1st Brigade, Hincks's Colored Division, XVIII Corps, Army of the James, Department of Virginia and North Carolina, to June 1864. 1st Brigade, 3d Division, XVIII Corps, to July 1864. Unattached, XVIII Corps, to August 1864. 3d Brigade, 3d Division, XVIII Corps, to December 1864. 3d Brigade, 1st Division, XXV Corps, to January 1865. 3d Brigade, 3d Division, XXV Corps, January 1865. Attached Brigade, 1st Division, XXV Corps, to June 1865. Department of Texas, to May 1866.

Engagements and Campaigns
Camp near Crany Island, to January 12, 1864.

Moved to Drummondstown, eastern shore of Virginia, and duty there until April. At Yorktown, Virginia, to May. Gen. Benjamin F. Butler's operations on south side of James River and against Petersburg and Richmond, May 4–June 15. Capture of Fort Powhatan, May 5. Wilson's Wharf, May 24 (detachment). At Fort Powhatan, to July 6. On Bermuda Hundred front in operations against Petersburg and Richmond, to August 27. At City Point, Virginia, to April 2, 1865. Moved to Bermuda Hundred, then to Richmond, April 2–3. Return to City Point, April 6, and duty there until June 1.

11th Regiment, United States Colored Infantry (new organization)

Date Raised
January 23, 1865

Muster Point(s)
Organized from 7th United States Colored Heavy Artillery

Date Disbanded
January 12, 1866

Place Disbanded
Department of the Tennessee

Movement Orders and Attachments
Attached to post and defenses of Memphis, Tennessee, District of West Tennessee, to July 1865. 2d Infantry Brigade, District of West Tennessee, to September 1865. Department of the Tennessee, to January 1866.

Engagements and Campaigns
Duty at Memphis and in District of West Tennessee, Department of the Tennessee, to January 1866.

11th Regiment, United States Colored Infantry (old organization)

Date Raised
December 19, 1863–March 3, 1864

Muster Point(s)
Fort Smith, Arkansas

Date Disbanded
April 22, 1865

Movement Orders and Attachments
Attached to 2d Brigade, District of the Frontier, VII Corps, Department of Arkansas, to January 1865. Colored Brigade, VII Corps, to February 1865. 2d Brigade, 1st Division, VII Corps, to April 1865. Consolidated with 112th and 113th Regiments to form new 113th Regiment, United States Colored Troops.

Engagements and Campaigns
Post and garrison duty at Fort Smith, to November 1864. Action at Fort Smith, August 24. Moved to Little Rock, Arkansas, November 1864. Action at Boggs' Mill, January 24, 1865. Duty at Little Rock and Lewisburg, Arkansas, to April 1865.

12th Regiment, United States Colored Infantry

Date Raised
July 24–August 14, 1863

Muster Point(s)
Tennessee

Date Disbanded
January 1866

Place Disbanded
Department of the Cumberland

Total Casualties
Regiment lost 4 officers and 38 enlisted men killed and mortally wounded, and 242 enlisted men to disease. Total: 284.

Movement Orders and Attachments
Attached to defenses of Nashville Camp, Northwestern Railroad, Department of the Cumberland, to October 1864. 2d Colored Brigade, District of the Etowah, Department of the Cumberland, to January 1865. Defenses of Nashville Camp, Northwestern Railroad, District of Middle Tennessee, to May 1865. 3d Subdistrict, District of Middle Tennessee, Department of the Cumberland, to January 1866.

Engagements and Campaigns
Railroad guard duty at various points in Tennessee and Alabama on line of Nashville Camp, Northwestern Railroad, to December 1864. Repulse of Gen. John Bell Hood's attack on Johnsonville, November 2 and 4–5. Action at Buford's Station, Section 37, Nashville Camp, Northwestern Railroad, November 24. March to Clarksville, Tennessee, and skirmish near that place, December

2. Battle of Nashville, December 15–16. Pursuit of Hood to Tennessee River, December 17–28. Action at Decatur, Alabama, December 27–28. Railroad guard and garrison duty in Department of the Cumberland, to January, 1866.

13th Regiment, United States Colored Infantry

Date Raised
November 19, 1863

Muster Point(s)
Nashville, Tennessee

Date Disbanded
January 10, 1866

Place Disbanded
Department of the Cumberland

Total Casualties
Regiment lost 4 officers and 86 enlisted men killed and mortally wounded, and 265 enlisted men to disease. Total: 355.

Movement Orders and Attachments
Attached to defenses of Nashville Camp, Northwestern Railroad, Department of the Cumberland, to November 1864. 2d Colored Brigade. District of the Etowah, Department of the Cumberland, to January 1865. Defenses, Nashville Camp, Northwestern Railroad, District of Middle Tennessee, Department of the Cumberland, to May 1865. 3d Subdistrict, District of Middle Tennessee, Department of the Cumberland, to January 1866.

Engagements and Campaigns
Railroad guard duty in Tennessee and Alabama on line of Nashville Camp, Northwestern Railroad, to December 1864. Repulse of Gen. John Bell Hood's attack on Johnsonville, Tennessee, September 25, and November 4–5. Eddyville, Kentucky, October 17 (detachment). Battle of Nashville, December 15–16. Pursuit of Hood to Tennessee River, December 17–18. Railroad guard and garrison duty in Department of the Cumberland, to January 1866.

14th Regiment, United States Colored Infantry

Date Raised
November 16, 1863–January 8, 1864

Muster Point(s)
Gallatin, Tennessee

Date Disbanded
March 26, 1866

Place Disbanded
At Greenville and in Department of the Tennessee

Movement Orders and Attachments
Attached to post of Gallatin, to January 1864. Post of Chattanooga, Tennessee, Department of the Cumberland, to November 1864. Unattached, District of the Etowah, Department of the Cumberland, to December 1864. 1st Colored Brigade, District of the Etowah, to May 1865. District of East Tennessee, to August 1865. Department of the Tennessee and Department of Georgia, to March 1866.

Engagements and Campaigns
Garrison duty at Chattanooga, to November 1864. March to relief of Dalton, Georgia, August 14. Action at Dalton, August 14–15. Siege of Decatur, Alabama, October 27–30. Battle of Nashville, Tennessee, December 15–16. Overton's Hill, December 16. Pursuit of Gen. John Bell Hood to Tennessee River, December 17–28. Duty at Chattanooga and in District of East Tennessee, to July 1865. At Greenville and in Department of the Tennessee, to March 1866.

15th Regiment, United States Colored Infantry

Date Raised
December 2, 1863–March 11, 1864

Muster Point(s)
Nashville, Tennessee

Date Disbanded
April 7, 1866

Place Disbanded
District of Middle Tennessee

Movement Orders and Attachments
Attached to post and District of Nashville, Department of the Cumberland, to August 1864. Post of Springfield, District of Nashville, Department of the Cumberland, to March 1865. 5th Subdistrict, District of Middle Tennessee, Department of the Cumberland, to April 1866.

Engagements and Campaigns
Garrison and guard duty at Nashville, Columbia, and Pulaski, Tennessee, to June 1864. Post duty at Springfield, Tennessee, and in District of Middle Tennessee, to April 1866.

16th Regiment, United States Colored Infantry

Date Raised
December 4, 1863–February 13, 1864

Muster Point(s)
Nashville, Tennessee

Date Disbanded
April 30, 1866

Place Disbanded
Middle and East Tennessee

Movement Orders and Attachments
Attached to post of Chattanooga, Department of the Cumberland, to November 1864. Unattached, District of the Etowah, Department of the Cumberland, to December 1864. 1st Colored Brigade, District of the Etowah, Department of the Cumberland, to January 1865. Unattached, District of the Etowah, to March 1865. 1st Colored Brigade, Department of the Cumberland, to April 1865. 5th Subdistrict, District of Middle Tennessee, to July 1865. 2d Brigade, 4th Division, District of East Tennessee and Department of the Cumberland, to April 1866.

Engagements and Campaigns
Duty at Chattanooga, Tennessee, to November 1864. Battle of Nashville, December 15–16. Overton Hill, December 16. Pursuit of Gen. John Bell Hood to Tennessee River, December 17–28. Duty at Chattanooga and in Middle and East Tennessee, to April 1866.

17th Regiment, United States Colored Infantry

Date Raised
December 12–21, 1863

Muster Point(s)
Nashville, Tennessee

Date Disbanded
April 25, 1866

Place Disbanded
Department of Tennessee

Movement Orders and Attachments
Attached to post of Murfreesboro, Tennessee, Department of the Cumberland, to April 1864. Post and District of Nashville, Department of the Cumberland, to December 1864. 1st Colored Brigade, District of the Etowah, Department of the Cumberland, to January 1865. Post and District of Nashville, Department of the Cumberland, to April 1866.

Engagements and Campaigns
Duty at McMinnville and Murfreesboro, to November 1864. Battle of Nashville, December 15–16. Overton Hill, December 16. Pursuit of Gen. John Bell Hood to Tennessee River, December 17–27. Decatur, December 28–30. Duty at post of Nashville and in Department of Tennessee, to April 1866.

18th Regiment, United States Colored Infantry

Date Raised
February 1–September 28, 1864

Muster Point(s)
Missouri

Date Disbanded
February 21, 1866

Place Disbanded
District of East Tennessee

Movement Orders and Attachments
Attached to District of St. Louis, Missouri, Department of Missouri, to December 1864. Unassigned, District of the Etowah, Department of the Cumberland, December 1864. 1st Colored Brigade, District of the Etowah, Department of the Cumberland, to January 1865. Unassigned, District of the Etowah, Department of the Cumberland, to March 1865. 1st Colored Brigade, Department of the Cumberland, to July 1865. 2d Brigade, 4th Division, District of East Tennessee and Department of the Tennessee, to February 1866.

Engagements and Campaigns
Duty in District of St. Louis and at St. Louis, to November 1864. Ordered to Nashville, Tennessee, November 7. Moved to Paducah, Kentucky,

November 7–11, then to Nashville. Occupation of Nashville during Gen. John Bell Hood's investment, December 1–15. Battle of Nashville, December 15–16. Pursuit of Hood to Tennessee River, December 17–28. At Bridgeport, Alabama, guarding railroad to February 1865. Action at Elrod's Tan Yard, January 27. At Chattanooga, Tennessee, and in District of East Tennessee, to February 1866.

19th Regiment, United States Colored Infantry

Date Raised
December 25, 1863–January 16, 1864

Muster Point(s)
Camp Stanton, Maryland

Date Disbanded
January 15, 1867

Place Disbanded
Rio Grande, Texas

Movement Orders and Attachments
Duty at Camp Stanton, Benedict, Maryland, to March 1864, and at Camp Birney, to April. Attached to 2d Brigade, 4th Division, IX Corps, Army of the Potomac, April–September 1864. 2d Brigade, 3d Division, IX Corps, to December 1864. 3d Brigade, 3d Division, XXV Corps, to January 1865. 3d Brigade, 1st Division, XXV Corps, to January 1866. Department of Texas, to January 1867.

Engagements and Campaigns
Campaign from Rapidan to James River, Virginia, May–June 1864. Guard trains through the Wilderness. Before Petersburg, Virginia, June 15–18. Siege operations against Petersburg and Richmond, Virginia, June 16, 1864–April 2, 1865. Mine explosion at Petersburg, July 30, 1864. Weldon Railroad, August 18–21. Fort Sedgwick, September 28. Poplar Grove Church, September 29–30. Hatcher's Run, October 27–28. Actions on Bermuda Hundred front, November 17–18. Duty at Bermuda Hundred, to March 1865. Appomattox Campaign, March 28–April 9. Hatcher's Run, March 29–31. Assault and capture of Petersburg, April 2. Pursuit of Gen. Robert E. Lee, April 3–9. Appomattox Court House, April 9. Surrender of Lee and his army. Duty at Petersburg and City Point, to June. Moved to Texas, June 13–July 3. Duty at Brownsville and on Rio Grande, to January 1867.

20th Regiment, United States Colored Infantry

Date Raised
February 9, 1864

Muster Point(s)
Riker's Island, New York Harbor

Date Disbanded
October 7, 1865

Place Disbanded
Nashville, Tennessee

Movement Orders and Attachments
Attached to Department of the East, to March 1864. Defenses of New Orleans, Louisiana, Department of the Gulf, to December 1864. District of West Florida and Southern Alabama, Department of the Gulf, to February 1865. Defenses of New Orleans, to June 1865. District of LaFourche, Department of the Gulf, to October 1865.

Engagements and Campaigns
Ordered to Department of the Gulf, March 1864, arriving at New Orleans, March 20. Moved to Port Hudson, Louisiana, March 21, and to Pass Cavallo, Texas, April 21. In District of Carrollton, Louisiana, June. At Plaquemine, July. At Camp Parapet and Chalmette, August 1866. At Camp Parapet and in District of Carrollton, to December. Ordered to West Pascagoula, Florida, December 26. Return to New Orleans, February 1865, and duty there until June. At Nashville, August.

21st Regiment, United States Colored Infantry

Date Raised
March 14, 1864

Muster Point(s)
Organized from 3d and 4th Regiments, South Carolina Colored Infantry

Date Disbanded
October 7, 1866

Place Disbanded
South Carolina and Georgia

Movement Orders and Attachments
Attached to 3d Brigade, Vogdes's Division, District of Florida, Department of the South, to April 1864.

Morris Island, South Carolina, Northern District, Department of the South, to October 1864. 1st Separate Brigade, Department of the South, to February 1865. Garrison of Charleston, South Carolina, Department of the South, to August 1865. Department of the South, to October 1866.

Engagements and Campaigns
Duty at Jacksonville, Florida, to April 1864. Moved to Hilton Head, South Carolina, then to Folly Island, South Carolina, April 18. Duty on Folly Island, Morris Island, and Coles Island operating against Charleston, to February 1865. Expedition to James Island, South Carolina, June 30–July 10. Action on James Island, July 2. Occupation of Charleston, February 18. Garrison duty at Charleston and Mt. Pleasant, South Carolina, to August 1865, and at various points in South Carolina and Georgia, to October 1866.

22d Regiment, United States Colored Infantry

Date Raised
January 10–29, 1864

Muster Point(s)
Philadelphia, Pennsylvania

Date Disbanded
October 16, 1865

Place Disbanded
Rio Grande, Texas

Total Casualties
Regiment lost 2 officers and 70 enlisted men killed and mortally wounded, and 1 officer and 144 enlisted men to disease. Total: 217.

Movement Orders and Attachments
Ordered to Yorktown, Virginia, January 1864. Attached to U.S. forces, Yorktown, Department of Virginia and North Carolina, to April 1864. 1st Brigade, Hincks's Division (Colored), XVIII Corps, Army of the James, to June 1864. 1st Brigade, 3d Division, XVIII Corps, June 1864. 2d Brigade, 3d Division, XVIII Corps, to August 1864. 1st Brigade, 3d Division, XVIII Corps, August 1864. 1st Brigade, 3d Division, X Corps, to September 1864. 1st Brigade, 3d Division, XVIII Corps, to December 1864. 1st Brigade, 3d Division, XXV Corps, December 1864. 1st Brigade, 1st Division, XXV Corps, and Department of Texas, to October 1865.

Engagements and Campaigns
Duty near Yorktown, to May 1864. Expedition to King and Queen County, March 9–12. Gen. Benjamin F. Butler's operations south of James River and against Petersburg and Richmond, May 4–June 15. Duty at Wilson's Wharf, James River, protecting supply transports, then constructing works near Fort Powhatan, to June. Attack on Fort Powhatan, May 21. Before Petersburg, June 15–18. Siege operations against Petersburg and Richmond, June 16, 1864–April 2, 1865. Deep Bottom, August 24. Dutch Gap, August 24. Demonstration north of James River, September 28–30. Battle of Chaffin's Farm, New Market Heights, September 29–30. Fort Harrison, September 29. Battle of Fair Oaks, October 27–28. Chaffin's Farm, November 4. In trenches before Richmond, to April 1865. Occupation of Richmond, April 3. Moved to Washington, D.C., and participated in obsequies of President Abraham Lincoln, and afterward to eastern shore of Maryland and along lower Potomac River in pursuit of assassins. Rejoined XXV Corps, May 1865. Moved to Texas, May 24–June 6. Duty along Rio Grande, to October 1865.

23d Regiment, United States Colored Infantry

Date Raised
November 23, 1863–June 30, 1864

Muster Point(s)
Camp Casey, Virginia

Date Disbanded
November 30, 1865

Place Disbanded
Rio Grande, Texas

Total Casualties
Regiment lost 4 officers and 82 enlisted men killed and mortally wounded, and 1 officer and 165 enlisted men to disease. Total: 252.

Movement Orders and Attachments
Attached to 2d Brigade, 4th Division, IX Corps, Army of the Potomac, April–September 1864. 2d Brigade, 3d Division, IX Corps, to December 1864. 3d Brigade, 3d Division, XXV Corps, December

1865. 3d Brigade, 1st Division, XXV Corps, and Department of Texas, to November 1865.

Engagements and Campaigns
Campaign from Rapidan to James River, Virginia, May–June 1864. Guarding wagon trains of Army of the Potomac through the Wilderness. Before Petersburg, June 15–18. Siege of Petersburg and Richmond, June 16, 1864–April 2, 1865. Mine explosion at Petersburg, July 30, 1864. Weldon Railroad, August 18–21. Fort Sedgwick, September 28. Poplar Grove Church, September 29–30. Boydton Plank Road, Hatcher's Run, October 27–28. Bermuda Hundred, December 13. Duty on Bermuda Hundred front, to March 1865. Appomattox Campaign, March 28–April 9. Hatcher's Run, March 29–31. Fall of Petersburg, April 2. Pursuit of Gen. Robert E. Lee, April 3–9. Appomattox Court House, April 9. Surrender of Lee and his army. Duty in Department of Virginia, to May. Moved to Texas, May–June. Duty at Brownsville and along Rio Grande, Texas, to November.

24th Regiment, United States Colored Infantry

Date Raised
January 30–March 30, 1865

Muster Point(s)
Camp William Penn, Philadelphia, Pennsylvania

Date Disbanded
October 1, 1865

Place Disbanded
Richmond, Virginia

Movement Orders and Attachments
Moved to Washington, D.C., May 5, and duty at Camp Casey, to June 1. At Point Lookout, Maryland, guarding prisoners, to July 16. Moved to Richmond and duty in Subdistrict of Roanoke, Headquarters at Burkesville, to September. Moved to Richmond.

25th Regiment, United States Colored Infantry

Date Raised
January 3–February 12, 1864

Muster Point(s)
Philadelphia, Pennsylvania

Date Disbanded
December 6, 1865

Place Disbanded
Fort Pickens, Pensacola Harbor

Movement Orders and Attachments
Sailed for New Orleans, Louisiana, on steamer *Suwahnee,* March 15, 1864 (right wing). Vessel sprung a leak off Hatteras and put into harbor at Beaufort, North Carolina. Duty there in defenses, under Gen. Henry Wessells, to April, then proceeded to New Orleans, arriving May 1. Left wing in camp at Carrollton. Attached to defenses of New Orleans, Department of the Gulf, May–July 1864. District of Pensacola, Florida, Department of the Gulf, to October 1864. 1st Brigade, 3d Division, United States Colored Troops, Department of the Gulf, October 1864. 1st Brigade, District of West Florida, to January 1865. 3d Brigade, 1st Division, United States Colored Troops, District of West Florida, to February 1865. 1st Brigade, 1st Division, United States Colored Troops, District of West Florida, to April 1865. Unattached, District of West Florida, to July 1865. Department of Florida, to December 1865.

Engagements and Campaigns
Duty in defenses of New Orleans, to July 1864. Garrison at post of Barrancas, Florida (six companies), and at Fort Pickens, Pensacola Harbor (four companies), to December 1865.

26th Regiment, United States Colored Infantry

Date Raised
February 27, 1864

Muster Point(s)
Riker's Island, New York Harbor

Date Disbanded
August 28, 1865

Place Disbanded
Beaufort, South Carolina

Total Casualties
Regiment lost 2 officers and 28 enlisted men killed and mortally wounded, and 3 officers and 112 enlisted men to disease. Total: 145.

Movement Orders and Attachments
Ordered to Department of the South, April 1864.

Attached to District of Beaufort, Department of the South, to October 1864. 2d Separate Brigade, Department of the South, to January 1865. 1st Separate Brigade, Department of the South, to February 1865. 2d Separate Brigade, Department of the South, to June 1865. Department of the South, to August 1865.

Engagements and Campaigns
Reported at Beaufort, April 13, 1864, and post duty there until November 27. Expedition to John's and James Islands, July 2–10. Operations against Battery Pringle, July 4–9. Actions on John's Island, July 5 and 7. Burden's Causeway, July 9. Battle of Honey Hill, November 30. Demonstration on Charleston & Savannah Railroad, December 6–9. Action at Devaux's Neck, December 6. Tillifinny Station, December 9. McKay's Point, December 22. Ordered to Beaufort, January 2, 1865, and duty there until August.

27th Regiment, United States Colored Infantry

Date Raised
January 16, 1864

Muster Point(s)
Camp Delaware, Ohio

Date Disbanded
September 21, 1865

Place Disbanded
Department of North Carolina

Movement Orders and Attachments
Ordered to Annapolis, Maryland. Attached to 1st Brigade, 4th Division, IX Corps, Army of the Potomac, to September 1864. 1st Brigade, 3d Division, IX Corps, to December 1864. 1st Brigade, 1st Division, XXV Corps, to December 1864. 1st Brigade, 3d Division, XXV Corps, to January 1865. 3d Brigade, 3d Division, XXV Corps, to March 1865. 3d Brigade, 3d Division, X Corps, Department of North Carolina, to July 1865. Department of North Carolina, to September 1865.

Engagements and Campaigns
Campaign from Rapidan to James River, Virginia, May–June, 1864. Guard trains of Army of the Potomac through the Wilderness. Before Petersburg, June 15–19. Siege of Petersburg and Richmond, June 16–December 7, 1864. Mine explosion at Petersburg, July 30, 1864. Weldon Railroad, August 18–21. Poplar Grove Church, September 29–October 1. Boydton Plank Road, Hatcher's Run, October 27–28. On Bermuda Hundred front, to December 1. First expedition to Fort Fisher, North Carolina, December 7–27. Second expedition to Fort Fisher, January 7–15, 1865. Bombardment of Fort Fisher, January 13–15. Assault and capture of Fort Fisher, January 15. Sugar Loaf Hill, January 19. Federal Point, February 11. Fort Anderson, February 18–20. Capture of Wilmington, February 22. Northeast Ferry, February 22. Campaign of the Carolinas, March 1–April 26. Advance on Kinston and Goldsboro, March 6–21. Cox's Bridge, March 23–24. Advance on Raleigh, April 9–14. Occupation of Raleigh, April 14. Bennett's House, April 26. Surrender of Gen. Joseph E. Johnston and his army. Duty in Department of North Carolina, to September.

28th Regiment, United States Colored Infantry

Date Raised
December 24, 1863–March 31, 1864

Muster Point(s)
Indianapolis, Indiana

Date Disbanded
November 8, 1865

Place Disbanded
Corpus Christi, Texas

Total Casualties
Regiment lost 2 officers and 45 enlisted men killed and mortally wounded, and 1 officer and 164 enlisted men to disease. Total: 212.

Movement Orders and Attachments
Left Indianapolis for Washington, D.C., April 24, then moved to Alexandria, Virginia. Attached to defenses of Washington, D.C., XXII Corps, April–June 1864. White House, Virginia, Abercrombie's command, to July 1864. 2d Brigade, 4th Division, IX Corps, Army of the Potomac, to September 1864. 2d Brigade, 3d Division, IX Corps, to December 1864. 3d Brigade, 2d Division, XXV Corps, to April 1865. Attached 1st Brigade, 1st Division, XXV Corps, to April 1865. District of St.

Mary's, XXII Corps, to May 1865. Department of Texas, to November 1865.

Engagements and Campaigns
Duty at Alexandria, to June 1864. Moved to White House, June 2. Engaged, June 21. Accompanied Gen. Philip H. Sheridan's cavalry through Chickahominy Swamps to Prince George Court House, with several skirmishes. Siege operations against Petersburg and Richmond, July 1864–April 1865. Mine explosion at Petersburg, July 30, 1864. Weldon Railroad, August 18–21. Poplar Grove Church, September 29–October 1. Boydton Plank Road, Hatcher's Run, October 27–28. On Bermuda Hundred front and before Richmond, to April 1865. Occupation of Richmond, April 3. At City Point, Virginia, and St. Mary's, Maryland, in charge of prisoners, April 6–May 12. Moved to City Point, then to Texas, June 10–July 1. Duty at Brazos Santiago and Corpus Christi, to November.

29th Regiment, United States Colored Infantry

Date Raised
April 24, 1864

Muster Point(s)
Quincy, Illinois

Date Disbanded
November 6, 1865

Place Disbanded
Rio Grande, Texas

Total Casualties
Regiment lost 3 officers and 43 enlisted men killed and mortally wounded, and 188 enlisted men to disease. Total: 234.

Movement Orders and Attachments
Ordered to Annapolis, Maryland, May 27, 1864, then to Alexandria, Virginia. Attached to defenses of Washington, D.C., XXII Corps, to June 1864. 2d Brigade, 4th Division, IX Corps, Army of the Potomac, to September 1864. 2d Brigade, 3d Division, IX Corps, to December 1864. 3d Brigade, 2d Division, XXV Corps, and Department of Texas, to November 1865.

Engagements and Campaigns
Duty at Alexandria, to June 15, 1864. Moved to White House, Virginia, then to Petersburg, Virginia. Siege operations against Petersburg and Richmond, June 19, 1864–April 3, 1865. Mine explosion at Petersburg, July 30, 1864. Weldon Railroad, August 18–21. Poplar Grove Church, September 29–October 1. Boydton Plank Road, Hatcher's Run, October 27–28. On Bermuda Hundred front and before Richmond, to April 1865. Appomattox Campaign, March 28–April 9. Duty in Department of Virginia, to May. Moved to Texas, May–June, and duty on Rio Grande, to November.

29th Regiment, Connecticut Infantry (Colored)

Date Raised
March 8, 1864

Muster Point(s)
Fair Haven

Date Disbanded
November 25, 1865

Place Disbanded
New Haven, Connecticut

Total Casualties
Regiment lost 1 officer and 44 enlisted men killed and mortally wounded, and 1 officer and 152 enlisted men to disease. Total: 198.

Movement Orders and Attachments
Left for Annapolis, Maryland, March 19. Moved to Beaufort, South Carolina, April 8–13, and duty there until August 8. Attached to District of Beaufort, Department of the South, April–August 1864. 1st Brigade, 3d Division, X Corps, Army of the James, Department of Virginia and North Carolina, to December 1864. 2d Brigade, 3d Division, XXV Corps, to January 1865. 2d Brigade, 1st Division, XXV Corps, to April 1865, District of St. Mary's, XXII Corps, Department of Washington, to May 1865. 2d Brigade, 1st Division, XXV Corps, Department of Texas, to October 1865.

Engagements and Campaigns
Moved from Beaufort to Bermuda Hundred, Virginia, August 8–13, 1864. Siege operations against Petersburg and Richmond, August 13, 1864–April 2, 1865. Demonstration on north side of James River, August 13–20, 1864. Deep Bottom, Strawberry Plains, August 14–18. Duty in trenches before Petersburg, August 25–September 24. New

Market Heights and Fort Harrison, September 28–29. Chaffin's Farm, September 29–30. Darbytown Road, October 13. Battle of Fair Oaks, October 27–28. Duty in trenches before Richmond, to April 1865. Occupation of Richmond, April 3 (first infantry regiment to enter city). Moved to City Point, April 18, then to Point Lookout, Maryland, and duty there guarding prisoners until May 28. Moved to City Point, May 28–30, then sailed for Texas, June 10, arriving at Brazos Santiago, July 3. Marched to Brownsville and duty there until October.

30th Regiment, United States Colored Infantry

Date Raised
February 12–March 18, 1864

Muster Point(s)
Camp Stanton, Maryland

Date Disbanded
December 10, 1865

Place Disbanded
North Carolina

Total Casualties
Regiment lost 3 officers and 48 enlisted men killed and mortally wounded, and 2 officers and 177 enlisted men to disease. Total: 230.

Movement Orders and Attachments
Attached to 1st Brigade, 4th Division, IX Corps, Army of the Potomac, to September 1864. 1st Brigade, 3d Division, IX Corps, to December 1864. 1st Brigade, 1st Division, XXV Corps, to December 1864. 1st Brigade, 3d Division, XXV Corps, to March 1865. 1st Brigade, 3d Division, X Corps, Department of North Carolina, to July 1865. Department of North Carolina to December 1865.

Engagements and Campaigns
Campaign from Rapidan to James River, Virginia, May–June 1864. Guard trains of Army of the Potomac through the Wilderness and to Petersburg. Before Petersburg, June 15–18. Siege operations against Petersburg and Richmond, June 16–December 7, 1864. Mine explosion at Petersburg, July 30. Weldon Railroad, August 18–21. Poplar Grove Church, September 29–October 1. Boydton Plank Road, Hatcher's Run, October 27–28. First expedition to Fort Fisher, North Carolina, December 7–27. Second expedition to Fort Fisher, January 7–15, 1865. Bombardment of Fort Fisher, January 13–15. Assault and capture of Fort Fisher, January 15. Sugar Loaf Hill, January 19. Federal Point, February 11. Fort Anderson, February 18–20. Capture of Wilmington, February 22. Northeast Ferry, February 22. Campaign of the Carolinas, March 1–April 26. Advance on Kinston and Goldsboro, March 6–21. Action at Cox's Bridge, March 23–24. Advance on Raleigh, April 9–14. Occupation of Raleigh, April 14. Bennett's House April 26. Surrender of Gen. Joseph E. Johnston and his army. Duty at various points in North Carolina until December.

31st Regiment, United States Colored Infantry

Date Raised
April 29, 1864

Muster Point(s)
Hart's Island, New York

Date Disbanded
November 7, 1865

Place Disbanded
Rio Grande, Texas

Total Casualties
Regiment lost 3 officers and 48 enlisted men killed and mortally wounded, and 1 officer and 123 enlisted men to disease. Total: 175.

Movement Orders and Attachments
Attached to 2d Brigade, 4th Division, IX Corps, Army of the Potomac, to September 1864. 2d Brigade, 3d Division, IX Corps, to December 1864. 3d Brigade, 2d Division, XXV Corps, and Department of Texas, to November 1865.

Engagements and Campaigns
Campaign from Rapidan to James River, Virginia, May–June 1864. Guard trains of Army of the Potomac through the Wilderness. Battles of Cold Harbor, June 2–12. Before Petersburg, June 15–19. Siege operations against Petersburg and Richmond, June 16, 1864–April 2, 1865. Mine explosion at Petersburg, July 30, 1864. Weldon Railroad, August 18–21. Fort Sedgwick, September 28. Hatcher's Run, October 27–28. On Bermuda Hundred front,

to March 1865. Moved to Hatcher's Run, March 26–28. Appomattox Campaign, March 28–April 9. Hatcher's Run, March 29–31. Fall of Petersburg, April 2. Pursuit of Gen. Robert E. Lee, April 3–9. Appomattox Court House, April 9. Surrender of Lee and his army. Duty in Department of Virginia, to May. Moved to Texas, May–June, and duty on Rio Grande, to November.

32d Regiment, United States Colored Infantry

Date Raised
February 7–March 7, 1864

Muster Point(s)
Camp William Penn, Philadelphia, Pennsylvania

Date Disbanded
August 22, 1865

Place Disbanded
Hilton Head, South Carolina

Total Casualties
Regiment lost 2 officers and 35 enlisted men killed and mortally wounded, and 113 enlisted men to disease. Total: 150.

Movement Orders and Attachments
Ordered to Hilton Head, South Carolina, April 1864, arriving April 27. Attached to Bailey's Brigade, District of Hilton Head, Department of the South, to June 1864. Morris Island, South Carolina, Northern District, Department of the South, to October 1864. 3d Separate Brigade, Hilton Head, Department of the South, to November 1864. 2d Brigade, Coast Division, Department of the South, to December 1864. 2d Separate Brigade, Department of the South, to June 1865. Department of the South, to August 1865.

Engagements and Campaigns
Ordered to Hilton Head, April 1864, and duty there until June. Moved to Morris Island and duty there operating against Charleston, South Carolina, to November. Expedition to Boyd's Neck, November 28–30. Battle of Honey Hill, November 30. Demonstration on Charleston Camp, Savannah Railroad, December 6–9. Devaux's Neck, December 6. James Island, February 14, 1865. Occupation of Charleston, February 18. Potter's Expedition, April 5–25. Dingle's Mills, April 9. Statesboro, April 15. Occupation of Camden, April 17. Boydkin's Mills, April 18. Beach Creek near Statesburg and Denken's Mills, April 19. Garrison duty at Charleston, Beaufort, and Hilton Head, to August.

33d Regiment, United States Colored Infantry

Date Raised
February 8, 1864

Muster Point(s)
Organized from 1st South Carolina Colored Infantry

Date Disbanded
January 31, 1866

Place Disbanded
Department of the South

Movement Orders and Attachments
Attached to U.S. forces, Port Royal Island, South Carolina, X Corps, Department of the South, to April 1864. District of Beaufort, South Carolina, Department of the South, to July 1864. Folly Island, South Carolina, Northern District, Department of the South, to October 1864. 1st Separate Brigade, Department of the South, to March 1865. District of Savannah, Georgia, and Department of the South, to January 1866.

Engagements and Campaigns
Duty at Port Royal Island, District of Beaufort, to July 1864. Expedition to James Island, South Carolina, June 30–July 10. James Island near Secessionville, July 2. Duty on Folly and Morris Islands operating against Charleston, South Carolina, to November. Demonstration on Charleston Camp, Savannah Railroad, December 6–9. Devaux's Neck, December 6. Tillifinny Station, December 9. Ordered to Folly Island, December 9. Near Pocotaligo Road, December 20. At Pocotaligo, South Carolina, to February 1865. Occupation of Charleston, to March 8. Moved to Savannah, March 8, and duty there until June 6. Moved to Augusta, Georgia. Duty there and at various points in Department of the South, to January 1866.

34th Regiment, United States Colored Infantry

Date Raised
February 8, 1864

Muster Point(s)
Organized from 2d South Carolina Colored Infantry

Date Disbanded
February 28, 1866

Place Disbanded
Florida

Movement Orders and Attachments
Attached to Montgomery's Brigade, District of Florida, Department of the South, February 1864. 3d Brigade, Vogdes's Division, District of Florida, Department of the South, to April 1864. Morris Island, South Carolina, Northern District, Department of the South, to June 1864. District of Beaufort, South Carolina, Department of the South, to August 1864. District of Florida, Department of the South, to October 1864. 4th Separate Brigade, Department of the South, to November 1864. 1st Brigade, Coast Division, Department of the South, to December 1864. 2d Brigade, Coast Division, Department of the South, to January 1865. 4th Separate Brigade, District of Florida, Department of the South, and Department of Florida, to February 1866.

Engagements and Campaigns
Provost duty at Jacksonville, Florida, to March 30, 1864. Moved to Palatka, Florida, March 30–31, and to Picolata, April 12. Ordered to Folly Island, South Carolina, April 13, then to Morris Island and duty there, operating against Charleston until May 20. Moved to St. Augustine, Florida, May 20, then to Tybee Island, South Carolina, May 22. Expedition to Ashepoo River, May 24–27. Action at Ashepoo River, May 26. Moved to Hilton Head, South Carolina, June 30. Expedition to James Island, South Carolina, July 1–10. Near Winter's Point, July 3. King's Creek, July 3. Actions on James Island, July 3, 9–10. Burden's Causeway, July 9. Return to Jacksonville, July 31. Expedition to Enterprise, August 2–5. Raid on Florida Railroad, August 15–18. Action at Gainesville, August 17. Duty at Jacksonville, Palatka, and Magnolia Springs, to November. Ordered to Hilton Head, November 25. Expedition to Boyd's Neck, South Carolina, November 28–30. Battle of Honey Hill, November 30. Expedition to Devaux's Neck, December 1–6. Action at Devaux's Neck, December 6. Moved to Hilton Head, then returned to Jacksonville, January 1865. Duty at Jacksonville and at various points in Florida, to February 1866.

35th Regiment, United States Colored Infantry

Date Raised
February 8, 1864

Muster Point(s)
Organized from 1st North Carolina Colored Infantry

Date Disbanded
June 1, 1866

Place Disbanded
Department of the South

Total Casualties
Regiment lost 4 officers and 49 enlisted men killed and mortally wounded, and 1 officer and 151 enlisted men to disease. Total: 205.

Movement Orders and Attachments
Attached to Montgomery's Brigade, District of Florida, Department of the South, February 1864. 2d Brigade, Vogdes's Division, District of Florida, Department of the South, to April 1864. District of Florida, Department of the South, to October 1864. 4th Separate Brigade, Department of the South, to November 1864. 2d Brigade, Coast Division, Department of the South, to December 1864. 4th Separate Brigade, Department of the South, to March 1865. 1st Separate Brigade, Department of the South, to August 1865. Department of the South, to June 1866.

Engagements and Campaigns
Expedition to Lake City, Florida, February 14–22, 1864. Battle of Olustee, February 20. Duty at Jacksonville, Florida, to November. Operations on St. John's River, May 19–27. Horse Head Landing, May 23. (Four companies detached on expedition to James Island, South Carolina, July 1–10, and King's Creek, South Carolina, July 3.) Raid from Jacksonville on Baldwin, July 23–28. South Fork, Black Creek, July 24. Black Creek near Whitesides, July 27. Raid on Florida Railroad, August 15–19. Ordered from Jacksonville to Hilton Head, South Carolina, November 25, Expedition to Boyd's Neck,

November 28–30. Battle of Honey Hill, November 30. Return to Jacksonville and duty there until March 1865. Ordered to Charleston, South Carolina. Duty there and at various points in Department of the South, to June 1866.

36th Regiment, United States Colored Infantry

Date Raised
February 8, 1864

Muster Point(s)
Organized from 2d North Carolina Colored Infantry

Date Disbanded
October 28, 1866

Place Disbanded
Texas

Movement Orders and Attachments
Attached to U.S. forces, Norfolk and Portsmouth, Department of Virginia and North Carolina, to April 1864. District of St. Mary's, Department of Virginia and North Carolina, to June 1864. Unattached, Army of the James, to August 1864. 2d Brigade, 3d Division, XVIII Corps, to December 1864. 1st Brigade, 3d Division, XXV Corps, to December 1864. 1st Brigade, 1st Division, XXV Corps, and Department of Texas, to October 1866.

Engagements and Campaigns
Duty at Norfolk and Portsmouth, Virginia, to April 1864. At Point Lookout, Maryland, District of St. Mary's, guarding prisoners until July 1864. Expedition from Point Lookout to Westmoreland County, April 12–14. Expedition from Point Lookout to Rappahannock River, May 11–14, and to Pope's Creek, June 11–21. Moved from Point Lookout to Bermuda Hundred, Virginia, July 1–3. Siege operations against Petersburg and Richmond, Virginia, July 3, 1864–April 2, 1865. Battle of Chaffin's Farm, New Market Heights, September 29–30. Battle of Fair Oaks, October 27–28. Dutch Gap, November 17. Indiantown, Sandy Creek, North Carolina, December 18 (detachment). Duty north of James River before Richmond, to March 27, 1865. Appomattox Campaign, March 27–April 9. Occupation of Richmond, April 3. Duty in Department of Virginia, to May. Moved to Texas, May 24–June 6. Duty along Rio Grande and at various points in Texas, to October 1866.

37th Regiment, United States Colored Infantry

Date Raised
February 3, 1864

Muster Point(s)
Organized from 3d North Carolina Colored Infantry

Date Disbanded
February 11, 1867

Place Disbanded
Department of the South

Movement Orders and Attachments
Attached to U.S. forces, Norfolk and Portsmouth, Virginia, Department of Virginia and North Carolina, to April 1864. 1st Brigade, Hincks's Colored Division, XVIII Corps, Army of the James, to June 1864. 1st Brigade, 3d Division, X Corps, to July 1864. Unattached, Army of the James, to August 1864. 1st Brigade, 3d Division, XVIII Corps, to December 1864. 3d Brigade, 3d Division, XXV Corps, to January 1865. 3d Brigade, 3d Division, Terry's Provisional Corps, Department of North Carolina, to March 1865. 2d Brigade, 3d Division, X Corps, Department of North Carolina, to August 1865. Department of North Carolina, to February 1867.

Engagements and Campaigns
Duty at Norfolk and Portsmouth, to April 1864. Expedition to Westmoreland County, April 12–14. Gen. Benjamin F. Butler's operations on south side of James River and against Petersburg and Richmond, May 4–June 15. Capture of Fort Powhatan, May 5. Duty there and at Wilson's Wharf, to September 28. Moved to Deep Bottom, September 28–29. Battle of Chaffin's Farm, New Market Heights, September 29–30. Battle of Fair Oaks, October 27–28. In trenches before Richmond, to December 7. First expedition to Fort Fisher, North Carolina, December 7–27. Second expedition to Fort Fisher, January 7–15, 1865. Bombardment of Fort Fisher, January 13–15. Assault and capture of Fort Fisher, January 15.

Sugar Loaf Hill, January 19. Federal Point, February 11. Fort Anderson, February 18–20. Capture of Wilmington, February 22. Northeast Ferry, February 22. Campaign of the Carolinas, March 1–April 26. Advance on Kinston and Goldsboro, March 6–21. Cox's Bridge, March 23–24. Advance on Raleigh, April 9–14. Occupation of Raleigh, April 14. Bennett's House, April 26. Surrender of Gen. Joseph E. Johnston and his army. Duty at various points in North Carolina and in Department of the South, to February 1867.

38th Regiment, United States Colored Infantry

Date Raised
January 23, 1864

Muster Point(s)
Virginia

Date Disbanded
January 25, 1867

Place Disbanded
Texas

Total Casualties
Regiment lost 1 officer and 42 enlisted men killed and mortally wounded, and 2 officers and 192 enlisted men to disease. Total: 237.

Movement Orders and Attachments
Attached to U.S. forces, Norfolk and Portsmouth, Virginia, Department of Virginia and North Carolina, to June 1864. Unattached, Department of Virginia and North Carolina, to August 1864. 2d Brigade, 3d Division, XVIII Corps, Army of the James, to December 1864. 1st Brigade, 3d Division, XXV Corps, to December 1864. 1st Brigade, 1st Division, XXV Corps, and Department of Texas, to January 1867.

Engagements and Campaigns
Duty at Norfolk and Portsmouth, to June 1864. Operations against Petersburg and Richmond, June 1864–April 1865. Battle of Chaffin's Farm, New Market Heights, September 29–30. Deep Bottom, October 1. Battle of Fair Oaks, October 27–28. Duty in trenches north of James River before Richmond, to April 1865. Occupation of Richmond, April 3, 1865. Duty in Department of Virginia, to May. Moved to Texas, May 24–June 6. Duty at Brownsville and at various points on Rio Grande and at Brazos Santiago, Indianola, and Galveston, Texas, to January 1867.

39th Regiment, United States Colored Infantry

Date Raised
March 22–31, 1864

Muster Point(s)
Baltimore, Maryland

Date Disbanded
December 4, 1865

Place Disbanded
Department of North Carolina

Total Casualties
Regiment lost 38 enlisted men killed and mortally wounded, and 3 officers and 239 enlisted men to disease. Total: 280.

Movement Orders and Attachments
Attached to 1st Brigade, 4th Division, IX Corps, Army of the Potomac, to September 1864. 1st Brigade, 3d Division, IX Corps, to December 1864. 2d Brigade, 1st Division, XXV Corps, to December 1864. 2d Brigade, 3d Division, XXV Corps, to January 1865. 2d Brigade, 3d Division, Terry's Provisional Corps, Department of North Carolina, to March 1865. 2d Brigade, 3d Division, X Corps, Department of North Carolina, to August 1865. Department of North Carolina, to December 1865.

Engagements and Campaigns
Campaign from Rapidan to James River, Virginia, May–June 1864. Guard trains of Army of the Potomac through the Wilderness and to Petersburg. Before Petersburg, June 15–19. Siege of Petersburg and Richmond, June 16–December 7. Mine explosion at Petersburg, July 30. Weldon Railroad, August 18–21. Poplar Grove Church, September 29–October 1. Boydton Plank Road, Hatcher's Run, October 27–28. On Bermuda Hundred front, to December. First expedition to Fort Fisher, North Carolina, December 7–27. Second expedition to Fort Fisher, January 7–15, 1865. Bombardment of Fort Fisher, January 13–15. Assault and capture of Fort Fisher, January 15. Sugar Loaf Hill, January 19. Federal Point, February 11. Fort Anderson, February 18–20. Capture of Wilmington, February 22.

Northeast Ferry, February 22. Campaign of the Carolinas, March 1–April 26. Advance on Kinston and Goldsboro, March 6–21. Cox's Bridge, March 23–24. Advance on Raleigh, April 9–14. Occupation of Raleigh, April 14. Bennett's House, April 26. Surrender of Gen. Joseph E. Johnston and his army. Duty at various points in Department of North Carolina, to December.

40th Regiment, United States Colored Infantry

Date Raised
February 29, 1864

Muster Point(s)
Nashville, Tennessee

Date Disbanded
April 25, 1866

Place Disbanded
District of East Tennessee

Movement Orders and Attachments
Attached to defenses of Louisville Camp, Nashville Railroad, Department of the Cumberland, to June 1864. Defenses of Nashville Camp, Northwestern Railroad, Department of the Cumberland, to December 1864. Defenses of Louisville & Nashville Railroad, Department of the Cumberland, to April 1865. 2d Brigade, 4th Division, District of East Tennessee, Department of the Cumberland, to July 1865. 1st Brigade, 4th Division, District of East Tennessee, to August 1865. Department of the Tennessee, to April 1866.

Engagements and Campaigns
Railroad guard duty entire term, Nashville & Louisville Railroad; Nashville Camp, Northwestern Railroad; and in District of East Tennessee. Action at South Tunnel, Tennessee, October 10, 1864.

41st Regiment, United States Colored Infantry

Date Raised
September 30–December 7, 1864

Muster Point(s)
Camp William Penn, Philadelphia, Pennsylvania

Date Disbanded
December 14, 1865

Place Disbanded
Philadelphia

Movement Orders and Attachments
Ordered to join Army of the James in Virginia, October 18, 1864. Attached to 1st Brigade, 3d Division, X Corps, to December 1864. 2d Brigade, 3d Division, XXV Corps, to January 1865. 2d Brigade, 1st Division, XXV Corps, to January 1865. 2d Brigade, 2d Division, XXV Corps, and Department of Texas, to December 1865.

Engagements and Campaigns
Guard duty at Deep Bottom, Virginia, to October 20, 1864. Moved to Fort Burnham on line north of James River, before Richmond, October 27. Battle of Fair Oaks, October 27–28. In trenches before Richmond and picket duty on Chaffin's Farm, to January 1, 1865. Near Fort Burnham, to March 27. Moved to Hatcher's Run, March 27–28. Appomattox Campaign, March 28–April 9. Hatcher's Run, March 29–31. Fall of Petersburg, April 2. Pursuit of Gen. Robert E. Lee, April 3–9. Appomattox Court House, April 9. Surrender of Lee and his army. Moved to Petersburg, April 11, and duty there until May 25. Embarked for Texas, May 25, arriving at Brazos Santiago, June 3. Moved to Edenburg and guard and provost duty there until November. Consolidated to a battalion of four companies, September 30. Mustered out at Brownsville, Texas, November 10, 1865.

42d Regiment, United States Colored Infantry

Date Raised
April 20, 1864

Muster Point(s)
Chattanooga and Nashville, Tennessee

Date Disbanded
January 31, 1866

Place Disbanded
Department of Georgia

Movement Orders and Attachments
Attached to District of Chattanooga, Department of the Cumberland, to November 1864. Unattached, District of the Etowah, Department of the Cumberland, to December 1864. 1st Colored Brigade, District of the Etowah, to January 1865.

Unattached, District of the Etowah, to March 1865. 1st Colored Brigade, Department of the Cumberland, to July 1865. 2d Brigade, 4th Division, District of East Tennessee, July 1865. Department of Georgia, to January 1866.

Engagements and Campaigns
Guard and garrison duty at Chattanooga in District of East Tennessee, and in Department of the Cumberland and Department of Georgia during entire term.

43d Regiment, United States Colored Infantry

Date Raised
March 12–June 3, 1864

Muster Point(s)
Philadelphia, Pennsylvania

Date Disbanded
November 30, 1865

Place Disbanded
Philadelphia

Total Casualties
Regiment lost 3 officers and 48 enlisted men killed and mortally wounded, and 188 enlisted men to disease. Total: 239.

Movement Orders and Attachments
Moved to Annapolis, Maryland, April 18. Attached to 1st Brigade, 4th Division, IX Corps, Army of the Potomac, to September 1864. 1st Brigade, 3d Division, IX Corps, to December 1864. 3d Brigade, 3d Division, XXV Corps, to January 1865. 3d Brigade, 1st Division, XXV Corps and Department of Texas, to October 1865.

Engagements and Campaigns
Campaign from Rapidan to James River, Virginia, May–June 1864. Guard trains of Army of the Potomac through the Wilderness and to Petersburg. Before Petersburg, June 15–19. Siege operations against Petersburg and Richmond, June 16, 1864–April 2, 1865. Mine explosion at Petersburg, July 30, 1864. Weldon Railroad, August 18–21. Poplar Grove Church, September 29–October 1. Boydton Plank Road, Hatcher's Run, October 27–28. On Bermuda Hundred front and before Richmond, to March 1865. Moved to Hatcher's Run, March 27–28. Appomattox Campaign, March 28–April 9. Hatcher's Run, March 29–31. Fall of Petersburg, April 2. Pursuit of Gen. Robert E. Lee, April 3–9. Appomattox Court House, April 9. Surrender of Lee and his army. Duty at Petersburg and City Point, to May 30. Moved to Texas, May 30–June 10. Duty on Rio Grande opposite Matamoras, Mexico, to October.

44th Regiment, United States Colored Infantry

Date Raised
April 7, 1864

Muster Point(s)
Chattanooga, Tennessee

Date Disbanded
April 30, 1866

Place Disbanded
Department of Georgia

Movement Orders and Attachments
Attached to District of Chattanooga, Department of the Cumberland, to November 1864. Unattached, District of the Etowah, Department of the Cumberland, to December 1864. 1st Colored Brigade, District of the Etowah, Department of the Cumberland, to January 1865. Unattached, District of the Etowah, to March 1865. 1st Colored Brigade, Department of the Cumberland, to July 1865. 2d Brigade, 4th Division, District of East Tennessee, July 1865. Department of the Cumberland and Department of Georgia, to April 1866.

Engagements and Campaigns
Post and garrison duty at Chattanooga, to November 1864. Action at Dalton, Georgia, October 13, 1864. Battle of Nashville, Tennessee, December 15–16. Pursuit of Gen. John Bell Hood to Tennessee River, December 17–28. Post and garrison duty at Chattanooga in District of East Tennessee, and in Department of Georgia, to April 1866.

45th Regiment, United States Colored Infantry

Date Raised
June 13–August 19, 1864

Muster Point(s)
Philadelphia, Pennsylvania

Date Disbanded
November 4, 1865

Place Disbanded
Brownsville, Texas

Movement Orders and Attachments
Moved to Washington, D.C. (four companies), July 1864. Attached to Provisional Brigade, Casey's Division, XXII Corps, and garrison duty at Arlington Heights, Virginia, to March 1865. Rejoined regiment at Chaffin's Farm, Virginia, March 14, 1865.

Six companies moved to City Point, Virginia, September 20, 1864. Attached to 2d Brigade, 3d Division, X Corps, Army of the James, to December 1864. 2d Brigade, 2d Division, XXV Corps, and Department of Texas, to November 1865.

Engagements and Campaigns
Demonstration on north side of James River and battle of Chaffin's Farm, New Market Heights, September 28–30, 1864. Fort Harrison, September 29. Darbytown Road, October 13. Battle of Fair Oaks, October 27–28. In trenches before Richmond, to March 1865. Moved to Hatcher's Run, March 27–28. Appomattox Campaign, March 28–April 9. Hatcher's Run, March 29–31. Fall of Petersburg, April 2. Pursuit of Gen. Robert E. Lee, April 3–9. Appomattox Court House, April 9. Surrender of Lee and his army. Duty at Petersburg and City Point, to May. Moved to Texas, May–June. Duty at Edinburg on Mexican frontier, to September 8, and at Brownsville, to November.

46th Regiment, United States Colored Infantry

Date Raised
May 11, 1864

Muster Point(s)
Organized from 1st Arkansas Infantry (African Descent)

Date Disbanded
January 30, 1866

Place Disbanded
Rio Grande, Texas

Movement Orders and Attachments
Attached to post of Milliken's Bend, Louisiana, District of Vicksburg, Mississippi, to November 1864. 2d Brigade, 1st Division, United States Colored Troops, District of Vicksburg, to January 1865. 2d Brigade, post and defenses of Memphis, Tennessee, District of West Tennessee, to February 1865. New Orleans, Louisiana, Department of the Gulf, to May 1865. Department of Texas, to January 1866.

Engagements and Campaigns
Post and garrison duty at Milliken's Bend and at Haynes Bluff, Mississippi, to January 1865. Actions at Mound Plantation, Mississippi, June 24 and 29, 1864. Ordered to Memphis, January 1865, and garrison duty there until February 1865. Ordered to New Orleans, February 23, and duty there until May 4. Ordered to Brazos Santiago, Texas, May 4. Duty at Clarksville and Brownsville on Rio Grande, to January 1866.

47th Regiment, United States Colored Infantry

Date Raised
March 11, 1864

Muster Point(s)
Organized from 8th Louisiana Infantry (African Descent)

Date Disbanded
January 5, 1866

Place Disbanded
Texas

Total Casualties
Regiment lost 1 officer and 30 enlisted men killed and mortally wounded, and 3 officers and 398 enlisted men to disease. Total: 432.

Movement Orders and Attachments
Attached to 2d Brigade, 1st Division, United States Colored Troops, District of Vicksburg, Mississippi, to October 1864. 2d Brigade, 4th Division, XVI Corps, to November 1864. 2d Brigade, 1st Division, United States Colored Troops, District of Vicksburg, to February 1865. 2d Brigade, 1st Division, United States Colored Troops, Military Division of West Mississippi, to June 1865. Department of the Gulf, to January 1866.

Engagements and Campaigns
Post and garrison duty at Vicksburg, Mississippi, to October 1864. Expedition from Haines Bluff up Yazoo River, April 19–23. Near Mechanicsburg,

April 20. Lake Providence, May 27. Moved to mouth of White River, Arkansas, October 15. Duty there and at Vicksburg, to February 1865. Ordered to Algiers, Louisiana, February 26, then to Barrancas, Florida. March from Pensacola, Florida, to Blakely, Alabama, March 20–April 1. Siege of Fort Blakely, April 1–9. Assault and capture of Fort Blakely, April 9. Occupation of Mobile, April 12. March to Montgomery, April 13–25. Return to Mobile and duty there until June. Moved to New Orleans, Louisiana, then to Texas, and duty on Rio Grande and at various points in Texas, to January 1866.

48th Regiment, United States Colored Infantry

Date Raised
March 11, 1864

Muster Point(s)
Organized from 10th Louisiana Infantry (African Descent)

Date Disbanded
January 4, 1866

Place Disbanded
Texas

Total Casualties
Regiment lost 3 officers and 59 enlisted men killed and mortally wounded, and 1 officer and 464 enlisted men to disease. Total: 527.

Movement Orders and Attachments
Attached to 1st Colored Brigade, District of Vicksburg, Mississippi, to April 1864. 1st Brigade, 1st Division, United States Colored Troops, District of Vicksburg, to February 1865. 3d Brigade, 1st Division, United States Colored Troops, Military Division of West Mississippi, to May 1865. 1st Brigade, 1st Division, United States Colored Troops, District of West Florida, to June 1865. Department of the Gulf, to January 1866.

Engagements and Campaigns
Garrison duty at Vicksburg, Mississippi, to February 1865. Expedition from Vicksburg to Rodney and Fayette, September 29–October 3, 1864. Ordered to Algiers, Louisiana, February 26, 1865; then to Barrancas, Florida. March from Pensacola, Florida, to Blakely, Alabama, March 20–April 1. Siege of Fort Blakely, April 1–9. Assault and capture of Fort Blakely, April 9. Occupation of Mobile, April 12. March to Montgomery, April 13–25. Duty there and at Mobile until June. Moved to New Orleans, Louisiana, then to Texas. Duty at various points on Rio Grande, to January 1866.

49th Regiment, United States Colored Infantry

Date Raised
March 11, 1864

Muster Point(s)
Organized from 11th Louisiana Infantry (African Descent)

Date Disbanded
March 27, 1866

Place Disbanded
Department of Mississippi

Movement Orders and Attachments
Attached to 1st Colored Brigade, District of Vicksburg, Mississippi, to April 1864. 1st Brigade, 1st Division, United States Colored Troops, District of Vicksburg, April 1864. 2d Brigade, 1st Division, United States Colored Troops, District of Vicksburg, to October 1864. 1st Brigade, 4th Division, XVI Corps, to November 1864. 1st Brigade, 1st Division, United States Colored Troops, District of Vicksburg, to June 1865. Department of Mississippi, to March 1866.

Engagements and Campaigns
Post and garrison duty at Vicksburg, Mississippi, and at various points in Department of Mississippi for entire term.

50th Regiment, United States Colored Infantry

Date Raised
March 11, 1864

Muster Point(s)
Organized from 12th Louisiana Infantry (African Descent)

Date Disbanded
March 20, 1866

Place Disbanded
Department of the Gulf

Movement Orders and Attachments
Attached to 2d Brigade, 1st Division, United States Colored Troops, District of Vicksburg, Mississippi, to October 1864. 2d Brigade, 4th Division, XVI Corps, to November 1864. 2d Brigade, 1st Division, United States Colored Troops, District of Vicksburg, to February 1865. 2d Brigade, 1st Division, United States Colored Troops, Military Division of West Mississippi, to June 1865. Department of the Gulf, to March 1866.

Engagements and Campaigns
Post and garrison duty at Vicksburg, Mississippi, to February 1865. Expedition from Haines Bluff to Yazoo River, April 19–23, 1864. Near Mechanicsburg, April 20. Expedition from Vicksburg to Rodney and Fayette, September 29–October 3. Ordered to Algiers, Louisiana, February 26, then to Barrancas, Florida. March from Pensacola, Florida, to Blakely, Alabama, March 20–April 1. Siege of Fort Blakely, April 1–9. Assault and capture of Fort Blakely, April 9. Occupation of Mobile, April 12. March to Montgomery, April 13–25. Duty there and at Mobile until June. Moved to New Orleans, Louisiana. At Greenville, June 16. Duty at various points in Department of the Gulf until March 1866.

51st Regiment, United States Colored Infantry

Date Raised
March 11, 1864

Muster Point(s)
Organized from 1st Mississippi Infantry (African Descent)

Date Disbanded
June 16, 1866

Place Disbanded
Texas

Movement Orders and Attachments
Attached to post of Goodrich Landing, District of Vicksburg, Mississippi, to December 1864. 1st Brigade, 1st Division, United States Colored Troops, District of Vicksburg, to Feburary 1865. 2d Brigade, 1st Division, Steele's Command, Military District of West Mississippi, to June 1865. Department of the Gulf, to June 1866.

Engagements and Campaigns
At Lake Providence, to May 1864. Post and garrison duty at Goodrich Landing, Louisiana, to December 1864. Action at Langley's Plantation, Issaquena County, March 22, 1864. Flod, Louisiana, July 2. Waterford, August 16–17. Duty at Vicksburg, Mississippi, to February 1865. Moved to Algiers, Louisiana, February 26; then to Barrancas, Florida. March from Pensacola, Florida, to Blakely, Alabama, March 20–April 1. Siege of Fort Blakely, April 1–9. Assault and capture of Fort Blakely, April 9. Occupation of Mobile, April 12. March to Montgomery, April 13–25. Duty there and at Mobile, to June. Ordered to New Orleans, then to Texas. Duty on Rio Grande and at various points in Texas, to June 1866.

52d Regiment, United States Colored Infantry

Date Raised
March 11, 1864

Muster Point(s)
Organized from 2d Mississippi Infantry (African Descent)

Date Disbanded
May 5, 1866

Place Disbanded
Departments of Mississippi and the Gulf

Movement Orders and Attachments
Attached to 2d Brigade, 1st Division, United States Colored Troops, District of Vicksburg, Mississippi, to October 1864. 2d Brigade, 4th Division, XVI Corps, to November 1864. 2d Brigade, 1st Division, United States Colored Troops, District of Vicksburg, to February 1865. Maltby's Brigade, District of Vicksburg, and Department of Mississippi, to May 1866.

Engagements and Campaigns
Post and garrison duty at Vicksburg, Mississippi, to June 1865. Action at Coleman's Plantation, Port Gibson, July 4, 1864. Bayou Liddell, October 15. Duty at various points in Departments of Mississippi and the Gulf, to May 1866.

53d Regiment, United States Colored Infantry

Date Raised
March 11, 1864

Muster Point(s)
Organized from 3d Mississippi Infantry (African Descent)

Date Disbanded
March 8, 1866

Place Disbanded
Department of Mississippi

Movement Orders and Attachments
Attached to 1st Brigade, 1st Division, United States Colored Troops, District of Vicksburg, Mississippi, to October 1864. 1st Brigade, 4th Division, XVI Corps, to November 1864. Department of Arkansas, to February 1865. District of Vicksburg and Department of Mississippi, to March 1866.

Engagements and Campaigns
Post and garrison duty at Haines Bluff, District of Vicksburg, to October 1864. Expedition to Grand Gulf, March 12–14. Action at Grand Gulf, July 16. Moved to St. Charles, Arkansas, on White River, October 1864, and duty there until February 1865. Action on White River, near St. Charles, October 22, 1864. Moved to Vicksburg, Mississippi, February 1865, and duty there; at Macon, Meridian, and other points in Department of Mississippi, to March 1866.

54th Regiment, United States Colored Infantry

Date Raised
March 11, 1864

Muster Point(s)
Organized from 2d Arkansas Infantry (African Descent)

Date Disbanded
August 8–December 31, 1866

Place Disbanded
Department of Arkansas

Movement Orders and Attachments
Attached to 2d Brigade, Frontier Division, VII Corps, Department of Arkansas, to February 1865. 2d Brigade, 1st Division, VII Corps, to August 1865. Department of Arkansas, to December 1866.

Engagements and Campaigns
Duty at Helena, Arkansas, to May 1864. Ordered to Fort Smith, Arkansas, and duty there until January 1865. Actions at Fort Gibson, September 16, 1864. Cabin Creek, September 19. Cow Creek, Kansas, November 14 and 28. Ordered to Little Rock, Arkansas, January 1865. Action on Arkansas River, January 18. Duty at Little Rock and at various points in Department of Arkansas, to December 1866.

54th Regiment, Massachusetts Infantry (Colored)

Date Raised
May 13, 1863

Muster Point(s)
Readville, Massachusetts

Date Disbanded
September 1, 1865

Place Disbanded
Boston, Massachusetts

Total Casualties
Regiment lost 5 officers and 104 enlisted men killed and mortally wounded, and 1 officer and 160 enlisted men to disease. Total: 270.

Movement Orders and Attachments
Left Boston on steamer *De Molay* for Hilton Head, South Carolina, May 28, arriving there June 3. Attached to U.S. forces at St. Helena Island, South Carolina, X Corps, Department of the South, to July 1863. 3d Brigade, 1st Division, Morris Island, South Carolina, X Corps, July 1863. 3d Brigade, Morris Island, to August 1863. 4th Brigade, Morris Island, to November 1863. 3d Brigade, Morris Island, to January 1864. Montgomery's Brigade, District of Hilton Head, to February 1864. Montgomery's Brigade, District of Florida, February 1864. 3d Brigade, Ames's Division, District of Florida, to April 1864. Folly and Morris Islands, Northern District, Department of the South, to October 1864. 1st Separate Brigade, Department of the South, to November 1864. 2d Brigade, Coast Division, Department of the South, to February 1865. 1st Separate Brigade, Northern District, Department of the South, to March 1865. 1st Separate Brigade, District of Charleston, South Carolina, Department of the South, to June 1865. 3d Subdistrict, District of Charleston, Department of South Carolina, to August 1865.

Engagements and Campaigns
At Thompson's Plantation near Beaufort, South Carolina, June 4–8, 1863. Moved to St. Simon's Island, June 8–9. Expedition up Altamaha River, June 10–11. At St. Simon's Island, June 12–24. At St. Helena Island, June 25–July 8. To Stono Inlet, July 8. Expedition against James Island, July 9–16. Affair Legaresville, July 13. Secessionville, July 16. Moved to Morris Island, July 16–18. Assault on Fort Wagner, July 18. Siege operations against Forts Wagner and Gregg, Morris Island, July 18–September 7, and against Fort Sumter and Charleston, September 7, 1863–January 28, 1864. Capture of Forts Wagner and Gregg, September 7, 1863. Moved to Hilton Head, January 28, 1864. Expedition to Jacksonville, Florida, February 5–7. Capture of Jacksonville, February 6. Expedition to Lake City, Florida, February 7–22. Battle of Olustee, February 20. Duty at Jacksonville, to April 17. Moved to Morris Island, April 17–18. Duty on Morris and Folly Islands, to November 1864. Expedition to James Island, June 30–July 10. Actions on James Island, July 2 and 9–10. Six companies in charge of rebel prisoners under fire of Charleston Batteries, September 7–October 20. Eight companies moved to Hilton Head, November 27. (Companies B and F at Morris Island until February 1865.) Expedition to Boyd's Neck, South Carolina, November 29–30. Boyd's Landing, November 29. Battle of Honey Hill, November 30. Demonstration on Charleston Camp, Savannah Railroad, December 6–9. Moved to Graham's Neck, December 20. Connect with Gen. William T. Sherman's army at Pocotaligo, South Carolina, January 15, 1865. March to Charleston, January 15–February 23, skirmishing all the way. (Companies B and F occupy Charleston, February 18.) Regiment on duty at Charleston, February 27–March 12. At Savannah, Georgia, March 13–27. At Georgetown, South Carolina, March 31–April 5. Potter's Expedition to Camden, April 5–25. Seven Mile Bridge, April 6. Destruction of Eppes' Bridge, Black River, April 7. Dingle's Mills, April 9. Destruction of Rolling Stock at Wateree Junction, April 11. Singleton's Plantation, April 12. Statesburg, April 15. Occupation of Camden, April 17. Boykin's Mills, April 18. At Georgetown, April 25. Duty at Georgetown, Charleston, and various points in South Carolina, April 25–August 17. Mustered out at Mount Pleasant, South Carolina, August 20, 1865.

55th Regiment, United States Colored Infantry

Date Raised
March 11, 1864

Muster Point(s)
Organized from 1st Alabama Infantry (African Descent)

Date Disbanded
December 31, 1865

Place Disbanded
Louisiana

Movement Orders and Attachments
Attached to 1st Colored Brigade, District of Memphis, Tennessee, XVI Corps, to April 1864. Fort Pickering, Memphis, District of West Tennessee, to June 1864. 3d Brigade, Infantry Division, Sturgis's Expedition, to June 1864. 1st Colored Brigade, District of Memphis, District of West Tennessee, to January 1865. 2d Brigade, post and defenses of Memphis, to February 1865. 2d Brigade, United States Colored Troops, District of Morganza, Louisiana, Department of the Gulf, to April 1865. District of Port Hudson, Louisiana, Department of the Gulf, to December 1865.

Engagements and Campaigns
Post and garrison duty at Memphis, to June 1, 1864. Sturgis's Expedition from Memphis into Mississippi, June 1–13. Battle of Brice's Cross Roads near Guntown, June 10. Ripley, June 11. Davis' Mills, June 12. Duty at Memphis, to August 1. Smith's Expedition to Oxford, Mississippi, August 1–30. Action at Waterford, August 16–17. Garrison duty at Memphis, to February 1865. Ordered to New Orleans, Louisiana, February 23; then to Morganza, February 28, and duty there until April. Garrison duty at Port Hudson, Baton Rouge, and other points in Louisiana until December 1865.

55th Regiment, Massachusetts Infantry (Colored)

Date Raised
June 22, 1863

Muster Point(s)
Readville, Massachusetts

Date Disbanded
September 23, 1865

Place Disbanded
Boston, Massachusetts

Total Casualties
Regiment lost 3 officers and 64 enlisted men killed and mortally wounded, and 2 officers and 128 enlisted men to disease. Total: 197.

Movement Orders and Attachments
Left for Newberne, North Carolina, July 21, 1863, arriving there July 25. Moved to Folly Island, South Carolina, July 30–August 3. Attached to Wild's African Brigade, Vogde's Division, North End, Folly Island, X Corps, Department of the South, to October 1863. 3d Brigade, Vogde's Division, Folly Island, X Corps, to February 1864. 3d Brigade, Ames's Division, District of Florida, to April 1864. Folly and Morris Islands, Northern District, Department of the South, to November 1864. 2d Brigade, Coast Division, Department of the South, to January 1865. 1st Separate Brigade, Department of the South, to March 1865. 1st Separate Brigade, District of Charleston, Department of the South, to June 1865. District of Charleston, Department of South Carolina, to August 1865.

Engagements and Campaigns
Fatigue duty on north end of Folly Island and in trenches on Morris Island, August 9–September 5, 1863. Fatigue duty on Forts Wagner and Gregg, Morris Island, and operations against Fort Sumter and Charleston, September 17–October 28. Camp on Folly Island, to February 1864. Expedition to John's Island, February (Company F). Moved to Jacksonville, Florida, February 13–16, and provost duty there until March 11. Advance to Baldwin, February 19–20. (Company F detached as garrison at Fort Fribley, Jacksonville, February–April.) Companies B and I at Yellow Bluff, February 28–April 17. Regiment ordered to Palatka, Florida, March 11, and duty there until April 17. Moved to Folly Island, April 17–18. Duty there until November 27. Demonstration on James Island, May 21–22. Expedition to James Island, June 30–July 10. Action on James Island, July 2. Moved to Hilton Head, South Carolina, November 27–28. (Company G detached at battery on Long Island, and Company H at Fort Delafield, Stono Inlet, to February 12, 1865.) Hatch's Expedition up Broad River to Boyd's Neck, November 29–30. Battle of Honey Hill, November 30. Demonstration on Charleston Camp, Savannah Railroad, December 6–9. Devaux's Neck, December 6. At Boyd's Landing, to January 11, 1865. Moved to Hilton Head, then to Fort Thunderbolt, near Savannah, Georgia, January 11–13. Duty at Forts Jackson, Bartow, and Battery Lee, to February 1. Moved to Hilton Head, then to Beaufort, South Carolina, February 1. Expedition up South Edisto River, February 1–6. Moved to Stono Inlet, February 6. Expedition to James Island, February 9–10. Expedition to Bull's Bay, February 11–15. Moved to Mount Pleasant, February 19–20. Expedition to Santee River, February 21–March 10. Duty at and near Charleston, to May 7. Expedition to Eutaw Springs, April 6–12. Moved to Sumpterville, May 7–8; then to Orangeburg, May 19, and provost duty there until August. Mustered out August 29, 1865.

56th Regiment, United States Colored Infantry

Date Raised
March 11, 1864

Muster Point(s)
Organized from 3d Alabama Infantry (African Descent)

Date Disbanded
September 15, 1866

Place Disbanded
Arkansas

Total Casualties
Regiment lost 4 officers and 21 enlisted men killed and mortally wounded, and 2 officers and 647 enlisted men to disease. Total: 674.

Movement Orders and Attachments
Attached to District of Eastern Arkansas, VII Corps, Department of Arkansas, to August 1865. Department of Arkansas, to September 1866.

Engagements and Campaigns
Post and garrison duty at Helena, Arkansas, to February 1865. Action at Indian Bay, April 13, 1864. Muffleton Lodge, June 29. Operations in Arkansas, July 1–31. Wallace's Ferry, Big Creek, July 26.

Expedition from Helena up White River, August 29–September 3. Expedition from Helena to Friar's Point, Mississippi, February 19–22, 1865. Duty at Helena and other points in Arkansas until September 1866.

57th Regiment, United States Colored Infantry

Date Raised
March 11, 1864

Muster Point(s)
Organized from 4th Arkansas Infantry (African Descent)

Date Disbanded
December 31, 1866

Place Disbanded
Department of Arkansas

Movement Orders and Attachments
Attached to District of Eastern Arkansas, VII Corps, Department of Arkansas, to May 1864. 1st Brigade, 2d Division, VII Corps, to January 1865. Colored Brigade, VII Corps, to February 1865. 2d Brigade, 1st Division, VII Corps, to August 1865. Department of Arkansas, to December 1866.

Engagements and Campaigns
Garrison duty at Helena and Little Rock, Arkansas, to August 1864. (A detachment on Steele's Camden Expedition, March 23–May 3, 1864, as bridge train guard.) Skirmish near Little Rock, April 26, 1864. Operations against Shelby, north of Arkansas River, May 13–31. Skirmishes near Little Rock, May 24 and 28. March to Brownsville, Arkansas, August 23, and to Duvall's Bluff, August 29. Duty there and at Little Rock until June 1865; then at various points in Department of Arkansas guarding property and on post duty until December 1866.

58th Regiment, United States Colored Infantry

Date Raised
March 11, 1864

Muster Point(s)
Organized from 6th Mississippi Infantry (African Descent)

Date Disbanded
April 30, 1866

Place Disbanded
Department of Mississippi

Movement Orders and Attachments
Attached to post of Natchez, Mississippi, District of Vicksburg, to April 1866.

Engagements and Campaigns
Post and garrison duty at Natchez and in Department of Mississippi for entire term. Expedition from Natchez to Gillespie's Plantation, Louisiana, August 4–6, 1864.

59th Regiment, United States Colored Infantry

Date Raised
March 11, 1864

Muster Point(s)
Organized from 1st Tennessee Infantry (African Descent)

Date Disbanded
January 31, 1866

Place Disbanded
District of West Tennessee

Movement Orders and Attachments
Attached to 1st Colored Brigade, District of Memphis, Tennessee, Department of Tennessee, to June 1864. 3d Brigade, Infantry Division, Sturgis's Expedition, to June 1864. 1st Colored Brigade, District of Memphis, District of West Tennessee, to February 1865. Fort Pickering, Memphis, District of West Tennessee, to July 1865. 2d Brigade, District of West Tennessee, to September 1865. Department of Tennessee, to January 1866.

Engagements and Campaigns
Post and garrison duty at Memphis, Tennessee, to June 1864. Sturgis's Expedition from Memphis into Mississippi, June 1–13. Battle of Brice's Cross Roads, Guntown, June 10. Ripley, June 11. Davis' Mill, June 12. Smith's Expedition to Tupelo, Mississippi, July 5–21. Near Ripley, July 7. Pontotoc, July 11–12. Camargo's Cross Roads, Harrisburg, July 13. Tupelo, July 14–15. Old Town Creek, July 15. Post and garrison duty at Memphis and in District of West Tennessee, to January 1866.

Repulse of Gen. Nathan Bedford Forrest's attack on Memphis, August 21, 1864.

60th Regiment, United States Colored Infantry

Date Raised
March 11, 1864

Muster Point(s)
Organized from 1st Iowa Colored Infantry

Date Disbanded
October 15, 1865

Place Disbanded
Duvall's Bluff, Arkansas

Movement Orders and Attachments
Attached to District of Eastern Arkansas, VII Corps, Department of Arkansas, to April 1865. 2d Brigade, 1st Division, VII Corps, to August 1865. Department of Arkansas, to October 1865.

Engagements and Campaigns
Post and garrison duty at Helena, Arkansas, to April 1865. Expedition from Helena to Big Creek, July 25, 1864. Action at Wallace's Ferry, Big Creek, July 26. Expedition to Kent's Landing, August 11–13. Expedition up White River, August 29–September 3 (Companies C and F). Scout to Alligator Bayou, September 9–14 (detachment). Scouts to Alligator Bayou, September 22–28 and October 1–4. Expedition to Harbert's Plantation, Mississippi, January 11–16, 1865 (Company C). Moved to Little Rock, Arkansas, April 8, 1865, and duty there until August 20. Moved to Duvall's Bluff, then to Jacksonport, Arkansas. Duty there and at various points in Subdistrict of White River in White, Augusta, Franklin, and Fulton Counties; Powhatan on Black River; and Batesville, to September.

61st Regiment, United States Colored Infantry

Date Raised
March 11, 1864

Muster Point(s)
Organized from 2d Tennessee Infantry (African Descent)

Date Disbanded
December 30, 1865

Place Disbanded
District of Alabama

Total Casualties
Regiment lost 1 officer and 37 enlisted men killed and mortally wounded, and 2 officers and 316 enlisted men to disease. Total: 356.

Movement Orders and Attachments
Attached to District of Memphis, Tennessee, XVI Corps, Department of Tennessee, to June 1864. 1st Colored Brigade, Memphis, Tennessee, District of West Tennessee, to February 1865. 1st Brigade, United States Colored Troops, District of Morganza, Department of the Gulf, to April 1865. 1st Brigade, 1st Division, United States Colored Troops, District of West Florida, to June 1865. Department of Alabama, to December 1865.

Engagements and Campaigns
Post and garrison duty at Memphis, to July 1864. Smith's Expedition to Tupelo, Mississippi, July 5–21. Camargo's Cross Roads, July 13. Tupelo, July 14–15. Old Town Creek, July 15. Smith's Expedition to Oxford, Mississippi, August 1–30. Repulse of Gen. Nathan Bedford Forrest's attack on Memphis, August 21. Near Memphis, August 24. Eastport, October 10. Moscow Station, December 2–3. Duty at Memphis, to February 1865. Ordered to New Orleans, Louisiana, February 23; then to Morganza, Louisiana. Ordered to Barrancas, Florida, March 17. Ordered to Blakely, Alabama, April 15. Duty there and in District of Alabama until December.

62d Regiment, United States Colored Infantry

Date Raised
March 11, 1864

Muster Point(s)
Organized from 1st Missouri Colored Infantry

Date Disbanded
March 31, 1866

Place Disbanded
St. Louis, Missouri

Movement Orders and Attachments
Attached to District of St. Louis, Department of Missouri, to March 1864. District of Baton Rouge, Louisiana, Department of the Gulf, to June 1864. Provisional Brigade, District of Morganza,

Department of the Gulf, to September 1864. 2d Brigade, 1st Division, United States Colored Troops, District of Morganza, Department of the Gulf, to September 1864. Port Hudson, Louisiana, Department of the Gulf, to September 1864. Brazos Santiago, Texas, to October 1864. 1st Brigade, 2d Division, United States Colored Troops, Department of the Gulf, to December 1864. Brazos Santiago, to June 1865. Department of Texas, to March 1866.

Engagements and Campaigns
Ordered to Baton Rouge, March 23, 1864, and duty there until June. Ordered to Morganza, and duty there until September. Expedition from Morganza to Bayou Sara, September 6–7. Ordered to Brazos Santiago, September, and duty there until May 1865. Expedition from Brazos Santiago, May 11–14. Action at Palmetto Ranch, May 12–13. White's Ranch, May 13. Last action of war. Duty at various points in Texas until March 1866. Ordered to St. Louis via New Orleans, Louisiana.

63d Regiment, United States Colored Infantry

Date Raised
March 11, 1864

Muster Point(s)
Organized from 9th Louisiana Infantry (African Descent)

Date Disbanded
January 9, 1866

Place Disbanded
Memphis, Tennessee

Movement Orders and Attachments
Attached to post of Natchez, Mississippi, District of Vicksburg, Mississippi, to February 1865. Subdistrict of Vidalia, District of Natchez, Department of Mississippi, to January 1866.

Engagements and Campaigns
Post and garrison duty at Natchez, to February 1865. Skirmish at Waterproof, Louisiana, April 20, 1864. Ashwood, Mississippi, June 25. Camp Marengo, September 4. Bullitt's Bayou, September 14 (Companies B and G). Post and garrison duty at Vidalia and Bullitt's Bayou, to January 1866. (A detachment at Helena, Arkansas, District of Eastern Arkansas, Department of Arkansas, to February 1865. Companies B and K at Memphis, February 1865.)

64th Regiment, United States Colored Infantry

Date Raised
March 11, 1864

Muster Point(s)
Organized from 7th Louisiana Infantry (African Descent)

Date Disbanded
March 13, 1866

Place Disbanded
Department of Mississippi

Movement Orders and Attachments
Attached to 1st Division, Unassigned, United States Colored Troops, District of Vicksburg, Mississippi, to May 1864. District of Natchez, Mississippi, District of Vicksburg, to September 1864. Davis' Bend, Mississippi, District of Vicksburg, to December 1864. Unattached, 1st Division, United States Colored Troops, District of Vicksburg, to February 1865. Post of Vicksburg and Department of Mississippi, to March 1866.

Engagements and Campaigns
Post and garrison duty at Vicksburg, Mississippi, to May 1864. Actions at Ashwood Landing, Louisiana, May 1 and 4. Post and garrison duty at Davis' Bend and Natchez, Mississippi, to February 1865. Action at Davis' Bend, June 2, 1864. Point Pleasant, June 25. Davis' Bend, June 29. (Pine Bluff, Arkansas, July 2, 1864; Helena, Arkansas, August 2, 1864, as a detachment.) Duty at Vicksburg, to April 1865. At Davis' Bend and in Department of Mississippi until March 1866.

65th Regiment, United States Colored Infantry

Date Raised
March 11, 1864

Muster Point(s)
Organized from 2d Missouri Colored Infantry

Date Disbanded
January 8, 1867

Place Disbanded
Northern District of Louisiana

Total Casualties
Regiment lost 6 officers and 749 enlisted men to disease. Total: 755.

Movement Orders and Attachments
Attached to Department of Missouri, to June 1864. Provisional Brigade, District of Morganza, Louisiana, Department of the Gulf, to September 1864. 2d Brigade, 1st Division, United States Colored Troops, District of Morganza, Department of the Gulf, to February 1865. 1st Brigade, 1st Division, United States Colored Troops, District of Morganza, Department of the Gulf, to May 1865. Northern District of Louisiana and Department of the Gulf, to January 1867.

Engagements and Campaigns
Garrison duty at Morganza, Louisiana, to May 1865. Ordered to Port Hudson, Louisiana. Garrison duty there and at Baton Rouge and in Northern District of Louisiana until January 1867.

66th Regiment, United States Colored Infantry

Date Raised
March 11, 1864

Muster Point(s)
Organized from 4th Mississippi Infantry (African Descent)

Date Disbanded
March 20, 1866

Place Disbanded
Department of Mississippi

Movement Orders and Attachments
Attached to post of Goodrich Landing, District of Vicksburg, Mississippi, Departments of the Tennessee and Mississippi, to February 1865. Little Rock, Arkansas, Unattached, 2d Division, VII Corps, Department of Arkansas, to February 1865. Unattached, District of Vicksburg and Department of Mississippi, to March 1866.

Engagements and Campaigns
Post and garrison duty at Goodrich Landing and at Lake Providence, Louisiana, to February 1865. Actions at Issaquena County, March 22, 1864. Goodrich Landing, March 24. Bayou Mason, July 2. Issaquena County, July 10. Goodrich Landing, July 16. Bayou Tensas, July 30. Issaquena County, August 17. Bayou Tensas, August 26. Post and garrison duty at Little Rock, to March 1865, and at Vicksburg, Mississippi, and in Department of Mississippi until March 1866.

67th Regiment, United States Colored Infantry

Date Raised
March 11, 1864

Muster Point(s)
Organized from 3d Missouri Colored Infantry

Date Disbanded
July 12, 1865

Movement Orders and Attachments
Attached to Department of Missouri, to March 1864. District of Port Hudson, Louisiana, Department of the Gulf, to June 1864. Provisional Brigade, District of Morganza, Department of the Gulf, to September 1864. 2d Brigade, 1st Division, United States Colored Troops, District of Morganza, Department of the Gulf, to February 1865. 1st Brigade, 1st Division, United States Colored Troops, District of Morganza, Department of the Gulf, to May 1865. Northern District of Louisiana, Department of the Gulf, to July 1865.

Engagements and Campaigns
Moved from Benton Barracks, Missouri, to Port Hudson, Louisiana, arriving March 19, 1864, and duty there until June. Moved to Morganza, Louisiana, and duty there until June 1865. Action at Mt. Pleasant Landing, Louisiana, May 15, 1864 (detachment). Expedition from Morganza to Bayou Sara, September 6–7, 1864. Moved to Port Hudson, June 1, 1865. Consolidated with 65th Regiment, United States Colored Troops, July 12, 1865.

68th Regiment, United States Colored Infantry

Date Raised
March 11, 1864

Muster Point(s)
Organized from 4th Missouri Colored Infantry

Date Disbanded
February 5, 1866

Place Disbanded
Texas

Movement Orders and Attachments
Attached to District of Memphis, Tennessee, XVI Corps, Department of the Tennessee, to June 1864. 1st Colored Brigade, Memphis, Tennessee, District of West Tennessee, to December 1864. Fort Pickering, defenses of Memphis, District of West Tennessee, to February 1865. 3d Brigade, 1st Division, United States Colored Troops, Military Division of West Mississippi, to May 1865. 1st Brigade, 1st Division, United States Colored Troops, District of West Florida, to June 1865. Department of Texas, to February 1866.

Engagements and Campaigns
At St. Louis, Missouri, to April 27, 1864. Ordered to Memphis and duty in defenses of that city until February 1865. Smith's Expedition to Tupelo, Mississippi, July 5–21, 1864. Camargo's Cross Roads, near Harrisburg, July 13. Tupelo, July 14–15. Old Town Creek, July 15. At Fort Pickering, defenses of Memphis, to February 1865. Ordered to New Orleans, Louisiana, then to Barrancas, Florida. March from Pensacola, Florida, to Blakely, Alabama, March 20–April 1. Siege of Fort Blakely, April 1–9. Assault and capture of Fort Blakely, April 9. Occupation of Mobile, April 12. March to Montgomery, April 13–25. Duty there and at Mobile until June. Moved to New Orleans, then to Texas. Duty on Rio Grande and at various points in Texas until February 1866.

69th Regiment, United States Colored Infantry

Date Raised
December 14, 1864–March 17, 1865

Muster Point(s)
Pine Bluff, Duvall's Bluff, and Helena, Arkansas; Memphis, Tennessee

Date Disbanded
September 20, 1865

Movement Orders and Attachments
On duty at these points in Department of Arkansas and District of West Tennessee until September 1865.

70th Regiment, United States Colored Infantry

Date Raised
April 23–October 1, 1864

Muster Point(s)
Natchez, Mississippi

Date Disbanded
March 7, 1866

Place Disbanded
Department of Mississippi

Movement Orders and Attachments
Attached to District of Natchez, Mississippi, and District of Vicksburg, Mississippi, Departments of the Tennessee and Mississippi, to March 1867.

Engagements and Campaigns
Post and garrison duty at Natchez, to April 1865, and at Rodney and other points in Department of Mississippi until March 1866.

71st Regiment, United States Colored Infantry

Date Raised
March 3–August 13, 1864

Muster Point(s)
Black River Bridge and Natchez, Mississippi; Alexandria, Louisiana

Date Disbanded
November 8, 1864

Movement Orders and Attachments
Attached to District of Natchez, Mississippi, District of Vicksburg, Mississippi. Consolidated with 70th Regiment, United States Colored Troops, November 8, 1864.

Engagements and Campaigns
Post and garrison duty at Natchez, to November 1864. Expedition from Natchez to Buck's Ferry and skirmishes, September 19–22.

72d Regiment, United States Colored Infantry

Date Raised
April 18, 1865

Muster Point(s)
Covington, Kentucky

Date Disbanded
May 3, 1865

Place Disbanded
Covington

73d Regiment, United States Colored Infantry

Date Raised
April 4, 1864

Muster Point(s)
Organized from I Corps d'Afrique Infantry

Date Disbanded
September 27, 1865

Place Disbanded
Department of the Gulf

Total Casualties
Regiment lost 4 officers and 42 enlisted men killed and mortally wounded, and 1 officer and 173 enlisted men to disease. Total: 220.

Movement Orders and Attachments
Attached to 1st Brigade, 1st Division, Corps d'Afrique, Department of the Gulf, to March 1865. 1st Brigade, 1st Division, United States Colored Troops, District of West Florida, to May 1865. 3d Brigade, 1st Division, United States Colored Troops, District of West Florida, to June 1865. Department of the Gulf, to September 1865. Consolidated with 96th Regiment, United States Colored Troops, September 27, 1865.

Engagements and Campaigns
Duty at Port Hudson, Louisiana, to March 1864. Red River Campaign, March 10–May 22. Advance from Franklin to Alexandria, March 14–26. Retreat from Alexandria to Morganza, May 13–20. Mansura, May 16. Near Moreauville and Yellow Bayou, May 17. Yellow Bayou, May 18. Near Morganza, May 24. Duty at Port Hudson until July, and at Morganza until February 1865. Moved to Algiers, Louisiana, February 26; then to Barrancas, Florida. March from Pensacola, Florida, to Blakely, Alabama, March 20–April 1. Siege of Fort Blakely, April 1–9. Assault and capture of Fort Blakely, April 9. Occupation of Mobile, April 12. March to Montgomery, April 13–25. Detached as guard to transports, April 28, and return to Mobile. Duty there until June. Moved to New Orleans, Louisiana, June 10; then to Greenville, Louisiana. Duty there and in Department of the Gulf until September.

74th Regiment, United States Colored Infantry

Date Raised
April 4, 1864

Muster Point(s)
Organized from II Corps d'Afrique Infantry

Date Disbanded
October 11, 1865

Movement Orders and Attachments
Attached to defenses of New Orleans, Department of the Gulf, to October 1864. 3d Brigade, 3d Division, United States Colored Troops, Department of the Gulf, to November 1864. Defenses of New Orleans, Department of the Gulf, to October 1864. Garrison duty at Ship Island, Mississippi, for entire term. Expedition from Fort Pike to Pearl River, September 9–12, 1864. Expedition from Fort Pike to Bayou Bonforica, January 31–February 1, 1865 (detachment). Expedition from Fort Pike to Bayou St. Louis, March 28–30 (detachment).

75th Regiment, United States Colored Infantry

Date Raised
April 4, 1864

Muster Point(s)
Organized from III Corps d'Afrique Infantry

Date Disbanded
November 25, 1865

Movement Orders and Attachments
Attached to 1st Brigade, 1st Division, Corps d'Afrique, Department of the Gulf, to February 1865. District of LaFourche, Department of the Gulf, to November 1865.

Engagements and Campaigns
Red River Campaign, March 10–May 22, 1864. Advance from Franklin to Alexandria, Louisiana, March 14–26. Retreat from Alexandria to Morganza, May 13–20. Mansura, May 16. Near Moreauville, May 17. Yellow Bayou, May 18. Duty at Morganza until February 1865. Ordered to Terre Bonne, February 26. Duty there and in District of LaFourche until November 1865. Expedition to Lake Verret, Grand Lake, and the Park, April 2–10, 1865. Operations around Brashear City, April 30–May 12.

76th Regiment, United States Colored Infantry

Date Raised
April 4, 1864

Muster Point(s)
Organized from IV Corps d'Afrique Infantry

Date Disbanded
December 31, 1865

Place Disbanded
Texas

Movement Orders and Attachments
Attached to 2d Brigade, 1st Division, Corps d'Afrique, Department of the Gulf, to July 1864. Post of Port Hudson, Louisiana, Department of the Gulf, to October 1864. 1st Brigade, 2d Division, United States Colored Troops, Department of the Gulf, to February 1865. 3d Brigade, 1st Division, United States Colored Troops, District of West Florida, to May 1865. 1st Brigade, 1st Division, United States Colored Troops, District of West Florida, Department of the Gulf, to June 1865. Department of the Gulf, to December 1865.

Engagements and Campaigns
Garrison duty at Port Hudson, to February 1865. Ordered to Algiers, Louisiana, February 21; then to Barrancas, Florida. March from Pensacola, Florida, to Blakely, Alabama, March 20–April 1. Siege of Fort Blakely, April 1–9. Assault and capture of Fort Blakely, April 9. Occupation of Mobile, April 12. March to Montgomery, April 13–25. Duty there and at various points in Alabama until June 1865. Ordered to New Orleans, Louisiana, then to Texas and duty on Rio Grande until December.

77th Regiment, United States Colored Infantry

Date Raised
April 4, 1864

Muster Point(s)
Organized from V Corps d'Afrique Infantry

Date Disbanded
October 18, 1865

Place Disbanded
Louisiana

Movement Orders and Attachments
Attached to defenses of New Orleans, Louisiana, Department of the Gulf, to October 1864. 3d Brigade, 3d Division, United States Colored Troops, Department of the Gulf, to November 1864. Defenses of New Orleans, Department of the Gulf, to October 1865. Consolidated with 10th Regiment, United States Colored Heavy Artillery, October 18, 1865.

Engagements and Campaigns
Duty in defenses of New Orleans at Fort St. Phillip, Jefferson City, and other points until October 1865.

78th Regiment, United States Colored Infantry

Date Raised
April 4, 1864

Muster Point(s)
Organized from VI Corps d'Afrique Infantry

Date Disbanded
January 6, 1866

Place Disbanded
Department of the Gulf

Movement Orders and Attachments
Attached to 2d Brigade, 2d Division, Corps d'Afrique, Department of the Gulf, to July 1864. Post of Port Hudson, Louisiana, Department of the Gulf, to October 1864. 2d Brigade, 2d Division, United States Colored Troops, Department of the Gulf, to October 1864. Post of Port Hudson, Department of the Gulf, to April 1865. District of LaFourche, Department of the Gulf, to January 1866.

Engagements and Campaigns
Post and garrison duty at Port Hudson, until April 1865; and at Donaldsonville, Thibodeaux, and other points in District of LaFourche, Department of the Gulf, to January 1866.

79th Regiment, United States Colored Infantry (old organization)

Date Raised
April 4, 1864

Muster Point(s)
Organized from VII Corps d'Afrique Infantry

Date Disbanded
July 28, 1864

Place Disbanded
New Orleans, Louisiana

Movement Orders and Attachments
Attached to 2d Brigade, 1st Division, Corps d'Afrique, Department of the Gulf, to June 1864. 2d Brigade, 2d Division, Corps d'Afrique, Department of the Gulf, to July 1864. Transferred to 75th Regiment, United States Colored Troops, July 28, 1864.

Engagements and Campaigns
Post and garrison duty at Port Hudson, Louisiana, until April 17, 1864, and at Fort Pike and Fort Macomb, defences of New Orleans, until July 1864.

79th Regiment, United States Colored Infantry (new organization)

Date Raised
December 13, 1864

Muster Point(s)
Organized from 1st Kansas Colored Infantry

Date Disbanded
October 30, 1865

Place Disbanded
Pine Bluff, Arkansas

Total Casualties
Regiment lost 5 officers and 183 enlisted men killed and mortally wounded, and 1 officer and 165 enlisted men to disease. Total: 354.

Movement Orders and Attachments
Attached to 2d Brigade, District of the Frontier, VII Corps, Department of Arkansas, to January 1865. Colored Brigade, VII Corps, to February 1865. 2d Brigade, 1st Division, VII Corps, to August 1865. Department of Arkansas, to October 1865.

Engagements and Campaigns
Duty at Fort Smith, Arkansas, until January 1865. Skirmish at Ivey's Ford, January 8. Ordered to Little Rock, Arkansas, January 16. Skirmish at Clarksville, Arkansas, January 18. Duty at Little Rock until July, and at Pine Bluff until October.

80th Regiment, United States Colored Infantry

Date Raised
September 1, 1863

Muster Point(s)
Port Hudson, Louisiana

Date Disbanded
April 4, 1864

Place Disbanded
Port Hudson

Movement Orders and Attachments
Attached to Ullman's Brigade, Corps d'Afrique, Department of the Gulf, to December 1863. 2d Brigade, 1st Division, Corps d'Afrique, to March 1864. Garrison, Port Hudson, to April 1864.

Engagements and Campaigns
Garrison duty at Port Hudson until April 1864. Designation of regiment changed to 80th United States Colored Troops, April 4, 1864.

81st Regiment, United States Colored Infantry

Date Raised
April 4, 1864

Muster Point(s)
Organized from IX Corps d'Afrique Infantry

Date Disbanded
January 30, 1866

Place Disbanded
Department of the Gulf

Movement Orders and Attachments
Attached to 2d Brigade, 1st Division, Corps

d'Afrique, Department of the Gulf, to July 1864. Consolidated with 88th and 89th Regiments, United States Colored Troops, July 6, 1864, to form 77th United States Colored Troops. Reorganized July 1864, by consolidation of 87th and 95th United States Colored Troops. Attached to Engineer Brigade, Department of the Gulf, to September 1864. 2d Brigade, 2d Division, United States Colored Troops, Department of the Gulf, to February 1865. Garrison of Port Hudson, Louisiana, Department of the Gulf, to July 1865. Department of the Gulf, to January 1866.

Engagements and Campaigns
Post and garrison duty at Port Hudson and in Department of the Gulf for entire term.

82d Regiment, United States Colored Infantry

Date Raised
April 4, 1864

Muster Point(s)
Organized from X Corps d'Afrique Infantry

Date Disbanded
September 10, 1866

Place Disbanded
District of Florida

Movement Orders and Attachments
Attached to 2d Brigade, 1st Division, Corps d'Afrique, Department of the Gulf, to July 1864. Consolidated with 80th Regiment, United States Colored Troops, July 6, 1864, to form new 79th Regiment, United States Colored Troops. Reorganized July 1864, by consolidation of 97th and 99th Regiments, United States Colored Troops. Attached to Pensacola, Florida, District of West Florida, Department of the Gulf, to October 1864. 1st Brigade, 3d Division, United States Colored Troops, Department of the Gulf, to October 1864. 1st Brigade, District of West Florida, to January 1865. 3d Brigade, District of West Florida, to March 1865. 1st Brigade, 1st Division, District of West Florida, to May 1865. Pensacola, District of West Florida and Department of Florida, to muster out.

Engagements and Campaigns
Duty at Port Hudson, Louisiana, until April 17, 1864. Moved to Fort Barrancas, Florida, and duty there until March 1865. Expedition toward Pollard, Alabama, July 21–25, 1864. Camp Gonzales, Florida, July 22. Near Pollard, July 23. Expedition from Fort Barrancas, August 15–19. Expedition to Marianna, September 18–October 4. Euchee Anna Court House, September 23. Marianna, September 27. Expedition up Blackwater Bay, October 25–28. Near Milton, October 26. Expedition to Pollard, December 13–19. Mitchell's Creek, December 15–16. Pine Barren Ford, December 17–18. March from Pensacola to Blakely, Alabama, March 20–April 1, 1865. Siege of Fort Blakely, April 1–9. Assault and capture of Fort Blakely, April 9. Occupation of Mobile, April 12. March to Montgomery, April 13–25. Duty there until May. Moved to Mobile, then to Barrancas, May 23. Expedition to Appalachicola, May 31–June 6. Duty at Appalachicola and in District of Florida until September 1866.

83d Regiment, United States Colored Infantry (old organization)

Date Raised
April 4, 1864

Muster Point(s)
Organized from XI Corps d'Afrique Infantry

Date Disbanded
July 28, 1864

Place Disbanded
Department of the Gulf

Movement Orders and Attachments
Attached to 1st Brigade, 1st Division, Corps d'Afrique, Department of the Gulf, to July 1864. Garrison duty at Port Hudson, Louisiana.

83d Regiment, United States Colored Infantry (new organization)

Date Raised
December 13, 1864

Muster Point(s)
Organized from 2d Kansas Colored Infantry

Date Disbanded
November 27, 1865

Place Disbanded
Leavenworth, Kansas

Total Casualties
Regiment lost 2 officers and 32 enlisted men killed and mortally wounded, and 211 enlisted men to disease. Total: 245.

Movement Orders and Attachments
Attached to 2d Brigade, District of the Frontier, VII Corps, Department of Arkansas, to January 1865. Colored Brigade, VII Corps, Department of Arkansas, to February 1865. 2d Brigade, 1st Division, VII Corps, Department of Arkansas, to August 1865. Department of Arkansas, to October 1865.

Engagements and Campaigns
Duty at Fort Smith, Arkansas, until January 1865. Moved to Little Rock, Arkansas, January 15–February 4, and duty there until August. Moved to Camden, Arkansas, August 1–10, and duty there until October 9. Mustered out October 9, 1865.

84th Regiment, United States Colored Infantry

Date Raised
April 4, 1864

Muster Point(s)
Organized from XII Corps d'Afrique Infantry

Date Disbanded
March 14, 1866

Place Disbanded
Department of the Gulf

Movement Orders and Attachments
Attached to 1st Brigade, 1st Division, Corps d'Afrique, Department of the Gulf, to February 1865. 2d Brigade, 1st Division, United States Colored Troops, Department of the Gulf, to May 1865. Northern District of Louisiana, Department of the Gulf, to March 1866.

Engagements and Campaigns
Red River Campaign, March 10–May 22, 1865. Advance from Franklin to Alexandria, March 14–26. Retreat from Alexandria to Morganza, May 13–20. Mansura, May 16. Near Moreauville, May 17. Yellow Bayou, May 18. Duty at Morganza until May 1865. Action near Morganza, November 23, 1864. Duty in Northern District of Louisiana and Department of the Gulf, to March 1866.

85th Regiment, United States Colored Infantry

Date Raised
April 4, 1864

Muster Point(s)
Organized from XIII Corps d'Afrique Infantry

Date Disbanded
May 24, 1864

Movement Orders and Attachments
Attached to a Provisional Brigade, XIII Corps, Texas, Department of the Gulf, to May 1864. Mustered out by consolidation with 77th Regiment, United States Colored Troops.

Engagements and Campaigns
Duty at Brownsville and other points in Texas until May 1864.

86th Regiment, United States Colored Infantry

Date Raised
April 4, 1864

Muster Point(s)
Organized from XIV Corps d'Afrique Infantry

Date Disbanded
April 10, 1866

Place Disbanded
Department of Florida

Movement Orders and Attachments
Attached to District of West Florida, Department of the Gulf, to October 1864. 1st Brigade, 3d Division, United States Colored Troops, Department of the Gulf, to November 1864. 1st Brigade, District of West Florida, to January 1865. 3d Brigade, District of West Florida, to January 1865. 3d Brigade, District of West Florida, to March 1865. 1st Brigade, 1st Division, United States Colored Troops, Steele's Command, to May 1865. District of West Florida, to July 1865. Department of Florida, to April 1866.

Engagements and Campaigns
Duty at Barrancas, Florida, until March 1865. March from Pensacola, Florida, to Blakely, Alabama, March 20–April 1. Siege of Fort Blakely, April 1–9.

Assault and capture of Fort Blakely, April 9. Occupation of Mobile, April 12. March to Montgomery, April 13–25. Duty there and at Mobile until May 19. Garrison at Fort Morgan, May 19–July. Duty at Pensacola and other points in Department of Florida until April 1866.

87th Regiment, United States Colored Infantry (old organization)

Date Raised
April 4, 1864

Muster Point(s)
Organized from XVI Corps d'Afrique Infantry

Date Disbanded
July 6, 1864

Movement Orders and Attachments
Attached to 2d Division, XIII Corps, to June 1864. Colored Brigade, U.S. forces, Texas, to July 1864. Consolidated with 95th Regiment, United States Colored Troops, to form new 81st Regiment, United States Colored Troops.

Engagements and Campaigns
Duty at Brazos Santiago, Point Isabel, and Brownsville, Texas, until July 1864. Consolidated with 95th United States Colored Troops, July 6, 1864, to form new 81st Regiment, United States Colored Troops. Redesignated 87th (new) Regiment, December 10, 1864.

87th Regiment, United States Colored Infantry (new organization)

Date Raised
November 26, 1864

Muster Point(s)
Organized by consolidation of 87th (old) and 96th Regiments, United States Colored Troops

Date Disbanded
August 14, 1865

Movement Orders and Attachments
Attached to U.S. forces, Texas, Department of the Gulf, to August 1865. Consolidated with 84th Regiment, United States Colored Troops, August 14, 1865.

Engagements and Campaigns
Duty at Brazos Santiago and other points in Texas until August 1865.

88th Regiment, United States Colored Infantry (old organization)

Date Raised
April 4, 1864

Muster Point(s)
Organized from XVII Corps d'Afrique Infantry

Date Disbanded
July 28, 1864

Movement Orders and Attachments
Duty at Port Hudson, Louisiana, until July 1864.

88th Regiment, United States Colored Infantry (new organization)

Date Raised
February 20, 1865

Muster Point(s)
Memphis, Tennessee

Date Disbanded
December 16, 1865

Movement Orders and Attachments
Attached to post and defenses of Memphis, District of West Tennessee, to July 1865. 2d Infantry Brigade, District of West Tennessee, to September 1865. Department of Tennessee, to December 1865. Consolidated with 3d Regiment, United States Colored Heavy Artillery.

Engagements and Campaigns
Duty at Memphis and in District of West Tennessee until December 1865.

89th Regiment, United States Colored Infantry

Date Raised
April 4, 1864

Muster Point(s)
Organized from XVIII Corps d'Afrique Infantry

Date Disbanded
July 28, 1864

Place Disbanded
Port Hudson, Louisiana

Movement Orders and Attachments
Duty at Port Hudson, until July 1864.

90th Regiment, United States Colored Infantry

Date Raised
April 4, 1864

Muster Point(s)
Organized from XIX Corps d'Afrique Infantry

Date Disbanded
July 28, 1864

Place Disbanded
Lakeport, Louisiana

Movement Orders and Attachments
Duty at Madisonville and Lakeport, Louisiana, until July 1864.

91st Regiment, United States Colored Infantry

Date Raised
April 4, 1864

Muster Point(s)
Organized from XX Corps d'Afrique Infantry

Date Disbanded
July 7, 1864

Movement Orders and Attachments
Garrison duty at Fort Pike, defenses of New Orleans, Louisiana, until July 1864. Pearl River Expedition, April 1–10 (Companies C, D, E, and F). Consolidated with 74th Regiment, United States Colored Troops, July 1864.

92d Regiment, United States Colored Infantry

Date Raised
April 4, 1864

Muster Point(s)
Organized from XXII Corps d'Afrique Infantry

Date Disbanded
December 31, 1865

Place Disbanded
Department of the Gulf

Engagements and Campaigns
Red River Campaign, March 10–May 22, 1864. Advance from Franklin to Alexandria, March 14–26. Retreat from Alexandria to Morganza, May 18–20. Mansura, May 16. Near Moreauville, May 17. Yellow Bayou, May 18. Duty at Morganza until June 1865. Operations near Morganza, September 16–25, 1864. Expedition from Morganza until June 1865. Operations near Morganza, September 16–25, 1864. Expedition from Morganza to Atchafalaya River, December 16–19, 1864. Duty in Northern District, Department of the Gulf, to December 1865.

93d Regiment, United States Colored Infantry

Date Raised
April 4, 1864

Muster Point(s)
Organized from XXVI Corps d'Afrique Infantry

Date Disbanded
June 23, 1865

Place Disbanded
Department of the Gulf

Movement Orders and Attachments
Attached to District of LaFourche, Department of the Gulf, to October 1864. 2d Brigade, 3d Division, United States Colored Troops, Department of the Gulf, to November 1864. District of LaFourche, Department of the Gulf, to June 1865.

Engagements and Campaigns
Duty at Brashear City until June 1864. At Brashear City and Berwick until June 1865. Expedition from Brashear City to Pattersonville, August 2, 1864. Expedition from Brashear City to Belle River, October 22–24, 1864 (detachment). Skirmish at Lake Fausse Point, November 18 (detachment). Skirmish at Lake Fausse Point, November 18 (detachment). Expedition from Brashear City to Lake Verret, February 10–11, 1865 (detachment). Expedition from Brashear City to Bayou Pigeon, March 20–22 (detachment). Bayou Teche, March 21 (detachment). Expedition from Brashear City to Indian Bend, March 15–27 (detachment).

Expedition from Brashear City to Oyster Bayou, March 25–28 (detachment). Expedition to Lake Verret, Grand Bayou, and the Park, April 2–10 (detachment). Operations around Brashear City, April 30–May 2.

94th Regiment, United States Colored Infantry

Date Raised
Failed to complete organization

95th Regiment, United States Colored Infantry

Date Raised
April 4, 1864

Muster Point(s)
Organized from I Corps d'Afrique Engineers

Date Disbanded
November 26, 1864

Movement Orders and Attachments
Attached to Engineers Brigade, XIII Corps, Department of the Gulf, to June 1864. Colored Brigade, U.S. forces, Texas, Department of the Gulf, to November 1864. Consolidated with 87th Regiment, United States Colored Troops.

Engagements and Campaigns
Duty at Brazos Santiago, Point Isabel, Brownsville, Arkansas Pass, and other points in Texas until November 1864.

96th Regiment, United States Colored Infantry

Date Raised
April 4, 1864

Muster Point(s)
Organized from II Corps d'Afrique Engineers

Date Disbanded
January 29, 1866

Place Disbanded
Department of the Gulf

Movement Orders and Attachments
Attached to Provisional Brigade, XIII Corps, Department of the Gulf, to June 1864. Engineer Brigade, Department of the Gulf, to October 1864. 1st Brigade, 3d Division, United States Colored Troops, Department of the Gulf, to November 1864. U.S. forces, Mobile Bay, Department of the Gulf, to December 1864. District of Southern Alabama, Department of the Gulf, to March 1865. Engineer Brigade, XIII Corps, Military Division of West Mississippi, to June 1865. Unassigned, Department of the Gulf, to January 1866.

Engagements and Campaigns
Garrison at Fort Esperanza and engineer duty on Matagorda Peninsula, Texas, until May 1864. Ordered to New Orleans, Louisiana, May 27; then to Port Hudson, Louisiana, and duty there until July 27. Moved to New Orleans, then to Mobile Bay, Alabama. Siege operations against Fort Gaines and Morgan, August 2–23. Duty at Mobile Point until November. At East Pascagoula until February 1865. Campaign against Mobile and its defenses, February–April. Siege of Spanish Fort and Fort Blakely, March 17–April 9. Duty on fortifications at Mobile and at various points in Department of the Gulf until January 1866.

97th Regiment, United States Colored Infantry

Date Raised
April 4, 1864

Muster Point(s)
Organized from III Corps d'Afrique Engineers

Date Disbanded
April 6, 1866

Place Disbanded
Department of the Gulf

Movement Orders and Attachments
Attached to Provisional Brigade, XIII Corps, Texas, Department of the Gulf, to February 1864. Engineer Brigade, Department of the Gulf, to October 1864. U.S. forces, Mobile Bay, Department of the Gulf, to November. 1st Brigade, District of West Florida, to February 1865. 3d Brigade, District of West Florida, to March 1865. Engineer Brigade, Military Division of West Mississippi, to June 1865. Unattached, Department of the Gulf, to April 1866.

Engagements and Campaigns
Red River Campaign, to May 22, 1864. Built bridge

over Red River at Grand Ecore, April 12. Constructed rifle pits and abatis around Grand Ecore, April 13–19. Repaired road from Grand Ecore to Cane River, and crossing over Cane River, April 19–20. Lower Crossing of Cane River, April 22. At Alexandria, constructing works and dam, April 25–May 13. Retreat to Morganza, May 13–22. Marksville, May 16. Operations around Yellow Bayou, May 17–20. Fatigue duty at Morganza until June 20. Ordered to New Orleans, Louisiana, June 20. Duty in District of Carrollton until August. Moved to Mobile Bay, Alabama, August 20. Duty at Mobile Point and Dauphin Island until February 1865. In District of Florida until March 1865. Campaign against Mobile and its defenses, March 17–April 12. Siege of Spanish Fort and Fort Blakely, March 26–April 9. Duty in fortifications of Mobile and at various points in Department of the Gulf until April 1866.

98th Regiment, United States Colored Infantry

Date Raised
April 4, 1864

Muster Point(s)
Organized from IV Corps d'Afrique Engineers

Date Disbanded
August 26, 1865

Movement Orders and Attachments
Attached to Engineer Brigade, Department of the Gulf, to July 1864. Defenses of New Orleans, Department of the Gulf, to October 1864. 2d Brigade, 3d Division, United States Colored Troops, Department of the Gulf, to November 1864. District of LaFourche, Department of the Gulf, to August 1865. Consolidated with 78th Regiment, United States Colored Troops.

Engagements and Campaigns
Stationed at Brashear City, Berwick City, and New Orleans until June 1864. In District of Carrollton until July 1864. At Greenville until September 1864. At Plaquemine until February 1865. At Brashear City and in District of LaFourche until August 1865.

99th Regiment, United States Colored Infantry

Date Raised
April 4, 1864

Muster Point(s)
Organized from V Corps d'Afrique Engineers

Date Disbanded
April 23, 1866

Place Disbanded
Department of Florida

Movement Orders and Attachments
Attached to Engineer Brigade, Department of the Gulf, to October 1864. 2d Brigade, 1st Division, United States Colored Troops, Department of the Gulf, to February 1865. District of Key West, Florida, to July 1865. Department of Florida, to April 1866.

Engagements and Campaigns
Red River Campaign, to May 22, 1864. Built bridges at Grand Ecore, April 12. Built fortifications at Grand Ecore, April 13–19. Repaired road and crossing over Cane River, April 19–20. Lower Crossing of Cane River, April 22. At Alexandria, constructing works and dam, April 25–May 13. Retreat to Morganza, May 18–22. Marksville, May 16. Operations around Yellow Bayou, May 17–20. Fatigue duty at Morganza until June 20. Ordered to New Orleans, June 20. Duty at New Orleans and Plaquemine, Louisiana, until December 1864. At Key West and Tortugas, Florida, and in Department of Florida until April 1866. Operations near St. Marks, Florida, February 21–March 7, 1865. Newport Bridge, March 5–6. Natural Bridge, March 6.

100th Regiment, United States Colored Infantry

Date Raised
May 3–June 1, 1864

Muster Point(s)
Kentucky

Date Disbanded
December 26, 1865

Place Disbanded
Nashville

Movement Orders and Attachments
Attached to defenses of Nashville & Northwestern Railroad, Department of the Cumberland, to December 1864. 2d Colored Brigade, District of the Etowah, Department of the Cumberland, to January 1865. Defenses of Nashville & Northwestern Railroad, Department of the Cumberland, to January 1865. Defenses of Nashville & Northwestern Railroad, Department of the Cumberland, to December 1865.

Engagements and Campaigns
Guard duty on Nashville & Northwestern Railroad in Tennessee until December 1864. Skirmish on Nashville & Northwestern Railroad, September 4. Action at Johnsonville, November 4–5. Battle of Nashville, Tennessee, December 15–16. Overton Hill, December 16. Pursuit of Gen. John Bell Hood to Tennessee River, December 17–28. Again assigned to guard duty on Nashville & Northwestern Railroad, January 16, 1865, and continued until December 1865.

101st Regiment, United States Colored Infantry

Date Raised
September 16, 1864

Muster Point(s)
Tennessee

Date Disbanded
January 21, 1866

Place Disbanded
Larkinsville, Alabama

Movement Orders and Attachments
Attached to defenses of Louisville & Nashville Railroad, Department of the Cumberland, to March 1865. Department of the Tennessee, to January 1866.

Engagements and Campaigns
Duty at Nashville, Tennessee, until October 1864; then guard of Louisville & Nashville Railroad, and duty in Tennessee and Alabama until mustered out. Affairs at Scottsboro and Larkinsville, January 8, 1865.

102d Regiment, United States Colored Infantry

Date Raised
May 23, 1864

Muster Point(s)
Organized from 1st Michigan Colored Infantry

Date Disbanded
September 30, 1865

Place Disbanded
Charleston

Movement Orders and Attachments
Attached to District of Hilton Head, South Carolina, Department of the South, and District of Beaufort, South Carolina, Department of the South, to August 1864. District of Florida, Department of the South, to October 1864. 2d Separate Brigade, Department of the South, to November 1864. 2d Brigade, Coast Division, Department of the South, to February 1865. 2d Separate Brigade, Department of the South, to March 1865. 1st Separate Brigade and Department of the South, to September 1865.

Engagements and Campaigns
Garrison at Port Royal, South Carolina, until June 15. Moved to Beaufort, South Carolina, and garrison duty there until August 1. Moved to Jacksonville, Florida, August 1–3. Picket duty at Baldwin until August 15. Attack on Baldwin, August 11–12. Raid on Florida Central Railroad, August 15–19. At Magnolia until August 29. Moved to Beaufort, August 29–31, and duty there until January 1865. Engaged in outpost and picket duty at Port Royal, Lady's Island, and Coosa Island. (A detachment at Honey Hill, November 30, 1864. Demonstration on Charleston & Savannah Railroad, December 6–9. Devaux's Neck, Tillifinny River, December 6 and 9.) Detachment at Beaufort; rejoined other detachment at Devaux's Neck, South Carolina, January 24, 1865. Moved to Pocotaligo, February 28. Advance on Charleston, February 7–23. Skirmish at Cuckwold Creek, February 8 (Companies B, E, and I). Duty at Charleston Neck

until March 9. Moved to Savannah, Georgia, March 9–16. Moved to Georgetown, March 28–April 1. (Right wing of regiment, under Chapman, moved to Charleston, April 7–9, then march to join Potter at Nelson's Ferry, April 11–18.) Potter's Expedition from Georgetown to Camden, April 5–29. Statesburg, April 15. Occupation of Camden, April 17. Boykin's Mills, April 18. Bradford Springs, April 18 (right wing). Dingle's Mills, April 19. Singleton's Plantation, April 19. Beech Creek, near Statesburg, April 19. Moved to Charleston, April 29, then to Summerville, May 7–8, to Branchville, May 18, to Orangeburg, May 25, and provost duty there until July 28. March to Winsboro, July 28–August 3, and duty there until September.

103d Regiment, United States Colored Infantry

Date Raised
March 10, 1865

Muster Point(s)
Hilton Head, South Carolina

Date Disbanded
April 15–20, 1866

Place Disbanded
South Carolina

Movement Orders and Attachments
Attached to District of Savannah, Georgia, Department of the South, to June 1865. Department of the South, to April 1866.

Engagements and Campaigns
Garrison and guard duty at Savannah and various points in Georgia and South Carolina for entire term.

104th Regiment, United States Colored Infantry

Date Raised
April 28–June 25, 1865

Muster Point(s)
Beaufort, South Carolina

Date Disbanded
February 5, 1866

Movement Orders and Attachments
Attached to Department of the South. Garrison and guard duty at various points in South Carolina until February 1866.

105th Regiment, United States Colored Infantry

Date Raised
Failed to complete organization

106th Regiment, United States Colored Infantry

Date Raised
May 16, 1864

Muster Point(s)
Organized from 4th Alabama Colored Infantry

Date Disbanded
November 7, 1865

Movement Orders and Attachments
Attached to District of North Alabama, Department of the Cumberland, to February 1865. Defenses of Nashville & Northwestern Railroad, Department of the Cumberland, to November 1865. Consolidated with 40th Regiment, United States Colored Troops.

Engagements and Campaigns
Garrison at Pulaski and railroad guard duty for entire term. Gen. Nathan Bedford Forrest's attack on Athens, Alabama, September 23–24, 1864.

107th Regiment, United States Colored Infantry

Date Raised
May 3–September 15, 1864

Muster Point(s)
Louisville, Kentucky

Date Disbanded
November 22, 1866

Place Disbanded
Department of the South

Movement Orders and Attachments
Attached to Military District of Kentucky, Department of the Ohio, to October 1864. Provisional Brigade, 3d Division, XVIII Corps, Army of the James, to December 1864. 3d Brigade, 1st Division, XXV Corps, to December 1864. 3d Brigade, 3d

Division, XXV Corps, to January 1865. 1st Brigade, 3d Division, XXV Corps, to March 1865. 1st Brigade, 3d Division, X Corps, Department of North Carolina, to August 1865. Department of North Carolina and Department of the South, to November 1866.

Engagements and Campaigns
Duty in Kentucky until October 1864. Ordered to Baltimore, Maryland, then to City Point, Virginia, October 26. Siege of Petersburg, November 3–December 7. First expedition to Fort Fisher, North Carolina, December 7–27. Second expedition to Fort Fisher, January 7–15, 1865. Bombardment of Fort Fisher, January 13–15. Assault and capture of Fort Fisher, January 15. Sugar Loaf Hill, January 19. Federal Point, February 11. Fort Anderson, February 18–20. Capture of Wilmington, February 22. Northeast Ferry, February 22. Campaign of the Carolinas, March 1–April 26. March on Kinston and Goldsboro, March 6–21. Action at Cox's Bridge, March 23–24. Advance on Raleigh, April 9–14. Occupation of Raleigh, April 14. Bennett's House, April 26. Surrender of Gen. Joseph E. Johnston and his army. Duty at various points in North Carolina and in Department of the South until November 1866.

108th Regiment, United States Colored Infantry

Date Raised
June 20, 1864

Muster Point(s)
Louisville, Kentucky

Date Disbanded
March 21, 1866

Place Disbanded
Department of Mississippi

Movement Orders and Attachments
Attached to 1st Brigade, 2d Division, District of Kentucky, 5th Division, XXIII Corps, Department of the Ohio, to January 1865. Military District of Kentucky, to May 1865. Department of Mississippi and Department of the Gulf, to March 1866.

Engagements and Campaigns
Garrison and guard duty at various points in Kentucky until January 1865. Action at Owensboro, Kentucky, October 22, 1864. Guard duty at Rock Island, Illinois, January–May 1865. Duty in Department of Mississippi until March 1866.

109th Regiment, United States Colored Infantry

Date Raised
July 5, 1864

Muster Point(s)
Louisville, Kentucky

Date Disbanded
March 21, 1866

Place Disbanded
Texas

Movement Orders and Attachments
Attached to 3d Brigade, 1st Division, District of Kentucky, 5th Division, XXIII Corps, Department of the Ohio, to October 1864. Martindale's Provisional Brigade, XVIII Corps, Army of the James, to December 1864. 1st Brigade, 2d Division, XXV Corps and Department of Texas, to March 1866.

Engagements and Campaigns
Duty at Louisville and Louisa, Kentucky, until October 1864. Ordered to join Army of the Potomac before Petersburg and Richmond, Virginia. Duty at Deep Bottom and in trenches before Richmond, north of James River, until March 1865. Actions at Fort Harrison, December 10, 1864, and January 23, 1865. Moved to Hatcher's Run, March 27–28. Appomattox Campaign, March 28–April 9. Boydton Road, Hatcher's Run, March 29–31. Fall of Petersburg, April 2. Pursuit of Gen. Robert E. Lee, April 3–9. Appomattox Court House, April 9. Surrender of Lee and his army. Duty at Petersburg and City Point until May. Embarked for Texas, May 25, arriving at Indianola, Texas, June 25. Duty there and on Rio Grande, Texas, until March 1866.

110th Regiment, United States Colored Infantry

Date Raised
June 25, 1864

Muster Point(s)
Organized from 2d Alabama Colored Infantry

Date Disbanded
February 6, 1866

Place Disbanded
Department of Tennessee

Movement Orders and Attachments
Attached to District of North Alabama, Department of the Cumberland, to February 1865. Defenses of Nashville & Northwestern Railroad, to March 1865. 3d Subdistrict, District of Middle Tennessee, to September 1865. Department of the Tennessee, to February 1866.

Engagements and Campaigns
Garrison duty at Pulaski, Tennessee, and guard duty on railroad in North Alabama until February 1865. Gen. Nathan Bedford Forrest's attack on Athens, Alabama, September 23–24, 1864. Larkinsville, Alabama, January 8, 1865 (detachment of Company E). Guard Nashville & Northwestern Railroad until June 1865. At Gallatin, Tennessee, and at various points in Department of the Tennessee, until February 1866.

111th Regiment, United States Colored Infantry

Date Raised
June 25, 1864

Muster Point(s)
Organized from 3d Alabama Colored Infantry

Date Disbanded
April 30, 1866

Place Disbanded
Middle Tennessee

Movement Orders and Attachments
Attached to garrison at Pulaski, Tennessee, District of North Alabama, Department of the Cumberland, to February 1865. Defenses of Nashville & Northwestern Railroad, Department of the Cumberland, to March 1865. 3d Subdistrict, District of Middle Tennessee, to July 1865. Department of the Tennessee, to April 1866.

Engagements and Campaigns
Duty at Pulaski and Athens, Alabama, District of North Alabama, until September 1864. Action at Athens with Gen. Nathan Bedford Forrest, September 23–24 (most of regiment captured). Sulphur Branch Trestle, September 25 (detachment). Duty at Pulaski until January 1865. Guard duty on Nashville & Northwestern Railroad and in Middle Tennessee until April 1866.

112th Regiment, United States Colored Infantry

Date Raised
April 23–November 8, 1864

Muster Point(s)
Little Rock, Arkansas, from 5th Arkansas Colored Infantry

Date Disbanded
April 1, 1865

Movement Orders and Attachments
Attached to 1st Division, VII Corps, Department of Arkansas, June 1864–January 1865. Colored Brigade, VII Corps, to February 1865. 2d Brigade, 1st Division, VII Corps, to April 1865. Transferred to 113th Regiment, United States Colored Troops (new).

Engagements and Campaigns
Post and garrison duty at Little Rock for entire term.

113th Regiment, United States Colored Infantry (new organization)

Date Raised
April 1, 1864

Muster Point(s)
Organized by consolidation of 11th Regiment, United States Colored Troops (old), 112th Regiment, United States Colored Troops, and 113th Regiment, United States Colored Troops (old).

Date Disbanded
April 9, 1866

Place Disbanded
Department of Arkansas

Movement Orders and Attachments
Attached to 2d Brigade, 1st Division, VII Corps, Department of Arkansas, to August 1865. Department of Arkansas, to April 1866.

Engagements and Campaigns
Duty in Department of Arkansas.

113th Regiment, United States Colored Infantry (old organization)

Date Raised
June 25, 1864

Muster Point(s)
Organized from 6th Arkansas Colored Infantry

Date Disbanded
April 1, 1865

Movement Orders and Attachments
Attached to 1st Division, VII Corps, Department of Arkansas, to January 1865. Colored Brigade, VII Corps, to February 1865. 2d Brigade, 1st Division, VII Corps, to April 1865. Consolidated with 11th Regiment, United States Colored Troops (old), and 112th Regiment, United States Colored Troops, to form 113th Regiment, United States Colored Troops (new), April 1865.

Engagements and Campaigns
Post and garrison duty at Little Rock, Arkansas, for entire term.

114th Regiment, United States Colored Infantry

Date Raised
July 4, 1864

Muster Point(s)
Camp Nelson, Kentucky

Date Disbanded
April 2, 1867

Place Disbanded
Texas

Movement Orders and Attachments
Attached to Military District of Kentucky, Department of the Ohio, to January 1865. 3d Brigade, 1st Division, XXV Corps, Department of Virginia, to April 1865. 2d Brigade, 1st Division, XXV Corps and Department of Texas, to April 1867.

Engagements and Campaigns
Duty at Camp Nelson and Louisa, Kentucky, until January 1865. Ordered to Department of Virginia, January 3, 1865. Siege operations against Petersburg and Richmond on Bermuda Hundred front until March 1865. Appomattox Campaign, March 28–April 9. Hatcher's Run, March 29–31. Fall of Petersburg, April 2. Pursuit of Gen. Robert E. Lee, April 3–9. Appomattox Court House, April 9. Surrender of Lee and his army. Duty at Petersburg and City Point until June. Moved to Texas, June–July. Duty at Brownsville and other points on Rio Grande, Texas, until April 1867.

115th Regiment, United States Colored Infantry

Date Raised
July 15–October 21, 1864

Muster Point(s)
Bowling Green, Kentucky

Date Disbanded
February 10, 1866

Place Disbanded
Texas

Movement Orders and Attachments
Attached to 2d Brigade, 2d Division, District of Kentucky, 5th Division, XXIII Corps, Department of the Ohio, to January 1865. 1st Brigade, 2d Division, XXV Corps, Department of Virginia, to March 1865. 2d Brigade, 1st Division, XXV Corps and Department of Texas, to February 1866.

Engagements and Campaigns
Garrison duty at Lexington, Kentucky, until December 1864. Ordered to Virginia. Siege operations against Petersburg and Richmond, January–April 1865. Occupation of Richmond, April 3. Duty in Department of Virginia until May. Sailed for Texas, May 20. Duty in District of the Rio Grande until February 1866.

116th Regiment, United States Colored Infantry

Date Raised
June 6–July 12, 1864

Muster Point(s)
Camp Nelson, Kentucky

Date Disbanded
January 17, 1867

Place Disbanded
Louisville, Kentucky

Movement Orders and Attachments
Attached to Military District of Kentucky, Department of the Ohio, to September 1864. Unattached, X Corps, Army of the James, to November 1864. 1st Brigade, 3d Division, X Corps, to December 1864. 1st Brigade, 2d Division, XXV Corps, to April 1865. 3d Brigade, 2d Division, XXV Corps and Department of Texas, to September 1866. Department of the Gulf, to January 1867.

Engagements and Campaigns
Duty at Camp Nelson until September 1864. Defense of Camp Nelson and Hickman's Bridge against Gen. Nathan Bedford Forrest's attack. Ordered to join Army of the James in Virginia, reporting to Gen. Benjamin F. Butler, September 27. Duty at City Point, Virginia, until October. Moved to Deep Bottom, October 23. Siege operations against Petersburg and Richmond, October 23, 1864–April 2, 1865. Operations on north side of James River before Richmond, October 27–28, 1864. Fatigue duty at Deep Bottom, Dutch Gap, and in trenches before Richmond until March 1865. Moved to Hatcher's Run, March 27–28. Appomattox Campaign, March 28–April 9. Boydton Road, Hatcher's Run, March 29–31. Fall of Petersburg, April 2. Pursuit of Gen. Robert E. Lee, April 3–9. Appomattox Court House, April 9. Surrender of Lee and his army. Duty at Petersburg until May 25. Embarked at City Point for Texas, May 25, arriving at Brazos Santiago, June 22. March to White's Ranch, June 24. Duty at Rome, Texas, until February 1866. In Subdistrict, Lower Rio Grande, until September 1866, and at New Orleans, Louisiana, until January 1867.

117th Regiment, United States Colored Infantry

Date Raised
July 18–September 27, 1864

Muster Point(s)
Covington, Kentucky

Date Disbanded
August 10, 1867

Place Disbanded
Rio Grande, Texas

Movement Orders and Attachments
Attached to Military District of Kentucky, Department of the Ohio, to October 1864. Provisional Brigade, XVIII Corps, Army of the James, to December 1864. 1st Brigade, 1st Division, XXV Corps and Department of Texas, to August 1867.

Engagements and Campaigns
Duty at Camp Nelson, Kentucky, until October 1864. Ordered to Baltimore, Maryland, then to City Point, Virginia, October 21. Siege operations against Petersburg and Richmond until March 1865. Appomattox Campaign, March 28–April 9. Hatcher's Run, March 29–31. Fall of Petersburg, April 2. Pursuit of Gen. Robert E. Lee, April 3–9. Appomattox Court House, April 9. Surrender of Lee and his army. Duty at Petersburg and City Point until June. Moved to Brazos Santiago, Texas, June–July. Duty at Brownsville and on Rio Grande until August 1867.

118th Regiment, United States Colored Infantry

Date Raised
October 19, 1864

Muster Point(s)
Baltimore, Maryland

Date Disbanded
February 6, 1866

Place Disbanded
Texas

Movement Orders and Attachments
Moved to City Point, Virginia, October 26, 1864. Attached to Provisional Brigade, 3d Division, XVIII Corps, Army of the James, to December 1864. 1st Brigade, 1st Division, XXV Corps and Department of Texas, to February 1866.

Engagements and Campaigns
Siege operations against Petersburg and Richmond, November 1864–April 1865. Occupation of Richmond, April 3, 1865. Duty in Department of Virginia until June. Moved to Brazos Santiago, Texas, June–July. Duty at Brownsville and various points on Rio Grande until February 1866.

119th Regiment, United States Colored Infantry

Date Raised
January 18–May 16, 1865

Muster Point(s)
Camp Nelson, Kentucky

Date Disbanded
April 27, 1866

Place Disbanded
Department of Kentucky

Movement Orders and Attachments
Attached to Department of Kentucky and duty at various points in Kentucky until April 1866.

120th Regiment, United States Colored Infantry

Date Raised
November 1864

Muster Point(s)
Henderson, Kentucky

Date Disbanded
June 21, 1865

Place Disbanded
Department of Kentucky

Movement Orders and Attachments
Garrison and guard duty at various points in Military District and Department of Kentucky until June 1865.

121st Regiment, United States Colored Infantry

Date Raised
October 8, 1864

Muster Point(s)
Maysville, Kentucky

Date Disbanded
June 30, 1865

Place Disbanded
Department of Kentucky

Movement Orders and Attachments
Garrison and guard duty at various points in Military District and Department of Kentucky until June 1865.

122d Regiment, United States Colored Infantry

Date Raised
December 31, 1864

Muster Point(s)
Louisville, Kentucky

Date Disbanded
February 8, 1866

Place Disbanded
Texas

Movement Orders and Attachments
Ordered to Virginia, January 12, 1865. Attached to XXV Corps, Army of the James. Unassigned, to April 1865. Department of Texas, to February 1866.

Engagements and Campaigns
Duty in defenses of Portsmouth, Virginia, until February 1865. Siege operations against Petersburg and Richmond, Virginia, February–April 1865. Fall of Petersburg and Richmond, April 2–3. Duty in Department of Virginia until June 1865. Moved to Brazos Santiago, Texas, June–July. Duty at Brownsville and various points on Rio Grande until February 1866.

123d Regiment, United States Colored Infantry

Date Raised
December 2, 1864

Muster Point(s)
Louisville, Kentucky

Date Disbanded
October 24, 1865

Place Disbanded
Department of Kentucky

Movement Orders and Attachments
Duty at Louisville and other points in Department of Kentucky until October 1865.

124th Regiment, United States Colored Infantry

Date Raised
January 1–April 27, 1865

Muster Point(s)
Camp Nelson, Kentucky

Date Disbanded
December 20, 1867

Place Disbanded
Department of Kentucky

Movement Orders and Attachments
Garrison and guard duty at various points in Department of Kentucky until December 1867.

125th Regiment, United States Colored Infantry

Date Raised
February 12–June 2, 1865

Muster Point(s)
Louisville, Kentucky

Date Disbanded
December 20, 1867

Place Disbanded
Department of Kentucky

Movement Orders and Attachments
Garrison and guard duty at Louisville and other points in Department of Kentucky until December 1867.

127th Regiment, United States Colored Infantry

Date Raised
August 23–September 10, 1864

Muster Point(s)
Camp William Penn, Philadelphia, Pennsylvania

Date Disbanded
October 20, 1865

Place Disbanded
Texas

Movement Orders and Attachments
Ordered to City Point, Virginia, September 1864. Attached to 1st Brigade, 3d Division, X Corps, Army of the James, to November 1864. 2d Brigade, 3d Division, X Corps, to December 1864. 2d Brigade, 2d Division, XXV Corps and Department of Texas, to October 1865.

Engagements and Campaigns
Siege operations against Petersburg and Richmond, Virginia, September 1864–April 1865. Chaffin's Farm, New Market Heights, September 29–30. Fort Harrison, September 29. Darbytown Road, October 13. Battle of Fair Oaks, October 27–28. Duty in trenches north of James River before Richmond until March 1865. Moved to Hatcher's Run, March 27–28. Appomattox Campaign, March 28–April 9. Hatcher's Run, March 29–31. Fall of Petersburg, April 2. Pursuit of Gen. Robert E. Lee, April 3–9. Appomattox Court House, April 9. Surrender of Lee and his army. Duty at Petersburg and City Point until June. Moved to Brazos Santiago, Texas, June–July. Duty at various points on Rio Grande until October.

128th Regiment, United States Colored Infantry

Date Raised
April 1865

Muster Point(s)
Hilton Head, South Carolina

Date Disbanded
October 20, 1865

Place Disbanded
Department of the South

Movement Orders and Attachments
Duty in Department of the South until October 1865.

135th Regiment, United States Colored Infantry

Date Raised
March 28, 1865

Muster Point(s)
Goldsboro, North Carolina

Date Disbanded
October 23, 1865

Place Disbanded
Department of North Carolina

Movement Orders and Attachments
Duty in Department of North Carolina until October 1865.

136th Regiment, United States Colored Infantry

Date Raised
July 15, 1865

Muster Point(s)
Atlanta, Georgia

Date Disbanded
January 4, 1866

Place Disbanded
Department of Georgia

Movement Orders and Attachments
Duty in Department of Georgia.

137th Regiment, United States Colored Infantry

Date Raised
April 8, 1865

Muster Point(s)
Macon, Georgia

Date Disbanded
January 15, 1866

Place Disbanded
Department of Georgia

Movement Orders and Attachments
Duty in Department of Georgia until January 1866.

138th Regiment, United States Colored Infantry

Date Raised
July 15, 1865

Muster Point(s)
Atlanta, Georgia

Date Disbanded
January 6, 1866

Place Disbanded
Department of Georgia

Movement Orders and Attachments
Duty in Department of Georgia.

References and Further Reading

Beecham, Robert K. *As If It Were Glory: Robert Beecham's Civil War from the Iron Brigade to the Black Regiments,* ed. Michael E. Stevens. Madison, WI: Madison House, 1998.

Blatt, Martin Henry, Thomas J. Brown, and Donald Yacovone, eds. *Hope and Glory: Essays on the Legacy of the 54th Massachusetts Regiment.* Amherst: University of Massachusetts Press, 2000.

Callum, Agnes Kane. *Colored Volunteers of Maryland: Civil War—7th Regiment United States Colored Troops, 1863–1866.* Baltimore: Mullac Publishers, 1990.

Cornish, Dudley Taylor. *The Sable Arm: Black Troops in the Union Army, 1861–1865.* Lawrence: University Press of Kansas, 1987.

Current, Richard Nelson. *Lincoln's Loyalists: Union Soldiers from the Confederacy.* New York: Oxford University Press, 1992.

Denney, Robert E. *The Civil War Years: A Day-by-Day Chronicle.* New York: Gramercy Books, 1992.

Dyer, Frederick H. *A Compendium of the War of the Rebellion.* 3 Vols. New York: Thomas Yoseloff, 1959.

Gladstone, William A. *United States Colored Troops, 1863–1867.* Gettysburg, PA: Thomas Publications, 1990.

Glatthaar, Joseph T. *Forged in Battle: The Civil War Alliance of Black Soldiers and White Officers.* Baton Rouge: Louisiana State University Press, 2000.

Hansen, Joyce. *Between Two Fires: Black Soldiers in the Civil War.* New York: Franklin Watts, 1993.

Higginson, Thomas Wentworth. *Army Life in a Black Regiment.* Williamstown, MA: Corner House Publishers, 1984.

Hollandsworth, James G. *The Louisiana Native Guards: The Black Military Experience during the Civil War.* Baton Rouge: Louisiana State University Press, 1995.

McPherson, James M. *Marching toward Freedom: Blacks in the Civil War, 1861–1865.* New York: Knopf, 1968.

———. *The Negro's Civil War: How American Blacks Felt and Acted during the War for the Union.* New York: Pantheon, 1965.

Miller, Edward A., Jr. *The Black Civil War Soldiers of Illinois: The Story of the Twenty-Ninth U.S. Colored Infantry.* Columbia: University of South Carolina Press, 1998.

Nankivell, John. *Buffalo Soldier Regiment: History of the Twenty-Fifth United States Infantry, 1869–1926.* Introduction by Quintard Taylor. Lincoln: University of Nebraska Press, 2001.

Paradis, James M. *Strike the Blow for Freedom: The*

6th United States Colored Infantry in the Civil War. Shippensburg, PA: White Mane, 1998.

Quarles, Benjamin. *The Negro in the Civil War.* New York: Da Capo Press, 1953.

Redkey, Edwin S., ed. *A Grand Army of Black Men: Letters from African American Soldiers in the Union Army, 1861–1865.* New York: Cambridge University Press, 1992.

Washington, Versalle F. *Eagles on Their Buttons: A Black Infantry Regiment in the Civil War.* Columbia: University of Missouri Press, 1999.

Wilson, Joseph T. *The Black Phalanx: A History of the Negro Soldiers of the United States in the Wars of 1775–1812, 1861–1865.* 1890. Reprint, Salem, NH: Ayer Company Publishers, 1992.

UNITED STATES COLORED TROOPS, BATTLES OF

Major battles and engagements are listed from 1861 to 1865. Dates are followed by battle location, units engaged/state of origin, and notes on the battle. It should be noted that many of the units were renamed during the war from their original state designations to USCT designations after the establishment of the Bureau of Colored Troops on May 22, 1863 (General Order No. 143). In many cases the USCT, USCC, or other African American units were unattached; in other words, they were not brigaded or placed into a division.

Abbreviations

USCC—United States Colored Cavalry Regiment
USCHA—United States Colored Heavy Artillery Regiment
USCLA—United States Colored Light Artillery Regiment
USCT—United States Colored Troops (Infantry Regiment)

October 27–28, 1862
Island Mound, Missouri
79th USCT (new), Kansas
Formerly the 1st Kansas Colored Volunteers. This was the first engagement in which African American soldiers engaged and defeated Confederate forces in combat and in which an African American officer (Lt. Patrick Minor) commanded African American soldiers (Company D) in combat.

January 26, 1863
Township, Florida
33d USCT, South Carolina
Formerly the 1st South Carolina Colored Infantry. The Battle of Township is rated as a skirmish.

March 29, 1863
Jacksonville, Florida
33d USCT, South Carolina
Operations near Jacksonville, March 23–31.

April 9, 1863
East Pascagoula, Missouri
74th USCT, Louisiana
Formerly the 2d Louisiana Native Guards and II Corps d'Afrique Infantry.

May 1–July 4, 1863
Vicksburg, Mississippi (including Port Gibson, Raymond, Jackson, Champion's Hill/Baker's Creek, Big Black Bridge)
African Brigade (Col. Isaac Fitzgerald Shepard)
At Millikens Bend—Col. Hiram Schofield: 8th Louisiana Colored Infantry Regiment (Col. Hiram Schofield); 9th Louisiana Colored Infantry Regiment (Col. Herman Leib, Maj. Erastus N. Owen and Lt. Col. C. J. Paine); 11th Louisiana Colored Infantry Regiment (Col. Edwin W. Chamberlain and Lt. Col. Cyrus Sears); 13th Louisiana Colored Infantry Regiment (Lt. H. Knoll); 1st Mississippi Colored Infantry Regiment (Lt. Col. A. W. Weber); 3d Mississippi Colored Infantry Regiment (Col. Richard H. Ballinger).

At Goodrich's Landing—Col. William F. Wood: 1st Arkansas Colored Infantry Regiment (Lt. Col. J. W. Campbell); 10th Louisiana Colored Infantry Regiment (Lt. Col. F. M. Carandall).

May 18, 1863
Sherwood, Missouri
79th USCT (new), Kansas
Formerly the 1st Kansas Colored Infantry. Forty-seven soldiers of the 79th USCT are buried at Fort Scott National Cemetery.

May 22–July 8, 1863
Port Hudson, Louisiana
75th USCT, Louisiana; 78th USCT, Louisiana; 79th USCT (old), Louisiana; 80th USCT, Louisiana; 81st USCT, Louisiana; 82d USCT, Louisiana; 95th USCT, Louisiana
Formerly 3d Louisiana Native Guards and III Corps d'Afrique Infantry (75th USCT), VI Corps d'Afrique Infantry (78th USCT), VII Corps d'Afrique Infantry (79th USCT), VIII Corps d'Afrique Infantry (80th USCT), IX Corps d'Afrique Infantry (81st USCT), X Corps d'Afrique Infantry (82d USCT), I Corps d'Afrique Engineers (95th USCT).

Gen. Nathaniel P. Banks laid siege to Port Hudson, and gathered there all the available forces in his department. Among these were the 1st and 3d Infantry Regiments (Louisiana Native Guards) of the "Black Phalanx." On May 23, Union forces, having completely invested the enemy's works, made a general assault along the whole line. The attack failed.

May 27, 1863
Lake Providence, Louisiana
47th USCT, Louisiana
Formerly the 8th Louisiana Infantry (African Descent). Part of Gen. Ulysses S. Grant's operations against Vicksburg (1863). Regimental casualties were one killed and one wounded.

June 5–7, 1863
Milliken's Bend, Louisiana
5th USCHA, Mississippi; 49th USCT, Louisiana; 51st USCT, Massachusetts
Formerly the 1st Mississippi Heavy Artillery (African Descent) (5th USCHA), 11th Louisiana Infantry (African Descent) (49th USCT), 1st Mississippi Infantry (African Descent) (51st USCT). A bitter engagement as Union troops (commanded by Col. Hermann Leib) held off a determined Confederate assault. Union casualties: 154 killed, 223 wounded, 115 missing. Confederate casualties: 125 killed, 400 wounded, 200 missing.

June 29, 1863
Mound Plantation, Louisiana
49th USCT, Louisiana; 51st USCT, Massachusetts
Part of Gen. Ulysses S. Grant's operations against Vicksburg (1863).

July 1–2, 1863
Cabin Creek, Cherokee Nation (Oklahoma)
79th USCT (new), Kansas
After a two-hour engagement, the Confederates were dislodged and driven from their position in great disorder, with a loss of 100 killed and wounded and 8 prisoners. Union loses were 8 killed and 25 wounded, including Capt. Ethan Earl of the 79th USCT, who was wounded at the head of his company.

July 10, 1863
Milltown Bluff, South Carolina
33d USCT, South Carolina
Expedition to James Island, South Carolina, June 30–July 10.

July 16, 1863
Sol Legare Island, South Carolina
54th Massachusetts Volunteers, Massachusetts
Three companies engaged.

July 17, 1863
Honey Springs, Indian Territory (Oklahoma)
79th USCT (new), Kansas
The Union troops fooled the Confederates into believing they were in full retreat. The Texans fell for the trap and ran directly into the heavy musket fire of the 1st Kansas Colored Infantry (1st Division commanded by Brig. Gen. James G. Blunt; 1st Brigade under Col. William R. Judson). Seeing that the battle was nearing an end, Confederate general Douglas H. Cooper ordered a controlled retreat south to the Confederate depot. The Union troops followed the Confederates for over a mile, but were unable to overwhelm them. The exhausted Northern soldiers ended the attack, and the Confederate army retreated from the field, defeated but intact. Union casualties: 17 killed, 60 wounded. Confederate casualties: 150 killed, 400 wounded.

July 18, 1863
Fort Wagner, South Carolina
54th Massachusetts Volunteers, Massachusetts

July 10–September 6: Siege of Fort Wagner, Morris Island, South Carolina. Union casualties: 1,757 killed, wounded, and missing. Confederate casualties: 561 killed, wounded, and missing.

4th Brigade (Col. James Montgomery), 54th Massachusetts Infantry Regiment (Col. M. S. Littlefield), 2d South Carolina (U.S.) Infantry Regiment (Lt. Col. W. W. Marple), 3d USCT (Col. B. C. Tilghman).

July 27, 1863
Lawrence, Kansas
79th USCT (new), Kansas

August 3, 1863
Jackson, Louisiana
75th USCT, Louisiana; 78th USCT, Louisiana
Union casualties: 2 killed, 2 wounded, 27 missing. The 73d USCT are also listed in some sources.

August 10, 1863
Bayou Tensas, Louisiana
48th USCT, Louisiana
Formerly the 10th Louisiana Infantry (African Descent).

August 26, 1863
Fort Wagner, South Carolina
3d USCT, Pennsylvania
Other troops deployed at north end of Folly Island under Brig. Gen. Israel Vodges: African Brigade (Brig. Gen. Edward A. Wild), 55th Massachusetts Infantry Regiment (Col. Norwood P. Hallowell), 1st North Carolina (U.S.) Infantry Regiment (Col. James C. Beecher), one company, 2d North Carolina (U.S.) Infantry (Col. Alonzo G. Draper), one company, 3d North Carolina (U.S.) Infantry (Capt. John Wilder).

August 27, 1863
Vicksburg, Mississippi
5th USCHA, Mississippi
Actions during garrison duties.

September 6, 1863
Fort Wagner, South Carolina
54th Massachusetts Volunteers, Massachusetts

October 6, 1863
Baxter Springs, Kansas
83d USCT (new), Kansas
William Quantrill's attack on the escort of Maj. Gen. James G. Blunt at Baxter Springs, Arkansas, robbing and murdering the prisoners. Union casualties: fifty-four killed, eighteen wounded, five missing.

November 9, 1863
Bayou Tunica, Louisiana
73d USCT, Louisiana
Formerly the 1st Louisiana Native Guards and I Corps d'Afrique Infantry. Battle considered a skirmish.

November 11, 1863
Natchez, Mississippi
58th USCT, Mississippi
Formerly the 6th Mississippi Infantry (African Descent). Union casualties: four killed, six wounded. Confederate casualties: four killed, eight wounded.

November 17, 1863
Bayou St Louis, Mississippi
91st USCT, Louisiana
Formerly XX Corps d'Afrique Infantry.

November 24, 1863
Hall Island (Cunningham's Bluff), South Carolina
33d USCT, South Carolina
Expedition to Pocotaligo, South Carolina, November 23–25 (Companies E and K). Skirmish near Cunningham's Bluff, November 24.

November 28, 1863
Plymouth, North Carolina
10th USCT, Virginia

December 4, 1863
Moscow Station, Tennessee
61st USCT, Tennessee
Formerly the 2d Tennessee Infantry (African Descent). Ripley and Moscow Station, Mississippi, and Salisbury, Tennessee. Union casualties: 175 killed and wounded. Confederate casualties: 15 killed, 40 wounded.

December 13, 1863
Bayou Boeuf, Arkansas
3d USCT, Mississippi
1st Mississippi Cavalry (African Descent), Mississippi.

"The conduct of the First Mississippi Cavalry (African Descent) could not have been excelled by veterans, wounded men refusing to go to the rear. It was the first fight for most of them, but, in the language of Major Cook, their commanding officer, 'I could have held them till the last man was shot.'" E. D. Osband, colonel, 1st Mississippi Cavalry (African Descent), Commanding Post.

December 18, 1863
Sandy Swamp, North Carolina
5th USCT, Ohio
Formerly the127th Ohio Volunteer Infantry. The unit's first engagement, it was part of Wild's Expedition to South Mills and Camden Court House, North Carolina.

December 18, 1863
Indiantown, North Carolina
36th USCT, North Carolina
Formerly the 2d North Carolina Colored Infantry.

January 20, 1864
Island No. 76, Mississippi
Battery E, 2d USCLA, Louisiana
Union casualties: three missing.

February 3, 1864
Haynes Bluff, Mississippi
53d USCT, Mississippi
Formerly the 3d Mississippi Infantry (African Descent).

February 3, 1864
Liverpool Heights, Mississippi
47th USCT, Louisiana
Expedition up Yazoo River, February 1–March 8, 1864.

February 4, 1864
Columbia, Louisiana
66th USCT, Mississippi
Formerly the 4th Mississippi Infantry (African Descent). While on post and garrison duty at Goodrich's Landing and Lake Providence, Louisiana.

February 7, 1864
Vidalia, Louisiana
64th USCT, Louisiana; 6th USCHA, Mississippi (formerly the 2d Mississippi Heavy Artillery [African Descent])
While on post and garrison duty at Davis' Bend and Natchez, Mississippi.

February 13, 1864
Vicksburg, Mississippi
52d USCT, Mississippi
Formerly the 2d Mississippi Infantry (African Descent). While on post and garrison duty.

February 14, 1864
Ross' Landing, Arkansas
51st USCT, Mississippi
Union casualties: thirteen killed, seven wounded.

February 14–15, 1864
Waterproof, Louisiana
49th USCT, Louisiana
Formerly the 11th Louisiana Infantry (African Descent). Union casualties: eight killed, fourteen wounded. Confederate casualties: fifteen killed.

February 17, 1864
Horse-Head Creek, Arkansas
79th USCT (new), Kansas

February 20, 1864
Olustee, Florida
8th USCT, Pennsylvania; 35th USCT, North Carolina
54th Massachusetts Volunteers, Massachusetts
Olustee or Silver Lake, Florida. The 8th USCT is listed as part of Hawley's Brigade (Col. Joseph R. Hawley). Union casualties: 193 killed, 1,175 wounded, 460 missing. Confederate casualties: 100 killed, 400 wounded.

February 28, 1864
Yazoo Expedition, Mississippi
3d USCT, Mississippi
Expedition up the Yazoo River, Mississippi, February 1–March 8. Union casualties: 35 killed, 121 wounded. Confederate casualties: 35 killed, 90 wounded.

March 2, 1864
New Kent Court House, Virginia
5th USCT, Ohio
Expedition to New Kent Court House in aid of Gen. Judson Kilpatrick's cavalry, March 1–4.

March 4, 1864
Williamsburg, Virginia
6th USCT, Pennsylvania
Expedition to New Kent Court House in aid of Gen. Judson Kilpatrick's cavalry, March 1–4.

March 5, 1864
Yazoo City, Mississippi
3d USCC, Mississippi; 47th USCT, Louisiana
Formerly the 1st Mississippi Cavalry (African Descent). *See* Yazoo Expedition (February 28)

March 9, 1864
Suffolk, Virginia
2d USCC, Virginia
Union casualties: eight killed, one wounded. Confederate casualties: twenty-five wounded.

March 20, 1864
Pass Manchas, Louisiana
10th USCHA, Louisiana
Formerly I Corps d'Afrique Heavy Artillery.

March 20, 1864
Roseville Creek, Arkansas
79th USCT (new), Kansas
On April 5, 1864, there was another encounter here involving detachments of the 2d and 6th Kansas Cavalry (seventy-five men), with four killed and ten wounded. Confederate strength unknown, but casualties were six killed, twenty wounded, and eleven missing.

March 24, 1864
Goodrich's Landing, Louisiana
66th USCT, Mississippi
While on post and garrison duty at Goodrich's Landing and Lake Providence, Louisiana, until February 1865.

March 25, 1864
Fort Anderson, Paducah, Kentucky
8th USCHA, Kentucky
Union casualties: fourteen killed, forty-six wounded. Confederate casualties: ten killed, forty wounded.

March 31, 1864
Roache's Plantation, Mississippi
3d USCC, Mississippi
Near Snydersville, Mississippi. Union casualties: sixteen killed, three wounded. Confederate casualties: three killed, seven wounded. Alternate date given as March 30. Battle of Snyder's Bluff, Mississippi.

April 1864
Haynes Bluff, Mississippi
3d USCC, Mississippi
Expedition from Haynes Bluff up the Yazoo River, April 19–28.

April 1, 1864
Plymouth, North Carolina
37th USCT, North Carolina
Gen. Benjamin F. Butler's operations on the south side of the James River and against Petersburg and Richmond, May 4–June 15.

April 9, 1864
Pleasant Hill, Louisiana
75th USCT, Louisiana
Pleasant Hill was the last major battle of the Louisiana phase of the Red River Campaign. Although Gen. Nathaniel P. Banks won this battle, he retreated, wishing to get his army out of western Louisiana before any greater calamity occurred. The Battles of Mansfield and Pleasant Hill jointly influenced Banks to forget his objective of capturing Shreveport.

April 12, 1864
Fort Pillow, Tennessee
Battery F, 2d USCLA, Tennessee; 11th USCT (new), Alabama
Union troops suffered 231 killed, 100 wounded, and 226 captured. African American units suffered 64 percent killed; white units only 33 percent. The attacking Confederates suffered only 14 killed and 86 wounded.

April 13, 1864
Indian Bay, Arkansas
56th USCT, Arkansas
Formerly the 3d Arkansas Infantry (African Descent).

April 13, 1864
Prairie D'Ann, Arkansas
79th USCT (new), Kansas 83d USCT (new), Kansas
Part of Arkansas Campaign, April 10–13. Union casualties: 100 killed and wounded. Confederate casualties: 50 killed and wounded.

April 18, 1864
Plymouth, North Carolina
10th USCT, Virginia
A detachment of the 10th USCT in addition to 37th USCT and 2d USCC are listed as part of the Subdistrict of the Albemarle, XVIII Corps, commanded by Gen. Henry Walton Wessells. Union casualties: 20 killed, 80 wounded, 1,500 missing. Confederate casualties: 500 killed, wounded, and missing.

April 18, 1864
Poison Springs, Arkansas
79th USCT (new), Kansas
Poison Springs located eight miles from Camden, Arkansas. Maj. Richard G. Ward commanded the 79th USCT. Union casualties: 113 killed, 88 wounded, 68 missing.

April 20, 1864
Waterproof, Louisiana
63d USCT, Louisiana
Formerly the 9th Louisiana Infantry (African Descent). Another encounter on February 14–15 involved the 49th USCT and the USS *Forest Rose*. Casualties were eight killed and fourteen wounded. Colonel Harrison commanded the Confederates, losing fifteen killed.

April 24, 1864
Camden, Arkansas
57th USCT, Arkansas
Formerly the 4th Arkansas Infantry (African Descent). Part of the 1864 Arkansas Campaign. A detachment on Steele's Camden Expedition, March 23–May 3, as bridge train guard.

April 25, 1864
Natchez, Mississippi
98th USCT, Louisiana
Formerly IV Corps d'Afrique Engineers. While attached to the Engineer Brigade, Department of the Gulf.

April 26, 1864
Berwick, Louisiana
98th USCT, Louisiana
While stationed in Berwick.

April 26 and 28, 1864
Little Rock, Arkansas
57th USCT, Arkansas
The regiment also engaged in two separate skirmishes during operations against Gen. Joseph Shelby north of the Arkansas River, May 13–31.

April 30, 1864
Jenkins' Ferry, Arkansas
79th USCT (new), Kansas; 83d USCT (new), Kansas
On the afternoon of April 29, Union forces reached Jenkins' Ferry and began crossing the Saline River, which was swollen by heavy rain. Rebel forces arrived on April 30 and attacked repeatedly. The Union troops repulsed the attacks and finally crossed with all their men and supply wagons, many of which they were compelled to abandon in the swamp north of the Saline. The Confederates bungled a good chance to destroy Maj. Gen. Fred Steele's army, which after crossing the river, regrouped at Little Rock. 2d Brigade (Col. Charles W. Adams): 1st Kansas Colored Infantry Regiment (Col. James M. Williams), 2d Kansas Colored Infantry Regiment (Col. Samuel Crawford), 12th Kansas Infantry Regiment (Lt. Col. Josiah E. Hayes), 1st Battery, Arkansas Light Artillery (Capt. Denton D. Stark). Union casualties: 200 killed, 955 wounded. Confederate casualties: 300 killed, 800 wounded.

May 1, 1864
Jacksonville, Florida
7th USCT, Maryland
Duty at Jacksonville until June 1864. Union casualties: one killed.

May 1–4, 1864
Ashwood Landing, Louisiana
64th USCT, Louisiana
Formerly the 7th Louisiana Infantry (African Descent). Regimental casualties were seven killed, wounded, and missing. Part of the Red River Campaign of l864.

May 1–12, 1864
Cold Harbor, Virginia (including Gaines' Mills, Salem Church, and Haw's Shop)
4th Division (Brig. Gen. Edward Ferrero)
1st Brigade (Col. Joshua K. Siegfried): 27th USCT (Col. Charles J. Wright), 30th USCT (Col. Delvan Bates), 39th USCT (Col. Ozora P. Stearns), 43d USCT (Lt. Col. H. Seymour Hall). 2d Brigade (Col. Henry G. Thomas): 19th USCT (Lt. Col. Joseph G.

Perkins), 23d USCT (Lt. Col. Cleveland J. Campbell), 31st USCT (Maj. Theophilus H. Rockwood).

May 3, 1864
City Belle, *steamer, Louisiana*
73d USCT, Louisiana
While at Alexandria, Louisiana.

May 4, 1864
Jenkins' Ferry, Arkansas
83d USCT (new), Kansas
While on duty at Fort Smith, Arkansas, until January 1865.

May 4, 1864
Bermuda Hundred, Virginia
4th USCT, Maryland
On May 9, Gen. Benjamin F. Butler made a thrust toward Petersburg and was met by Gen. Bushrod Johnson's division at Swift Creek. A premature Confederate attack at Arrowfield Church was driven back with heavy losses, but Union forces did not follow up. After skirmishing, Butler tore up the railroad tracks and did not press the defenders. Five federal gunboats steamed up the Appomattox River to bombard Fort Clifton, while Hincks's USCT infantry division struggled through marshy ground from the land side. The gunboats were quickly driven off, and the infantry attack was abandoned.

May 4, 1864
Saline River, Arkansas
83d USCT (new), Kansas
While on duty at Fort Smith, Arkansas, until January 1865.

May 5–7, 1864
Wilderness, Virginia
1st USCC, Virginia; 2d USCC, Virginia
1st USCC (Maj. Harvey W. Brown) and 2d USCC (Col. George W. Cole) were both unattached.

May 6, 1864
City Point, Virginia
5th USCT, Ohio
Gen. Benjamin F. Butler's operations on the south side of the James River and against Petersburg and Richmond, May 4–June 15. Capture of City Point, May 4.

May 7–20, 1864
Spotsylvania, Virginia
4th Division (Brig. Gen. Edward Ferrero of Gen. Ambrose E. Burnside's IX Corps); 3d Division (Brig. Gen. Edward W. Hincks of Maj. Gen. William Farr's XXIII Corps)
For 4th Division, see Ny River (May 10).

3d Division—1st Brigade (Brig. Gen. Edward A. Wild): 1st USCT (Col. John H. Holman), 10th USCT (Lt. Col. Edward H. Powell), 22d USCT (Col. Joshua B. Kiddo), 37th USCT (Lt. Col. A. G. Chamberlain).

3d Division—2d Brigade (Col. Samuel A. Duncan): 4th USCT (Lt. Col. George Rogers), 5th USCT (Col. James W. Conine), 6th USCT (Col. John W. Ames).

May 9–10, 1864
Swift Creek, Virginia (Arrowfield Church)
Battery B, 2d U.S. Artillery; 1st USCT, District of Columbia; 2d USCT, Virginia
Commanded by Capt. Francis C. Choate and attached to 3d Division (Brig. Gen. Edward W. Hincks) of XVIII Corps (Maj. Gen. William F. Smith).

May 10, 1864
Drewry's Bluff, Virginia
2d USCC, Virginia
Also known as Fort Darling. The 1st USCT (Maj. Harvey W. Brown) and 2d USCT (Col. George W. Cole) are also listed as unattached.

May 10, 1864
Ny River, Virginia (Spotsylvania Court House)
4th Division (Brig. Gen. Edward Ferrero of Gen. Ambrose E. Burnside's IX Corps)
1st Brigade (Col. Joshua K. Siegfried): 27th USCT (Lt. Col. Charles J. Wright), 30th USCT (Col. Delvan Bates), 39th USCT (Col. Osora P. Steams), 43d USCT (Lt. Col. Cleveland J. Campbell).

May 13, 1864
Pulaski, Tennessee
111th USCT, Alabama
Duty at Pulaski, Tennessee, and Athens, Alabama, District of North Alabama, until September 1864.

May 13, 1864
Point Lookout, Virginia

36th USCT, North Carolina
Expedition from Point Lookout to Rappahannock River, May 11–14.

May 13, 1864
Yazoo City, Mississippi
3d USCC, Mississippi
The Yazoo Expedition lasted from May 4–13 and included engagements at Benton and Vaughn.

May 15, 1864
Mount Pleasant Landing, Louisiana
67th USCT, Missouri
During the Red River Campaign (1864). The date of April 15 is given in some sources. Formerly the 3d Missouri Colored Infantry. Union casualties: three killed, five wounded.

May 16, 1864
Drewry's Bluff, Virginia
2d USCC, Virginia
Operations against Fort Darling, May 12–16. Actions at Drewry's Bluff, May 10, and 14–16. 1st USCC is also credited as being present.

May 18, 1864
Morganza, Louisiana (Yellow Bayou, Bayou DeGlaize, or Norwood's Plantation)
73d USCT, Louisiana
About 40,000 Union troops were stationed here, most of whom were former slaves. They were called "General Ullmann's Corps d'Afrique." The fort was abandoned due to malaria and cholera epidemics. Corps d'Afrique—Col. William H. Dickey: 1st Brigade, 1st Division—(Col. William H. Dickey): 1st Infantry (73d USCT)—Maj. Hiram E. Perkins; 3d Infantry (75th USCT)—Col. Henry W. Fuller; 12th Infantry (84th USCT)—Capt. James H. Corrin; 27th Infantry (92d USCT)—Col. Henry N. Frisbie.

May 18–20, 1864
Red River Expedition, Louisiana (retreat from Alexandria to Morganza)
92d USCT, Louisiana
Formerly XXII Corps d'Afrique Infantry. The 92d USCT had advanced from Franklin to Alexandria, March 14–26.

May 20, 1864
Drewry's Bluff, Virginia
2d USCC, Virginia
See Drury's Bluff (May 10).

May 20, 1864
Bermuda Hundred, Virginia
1st USCC, Virginia
Bermuda Hundred, Virginia, May 16–30. Union casualties: 200 killed, 1,000 wounded. Confederate casualties: 3,000 killed, wounded, and missing.

May 21, 1864
James Island, South Carolina
55th Massachusetts Volunteers, Massachusetts
Demonstration on James Island, May 21–22.

May 23, 1864
St. John's River, South Carolina
35th USCT, North Carolina
Operations on St. John's River, May 19–27.

May 23–27, 1864
North Ana River, Virginia
4th Division (Brig. Gen. Edward Ferrero of Gen. Ambrose E. Burnside's IX Corps)
See Ny River (May 10). Includes Battle of Totopotomoy, Virginia, May 26–30. The 3d Division (Brig. Gen. Edward W. Hincks) was also present.

May 24, 1864
Nashville, Tennessee
15th USCT, Tennessee
Garrison and guard duty at Nashville, Columbia, and Pulaski, Tennessee, until June 1864. Union casualties: four killed, eight wounded.

May 24, 1864
Wilson's Wharf, Virginia
Battery B, 2d USCLA, Virginia; 1st USCT, District of Columbia; 10th USCT, Virginia
At noon, about 2,500 Confederate cavalry initiated action at Wilson's Wharf, which was manned by a force of about 1,400 soldiers. The attack began with a mounted charge on Union pickets, and then a dismounted attack on the fort. To attack the fort it was necessary to cross through a clearing. Attempts at the center failed and lines of skirmishers were deployed to attack from the eastern side of the fort. Maj. Gen. Fitzhugh Lee sent a surrender demand that Brig. Gen. Edward A. Wild quickly declined. Union troops, reinforced by two gunboats in the

James River, returned fire and repulsed all attacks until the battle ended at six o'clock that evening. Reports of casualties are conflicting, but can be estimated at 20 for the Union and 100 for the Confederates, including dead, wounded, and captured.

May 26, 1864
Ashepoo River, South Carolina
34th USCT, South Carolina
Formerly the 2d South Carolina Colored Infantry. Expedition to Ashepoo River, May 24–27.

May 28, 1864
Jacksonville, Florida
7th USCT, Maryland
Duty at Jacksonville until June 1864.

May 31, 1864
Dallas, Georgia
110th USCT, Alabama
Formerly the 2d Alabama Colored Infantry.

June ? 1864
City Point, Virginia
Battery B, 2d USCLA, Virginia
During garrison duties.

June 2, 1864
Davis' Bend, Louisiana
64th USCT, Louisiana
During post and garrison duty at Davis' Bend and Natchez, Mississippi, until February 1865.

June 4, 1864
Vicksburg, Mississippi
3d USCC, Mississippi
Duty at Vicksburg, Mississippi, and in the District of Vicksburg until December 1864.

June 7, 1864
Ripley, Mississippi
55th USCT, Alabama
Formerly the 1st Alabama Infantry (African Descent). During Sturgis's Expedition from Memphis into Mississippi, June 1–13.

June 9, 1864
Point of Rocks, Virginia (or Maryland)
2d USCC, Virginia
During duty in trenches at Bermuda Hundred until June 13. Union casualties: two killed.

June 10, 1864
Brice's Cross Roads, Mississippi (Tishimingo Creek)
Battery F, 2d USCLA, Tennessee; 55th USCT, Alabama; 59th USCT, Tennessee (formerly the 1st Tennessee Infantry [African Descent])
Brice's Cross Roads near Guntown, Mississippi. The Confederates initiated a full-frontal attack on weary Union lines, which soon gave way and began retreating. The retreat quickly became a rout as the Union forces fled back to the safety of Memphis. Union casualties: 223 killed, 394 wounded, 1,623 missing. Confederate casualties: 131 killed, 475 wounded.

June 11, 1864
Wilson's Landing, Virginia
1st USCC, Virginia
During duties in trenches at Bermuda Hundred until June 18.

June 15, 1864
Moscow, Tennessee
55th USCT, Alabama
While on duty at Memphis, Tennessee, until August 1.

June 15, 1864–April 2, 1865
Petersburg, Virginia
5th Massachusetts Cavalry, Massachusetts; 1st USCT, District of Columbia; 4th USCT, Maryland; 5th USCT, Ohio; 6th USCT, Pennsylvania; 7th USCT, Maryland; 10th USCT, Virginia; 19th USCT, Maryland; 22d USCT, Pennsylvania; 23d USCT, Virginia; 27th USCT, Ohio; 28th USCT, Indiana; 29th USCT, Illinois; 29th Connecticut Infantry, Connecticut; 30th USCT, Maryland; 31st USCT, New York; 36th USCT, North Carolina; 39th USCT, Maryland; 41st USCT, Pennsylvania; 43d USCT, Pennsylvania; 45th USCT, Pennsylvania; 116th USCT, Kentucky
The siege of Petersburg, Virginia, commences on June 15–19 and continues until the city's fall on April 2, 1865. USCT troops made up XXV Corps, which was almost exclusively African American. Union casualties: 1,298 killed, 7,474 wounded, 1,814 missing.

June 16, 1864
Pierson's Farm, Virginia

36th USCT, North Carolina
Expedition to Pope's Creek, June 11–21.

June 22–30, 1864
Weldon Railroad Raid, Virginia
1st USCT, District of Columbia; 2d USCT, Virginia
Part of the Petersburg Campaign. The two USCT units were unattached but under the command of Gen. Philip H. Sheridan's 3d Division (Brig. Gen. James H. Wilson).

June 23, 1864
Jones' Bridge, Virginia
28th USCT, Indiana
Jones' Bridge and Samaria Church, Virginia. Union casualties: 54 killed, 235 wounded, 300 missing. Confederate casualties: 250 killed and wounded.

June 24, 1864
New Market Heights, Virginia
22d USCT, Pennsylvania
Demonstration north of the James River, September 28–30.

June 25, 1864
Ashwood, Mississippi
63d USCT, Louisiana
The 64th USCT is also credited as having taken part.

June 25, 1864
Point Pleasant, Louisiana
64th USCT, Louisiana
Attached to District of Natchez, Mississippi, until September 1864.

June 25, 1864
Staunton River Bridge, Virginia
1st USCT, District of Columbia; 2d USCT, Virginia
Part of the Richmond and Petersburg Campaign. Also known as Blacks and Whites or Old Men and Young Boys. The two USCT units were unattached.

June 27–29, 1864
Meffleton Lodge, Arkansas
56th USCT, Arkansas
Prior to operations in Arkansas, July 1–31.

June 29, 1864
Davis' Bend, Louisiana
64th USCT, Louisiana
At Davis' Bend and in the Department of Mississippi until March 1866.

July 1 and 2, 1864
James Island, South Carolina
33d USCT, South Carolina; 55th Massachusetts Infantry, Massachusetts
On July 2, the 55th Massachusetts Infantry Regiment was brigaded with the 103d New York and the 33d USCT, and ordered to attack Fort Lamar, a large rebel earthwork fortification on James Island, South Carolina. Although the fort was not taken during this skirmish (known as the Battle of River's Causeway), two brass twelve-pound Napoleon guns were captured by the 55th from a Confederate artillery group that had been stationed about a mile in front of Fort Lamar.

July 2, 1864
Bayou Mason, Mississippi
66th USCT, Mississippi
Post and garrison duty at Goodrich's Landing and Lake Providence, Louisiana, until February 1865.

July 2, 1864
Floyd, Louisiana
51st USCT, Mississippi
Post and garrison duty at Goodrich's Landing, Louisiana, until December 1864.

July 2, 1864
Pine Bluff, Arkansas
64th USCT, Louisiana
Ten companies of the 5th Kansas Colored Cavalry (Lt. Col. Wilton A. Jenkins) were stationed at Pine Bluff during the Arkansas Campaign.

July 4, 1864
Vicksburg, Mississippi
48th USCT, Louisiana
Regimental loses: one killed, seven wounded.

July 4–5, 1864
Coleman's Plantation, Mississippi (near Port Gibson)
52d USCT, Mississippi
Post and garrison duty at Vicksburg, Mississippi, until June 1865. Regimental loses: six killed, eighteen wounded.

July 5, 1864
Jackson, Mississippi
3d USCC, Mississippi
Expedition from Vicksburg, Mississippi, to Pearl River, July 2–10.

July 5–7, 1864
James Island, South Carolina
7th USCT, Maryland
Expedition to North Edisto River and John's and James Islands, July 2–10.

July 5–7, 1864
John's Island, South Carolina
26th USCT, New York
Expedition to John's and James Islands, July 2–10. Operations against Battery Pringle, July 4–9. Actions on John's Island July 5 and 7. Union casualties: sixteen killed, eighty-two wounded. Confederate casualties: twenty killed, eighty wounded.

July 6, 1864
Little Blue, Missouri
2d USCC, Virginia
Expedition from Vicksburg, Mississippi, to Pearl River, July 2–10. Regimental loses: eight killed, one wounded.

July 9, 1864
John's Island, South Carolina
7th USCT, Maryland; 34th USCT, South Carolina
Also known as Bloody Bridge (Burden's Causeway), July 7–9, 1864. Union troops consisted of Brig. Gen. John P. Hatch's command of Saxton's Brigade (Brig. Gen. Rufus Saxton): 9th USCT, 26th USCT, 56th New York Infantry Regiment, 114th Pennsylvania Infantry Regiment (Col. W. W. H. Davis), 4th Massachusetts Cavalry, and Wildt's Battery.

Montgomery's Brigade (Col. James Montgomery): 8th USCT, 34th USCT.

July 10, 1864
Issaquena County, Mississippi
66th USCT, Mississippi
Post and garrison duty at Goodrich's Landing and Lake Providence, Louisiana, until February 1865.

July 13–15, 1864
Tupelo, Mississippi
59th USCT, Tennessee; 61st USCT, Tennessee; 68th USCT, Missouri
Formerly the 4th Missouri Colored Infantry (68th USCT). Gen. A. J. Smith's Tupelo Expedition, July 5–18, 1864.

July 16, 1864
Goodrich's Landing, Louisiana
66th USCT, Mississippi
Post and garrison duty at Goodrich's Landing and Lake Providence, Louisiana, until February 1865.

July 16–17, 1864
Grand Gulf, Mississippi (also Port Gibson)
53d USCT, Mississippi
Other Union forces present were the 17th and 76th Illinois and the 2d Wisconsin. On post and garrison duty at Haynes Bluff, District of Vicksburg, Mississippi, until October 1864.

July 22, 1864
Barrancas, Florida
82d USCT, Louisiana
Moved to Fort Barrancas, Florida, and on duty there until March 1865. Expedition toward Pollard, Alabama, July 21–25, 1864.

July 22, 1864
Vidalia, Louisiana
6th USCHA, Kentucky
Formerly the 2d Mississippi Heavy Artillery (African Descent). Battle rated as a skirmish.

July 26, 1864
Wallace's Ferry, Arkansas
56th USCT, Arkansas
Operations in Arkansas, July 1–31. Union casualties: 16 killed, 32 wounded. Confederate casualties: 150 wounded.

July 26, 1864
Big Creek, Arkansas
Battery E, 2d USCLA, Arkansas; 60th USCT, Iowa
Formerly the 1st Iowa Colored Infantry (60th USCT). The 56th USCT is also credited as being present. Operations in Arkansas, July 1–31.

July 27, 1864
Black Creek, Florida

35th USCT, North Carolina
Raid from Jacksonville on Baldwin, Florida, July 23–28. South Fork, Black Creek, July 24. Black Creek near Whitesides, July 27.

July 30, 1864
Bayou Tensas, Louisiana
66th USCT, Mississippi
On post and garrison duty at Goodrich's Landing and Lake Providence, Louisiana, until February 1865.

May 24, 1864
Fort Pocahontas, Virginia
1st USCC, Virginia
Fort Pocahontas was a supply depot built and manned by hundreds of USCT under the direct command of Brig. Gen. Edward A. Wild.

August 2, 1864
Helena, Arkansas
64th USCT, Louisiana
The engagement is alternatively dated July 4, 1863. The 54th USCT (2d Arkansas Colored Infantry) was an unattached unit of the 1st Division (Brig. Gen. Frederick Salomon) of Maj. Gen. Benjamin Prentiss' XIII Corps (57 killed, 146 wounded, and 36 missing).

August 2–8, 1864
Fort Gaines, Alabama
96th USCT, Louisiana
Formerly II Corps d'Afrique Engineers. Part of siege operations against Fort Gaines and Fort Morgan, August 2–23.

August 5, 1864
Concordia Bayou, Louisiana
6th USCHA, Mississippi
Expedition from Natchez to Gillespie's Plantation, Louisiana, August 4–6, 1864.

August 5, 1864
Cabin Point, Virginia
1st USCC, Virginia

August 6, 1864
Indian Village, Louisiana
11th USCHA, Rhode Island
Formerly the14th Rhode Island Colored Heavy Artillery.

August 8, 1864
Point Isabel, Texas
Corps d'Afrique 9th Infantry (later 81st USCT)
Detachment of the Corps d'Afrique 9th Infantry (later 81st USCT) (seventy-five men) under Captain Jordan.

August 14–18, 1864
Deep Bottom, Virginia
7th USCT, Maryland; 9th USCT, Maryland
In some reports, the 1st USCT (Maj. Harvey W. Brown) and the 2d USCT (Col. George W. Cole) are also listed. This was part of the New Market Heights engagement.

August 15–16, 1864
Dalton, Georgia
14th USCT, Tennessee
The 14th USCT seemed to be attached to the 3d Cavalry Brigade under Col. John T. Wilder, part of the 2d Cavalry Division commanded by Brig. Gen. Kenner Garrard. Engagement was part of the Atlanta Campaign.

August 16–17, 1864
Waterford, Mississippi
55th USCT, Alabama; 61st USCT, Tennessee
Smith's Expedition to Oxford, Mississippi, August 1–30.

August 17, 1864
Issaquena County, Mississippi
66th USCT, Mississippi

August 18, 1864
Decatur, Tennessee
1st USCHA, Tennessee

August 21, 1864
Memphis, Tennessee
61st USCT, Tennessee
Union forces were commanded by Maj. Gen. C. C. Washburn. Total casualties were 160. This was an encounter in Gen. Nathan Bedford Forrest's defense of Mississippi. Confederate troop strength was around 4,000, with 34 casualties.

August 21, 1864
Fort Taylor, Florida
2d USCT, Virginia

While attached to the District of Key West, Florida, Department of the Gulf, February 1864–July, 1865.

August 24, 1864
Fort Smith, Arkansas
11th USCT (old), Arkansas
Post and garrison duty at Fort Smith, Arkansas, until November 1864. Union casualties: one killed, thirteen wounded.

August 24, 1864
Dutch Gap, Virginia
22d USCT, Pennsylvania
In support of a naval engagement on the James River, during siege operations against Petersburg and Richmond, June 16, 1864–April 2, 1865.

August 24–25, 1864
Bermuda Hundred, Virginia
7th USCT, Maryland
Siege operations against Petersburg and Richmond, August 1864–April 1865. Union casualties: thirty-one wounded. Confederate casualties: sixty-one missing.

August 25, 1864
Clinton, Louisiana (Olive Branch, Comite River)
4th USCC, Louisiana
Formerly I Corps d'Afrique Cavalry. Expedition to Clinton, August 23–29.

August 26, 1864
Bayou Tensas, Louisiana
66th USCT, Mississippi
Post and garrison duty at Goodrich's Landing and Lake Providence, Louisiana, until February 1865.

August 27, 1864
Owensboro, Kentucky
108th USCT, Kentucky
Garrison and guard duty at various posts in Kentucky until January 1865.

August 27–28, 1864
Holly Springs, Mississippi
11th USCT (new), Alabama
The 14th Iowa Infantry Regiment and 10th Missouri Cavalry Regiment were also present. Union casualties: one killed, two wounded. On post and garrison duty at Fort Smith, Arkansas, until November 1864.

August 29, 1864
Ghent, Kentucky
117th USCT, Kentucky
During duty at Camp Nelson, Kentucky, until October 1864.

August 30, 1864
Smithfield, Virginia
1st USCC, Virginia
During siege of Petersburg. Union casualties: 10 killed, 90 wounded. Confederate casualties: 200 killed and wounded.

September 2, 1864
Deep Bottom, Virginia
2d USCC, Virginia
Siege of Petersburg and Richmond, June 16, 1864–February 18, 1865. Moved to Deep Bottom, July 25.

September 4, 1864
Nashville & Northwestern Railroad, Tennessee
100th USCT, Kentucky
Guard duty with Nashville & Northwestern Railroad in Tennessee until December 1864.

September 6, 1864
Deep Bottom, Virginia
2d USCC, Virginia
See Deep Bottom (September 2).

September 7, 1864
Dutch Gap, Virginia
4th USCT, Maryland
Siege operations against Petersburg and Richmond, June 16–December 7.

September 14, 1864
Camp Marengo, Louisiana
63d USCT, Louisiana
On post and garrison duty at Natchez, Mississippi, until February 1865.

September 16 and 18, 1864
Fort Gibson, Cherokee Nation (Oklahoma)
79th USCT (new), Kansas; 54th USCT, Alabama
Union casualties: thirty-eight killed, forty-eight missing.

September 23–24, 1864
Athens, Alabama

106th USCT, Alabama (formerly the 4th Alabama Colored Infantry); 110th USCT, Alabama; 111th USCT, Alabama
During Gen. Nathan Bedford Forrest's attacks on Athens. Union casualties: 950 missing. Confederate casualties: 5 killed, 25 wounded. Some sources state that it was the 114th USCT, not the 111th USCT. This is unlikely because the 114th USCT was engaged in siege operations against Petersburg and Richmond on the Bermuda Hundred front until March 1865. In fact, most of the 111 USCT was captured at this battle.

September 25, 1864
Johnsonville, Tennessee
13th USCT, Tennessee
This may have been in defense of the supply depot here during one of Gen. Nathan Bedford Forrest's raids or Gen. John Bell Hood's attack on Johnsonville. The 13th USCT was engaged in railroad guard duty in Tennessee and Alabama for the Nashville Camp, Northwestern Railroad, until December 1864.

September 25, 1864
Sulphur Branch Trestle, Alabama
111th USCT, Alabama
Only a detachment fought here. *See* Athens (September 23–24).

September 26, 1864
Richland, Tennessee
111th USCT, Alabama
Only a detachment fought here. *See* Athens (September 23–24).

September 27, 1864
Marianna, Florida
82d USCT, Louisiana
Expedition to Marianna, September 18–October 4. Also present were the 7th Vermont Infantry and 2d Maine Cavalry. Union casualties: 32 dead and wounded. Confederate casualties: 81 dead and wounded.

September 29–30, 1864
Chaffin's (Chapin's) Farm, Virginia
2d USCC, Virginia; 1st USCT, District of Columbia; 4th USCT, Maryland; 5th USCT, Ohio; 6th USCT, Pennsylvania; 7th USCT, Maryland; 8th USCT, Pennsylvania; 9th USCT, Maryland; 22d USCT, Pennsylvania; 29th Connecticut Infantry, Connecticut; 36th USCT, North Carolina/Virginia; 37th USCT, North Carolina/Virginia (formerly the 3d North Carolina Colored Infantry); 38th USCT, Virginia

October 1, 1864
Deep Bottom, Virginia
38th USCT, Virginia
Operations against Petersburg and Richmond, June 1864–April 1865.

October 2, 1864
Saltville, Virginia
5th USCC, Kentucky; 6th USCC, Kentucky
Stoneman's Raid into southwestern Virginia, December 10–29. Union casualties: 54 killed, 190 wounded, 104 missing. Confederate casualties: 18 killed, 71 wounded, 21 missing.

October 4, 1864
Fillmore, Virginia
1st USCT, District of Columbia

October 5, 1864
Fort Adams, Louisiana
3d USCC, Mississippi
Expedition from Natchez to Woodville, Mississippi, October 4–11.

October 10, 1864
Dalton, Georgia
44th USCT, Georgia
Under the command of Colonel Johnson, some 400 men were captured.

October 10, 1864
Eastport (or East Point), Mississippi
61st USCT, Tennessee
Union casualties: 16 killed, 20 wounded.

October 10, 1864
South Tunnel, Tennessee
40th USCT, Tennessee
Guard duty for entire term on Nashville & Louisville Railroad and Nashville Camp, Northwestern Railroad, and in the District of East Tennessee.

October 11, 1864
Fort Donelson, Tennessee
4th USCHA, Mississippi
Formerly the 2d Tennessee Heavy Artillery (African Descent). In October 1864, the 119th USCT and the 4th Colored Artillery (Heavy) skirmished near Fort Donelson. Union casualties: four killed, nine wounded. Confederate casualties: three killed, twenty-three wounded.

October 13, 1864
Darbytown Road, Virginia
7th USCT, Maryland; 8th USCT, Pennsylvania; 9th USCT, Maryland; 29th Connecticut Infantry, Connecticut
Part of the Petersburg Campaign. Union casualties: 109 killed, 502 wounded, 200 missing. Confederate casualties: 1,100 killed and wounded, 350 missing.

October 15, 1864
Bayou Liddell, Louisiana
52d USCT, Mississippi

October 15, 1864
Glasgow, Missouri
62d USCT, Missouri
Formerly the 1st Missouri Colored Infantry. Only a detachment of the 62d USCT was present, accompanied by the 43d Illinois Infantry and detachments from three other regiments. Union casualties: 400 missing. Confederate casualties: 50 killed and wounded.

October 20, 1864
Waterloo, Louisiana
75th USCT, Louisiana
Unit later ordered to Terrebonne, Louisiana, February 26, 1864. Duty there and in the District of LaFourche until November 1865.

October 21, 1864
Bryan's Plantation, Florida
3d USCT, Pennsylvania
Attached to District of Florida, Department of the South, to October 1864.

October 21, 1864
Harrodsburg, Kentucky
5th USCC, Kentucky
Follows the unit's participation in Burbridge's Raid from Kentucky into southwestern Virginia, September 20–October 17, 1864. The 9th Kentucky Cavalry Regiment (Lt. Col. Boyle) fought here on October 10, 1862.

October 22, 1864
White River, Arkansas
53d USCT, Mississippi
Unit moved to St. Charles, Arkansas, on the White River on October 1864, and remained there until February 1865.

October 27–28, 1864
Fair Oaks, Virginia
1st USCT, District of Columbia; 5th USCT, Ohio; 9th USCT, Maryland; 22d USCT, Pennsylvania; 29th Connecticut Infantry, Connecticut; 37th USCT, North Carolina
Union casualties: 120 killed, 783 wounded, 400 missing. Confederate casualties: 60 killed, 311 wounded, 80 missing. The 1st USCT (Maj. Harvey W. Brown) and 2d USCT (Col. George W. Cole) are both listed as unattached.

October 27–28, 1864
Hatcher's Run, Virginia
27th USCT, Ohio; 39th USCT, Maryland; 41st USCT, Pennsylvania; 43d USCT, Pennsylvania; 45th USCT, Pennsylvania
Part of the Petersburg Campaign. Union casualties: 156 killed, 1,047 wounded, 699 missing. Confederate casualties: 200 killed, 600 wounded, 200 missing.

October 28–29, 1864
Decatur, Alabama
14th USCT, Tennessee
Part of the Franklin-Nashville Campaign, 1864. Forces under Brig. Gen. Robert S. Granger. Union casualties: 10 killed, 45 wounded, 100 missing.

October 28–29, 1864
Richmond, Virginia
2d USCC, Virginia; 7th USCT, Maryland
In trenches before Richmond until March 27, 1865.

October 31, 1864
Deep Bottom, Virginia
127th USCT, Pennsylvania
Duty in trenches north of the James River before Richmond until March 1865.

November 1, 1864
Black River, Louisiana
6th USCHA, Mississippi

November 4, 1864
Chaffin's Farm, Virginia
22d USCT, Pennsylvania
Second battle.

November 14, 1864
Cow Creek, Kansas
54th USCT, Arkansas
Formerly the 2d Arkansas Infantry (African Descent). Battles at Cow Creek, Kansas, November 14 and 28.

November 17, 1864
Dutch Gap, Virginia
36th USCT, North Carolina
Siege operations against Petersburg and Richmond, Virginia, July 3, 1864–April 2, 1865.

November 19, 1864
Ash Bayou, Louisiana
93d USCT, Louisiana
May actually refer to skirmish at Lake Fausse Point, November 18. Only a detachment of 93d USCT, formerly XXVI Corps d'Afrique Infantry.

November 19, 1864
Timber Hill, Cherokee Nation (Oklahoma)
79th USCT (new), Kansas

November 22, 1864
Rolling Fork, Mississippi
3d USCC, Mississippi
Alternate date given as November 11.

November 23, 1864
Morganza, Louisiana
84th USCT, Louisiana
Formerly XII Corps d'Afrique Infantry. Duty at Morganza until May 1865.

November 24, 1864
Section 37, Nashville & Northwestern Railroad, Tennessee
12th USCT, Tennessee
Action at Buford's Station, Section 37, Nashville & Northwestern Railroad.

November 26, 1864
Madison Station, Alabama
101st USCT, Tennessee
Unit set to guard Louisville & Nashville Railroad, and duties in Tennessee and Alabama.

November 30, 1864
Bermuda Hundred, Virginia
19th USCT, Maryland
Unit also saw action on the Bermuda Hundred front, November 17–18. On duty at Bermuda Hundred until March 1865.

November 30, 1864
Honey Hill, South Carolina
32d USCT, Pennsylvania; 35th USCT, North Carolina; 54th Massachusetts Volunteers, Massachusetts 55th Massachusetts Volunteers, Massachusetts 102d USCT, Michigan
Honey Hill or Grahamsville, South Carolina. 1st Brigade (Gen. E. E. Potter): 56th New York, 127th New York, 144th New York, 157th New York, 25th Ohio, 32d USCT, 34th USCT, and 35th USCT Regiments.

2d Brigade (Col. A. S. Hartwell): 54th Massachusetts, 55th Massachusetts, 26th USCT, and 102d USCT Regiments. Union casualties: 66 killed, 645 wounded.

December 1, 1864
Bermuda Hundred, Virginia
39th USCT, Maryland

December 2, 1864
Nashville, Tennessee (Block House # 2, Nashville & Chattanooga Railroad)
44th USCT, Georgia
Also known as Mill Creek, Chattanooga, December 2–3. Union troops consisted of the 44th USCT, two companies of the 14th USCT, and a detachment of the 115th Ohio Infantry Regiment.

December 4, 1864
Bermuda Hundred, Virginia
19th USCT, Maryland
Stationed on the Bermuda Hundred front until December 7.

December 5, 1864
Gregory's Farm, South Carolina

26th USCT, New York
Prior to demonstration on Charleston & Savannah Railroad, December 6–9.

December 7, 1864
Nashville, Tennessee
18th USCT, Missouri
Occupation of Nashville during Gen. John Bell Hood's investment, December 1–15.

December 6–9, 1864
Devaux's Neck, South Carolina
32d USCT, Pennsylvania; 34th USCT, South Carolina; 55th Massachusetts Volunteers, Massachusetts; 102d USCT, Michigan
Expedition to Devaux's Neck, December 1–6. Union casualties: 39 killed, 390 wounded, 200 missing. Confederate casualties: 400 killed and wounded. Alternate listing: 26th USCT, 33d USCT, 34th USCT, 102d USCT, 54th Massachusetts (Colored) Infantry, 55th Massachusetts (Colored) Infantry.

December 9, 1864
Gregory's Farm, South Carolina
26th USCT, New York
Battle also called Tillifinny Station.

December 10, 1864
Fort Burnham, Virginia
41st USCT, Pennsylvania
Unit moved to Fort Burnham north of the James River, before Richmond, October 27.

December 12, 1864
Hopkinsville, Kentucky
5th USCC, Kentucky
Stoneman's Raid into southwestern Virginia, December 10–29.

December 13, 1864
Bermuda Hundred, Virginia
23d USCT, Virginia
Unit on duty at the Bermuda Hundred front until March 1865.

December 15–16, 1864
Nashville, Tennessee
12th USCT, Tennessee; 13th USCT, Tennessee; 14th USCT, Tennessee; 17th USCT, Tennessee; 18th USCT, Missouri; 100th USCT, Kentucky
Union casualties: 400 killed, 1,740 wounded. Confederate casualties: 4,462 missing.

Alternate listing: 1st Colored Brigade (Col. Thomas J. Morgan): 14th USCT (Lt. Col. H. C. Corbin), 16th USCT (Col. William B. Gaw), 17th USCT (Col. William R. Shafter), 44th USCT (Col. Lewis Johnson), 18th USCT (Maj. Lewis D. Joy). Casualties: 21 killed, 118 wounded, 25 missing. 2d Colored Brigade (Col. Charles R. Thompson): 12th USCT (Lt. Col. William R. Sellon), 13th USCT (Col. J. A. Hottenstein), 100th USCT (Maj. Collin Ford), 1st Battery, Kansas Light Artillery (Capt. Marcus D. Tenney). Casualties: 77 killed, 390 wounded, 1 missing.

December 17, 1864
Mitchell's Creek, Florida
82d USCT, Louisiana
Mitchell's Creek, Florida, and Pine Barren Creek, Alabama. Union casualties: nine killed, fifty-three wounded, eleven missing. Pine Barren Ford and Pine Barren Creek were part of the same action in the expedition to Pollard, Alabama, December 13–19.

December 17–18, 1864
Pine Barren Ford, Florida
82d USCT, Louisiana
Expedition to Pollard, Alabama, December 13–19.

December 17–19, 1864
Pine Barren Creek, Alabama
97th USCT, Louisiana
Formerly III Corps d'Afrique Engineers. Expedition to Pollard, Alabama, December 13–19.

December 17–18, 1864
Marion, Virginia
6th USCC, Kentucky
Part of Stoneman's Raid into southwestern Virginia.

December 18, 1864
Arkansas River, Arkansas
54th USCT, Arkansas
Date may have been January 18, 1865, because the 54th USCT was not ordered to Little Rock until January.

December 19, 1864
Rector's Farm, Arkansas
83d USCT (new), Kansas
On duty at Fort Smith, Arkansas, until January 1865.

December 20, 1864
Saltville, Virginia
5th USCC, Kentucky
Part of Stoneman's Raid into Virginia and Tennessee, December 12–21, 1864.

December 21, 1864
Nashville, Tennessee
44th USCT, Georgia
Pursuit of Gen. John Bell Hood to the Tennessee River, December 17–28.

December 22, 1864
McKay's Point, South Carolina
26th USCT, New York
Following this engagement, the unit was ordered to Beaufort, South Carolina, January 2, 1865, and remained on duty there until August.

December 24, 1864
Murfreesboro, Tennessee
12th USCT, Tennessee
After this, the unit was given railroad guard and garrison duty in the Department of the Cumberland until January 1866.

December 24, 1864
Fort Smith, Arkansas
83d USCT (new), Kansas
Duty at Fort Smith until January 1865.

December 27–28, 1864
Decatur, Alabama
17th USCT, Tennessee
Unit involved in pursuit of Gen. John Bell Hood to the Tennessee River, December 17–27; therefore, alternate Battle of Decatur dates may be December 28–30.

December 28, 1864
Egypt Station, Mississippi
3d USCC, Mississippi
Expedition from Memphis, Tennessee, to destroy Mobile & Ohio Railroad, December 21, 1864–January 5, 1865. Union casualties: 23 killed, 88 wounded. Confederate casualties: 500 captured.

January 2, 1865
Franklin, Mississippi
3d USCC, Mississippi
Expedition from Memphis, Tennessee, to destroy Mobile & Ohio Railroad, December 21, 1864–January 5, 1865. Union casualties: four killed, nine wounded. Confederate casualties: twenty killed, thirty wounded. Union forces consisted of 3d USCC, 4th Illinois Cavalry Regiment, and 11th Illinois Cavalry Regiment.

January 5, 1865
Mud Creek, Alabama
106th USCT, Alabama

January 5, 1865
Smithfield, Kentucky
6th USCC, Kentucky
Unit at Louisville, Kentucky, and Helena, Arkansas, until January 1866.

January 7, 1865
Magnolia, Tennessee
15th USCT, Tennessee
Unit on post duty at Springfield, Tennessee, and in the District of Middle Tennessee until April 1866.

January 8, 1865
Scottsboro, Alabama
101st USCT, Tennessee
Unit on duty at Nashville, Tennessee, until October 1864. Then assigned to guard Louisville & Nashville Railroad, and stationed in Tennessee and Alabama until mustered out. Involved in two skirmishes at Scottsboro and Larkinsville, Alabama, on January 8, 1865.

January 8, 1865
Ivey's Ford, Arkansas
79th USCT (new), Kansas
Battle rated as a skirmish.

January 13–15, 1865
Fort Fisher, North Carolina
3d Division, XXV Corps (Brig. Gen. Charles J. Paine): 2d Brigade (Col. John W. Ames)
4th USCT (Lt. Col. George Rogers), 6th USCT (Maj. William R. Brazie), 10th USCT (Lt. Col. Edward H. Powell), 27th USCT (Col. A. H. Blackman), 37th USCT (Col. Nathan Goff, Jr.).
First expedition to Fort Fisher, North Carolina, took place December 7–27. Second expedition to Fort Fisher occurred January 7–15, 1865. Bombardment

of Fort Fisher, January 13–15. Assault and capture of Fort Fisher, January 15. Accounts also state that the 107th USCT was present.

January 15–April 26, 1865
North Carolina and South Carolina
110th USCT, Alabama
Campaign of the Carolinas. 110th USCT unassigned.

January 17, 1865
Lotus *steamer, Arkansas*
83d USCT (new), Kansas
Capture of vessel.

January 18, 1865
Clarksville, Arkansas
79th USCT (new), Kansas
Battle designated as a skirmish.

January 19, 1865
Sugar Loaf Hill, North Carolina
6th USCT, Pennsylvania; 107th USCT, Kentucky

January 24, 1865
Boggs' Mills, Arkansas
11th USCT (old), Arkansas
Unit moved to Little Rock, Arkansas, in November 1864.

January 24, 1865
Fort Brady, Virginia
118th USCT, Kentucky
Siege operations against Petersburg and Richmond, November 1864–April 1865.

January 24, 1865
Fort Burnham, Virginia
7th USCT, Maryland
In trenches before Richmond until March 27, 1865.

January 25, 1865
Simpsonville, Kentucky
5th USCC, Kentucky
Unit served at Ghent, Paducah, LaGrange, Crab Orchard, and Camp Nelson, Kentucky, until August 1865.

January 25, 1865
Powhatan, Virginia
1st USCC, Virginia
Company E, 1st USCC (Capt. Charles W. Emerson) was posted at Harrison's Landing under Col. William J. Sewell.

January 27, 1865
Elrod's Tan Yard, Tennessee
18th USCT, Missouri
Unit based in Bridgeport, Alabama, guarding railroad until February 1865.

February 9, 1865
Salkehatchie, South Carolina
102d USCT, Michigan
Battle dates given as January 25–February 9, 1865. Engagement also known as Combahee River or Rivers Bridge. Action part of advance on Charleston, February 7–23. Skirmish at Cuckwold Creek, February 8 (Companies B, E, and I). Then on duty at Charleston Neck until March 9.

February 10, 1865
James Island, South Carolina
55th Massachusetts Volunteers, Massachusetts
55th Massachusetts Infantry Regiment involved in yet another attack on James Island. Known as the Battle of Grimball's Causeway or the Last Fight for Charleston, each side would retreat after the brief skirmish with no sufficient gains made. Union casualties: twenty killed, seventy-six wounded. Confederate casualties: twenty killed, seventy wounded. Expedition to John's Island in February only involved Company F.

February 11, 1865
Federal Point, North Carolina
39th USCT, Maryland
Part of a series of battles including Sugar Loaf Hill and Federal Point, North Carolina. Union casualties: 14 killed, 114 wounded.

February 11, 1865
Sugar Loaf Hill, North Carolina
4th USCT, Maryland; 6th USCT, Pennsylvania; 30th USCT, Maryland
Part of a series of battles including Sugar Loaf Hill and Federal Point, North Carolina. Union casualties: 14 killed, 114 wounded.

February 16, 1865
Cedar Keys, Florida

2d USCT, Virginia
May have actually have been Station No. 4, February 13, 1865.

February 17, 1865
Chippewa *steamer, Arkansas*
83d USCT (new), Kansas
Capture of vessel.

February 18, 1865
Fort Jones, Kentucky
12th USCHA, Kentucky
Assigned to garrison duty in District of Kentucky at Bowling Green, Camp Nelson, and other posts until April 1866.

February 20, 1865
Town Creek, North Carolina
1st USCT, District of Columbia
A number of encounters around Wilmington, North Carolina, during February 18–22, 1865, including Fort Anderson and Town Creek.

February 22, 1865
Wilmington, North Carolina
1st USCT, District of Columbia
Listed as being present was the 3d Division, XXV Corps (Brig. Gen. Charles J. Paine): 2d Brigade (Col. John W. Ames): 4th USCT (Lt. Col. George Rogers), 6th USCT (Maj. William R. Brazie), 10th USCT (Lt. Col. Edward H. Powell), 27th USCT (Col. A. H. Blackman), 37th USCT (Col. Nathan Goff, Jr.).

February 25, 1865
Briggen Creek, South Carolina
55th Massachusetts Volunteers, Massachusetts
Expedition to Santee River, February 21–March 10.

March 1, 1865
St. Stephen's, South Carolina
55th Massachusetts Volunteers, Massachusetts
Expedition to Santee River, February 21–March 10.

March 6, 1865
Natural Bridge, Florida
2d USCT, Virginia; 99th USCT, Louisiana
Formerly V Corps d'Afrique Engineers (99th USCT). Operations in the vicinity of St. Mark's, Florida, February 21–March 7, under the command of Maj. Gen. John Newton. Casualties: 148 killed and wounded.

March 8, 1865
Alliance *steamer, Florida*
99th USCT, Louisiana
Operations near St Mark's, Florida.

March 10, 1865
Marion County, Florida
3d USCT, Pennsylvania
Unit on duty in Jacksonville, Florida, as Heavy Artillery until May 1865. (One company at Fernandina, Florida.)

March 15, 1865
Yazoo City, Mississippi
3d USCC, Mississippi
Following the occupation of Yazoo City, February 9–March 6.

March 18, 1865
Boyd's Station, Alabama
101st USCT, Tennessee
During duty in Tennessee and Alabama.

March 18, 1865
Amite River, Louisiana
77th USCT, Louisiana
V Corps d'Afrique Infantry.

March 24, 1865
Cox's Bridge, North Carolina
30th USCT, Maryland
Campaign of the Carolinas, March 1–April 26.

March 25, 1865
Brawley Fork, Tennessee
17th USCT, Tennessee
Unit posted to Nashville, Tennessee, and in the Department of Tennessee until April 1866.

March 27–April 8, 1865
Spanish Fort, Alabama
68th USCT, Missouri
During march from Pensacola, Florida, to Blakely, Alabama, March 20–April 1. Union casualties: 657. Confederate casualties: 744. Part of the Mobile Campaign under Maj. Gen. Edward Richard Sprigg Canby.

March 31, 1865
White Oak Road, Virginia
29th USCT, Illinois
Appomattox Campaign, March 28–April 9.

March 31–April 9, 1865
Fort Blakely, Alabama
47th USCT, Louisiana; 48th USCT, Louisiana; 50th USCT, Louisiana; 51st USCT, Mississippi; 68th USCT, Missouri; 73d USCT, Louisiana; 76th USCT, Louisiana; 82d USCT, Louisiana; 86th USCT, Louisiana
Formerly the 12th Louisiana Infantry (African Descent) (50th USCT), the 4th Louisiana Native Guards and IV Corps d'Afrique Infantry (76th USCT), and XIV Corps d'Afrique Infantry (86th USCT). Mobile Campaign, 1865, with 55,000 Union troops involved during the months of March and April. Up to 10,000 Confederates were stationed throughout the Mobile area, some 2,500 defending the city of Mobile while the rest were found at Fort Blakely and Spanish Fort. At least 32,000 Union soldiers marched through the entire length of Baldwin County up the eastern shore, while 14,000 Union troops came out of Pensacola, traveled due north, then turned back south in a surprise movement to invest Blakely.

April 4, 1865
Jacksonville, Florida
3d USCT, Pennsylvania
Expedition from Jacksonville to Camp Milton, May 31–June 3, 1864.

April 6, 1865
Warsaw, North Carolina
1st USCT, District of Columbia

April 7, 1865
Raleigh, North Carolina
1st USCT, District of Columbia; 5th USCT, Ohio
Advance on Raleigh, April 9–13, and occupation of Raleigh, April 13.

April 8, 1865
Eppes' Ferry, South Carolina (Potter's South Carolina Raid)
54th Massachusetts Volunteers, Massachusetts
Companies A and H, 54th Massachusetts Infantry under Brig. Gen. Edward E. Potter. Potter's Expedition to Camden, April 5–25. Seven Mile Bridge, April 6. Destruction of Eppes' Bridge, Black River, April 7. Dingle's Mills, April 9. Destruction of Rolling Stock at Wateree Junction, April 11. Singleton's Plantation, April 12. Statesburg, April 15. Occupation of Camden, April 17. Boykin's Mills, April 18.

April 9, 1865
Appomattox Court House, Virginia
41st USCT, Pennsylvania
Pursuit of Gen. Robert E. Lee, April 3–9. Union casualties: 200 killed and wounded. Confederate casualties: 500 killed.

April 11, 1865
Sumterville, South Carolina (Potter's South Carolina Raid)
54th Massachusetts Volunteers, Massachusetts
See Eppes' Ferry (April 8). Operating with the 4th Massachusetts Infantry Regiment.

April 13, 1865
Manchester, South Carolina (Potter's South Carolina Raid)
54th Massachusetts Volunteers, Massachusetts
See Eppes' Ferry (April 8). Losses unknown, regiment now commanded by Col. Henry N. Hooper.

April 14, 1865
Swiss Creek, South Carolina (Potter's South Carolina Raid)
54th Massachusetts Volunteers, Massachusetts; 32d USCT, Pennsylvania
See Eppes' Ferry (April 8). Another battle took place here on April 16, which not only involved the 54th, but also the 3d USCT and the 102d USCT.

April 18, 1865
Boykin's Mills, South Carolina
54th Massachusetts Volunteers, Massachusetts; 102d USCT, Michigan
See Eppes' Ferry (April 8). Regimental casualties: two killed, eighteen wounded.

April 18, 1865
Bradford Springs, South Carolina
102d USCT, Michigan
Formerly the 1st Michigan Colored Infantry. Potter's Expedition from Georgetown to Camden, April

5–29. Statesburg, April 15. Occupation of Camden, April 17. Boykin's Mills, April 18. Bradford Springs, April 18 (right wing). Dingle's Mills, April 19. Singleton's Plantation, April 19. Beech Creek, near Statesburg, April 19.

April 18, 1865
Taylorsville, Kentucky
119th USCT, Kentucky
Attached to the Department of Kentucky until April 1866.

April 19, 1865
Swift's Creek, South Carolina (Dingle's Mills)
102d USCT, Michigan
See Bradford Springs (April 18).

April 30 , 1865
Saline River, Arkansas
54th USCT, Arkansas
Attached to the Department of Arkansas until December 1866.

May 15, 1865
Palmetto Ranch, Texas
62d USCT, Missouri
Battle alternately dated May 12–13, 1865. Union troops commanded by Lieutenant Colonel Bronson. Union casualties: 118 killed and wounded. Expedition from Brazos Santiago, Texas, May 11–14.

November 4, 1865
Cabin Creek, Cherokee Nation (Oklahoma)
54th USCT, Arkansas
Union casualties: twenty-three killed, wounded, and missing. Confederate casualties: sixty-five killed, wounded, and missing.

References and Further Reading

Dyer, Frederick H. *A Compendium of the War of the Rebellion.* 3 vols. New York: Thomas Yoseloff, 1959.

Gladstone, William A. *United States Colored Troops, 1863–1867.* Gettysburg, Pa.: Thomas Publications, 1990.

Wilson, Joseph T. *The Black Phalanx: A History of the Negro Soldiers of the United States in the Wars of 1775–1812, 1861–1865.* 1890. Reprint, Salem, NH: Ayer, 1992.

Buffalo Soldier Postings, 1865–1917

The Buffalo Soldiers (9th and 10th Cavalry Regiments and 24th and 25th Infantry Regiments) were often stationed in isolated garrisons along the western frontier. Based on the latest research available, these listings seek to indicate the postings during the period between the end of the Civil War and the beginning of World War I. Many of the posts were temporary structures, and in only a handful of cases are there any material remains of the installations.

Forts Occupied by the 9th Cavalry Regiment, 1865–1917

New Orleans, LA (HQ)
  September 9, 1866–March 9, 1867
Carrollton, LA (HQ)
  March 9, 1867–March 27, 1867
San Antonio, TX (HQ)
  April 1867–June 1867
Camp Stockton, TX (HQ)
  July 7, 1867–September 9, 1868
Fort Davis, TX (HQ)
  October 3, 1868–January 21, 1871
Fort Stockton, TX (HQ)
  January 23, 1871–April 16, 1872
Fort Clark, TX (HQ)
  April 27, 1872–January 23, 1873
  July 1, 1875–October 19, 1875
Ringgold Barracks, TX (HQ)
  February 7, 1873–June 10, 1875
Fort Union, NM (HQ)
  December 3, 1875–February 15, 1876
Santa Fe, NM (HQ)
  February 18, 1876–November 6, 1881
Fort Riley, KS (HQ)
  November 8, 1881–June 14, 1885
Fort McKinney, WY (HQ)
  August 17, 1885–May 1887
Fort Robinson, NE (HQ)
  May 16, 1887–April 2, 1898
Chickamauga Park, GA
  April 23, 1893–April 30, 1889
Port Tampa, FL
  May 2, 1898–June 13, 1898
Cuba
  June 20, 1898–August 14, 1898
Camp Wikoff, NY
  August 20, 1898–September 27, 1898
Fort Grant, AZ
  October 5, 1898– July 28, 1900
Philippines
  October 5, 1889–July 28, 1900
  October 6, 1900–September 20, 1902
  June 2, 1907–May 15, 1909
  February 6, 1916–December 31, 1916
Fort Walla Walla, WA
  October 24, 1902–October 19, 1904
Fort Riley, KS
  October 23, 1904–April 29, 1907
Fort D. A. Russell, WY
  June 15, 1909–March 11, 1911
San Antonio, TX
  March 15, 1911–July 9, 1911
Douglas, AZ
  September 13, 1912–December 25, 1915

Detachments

Fort Garland, NM
Fort Lancaster, TX
Fort Elliott, KS
Fort Duncan, TX
Fort Hays, KS
Fort Sill, OK

Fort Quitman, TX
Fort Reno, NE
Fort Supply, OK
Fort Bayard, NM
Fort McRae, NM
Fort Duchesne, UT
Fort Wingate, NM
Fort McKinney, WY
Fort Stanton, NM
Fort Niobrara, NE
Fort Union, NM
Fort Seldon, NM

Forts Occupied by the 10th Cavalry Regiment, 1865–1917

Fort Leavenworth, KS (HQ)
September 24, 1866–August 5, 1867
Fort Riley, KS (HQ)
August 7, 1867–April 17, 1868
Fort Gibson, Indian Territory (HQ)
May 4, 1868–March 31, 1869
June 11, 1872–June 5, 1872
Camp Wichita/Fort Sill, OK (HQ)
April 12, 1869–June 5, 1872
May 4, 1873–March 27, 1875
Fort Concho, TX (HQ)
April 17, 1875–July 18, 1882
Fort Davis, TX (HQ)
July 29, 1882–April 11, 1885
Whipple Barracks, AZ (HQ)
May 20, 1885–July 11, 1886
Fort Grant, TX (HQ)
July 22, 1886–November 28, 1886
September 27, 1890–April 25, 1892
Santa Fe, NM (HQ)
November 1886–December 6, 1888
Fort Apache, AZ (HQ)
December 11, 1888–September 21, 1890
Fort Custer, MT (HQ)
May 5, 1892–November 1894
Fort Assiniboine, MT (HQ)
November 21, 1894–April 19, 1898
Chickamauga Park, GA
April 25, 1898–May 14, 1898
Lakeland, FL
May 16, 1898–June 7, 1898
Tampa, FL
June 7, 1898–June 14, 1898
Cuba
June 23, 1889–August 13, 1889
May 7, 1899–April 24, 1902
Camp Wikoff, NY
August 21, 1898–October 6, 1898
Camp Forse, AL
October 11, 1898–January 29, 1899
Fort Sam Houston, TX
February 4, 1899–April 28, 1899
Fort Robinson, NE
May 4, 1902–March 1, 1907
Philippines
April 3, 1907–May 15, 1909
Fort Ethan Allen, VT
July 28, 1909–December 5, 1913
Fort Huachuca, AZ
December 19, 1913–March 9, 1916

Detachments
Fort McKavett, TX
Fort Stockton, TX
Fort Arbuckle, KS
Fort Hays, KS
Fort Harker, KS
Fort Larned, KS
Fort Richardson, TX
Fort Verde, AZ
Fort Duncan, TX
Fort Bowie, AZ
Fort Cobb, Indian Territory
Fort Thomas, AZ
Fort Lyon, CO
Fort Dodge, IA
Fort Supply, OK
Fort Griffin, TX
Fort Keogh, MT
Fort Bayard, NM

In the immediate aftermath of the Civil War, there were four African American infantry regiments, the 38th, 39th, 40th, and 41st. The 38th was stationed in Kansas and New Mexico and the 39th in Louisiana and Mississippi; details of the postings are unknown. The 41st was based at Fort McKavett, Texas. More is known about the stations occupied by the 40th, although much of the detail is unavailable. In 1869 these four regiments were reorganized into the 24th and 25th Infantry Regiments.

Posts and Regimental Headquarters for the 40th Infantry

Fort Kuston
Camp Distribution,VA
Fort Plymouth
Sullivan's Island,SC
Fort Goldsboro
Smithville, NC(HQ)
Raleigh, NC (HQ)
Castle Pinckney, SC
Fort Macon, NC
Walterboro,SC
Fort Hatteras, NC
Orangeburg, SC
Fort Fisher, NC
Hilton Head, SC
Fort Caswell, NC

Forts Occupied by the 24th Infantry Regiment, 1865–1917

Fort McKavett, TX (HQ)
  November 1, 1869–August 7, 1872
Fort Brown, TX (HQ)
  September 1, 1872–July 18, 1873
  October 30, 1874–June 1, 1876
Fort Duncan, TX (HQ)
  August 1, 1873–October 15, 1874
  September 19, 1876–December 14, 1876
  February 11, 1878–March 13, 1879
  April 3, 1879–April 29, 1880
Fort Clark, TX (HQ)
  December 16, 1876–February 9, 1878
  March 14, 1879–April 2, 1879
Fort Davis, TX (HQ)
  June 18, 1880–October 15, 1880
Fort Supply, OK (HQ)
  December 16, 1880–October 5, 1887
  April 17, 1888–June 1, 1888
Fort Sill, OK (HQ)
  October 17, 1887–April 9, 1888
Fort Bayard, NM (HQ)
  June 4, 1888–October 19, 1896
Fort Douglas, UT (HQ)
  October 22, 1896–April 20, 1898
Chickamauga Park, GA
  April 24, 1898–April 30, 1898
Tampa, FL
  May 2, 1898–June 9, 1898
Cuba
  June 25, 1898–August 26, 1898
Camp Wikoff, NY
  September 3, 1898–September 23, 1898
Fort Douglas, UT
  October 1, 1898–April 5, 1899
Presidio of San Francisco, CA
  April 7, 1899–July 15, 1899
Philippines
  August 19, 1899–June 28, 1902
  February 24, 1906–February 8, 1908
  January 1, 1912–September 14, 1915
Fort Harrison, MT
  August 16, 1902–December 23, 1905
Madison Barracks, NY
  March 25, 1908–November 28, 1911
San Francisco, CA
  November 14, 1915–February 25, 1916
Fort D. A. Russell, WY
  February 28, 1916–March 23, 1916
Mexican border
  March 26, 1916–October 5, 1922

Detachments

Fort Apache, NM
Fort Stockton, TX
Fort Grant, AZ
Fort Concho, TX
Fort Huachuca, AZ
Fort San Carlos, FL
Fort Ringgold, TX
Fort Thomas, AZ
Fort Duncan, TX
Fort Bowie, AZ
Fort Elliott, TX

Forts Occupied by the 25th Infantry Regiment, 1865–1917

New Orleans, LA (HQ)
  April 20, 1869–May 1870
Fort Clark, TX (HQ)
  July 2, 1870–May 6, 1872
Fort Davis, TX (HQ)
  May 26, 1872–May 17, 1880
Fort Randall, SD (RH)
  June 29, 1880–November 17, 1882
Fort Snelling, MN (HQ)
  November 20, 1882–May 23, 1888

Fort Missoula, MT (HQ)
May 26, 1888–April 10, 1898
Chickamauga Park, GA
April 15, 1898–May 6, 1898
Tampa, FL
May 7, 1898–June 6, 1898
Cuba
June 22, 1898–August 13, 1898
Camp Wikoff, NY
August 22, 1898–September 29, 1898
Fort Logan, CO
October 3, 1898–June 27, 1899
Philippines
October 31, 1899–July 6, 1902
September 17, 1907–September 6, 1909
Fort Niobrara, NE
August 27, 1902–July 23, 1906
Fort Bliss, TX
July 28, 1906–June 12, 1907
Fort Lawton, WA
October 5, 1909–January 1, 1913
Schofield Barracks, HI
January 15, 1913–August 18, 1918

Detachments
Fort Hale, SD
Fort Meade, SD
Fort Quitman, TX
Fort McKavett, TX
Fort Duncan, TX
Fort Stockton, TX
Fort Shaw, MO
Fort Bliss, TX
Fort Custer, MT
Fort Sam Houston, TX
Fort Keogh, MT
Fort Gibson, OK
Fort Buford, ND
Fort Sill, OK

References and Further Reading

Carroll, John M., ed. *The Black Military Experience in the American West.* New York: Liveright, 1971.

Schubert, Frank N. *On the Trail of the Buffalo Soldier.* Wilmington, DE: Scholarly Resources, 1995.

Schubert, Frank N. *Black Valor: Buffalo Soldiers and the Medal of Honor, 1870–1898.* Wilmington, DE: Scholarly Resources, 1997.

World War I
Recruitment Camps and Postings, African American Troops

The U.S. Army's rapid expansion arising out of the recruitment for World War I required the creation of some thirty-two training camps each capable of housing around 40,000 men. Ten of the camps later became permanent installations used by the army. The information on each of the training camps details the African American units recruited and stationed there during this period.

Camp Alexander *(Newport News, VA)*
Pioneer Infantry Battalions: 801st, 808th, 813th, 816th
Labor Battalions: 313th, 316th, 317th, 319th, 320th, 325th, 339th, 340th, 341st, 342d, 343d, 346th, 347th
Engineer Service Battalions: 508th, 511th, 516th, 520th, 522d, 543d, 549th

Camp Beauregard *(Alexandria, LA)*
African American Enlistments, 1918:

May	6	September	86
June	13	October	998
July	13	November	769
August	14	December	241

Camp Bowie *(Fort Worth, TX)*
African American Enlistments, 1918:

September	310	November	1,671
October	2,808	December	1,354

Camp Cody *(Deming, NM)*
Infantry Regiment: 24th (2d Battalion)

African American Enlistments, 1917:

September	1	November	100
October	100	December	100

African American Enlistments, 1918:
Unknown

Camp Custer *(Battle Creek, MI)*
Labor Battalion: 324th
Engineer Service Battalion: 536th

African American Enlistments, 1917:

December	380

African American Enlistments, 1918:

January	383	July	827
February	142	August	3,670
March	161	September	1,702
April	180	October	2,033
May	926	November	1,053
June	1,427	December	295

Camp Devens *(Ayer, MS)*
Engineer Service Battalions: 519th, 520th, 534th, 537th

African American Enlistments, 1918:

January	1	July	600
February	3	August	3,959
March	0	September	3,252
April	249	October	3,244
May	1,976	November	1,588
June	4,367	December	2,933

Camp Dix *(Wrightstown, NJ)*
Field Artillery: 167th Brigade (less 351st), 349th, 350th
Pioneer Infantry Battalions: 807th, 811th, 813th
Engineer Battalions: 541st, 542d

African American Enlistments, 1917:

September	671	November	1
October	642	December	0

African American Enlistments, 1918:

January	1,374	July	5,236
February	1,416	August	8,084
March	1,415	September	7,162
April	1,649	October	6,280
May	2,712	November	5,379
June	1,601	December	2,533

Camp Dodge *(Des Moines, IA)*
Infantry Battalion: 366th (mobilizing)
Pioneer Infantry Battalions: 804th, 809th
Officers Training School for African American Candidates

African American Enlistments, 1917:

September	0	November	3,659
October	238	December	3,917

African American Enlistments, 1918:

January	4,905	July	6,772
February	3,636	August	7,354
March	3,697	September	6,802
April	3,597	October	4,682
May	6,378	November	3,867
June	3,184	December	2,053

Camp Fremont *(Palo Alto, CA)*
African American Enlistments, 1918:

May	4	September	4
June	4	October	1
July	5	November	1
August	4	December	1

Camp Furlong *(Columbus, NM)*
Infantry Regiment: 24th

Camp Gordon *(Augusta, GA)*
Engineer Service Battalions: 514th, 516th, 517th, 518th, 527th, 528th, 539th, 548th, 550th
Pioneer Battalions: 802d, 804th
Labor Battalions: 308th, 312th, 313th, 314th, 315th, 324th, 327th, 342d, 345th

African American Enlistments, 1917:

September	0	November	1,700
October	1,676	December	700

African American Enlistments, 1918:

January	3,936	July	6,962
February	820	August	10,494
March	3,574	September	6,624
April	5,154	October	5,769
May	8,793	November	5,123
June	7,078	December	1,944

Camp Grant *(Rockford, IL)*
Headquarters: 183d Infantry Brigade
Infantry Battalions: 365th, 370th (demobilizing)
Machine Gun Battalion: 350th (mobilizing for overseas)
Pioneer Infantry Battalion: 803d
Labor Battalions: 323d, 329th

African American Enlistments, 1917:

November	951	December	1,048

African American Enlistments, 1918:

January	1,041	July	5,769
February	1,159	August	6,026
March	3,081	September	10,124
April	7,865	October	13,898
May	3,543	November	12,851
June	3,285	December	6,595

Camp Greene *(Charlotte, NC)*
Labor Battalions: 344th–348th inclusive

African American Enlistments, 1918:

January	4	July	87
February	2	August	5,875
March	1	September	7,142
April	37	October	14,336
May	1	November	8,012
June	1	December	4,590

Fort Hancock *(Highlands, NJ)*
African American Enlistments, 1918:

May	0	September	3,168
June	532	October	2,564
July	1,274	November	2,778
August	1,594	December	3,041

Camp Hill *(Newport News, VA)*
Labor Battalions: 306th, 308th, 309th, 310th, 311th, 312th, 313th, 315th, 318th, 319th, 322d,

327th, 331st, 332d, 334th, 336th, 337th, 338th, 343d
Stevedore Regiments: 301st, 302d, 303d

Fort Huachuca *(Tombstone, AZ)*
Cavalry Regiment: 10th

Camp Humphries *(Alexandria, VA)*
Service Engineer Battalions: 516th, 520th–524th inclusive, 540th–550th inclusive

African American Enlistments, 1918:

January	0	July	2,174
February	0	August	5,306
March	0	September	6,051
April	114	October	5,511
May	3,148	November	3,956
June	2,767	December	2,732

Camp Jackson *(Columbia, SC)*
Headquarters: 186th Infantry Brigade
Infantry Battalion: 371st (mobilizing for overseas and demobilizing)
Engineer Battalions: 520d, 524th, 534th, 536th, 546th
Pioneer Infantry Battalion: 807th
Labor Battalions: 305th, 309th, 321st, 328th, 329th, 330th, 331st, 335th, 346th
Labor Companies: 301st–305th inclusive

African American Enlistments, 1917:

September	15	November	1,017
October	2,642	December	2,266

African American Enlistments, 1918:

January	62	July	6,704
February	2,819	August	7,795
March	3,240	September	3,633
April	788	October	3,667
May	2,819	November	3,951
June	3,295	December	4,590

Camp Kearney *(Linda Vista, CA)*
African American Enlistments, 1918:

November	4	December	1

Camp Lee *(Petersburg, VA)*
Pioneer Infantry Battalion: 808th
Labor Battalions: 304th, 320th, 321st, 323d, 330th, 338th, 339th, 344th, 347th, 348th
Engineer Service Battalions: 505th, 506th, 510th, 511th, 535th, 540th, 543d, 547th, 549th

African American Enlistments, 1917:

September	0	November	4,179
October	20	December	4,255

African American Enlistments, 1918:

January	4,899	July	8,988
February	5,772	August	6,303
March	4,230	September	7,433
April	477	October	6,637
May	1,919	November	5,663
June	4,740	December	5,455

Camp Lewis *(Washington, DC)*
Some 400 African Americans were posted here in the early months of the war.

Camp Lewis *(Tacoma, WA)*
African American Enlistments, 1917:

September	0	November	489
October	518	December	444

African American Enlistments, 1918:

January	862	July	14
February	425	August	1,093
March	21	September	880
April	11	October	566
May	61	November	537
June	75	December	250

Camp Stephen Little *(Nogales, AZ)*
Infantry Regiment: 25th

Camp Logan *(Houston, TX)*
Headquarters: 185th Infantry Brigade
Infantry Battalions: 370th (mobilizing for overseas)
Infantry Regiment: 24th (3d Battalion)

African American Enlistments, 1917:

September	177	November	2,189
October	1,722	December	0

African American Enlistments, 1918:

January	2,555	July	0
February	2,516	August	0
March	0	September	0
April	0	October	731
May	0	November	734
June	0	December	746

Camp MacArthur *(Waco, TX)*
Labor Battalion: 331st
Infantry Regiment: 24th (1st Battalion)

African American Enlistments, 1918:

January	0	July	1,163
February	0	August	2,347
March	3	September	1,388
April	3	October	1,376
May	341	November	959
June	1,164	December	1,059

Camp McClellan *(Anniston, AL)*
Labor Battalion: 326th

African American Enlistments, 1917:

November	99	December	140

African American Enlistments, 1918:

January	0	July	0
February	0	August	2,480
March	0	September	1,861
April	0	October	8,338
May	0	November	6,352
June	0	December	3,404

Camp Meade *(Baltimore, MD)*
Infantry Regiment: 368th
Field Artillery: 351st (training and mobilizing for overseas), 325th Signal Battalion
Headquarters: 184th Infantry Brigade (DHQ), 167th Field Artillery Brigade, 317th Train Headquarters and Military Police

African American Enlistments, 1917:

November	2,154	December	3,336

African American Enlistments, 1918:

January	6,082	July	10,596
February	5,951	August	5,126
March	7,946	September	6,169
April	4,799	October	7,921
May	7,969	November	3,586
June	8,971	December	3,033

Camp Merritt *(Jersey City, NJ)*
Headquarters: 184th Infantry Brigade
Field Signal Corps: 325th (staging)
Infantry Battalion: 369th (preparing to embark)
Pioneer Infantry Battalions: 801st, 812th, 815th
Engineer Service Battalions: 505th, 506th, 545th, 547th–550th inclusive
Labor Battalions: 318th, 321st

Camp Mills *(Long Island, NY)*
Headquarters: 167th Field Artillery Brigade
Field Artillery: 351st (staging)
Engineer Service Battalions: 515th, 532d, 537th, 548th, 550th
Pioneer Infantry Battalions: 802d, 804th, 806th, 809th, 811th, 813th, 814th

African American Enlistments, 1918:

May	50	September	2,044
June	636	October	748
July	636	November	1,476
August	673	December	1,472

Norfolk, VA *(establishments around this area)*
Engineer Service Battalions: 525th, 526th, 546th, 547th
Pioneer Infantry Battalions: 803d, 807th
Labor Battalions: 316th

Fort Oglethorpe *(Rossville, GA)*
Infantry Battalion: 366th (demobilizing)

Camp Pike *(Little Rock, AR)*
Engineer Service Battalions: 508th, 512th, 523d, 524th, 525th, 526th, 533d
Labor Battalions: 309th, 322d, 334th, 335th

African American Enlistments, 1917:

September	0	November	2,932
October	1,432	December	2,959

African American Enlistments, 1918:

January	1,955	July	9,381
February	3,229	August	9,504
March	5,479	September	9,484
April	5,205	October	11,267
May	11,288	November	10,399
June	10,014	December	5,363

Fort Riley *(Junction City, KS)*
Headquarters: 349th Machine Gun Battalion
Engineer Service Battalions: 529th, 530th
Pioneer Infantry Battalions: 805th, 806th, 815th, 816th
Labor Battalion: 325th

African American Enlistments, 1917:

September	7	November	7
October	7	December	2

African American Enlistments, 1918:

January	2,707	April	2,671
February	2,661	May	2,050
March	2,454	June	3,706

July	9,765	October	9,134
August	9,969	November	7,576
September	9,459	December	3,974

Schofield Barracks *(Oahu, HI)*
Infantry Regiment: 25th

Camp Sevier *(Greenville, SC)*
Labor Battalion: 321st

African American Enlistments, 1918:

May	0	September	4,786
June	4	October	5,327
July	0	November	2,895
August	1,747	December	2,795

Camp Shelby *(Hattiesburg, MS)*
Field Artillery: 317th Trench Mortar Battery (demobilizing)
Pioneer Infantry Battalions: 805th, 806th, 816th
Labor Battalions: 310th, 318th, 319th, 325th, 326th, 329th, 334th, 335th, 340th

African American Enlistments, 1918:

January	0	July	1,469
February	0	August	2,225
March	0	September	3,378
April	49	October	2,332
May	307	November	1,536
June	115	December	1,779

Camp Sheridan *(Montgomery, AL)*
National Guard: 9th Separate Battalion of Ohio

African American Enlistments, 1918:

May	0	September	1,680
June	56	October	941
July	1,000	November	984
August	3,109	December	975

Camp Sherman *(Chillicothe, OH)*
Engineer Battalion: 317th (mobilizing for overseas and demobilizing)
Field Signal Battalion: 325th (mobilizing for overseas)
Infantry Battalion: 372d (demobilizing)
Pioneer Infantry Battalions: 802d, 809th, 813th

African American Enlistments, 1917:

September	4	November	2,032
October	0	December	3,314

African American Enlistments, 1918:

January	3,521	July	3,695
February	3,933	August	5,884
March	2,414	September	6,070
April	2,219	October	7,817
May	2,819	November	7,868
June	3,777	December	3,779

Fort Sill *(Lawton, OK)*
A handful of African American officers were trained here.

African American Enlistments, 1918:

January	1	April	1
February	1	July	2
March	1	August	2

Camp Stuart *(Newport News, VA)*
Headquarters: 185th Infantry Brigade (less 369th Infantry) (preparing to embark)
Engineer Service Battalions: 513th, 514th, 523d, 524th, 532d
Pioneer Infantry Battalion: 815th
Labor Battalions: 314th, 335th, 339th, 347th

Camp Stotsenburg *(Luzon, Philippines)*
Cavalry Regiment: 9th

Camp Taylor *(Louisville, KY)*
Machine Gun Battalion: 349th. Trains: 317th Ammunition, 317th Supply, 317th Sanitation (demobilizing)

African American Enlistments, 1917:

November	15	December	34

African American Enlistments, 1918:

January	81	July	6,308
February	137	August	8,267
March	206	September	5,258
April	3,262	October	4,934
May	2,101	November	4,490
June	2,544	December	3,601

Camp Travis *(San Antonio, TX)*
Engineer Service Battalions: 507th, 509th, 513th, 531st, 537th
Pioneer Infantry Battalion: 815th
Labor Battalions: 322d, 331st, 332d

African American Enlistments, 1917:

November	7,623	December	7,100

African American Enlistments, 1918:

January	3,964	July	8,067
February	1,645	August	7,765
March	1,414	September	7,139
April	5,301	October	7,065
May	5,790	November	2,929
June	5,111	December	3,120

Camp Upton *(Yaphank, NY)*

Headquarters: 183d Infantry Brigade, 366th Infantry Brigade

Infantry Brigades: 183d (less 366th), 184th (less 368th)

Infantry Battalions: 367th, 368th, 369th (demobilizing), 370th, 371st, 372d (latter three staging)

Field Signal Battalion: 325th

Trains: 317th Training Headquarters and Military Police, 317th Ammunition, 317th Supply (preparing to embark), 317th Sanitary (staging), 317th Engineering (demobilizing)

Field Artillery Brigades: 349th, 350th, 317th Trench Mortar Battery

Machine Gun Battalion: 349th

Engineer Service Battalions: 509th, 512th, 513th, 514th, 527th–531st inclusive, 534th, 535th, 536th, 539th, 540th, 542d

Pioneer Infantry Battalions: 803d, 804th, 805th, 806th, 809th, 814th, 816th

Labor Battalions: 307th, 312th, 321st, 323d, 325th, 329th, 333d, 344th, 345th

African American Enlistments, 1917:

September	606	November	604
October	604	December	0

African American Enlistments, 1918:

January	3,345	July	7,193
February	3,351	August	7,721
March	3,409	September	4,833
April	3,591	October	3,072
May	4,431	November	2,289
June	2,657	December	1,403

Camp Wadsworth *(Spartanburg, SC)*

Labor Battalion: 330th

African American Enlistments, 1917:

September	0	November	0
October	1,258	December	0

African American Enlistments, 1918:

January	0	July	3,299
February	0	August	5,664
March	0	September	1,734
April	0	October	2,687
May	0	November	1,401
June	0	December	1,347

Camp Wheeler *(Macon, GA)*

Labor Battalion: 327th

African American Enlistments, 1918:

January	0	July	872
February	0	August	3,884
March	199	September	2,352
April	190	October	5,426
May	1,392	November	3,394
June	1,467	December	986

References and Further Reading

Barbeau, Arthur E., and Florette Henri. *The Unknown Soldiers: Black American Troops in World War I.* Philadelphia: Temple University Press, 1974.

Henri, Florette. *Bitter Victory: A History of Black Soldiers in World War I.* Garden City, NY: Doubleday, 1970.

Johnson, Charles, Jr. *African American Soldiers in the National Guard: Recruitment and Deployment.* Westport, CT: Greenwood, 1992.

Scott, Emmett J. *Scott's Official History of the American Negro in the World War.* N.p., 1919.

Sweeney, W. Allison. *History of the American Negro in the Great World War.* New York: Johnson, 1970.

Woodson, Carter G. *The Negro in Our History.* Washington, DC: Associated Publishers, 1922.

World War II and Korean War Recruitment Camps, African American Troops

World War II saw the beginning of the end of segregated units in the U.S. military. However, during this period there are a large number of military installations associated with African Americans. In part, this is due to the enormous increase in the number of African American units that were created by the services starting in December 1941.

The allocation or establishment of facilities suitable for African American units had a number of key considerations:

- availability of housing and facilities on the post
- proportions of white and African American troops at the post
- proximity to civilian centers of African American population with good recreational facilities that could absorb sizable numbers of men on leave or with passes
- attitude of the nearby citizen community to the presence of African American troops
- division of large units into smaller units and training at different bases

U.S. Army

2d Cavalry Division (Horse)
Activated at Fort Clark, Texas, and staged at Camp Patrick Henry, Virginia. Consisting of 4th, 5th Cavalry Brigades HHT 9th, 10th, 27th, 28th Cavalry Regiments; HHB Division Artillery 77th, 79th, 159th Field Artillery Battalions; Headquarters Troop 162d Engineer Squadron; 3d Medical Squadron; 35th Cavalry Reconnaissance Squadron, Mechanized; Maintenance Company 114th Ordinance Medium; 20th Cavalry Quartermaster Military Police, 2d Cavalry Squadron.

92d Infantry Division
Activated at Fort McClellan, Alabama, and moved to Fort Huachuca, Arizona. Staged at Camp Patrick Henry, Virginia. Consisting of 365th, 370th, 371st, Infantry Regiments (442d, 473d attached); 597th, 598th, 599th, 600th Field Artillery Battalions; HHB Division Artillery; 92d Reconnaissance Troop 317th, Engineer Combat Battalion; 317th Medical Battalion; Headquarters Special Troops Headquarters Company; Military Police Platoon; 792d Ordnance Light Maintenance Company; 92d Quartermaster Company; 92d Signal Company.

93d Infantry Division
Activated at Fort Huachuca, Arizona, and staged at Camp Stoneman, California. Consisting of 25th, 368th, 369th Infantry Regiments; 593d, 594th, 595th, 596th Field Artillery Battalions; HHB Division Artillery; 93d Reconnaissance Troop, Mechanized; 318th Engineer Combat Battalion; 318th Medical Battalion; 93d Counterintelligence Corps; Headquarters Special Troops; Headquarters Company; Military Police Platoon; 793d Ordnance Light Maintenance Company; 93d Quartermaster Company; 93d Signal Company.

24th Infantry Regiment
Stationed at Fort Benning, Georgia.

25th Infantry Regiment
Stationed at Fort Huachuca, Arizona; attached to Third Army, then to 93d Infantry Division.

364th Infantry Regiment
Formerly the 367th, activated at Camp Claiborne, Louisiana. Moved to Phoenix, Arizona; staged at Fort Lawton, Washington.

366th Infantry Regiment
Activated at Fort Devens, Massachusetts; moved to Fort A. P. Hill, Virginia, and Camp Atterbury, Indiana. Staged at Camp Patrick Henry, Virginia.

367th Infantry Regiment
Activated at Camp Claiborne, Louisiana; staged in Charleston, South Carolina. Redesignated the 364th.

368th Infantry Regiment
Activated at Fort Huachuca, Arizona, and assigned to 93d Infantry.

369th Infantry Regiment
Activated at Fort Huachuca, Arizona, and assigned to 93d Infantry.

370th Infantry Regiment
Activated at Camp Breckinridge, Kentucky, and assigned to 92d Infantry Division.

371st Infantry Regiment
Activated at Camp Joseph T. Robinson, Arkansas, and assigned to 92d Infantry Division.

372d Infantry Regiment
Inducted into federal service from Washington, D.C.; New Jersey; Columbus, Ohio; and Boston, Massachusetts. Moved to Fort Dix, New Jersey. Transferred to Camp Breckinridge, Kentucky, and Fort Huachuca, Arizona. Staged at Fort Lawton, Washington.

367th Armored Infantry Battalion
Formed at Camp Davis, North Carolina.

555th Parachute Infantry Battalion
Formed at Camp Mackall, North Carolina.

5th Armored Group
Activated at Camp Claiborne, Louisiana, as 5th Tank Group. Moved to Fort Hood, Texas. Moved to Fort Huachuca, Arizona, and returned to Fort Hood, Texas.

758th Light Tank Battalion
Formed at Fort Knox, Kentucky.

761st Tank Battalion
Formed at Camp Claiborne, Louisiana.

748th Tank Battalion
Formed at Camp Claiborne, Louisiana. Moved to Camp Kilmer, New Jersey.

4th Cavalry Brigade
Activated at Fort Riley, Kansas. Moved to Camp Lockett, California. Staged at Camp Patrick Henry, Virginia.

5th Calvary Brigade
Activated at Fort Clark, Texas, and staged at Camp Patrick Henry, Virginia. Elements became the 6400th Ordnance Ammunition Battalion.

9th Cavalry Regiment
Stationed at Fort Riley, Kansas. Transferred to Fort Clark, Texas, and then staged at Camp Patrick Henry, Virginia. Under 2d Cavalry Division.

10th Cavalry Regiment
Stationed at Fort Leavenworth, Kansas. Moved to Fort Riley, Kansas. Moved to Camp Lockett, California, and then staged at Camp Patrick Henry, Virginia. Also under 2d Cavalry Division.

27th Cavalry Regiment
Activated at Fort Clark, Texas. Transferred to 2d Cavalry Division.

28th Cavalry Regiment
Activated at Camp Lockett, California, as part of 2d Cavalry Division.

U.S. Military Academy Cavalry Squadron
Formed at West Point, New York.

5th Reconnaissance Squadron
Formed at Fort Clark, Texas. Assigned to 2d Cavalry Division.

35th Cavalry Reconnaissance Squadron (Mechanized)
Formed at Fort Clark, Texas. Assigned to 2d Cavalry Division.

614th Tank Destroyer Battalion
Formed at Camp Carson, Colorado. Moved to Camp Kilmer, New Jersey.

649th Tank Destroyer Battalion
Formed at Camp Bowie, Texas.

659th, 669th Tank Destroyer Battalions
Formed at Camp Hood, Texas.

679th Tank Destroyer Battalion
Formed at Camp Hood, Texas. Moved to Camp Kilmer, New Jersey.

795th Tank Destroyer Battalion
Formed at Fort Custer, Michigan, as Heavy Self-Propelled.

827th Tank Destroyer Battalion
Formed at Camp Forrest, Tennessee. Moved to Camp Patrick Henry, Virginia.

828th Tank Destroyer Battalion
Formed at Fort Knox, Kentucky, and moved to Fort Huachuca, Arizona.

829th Tank Destroyer Battalion
Formed at Camp Gruber, Oklahoma, as Heavy Self-Propelled. Moved to Camp Hood, Texas.

846th Tank Destroyer Battalion
Formed at Camp Livingston, Louisiana, and moved to Camp Swift, Texas.

46th Field Artillery Brigade
Activated at Camp Livingston, Louisiana, and assigned to Third Army. Redesignated HHB, 46th Field Artillery Group.

333d Field Artillery Group (Motorized)
Redesignated from HHB 333d Field Artillery Regiment at Camp Gruber, Oklahoma. Staged at Camp Shanks, New York. 1st and 2d Battalions redesignated 333d and 969th Field Artillery Battalions.

349th Field Artillery Group (Motorized)
Redesignated from 349th Field Artillery Regiment at Fort Sill, Oklahoma. Moved to Camp Hood, Texas. Staged at Camp Myles Standish, Massachusetts. 1st and 2d Battalions redesignated 3498th and 686th Field Artillery Battalions.

350th Field Artillery Group (Motorized)
Redesignated from HHB 350th Field Artillery Regiment at Camp Livingston, Louisiana. 1st and 2d Battalions redesignated 350th and 971st Field Artillery Battalions.

351st Field Artillery Group (Motorized)
Redesignated from HHB 351st Field Artillery Regiment at Camp Livingston, Louisiana. Moved to Fort Sill, Oklahoma, and Camp Gruber, Oklahoma. Staged at Camp Myles Standish, Massachusetts. 1st and 2d Battalions redesignated 351st and 973d Field Artillery Battalions.

353d Field Artillery Group (Motorized)
Formed at Camp Livingston, Louisiana. 1st and 2d Battalions redesignated 353d and 993d Field Artillery Battalions.

184th Field Artillery Regiment
Inducted into federal service from Illinois National Guard at Chicago, Illinois. Moved to Fort Custer, Michigan, and assigned to Second Army. 1st and 2d Battalions redesignated 930th and 931st Field Artillery Battalions.

578th Field Artillery Regiment (Motorized)
Activated at Fort Bragg, North Carolina. Redesignated HHB 578th Field Artillery; 1st and 2d Battalions redesignated 578th and 999th Field Artillery Battalions.

77th, 79th Field Artillery Battalions
Formed at Fort Clark, Texas. Assigned to 2d Cavalry Division.

159th Field Artillery Battalion
Formed at Fort Clark, Texas. Assigned to 2d Cavalry Division.

593d, 594th, 595th, 596th Field Artillery Battalions
Formed at Fort Huachuca, Arizona. Moved to Camp Stoneman, California.

597th Field Artillery Battalion
Formed at Camp Atterbury, Indiana. Moved to Camp Myles Standish, Massachusetts.

598th Field Artillery Battalion
Formed at Camp Breckinridge, Kentucky, and staged at Camp Myles Standish, Massachusetts.

599th Field Artillery Battalion
Formed at Camp Joseph T. Robinson, Arkansas. Staged at Camp Myles Standish, Massachusetts.

600th Field Artillery Battalion
Formed at Fort McClellan, Alabama. Staged at Camp Myles Standish, Massachusetts.

732d Field Artillery Battalion
Formed at Fort Bragg, North Carolina. Redesignated 1695th Combat Engineer Battalion.

777th Field Artillery Battalion
Formed at Camp Beale, California.

795th Field Artillery Battalion
Formed at Fort Bragg, North Carolina. Redesignated 1700th Combat Engineer Battalion.

54th Coast Artillery Regiment
Activated at Camp Wallace, Texas. Moved to Camp Davis, North Carolina; Fort Fisher, North Carolina; and back to Camp Davis. Transferred to Fort Cronkhite, California, and Fort Ord, California. HHB unit redesignated HHB 152d Coast Artillery Group; then 1st–3d Battalions redesignated 606th, 49th, 607th Coast Artillery Battalions.

76th Coast Artillery Regiment
Activated at Fort Bragg, North Carolina. Transferred to Burbank, California, and Philadelphia, Pennsylvania. HHB redesignated HHB 76th AAA Group; 1st and 2d Battalions redesignated 76th and 933d AAA Battalions.

77th Coast Artillery Regiment
Activated at Fort Bragg, North Carolina, and moved to Hartford, Connecticut. Staged at Fort Dix, New Jersey. HHB redesignated HHB 77th AAA Group; 1st–3d Battalions redesignated 77th AAA Gun, 938th AAA Auto-Weapons, and 374th Searchlight Battalions.

90th Coast Artillery Regiment
Activated at Camp Stewart, Georgia, and staged at Fort Dix, New Jersey. HHB redesignated HHB 90th AAA Group; 1st–3d Battalions redesignated 90th AAA Gun, 897th AAA Auto-Weapons, and 334th Searchlight Battalions.

99th Coast Artillery Regiment.
Activated at Camp Davis, North Carolina. 1st–3d Battalions redesignated 99th AA Gun, 871st AAA Auto-Weapons, and 338th Searchlight Battalions.

100th Coast Artillery Regiment
Activated at Camp Davis, North Carolina, and moved to Fort Custer, Michigan. Also moved to Fort Brady, Michigan, and Fort Stewart, Georgia. 1st and 2d Battalions redesignated 100th AAA Gun and 538th AAA Auto-Weapons Battalions.

369th Coast Artillery Regiment
Inducted into federal service in New York. Moved to Fort Ontario, New York, and then transferred to Camp Edwards, Massachusetts, and Los Angeles, California. HHB redesignated HHB 369th AAA Group; 1st and 2d Battalions redesignated 369th AAA Gun and 870th Auto-Weapons Battalions.

612th Coast Artillery Regiment
Activated at Fort Stewart, Georgia. HHB redesignated HHB 121st Coast Artillery Group; 1st–3d Battalions redesignated 741st, 207th, and 234th Coast Artillery Battalions.

613th Coast Artillery Regiment
Activated at Fort Stewart, Georgia. HHB redesignated HHB 122d Coast Artillery Group; 1st–3d Battalions redesignated 742d, 208th, and 235th Coast Artillery Battalions.

318th, 319th, 320th, 321st Balloon Battalions
Formed at Camp Tyson, Tennessee.

361st AAA Searchlight Battalion
1st Platoon, Battery A, formed at Fort Jackson, South Carolina.

450th AAA Auto Weapons Battalion
Formed at Camp Davis, North Carolina.

452d, 458th, 466th, 477th, 484th, 492d, 493d, 538th AAA Auto-Weapons Battalions
Formed at Camp Stewart, Georgia.

846th AAA Auto-Weapons Battalion
Formed at Camp Stewart, Georgia.

41st Engineer General Service Regiment
Activated at Fort Bragg, North Carolina. Designated parent unit of 358th Engineer Regiment.

45th Engineer General Service Regiment
Activated at Camp Blanding, Florida.

91st Engineer Battalion
Formed at Camp Shelby, Mississippi. Redesignated a regiment at Camp Forrest, Tennessee.

92d Engineer Battalion
Formed at Fort Leonard Wood, Missouri. Redesignated a regiment at Camp Forrest, Tennessee.

93d Engineer General Service Regiment
Redesignated from the 93d Engineer Battalion (Separate) at Camp Livingston, Louisiana.

94th Engineer General Service Regiment
Redesignated from the 94th Engineer Battalion (Separate) at Fort Custer, Michigan. Moved to Fort Dix, New Jersey.

95th Engineer General Service Regiment
Redesignated from the 95th Engineer Battalion (Separate) at Fort Belvoir, Virginia, and moved to Fort Bragg, North Carolina.

96th Engineer General Service Regiment
Formerly 96th Engineer Battalion formed at Fort Bragg, North Carolina.

97th Engineer General Service Regiment
Redesignated from the 97th Engineer Battalion (Separate) at Eglin Field, Florida.

98th Engineer General Service Regiment
Redesignated from the 98th Engineer Battalion (Separate) at Camp Claiborne, Louisiana.

224th, 226th Engineer General Service Regiments
Formed from the 366th Infantry Regiment.

350th Engineer General Service Regiment
Activated at Camp Shelby, Mississippi.

352d Engineer General Service Regiment
Activated at Camp Gordon, Georgia. Transferred to Indiantown Gap, Pennsylvania.

354th Engineer General Service Regiment
Activated at Camp Maxey, Texas. Staged at Camp Shanks, New York.

356th Engineer General Service Regiment
Activated at Camp Shelby, Mississippi. Staged at Camp Shanks, New York.

357th Engineer General Service Regiment
Activated at Camp Pickett, Virginia. Transferred to Camp Claiborne, Louisiana.

362d Engineer General Service Regiment
Activated at Camp Claiborne, Louisiana.

364th Engineer General Service Regiment
Activated at Camp Swift, Texas. Transferred to Camp Claiborne, Louisiana. Staged at Camp Shanks, New York.

365th Engineer General Service Regiment
Activated at Camp Campbell, Kentucky. Transferred to Camp Claiborne, Louisiana. Staged at Camp Shanks, New York.

366th Engineer General Service Regiment
Activated at Camp Phillips, Kansas. Transferred to Camp Forrest, Tennessee. Staged at Camp Shanks, New York.

374th Engineer General Service Regiment
Redesignated from the 374th Engineer Battalion (Separate) at Camp Hood, Texas, and assigned to Eighth Service Command. Staged at Camp Shanks, New York. Battalion formed at Camp Gordon, Georgia.

375th Engineer General Service Regiment
Redesignated from the 375th Engineer Battalion (Separate) at Fort Knox, Kentucky. Staged at Camp Shanks, New York. Battalion formed at Camp Sutton, North Carolina.

376th Engineer Battalion
Formed at Camp Polk, Louisiana. Staged at Camp Myles Standish, Massachusetts.

377th Engineer General Service Regiment
Redesignated from the 377th Engineer Battalion (Separate) at Fort Knox, Kentucky, and assigned to Fifth Service Command. Staged at Camp Shanks, New York. Battalion formed at Camp Pickett, Virginia.

378th, 379th, 383d Engineer Battalions
Formed at Camp Shelby, Mississippi. The 383d became the 1349th Engineer Regiment.

382d, 386th Engineer Battalions
Formed at Fort Knox, Kentucky. Staged at Camp Kilmer, New Jersey.

384th Engineer Battalion
Formed at Fort Bragg, North Carolina.

385th Engineer Battalion
Formed at Camp Edwards, Massachusetts, and staged at Camp Myles Standish, Massachusetts.

387th Engineer Battalion
Formed at Fort Meade, Maryland.

388th Engineer General Service Regiment
Redesignated from the 388th Engineer Battalion (Separate) at Waterways, Alberta, Canada. Transferred to Camp Sutton, North Carolina. Staged at Camp Myles Standish, Massachusetts. Battalion formed at Camp Claiborne, Louisiana.

389th Engineer General Service Regiment
Redesignated from the 389th Engineer Battalion (Separate) at Camp Young, California, and transferred to Camp Butner, North Carolina. Staged at Camp Shanks, New York. Battalion formed at Camp Gordon, Georgia.

390th Engineer General Service Regiment
Activated at Camp Claiborne, Louisiana, and staged at Camp Shanks, New York.

392d Engineer General Service Regiment
Activated at Camp Joseph T. Robinson, Arkansas, and moved to Camp Claiborne, Louisiana. Staged at Camp Shanks, New York.

393d Engineer General Service Regiment
Activated at Camp Claiborne, Louisiana, and returned after a short stay at Camp Joseph T. Robinson, Arkansas. Staged at Camp Patrick Henry, Virginia.

398th Engineer General Service Regiment
Activated at Camp Claiborne, Louisiana, and staged at Camp Shanks, New York.

810th, 812th, 838th, 847th, 849th Engineer Aviation Battalions
Formed at MacDill Field, Florida. 847th was staged at Camp Kilmer, New Jersey.

811th, 822d, 823d Engineer Aviation Battalions
Formed at Langley Field, Virginia.

827th Engineer Aviation Battalion
Formed at Savannah, Georgia.

828th, 839th Engineer Aviation Battalions
Formed at Will Rogers Field, Oklahoma. Staged at Fort Lewis, Washington.

829th, 870th Engineer Aviation Battalions
Formed at Dale Mabry Field, Florida. Staged at Camp Myles Standish, Massachusetts.

837th, 848th Engineer Aviation Battalions
Formed at Greenville, South Carolina. 848th staged at Camp Kilmer, New Jersey.

855th, 856th Engineer Aviation Battalions
Formed at March Field, California, and staged at Camp Stoneman, California.

857th, 867th Engineer Aviation Battalions
Formed at Eglin Field, Florida.

858th Engineer Aviation Battalion
Formed at Avon Park, Florida.

868th, 869th, 927th Engineer Aviation Regiments
Activated at MacDill Field, Florida.

923d Engineer Aviation Regiment
Activated at Eglin Field, Florida. 1st Battalion redesignated the 859th Engineer Aviation Battalion, 2d Battalion redesignated the 1882d, and the 3d Battalion redesignated the 1883d. Staged at Camp Kilmer, New Jersey.

929th Engineer Aviation Regiment
Activated at Davis-Monthan Field, Arizona. Staged at Camp Stoneman, California.

932d Engineer Aviation Regiment
Activated at Eglin Field, Florida.

1310th, 1311th, 1312th, 1313th, 1314th, 1315th, 1316th Engineer General Service Regiments
Activated at Camp Claiborne, Louisiana. 1310th and 1314th staged at Camp Shanks, New York. 1311th and 1312th staged at Camp Stoneman, California. 1313th staged at Camp Myles Standish, Massachusetts. 1315th transferred to Camp Sutton, North Carolina. 1316th transferred to Camp Sutton and Fort Huachuca. Staged at Fort Lawton, Washington.

1317th Engineer General Service Regiment
Activated at Camp Ellis, Illinois. Staged at Camp Shanks, New York.

1318th, 1319th, 1321st Engineer General Service Regiments
Activated at Camp Butler, North Carolina. 1318th staged at Camp Shanks, New York. 1319th staged at Vancouver Barracks, Washington. 1321st staged at Camp Myles Standish, Massachusetts.

1320th, 1322d, 1323d Engineer General Service Regiments
Activated at Camp Swift, Texas. 1320th and 1322d staged at Camp Stoneman, California. 1323d staged at Camp Myles Standish, Massachusetts.

1324th, 1325th, 1326th, 1327th, 1329th, 1330th, 1331st Engineer General Service Regiments
Redesignated as battalions at Camp Claiborne, Louisiana. 1324th, 1329th, 1330th, and 1331st staged at Camp Shanks, New York. 1325th and 1326th staged at Camp Kilmer, New Jersey. 1327th divided into units from Los Angeles and Miami Port.

1332d, 1333d Engineer General Service Regiments
Redesignated battalions at Camp Ellis, Illinois. 1332d staged at Camp Shanks, New York. 1333d departed New York.

1334th, 1553d, 1554th Engineer Construction Battalions
Not created in United States.

1349th Engineer General Service Regiment
Redesignated from 383d Engineer Battalion in England.

1749th, 2822d Engineer General Service Regiments
Activated at Fort Lewis, Washington.

317th Engineer Combat Battalion
Formed at Fort McClellan, Alabama.

318th Engineer Combat Battalion
Formed at Fort Huachuca, Arizona, and moved to Camp Stoneman, California.

1692d Engineer Combat Battalion
Formed at Camp Livingston, Louisiana.

1693d, 1694th Engineer Combat Battalions
Formed at Camp Livingston, Louisiana.

1695th Engineer Combat Battalion
Formed at Camp Pickett, Virginia.

1696th Engineer Combat Battalion
Formed at Camp Swift, Texas.

1697th Engineer Combat Battalion
Formed at Camp Van Dorn, Mississippi.

1698th Engineer Combat Battalion
Formed at Camp Gordon, Georgia.

1699th Engineer Combat Battalion
Formed at Camp Butner, North Carolina.

1700th Engineer Combat Battalion
Formed at Camp Jackson, South Carolina.

1862d, 1863d Engineer Aviation Battalions
Formed at Gulfport Army Air Field, Mississippi.

1864th, 1870th Engineer Aviation Battalions
Formed at Drew Field, Florida.

1865th Engineer Aviation Battalion
Formed at Avon Park, Florida.

1866th Engineer Aviation Battalion
Formed at Columbia Army Air Base, South Carolina.

1867th Engineer Aviation Battalion
Formed at Key Field, Mississippi.

1868th, 1871st, 1882d, 1895th, 1908th Engineer Aviation Battalions
Formed at Greenville Army Air Base, South Carolina.

1869th, 1909th Engineer Aviation Battalions
Formed at Dale Mabry Field, Florida.

1872d, 1873d, 1889th Engineer Aviation Battalions
Formed at Davis-Monthan Field, Arizona.

1883d, 1898th Engineer Aviation Battalions
Formed at Eglin Field, Florida.

1887th, 1890th Engineer Aviation Battalions
Formed at March Field, California.

1888th, 1894th, 1899th, 1916th, 1917th Engineer Aviation Battalions
Formed at MacDill Field, Florida.

6486th, 6487th, 6495th, 6496th Engineer Construction Battalions
Not created or served in the United States.

U.S. Army Air Forces

332d Fighter Group
Tuskegee Air Field, Alabama; Selfridge, Michigan; and Oscoda, Michigan. Squadrons included 99th, 100th, 301st, 302d.

477th Composite Group (Bombardment Group [Medium])
MacDill Field, Florida; Selfridge, Michigan; Godman Field, Kentucky; and Lockbourne Army Air Base, Ohio. Squadrons included 99th Fighter, 616th Bombardment, 617th Bombardment, 618th Bombardment, 619th Bombardment. (553d Fighter Squadron formed to provide replacement for the 477th; trained at Walterboro Air Field, South Carolina.)

Army Air Corps Aviation Squadrons (Separate)
In 1941, nine aviation squadrons of 250 men each serving at Langley Field, Virginia; Maxwell Field, Alabama; Daniels Field and Savannah, Georgia; Barksdale Field, Louisiana; Camp Livingston, Louisiana; Dale Mabry and MacDill Fields, Florida; and Jackson, Mississippi. As more African Americans joined, air base defense units formed. In September 1942, some 37,223 African American men and officers in the Army Air Corps. Reached peak of 145,025 in December 1943; at end of war (December 1945) numbered 69,016.

U.S. Marine Corps

Camp Montford Point, Jacksonville, North Carolina (training center).
Camp Lejeune, Onslow County, North Carolina.
Marine Corps Base, Quantico, Virginia.

U.S. Navy

Educational and Training Facilities
Great Lakes Naval Training Station, Illinois (segregated Camps Robert Smalls, Moffett, and Lawrence); Hampton Institute, Virginia (Specialized Training); Navy Technical Training Station, Memphis, Tennessee (Aviation Machinist School); Camp May, New Jersey (Soundman School); Messman School, Bainbridge, Maryland.

Construction Battalions
Camp Bradford, Norfolk, Virginia; Camp Allen, Norfolk, Virginia.

Shoremen
Large number of different facilities and stations, perhaps most significant being Port Chicago.

Officers
Great Lakes Naval Training Station, Illinois (segregated).
Women's Reserve U.S. Naval Training Station, Hunter College, New York City.

U.S. Coast Guard

Coast Guard Training Center, Manhattan Beach, New York.

References and Further Reading

Osur, Alan M. *Blacks in the Army Air Forces during World War II: The Problem of Race Relations.* Washington, D.C.: Office of Air Force History, 1977.

Smith, Steven D., Keith Krawczynski, and Robert F. Jefferson. "Victory and Context: Recognition of African American Contributions to American Military History." In *A Historic Context for the African-American Military Experience,* ed. Steven D. Smith and James A. Ziegler. https://www.denix.osd.mil/denix/Public/ES-Programs/Conservation/Legacy/AAME/aame4c.html (accessed September 18, 2003).

Stanton, Shelby L. *Order of Battle: U.S. Army, World War II.* Novato, CA: Presidio Press, 1984.

Desegregation of the Armed Forces: Chronology, 1945–1953

September 1945 Robert P. Patterson, the secretary of war, appoints a board of three general officers to investigate the U.S. Army's policy with respect to African Americans. The board is to prepare a new policy for the integrated and efficient use of African Americans. Heading the board as chairman is Gen. Alvan C. Gillem Jr. The board will become known as the Gillem Board.

October 1, 1945 The Gillem Board holds its first meeting and continues its deliberations for the next four months.

February 1946 South Carolina police officers violently attack an African American World War II veteran, Isaac Woodard, in Aitken. Woodward is blinded as a result of the attack after an argument with a bus driver.

April 1946 The Gillem Board publishes its report, *Utilization of Negro Manpower in the Postwar Army Policy.* The report recommends that the U.S. Army's future policy should "eliminate, at the earliest practicable moment, any special consideration based on race." African American commentators and activists are stunned that the board does not challenge the issue of segregation in the army. Later, Kenneth Royall, the secretary of the army, will describe the proposed policy as "equality of opportunity on the basis of segregation."

July 1946 In Monroe, Georgia, two African American veterans and their wives are dragged from their car; a white mob riddles their bodies with sixty bullets.

July 30, 1946 Attorney General Tom Clark announces that President Harry S. Truman has instructed the Justice Department to "proceed with all its resources to investigate [the atrocity in Monroe, Georgia atrocity] and other crimes of oppression so as to ascertain if any Federal statute can be applied."

September 12, 1946 President Truman writes to the National Urban League, stating that government has "an obligation to see that the civil rights of every citizen are fully and equally protected."

December 6, 1946 The President's Committee on Civil Rights is established.

May 1947 President Truman is presented with a report from the President's Advisory Commission on Universal Training. It concludes that "nothing could be more tragic for the future attitude of our people, and for the unity of our Nation, than a program [the proposed Universal Military Training program] in which our Federal Government forced our young manhood to live for a period of time in an atmosphere which emphasized or bred class or racial difference."

October 29, 1947 The President's Committee on Civil Rights issues its report, *To Secure These Rights.* The committee roundly condemns segregation, specifically in the armed forces. The report concludes with the opinion that only legislative or administrative action will be able "to end immediately all discrimination and segregation based on race, color, creed or national origin in . . . all branches of the Armed Services."

November 1947 President Truman receives a memorandum from Clark Clifford, special counsel to the president (1946–1950), stating his opinion that the president, in order to win the 1948 presidential election, will have to focus on civil rights and the issues affecting African Americans in particular.

November 1947 The Committee Against Jim Crow in Military Service and Training is established by union and civil rights leader A. Philip Randolph and black New York Republican Grant Reynolds.

January 1948 After considering his options, President Truman determines that segregation in the armed forces and the civil service can only be ended by administrative action in the form of an executive order, rather than through the legislative process.

February 2, 1948 President Truman tells Congress that he has given instructions to the secretary of defense to end discrimination in the armed forces as soon as is practicable.

March 22, 1948 President Truman has a meeting with leading African Americans who try to convince him to insist on desegregation amendments to legislation being considered in Congress regarding the reintroduction of the draft.

March 27, 1948 The "Declaration of Negro Voters" is issued by twenty African American organizations meeting in New York. The declaration demands "that every vestige of segregation and discrimination in the armed forces be forthwith abolished."

March 30, 1948 As the representative of the Committee Against Jim Crow in Military Service and Training, Randolph testifies before the Senate Armed Services Committee. He contends that African Americans will refuse to serve in the armed forces if legislation does not end segregation.

April 26, 1948 A delegation of some sixteen African American leaders informs James V. Forrestal, the secretary of defense, that African Americans are likely to react very aggressively if segregation is not outlawed in the armed forces.

May 1948 President Truman's staff considers advising him that it may be prudent to establish a committee to oversee the integration program in the armed forces.

June 25, 1948 The creation of the League for Nonviolent Civil Disobedience Against Military Segregation is announced by Randolph.

June 29, 1948 Randolph tells President Truman that unless he issues an executive order to end segregation in the armed forces, it is probable that African Americans will seek to resist the draft.

July 13, 1948 Minneapolis mayor Hubert H. Humphrey, a member of the platform committee at the Democratic National Convention, proposes that the party call for the abolition of segregation in the armed forces. The proposal is rejected, despite the support of President Truman and his advisors. A more moderate stance is adopted in order not to alienate the Southern delegates and supporters.

July 14, 1948 Much to the astonishment of the Democratic Party leadership, delegates at the Democratic National Convention overwhelmingly vote to overrule the platform committee and the Truman administration's moderate approach. They vote for a more liberal policy that incorporates the desegregation of the armed forces. President Truman's staff works on drafting an executive order to end segregation, while the president decides to follow the suggestion of his advisors and set up a committee to oversee the desegregation program in the armed forces.

July 26, 1948 President Truman signs Executive Order 9981, which states: "It is hereby declared to be the policy of the President that there shall be equality of treatment and opportunity for all persons in the armed services without regard to race, color, religion, or national origin." The order establishes the President's Committee on Equality of Treatment and Opportunity in the Armed Services as the overseeing body to monitor the implementation of the desegregation program.

July 26, 1948 Due to the ambiguity of the executive order, some army staff officers leak to the press that they do not consider that 9981 forbids segregation.

July 27, 1948 Gen. Omar N. Bradley, the U.S. Army Chief of Staff, states that in his opinion a desegregated army will only come into existence when American society is no longer segregated itself.

July 29, 1948 President Truman is forced to make it clear at a press conference that Executive Order 9981's primary purpose is to end segregation in the armed forces.

August 2, 1948 Randolph and other representatives of the League for Nonviolent Civil Disobedience Against Military Segregation meet with J. Howard McGrath, the chairman of the Democratic National Committee. McGrath assures them that the President's Committee on Equality of Treatment and Opportunity in the Armed Services will end segregation in the armed forces as intended by Executive Order 9981. Convinced of his sincerity and give reassurances, Randolph and the other representatives issue a statement ending the organization's civil disobedience campaign.

August 14, 1948 Secretary of the Army Royall admits to the press that "segregation in the Army must go." He is not convinced that it will happen immediately.

September 18, 1948 The members of the President's Committee on Equality of Treatment and Opportunity in the Armed Services are announced by the White House. The chairman is Charles Fahy and subsequently the committee is known as the Fahy Committee. The body will have five members, two of whom are African American.

October 9, 1948 Preemptively, the U.S. Navy announces that it will be continuing and extending its policy of integration that it began in the last few months of World War II.

December 1948 James V. Forrestal, secretary of defense, receives a proposal from Kenneth Royall, the secretary of the army, that an experimental integrated unit be established in the U.S. Army. In this way, the army could assess the process and effects of integration. Stuart Symington, the secretary of the air force, presents President Truman with an integration plan for the U.S. Air Force. It proposes to assign African Americans to units on the basis of merit and not on the basis of color or creed.

January 12, 1949 President Truman has his first meeting with the Fahy Committee. Also present are the secretaries of the army, navy, air force, and defense. Truman states to them all that: "I want the job done and I want it done in a way so that everyone will be happy to cooperate to get it done."

January 13, 1949 Representatives of the armed services are called to the first of the hearings set up by the Fahy Committee. Secretary of the Army Kenneth Royall defends the U.S. Army's segregation policy; the U.S. Marine Corps follows suit and admits that only one 1 of its 8,200 officers is African American. Secretary of the Navy John L. Sullivan admits that only 5 of their 45,000 officers are African American, but states that the navy is committed to a policy of integration. Secretary of the Air Force Stuart Symington also agrees to institute a policy of desegregation.

January 22, 1949 The U.S. Air Force prematurely announces to the press that it has completed its plans for a desegregated service.

March 28, 1949 The Fahy Committee calls the secretaries of the three services—army, navy, and air force—to testify. Stuart Symington (air force) and John L. Sullivan (navy) testify that they are opposed to segregation in their services and confirm that policies are in place or are being developed to achieve integration. Kenneth Royall (Army) testifies that he wishes to maintain a segregated service and further states that the U.S. Army is "not an instrument for social evolution."

April 1, 1949 Secretary of Defense Louis Johnson issues directives to Symington, Sullivan, and Royall clearly stating his department's commitment to equality of opportunity and employment in the armed services. He tells them "qualified Negro personnel shall be assigned to fill any type of position . . . without regard to race."

May 11, 1949 Secretary of Defense Louis Johnson decides to approve the U.S. Air Force's integration plan but flatly rejects those proposed by Sullivan and Royall for the U.S. Navy and U.S. Army, respectively. The Fahy Committee makes additional recommendations to the U.S. Army and U.S. Navy, among which are the recommendations that the army end its 10 percent African American enlistment quota and that it desegregate all of its units.

June 7, 1949 The revised U.S. Navy integration plan is accepted by Louis Johnson, secretary of defense. The U.S. Army revised army plan is rejected once more and Johnson makes a formal statement to the U.S. Army insisting that it incorporates the recommendations of the Fahy Committee before he approves the plan.

July 5, 1949 Gordon Gray, the new secretary of the army, and Army Chief of Staff General Omar N.

Bradley make the formal presentation of the revised U.S. Army plan to the Fahy Committee. The U.S. Army still proposes to maintain segregation and the 10 percent African American recruitment quota.

July 25 and 27, 1949 Speaking as the representative of the Fahy Committee, Charles Fahy tells President Truman, Secretary of Defense Louis Johnson, and Secretary of the Army Gordon Gray that the U.S. Army plan for integration will not be accepted until the army embraces the spirit of Executive Order 9981.

August–September, 1949 Fruitless discussions continue between the Fahy Committee and representatives of the U.S. Army to resolve the disparity between the army's integration plan and those of the other two services.

September 27, 1949 The U.S. Army sends a copy of their revised plan to Louis Johnson, the secretary of defense. The Fahy Committee is apprised of the dispatch, but does not receive a copy of its own.

September 30, 1949 Louis Johnson approves the revised U.S. Army plan, which still incorporates the maintaining of segregated units and the 10 percent African American enlistment quota.

October 6, 1949 For public relations purposes, President Truman announces to the press that the U.S. Army plan is a "a progress report" and not a completed and approved document. He reaffirms his commitment to ensuring that the U.S. Army follows the lead of the other two services and ends segregation.

October 11, 1949 President Truman receives a letter from Charles Fahy stating that the revised U.S. Army plan would not end segregation in the service.

November 1949 The U.S. Army again revises its integration plan, which still includes segregated units and the 10 percent recruitment quota. The Fahy Committee warns the U.S. Army that it has no hope of having the plan approved and that it is the intention of the committee to release a statement to the press roundly condemning the plan.

December 1949 President Truman and the White House request the Fahy Committee not to issue the a condemnation of the U.S. Army plan to the press. Instead, they ask that the Fahy Committee reissue recommendations to the U.S. Army with advice as to steps needed to modify the plan to achieve the goal of approval.

December 15, 1949 The White House is presented with the Fahy Committee's recommendations and suggested modifications to the U.S. Army integration plan. The Fahy Committee stands by the phasing out of segregation and the termination of the recruitment quota.

December 27, 1949 Secretary of the Army Gordon Gray and Charles Fahy meet and discuss the issue. Gray concedes on the point of segregated units, but reserves the right to institute this as a rolling program over a period of time.

January 14, 1950 The U.S. Army's integration plan is finally approved by the Fahy Committee. The question of the 10 percent African American recruitment quota remains an issue to be dealt with at a later date.

January 16, 1950 President Truman is apprised of the approval of the U.S. Army's integration plan by the Fahy Committee. The plan is officially issued as Special Regulations No. 600-629-1 by the U.S. Army.

February 1, 1950 The continuing operation of the Fahy Committee is approved by President Truman until the U.S. Army formally accepts the abolition of the 10 percent recruitment quota for African American enlistments.

March 1, 1950 Secretary of the Army Gordon Gray discusses the matter of the 10 percent recruitment quota with President Truman. He tells the president that as he understands it, the U.S. Army will abolish the 10 percent recruitment quota, but that if there is a larger than 10 percent influx of African Americans into the U.S. Army, the president has already stated that the U.S. Army would have the right to reinstate the quota. He bases his assumptions on the long discussions held over the past several months with the president on this issue.

March 13, 1950 Seemingly reassured by President Truman's conversation with Gordon Gray, the U.S. Army agrees to abolish its 10 percent recruitment quota for African Americans. The change of policy will come into effect in April 1950.

March 27, 1950 President Truman thanks Gordon

Gray for the change of policy and tells him: "I am sure everything will work out as it should."

May 22, 1950 *Freedom to Serve,* the last report of the Fahy Committee, is published and submitted to President Truman. In thanking the committee, the president expresses hopes that the recommendations are carried out and "within the reasonably near future, equality of treatment and opportunity for all persons within the armed services would be accomplished." With this, the Fahy Committee effectively completes its work.

June 1950 The U.S. Army encounters severe difficulties as it tries to predict the levels of recruitment for African Americans. Training camps are told, unofficially, that training should be integrated. Meanwhile, in Korea, the problem of replacing white casualties in combat units and the sudden influx of African American recruits speeds up the integration process as African American replacements are assigned to previously segregated, white-only units.

July 6, 1950 President Truman officially winds up the operations of the Fahy Committee, despite the fact that members of the committee feel that there is still work to be done in monitoring the implementation of the integration plans in the three services. President Truman writes: "The necessary programs having been adopted, I feel that the Armed Services should now have an opportunity to work out in detail the procedures which will complete the steps so carefully initiated by the Committee."

January 1951 In Korea, the Eighth Army unofficially adopts the policy of integrating African Americans into white-only units once the all–African American units have reached official combat strength.

March 18, 1951 The Department of Defense announces that all basic training in the armed services will be integrated from this point onward.

April 1951 The commander of the United Nations Command in Korea, Gen. Matthew B. Ridgway, requests that the U.S. Army approve the integration of African Americans into all units under his command.

July 26, 1951 The army approves Ridgway's request and makes an announcement that within six months all units assigned to Japan, Korea, and Okinawa will be integrated.

October 1953 The U.S. Army makes an official announcement that 95 percent of African Americans serving in the army are now in fully integrated units.

References and Further Reading

Dalfiume, Richard M. *Desegregation of the U.S. Armed Forces, Fighting on Two Fronts, 1939–1953.* Columbia: University of Missouri Press, 1969.

MacGregor, Morris J., Jr. *Integration of the Armed Forces 1940–1965.* Washington, DC: Center of Military History, United States Army, 1989.

Medal of Honor

The congressional bill establishing the U.S. Navy Medal of Honor as being awarded to noncommissioned officers and enlisted men of the navy and Marine Corps for "extraordinary bravery" was approved by President Abraham Lincoln on December 21, 1861. On July 12, 1862, he approved the joint resolution of Congress that authorized the preparation of 2,000 Medals of Honor to be presented to noncommissioned officers and privates of the army and volunteer forces for "gallantry in action" and other "soldier-like qualities." Originally the U.S. Army was not included, as General Winfield Scott, then commander in chief of the Union Army, thought it inappropriate. Shortly after, however, it was extended to the army and became the standard decoration in 1863.

On April 16, 1864, General Order 32, Navy Department, announced the first Medal of Honor ever awarded to a black enlisted man of the U.S. Navy. It was not until April 6, 1865, that black privates and noncommissioned officers of the United States Colored Troops were awarded the Medal of Honor.

Civil War (1861–1865)

Anderson, Bruce
Rank and Unit Private, Company K, 142d New York Infantry
Born June 19, 1845; Mexico, Oswego County, New York
Entered Service Albany/Ephratah, New York
Place and Date of Award Fort Fisher, North Carolina; January 15, 1865
Date of Issue December 28, 1914 (posthumously)
Citation Voluntarily advanced with the head of the column and cut down the palisading.

Barnes, William Henry
Rank and Unit Private, Company C, 38th United States Colored Troops
Born 1845; St. Mary's County, Maryland
Entered Service Norfolk, Virginia
Place and Date of Award Chaffin's Farm, Virginia; September 29, 1864
Date of Issue April 6, 1865
Citation Among the first to enter the enemy's works; although wounded.

Beaty, Powhatan
Rank and Unit First Sergeant, Company G, 5th United States Colored Troops
Born October 8, 1837; Richmond, Virginia
Entered Service Cincinnati/Delaware County, Ohio
Place and Date of Award Chaffin's Farm, Virginia; September 29, 1864
Date of Issue April 6, 1865
Citation Took command of his company, all the officers having been killed or wounded, and gallantly led it.

Blake, Robert
Rank and Unit Contraband, U.S. Navy
Born Virginia
Entered Service Port Royal, Virginia
Place and Date of Award Onboard the steam gunboat USS *Marblehead* off Legareville, Stono River, in an engagement with the enemy on John's Island; December 25, 1863
Date of Issue April 16, 1864
Citation Serving the rifle gun, Blake, an escaped slave, carried out his duties bravely throughout the engagement which resulted in the enemy's abandonment of positions, leaving a caisson and one gun behind.

Bronson, James H.
Rank and Unit First Sergeant, Company D, 5th United States Colored Troops
Born 1838; Indiana County, Pennsylvania
Entered Service Trumbull County/Delaware County, Ohio
Place and Date of Award Chaffin's Farm, Virginia; September 29, 1864
Date of Issue April 6, 1865
Citation Took command of his company, all the officers having been killed or wounded, and gallantly led it.

Brown, William H.
Rank and Unit Landsman, U.S. Navy
Born 1836; Baltimore, Maryland
Entered Service Maryland
Place and Date of Award Onboard the USS *Brooklyn* during successful attacks against Fort Morgan, rebel gunboats, and the ram CSS *Tennessee* in Mobile Bay; August 5, 1864
Date of Issue December 31, 1864
Citation Stationed in the immediate vicinity of the shell whips which were twice cleared of men by bursting shells, Brown remained steadfast at his post and performed his duties in the powder division throughout the furious action which resulted in the surrender of the prize rebel ram *Tennessee* and in the damaging and destruction of batteries at Fort Morgan.

Brown, Wilson
Rank and Unit Landsman, U.S. Navy
Born 1841; Natchez, Mississippi
Entered Service Mississippi River, Mississippi
Place and Date of Award Onboard the flagship USS *Hartford* during successful attacks against Fort Morgan, rebel gunboats, and the ram CSS *Tennessee* in Mobile Bay; August 5, 1864
Date of Issue December 31, 1864
Citation Knocked unconscious into the hold of the ship when an enemy shell burst fatally wounded a man on the ladder above him, Brown, upon regaining consciousness, promptly returned to the shell whip on the berth deck and zealously continued to perform his duties although 4 of the 6 men at this station had been either killed or wounded by the enemy's terrific fire.

Carney, William Harvey
Rank and Unit Sergeant, Company C, 54th Massachusetts Infantry
Born February 29, 1840; Norfolk, Virginia
Entered Service New Bedford, Massachusetts
Place and Date of Award Fort Wagner, South Carolina; July 18, 1863
Date of Issue May 23, 1900
Citation When the color sergeant was shot down, this soldier grasped the flag, led the way to the parapet, and planted the colors thereon. When the troops fell back he brought off the flag, under a fierce fire in which he was twice severely wounded.

Dorsey, Decatur
Rank and Unit Sergeant, Company B, 39th United States Colored Troops
Born 1836; Howard County, Maryland
Entered Service Baltimore County, Maryland
Place and Date of Award Petersburg, Virginia; July 30, 1864
Date of Issue November 8, 1865
Citation Planted his colors on the Confederate works in advance of his regiment, and when the regiment was driven back to the Union works he carried the colors there and bravely rallied the men.

Fleetwood, Christian A.
Rank and Unit Sergeant Major, 4th United States Colored Troops
Born July 21, 1840; Baltimore, Maryland
Entered Service Baltimore, Maryland
Place and Date of Award Chaffin's Farm, Virginia; September 29, 1864
Date of Issue April 6, 1865
Citation Seized the colors, after 2 color bearers had been shot down, and bore them nobly through the fight.

Gardiner, James (Gardner, James Daniel)
Rank and Unit Private, Company I, 36th United States Colored Troops
Born September 16, 1839; Gloucester, Virginia
Entered Service Yorktown, Virginia
Place and Date of Award Chaffin's Farm, Virginia; September 29, 1864
Date of Issue April 6, 1865

Citation Rushed in advance of his brigade, shot a rebel officer who was on the parapet rallying his men, and then ran him through with his bayonet.

Harris, James H.
Rank and Unit Sergeant, Company B, 38th United States Colored Troops
Born 1828; St. Mary's County, Maryland
Entered Service Great Mills, Maryland
Place and Date of Award New Market Heights, Virginia; September 29, 1864
Date of Issue February 18, 1874
Citation Gallantry in the assault.

Hawkins, Thomas R.
Rank and Unit Sergeant Major, 6th United States Colored Troops
Born 1840; Cincinnati, Ohio
Entered Service Philadelphia, Pennsylvania
Place and Date of Award Chaffin's Farm, Virginia; September 29, 1864
Date of Issue February 8, 1870
Citation Rescue of regimental colors.

Hilton, Alfred B.
Rank and Unit Sergeant, Company H, 4th United States Colored Troops
Born 1842; Harford County, Maryland
Entered Service Baltimore, Maryland
Place and Date of Award Chaffin's Farm, Virginia; September 29, 1864
Date of Issue April 6, 1865 (posthumously)
Citation When the regimental color bearer fell, this soldier seized the color and carried it forward, together with the national standard, until disabled at the enemy's inner line.

Holland, Milton Murray
Rank and Unit Sergeant Major, 5th United States Colored Troops
Born August 1, 1844; Austin, Texas
Entered Service Athens/Albany, Ohio
Place and Date of Award Chaffin's Farm, Virginia; September 29, 1864
Date of Issue April 6, 1865
Citation Took command of Company C, after all the officers had been killed or wounded, and gallantly led it.

James, Miles
Rank and Unit Corporal, Company B, 36th United States Colored Troops
Born 1829; Princess Anne County, Virginia
Entered Service Portsmouth/Norfolk, Virginia
Place and Date of Award Chaffin's Farm, Virginia; September 30, 1864
Date of Issue April 6, 1865
Citation Having had his arm mutilated, making immediate amputation necessary, he loaded and discharged his piece with one hand and urged his men forward; this within 30 yards of the enemy's works.

Kelly, Alexander
Rank and Unit First Sergeant, Company F, 6th United States Colored Troops
Born April 7, 1840; Pennsylvania
Entered Service Allegheny, Pennsylvania
Place and Date of Award Chaffin's Farm, Virginia; September 29, 1864
Date of Issue April 6, 1865
Citation Gallantly seized the colors, which had fallen near the enemy's lines of abatis, raised them and rallied the men at a time of confusion and in a place of the greatest danger.

Lawson, John
Rank and Unit Landsman, U.S. Navy
Born June 16, 1837; Philadelphia, Pennsylvania
Entered Service Pennsylvania
Place and Date of Award Onboard the flagship USS *Hartford* during successful attacks against Fort Morgan, rebel gunboats, and the ram CSS *Tennessee* in Mobile Bay; August 5, 1864
Date of Issue December 31, 1864
Citation Wounded in the leg and thrown violently against the side of the ship when an enemy shell killed or wounded the 6-man crew as the shell whipped on the berth deck, Lawson, upon regaining his composure, promptly returned to his station and, although urged to go below for treatment, steadfastly continued his duties throughout the remainder of the action.

Mifflin, James
Rank and Unit Engineer's Cook, U.S. Navy
Born 1839; Richmond, Virginia

Entered Service Virginia
Place and Date of Award Onboard the USS *Brooklyn* during successful attacks against Fort Morgan, rebel gunboats, and the ram CSS *Tennessee* in Mobile Bay; August 5, 1864
Date of Issue December 31, 1864
Citation Stationed in the immediate vicinity of the shell whips which were twice cleared of men by bursting shells, Mifflin remained steadfast at his post and performed his duties in the powder division throughout the furious action which resulted in the surrender of the prize rebel ram *Tennessee* and in the damaging and destruction of batteries at Fort Morgan.

Pease, Joachim
Rank and Unit Seaman, U.S. Navy
Born 1842; Long Island, New York
Entered Service New York
Place and Date of Award Onboard the USS *Kearsarge* when she destroyed the CSS *Alabama* off Cherbourg, France; June 19, 1864
Date of Issue December 31, 1864
Citation Acting as loader on the No. 2 gun during this bitter engagement, Pease exhibited marked coolness and good conduct and was highly recommended by the divisional officer for gallantry under fire.

Pinn, Robert A.
Rank and Unit First Sergeant, Company I, 5th United States Colored Troops
Born March 1, 1843; Stark County, Ohio
Entered Service Massillon, Ohio
Place and Date of Award Chaffin's Farm, Virginia; September 29, 1864
Date of Issue April 6, 1865
Citation Took command of his company after all the officers had been killed or wounded and gallantly led it in battle.

Ratcliff, Edward
Rank and Unit First Sergeant, Company C, 38th United States Colored Troops
Born February 8, 1835; James County, Virginia
Entered Service Yorktown, Virginia
Place and Date of Award Chaffin's Farm, Virginia; September 29, 1864
Date of Issue April 6, 1865
Citation Commanded and gallantly led his company after the commanding officer had been killed; was the first enlisted man to enter the enemy's works.

Sanderson, Aaron (Anderson Aaron)
Rank and Unit Landsman, U.S. Navy
Born 1811; North Carolina
Entered Service Philadelphia, Pennsylvania
Place and Date of Award Onboard the USS *Wyandank* at Mattox Creek, Virginia; March 17, 1865
Date of Issue June 22, 1865
Citation Participating with a boat crew in the clearing of Mattox Creek, L/man Anderson carried out his duties courageously in the face of a devastating fire which cut away half the oars, pierced the launch in many places and cut the barrel off a musket being fired at the enemy.

Smith, Andrew Jackson
Rank and Unit Corporal, 55th Massachusetts Infantry
Born September 3, 1842; Grand Rivers, Kentucky
Entered Service Clinton, Illinois
Place and Date of Award Honey Hill, South Carolina; November 30, 1864
Date of Issue January 16, 2001 (posthumously)
Citation For conspicuous gallantry and intrepidity at the risk of his life above and beyond the call of duty.

Veal, Charles (Veale, Charles)
Rank and Unit Private, Company D, 4th United States Colored Troops
Born 1838; Portsmouth, Virginia
Entered Service Baltimore, Maryland
Place and Date of Award Chaffin's Farm, Virginia; September 29, 1864
Date of Issue April 6, 1865
Citation Seized the national colors after 2 color bearers had been shot down close to the enemy's works, and bore them through the remainder of the battle.

Indian Wars (1861–1898)

Boyne, Thomas
Rank and Unit Sergeant, Company C, 9th U.S. Cavalry
Born 1849; Prince Georges County, Maryland
Entered Service Norfolk, Virginia

Place and Date of Award Mimbres Mountains, New Mexico; May 29, 1879; and Cuchillo Negro River near Ojo Caliente, New Mexico; September 27, 1879
Date of Issue January 6, 1882
Citation Bravery in action.

Brown, Benjamin
Rank and Unit Sergeant, Company C, 24th U.S. Infantry
Born 1859; Spotsylvania County, Virginia
Entered Service Harrisburg, Pennsylvania
Place and Date of Award Arizona; May 11, 1889
Date of Issue February 19, 1890
Citation Although shot in the abdomen, in a fight between a paymaster's escort and robbers, did not leave the field until again wounded through both arms.

Denny, John
Rank and Unit Sergeant, Company C, 9th U.S. Cavalry
Born Big Flats, New York
Entered Service 1867; Elmira, New York
Place and Date of Award Las Animas Canyon, New Mexico; September 18, 1879
Date of Issue November 27, 1891
Citation Removed a wounded comrade, under a heavy fire, to a place of safety.

Factor, Pompey
Rank and Unit Private, Indian Scouts
Born 1849; Arkansas
Entered Service Fort Duncan, Texas
Place and Date of Award Pecos River, Texas; April 25, 1875
Date of Issue May 28, 1875
Citation With 3 other men, he participated in a charge against 25 hostiles while on a scouting patrol.

Greaves, Clinton
Rank and Unit Corporal, Company C, 9th U.S. Cavalry
Born August 12, 1855; Madison County, Virginia
Entered Service Prince Georges County, Maryland
Place and Date of Award Florida Mountains, New Mexico; January 24, 1877
Date of Issue June 26, 1879
Citation While part of a small detachment to persuade a band of renegade Apache Indians to surrender, his group was surrounded. Cpl. Greaves in the center of the savage hand-to-hand fighting, managed to shoot and bash a gap through the swarming Apaches, permitting his companions to break free.

Johnson, Henry
Rank and Unit Sergeant, Company D, 9th U.S. Cavalry
Born June 11, 1850; Boynton, Virginia
Entered Service Detroit, Michigan
Place and Date of Award Milk River, Colorado; October 2–5, 1879
Date of Issue September 22, 1890
Citation Voluntarily left fortified shelter and under heavy fire at close range made the rounds of the pits to instruct the guards, fought his way to the creek and back to bring water to the wounded.

Jordan, George
Rank and Unit Sergeant, Company K, 9th U.S. Cavalry
Born 1847; Williamson County, Tennessee
Entered Service Nashville, Tennessee
Place and Date of Award Fort Tularosa, New Mexico; May 14, 1880; and Carrizo Canyon, New Mexico; August 12, 1881
Date of Issue May 7, 1890
Citation While commanding a detachment of 25 men at Fort Tularosa, N. Mex., repulsed a force of more than 100 Indians. At Carrizo Canyon, N. Mex., while commanding the right of a detachment of 19 men, on 12 August 1881, he stubbornly held his ground in an extremely exposed position and gallantly forced back a much superior number of the enemy, preventing them from surrounding the command.

Mays, Isaiah
Rank and Unit Corporal, Company B, 24th U.S. Infantry
Born February 16, 1858; Carters Bridge, Virginia
Entered Service Columbus Barracks, Ohio
Place and Date of Award Arizona; May 11, 1889
Date of Issue February 19, 1890
Citation Gallantry in the fight between Paymaster Wham's escort and robbers. Mays walked and crawled 2 miles to a ranch for help.

McBryar, William
Rank and Unit Sergeant, Company K, 10th U.S. Cavalry
Born February 14, 1861; Elizabethtown, North Carolina
Entered Service New York
Place and Date of Award Arizona; March 7, 1890
Date of Issue May 15, 1890
Citation Distinguished himself for coolness, bravery and marksmanship while his troop was in pursuit of hostile Apache Indians.

Paine, Adam (Payne, Adan)
Rank and Unit Private, Indian Scouts
Born 1843; Florida
Entered Service Fort Duncan, Texas
Place and Date of Award Canyon Blanco tributary of the Red River, Texas; September 26–27, 1874
Date of Issue October 13, 1875
Citation Rendered invaluable service to Col. R. S. Mackenzie, 4th U.S. Cavalry, during this engagement.

Payne, Isaac
Rank and Unit Trumpeter, Indian Scouts
Born 1854; Mexico
Entered Service Fort Duncan, Texas
Place and Date of Award Pecos River, Texas; April 25, 1875
Date of Issue May 28, 1875
Citation With 3 other men, he participated in a charge against 25 hostiles while on a scouting patrol.

Shaw, Thomas
Rank and Unit Sergeant, Company K, 9th U.S. Cavalry
Born 1846; Covington, Kentucky
Entered Service Baton Rouge, Louisiana
Place and Date of Award Carrizo Canyon, New Mexico; August 12, 1881
Date of Issue December 7, 1890
Citation Forced the enemy back after stubbornly holding his ground in an extremely exposed position and prevented the enemy's superior numbers from surrounding his command.

Stance, Emanuel
Rank and Unit Sergeant, Company F, 9th U.S. Cavalry
Born 1843; Carroll Parish, Louisiana
Entered Service East Carroll Parish, Louisiana
Place and Date of Award Kickapoo Springs, Texas; May 20, 1870
Date of Issue June 28, 1870
Citation Gallantry on scout after Indians.

Walley, Augustus
Rank and Unit Private, Company I, 9th U.S. Cavalry
Born March 10, 1868; Reistertown, Maryland
Entered Service Baltimore, Maryland
Place and Date of Award Cuchillo Negro Mountains, New Mexico; August 16, 1881
Date of Issue October 1, 1890
Citation Bravery in action with hostile Apaches.

Ward, John (Warrior, John)
Rank and Unit Sergeant, 24th U.S. Infantry Indian Scouts
Born 1847; Arkansas
Entered Service Fort Duncan, Texas
Place and Date of Award Pecos River, Texas; April 25, 1875
Date of Issue May 28, 1875
Citation With 3 other men, he participated in a charge against 25 hostiles while on a scouting patrol.

Williams, Moses
Rank and Unit First Sergeant, Company I, 9th U.S. Cavalry
Born 1845; Carrollton, Louisiana
Entered Service East Carroll Parish, Louisiana
Place and Date of Award Cuchillo Negro Mountains, New Mexico; August 16, 1881
Date of Issue November 12, 1896
Citation Rallied a detachment, skillfully conducted a running fight of 3 or 4 hours, and by his coolness, bravery, and unflinching devotion to duty in standing by his commanding officer in an exposed position under a heavy fire from a large party of Indians saved the lives of at least 3 of his comrades.

Wilson, William
Rank and Unit Sergeant, Company I, 4th U.S. Cavalry
Born Philadelphia, Pennsylvania
Entered Service Philadelphia, Pennsylvania

Place and Date of Award Colorado Valley, Texas; March 28, 1872; and Red River, Texas; September 29, 1872
Date of Issue April 27, 1872
Citation In pursuit of a band of cattle thieves from New Mexico. Distinguished conduct in action with Indians, Red River, Tex.

Wilson, William O.
Rank and Unit Corporal, Company I, 9th U.S. Infantry
Born 1867; Hagerstown, Maryland
Entered Service St. Paul, Maine
Place and Date of Award Sioux campaign; 1890
Date of Issue September 17, 1891
Citation Bravery.

Woods, Brent
Rank and Unit Sergeant, Company B, 9th U.S. Cavalry
Born 1850; Pulaski County, Kentucky
Entered Service Louisville, Kentucky
Place and Date of Award New Mexico, August 19, 1881
Date of Issue July 12, 1894
Citation Saved the lives of his comrades and citizens of the detachment.

Interim Period (1871–1898)

Atkins, Daniel
Rank and Unit Ship's Cook, First Class, U.S. Navy
Born 1867; Brunswick, Virginia
Entered Service Virginia
Place and Date of Award Onboard the USS *Cushing,* February 11, 1898
Date of Issue May 20, 1898
Citation Showing gallant conduct, Atkins attempted to save the life of the late Ens. Joseph C. Breckenridge, U.S. Navy, who fell overboard at sea from that vessel on this date.

Davis, John
Rank and Unit Ordinary Seaman, U.S. Navy
Born 1854; Kingston, Jamaica
Entered Service N.A.
Place and Date of Award Onboard the USS *Trenton,* Toulon, France; February 1881
Date of Issue October 18, 1884
Citation Jumping overboard, Davis rescued Augustus Ohlensen, coxswain, from drowning.

Johnson, John
Rank and Unit Seaman, U.S. Navy
Born 1839; Philadelphia, Pennsylvania
Entered Service Pennsylvania
Place and Date of Award Serving onboard the USS *Kansas* near Greytown, Nicaragua; April 12, 1872
Date of Issue July 9, 1872
Citation Johnson displayed great coolness and self-possession at the time Comdr. A. F. Crosman and others were drowned and, by extraordinary heroism and personal exertion, prevented greater loss of life.

Johnson, William
Rank and Unit Cooper, U.S. Navy
Born 1855; St. Vincent, West Indies
Entered Service New York
Place and Date of Award Serving onboard the USS *Adams* at the Navy Yard, Mare Island, California; November 14, 1879
Date of Issue October 18, 1884
Citation Johnson rescued Daniel W. Kloppen, a workman, from drowning.

Noil, Joseph B.
Rank and Unit Seaman, U.S. Navy
Born 1841; Nova Scotia, Canada
Entered Service New York
Place and Date of Award Serving onboard the USS *Powhatan* at Norfolk; December 26, 1872
Date of Issue N.A.
Citation Noil saved Boatswain J. C. Walton from drowning.

Smith, John
Rank and Unit Seaman, U.S. Navy
Born 1854; Bermuda
Entered Service New York
Place and Date of Award Serving onboard the USS *Shenandoah,* at Rio de Janeiro, Brazil; September 19, 1880
Date of Issue September 19, 1880
Citation For jumping overboard from the U.S.S. *Shenandoah,* at Rio de Janeiro, Brazil, 19 September 1880, and rescuing from drowning James Grady, first class fireman.

Sweeney, Robert Augustus
Rank and Unit Ordinary Seaman, U.S. Navy
Born February 20, 1853; Montreal, Canada
Entered Service New Jersey
Place and Date of Award Serving onboard the USS *Kearsage,* at Hampton Roads, Virginia; October 26, 1881
Date of Issue October 18, 1884
Citation Serving on board the U.S.S. *Kearsarge,* at Hampton Roads, Va., 26 October 1881, Sweeney jumped overboard and assisted in saving from drowning a shipmate who had fallen overboard into a strongly running tide.

Spanish-American War (1898)

Baker, Edward Lee, Jr.
Rank and Unit Sergeant Major, 10th U.S. Cavalry
Born Laramie County, Wyoming
Entered Service Cincinnati, Ohio
Place and Date of Award Santiago, Cuba; July 1, 1898
Date of Issue July 3, 1902
Citation Left cover and, under fire, rescued a wounded comrade from drowning.

Bell, Dennis
Rank and Unit Private, Troop H, 10th U.S. Cavalry
Born December 28, 1866; Washington, D.C.
Entered Service Washington, D.C.
Place and Date of Award Tayabacoa, Cuba; June 30, 1898
Date of Issue June 23, 1899
Citation Voluntarily went ashore in the face of the enemy and aided in the rescue of his wounded comrades; this after several previous attempts at rescue had been frustrated.

Lee, Fitz
Rank and Unit Private, Troop M, 10th U.S. Cavalry
Born June 1866; Dinwiddie County, Virginia
Entered Service Philadelphia, Pennsylvania
Place and Date of Award Tayabacoa, Cuba; June 30, 1898
Date of Issue June 23, 1899
Citation Voluntarily went ashore in the face of the enemy and aided in the rescue of his wounded comrades; this after several previous attempts had been frustrated.

Penn, Robert
Rank and Unit Fireman, First Class, U.S. Navy
Born October 10, 1872; City Point, Virginia
Entered Service Virginia
Place and Date of Award Serving onboard the USS *Iowa* at Santiago de Cuba, Cuba; July 20, 1898
Date of Issue December 14, 1898
Citation On board the U.S.S. *Iowa* off Santiago de Cuba, 20 July 1898. Performing his duty at the risk of serious scalding at the time of the blowing out of the manhole gasket on board the vessel, Penn halted the fire while standing on a board thrown across a coal bucket 1 foot above the boiling water which was still blowing from the boiler.

Thompkins, William H.
Rank and Unit Private, Troop G, 10th U.S. Cavalry
Born October 3, 1872; Paterson, New Jersey
Entered Service Paterson, New Jersey
Place and Date of Award Tayabacoa, Cuba; June 30, 1898
Date of Issue June 23, 1899
Citation Voluntarily went ashore in the face of the enemy and aided in the rescue of his wounded comrades; this after several previous attempts at rescue had been frustrated.

Wanton, George Henry
Rank and Unit Private, Troop M, 10th U.S. Cavalry
Born May 15, 1868; Paterson, New Jersey
Entered Service Paterson, New Jersey
Place and Date of Award Tayabacoa, Cuba; June 30, 1898
Date of Issue June 23, 1899
Citation Voluntarily went ashore in the face of the enemy and aided in the rescue of his wounded comrades; this after several previous attempts at rescue had been frustrated.

Girandy, Alphonse
Rank and Unit Seaman, U.S. Navy
Born January 21, 1868; Guadeloupe, West Indies
Entered Service Pennsylvania
Place and Date of Award Serving on board the USS *Petrel* at sea, March 31, 1901
Date of Issue March 22, 1902
Citation Serving on board the U.S.S. *Petrel,* for heroism and gallantry, fearlessly exposing his own life to danger for the saving of others, on the oc-

casion of the fire on board that vessel, 31 March 1901.

World War I (1914–1918)

Stowers, Freddie

Rank and Unit Corporal, Company C, 371st Infantry Regiment, 93d Infantry Division

Born 1896; Sandy Springs, Anderson County, South Carolina

Entered Service Anderson County, South Carolina

Place and Date of Award Hill 188, Champagne Marne Sector, France; September 28, 1918

Date of Issue April 24, 1991 (posthumously)

Citation Corporal Stowers, a native of Anderson County, South Carolina, distinguished himself by exceptional heroism on 28 September 1918, while serving as a squad leader in Company C, 371st Infantry Regiment, 93rd Infantry Division. His company was the lead company during the attack on Hill 188, Champagne Marne Sector, France, during World War I. A few minutes after the attack began, the enemy ceased firing and began climbing up onto the parapets of the trenches, holding up their arms as if wishing to surrender. The enemy's actions caused the American forces to cease fire and to come out into the open. As the company started forward and when within about 100 meters of the trench line, the enemy jumped back into their trenches and greeted Corporal Stowers' company with interlocking bands of machine gun fire and mortar fire causing well over fifty percent casualties. Faced with incredible enemy resistance, Corporal Stowers took charge, setting such a courageous example of personal bravery and leadership that he inspired his men to follow him in the attack. With extraordinary heroism and complete disregard of personal danger under devastating fire, he crawled forward leading his squad toward an enemy machine gun nest, which was causing heavy casualties to his company. After fierce fighting, the machine gun position was destroyed and the enemy soldiers were killed. Displaying great courage and intrepidity, Corporal Stowers continued to press the attack against a determined enemy. While crawling forward and urging his men to continue the attack on a second trench line, he was gravely wounded by machine gun fire. Although, Corporal Stowers was mortally wounded, he pressed forward, urging on the members of his squad, until he died. Inspired by the heroism and display of bravery of Corporal Stowers, his company continued the attack against incredible odds, contributing to the capture of Hill 188 and causing heavy enemy casualties. Corporal Stowers' conspicuous gallantry, extraordinary heroism and supreme devotion to his men were well above and beyond the call of duty, follow the finest traditions of military service and reflect the utmost credit on him and the United States Army.

World War II (1939–1945)

Baker, Vernon J.

Rank and Unit First Lieutenant, Company C, 370th Infantry, 92d Infantry Division

Born December 17, 1919; Cheyenne, Wyoming

Entered Service Cheyenne, Wyoming

Place and Date of Award Viareggio, Italy; April 5–6, 1945

Date of Issue January 13, 1997

Citation For extraordinary heroism in action on 5 and 6 April 1945, near Viareggio, Italy. Then Second Lieutenant Baker demonstrated outstanding courage and leadership in destroying enemy installations, personnel and equipment during his company's attack against a strongly entrenched enemy in mountainous terrain. When his company was stopped by the concentration of fire from several machine gun emplacements, he crawled to one position and destroyed it, killing three Germans. Continuing forward, he attacked an enemy observation post and killed two occupants. With the aid of one of his men, Lieutenant Baker attacked two more machine gun nests, killing or wounding the four enemy soldiers occupying these positions. He then covered the evacuation of the wounded personnel of his company by occupying an exposed position and drawing the enemy's fire. On the following night Lieutenant Baker voluntarily led a battalion advance through enemy mine fields and heavy fire toward the division objective. Second Lieutenant Baker's fighting spirit and daring leadership were an inspiration to his men and exemplify the highest traditions of the Armed Forces.

Carter, Edward A., Jr.
Rank and Unit Staff Sergeant, Company 1, 56th Armored Infantry, 12th Armored Division
Born 1916; Los Angeles, California
Entered Service Los Angeles, California
Place and Date of Award Speyer, Germany; March 23, 1945
Date of Issue January 13, 1997 (posthumously)
Citation For extraordinary heroism in action on 23 March 1945, near Speyer, Germany. When the tank on which he was riding received heavy bazooka and small arms fire, Sergeant Carter voluntarily attempted to lead a three-man group across an open field. Within a short time, two of his men were killed and the third seriously wounded. Continuing on alone, he was wounded five times and finally forced to take cover. As eight enemy riflemen attempted to capture him, Sergeant Carter killed six of them and captured the remaining two. He then crossed the field using as a shield his two prisoners from which he obtained valuable information concerning the disposition of enemy troops. Staff Sergeant Carter's extraordinary heroism was an inspiration to the officers and men of the Seventh Army Infantry Company Number 1 (Provisional) and exemplify the highest traditions of the Armed Forces.

Fox, John R.
Rank and Unit First Lieutenant, 366th Infantry, 92d Infantry Division
Born December 7, 1917
Entered Service Cincinnati, Ohio
Place and Date of Award Sommocolonia, Italy; December 26, 1944
Date of Issue January 13, 1997 (posthumously)
Citation For extraordinary heroism against an armed enemy in the vicinity of Sommocolonia, Italy, on 26 December 1944, while serving as a member of Cannon Company, 366th Infantry Regiment, 92d Infantry Division. During the preceding few weeks, Lieutenant Fox served with the 598th Field Artillery Battalion as a forward observer. On Christmas night, enemy soldiers gradually infiltrated the town of Sommocolonia in civilian clothes, and by early morning the town was largely in hostile hands. Commencing with a heavy barrage of enemy artillery at 0400 hours on 26 December 1944, an organized attack by uniformed German units began. Being greatly outnumbered, most of the United States Infantry forces were forced to withdraw from the town, but Lieutenant Fox and some other members of his observer party voluntarily remained on the second floor of a house to direct defensive artillery fire. At 0800 hours, Lieutenant Fox reported that the Germans were in the streets and attacking in strength. He then called for defensive artillery fire to slow the enemy advance. As the Germans continued to press the attack towards the area that Lieutenant Fox occupied, he adjusted the artillery fire closer to his position. Finally he was warned that the next adjustment would bring the deadly artillery right on top of his position. After acknowledging the danger, Lieutenant Fox insisted that the last adjustment be fired as this was the only way to defeat the attacking soldiers. Later, when a counterattack retook the position from the Germans, Lieutenant Fox's body was found with the bodies of approximately 100 German soldiers. Lieutenant Fox's gallant and courageous actions, at the supreme sacrifice of his own life, contributed greatly to delaying the enemy advance until other infantry and artillery units could reorganize to repel the attack. His extraordinary valorous actions were in keeping with the most cherished traditions of military service, and reflect the utmost credit on him, his unit, and the United States Army.

James, Willy F., Jr.
Rank and Unit Private, First Class, 413th Infantry, 104th Infantry Division
Born Kansas City, Missouri
Entered Service Kansas City
Place and Date of Award Lippoldsberg, Germany; April 7, 1945
Date of Issue January 13, 1997 (posthumously)
Citation For extraordinary heroism in action on 7 April 1945 near Lippoldsberg, Germany. As lead scout during a maneuver to secure and expand a vital bridgehead, Private First Class James was the first to draw enemy fire. He was pinned down for over an hour, during which time he observed enemy positions in detail. Returning to his platoon, he assisted in working out a new plan of maneuver. He then led a squad in the assault, accurately designating targets as he advanced, until he was killed by enemy machine gun fire while going to the aid of his fatally wounded platoon leader. Private First Class James' fearless, self-assigned ac-

tions, coupled with his diligent devotion to duty exemplified the finest traditions of the Armed Forces.

Rivers, Ruben
Rank and Unit Staff Sergeant, Company A, 761st Tank Battalion, Third Army
Born Hotulka, Oklahoma
Entered Service Tecumseh, Oklahoma
Place and Date of Award Guebling, France; November 15–19, 1944
Date of Issue January 13, 1997 (posthumously)
Citation For extraordinary heroism in action during the 15–19 November 1944, toward Guebling, France. Though severely wounded in the leg, Sergeant Rivers refused medical treatment and evacuation, took command of another tank, and advanced with his company in Guebling the next day. Repeatedly refusing evacuation, Sergeant Rivers continued to direct his tank's fire at enemy positions through the morning of 19 November 1944. At dawn, Company A's tanks began to advance towards Bougaktroff, but were stopped by enemy fire. Sergeant Rivers, joined by another tank, opened fire on the enemy tanks, covering Company A as they withdrew. While doing so, Sergeant River's tank was hit, killing him and wounding the crew. Staff Sergeant Rivers' fighting spirit and daring leadership were an inspiration to his unit and exemplify the highest traditions of military service.

Thomas, Charles L.
Rank and Unit Captain, Company C, 614th Tank Destroyer Battalion, 103d Division
Born Detroit, Michigan
Entered Service Detroit, Michigan
Place and Date of Award Climbach, Korea; December 14, 1944
Date of Issue January 13, 1997 (posthumously)
Citation For extraordinary heroism in action on 14 December 1944, near Climbach, France. While riding in the lead vehicle of a task force organized to storm and capture the village of Climbach, France, then First Lieutenant Thomas's armored scout car was subjected to intense enemy artillery, self-propelled gun, and small arms fire. Although wounded by the initial burst of hostile fire, Lieutenant Thomas signaled the remainder of the column to halt and, despite the severity of his wounds, assisted the crew of the wrecked car in dismounting. Upon leaving the scant protection which the vehicle afforded, Lieutenant Thomas was again subjected to a hail of enemy fire which inflicted multiple gunshot wounds in his chest, legs, and left arm. Despite the intense pain caused by these wounds, Lieutenant Thomas ordered and directed the dispersion and emplacement of two antitank guns which in a few moments were promptly and effectively returning the enemy fire. Realizing that he could no longer remain in command of the platoon, he signaled to the platoon commander to join him. Lieutenant Thomas then thoroughly oriented him on enemy gun dispositions and the general situation. Only after he was certain that his junior officer was in full control of the situation did he permit himself to be evacuated. First Lieutenant Thomas' outstanding heroism were an inspiration to his men and exemplify the highest traditions of the Armed Forces.

Watson, George
Rank and Unit Private, 29th Quartermaster Regiment
Born 1915; Birmingham, Alabama
Entered Service Birmingham, Alabama
Place and Date of Award Porloch Harbor, New Guinea; March 8, 1943
Date of Issue January 13, 1997 (posthumously)
Citation For extraordinary heroism in action on 8 March 1943. Private Watson was on board a ship which was attacked and hit by enemy bombers. When the ship was abandoned, Private Watson, instead of seeking to save himself, remained in the water assisting several soldiers who could not swim to reach the safety of the raft. This heroic action, which subsequently cost him his life, resulted in the saving of several of his comrades. Weakened by his exertions, he was dragged down by the suction of the sinking ship and was drowned. Private Watson's extraordinarily valorous actions, daring leadership, and self-sacrificing devotion to his fellow-man exemplify the finest traditions of military service.

Korean War (1950–1953)

Charlton, Cornelius H.
Rank and Unit Sergeant, U.S. Army, Company C, 24th Infantry Regiment, 25th Infantry Division

Born July 24, 1929; East Gulf, West Virginia
Entered Service Bronx County, New York
Place and Date of Award Chipo-ri, Korea; June 2, 1951
Date of Issue March 12, 1952 (posthumously)
Citation Sgt. Charlton, a member of Company C, distinguished himself by conspicuous gallantry and intrepidity above and beyond the call of duty in action against the enemy. His platoon was attacking heavily defended hostile positions on commanding ground when the leader was wounded and evacuated. Sgt. Charlton assumed command, rallied the men, and spearheaded the assault against the hill. Personally eliminating 2 hostile positions and killing 6 of the enemy with his rifle fire and grenades, he continued up the slope until the unit suffered heavy casualties and became pinned down. Regrouping the men he led them forward only to be again hurled back by a shower of grenades. Despite a severe chest wound, Sgt. Charlton refused medical attention and led a third daring charge which carried to the crest of the ridge. Observing that the remaining emplacement which had retarded the advance was situated on the reverse slope, he charged it alone, was again hit by a grenade but raked the position with a devastating fire which eliminated it and routed the defenders. The wounds received during his daring exploits resulted in his death but his indomitable courage, superb leadership, and gallant self-sacrifice reflect the highest credit upon himself, the infantry, and the military service.

Thompson, William Henry
Rank and Unit Private, First Class, U.S. Army, Company M, 24th Infantry Regiment, 25th Infantry Division
Born August 16, 1927; New York, New York
Entered Service Bronx County, New York
Place and Date of Award Haman, Korea; August 6, 1950
Date of Issue August 2, 1951 (posthumously)
Citation Pfc. Thompson distinguished himself by conspicuous gallantry and intrepidity above and beyond the call of duty in action against the enemy. While his platoon was reorganizing under cover of darkness, fanatical enemy forces in overwhelming strength launched a surprise attack on the unit. Pfc. Thompson set up his machine gun in the path of the onslaught and swept the enemy with withering fire, pinning them down momentarily thus permitting the remainder of his platoon to withdraw to a more tenable position. Although hit repeatedly by grenade fragments and small-arms fire, he resisted all efforts of his comrades to induce him to withdraw, steadfastly remained at his machine gun and continued to deliver deadly, accurate fire until mortally wounded by an enemy grenade. Pfc. Thompson's dauntless courage and gallant self-sacrifice reflect the highest credit on himself and uphold the esteemed traditions of military service.

Vietnam War (1964–1973)

Anderson, James, Jr.
Rank and Unit Private, First Class, U.S. Marine Corps, 2d Platoon, Company F, 2d Battalion, 3d Marines, 3d Marine Division
Born January 22, 1947; Los Angeles, California
Entered Service Los Angeles, California
Place and Date of Award Cam Lo, Republic of Vietnam; February 28, 1967
Date of Issue August 21, 1968 (posthumously)
Citation For conspicuous gallantry and intrepidity at the risk of his life above and beyond the call of duty. Company F was advancing in dense jungle northwest of Cam Lo in an effort to extract a heavily besieged reconnaissance patrol. Pfc. Anderson's platoon was the lead element and had advanced only about 200 meters when they were brought under extremely intense enemy small-arms and automatic weapons fire. The platoon reacted swiftly, getting on line as best they could in the thick terrain, and began returning fire. Pfc. Anderson found himself tightly bunched together with the other members of the platoon only 20 meters from the enemy positions. As the fire fight continued several of the men were wounded by the deadly enemy assault. Suddenly, an enemy grenade landed in the midst of the marines and rolled alongside Pfc. Anderson's head. Unhesitatingly and with complete disregard for his personal safety, he reached out, grasped the grenade, pulled it to his chest, and curled around it as it went off. Although several marines received shrapnel from the grenade, his body absorbed the major force of the explosion. In this singularly heroic act, Pfc. Anderson saved his comrades from serious injury and possible death. His per-

sonal heroism, extraordinary valor, and inspirational supreme self-sacrifice reflected great credit upon himself and the Marine Corps and upheld the highest traditions of the U.S. Naval Service. He gallantly gave his life for his country.

Anderson, Webster
Rank and Unit Sergeant, First Class, U.S. Army, Battery A, 2d Battalion, 320th Field Artillery, 101st Airborne Infantry Division (Airmobile)
Born July 15, 1933; Winnsboro, South Carolina
Entered Service Winnsboro, South Carolina
Place and Date of Award Tam Ky, Republic of Vietnam; October 15, 1967
Date of Issue November 24, 1969
Citation Sfc. Anderson (then S/Sgt.) distinguished himself by conspicuous gallantry and intrepidity in action while serving as chief of section in Battery A, against a hostile force. During the early morning hours Battery A's defensive position was attacked by a determined North Vietnamese Army infantry unit supported by heavy mortar, recoilless rifle, rocket propelled grenade and automatic weapon fire. The initial enemy onslaught breached the battery defensive perimeter. Sfc. Anderson, with complete disregard for his personal safety, mounted the exposed parapet of his howitzer position and became the mainstay of the defense of the battery position. Sfc. Anderson directed devastating direct howitzer fire on the assaulting enemy while providing rifle and grenade defensive fire against enemy soldiers attempting to overrun his gun section position. While protecting his crew and directing their fire against the enemy from his exposed position, 2 enemy grenades exploded at his feet knocking him down and severely wounding him in the legs. Despite the excruciating pain and though not able to stand, Sfc. Anderson valorously propped himself on the parapet and continued to direct howitzer fire upon the closing enemy and to encourage his men to fight on. Seeing an enemy grenade land within the gun pit near a wounded member of his gun crew, Sfc. Anderson heedless of his own safety, seized the grenade and attempted to throw it over the parapet to save his men. As the grenade was thrown from the position it exploded and Sfc. Anderson was again grievously wounded. Although only partially conscious and severely wounded, Sfc. Anderson refused medical evacuation and continued to encourage his men in the defense of the position. Sfc. Anderson by his inspirational leadership, professionalism, devotion to duty and complete disregard for his welfare was able to maintain the defense of his section position and to defeat a determined attack. Sfc. Anderson's gallantry and extraordinary heroism at the risk of his life above and beyond the call of duty are in the highest traditions of the military service and reflect great credit upon himself, his unit, and the U.S. Army.

Ashley, Eugene, Jr.
Rank and Unit Sergeant, First Class, U.S. Army, Company C, 5th Special Forces Group (Airborne), 1st Special Forces
Born October 12, 1931; Wilmington, North Carolina
Entered Service New York
Place and Date of Award Lang Vei, Republic of Vietnam; February 6–7, 1968
Date of Issue December 2, 1969 (posthumously)
Citation Sfc. Ashley distinguished himself by conspicuous gallantry and intrepidity while serving with Detachment A-101, Company C. Sfc. Ashley was the senior special forces advisor of a hastily organized assault force whose mission was to rescue entrapped U.S. special forces advisors at Camp Lang Vei. During the initial attack on the special forces camp by North Vietnamese army forces, Sfc. Ashley supported the camp with high explosive and illumination mortar rounds. When communications were lost with the main camp, he assumed the additional responsibility of directing air strikes and artillery support. Sfc. Ashley organized and equipped a small assault force composed of local friendly personnel. During the ensuing battle, Sfc. Ashley led a total of 5 vigorous assaults against the enemy, continuously exposing himself to a voluminous hail of enemy grenades, machine gun and automatic weapons fire. Throughout these assaults, he was plagued by numerous booby-trapped satchel charges in all bunkers on his avenue of approach. During his fifth and final assault, he adjusted air strikes nearly on top of his assault element, forcing the enemy to withdraw and resulting in friendly control of the summit of the hill. While exposing himself to intense enemy fire, he was seriously wounded by machine gun fire but continued his

mission without regard for his personal safety. After the fifth assault he lost consciousness and was carried from the summit by his comrades only to suffer a fatal wound when an enemy artillery round landed in the area. Sfc. Ashley displayed extraordinary heroism in risking his life in an attempt to save the lives of his entrapped comrades and commanding officer. His total disregard for his personal safety while exposed to enemy observation and automatic weapons fire was an inspiration to all men committed to the assault. The resolute valor with which he led 5 gallant charges placed critical diversionary pressure on the attacking enemy and his valiant efforts carved a channel in the overpowering enemy forces and weapons positions through which the survivors of Camp Lang Vei eventually escaped to freedom. Sfc. Ashley's bravery at the cost of his life was in the highest traditions of the military service, and reflects great credit upon himself, his unit, and the U.S. Army.

Austin, Oscar Palmer

Rank and Unit Private, First Class, U.S. Marine Corps, Company E, 2d Battalion, 7th Marines, 1st Marine Division (Rein), Fleet Marine Force (FMF)

Born January 15, 1948; Nacogdoches, Texas

Entered Service Phoenix, Arizona

Place and Date of Award West of Da Nang, Republic of Vietnam; February 23, 1969

Date of Issue April 20, 1970 (posthumously)

Citation For conspicuous gallantry and intrepidity at the risk of his life above and beyond the call of duty while serving as an assistant machine gunner with Company E, in connection with operations against enemy forces. During the early morning hours Pfc. Austin's observation post was subjected to a fierce ground attack by a large North Vietnamese Army force supported by a heavy volume of hand grenades, satchel charges, and small arms fire. Observing that 1 of his wounded companions had fallen unconscious in a position dangerously exposed to the hostile fire, Pfc. Austin unhesitatingly left the relative security of his fighting hole and, with complete disregard for his safety, raced across the fire-swept terrain to assist the marine to a covered location. As he neared the casualty, he observed an enemy grenade land nearby and, reacting instantly, leaped between the injured marine and the lethal object, absorbing the effects of its detonation. As he ignored his painful injuries and turned to examine the wounded man, he saw a North Vietnamese Army soldier aiming a weapon at his unconscious companion. With full knowledge of the probable consequences and thinking only to protect the marine, Pfc. Austin resolutely threw himself between the casualty and the hostile soldier, and, in doing, was mortally wounded. Pfc. Austin's indomitable courage, inspiring initiative and selfless devotion to duty upheld the highest traditions of the Marine Corps and the U.S. Naval Service. He gallantly gave his life for his country.

Bryant, William Maud

Rank and Unit Sergeant, First Class, U.S. Army, Company A, 5th Special Forces Group, 1st Special Forces

Born February 16, 1933; Cochran, Georgia

Entered Service Detroit, Michigan

Place and Date of Award Long Khanh Province, Republic of Vietnam; March 24, 1969

Date of Issue February 16, 1971 (posthumously)

Citation For conspicuous gallantry and intrepidity in action at the risk of his life above and beyond the call of duty. Sfc. Bryant, assigned to Company A, distinguished himself while serving as commanding officer of Civilian Irregular Defense Group Company 321, 2d Battalion, 3d Mobile Strike Force Command, during combat operations. The battalion came under heavy fire and became surrounded by the elements of 3 enemy regiments. Sfc. Bryant displayed extraordinary heroism throughout the succeeding 34 hours of incessant attack as he moved throughout the company position heedless of the intense hostile fire while establishing and improving the defensive perimeter, directing fire during critical phases of the battle, distributing ammunition, assisting the wounded, and providing the leadership and inspirational example of courage to his men. When a helicopter drop of ammunition was made to re-supply the beleaguered force, Sfc. Bryant with complete disregard for his safety ran through the heavy enemy fire to retrieve the scattered ammunition boxes and distributed needed ammunition to his men. During a lull in the intense fighting, Sfc. Bryant led a patrol outside the perimeter to obtain information of the enemy. The patrol came under intense automatic weapons fire and was pinned down. Sfc. Bryant single-handedly repulsed 1 enemy attack on his small force and by his heroic action inspired his men to fight off other assaults. Seeing a wounded enemy soldier some distance from the patrol location, Sfc. Bryant crawled forward alone under heavy fire to retrieve the soldier for intelligence purposes. Finding that the enemy soldier had expired, Sfc. Bryant crawled back to his patrol and led his men back to the company position where he again took command of the defense. As the siege continued, Sfc. Bryant organized and led a patrol in a daring attempt to break through the enemy encirclement. The patrol had advanced some 200 meters by heavy fighting when it was pinned down by the intense automatic weapons fire from heavily fortified bunkers and Sfc. Bryant was severely wounded. Despite his wounds he rallied his men, called for helicopter gunship support, and directed heavy suppressive fire upon the enemy positions. Following the last gunship attack, Sfc. Bryant fearlessly charged an enemy automatic weapons position, overrunning it, and single-handedly destroying its 3 defenders. Inspired by his heroic example, his men renewed their attack on the entrenched enemy. While regrouping his small force for the final assault against the enemy, Sfc. Bryant fell mortally wounded by an enemy rocket. Sfc. Bryant's selfless concern for his comrades, at the cost of his life above and beyond the call of duty, are in keeping with the highest traditions of the military service and reflect great credit upon himself, his unit, and the U.S. Army.

Davis, Rodney Maxwell

Rank and Unit Sergeant, U.S. Marine Corps, Company B, 1st Battalion, 5th Marines, 1st Marine Division

Born April 7, 1942; Macon, Georgia

Entered Service Macon, Georgia

Place and Date of Award Quang Nam Province, Republic of Vietnam; September 6, 1967

Date of Issue March 26, 1969 (posthumously)

Citation For conspicuous gallantry and intrepidity at the risk of his life above and beyond the call of duty while serving as the right guide of the 2d Platoon, Company B, in action against enemy forces. Elements of the 2d Platoon were pinned down by a numerically superior force of attacking North Vietnamese Army Regulars. Remnants of the platoon were located in a trench line where Sgt. Davis was directing the fire of his men in an attempt to repel the enemy attack. Disregarding the enemy hand grenades and high volume of small arms and mortar fire, Sgt. Davis moved from man to man shouting words of encouragement to each of them while firing and throwing grenades at the onrushing enemy. When an enemy grenade landed in the trench in the midst of his men, Sgt. Davis, realizing the gravity of the situation, and in a final valiant act of complete self-sacrifice, instantly threw himself upon the grenade, absorbing with his body the full and terrific force of the explosion. Through his extraordinary initiative and inspiring valor in the face of almost certain death, Sgt. Davis saved his comrades from injury and possible loss of life, enabled his platoon to hold its vital position, and upheld the highest traditions of the Marine Corps and the U.S. Naval Service. He gallantly gave his life for his country.

Jenkins, Robert H., Jr.

Rank and Unit Private, First Class, U.S. Marine Corps, 3d Reconnaissance Battalion, 3d Marine Division (Rein), FMF

Born June 1, 1948; Interlachen, Florida

Entered Service Jacksonville, Florida

Place and Date of Award Fire Support Base, Argonne, Republic of Vietnam; March 5, 1969

Date of Issue April 20, 1970 (posthumously)

Citation For conspicuous gallantry and intrepidity at the risk of his life above and beyond the call of duty while serving as a machine gunner with Company C, 3d Reconnaissance Battalion, in connection with operations against enemy forces. Early in the morning Pfc. Jenkins' 12-man reconnaissance team was occupying a defensive position at Fire Support Base Argonne south of the Demilitarized Zone. Suddenly, the marines were assaulted by a North Vietnamese Army platoon employing mortars, automatic weapons, and hand grenades. Reacting instantly, Pfc. Jenkins and another marine quickly moved into a 2-man fighting emplacement, and as they boldly delivered accurate machine gun fire against the enemy, a North Vietnamese soldier threw a hand grenade into the friendly emplacement. Fully realizing the inevitable results of his actions, Pfc. Jenkins quickly seized his comrade, and pushing the man to the ground, he leaped on top of the marine to shield him from the explosion. Absorbing the full impact of the detonation, Pfc. Jenkins was seriously injured and subsequently succumbed to his wounds. His courage, inspiring valor and selfless devotion to duty saved a fellow marine from serious injury or possible death and upheld the highest traditions of the Marine Corps and the U.S. Naval Service. He gallantly gave his life for his country.

Joel, Lawrence

Rank and Unit Specialist, Sixth Class, U.S. Army, Headquarters and Headquarters Company, 1st Battalion (Airborne), 503d Infantry, 173d Airborne Brigade

Born February 22, 1928; Winston-Salem, North Carolina

Entered Service New York

Place and Date of Award Republic of Vietnam; November 8, 1965

Date of Issue March 9, 1967

Citation For conspicuous gallantry and intrepidity at the risk of life above and beyond the call of duty. Sp6c. Joel demonstrated indomitable courage, determination, and professional skill when a numerically superior and well-concealed Viet Cong element launched a vicious attack which wounded or killed nearly every man in the lead squad of the company. After treating the men wounded by the initial burst of gunfire, he bravely moved forward to assist others who were wounded while proceeding to their objective. While moving from man to man, he was struck in the right leg by machine gun fire. Although painfully wounded his desire to aid his fellow soldiers transcended all personal feeling. He bandaged his own wound and self-administered morphine to deaden the pain enabling him to continue his dangerous undertaking. Through this period of time, he constantly shouted words of encouragement to all around him. Then, completely ignoring the warnings of others, and his pain, he continued his search for wounded, exposing himself to hostile fire; and, as bullets dug up the dirt around him, he held plasma bottles high while kneeling completely engrossed in his life saving mission. Then, after being struck a second time and with a bullet lodged in his thigh, he dragged himself over the battlefield and succeeded in treating 13 more men before his medical supplies ran out. Displaying resourcefulness, he saved the life of 1 man by placing a plastic bag over a severe chest wound to congeal the blood. As 1 of the platoons pursued the Viet Cong, an insurgent force in concealed positions opened fire on the platoon and wounded many more soldiers. With a new stock of medical supplies, Sp6c. Joel again shouted words of encouragement as he crawled through an intense hail of gunfire to the wounded men. After the 24 hour battle subsided and the Viet Cong dead numbered 410, snipers continued to harass the company. Throughout the long battle, Sp6c. Joel never lost sight of his mission as a medical aidman and continued to comfort and treat the wounded until his own evacuation was ordered. His meticulous attention to duty saved a large number of lives and his unselfish, daring example under most adverse conditions was an inspiration to all. Sp6c. Joel's profound concern for his fellow soldiers, at the risk of his life above and beyond the call of duty, are in the highest traditions of the U.S. Army and reflect great credit upon himself and the Armed Forces of his country.

Johnson, Dwight Hal

Rank and Unit Specialist, Fifth Class, U.S. Army, Company B, 1st Battalion, 69th Armor, 4th Infantry Division

Born May 7, 1947; Detroit, Michigan

Entered Service Detroit, Michigan

Place and Date of Award Near Dak To, Kontum Province, Republic of Vietnam; January 15, 1968

Date of Issue November 19, 1968

Citation For conspicuous gallantry and intrepidity at the risk of his life above and beyond the call of duty. Sp5c. Johnson, a tank driver with Company B, was a member of a reaction force moving to aid other elements of his platoon, which was in heavy contact with a battalion-size North Vietnamese force. Sp5c. Johnson's tank, upon reaching the point of contact, threw a track and became immobilized. Realizing that he could do no more as a driver, he climbed out of the vehicle, armed only with a .45 caliber pistol. Despite intense hostile fire, Sp5c. Johnson killed several enemy soldiers before he had expended his ammunition. Returning to his tank through a heavy volume of antitank rocket, small arms and automatic weapons fire, he obtained a submachine gun with which to continue his fight against the advancing enemy. Armed with this weapon, Sp5c. Johnson again braved deadly enemy fire to return to the center of the ambush site where he courageously eliminated more of the determined foe. Engaged in extremely close combat when the last of his ammunition was expended, he killed an enemy soldier with the stock end of his submachine gun. Now weaponless, Sp5c. Johnson ignored the enemy fire around him, climbed into his platoon sergeant's tank, extricated a wounded crewmember and carried him to an armored personnel carrier. He then returned to the same tank and assisted in firing the main gun until it jammed. In a magnificent display of courage, Sp5c. Johnson exited the tank and again armed only with a .45 caliber pistol, engaged several North Vietnamese troops in close proximity to the vehicle. Fighting his way through devastating fire and remounting his own immobilized tank, he remained fully exposed to the enemy as he bravely and skillfully engaged them with the tank's externally-mounted .50 caliber machine gun; where he remained until the situation was brought under control. Sp5c. Johnson's profound concern for his fellow soldiers, at the risk of his life above and beyond the call of duty, are in keeping with the highest traditions of the military service and reflect great credit upon himself and the U.S. Army.

Johnson, Ralph Henry

Rank and Unit Private, First Class, U.S. Marine Corps, Company A, 1st Reconnaissance Battalion, 1st Marine Division (Rein), FMF

Born January 11, 1949; Charleston, South Carolina

Entered Service Oakland, California

Place and Date of Award Quan Duc Valley, Republic of Vietnam; March 5, 1968

Date of Issue April 20, 1970 (posthumously)

Citation For conspicuous gallantry and intrepidity at the risk of his life above and beyond the call of duty while serving as a reconnaissance scout with Company A, in action against the North Vietnamese Army and Viet Cong forces. In the early morning hours during Operation ROCK, Pfc. Johnson was a member of a 15-man reconnaissance patrol manning an observation post on Hill 146 overlooking the Quan Duc Valley deep in enemy controlled territory. They were attacked by a platoon-size hostile force employing automatic weapons, satchel charges and hand grenades. Suddenly, a hand grenade landed in the 3-man fighting hole occupied by Pfc. Johnson and 2 fellow marines. Realizing the inherent danger to his 2 comrades, he shouted a warning and unhesitatingly hurled himself upon the explosive device. When the grenade exploded, Pfc. Johnson absorbed the tremendous impact of the blast and was killed instantly. His prompt and heroic act saved the life of 1 marine at the cost of his life and undoubtedly prevented the enemy from penetrating his sector of the patrol's perimeter. Pfc. Johnson's courage, inspiring valor and selfless devotion to duty, were in keeping with the highest traditions of the Marine Corps and the U.S. Naval Service. He gallantly gave his life for his country.

Langhorn, Garfield McConnell

Rank and Unit Private First Class, U.S. Army, Troop C, 7th Squadron (Airmobile), 17th Cavalry, 1st Aviation Brigade

Born September 10, 1948; Cumberland, Virginia

Entered Service Brooklyn, New York

Place and Date of Award Plei Djereng, Pleiku Province, Republic of Vietnam; January 15, 1969

Date of Issue April 7, 1970 (posthumously)

Citation For conspicuous gallantry and intrepidity in action at the risk of his life above and beyond the call of duty. Pfc. Langhorn distinguished himself while serving as a radio operator with Troop C, near Plei Djereng in Pleiku Province. Pfc. Langhorn's platoon was inserted into a landing zone to rescue 2 pilots of a Cobra helicopter shot down by enemy fire on a heavily timbered slope. He provided radio coordination with the command-and-control aircraft overhead while the troops hacked their way through dense undergrowth to the wreckage, where both aviators were found dead. As the men were taking the bodies to a pickup site, they suddenly came under intense fire from North Vietnamese soldiers in camouflaged bunkers to the front and right flank, and within minutes they were surrounded. Pfc. Langhorn immediately radioed for help from the orbiting gunships, which began to place minigun and rocket fire on the aggressors. He then lay between the platoon leader and another man, operating the radio and providing covering fire for the wounded who had been moved to the center of the small perimeter. Darkness soon fell, making it impossible for the gunships to give accurate support, and the aggressors began to probe the perimeter. An enemy hand grenade landed in front of Pfc. Langhorn and a few feet from personnel who had become casualties. Choosing to protect these wounded, he unhesitatingly threw himself on the grenade, scooped it beneath his body and absorbed the blast. By sacrificing himself, he saved the lives of his comrades. Pfc. Langhorn's extraordinary heroism at the cost of his life was in keeping with the highest traditions of the military service and reflect great credit on himself, his unit, and the U.S. Army.

Leonard, Matthew
Rank and Unit Sergeant, U.S. Army, Company B, 1st Battalion, 16th Infantry, 1st Infantry Division
Born November 26, 1929; Eutaw, Alabama
Entered Service Birmingham, Alabama
Place and Date of Award Near Suoi Da, Republic of Vietnam; February 28, 1967
Date of Issue December 19, 1968 (posthumously)
Citation For conspicuous gallantry and intrepidity in action at the risk of his life above and beyond the call of duty. His platoon was suddenly attacked by a large enemy force employing small arms, automatic weapons, and hand grenades. Although the platoon leader and several other key leaders were among the first wounded, P/Sgt. Leonard quickly rallied his men to throw back the initial enemy assaults. During the short pause that followed, he organized a defensive perimeter, redistributed ammunition, and inspired his comrades through his forceful leadership and words of encouragement. Noticing a wounded companion outside the perimeter, he dragged the man to safety but was struck by a sniper's bullet which shattered his left hand. Refusing medical attention and continuously exposing himself to the increasing fire as the enemy again assaulted the perimeter, P/Sgt. Leonard moved from position to position to direct the fire of his men against the well camouflaged foe. Under the cover of the main attack, the enemy moved a machine gun into a location where it could sweep the entire perimeter. This threat was magnified when the platoon machine gun in this area malfunctioned. P/Sgt. Leonard quickly crawled to the gun position and was helping to clear the malfunction when the gunner and other men in the vicinity were wounded by fire from the enemy machine gun. P/Sgt. Leonard rose to his feet, charged the enemy gun and destroyed the hostile crew despite being hit several times by enemy fire. He moved to a tree, propped himself against it, and continued to engage the enemy until he succumbed to his many wounds. His fighting spirit, heroic leadership, and valiant acts inspired the remaining members of his platoon to hold back the enemy until assistance arrived. P/Sgt. Leonard's profound courage and devotion to his men are in keeping with the highest traditions of the military service, and his gallant actions reflect great credit upon himself and the U.S. Army.

Long, Donald Russell
Rank and Unit Sergeant, U.S. Army, Troop C, 1st Squadron, 4th Cavalry, 1st Infantry Division
Born August 27, 1939; Blackfork, Ohio
Entered Service Ashland, Kentucky
Place and Date of Award Republic of Vietnam; June 30, 1966
Date of Issue February 8, 1968 (posthumously)
Citation For conspicuous gallantry and intrepidity in action at the risk of his life above and beyond the call of duty. Troops B and C, while conducting a reconnaissance mission along a road, were suddenly attacked by a Viet Cong regiment, supported by mortars, recoilless rifles and machine guns, from concealed positions astride the road. Sgt. Long abandoned the relative safety of his armored personnel carrier and braved a withering hail of enemy fire to carry wounded men to evacuation helicopters. As the platoon fought its way forward to resupply advanced elements, Sgt. Long repeatedly exposed himself to enemy fire at point blank range to provide the needed supplies. While assaulting the Viet Cong position, Sgt. Long inspired his comrades by fearlessly standing unprotected to repel the enemy with rifle fire and grenades as they attempted to mount his carrier. When the enemy threatened to overrun a disabled carrier nearby, Sgt. Long again disregarded his

own safety to help the severely wounded crew to safety. As he was handing arms to the less seriously wounded and reorganizing them to press the attack, an enemy grenade was hurled onto the carrier deck. Immediately recognizing the imminent danger, he instinctively shouted a warning to the crew and pushed to safety one man who had not heard his warning over the roar of battle. Realizing that these actions would not fully protect the exposed crewmen from the deadly explosion, he threw himself over the grenade to absorb the blast and thereby saved the lives of 8 of his comrades at the expense of his life. Throughout the battle, Sgt. Long's extraordinary heroism, courage and supreme devotion to his men were in the finest tradition of the military service, and reflect great credit upon himself and the U.S. Army.

Olive, Milton Lee, III

Rank and Unit Private, First Class, U.S. Army, Company B, 2d Battalion (Airborne), 503d Infantry, 173d Airborne Brigade

Born November 7, 1946; Chicago, Illinois

Entered Service Chicago, Illinois

Place and Date of Award Phu Cuong, Republic of Vietnam; October 22, 1965

Date of Issue April 21, 1966 (posthumously)

Citation For conspicuous gallantry and intrepidity at the risk of his life above and beyond the call of duty. Pfc. Olive was a member of the 3d Platoon of Company B, as it moved through the jungle to find the Viet Cong operating in the area. Although the platoon was subjected to a heavy volume of enemy gunfire and pinned down temporarily, it retaliated by assaulting the Viet Cong positions, causing the enemy to flee. As the platoon pursued the insurgents, Pfc. Olive and 4 other soldiers were moving through the jungle together when a grenade was thrown into their midst. Pfc. Olive saw the grenade, and then saved the lives of his fellow soldiers at the sacrifice of his by grabbing the grenade in his hand and falling on it to absorb the blast with his body. Through his bravery, unhesitating actions, and complete disregard for his safety, he prevented additional loss of life or injury to the members of his platoon. Pfc. Olive's extraordinary heroism, at the risk of his life above and beyond the call of duty are in the highest traditions of the U.S. Army and reflect great credit upon himself and the Armed Forces of his country.

Pitts, Riley Leroy

Rank and Unit Captain, U.S. Army, Company C, 2d Battalion, 27th Infantry, 25th Infantry Division

Born October 15, 1937; Fallis, Oklahoma

Entered Service Wichita, Kansas

Place and Date of Award Ap Dong, Republic of Vietnam; October 31, 1967

Date of Issue December 10, 1968 (posthumously)

Citation Distinguishing himself by exceptional heroism while serving as company commander during an airmobile assault. Immediately after his company landed in the area, several Viet Cong opened fire with automatic weapons. Despite the enemy fire, Capt. Pitts forcefully led an assault which overran the enemy positions. Shortly thereafter, Capt. Pitts was ordered to move his unit to the north to reinforce another company heavily engaged against a strong enemy force. As Capt. Pitts' company moved forward to engage the enemy, intense fire was received from 3 directions, including fire from 4 enemy bunkers, 2 of which were within 15 meters of Capt. Pitts' position. The severity of the incoming fire prevented Capt. Pitts from maneuvering his company. His rifle fire proving ineffective against the enemy due to the dense jungle foliage, he picked up an M-79 grenade launcher and began pinpointing the targets. Seizing a Chinese Communist grenade which had been taken from a captured Viet Cong's web gear, Capt. Pitts lobbed the grenade at a bunker to his front, but it hit the dense jungle foliage and rebounded. Without hesitation, Capt. Pitts threw himself on top of the grenade which, fortunately, failed to explode. Capt. Pitts then directed the repositioning of the company to permit friendly artillery to be fired. Upon completion of the artillery fire mission, Capt. Pitts again led his men toward the enemy positions, personally killing at least 1 more Viet Cong. The jungle growth still prevented effective fire to be placed on the enemy bunkers. Capt. Pitts, displaying complete disregard for his life and personal safety, quickly moved to a position which permitted him to place effective fire on the enemy. He maintained a continuous fire, pinpointing the enemy's fortified positions, while at the same time directing and urging his men forward, until he was mortally wounded. Capt. Pitts' conspicuous gallantry, extraordinary heroism, and intrepidity at the cost of his life, above and beyond the call of duty, are in the highest traditions of the U.S. Army and reflect great credit upon himself, his unit, and the Armed Forces of his country.

Rogers, Charles Calvin

Rank and Unit Lieutenant Colonel, U.S. Army, 1st Battalion, 5th Artillery, 1st Infantry Division

Born September 6, 1929; Claremont, West Virginia

Entered Service Institute, West Virginia

Place and Date of Award Fishhook, near Cambodian border, Republic of Vietnam; November 1, 1968

Date of Issue May 14, 1970

Citation For conspicuous gallantry and intrepidity in action at the risk of his life above and beyond the call of duty. Lt. Col. Rogers, Field Artillery, distinguished himself in action while serving as commanding officer, 1st Battalion, during the defense of a forward fire support base. In the early morning hours, the fire support base was subjected to a concentrated bombardment of heavy mortar, rocket and rocket propelled grenade fire. Simultaneously the position was struck by a human wave ground assault, led by sappers who breached the defensive barriers with bangalore torpedoes and penetrated the defensive perimeter. Lt. Col. Rogers with complete disregard for his safety moved through the hail of fragments from bursting enemy rounds to the embattled area. He aggressively rallied the dazed artillery crewmen to man their howitzers and he directed their fire on the assaulting enemy. Although knocked to the ground and wounded by an exploding round, Lt. Col. Rogers sprang to his feet and led a small counterattack force against an enemy element that had penetrated the howitzer positions. Although painfully wounded a second time during the assault, Lt. Col. Rogers pressed the attack killing several of the enemy and driving the remainder from the positions. Refusing medical treatment, Lt. Col. Rogers reestablished and reinforced the defensive positions. As a second human wave attack was launched against another sector of the perimeter, Lt. Col. Rogers directed artillery fire on the assaulting enemy and led a second counterattack against the charging forces. His valorous example rallied the beleaguered defenders to repulse and defeat the enemy onslaught. Lt. Col. Rogers moved from position to position through the heavy enemy fire, giving encouragement and direction to his men. At dawn the determined enemy launched a third assault against the fire base in an attempt to overrun the position. Lt. Col. Rogers moved to the threatened area and directed lethal fire on the enemy forces. Seeing a howitzer inoperative due to casualties, Lt. Col. Rogers joined the surviving members of the crew to return the howitzer to action. While directing the position defense, Lt. Col. Rogers was seriously wounded by fragments from a heavy mortar round which exploded on the parapet of the gun position. Although too severely wounded to physically lead the defenders, Lt. Col. Rogers continued to give encouragement and direction to his men in the defeating and repelling of the enemy attack. Lt. Col. Rogers' dauntless courage and heroism inspired the defenders of the fire support base to the heights of valor to defeat a determined and numerically superior enemy force. His relentless spirit of aggressiveness in action are in the highest traditions of the military service and reflects great credit upon himself, his unit, and the U.S. Army.

Sargent, Ruppert L.

Rank and Unit First Lieutenant, U.S. Army, Company B, 4th Battalion, 9th Infantry, 25th Infantry Division

Born January 6, 1938; Hampton, Virginia

Entered Service Richmond, Virginia

Place and Date of Award Hau Nghia Province, Republic of Vietnam; March 15, 1967

Date of Issue March 10, 1969 (posthumously)

Citation For conspicuous gallantry and intrepidity in action at the risk of his life above and beyond the call of duty. While leading a platoon of Company B, 1st Lt. Sargent was investigating a reported Viet Cong meeting house and weapons cache. A tunnel entrance which 1st Lt. Sargent observed was booby trapped. He tried to destroy the booby trap and blow the cover from the tunnel using hand grenades, but this attempt was not successful. He and his demolition man moved in to destroy the booby trap and cover which flushed a Viet Cong soldier from the tunnel, who was immediately killed by the nearby platoon sergeant.

1st Lt. Sargent, the platoon sergeant, and a forward observer moved toward the tunnel entrance. As they approached, another Viet Cong emerged and threw 2 hand grenades that landed in the midst of the group. 1st Lt. Sargent fired 3 shots at the enemy then turned and unhesitatingly threw himself over the 2 grenades. He was mortally wounded, and his 2 companions were lightly wounded when the grenades exploded. By his courageous and selfless act of exceptional heroism, he saved the lives of the platoon sergeant and forward observer and prevented the injury or death of several other nearby comrades. 1st Lt. Sargent's actions were in keeping with the highest traditions of the military services and reflect great credit upon himself and the U.S. Army.

Sasser, Clarence Eugene

Rank and Unit Specialist, Fifth Class (then Private, First Class), U.S. Army, Headquarters Company, 3d Battalion, 60th Infantry, 9th Infantry Division

Born September 12, 1947; Chenango, Texas

Entered Service Houston, Texas

Place and Date of Award Ding Tuong Province, Republic of Vietnam; January 10, 1968

Date of Issue March 7, 1969

Citation For conspicuous gallantry and intrepidity in action at the risk of his life above and beyond the call of duty. Sp5c. Sasser distinguished himself while assigned to Headquarters and Headquarters Company, 3d Battalion. He was serving as a medical aidman with Company A, 3d Battalion, on a reconnaissance in force operation. His company was making an air assault when suddenly it was taken under heavy small arms, recoilless rifle, machine gun and rocket fire from well fortified enemy positions on 3 sides of the landing zone. During the first few minutes, over 30 casualties were sustained. Without hesitation, Sp5c. Sasser ran across an open rice paddy through a hail of fire to assist the wounded. After helping 1 man to safety, was painfully wounded in the left shoulder by fragments of an exploding rocket. Refusing medical attention, he ran through a barrage of rocket and automatic weapons fire to aid casualties of the initial attack and, after giving them urgently needed treatment, continued to search for other wounded. Despite 2 additional wounds immobilizing his legs, he dragged himself through the mud toward another soldier 100 meters away. Although in agonizing pain and faint from loss of blood, Sp5c. Sasser reached the man, treated him, and proceeded on to encourage another group of soldiers to crawl 200 meters to relative safety. There he attended their wounds for 5 hours until they were evacuated. Sp5c. Sasser's extraordinary heroism is in keeping with the highest traditions of the military service and reflects great credit upon himself, his unit, and the U.S. Army.

Sims, Clifford Chester

Rank and Unit Staff Sergeant, U.S. Army, Company D, 2d Battalion (Airborne), 501st Infantry, 101st Airborne Division

Born June 18, 1942; Port St. Joe, Florida

Entered Service Jacksonville, Florida

Place and Date of Award Hue, Republic of Vietnam; February 21, 1968

Date of Issue December 2, 1969 (posthumously)

Citation For conspicuous gallantry and intrepidity in action at the risk of his life above and beyond the call of duty. S/Sgt. Sims distinguished himself while serving as a squad leader with Company D. Company D was assaulting a heavily fortified enemy position concealed within a dense wooded area when it encountered strong enemy defensive fire. Once within the woodline, S/Sgt. Sims led his squad in a furious attack against an enemy force which had pinned down the 1st Platoon and threatened to overrun it. His skillful leadership provided the platoon with freedom of movement and enabled it to regain the initiative. S/Sgt. Sims was then ordered to move his squad to a position where he could provide covering fire for the company command group and to link up with the 3d Platoon, which was under heavy enemy pressure. After moving no more than 30 meters S/Sgt. Sims noticed that a brick structure in which ammunition was stocked was on fire. Realizing the danger, S/Sgt. Sims took immediate action to move his squad from this position. Though in the process of leaving the area 2 members of his squad were injured by the subsequent explosion of the ammunition, S/Sgt. Sims' prompt actions undoubtedly prevented more serious casualties from occurring. While continuing through the dense woods amidst heavy enemy fire, S/Sgt. Sims and his squad were approaching a bunker when they heard the unmistakable noise of a concealed booby trap being triggered immediately to their front. S/Sgt. Sims warned his comrades of the danger and unhesitatingly hurled himself upon the device as it exploded, taking the full impact of the blast. In so protecting his fellow soldiers, he willingly sacrificed his life. S/Sgt. Sims' extraordinary heroism at the cost of his life is in keeping with the highest traditions of the military service and reflects great credit upon himself and the U.S. Army.

Warren, John Earl, Jr.

Rank and Unit First Lieutenant, U.S. Army, Company C, 2d Battalion (Mechanized), 22d Infantry, 25th Infantry Division

Born November 16, 1946; Brooklyn, New York

Entered Service New York

Place and Date of Award Tay Ninh Province, Republic of Vietnam; January 14, 1969

Date of Issue August 6, 1970

Citation For conspicuous gallantry and intrepidity in action at the risk of his life above and beyond the call of duty. 1st Lt. Warren distinguished himself at the cost of his life while serving as a platoon leader with Company C. While moving through a rubber plantation to reinforce another friendly unit, Company C came under intense fire from a well-fortified enemy force. Disregarding his safety, 1st Lt. Warren with several of his men began maneuvering through the hail of enemy fire toward the hostile positions. When he had come to within 6 feet of one of the enemy bunkers and was preparing to toss a hand grenade into it, an enemy grenade was suddenly thrown into the middle of his small group. Thinking only of his men, 1st Lt. Warren fell in the direction of the grenade, thus shielding those around him from the blast. His action, performed at the cost of his life, saved 3 men from serious or mortal injury. 1st Lt. Warren's ultimate action of sacrifice to save the lives of his men was in keeping with the highest traditions of the military service and reflects great credit on him, his unit, and the U.S. Army.

References and Further Reading

Above and Beyond: A History of the Medal of Honor from the Civil War to Vietnam. Boston: Boston Publishing Company, 1985.

Beyer, Walter F., O. F. Keydel, W. F. Beyer, Oscar Keydel, eds. *Deeds of Valor: How America's Civil War Heroes Won the Congressional Medal of Honor.* Stamford, CT: Longmeadow Press, 1992.

Congressional Medal of Honor Society. http://www.cmohs.com.

Converse, Elliott V. and Julius W. Becton, Jr. *The Exclusion of Black Soldiers from the Medal of Honor in World War II.* Jefferson, NC: McFarland, 1997.

Cooke, Donald Ewin. *For Conspicuous Gallantry: Winners of the Medal of Honor.* Maplewood, NJ: C. S. Hammond & Co., 1966.

Doherty, Kieran. *Congressional Medal of Honor Recipients.* Springfield, NJ: Enslow Publishers, 1998.

Donovan, Frank Robert. *The Medal: The Story of the Medal of Honor.* New York: Dodd, Mead, 1962.

Korea: The Names, the Deeds. New York: Dell, 1987.

Lang, George, Raymond L. Collins, and Gerard White. *Medal of Honor Recipients, 1863–1994.* New York: Facts on File, 1995.

Lee, Irvin H. *Negro Medal of Honor Men.* New York: Dodd, Mead, 1969.

Medal of Honor Citations: Vietnam War, 1964–1972. http://www.mishalov.com/Citations.html.

Murphy, Edward. *Vietnam Medal of Honor Heroes.* New York: Ballantine Books, 1987.

Schubert, Frank N. *Black Valor: Buffalo Soldiers and the Medal of Honor, 1870–1898.* Wilmington, Del.: Scholarly Resources, 1997.

U.S. Army Center of Military History: Full-text Listings of Medal of Honor Citations. http://www.army.mil/cmh-pg/moh1.htm.

World War II: The Names, the Deeds, A-L. Vol. 1. New York: Dell, 1986.

World War II: The Names, the Deeds, M-Z. Vol. 2. New York: Dell, 1986.

Historic Sites of African American Military Significance

Alabama

Fort Gaines, Mobile, Alabama
This is the site of the Battle of Mobile Bay (1862). Located at the east end of Bienville Boulevard on Dauphin Island, Fort Gaines was a key stronghold guarding Mobile Bay prior to and during the battle. Visitors can explore the battlements, living quarters, tunnels, and bastions of Fort Gaines. Cannon used during the battle are also on display.

Sulphur Trestle Fort Site,
near Elkmont, Alabama
This site commemorates the battle between the 11th United States Colored Troops, the 3d Tennessee Infantry, and the 9th Indiana Cavalry against Confederate forces under Nathan Bedford Forrest. The fort subsequently surrendered and was burned by Forrest. The site, situated one mile south of Elkmont, is currently used for agriculture.

Arizona

Tortilla Flats, Arizona
This site commemorates a battle involving Gen. George Crook's forces (including African American units) as part of a campaign to wipe out Apache renegades (1872–1873).

Fort Bowie, Bowie, Arizona
Fort Bowie is situated in Cochise County, about 13 miles south of Bowie. Commanding the eastern entrance of Apache Pass, Fort Bowie (1862) was a focal point in U.S. Army operations against the Chiricahua Apache in the 1860s and 1870s. A much-traveled mountain crossing of strategic value due to the presence of spring water, the pass served Apache peoples, as well as Spanish, Mexican, and American settlers in the Southwest.

Fort Grant, Bonita, Arizona
This is the site of the historic fort originally established as Fort Aravaipa and then changed to Fort Breckinridge. The camp was situated in the Aravaipa Canyon until a new site for the post was selected in 1872. The camp was destroyed on July 10, 1861, in order to keep its supplies out of Confederate hands. The post was reestablished on May 18, 1862, by the California Volunteers and renamed Camp Stanford for Governor Leland Stanford of California, before being changed back to Fort Breckinridge in October 1863. On November 1, 1865, the post was renamed Camp Grant in honor of Union General Ulysses S. Grant.

Fort Huachuca, Arizona
Today, Fort Huachuca is an active military base. It has numerous buildings and sites related to African American soldiers, including the Buffalo Soldiers, and contains exhibits on black military history in the West. Many of the nineteenth-century buildings are still standing. A museum displays the role of the military in the development of the Southwest.

Arkansas

Battle of Helena, Helena, Arkansas
Four sites commemorate the Battle of Helena (July 1863), in which the African American 2d Infantry took part in overcoming a Confederate siege of the city.

Battery A site is at the northwest junction of Adams and Columbia Streets, and is currently unoccupied land.

Battery B site is at the northeast junction of Liberty Street and Summit Road, and is also unoccupied land.

Battery C site, also known as Graveyard Hill, is at the junction of Clark and York Streets, and is a landscaped park.

Battery D site is also known as Hindman Hill and is currently a landscaped park.

California

Allensworth Historic District, Route 43, California
This site commemorates Allen Allensworth, a chaplain in the 24th Infantry Regiment. The 600-acre, 67-building site is in the town of Allensworth and currently consists of a religious structure, a school, and another dwelling.

Colorado

Beecher's Island Battlefield Monument, Colorado
Established in 1905, this memorial is located on the bank of the Arikaree River and is a joint Colorado-Kansas historical site. It is dedicated to the 10th Cavalry to commemorate the September 17–19, 1868, battle between Col. George A. Forsyth's scouts and a group of about 750 Indians. The monument is the second to be erected. The original 1905 monument was washed away in the 1935 Arikaree River flood. Only the engraved portion of the base of the original marker was recovered.

Connecticut

Jeff Liberty's Grave, Washington, Connecticut
This grave marks the final resting place of the former slave who served in the African American Connecticut Regiment during the American Revolution.

Prince Goodin Home, Canterbury, Connecticut
This is the house once owned by a freeman who fought in the French and Indian War, serving at Fort William Henry, where he was captured and then freed in 1760 when the British took Montreal.

District of Columbia

African American Civil War Memorial, Washington, D.C.
This memorial was erected and dedicated in March 1998 to the memory of the 186,000 African Americans who fought for the Union during the Civil War.

Black Revolutionary War Patriot Memorial, Washington, D.C.
This memorial is dedicated to the 5,000 African Americans who fought in the American Revolution.

Frederick Douglass House, Washington, D.C.
This historic landmark was the home of the prominent African American abolitionist, writer, and influential Civil War figure from 1877 to 1895. The Frederick Douglass Memorial and Historical Association was established in 1900 and the historic home opened in 1962. It was redesignated the Frederick Douglass National Historic Site on February 12, 1988. Visitors to the site will learn about his efforts to abolish slavery and his struggle for human rights, equal rights, and civil rights for all oppressed people.

Florida

Olustee Battlefield Historic State Park, Olustee, Florida
This battlefield site commemorates the place where the 8th United States Colored Troops and the 54th Massachusetts Regiment fought during the Civil War. It is Florida's first state park and is located on U.S. Highway 90, fifteen miles east of Lake City and fifty miles west of Jacksonville.

Illinois

Victory Monument, 35th Street and South Park Way, Chicago, Illinois
This monument was erected in 1927 and is also known as the Black Doughboy Monument. It commemorates the predominantly Illinois-based 369th Infantry Regiment.

Eighth Regiment Armory, Chicago, Illinois
Based at 3533 South Giles Avenue, this was the first armory to be constructed for the use of African American troops. It was built in 1914–1915 by J. B.

Dibelka. The "Fighting 8th" traces its roots to the formation of the volunteer Hannibal Guard militia in 1871. It later became a division of the Illinois National Guard, and during World War I was incorporated into the 370th Infantry Regiment.

Iowa

Fort Des Moines, Des Moines, Iowa
This historic fort commemorates the African American 24th and 25th Infantry and 9th and 10th Cavalry members who trained and graduated from there. After graduation in June 1917, the men assembled as the 92d Infantry Division and fought on the approaches to Metz, France, in World War I.

Kansas

Buffalo Soldier Monument,
Fort Leavenworth, Kansas
This memorial commemorates the contributions of the Buffalo Soldiers. Fort Leavenworth was the historic home of the 10th Cavalry. The monument, initiated by Gen. Colin Powell, was dedicated in July 1992 to the memory of the 9th and 10th Cavalry.

Fort Dodge, Dodge City, Kansas
This fort was much used by the 10th Cavalry during its operations against Native Americans in 1868–1869. The fort was established in 1859 near the 100th meridian (the Louisiana Purchase western border). It was the last U.S. Army fort located before the Civil War, and was the first fort opened (in 1865) after the war. Fort Dodge, intended to guard travelers on the Santa Fe Trail and to keep Indian and other predators at bay, quickly became an important military fortification.

Fort Scott National Historic Site, Fort Scott, Kansas
This site is associated with the formation of the 1st Kansas Colored Volunteers, the first African American unit to see action during the Civil War. Fort Scott was established in 1842 and served first as a frontier outpost and then as a Civil War garrison. During the war, the fort was a major focal point of African American troop activity and training. The fort was restored to its 1840s appearance and contains a Civil War museum.

Fort Wallace, Wallace, Kansas
A roadside marker shows the position of the fort that was used by African American troops in the latter part of the nineteenth century. Gen. William T. Sherman, while in command of the Military Division of the Missouri, arranged the construction of Fort Wallace—as well as Forts Riley, Harker, and Hays—for the protection for stagecoaches, wagon trains, railroad surveyors and laborers, and settlers. Fort Wallace, originally known as Camp Pond Creek, was the most western post in Kansas along the Smoky Hill Trail, and from 1865 to 1878 bore the brunt of the Indian wars in the state.

Kentucky

Camp Nelson Archaeological Sites,
Jessamine County, Kentucky
This is the site of a major recruitment camp for African American troops. It also has an important national cemetery.

Kentucky Military History Museum,
Frankfort, Kentucky
This museum has specific exhibits related to African Americans recruited from Kentucky during the Civil War. The museum is housed in the Old State Arsenal building, which formerly held the weapons and equipment of the Kentucky Militia. It is located on the corner of Main Street and Capitol Avenue, and displays uniforms, medals, flags, and weapons, including a collection of automatic arms and Kentucky rifles. Exhibits trace the state's involvement in military conflicts through two centuries.

Louisiana

Chalmette Battlefield, Jean Lafitte National Historic
Park and Preserve, Louisiana
This is the location of the Battle of New Orleans site where the so-called Free Men of Color fought during the War of 1812. The site is situated 6 miles to the southeast of New Orleans on St. Bernard Highway, and is adjacent to the Chalmette National Cemetery.

Port Hudson Siege Marker, Port Hudson, Louisiana
This site marks the Port Hudson siege involving African American troops during the Civil War.

Massachusetts

Crispus Attucks Monument, Boston Massacre Site, Massachusetts
This monument was erected to commemorate the prominent African American who died in the Boston Massacre (1770) prior to the American Revolution. The monument and burial place are located just off Boston Common.

Robert G. Shaw and 54th Massachusetts Memorial, Boston, Massachusetts
This memorial was erected in 1897 at the entrance to Boston Common at the junction of Beacon and Park Streets in Boston.

Mississippi

Black Confederate Memorial, Canton, Mississippi
This twenty-foot obelisk was erected in 1894 as a tribute to the African American slaves who went to battle with Confederate forces.

Montana

Fort Missoula, Missoula, Montana
This site was a home of the 25th Infantry Regiment. The unit tested bicycles to replace horses. Twelve buildings remain from the historic fort, and there are permanent exhibits, including material related to the black bicycle corps. The buildings are located on thirty-two acres at the center of what was Fort Missoula. The site includes former log quarters for noncommissioned officers, a U.S. Forest Service lookout, a school, a log cabin, a railroad depot, an army warehouse, a quartermaster warehouse, internment camp barracks, and a quartermaster root cellar.

Fort Shaw, Montana
This Montana fort was a home of the 25th Infantry Regiment. It is situated on the Sun River and was built in 1867. First named Camp Reynolds, it was changed in honor of Civil War colonel Robert Gould Shaw. It was established as a military post in 1876 and has been recognized as the "Queen of Montana's Posts" because one of the buildings was 125 feet long. Fort Shaw was used as an Indian school after being abandoned in 1890. Later, the Great Northern Railroad came through and Fort Shaw became part of the Vaughn-Augusta branch.

New Mexico

Fort Union National Monument, Watrous, New Mexico
This monument celebrates elements of the 9th Cavalry that were stationed at the post. Fort Union was established in 1851 by Lt. Col. Edwin V. Sumner to guard and protect the Santa Fe Trail. During its forty-year history, three different forts were constructed close together. The third and final Fort Union was the largest in the Southwest, and functioned as a military garrison, territorial arsenal, and military supply depot for the region.

New York

Fort Ticonderoga, Ticonderoga, New York
The fort memorializes the battle in which Ethan Allen's Green Mountain Boys, some of whom were African American (including Lemuel Haynes, Primus Black, and Epheram Blackman), defeated a British force. For most of the second half of the eighteenth century, this landmark was the military key to the Champlain Valley, New York City, the Hudson River Valley, western New England, and Montreal. This strategic location made the fort one of the most important military sites in the struggle for control of North America during the French and Indian War and the American Revolution.

369th Regiment Armory, New York
This armory was built around 1933 for the African American 369th Infantry Regiment, founded in 1918. The building is still used for arms storage.

Ohio

John Mercer Langston House, Oberlin, Ohio
This site was the home of John Mercer Langston, one of whose many activities was serving as a recruiter for the 54th and the 55th Massachusetts Regiments.

Charles Young Home, Xenia, Ohio
This is a registered National Historic Landmark and is scheduled to become the future site of the National Museum of African American Military History. Its unique history relives the days when it was a way station for the Underground Railroad.

Oklahoma

Fort Sill, Comanche, Oklahoma
Units of the 10th Cavalry and 24th Infantry served at Fort Sill. Troops stationed here were active in campaigns against Southern Plains tribes in the late nineteenth century. Virtually all of the original fort survives. It has been expanded and continues to play a significant role for the U.S. Army in the twentieth century.

Pennsylvania

Valley Forge National Historic Park, Valley Forge, Pennsylvania
This national historic park opened on July 4, 1976. It commemorates the Continental Army and its African American soldiers who stayed at Valley Forge during the winter of 1777. Of all the places associated with the American Revolution, perhaps none has come to symbolize perseverance and sacrifice more than Valley Forge. The hardships of the encampment claimed the lives of one in ten, nearly all from disease. Despite the privations suffered by the army at Valley Forge, George Washington and his generals built a professional military organization that ultimately enabled the Continental Army to triumph over the British.

Rhode Island

Black Regiment Memorial, Rhode Island
Situated to the west of Portsmouth, this memorial was erected to commemorate the contribution of the 1st Rhode Island Regiment in the Battle of Rhode Island during the American Revolution.

Battle of Rhode Island Site, Portsmouth, Rhode Island
African Americans played a major role in this victory over the British during the American Revolution. The site is situated on Lehigh Hill between Medley and Dexter Streets in Portsmouth and is currently a landscaped park.

South Carolina

Folly Island, South Carolina
This is the site of archaeological excavations of an abandoned cemetery of the 55th Massachusetts Regiment and 1st North Carolina Colored Infantry (35th United States Colored Troops). The site is now located within a residential housing development.

Robert Smalls's House, Beaufort, South Carolina
Located at 511 Prince Street in Beaufort, this site was named as a national historic landmark in 1973. It is now a private dwelling.

Fish Haul Archaeological Site, Hilton Head Island, South Carolina
This site was the location of Mitchellville, a village of freed slaves. Many freed slaves entered the U.S. Army as contraband or United States Colored Troops during the Civil War. It is a National Register site and is currently unoccupied land.

Tennessee

Fort Pillow State Park, Henning, Tennessee
This site contains well-preserved ruins of Civil War fortifications. The 1,642-acre Fort Pillow is located on the Chickasaw Bluffs overlooking the Mississippi River. The Union army seized the fort due to its strategic location and controlled it during most of the war.

Texas

Fort Davis, Texas
This site is a re-creation of the frontier military post. Exhibits include restored living quarters and a commissary. Fort Davis was a key U.S. Army fortification in West Texas, established to guard the San Antonio–El Paso route. Its peak strength was between 1879 and 1885.

Fort Concho, San Angelo, Texas
This site is the best preserved of all the Texas frontier forts, with eleven original buildings still standing. A home of the 10th Cavalry, there are exhibits on the fort's role on the frontier. Located at 630 South Oakes Street in San Angelo, the fort was established in 1867 to protect the Texas frontier and was active until 1889, when it was abandoned by the U.S. Army. Soldiers from the fort carried out campaigns against the Kiowa and Comanche in 1870–1875.

Archaeological Site 41HZ228, near Sierra Blanca, Texas
This is a possible burial site of soldiers killed in the

October 28, 1880, ambush by Apaches. It is a National Register site.

Archaeological Site 41HZ439, near Sierra Blanca, Texas
This National Register site is also located near Sierra Blanca and was the campsite of the 10th Cavalry.

Archaeological Site 41HZ227, near Sierra Blanca, Texas
Also near Sierra Blanca, this is a National Register site of a 10th Cavalry camp and could be the place where soldiers were ambushed by Apache on October 28, 1880.

Bullis Camp Site, Dryden, Texas
From 1877 to 1879, this site was the camp of the Seminole Negro Scouts. Also known as Camp Meyers or Fort Bullis, the National Register site is currently used for agriculture.

Utah

Fort Douglas, Salt Lake City, Utah
This site was once a home of the 24th Infantry Regiment. The U.S. Army was stationed here to maintain federal authority in the Mormon territory in the 1860s. The fort also represented an effort to protect transcontinental telegraph lines and mail and transportation routes.

Virginia

Great Bridge Battlefield Memorial, Virginia
This memorial is dedicated to commemorate the contribution of African Americans who fought in the Battle of Great Bridge (1775) during the American Revolution.

Richmond National Battlefield Park, Virginia
This site is where nine black regiments participated in fighting in 1864. Between 1861 and 1865, Union armies repeatedly set out to capture Richmond, the capital of the Confederacy, and thereby end the Civil War. This park commemorates eleven different sites associated with those campaigns, including the battlefields at Gaines' Mill, Malvern Hill, and Cold Harbor. Established in 1936, the park protects 763 acres of historic ground.

Petersburg National Battlefield Park, Virginia
This park is the location of the Battle of the Crater and the Siege of Petersburg, both events in which African Americans played prominent roles. Petersburg became the setting for the longest siege in American history when Union general Ulysses S. Grant failed to capture Richmond in the spring of 1864. The nine-and-a-half-month siege ended on April 2, 1865. The park contains a museum and interpretive center.

Wyoming

Fort Russell, Wyoming
Fort Russell is now called F. E. Warren Air Force Base. The fort area contains many well-preserved barracks and officers' quarters.

Fort Washakie Blockhouse, Wyoming
Fort Washakie was in military use from 1869 to 1909; the 9th and 10th cavalry were stationed there for some time. Originally called Camp Brown, it was renamed in 1878 after the last chief of the Shoshone tribe, who in the 1870s provided 150 men for General Crook's campaign against the Sioux and Cheyenne, which ended with the disaster at Little Big Horn (1876). When Washakie died (aged 100) in 1900, he was buried with full military honors. The site is on the Wind River Indian Reservation.

Bibliography

General

Achebe, Chinua. *Home and Exile.* Oxford and New York: Oxford University Press, 2001.

Adler, Bill, ed. *The Black Soldier: From the American Revolution to Vietnam.* New York: Morrow, 1971.

Ambrose, Stephen E. *Duty, Honor, Country: A History of West Point.* Baltimore, MD: Johns Hopkins University Press, 1996.

Aptheker, Herbert. *A Documentary History of the Negro People in the United States.* New York: Citadel Press, 1951.

Atkinson, Rick. *The Long Gray Line: West Point's Journey to Vietnam.* Glasgow: William Collins, 1990.

Barr, Aluyn. *Black Texans: A History of Negroes in Texas, 1528–1971.* Austin, TX: Jenkins Publishing, 1973.

Bennett, Lerone, Jr. *Before the Mayflower: A History of Black America.* New York: Penguin Books, 1982.

Berlin, Ira, ed. *The Black Military Experience.* New York: Cambridge University Press, 1983.

Binkin, Martin, and Mark J. Eitelberg. *Blacks and the Military.* Washington, DC: Brookings Institution, 1982.

Boston Publishing Company, ed. *Above and Beyond: A History of the Medal of Honor from the Civil War to Vietnam.* Boston: Boston Publishing Company/Time Life Education, 1985.

Carruth, Gorton. *The Encyclopaedia of American Facts and Dates.* New York: HarperCollins, 1993.

Christmas, Walter. *Negroes in Public Affairs and Government.* New York: Educational Heritage, 1966.

Cloyd, Iris, ed. *Who's Who among Black Americans.* Detroit, MI: Gale Research Inc, 1990.

Cooke, Donald Ewin. *For Conspicuous Gallantry: Winners of the Medal of Honor.* Union, NJ: Hammond World Atlas Corp., 1966.

Creamer, Maureen. *Black Women in America: An Historical Encyclopaedia.* Brooklyn, NY: Carlson Publishing, 1993.

David, Jay, and Elaine Crane, eds. *The Black Soldier: From the American Revolution to Vietnam.* New York: Morrow, 1971.

Davis, Benjamin O., Jr. *Benjamin O Davis Jr., American: An Autobiography.* Washington, DC: Smithsonian Institution Press, 1992.

Davis, Lenwood G., and George Hill. *Blacks in the American Armed Forces, 1776–1983: A Bibliography.* Westport, CT: Greenwood Press, 1985.

Doherty, Kieran. *Congressional Medal of Honor Recipients* Collective Biographies series. Berkeley Heights, NJ: Enslow Publishers, 1998.

Donaldson, Gary A. *The History of African-Americans in the Military.* Malabar, FL: Krieger, 1991.

Donovan, Frank Robert *The Medal; The Story of the Medal of Honor.* New York: Dodd Mead, 1962.

Douglass, Frederick. *The Narrative of the Life of Frederick Douglass, An American Slave.* Cambridge, MA: Belknap Press of Harvard University, 1960.

———. *Life and Times of Frederick Douglass.* New York: Collier Books, 1962.

———. *My Bondage and My Freedom.* New York: Dover Publications, 1969.

Douglass, Frederick, Philip Sheldon Foner, and Yuval Taylor. *Frederick Douglass.* Chicago: Lawrence Hill Books, 1999.

Douglass Sprague, Rosetta. *Anna Murray-Douglass, My Mother As I Recall Her.* The Frederick Douglass Papers, Library of Congress.

DuBois, W. E. B. *Dusk of Dawn. An Essay Toward an Autobiography of a Race Concept.* Somerset, NJ: Transaction Publications, 1991.

Dupuy, R. Ernest, and Trevor N. Dupuy. *Military Heritage of America.* New York: McGraw-Hill, 1956.

———. *The Encyclopaedia of Military History.* New York: Harper and Row, 1986.

Fabre, Michel. *From Harlem to Paris: Black American Writers in France.* Chicago: University of Illinois Press, 1991.

Fletcher, Marvin E. *America's First Black General: Benjamin O. Davis Sr. 1880–1970.* Lawrence: University Press of Kansas, 1989.

Foner, Eric, and John A. Garraty, eds. *The Readers' Companion to American History.* Boston: Houghton Mifflin, 1991.

Foner, Jack D. *Blacks and the Military in American History.* New York: Praeger, 1974.

Franklin, John Hope. *From Slavery to Freedom: A History of Negro Americans.* New York: Alfred A. Knopf, 1956.

Ganoe, William A. *The History of the United States Army.* New York: D Appleton & Co, 1924.

Grant, John, James L. Lynch, and Ronald H. Bailey. *West Point: The First 200 Years.* Guilford, CT: Globe Pequot Press, 2002.

Greene, Robert Ewell. *Black Defenders of America, 1775–1973.* Chicago: Johnson, 1974.

Guthrie, Chaplain James M. *Camp-fires of the Afro-American or, the Colored Man as a Patriot.* Philadelphia: Afro-American Pub., 1899.

Harlan, Lewis R. *Booker. T. Washington: The Making of a Black Leader, 1856–1901.* Oxford and New York: Oxford University Press, 1975.

Harley, Sharon. *The Timetables of African American History: A Chronology of the Most Important People and Events in African American History.* New York: Simon and Schuster, 1995.

Herr, John K., and Edward S. Wallace. *The Story of the US Cavalry.* Boston: Little Brown, 1953.

Horton, James Oliver, and Lois E. Horton, eds. *A History of the African American People.* London: Salamander Books, 1995.

Howard, Victor. *Black Liberation in Kentucky: Emancipation and Freedom, 1862–1884.* Lexington: University Press of Kentucky, 1983.

Huggins, Nathan Irvin. *Slave and Citizen: The Life of Frederick Douglass.* Boston: Little, Brown, 1980.

Johnson, Edward A. *Negro Race in America from 1619–1899.* New York: Isaac Goldman, 1891.

Johnson, Jesse J. *Black Armed Forces Officers, 1736–1971.* Hampton, VA: J. J. Johnson, 1971.

———. *Women in the Armed Forces 1942–1974: A Pictorial History.* Hampton, VA: J. J. Johnson, 1974.

Johnson, Jesse J., ed. *A Pictorial History of Black Soldiers (1619–1969) in Peace and War.* Hampton, VA: Hampton Institute, 1969.

Lane, Linda Rochelle. *Black Women in America: An Historical Encyclopaedia.* Brooklyn, NY: Carlson, 1993.

Lang, George, Raymond L. Collins, and Gerard White. *Medal of Honor Recipients, 1863–1994.* New York: Facts on File, 1996.

Lanning, Michael G. *The African American Soldier: From Crispus Attucks to Colin Powell.* Secaucus, NJ: Birch Lane Press, 1997.

Lee, E. Lawrence. *Indian Wars in North Carolina, 1663–1763.* Raleigh, NC: Carolina Charter Tercentenary Commission, 1963.

Lee, Irvin H. *Negro Medal of Honor Men.* New York: Dodd Mead, 1969.

Lee, Ulysses. *The Employment of Negro Troops.* Washington, DC: United States Army Center of Military History, 1966.

Lewis, David Levering. *W. E. B. DuBois: The Fight for Equality and the American Century, 1919–1963.* New York: Henry Holt, 2000.

Litwack, Leon F. *North of Slavery: The Negro in the Free States, 1790–1860.* Chicago: University of Chicago Press, 1961.

Logan, Rayford W., and Michael R. Winston, eds. *Dictionary of American Negro Biography.* New York: W. W. Norton, 1982.

Lucas, Marion Brunson. *A History of Blacks in Kentucky: From Slavery to Segregation, 1760–1891.* Frankfort: Kentucky Historical Society, 2001.

Matthews, Basil. *Booker T. Washington.* London: SCM Press, 1949.

McGuire, Phillip. *He, Too, Spoke for Democracy.* New York: Greenwood Press, 1988.

Morais, Herbert Montford. *History of the Negro in Medicine.* New York: New York Publishers, 1967.

Mullen, Robert F. *Blacks in America's Wars: The Shift in Attitudes from the Revolutionary War to Vietnam.* New York: Monad Press, 1974.

Nalty, Bernard C. *Strength for the Fight: A History of Black Americans in the Military.* New York: Free Press, 1986.

Nalty, Bernard C., and Maurice J. MacGregor. *Blacks in the Military: Essential Documents.* Wilmington, DE: Scholarly Resources, 1981.

Nash, Gary B. *The American People: Creating a Nation and a Society.* New York: Harper Collins, 1992.

Nelson, Dennis Denmark. *The Integration of the Negro into the United States Navy, 1776–1947, with a Brief Historical Introduction by Lieutenant (D) Dennis Denmark Nelson, U.S.N.R.* Washington, DC: Department of the Navy, 1948.

Quarles, Benjamin. *Frederick Douglass.* Washington, DC: Associated Publishers, 1948.

———. *The Negro in the Making of America.* New York: Collier Books, 1964.

Reef, Catherine. *Benjamin Davis Jr. (African American Soldiers).* Breckenridge, CO: Twenty First Century Books, 1992.

Schlesinger, Arthur M., Jr., ed. *The Almanac of American History.* New York: Perigee Books, 1983.

Sterne, Emma Gelders. *Blood Brothers: Four Men of Science.* New York: Knopf, 1959.

Steward, Theophilus Gould. *The Colored Regulars in the United States Army, Revolutionary War to 1899.* Philadelphia: A. M. E. Book Concern, 1904.

Townsend, Linda E., and Dupree Davenport. *A History of Blacks in the Coastguard from 1790.* Washington, DC: Department of Transportation, 1977.

Ware, Gilbert. *William Hastie: Grace under Pressure.* New York: Oxford University Press, 1984.

Washington, Booker T. *Up from Slavery: An Autobiography.* London: Thomas Nelson and Sons, 1901.

Willenz, June A. *Women Veterans: America's Forgotten Heroines.* New York: Continuum, 1983.

Pre–American Civil War

Alden, John R. *A History of the American Revolution.* New York: Knopf, 1969.

Altoff, Gerard T. *Among My Best Men: African Americans and the War of 1812.* Introduction by Joseph P. Reidy and illustrations by Robyn Opthoff Lile. Put-in-Bay, OH: Perry Group, 1996.

Beach, E. Merrill. *From Valley Forge to Freedom: A Story of a Black Patriot.* Chester, CT: Pequot Press, 1975.

Bennett, Lerone, Jr. *Before the Mayflower.* New York: Penguin Books, 1978.

Berlin, Ira, ed. *Slavery and Freedom in the Age of the American Revolution.* Blacks in the New World series. Urbana: United States Capitol Historical Society/University of Illinois Press, 1986.

Bobrick, Benson. *Angel in the Whirlwind: The Triumph of the American Revolution.* New York: Simon & Schuster, 1997.

Bradley, Patricia. *Slavery, Propaganda, and the American Revolution.* Jackson: University Press of Mississippi, 1998.

Buckley, Robert N. *Slaves in Red Coats: The British West India Regiments, 1795–1815.* New Haven, CT: Yale University, 1979.

Cox, Clinton. *Come All You Brave Soldiers: Blacks in the American Revolution.* New York: Scholastic Press, 1999.

Davis, Burke. *Black Heroes of the American Revolution.* New York: Harcourt Brace Jovanovich, 1976.

Foner, Philip S. *The Life and Writings of Frederick Douglass: Early Years 1817–1849.* New York: International Publishers, 1950.

———. *The Life and Writings of Frederick Douglass: Pre-Civil War Decade, 1850–1860.* New York: International Publishers, 1950.

———. *Blacks in the American Revolution.* Westport, CT: Greenwood Press, 1975.

Greene, Robert Ewell. *Black Courage, 1775–1783: Documentation of Black Participation in the American Revolution.* Washington, DC: National Society of Daughters of the American Revolution, 1984.

Gregory, P. Lampe. *Frederick Douglass—Freedom's Voice, 1818–1845.* East Lansing: Michigan State University Press, 1998.

Heatter, Basil. *A King in Haiti: The Story of Henri Christophe.* New York: Farrar, Straus and Giroux, 1972.

Hirschfeld, Fritz. *George Washington and Slavery: A Documentary Portrayal.* Columbia: University of Missouri Press, 1997.

Hoyt, Edwin Palmer. *The Amistad Affair.* New York: Abelard-Schuman, 1970.

Jones, Howard. *Mutiny on the Amistad: The Saga of a Slave Revolt and Its Impact on American Abolition, Law and Diplomacy.* New York: Oxford University Press, 1987.

Kaplan, Sidney, and Emma Nogrady Kaplan. *The Black Presence in the Era of the American Revolution, 1770–1800.* Greenwich, CT: New York Graphic Society, 1973. Reprint, Amherst: University of Massachusetts Press, 1989.

Kohn, Bernice. *The Amistad Mutiny.* New York: McCall Publishing, 1971.

Litwack, Leon F. *North of Slavery: The Negro in the Free States, 1790–1860.* Chicago: University of Chicago Press, 1970.

McGuire, Thomas J., Craig A. Benner, and Kyle R. Weaver. *Brandywine Battlefield Park: Pennsylvania Trail of History Guide.* Mechanicsburg, PA: Stackpole Books. 2001.

Millender, Dharanthula. *Crispus Attucks: Black Leader of Colonial Patriots.* Indianapolis: Merrill & Co, 1982.

Nell, William Cooper. *Colored Patriots of the American Revolution.* Salem, NH: Ayer, 1986.

Newman, Richard. *Black Preacher to White America.* Brooklyn, NY: Carlson Publishing, 1990.

Owens, William A. *Black Mutiny: The Revolt on the Schooner Amistad.* New York: J. Day, 1953.

Quarles, Benjamin. *The Negro in the American Revolution.* New York: W. W. Norton, 1973.

Stampp, Kenneth M. *The Peculiar Institution: Slavery in the Ante-Bellum South.* New York: Vintage, 1956.

Tuchman, Barbara W. *The First Salute, a View of the American Revolution.* New York: Ballantine Books, 1988.

Walters, Ronald G. *The Anti-Slavery Appeal: American Abolitionism after 1830.* Baltimore, MD: John Hopkins Press, 1976.

Wilson, Joseph T. *The Phalanx: A History of the Negro Soldier of the United States in the Wars of 1775–1812, 1861–1865.* Hartford, CT: American Publishing Company, 1890. Reprint, Manchester, NH: Ayer Company Publishers, 1992.

Wood, W. J. *Battles of the Revolutionary War, 1775–1781: Major Battles and Campaigns.* Chapel Hill, NC: Da Capo Press, 1990.

Zinert, Karen. *The Amistad Slave Revolt.* North Haven, CT: Linnet Books, 1997.

American Civil War

Adams, George W. *Doctors in Blue: The Medical History of the Union Army in the Civil War.* New York: Henry Schuman, 1952.

Auchincloss, Louis, ed. *The Hone & Strong Diaries of Old Manhattan.* New York: Abbeville Press, 1989.

Barrow, Charles Kelly, Segars, J.H., and Rosenburg, R.B., eds. *Forgotten Confederates: An Anthology about Black Southerners.* Atlanta, GA: Southern Heritage Press, 1995.

Beecham, Robert K., and Michael E. Stevens, eds. *As If It Were Glory: Robert Beecham's Civil War from the Iron Brigade to the Black Regiments.* Madison, WI: Madison House, 1998.

Bellard, Alfred. *Gone for a Soldier: The Civil War Memoirs of Private Alfred Bellard.* Boston: Little, Brown, 1975.

Berlin, Ira, Joseph P. Reidy, and Leslie S. Rowland. *Freedom: A Documentary History of Emancipation, 1861–1867.* 2 vols. New York: Cambridge University Press, 1982.

Beyer, Walter F., and O. F. Keydel, eds. *Deeds of Valor: How America's Civil War Heroes Won the Congressional Medal of Honor.* Stamford, CT: Longmeadow Press, 1992.

Blackerby, H.C. *Blacks in Blue and Gray: Afro-American Service in the Civil War.* Tuscaloosa, AL: Portals Press, 1979.

Blackett, R. J. M., ed. *Thomas Morris Chester, Black Civil War Correspondent.* Baton Rouge, Louisiana State University Press, 1989.

Bradford, Sarah. *Scenes in the Life of Harriet Tubman.* Salem, NH: Ayer, 1988.

Brewer, James. *Confederate Negro: Virginia's Craftsmen and Military Laborers.* Durham, NC: Duke, 1969.

Brown, William Wells. *The Negro in the American Rebellion: His Heroism and His Fidelity.* New York: Lee and Shepard, 1867. Reprint, New York: Kraus, 1969.

Burchard, Peter. *One Gallant Rush: Robert Gould Shaw and His Brave Black Regiment.* New York: St Martin's Press, 1965.

Coffman, Edward M. *The Old Army: A Portrait of the American Army in Peacetime, 1784–1898.* New York: Oxford University Press, 1986.

Cooper, Michael L. *From Slave to Civil War Hero:*

The Life and Times and Robert Smalls. New York: Lodestar Books, 1994.

Cornish, Dudley T. *The Sable Arm: Negro Troops in the Union Army, 1861–1865.* New York: Longmans Green & Co, 1956. Reprint, Lawrence: University Press of Kansas, 1987.

Cowden, Robert. *A Brief Sketch of the Organization and Services of the Fifty-Ninth Regiment of the United States Colored Infantry, and Biographical Sketches.* Dayton, OH: United Brethren, 1883.

Crawford, Samuel J. *Kansas in the Sixties.* Chicago: McClurg & Co, 1911.

Current, Richard Nelson. *Lincoln's Loyalists: Union Soldiers from the Confederacy.* New York: Oxford University Press, 1992.

Davis, W. C. "The Massacre at Saltville." *Civil War Times Illustrated* 9 (1971): 4–11, 43–48.

Dennett, George M. *History of the 9th USC Troops.* Philadelphia: King and Bair, 1886.

Denney, Robert E. *The Civil War Years: A Day-by-Day Chronicle.* New York: Gramercy Books, 1992.

Duncan, Russell, ed. *Blue-Eyed Child of Fortune: The Civil War Letters of Colonel Robert Gould Shaw.* Athens: University of Georgia Press, 1992.

Dyer, Frederick H. *A Compendium of the War of the Rebellion.* New York: Thomas Yoseloff, 1959.

Edelstein, Tilden G. *Strange Enthusiasm: A Life of Thomas Wentworth Higginson.* New Haven: Yale University Press, 1968.

Edmonds, David C. *The Guns of Port Hudson: The Investment, Siege, and Reduction.* 2 vols. Lafayette, LA: Arcadiana Press, 1984.

Emilio, Luis F. *The Assault on Fort Wagner, July 18th 1863: The Memorable Charge of the Fifty-Fourth Regiment of Massachusetts Volunteers.* Boston: Rand Avery, 1887.

———. *A Brave Black Regiment: History of the Fifty-Fourth Regiment of Massachusetts Volunteer Infantry.* Boston: Boston Book Co., 1894.

Fishel, Edwin C. *The Secret War for the Union.* Boston: Houghton Mifflin Co., 1996.

Fletcher, Marvin. *The Black Soldier and Officer in the United States Army, 1891–1917.* Colombia: University of Missouri Press, 1974.

Foner, Philip S. *The Life and Writings of Frederick Douglass: The Civil War 1861–1865.* New York: International Publishers, 1952.

Foote, Shelby. *The Civil War—A Narrative—Red River to Appomattox.* New York: Random House, 1974.

Ford, Worthington Chauncey, ed. *A Cycle of Adam's Letters, 1861–1865.* 2 vols. Boston: Houghton Mifflin, 1920.

Gladstone, William A. *Men of Color.* Gettysburg, PA: Thomas Publications, 1993.

Glatthaar, Joseph T. *Forged in Battle: The Civil War Alliance of Black Soldiers and White Officers.* Baton Rouge: Louisiana State University Press, 1990.

Hansen, Joyce. *Between Two Fires—Black Soldiers in the Civil War.* New York: Franklin Watts, 1993.

Henry, Robert. *Story of the Confederacy.* Indianapolis: Bobbs-Merrill, 1931.

Hewitt, Lawrence Lee. *Port Hudson: Confederate Bastion on the Mississippi River.* Baton Rouge: Louisiana State University Press, 1987.

Higginson, Thomas Wentworth. *Army Life in a Black Regiment.* Boston: Beacon Press, 1962.

Johnson, Robert Underwood, and Buel, Clarence Clough, eds. *Battles & Leaders of the Civil War: Volumes I–IV.* New York: Century, 1887.

Jordan, Ervin L. *Blacks Confederates and Afro-Yankees in Civil War Virginia.* Charlottesville: University of Virginia Press, 1995.

Kireker, Charles. *History of the 116th Regiment USC Infantry.* Philadelphia: King and Baird, 1866.

Kirkland, Frazer, pseud. [Devens, Richard Miller]. *The Pictorial Book of Anecdotes and Incidents of the War of the Rebellion, Civil, Military, Naval and Domestic.* Hartford, CT: Hartford Publishing, 1866.

Lawrence, R. de T. *History of Bill Yopp.* Atlanta, GA: N.p., 1920.

McPherson, James N. *The Negro's Civil War.* New York: Pantheon, 1965.

———. *For Cause and Comrades: Why Men Fought the Civil War.* Oxford University Press, 1997.

Markle, Donald E. *Spies and Spymasters of the Civil War.* New York: Hippocrene Books, 1995.

Marvel, W. "The Battle of Saltville: Massacre or Myth?" *Blue and Gray Magazine,* August 1991, pp. 10–19, 46–60.

Mays, Thomas D. *The Saltville Massacre.* Fort Worth, TX: Ryan Place Publishers, 1995.

Moebs, Thomas Truxton. *Black Soldiers—Black Sailors—Black Ink.* Chesapeake Bay, VA: Moebs Publishing, 1994.

National Archives, Record Group 94. *The Negro in the Military Service of the United States, 1607–1889.*

Newton, Alexander H. *Out of the Briars: An Autobiography and Sketch of the Twenty-Ninth Regiment Connecticut Volunteers.* Miami, FL: Mnemosyne, 1969.

Pinkerton, Allan. *The Spy of the Rebellion.* Chicago: A. G. Nettleton, 1883.

Priest, John Michael. *Into the Fight—Pickett's Charge at Gettysburg.* Shippensburg, PA: White Mane Books, 1998.

Quarles, Benjamin. *The Negro in the Civil War.* Boston: Little, Brown, 1953.

Redkey, Edwin S., ed. *A Grand Army of Black Men: Letters from African American Soldiers in the Union Army, 1861–1865.* Cambridge, UK: Cambridge University Press, 1992.

Robinson, Charles M. *Hurricane of Fire: The Union Assault on Fort Fisher.* Annapolis, MD: United States Naval Institute Press, 1998.

Rollin, Frank A. *Life and Public Services of Martin R. Delaney.* Boston: Lee and Shepard, 1868.

Ryan, David D. *A Yankee Spy in Richmond: The Civil War Diary of "Crazy Bet" Van Lew.* Mechanicsburg, PA: Stackpole Books, 1996.

Sandburg, Carl. *Abraham Lincoln: The War Years.* 4 vols. New York: Harcourt, Brace, 1939.

Sefton, James E. *The United States Army and Reconstruction, 1865–1877.* Baton Rouge: Louisiana State University Press, 1967.

Shannon, Fred A. *The Organization and Administration of the Union Army, 1861–65.* 2 vols. Gloucester, MA: Peter Smith, 1965.

Steiner, Paul E. *Medical History of a Civil War Regiment: Disease in the Sixty-Fifth US Colored Infantry.* Clayton, MO: Institute of Civil War Studies, 1977.

Stephens, George E. *A Voice of Thunder: The Civil War Letters of George E. Stephens.* Ed. Donald Yacovone. Urbana: University of Illinois Press, 1998.

Taylor, M. W. *Harriet Tubman.* New York: Chelsea House Publishers, 1991.

Trudeau, Noah Andre. *Like Men of War.* Boston: Little Brown & Co, 1998.

U.S. War Department. *The War of the Rebellion: A Compilation of the Official Records of the Union and Confederate Armies.* Washington, DC: Government Printing Office, 1880–1901.

Webb, Garrison. *Civil War Curiosities.* Nashville, TN: Rutledge Hill Press, 1994.

Wiley, Bell Irvin. *Southern Negroes, 1861–1865.* New Haven, CT: Yale University Press, 1938.

Williams, George Washington. *A History of the Negro Troops in the War of the Rebellion, 1861–1865, Preceded by a Review of the Military Service of Negroes in Ancient and Modern Times.* Reprint, New York: Negro Universities Press, 1969.

Wilson, Joseph T. *The Phalanx: A History of the Negro Soldier of the United States in the Wars of 1775–1812, 1861–1865.* Hartford, CT: American Publishing Company, 1890. Reprint, Manchester, NH: Ayer Company Publishers, Inc., 1992.

Yopp, Bill. *Bill Yopp: Ten Cent Bill.* Clarkston, GA: Charles W. Hampton, 1969.

Post–American Civil War to World War I

Amos, Preston E. *Above and Beyond in the West: Black Medal of Honor Winners 1807–1890.* Washington, DC: Potomac Corral, The Westerners, 1974.

Athearn, Robert C. *William Tecumseh Sherman and the Settlement of the West.* Norman: University of Oklahoma Press, 1956.

Berthrong, Donald J. *The Southern Cheyennes.* Norman: University of Oklahoma Press, 1963.

Billington, Monroe Lee. *New Mexico's Buffalo Soldiers, 1866–1900.* Boulder: University of Colorado Press, 1991.

Bourke, John G. *An Apache Campaign in the Sierra Madre.* New York: Scribner's, 1886.

Brady, Cyrus T. *Indian Fights and Fighters.* New York: McClure, Phillips and Co, 1904.

Brown, D. Alexander. *Grierson's Raid.* Urbana: University of Illinois Press, 1954.

Carroll, John M. *The Black Military Experience in the American West.* New York: Liveright, 1972.

Cashin, Herschel V. *Under Fire with the Tenth U.S. Cavalry.* New York: Arno Press, 1969.

Chew, Abraham. *A Biography of Colonel Charles Young.* Washington, DC: Pendleton 1923.

Clendenon, Clarence C. *Blood on the Border: United States Army and Mexican Irregulars.* New York: Macmillan, 1969.

Clum, Woodworth. *Apache Agent.* Boston: Houghton Mifflin, 1936.

Cohn, Michael. *Black Men of the Sea.* New York: Dodd Mead, 1978.

Connell, Evan S. *Son of the Morning Star.* New York: Harper and Row, 1984.

Cox, Clinton. *The Forgotten Heroes: The Story of the Buffalo Soldiers.* New York: Scholastic, 1993.

Dierks, Jack Cameron. *A Leap to Arms: The Cuban Campaign of 1898.* Philadelphia: Lippincott, 1970.

Downey, Fairfax. *The Buffalo Soldiers in the Indian Wars.* New York: McGraw-Hill, 1969.

Drinnon, Richard. *Facing West.* New York: New American Library, 1980.

Dunlay, Thomas W. *Wolves for the Blue Soldiers: Indian Scouts and Auxiliaries with the United States Army, 1860–1890.* Lincoln: University of Nebraska Press, 1982.

Dunn, J. P., Jr. *Massacres of the Mountains.* New York: Archer House, 1886.

Emmitt, Robert. *The Last War Trail: The Utes and the Settlement of Colorado.* Norman: University of Oklahoma Press, 1954.

Fletcher, Marvin E. *The Black Soldier and Officer in the United States Army, 1891–1917.* Columbia: University of Missouri Press, 1974.

Flipper, Henry Ossian. *The Colored Cadet at West Point: Autobiography of Lieutenant Henry Ossian Flipper, U.S.A., First Graduate of Color from the U. S. Military Academy.* Introduction by Quintard Taylor Jr. Lincoln: University of Nebraska Press, 1998.

———. *Black Frontiersman: The Memoirs of Henry O. Flipper, First Black Graduate of West Point.* Compiled and edited with introduction and notes by Theodore D. Harris. Fort Worth: Texas Christian University Press, 1997.

Foner, Eric. *Reconstruction: America's Unfinished Revolution, 1863–1877.* New York: Harper and Row, 1988.

Foner, Jack D. *The United States Soldier between Two Wars: Army Life and Reforms, 1865–1898.* New York: Humanities Press, 1970.

Foner, Philip S. *The Life and Writings of Frederick Douglass: Reconstruction and After.* New York: International Publishers, 1955.

Fowler, Arlen L. *The Black Infantry in the West, 1869–1891.* Westport, CT: Greenwood, 1971.

Frazer, Robert W. *Forts of the West.* Norman: University of Oklahoma Press, 1965.

Gatewood, William B., Jr. *Smoked Yankees and the Struggle for Empire: Letters from Negro Soldiers 1898–1902.* Fayetteville: University of Arkansas Press, 1987.

Glass, Edward L N. *The History of the Tenth Cavalry, 1866–1921.* Fort Collins, CO: Old Army Press, 1972.

Glatthaar, Joseph T. *Forged In Battle: The Civil War Alliance of Black Soldiers and White Officers.* Baton Rouge: Louisiana State University Press, 1990.

Gray, Valerie A. *The Court Martial Trial of West Point Cadet Johnson Whittaker: A Headline Court Case.* Berkeley Heights, NJ: Enslow Publishers, 2001.

Greene, Robert Ewell. *The Early Life of Colonel Charles Young, 1864–1899.* Washington, DC: Department of History, Howard University, 1973.

Griffin, Louis George III, and John M Carroll. *Buffalo Soldiers West.* Fort Collins, CO: Old Army Press, 1971.

Haynes, Robert V. *A Night of Violence: The Houston Riot of 1917.* Baton Rouge: Louisiana State University Press, 1976.

Herr, John K., and Edward S. Wallace. *The Story of the U.S. Cavalry.* Boston: Little Brown, 1953.

Higginson, Thomas Wentworth. *Army Life in a Black Regiment.* East Lansing: Michigan State University Press, 1960.

Hutton, Paul Andrew, ed. *Soldiers West: Biographies from the Military Frontier.* Lincoln: University of Nebraska Press, 1987.

Johnson, Harry. *Buffalo Soldiers: The Formation of the Ninth Cavalry Regiment, July 1866–1867.* Fort Leavenworth, KS: U.S. Army Command and General Staff College, 1991.

Katz, William Loren. *The Black West.* Garden City, NY: Doubleday, 1973.

Kelley, William F. *Pine Ridge, 1890: An Eyewitness Account of the Events Surrounding the Fighting at Wounded Knee.* San Francisco: Pierre Bovis, 1971.

Lane, Ann J. *The Brownsville Affair.* Port Washington, NY: National University, 1971.

Langellier, John P. *Men A-Marching: The African American Soldier in the West, 1866–1896.* Springfield, PA: Steven Wright, 1995.

Laughlin, David. *Buffalo Soldiers: An Illustrated 30 Year History of the 10th Regiment of the U.S. Cavalry.* Tucson, AZ: Blue Horse Productions, 1991.

Leckie, William H. *The Military Conquest of the Southern Plains.* Norman: University of Oklahoma Press, 1963.

———. *The Buffalo Soldiers, A Narrative of the Negro Cavalry in the West.* Norman: University of Oklahoma Press, 1967.

Logan, Rayford W. *The Betrayal of the Negro, from Rutherford B. Hayes to Woodrow Wilson.* New York: Macmillan, 1965.

Lynk, Miles V. *The Black Troopers or the Daring Heroism of the Negro Soldiers in the Spanish-American War.* New York: AMS, 1971.

McMiller, Anita Williams. *Buffalo Soldiers: The Formation of the Tenth Cavalry Regiment from September, 1866 to August, 1867.* Fort Leavenworth, KS: US Army Command and General Staff College, 1990.

Morris, Edmund. *The Rise of Theodore Roosevelt.* New York: Ballantine, 1979.

Muller, William G. *The Twenty Fourth Infantry Past and Present.* Fort Collins, CO: The Old Army Press, 1972.

Nankivel, John H. *A History of the Twenty Fifth Infantry, 1869–1926.* Fort Collins, CO: The Old Army Press, 1972.

Nofi, Albert A. *The Spanish American War of 1898.* New York: Da Capo, 1997.

Porter, Kenneth Wiggins. *The Negro on the American Frontier.* New York: Arno Press/New York Times, 1971.

Ransom, Mudge. *Seas of the Bear.* New York: Ayer Company Publishers, 1980.

Rickey, Don, Jr. *Forty Miles a Day on Beans and Hay: The Enlisted Soldier Fighting in the Indian Wars.* Norman: University of Oklahoma Press, 1963.

Rodenbough, Theodore F. *The Tenth Regiment of Cavalry.* New York: Maynard, Merill, 1896.

Roosevelt, Theodore. *The Rough Riders.* New ed. New York: Modern Library, 1999.

Samuels, Peggy, and Harold Samuels. *Teddy Roosevelt at San Juan.* College Station: Texas A&M University, 1997.

Savage, W. Sherman. *Blacks in The West.* Westport, CT: Greenwood, 1976.

Schubert, Frank N. *Buffalo Soldiers, Braves and the Brass: The Story of Fort Robinson, Nebraska.* Shippensburg, PA: White Mane, 1993.

———. *On the Trail of the Buffalo Soldier: Biographies of African Americans in the US Army 1860–1917.* Wilmington, DE: Scholarly Resources, 1995.

———. *Black Valor: Buffalo Soldiers and the Medal of Honor, 1870–1898.* Wilmington, DE: Scholarly Resources, 1997.

Scott, Edward van Zile. *The Unwept: Black American Soldiers and the Spanish-American War.* Montgomery, AL: Black Belt Press, 1995.

Sefton, James E. *The United States Army and Reconstruction, 1865–1877.* Baton Rouge: Louisiana State University Press, 1967.

Steward, Theophilus G. *The Colored Regulars in the United States Army.* Philadelphia: AME, 1904.

Toulmin, Harry A. *With Pershing in Mexico.* Harrisburg, PA: Military Service, 1935.

Utley, Robert M. *Frontier Regulars, The United States Army and the Indian, 1866–1891.* New York: Macmillan, 1974.

———. *The Indian Frontier of the American West 1846–1890.* Albuquerque: University of New Mexico Press, 1984.

Wolff, Leon. *Little Brown Brother: How the United States Purchased and Classified the Philippine Islands at the Century's Turn.* New York: Doubleday, 1961.

Wooster, Robert A. *The Military and United States Indian Policy, 1865–1903.* New Haven, CT: Yale University Press, 1988.

World War I and the Interwar Years

Badger, Reid. *A Life in Ragtime: A Biography of James Reese Europe.* Philadelphia: American Philological Association, 1995.

Barbeau, Arthur E., and Florette Henri. *The Unknown Soldiers.* New York: Da Capo, 1996.

Bradden, William S. *Under Fire with the 370th Infantry AEF.* Chicago: William Bradden, nd.

Bullard, Robert L. *Personalities and Reminiscences of the War.* New York: Doubleday, 1925.

———. *American Soldiers also Fought.* New York: Longmans, 1936.

Carisella, P. J., and James W. Ryan. *Black Swallow of Death.* Boston: Marlborough House, 1972.

Cobb, Irvin S. *The Glory of the Coming.* New York: Doran, 1918.

Farwell, Byron. *Over There.* New York: W W Norton, 1999.

Fish, Hamilton. *Memoir of an American Patriot.* Washington, DC: Regnery Gateway, 1991.

Fisher, Lillian M. *Brave Bessie: Flying Free.* Houston, TX: Hendrick Long Publishing, 1995.

Hagood, Johnson. *The Services of Supply.* Boston: Houghton Mifflin, 1927.

Heywood, Chester D. *Negro Combat Troops in the World War.* Worcester, MA: Commonwealth, 1928.

Kimball, Robert, and William Bolcom. *Reminiscing with Sissle and Blake.* New York: Viking, 1973.

Lewis, David Levering. *When Harlem Was in Vogue.* New York: Knopf, 1981.

Little, Arthur. *From Harlem to the Rhine.* New York: Corvici, 1936.

Mason, Monroe, and Arthur Furr. *The American Negro with the Red Hand of France.* Boston: Cornhill, 1920.

Miller, Warren H. *The Boys of 1917.* Boston: Page, 1939.

Nugent, John Peer. *The Black Eagle.* New York: Stein and Day, 1971.

Page, Arthur W. *Our 110 Days Fighting.* Garden City, NJ: Doubleday, 1920.

Patton, Gerald W. *War and Race: The Black Officer in the Military, 1915–1941.* Westport, CT: Greenwood, 1981.

Rich, Doris L. *Queen Bess: Daredevil Aviator.* Washington, DC: Smithsonian Institution Press, 1995.

Scott, Emmett J. *Scott's Official History of the American Negro in the World War.* Chicago: Homewood Press, 1919.

Stallings, Laurence. *The Dough Boys.* New York: Harper and Row, 1963.

Sweeney, W. Allison. *History of the American Negro in the Great World War.* Chicago: Cuneo-Henneberry, 1919.

World War II

Allen, Robert L. *The Port Chicago Mutiny.* New York: Warner Books, 1989.

Anderson, Trezzvant W. *Come out Fighting.* Long Island, NY: 761st Tank Battalion and Allied Veterans Association, 1979.

Baker, Vernon, and Ken Olsen. *Lasting Valor.* Columbus, MS: Genesis Press, 1997.

Byers, Jean. *A Study of the Negro in the Military Service.* Washington, DC: Department of the Navy, 1974.

Colley, David P. *The Road to Victory: The Untold Story of World War II's Red Ball Express.* Washington, DC: Brasseys, 2001.

Converse, Elliott V., and Julius W. Becton, Jr. *The Exclusion of Black Soldiers from the Medal of Honor in World War II.* Jefferson, NC: McFarland & Company, 1997.

Downey, Bill. *Uncle Sam Must Be Losing the War.* San Francisco: Strawberry Hill Press, 1982.

Duberman, Martin Bauml. *Paul Robeson.* New York: Knopf, 1988.

Earley, Charity Adams. *One Woman's Army: A Black Officer Remembers the WAC.* College Station: Texas A&M University, 1989.

Francis, Charles E. *The Tuskegee Airmen.* Boston: Branden, 1988.

Goodwin, Doris Kearns. *No Ordinary Time.* New York: Simon and Schuster, 1994.

Johnson, Jesse J. *Roots of Two Black Marine Sergeants Major.* Hampton, VA: Carver Publishing, 1978.

Lash, Joseph. *Eleanor and Franklin: The Story of Their Relationship, Based on Eleanor Roosevelt's Private Papers.* New York: W. W. Norton, 1971.

Litoff, Judy Barrett, and Davis Smith. *We're in This War Too: World War II Letters from American Women in Uniform.* New York: Oxford University Press, 1994.

Motley, Mary Penick. *The Invisible Soldier.* Detroit: Wayne State University Press, 1987.

O'Donnell, Patrick K. *Beyond Valor.* New York: Free Press, 2000.

Osur, Alan M. *The Blacks in the Army Air Forces During World War II.* Washington, DC: Office of Air Force History, 1977.

Purdon, Eric. *Black Company: The Story of Subchaser 1264.* Washington and New York: Robert B. Luce, 1972.

Putney, Martha S. *When the Nation Was in Need: Blacks in the Women's Army Corps during World War II.* Metuchen, NJ: Scarecrow Press, 1992.

Robeson, Paul. *Here I Stand.* Boston: Beacon, 1971.

Rowan, Carl T. *Breaking Barriers.* Boston: Little Brown, 1981.

Shaw, Henry I., Jr., and Ralph W. Donnelly. *Blacks in the Marine Corps.* Washington, DC: History and Museums Division, Headquarters U.S. Marine Corps, 1975.

Smith, Graham. *When Jim Crow Met John Bull.* New York: St Martin's Press, 1987.

Terkel, Studs. *The Good War.* New York: Ballantine, 1984.

Washburn, Patrick S. *A Question of Sedition.* New York: Oxford University Press, 1986.

Weston, Zak. *Biographical Sketch of Charity Edna Adams Earley.* Columbia: South Carolina Library, University of South Carolina.

Wilkins, Roy. *Standing Fast.* New York: Penguin Books, 1982.

World War II: The Names, the Deeds, A-L. Vol. 1. New York: Dell, 1986.

World War II: The Names, the Deeds, M–Z. Vol. 2. New York: Dell, 1986.

Korea

Bowers, William T., William M. Hammond, and George L. MacGarrigle. *Black Soldier—White Army: The Twenty Fourth Infantry Regiment in Korea.* Washington: Office of the Chief of Military History, United States Army, 1996.

Bussey, Charles M. *Firefight at Yechon: Courage and Racism in the Korean War.* Washington, DC: Brasseys, 1991.

Dalfiume, Richard M. *Desegregation of the U.S. Armed Forces: Fighting on Two Fronts 1939–1954.* Columbia: University of Missouri Press, 1969.

Gropman, Alan L. *The Air Force Integrates 1945–1964.* Washington, DC: Office of Air Force History, 1978.

Korea: The Names, the Deeds. New York: Dell, 1987.

MacGregor, Morris J. *Defense Studies: The Integration of the Armed Forces.* Washington, DC: Center of Military History, 1981.

Ridgway, Matthew B. *The Korean War. How We Met the Challenge: How All-Out Asian War Was Averted: Why Macarthur Was Dismissed: Why Today's War Objectives Must Be Limited.* Garden City, NY: Doubleday, 1967.

Vietnam

Gill, Gerald. "Black Soldiers' Perspectives on the War." In *A Vietnam Reader,* ed. Walter Capps. New York: Routledge, 1991.

Cash, John A. *Seven Firefights in Vietnam.* Washington, DC: Office of the Chief of Military History, United States Army, 1985.

Foster, John W. *Did Blacks Suffer More Deaths Than Whites in Vietnam?* Maxwell Air Force Base, AL: Air Command and Staff College, 1987.

Goff, Stanley, and Robert Sanders. *Brothers, Black Soldiers in the Nam.* Novato, CA: Presidio Press, 1982.

MacPherson, Myra. *Long Time Passing: Vietnam and the Haunted Generation.* Garden City, NY: Doubleday, 1984.

Murphy, Edward. *Vietnam Medal of Honor Heroes.* New York: Ballantine, 1987.

Obadele-Starks, Ernest M. B., and Amilcar Shabazz. "Blacks and the Vietnam War." In *The Vietnam War: Handbook of the Literature and Research,* ed. James S. Olson. Westport, CT: Greenwood Press, 1993.

Parks, David. *GI Diary.* New York: Harper and Row, 1968.

Phillips, William R., and William C. Westmoreland. *Night of the Silver Stars: The Battle of Lang Vei.* Washington, DC: U.S. Naval Institute, 1997.

Terry, Wallace. *Bloods: An Oral History of the Vietnam War by Black Veterans.* New York: Ballantine Books, 1984.

Vance, Samuel. *The Courageous and the Proud.* New York: W. W. Norton, 1970.

Westheider, James E. *Fighting on Two Fronts: African Americans and the Vietnam War.* New York: New York University Press, 1997.

Post-Vietnam

Atkinson, Rick. *Crusade.* Boston: Houghton Mifflin, 1993.

Buckley, Gail. *American Patriots: The Story of Blacks in the Military from the Revolution to Desert Storm.* New York: Random House, 2001.

Powell, Colin. *My American Journey.* New York: Random House, 1995.

Schwarzkopf, General H. Norman. *It Doesn't Take a Hero.* New York: Bantam Books, 1993.

Index

Military Units

Page numbers in **boldface** indicate main entries.

GENERAL INDEX